SOURCES IN CHINESE HISTORY

Praise for *Sources in Chinese History*

This book, in a word, is excellent. The use of visual sources is an extraordinarily effective device for "hooking" students and making the past much closer. Chapter introductions are cogent, as the Atwills have selected new or infrequently-utilized people and events. There is nothing humdrum here: the documents are compelling and important; and the commentary crackles with fresh and acute insights and analysis.

R. Keith Schoppa, Loyola College in Maryland

David and Yurong Atwill have done a valuable service to those of us who teach classes on the history of modern China. No other text has the diversity of voices and perspectives on the last 300 years of Chinese history. Combining text and images, this book offers a vivid set of accounts of China's turbulent transition from the late imperial period to the present day. Students will find an array of primary sources covering politics, economics, society and culture, education, foreign relations, gender and ethnicity, and much more.

Peter Worthing, Texas Christian University

This is a splendid selection of documents, superbly translated. It reflects the new changes and trends in the field of Chinese history and provides a much richer variety of materials than those found in other sourcebooks. It will be very useful to both beginning and advanced scholars of Chinese history. It is certainly a "must-have" for any modern Chinese history course or seminar.

Zvi Ben-Dor, New York University

This rich, well-written, and well-organized sourcebook in Chinese history, edited by David and Yurong Atwill, offers a unique selection of primary source documents from the Qing dynasty through the twenty-first century, organized chronologically and by topic. The Atwills' sourcebook not only includes all of the old standbys, such as Kangxi's Sacred Edict and Mao Zedong's "Bombard the Headquarters" poster, but also provides a rich bounty of materials relating to diverse topics and facets of modern Chinese history hitherto unexplored in similar collections. The book is a must for anyone seriously interested in the history of modern China.

Robert Cliver, Humboldt State University

This is the most up-to-date and comprehensive Chinese history sourcebook currently available. What is most valuable about this book is its extensive use of Chinese sources, which helps readers to understand Chinese perspectives in a new way.

Yufeng Mao, Washington University in St. Louis

SOURCES IN CHINESE HISTORY
Diverse Perspectives
from 1644 to the Present

Edited by

David G. Atwill

Yurong Y. Atwill
Pennsylvania State University

Prentice Hall

Upper Saddle River   London   Singapore
Toronto   Tokyo   Sydney   Hong Kong   Mexico City

Editorial Director: Leah Jewell
Editor-in-Chief: Priscilla McGeehon
Executive Editor: Charles Cavaliere
Editorial Assistant: Lauren Aylward
Director of Marketing: Brandy Dawson
Senior Marketing Manager: Sue
  Westmoreland
Marketing Assistant: Athena Moore
Senior Managing Editor: Ann Marie
  McCarthy
Project Manager: Debra Wechsler
Senior Operations Supervisor: Mary
  Ann Gloriande
Senior Art Director: Jayne Conte
Text and Cover Designer: Bruce Kenselaar
Manager, Visual Research: Beth Brenzel

Manager, Rights and Permissions: Zina
  Arabia
Image Permission Coordinator: Craig A.
  Jones
Manager, Cover Visual Research
  & Permissions: Karen Sanatar
Cover Art: (Boxer troops) Getty Images
  Inc. — Hulton Archive Photos; (1930s
  fertilizer ad) University of Minnesota
  Libraries
Full-Service Project Management: Bruce
  Hobart
Composition: Pine Tree Composition Co.
Printer/Binder: Hamilton Printing
  Company
Cover Printer: Coral Graphics Services

This book was set in Times Ten Roman.

Credits and acknowledgments borrowed from other sources and reproduced, with permission, in this textbook appear on page 369.

Library of Congress Cataloging-in-Publication Data
Sources in Chinese history / edited by David G. Atwill, Yurong Y. Atwill.
    p. cm.
Includes bibliographical references and index.
ISBN-13: 978-0-13-233089-3
ISBN-10: 0-13-233089-X
1.–China—History—Sources. I. Atwill, David G. II. Atwill, Yurong Y.
DS703.S68 2009
951–dc22

                                                            2008053093

10 9 8 7 6 5 4

Prentice Hall
is an imprint of

www.pearsonhighered.com   ISBN-10: 0-13-233089-X
                             ISBN-13: 978-0-13-233089-3

For Peter 杨维康 *and Kate* 杨维馨, *whose love of China has enhanced our own*

CONTENTS

CHAPTER 3   Mid-Nineteenth-Century Rebellions and Qing Responses

CHAPTER 4   The Deepening Crisis of Imperialism in China (1856–1890)

CHAPTER 8   China in the Twenties: The Struggle for Unity

CHAPTER 9   Fractured Visions: Manchuria, Nanjing, and Yan'an in the 1930s

CHAPTER 10 China at War (1937–1949)

PART THREE   POST-1949 CHINA (1949–PRESENT)

CHAPTER 11 New China – Finding a New Way

CHAPTER 14   Life in China Under Deng Xiaoping (1980s and 1990s)

CHAPTER 15   China in the Twenty-First Century

THEMATIC TABLE OF CONTENTS

Treaties, Diplomacy, and Foreign Relations

Military, War, and Aggression

PREFACE

Glance at any recent newspaper, magazine, or mainstream website and one will encounter some mention of China. The number of Americans and Europeans studying the Chinese language has soared in recent years. Foreign investment in China and Chinese exports to the world are increasing at a record pace. Western political leaders ponder how to join or combat the country's expanding influence. Yet, this emerging "discovery" of China should more correctly be described as a "rediscovery." European and American churches have sent missionaries to China for more than five centuries. Western traders and businesses have sought Chinese products and pursued new markets for their own goods for a commensurate period. Still, this newfound interest in China suggests there is a need for a sourcebook that goes beyond the narrow boundaries of political and intellectual thought: a sourcebook that explores the broad cultural, social, and ethnic trends that are the foundation of a twenty-first-century China.

Compiling a selection of documents accurately reflecting China's complex history was not an easy task. The greatest challenge was choosing diverse sources that reflect the various directions the field of studies has taken in recent years. While nearly every chapter contains conventional documents such as speeches, treaties, or imperial communications, we sought to pair such traditional offerings with other documents that would provide for a broader interpretation of their consequences for Chinese society. We also sought to pick documents that would pique students' and instructors' interests with such selections as the "Taiping Ten Commandments," *Time* magazine's positive spin on Warlord Wu Peifu, and the recent "sex rules" for students at Fudan University.

Topically, this collection includes a broad spectrum of perspectives and ideas. Within the scope of documents included we have chosen to emphasize three categories that are all significant but also often underemphasized. First, we have included an array of sources on women's topics like the education of women in late imperial China, women's role in China's revolutions, as well as the evolving notions of "modern love" and dating in twentieth-century China. Second, there is a significant sampling of Chinese literature that permits comparisons both across time and within a single era. Finally, we have given popular culture an important place among the documents by including translations of advertisements, movie dialogues, and wall posters.

One of our main goals when we set out to create a new sourcebook was to highlight inherent historiographical issues. As we compiled the documents we paid considerable attention to the types of documents and, in numerous instances, the manner in which we sequenced them in order to promote a greater awareness of the different ways history can be told and interpreted. For example, propaganda from various periods of the People's Republic of China and culturally prejudiced sources, both Western and Chinese from the nineteenth century, are included. By incorporating such obviously "loaded" source material, an immediacy and intimacy is brought to China's contentious past that is otherwise lost to the modern student.

One of the hardest aspects of creating a sourcebook is making difficult decisions about which documents to include and which to leave out. In general we focused on maintaining breadth over depth, and in several instances we sought to group documents into meaningful themes so that an instructor could sequence them across a particular course. Similarly, while it was often tempting to include complete documents, we chose to abbreviate, excerpt, and otherwise shorten documents.

This sourcebook is designed primarily for a single or two-semester course on Chinese history after 1600. The format of this sourcebook assumes the use of outside readings or a textbook, but for the more adventurous it could also be used as a stand-alone sourcebook with the instructor offering crucial information and context. Each chapter begins with a short introductory essay that examines a key event, personage, or theme from the period covered by the chapter. These are written to supplement, not replace, the accompanying textbook narratives. We have selected perspectives that help to orient the student to the issues, trends, and challenges of each particular period. We hope the different viewpoints presented will lead students to rethink the way in which historical events are commonly understood.

Every document included in the sourcebook is preceded by a short headnote. The headnotes serve different purposes: Some offer basic background information, others introduce key personages, and still others seek to highlight the significance of the document. They are not meant to be exhaustive or comprehensive. Rather they attempt to set a tone so the reader may correctly place the document in its historical context.

To encourage students to move beyond simply *reading* about history, each chapter is introduced by a visual document from the era to be examined. We have selected a variety of sources—including a Qing memorial to the throne, Cultural Revolution-era posters, as well as political cartoons and advertisements. Each visual source includes eight to ten comments that offer translations of any Chinese text, background information, and information that should allow students to begin to tease out significant issues "embedded" in the document.

Given the inherent limitations of any sourcebook, for instructors and students alike, we hope that this sourcebook is only the beginning of one's exploration of modern Chinese history, culture, and society. To that purpose, we have included several guides at the end of each of the three main parts of the book with suggested readings, specialized readers, and websites.

A NOTE ON ROMANIZATION, NAMES, AND DATES

All Chinese terms, people, and places in this book are romanized according to the *pinyin* system. In some instances, where the term or name might be better known by another romanization system, we have included its non-pinyin form in brackets after its first usage. While the decision to employ only pinyin is not without its own set of problems, we believe its use provides for consistency across all the documents, and removes a hindrance to understanding China's past.

Chinese names are given with their family name first, followed by their given name. Mao Zedong's family name is Mao and his given name is Zedong. Only in very rare instances do Chinese use only their first name. Chinese in the late Imperial and Republican eras often had multiple names or sobriquets (Sun Zhongshan was known by at least six different names). If a document employed a lesser-known name for an individual, we have included the more common name in brackets. Emperors during the Qing dynasty are referred to by their reign name.

Prior to 1911, China adhered almost exclusively to a lunar calendar. All dates have been converted to the solar calendar, though in some instances the original date remains with the solar date in brackets to retain the flavor of the document.

Following are a few hints for pronouncing Chinese words that are romanized using pinyin. Most of the consonants are close to the pronuciation of the corresponding English letter with the following exceptions:

Consonants

C = 'ts' (fits)
Q = 'ch' (cheat)
X = 'sh' (sheer)
ZH = 'j' (joe)

Vowels

(Vowel combinations with phonetic pronunciation followed by rhyming word in English)

A = 'ah' (car)
AI = 'eye' (pie)
AO = 'ow' (pow)
AN = 'an' (tan)
ANG = 'ong' (song)

E = 'uh' (duh)
EI = 'eh' (pay)
EN = 'un' (sun)
ENG = 'ung' (sung)

I = 'ee' (bee)
IA = 'ee-ya' (yea)
IAO = 'ee-ow' (meow)
IAN = 'ee-en' (mien)
IANG = 'ee-ang' (see song)
IE = 'ee-yeh' (ye-ah)
IN = 'een' (mean) plié
ING = 'eeng' (ding)
IONG = 'ee-yong' (boing)
IU = 'yo' (yo-yo)

O = 'w-oh' (woe)
OU = 'oo' (oh)
ONG = 'ohng' (tong)

U = 'ue' (rue)
UAI = 'why' (Kauai)
UAN = 'when' (when)
UANG = 'awng' (prolong)
UE = 'you-eh' (you way)
UI = 'eigh' (weigh)
UN = 'yew-n' (swoon)
UO = 'w-oh' (wo)

ACKNOWLEDGMENTS

In the years since we began writing this sourcebook we have relied on the advice, input, and support of numerous people, and we are happy to have this opportunity to thank them. The first phase of our research took place primarily at the University of Pittsburgh's East Asian Library supported financially by a University of Pittsburgh East Asian Library travel grant. Special thanks goes to the librarians there—Xu Hong, Zhang Haihui, and Zou Xiuying—who without fail pulled books from the shelves and out of storage in anticipation of our visits, tracked down hard-to-find sources, and responded to all queries happily.

At our home institution of Penn State, numerous people facilitated the writing of this book. Our supervisors, Sally McMurry, Rebecca Mugridge and Daniel Mack, as well as our deans, Susan Welch and Nancy Eaton, all provided both the time and the funds to help us carry out the research for this book. Helen Sheehy helped us with government documents. Fannie Mui, the Penn State East Asian cataloger, helped us acquire documents by scanning and e-mailing them to us while we were in China with mind-boggling speed, and never once protested that these "favors" fell well outside of her own job responsibilities. It was a pleasure to find an expert on the imperial examination system, Hoi K. Suen, in my own backyard who willingly shared his knowledge with us. Tijana Krstic served as a crucial sounding board and sympathetic listener. Heidi von Bernewitz and Rob Nairn patiently listened to our descriptions of past events sharing in both the frustrations and thrills of writing up the sourcebook. Despite the feelings of isolation that one has when writing a book of this nature, we came away from the process with a deep appreciation of the friends and colleagues at Penn State—we thank them all.

In China, we relied on several individuals to introduce us to the proper people in the proper places who then guided us through the complex process of getting permissions from Chinese publishers. Wang Tong from China International Book Trading Corporation and Zhang Ying from China National Publishing Industry Trading Corporation were particularly helpful. We are especially obliged to those people who listened to our explanation of the sourcebook and agreed to let us use out of date articles that contained "outdated facts and viewpoints which do not reflect the current situation of China" in order for the students who use this sourcebook come away with a far more nuanced understanding of China's past. The book is far more complete and much better because of their help. The staff at the National Library of China was accommodating and cooperative during our visit. Bu Tong and the staff of the various reading rooms and collections at Yunnan University were indefatigable in their assistance.

We would be remiss not to give our utmost thanks to the numerous friends and colleagues including Hsi-chu Bolick (University of North Carolina, Chapel Hill), Su Chen (Minnesota), Vicky Doll (Kansas University), John Israel (University of Virginia), Lisa Riddering (Penn State), Chaomin Lin (Yunnan University), Jing Liu (University of British Columbia), Wen-ling Liu (Indiana), Beth Notar (Trinity College), Eric Novotny (Penn State), Chengzhi Wang (Columbia), Peter M. Worthing (Texas Christian University), Diana Xu (University of Wisconsin), Zhaohui Xue (Stanford), and Yunshan Ye (Dickinson) who suggested documents, helped procure sources, read drafts of chapters or happily spoke with us about matters related to the sourcebook. Both Yang Yin and Long Ruihua willingly offered their own memories of events and served as a sounding board for our own understanding of the past as well as always being willing to host us at a moment's notice.

One of the unsung but most critical phases of writing any book is finding people who are both willing and able to offer constructive criticisms and suggestions to a manuscript at its various stages. We count ourselves extremely lucky to have had Zvi Ben-Dor (New York University), Wing Chung Ng (University of Texas at San Antonio), Robert Cliver (Humboldt State University), Louis G. Perez (Illinois State University), Keith Schoppa (Loyola College of Maryland), Harold M. Tanner (University of North Texas), Peter M. Worthing (Texas Christian University), Mao Yufeng (Washington University) and one anonymous reader who all offered pointed but always constructive comments on the project proposal and manuscript. As well, Dr. Donald P. King, Laura Clark Hull, John R. Atwill, and Sally Rodgers all looked over the manuscript polishing the prose and point-ing out inconsistencies. The sourcebook is much improved for all of their help.

From the earliest discussions with our editor, Charles Cavaliere, he remained pos-itive, helpful, and enthusiastic about our project. His benign neglect gave us the space and time to formulate our own voice for the sourcebook while offering increasingly urgent reminders that kept us moving forward. His guiding hand and insights to are vis-ible throughout this sourcebook. Despite numerous hiccups and delays, he displayed amazing *sangfroid* that helped keep the sourcebook on track and moving forward. We could not have asked for a better editor.

But no two people have lived with this book more than our son and daughter, Peter and Kate. Spending hours in libraries, traveling with us innumerable times between the United States and China, and patiently waiting while we wrote "just one more para-graph," they expressed an ongoing curiosity to what the book would be like. We are all pleased to see the finished product and it is with our deep love for them that we dedi-cate this book and with the hope that they will continue to visit, study and enjoy China.

ABOUT THE AUTHORS

David G. Atwill teaches Asian History at Pennsylvania State University. He is the author of *The Chinese Sultanate: Islam, Ethnicity and the Panthay Rebellion in Southwestern China, 1856–1873,* the recipient of two Fulbright fellowships, and most recently, an Andrew W. Mellon New Direction Fellowship.

Yurong Y. Atwill is the Asian Studies Librarian at Pennsylvania State University and the author of numerous articles on Chinese librarianship. She is active in the Council on East Asian Libraries.

PART ONE

LATE IMPERIAL CHINA
(1644–1911)

Timeline

World		China
	1368–1644	Ming dynasty
British East India Company established	1600	
	1644	Qing dynasty founded
	1692	Kangxi issues Edict of Toleration
	1720	Gonghang guild system established
Papal bull ends Jesuit mission in China	1740s	
	c.1740	Pu Songling's *Strange Tales* first published
	1757	All Western trade restricted to Guangzhou
Boston Tea Party	1773	
	1799	Qianlong emperor dies and Heshen sentenced to death
	c.1805	Shen Fu publishes *Six Chapters of a Floating Life*
Queen Victoria ascends British throne	1837	
	1839–1842	Opium War
	1842	Treaty of Nanjing
Communist Manifesto published	1848	
	1851–1864	Taiping Rebellion
	1860	Convention of Beijing signed/Yuanming Yuan burned
American Civil War	1861–1865	
	1861	Zongli Yamen founded
	1865	Jiangnan Arsenal created
Japan's Meiji Restoration	1868	
	1884–1885	Sino-French War
	1894–1895	Sino-Japanese War
	1898	Hundred Days Reform
	1900	Boxer Uprising
	1905	Sun Zhongshan forms Revolutionary Alliance
Henry Ford builds first Model T	1908	Cixi and Guangxu Emperor die
	1911	Wuchang Uprising
	1912	Republic of China established

CHAPTER 1
THE RISE OF THE QING (1644–1799)

VISUAL SOURCE
Yang Lin: "Memorial to Kangxi"

VERMILLION RESCRIPT: When the emperor wrote his comments on a memorial (typically called a "rescript"), his remarks were written in vermillion (red) a color reserved exclusively for the emperor. As a result of this, his comments at the end of the memorial are often referred to as his "vermillion rescripts."

RESCRIPT TRANSLATION: Kangxi begins his rescript (or comments) with the words "duly noted" (*zhidaole*) a commonly employed phrase to indicate that the emperor had read and understood the contents. Following that he wrote: "Westerners who come [to China] and are scholars or doctors should be sent directly to the capital."

DATE: Up until the early twentieth century, Chinese society adhered to a lunar calendar. Interestingly, there was no continuous numbering system for counting the years. Rather, the year indicated on most Chinese documents simply denoted the regnal year (e.g. number of years the current emperor had been on throne). In this memorial the date reads: the 27th day, 7th month of the 57th year of the Kangxi reign [August 23, 1718].

OVERSEAS CHINESE: It is easy to forget that by the beginning of the Qing dynasty in 1644, there were extensive overseas Chinese communities. This memorial refers to the Qing's efforts to curtail Chinese trade in the South China Sea and Euro-American ships aiding Chinese attempting to return to China.

HOW TO READ: Chinese was traditionally written (and read) from top to bottom, right to left. Also note that classical Chinese did not include any punctuation so the reader was expected to understand the beginning and end of sentences from grammatical construction.

STRUCTURE: All palace memorials had to comply with strict guidelines regarding the number of characters per line and the number of lines per page. The elevation of certain characters (usually those relating to the emperor or dynasty) had to be raised above the body of the communication. If the memorial contravened any of these guidelines they could be rejected, sent back to the sender (a serious breach of etiquette for which the author would not lightly forget).

EMPEROR'S WORKLOAD: Kangxi wrote fifty to a hundred rescripts a day. The Qing emperors often used the rescript to motivate, exhort and castigate his military and civil provincial officials. The exhilaration an official felt upon receiving a lengthy response (or even a terse endorsement of one's actions) made it a highly effective tool by which the emperor could spur on his officials.

FOREIGN TERMS: During the 17th and 18th centuries, contact between Chinese and Europeans increased. With this rising familiarity, there also inevitably emerged confusion over how to translate names, places, and terms. As a result, Chinese officials often simply created phonetic approximations. Such phonetic approximations were often indicated by the addition of a "mouth" radical (which looks like a square) to the upper-left of the Chinese character. In this memorial, the governor-general refers to a country called "Fu-lan-si" -- likely meaning France.

Walking along Beijing's trendy downtown shopping district today there is little to distinguish it from a modern western city. Glass-faced office buildings dominate the skyline and popular American restaurant chains such as Pizza Hut, KFC and Starbucks crowd the main streets. Given these superficial similarities, one might assume that modern China is unconcerned with its own past in its race to adopt the modern cultural features of the West. Yet this illusion is quickly dispelled by the imposing presence of the Forbidden City in the very center of the city. As the former residence of the Qing emperors (1644–1911), the Forbidden City occupies over two hundred and fifty acres of prime real estate in downtown Beijing. Now a museum, the 600-year old palace is a sprawling complex of some 800 halls and 9,000 rooms. Its presence offers a potent reminder of China's imperial past.

The Forbidden City is not merely a dusty relic retained out of nostalgia for China's past. The Qing emperors and their accomplishments are well known to most contemporary Chinese. The popularity and interest in the Qing dynasty is illustrated by the numerous television series fictionalizing the lives of the emperors and court life. Often more than 50 episodes long, the series are immensely popular among all age groups. Similarly, at most major tourist sites one can dress up in imperial costumes and have a souvenir picture taken. Numerous restaurants in many major cities have adopted "imperial" themes where the staff dresses in late imperial clothing, and specialty dishes from recipes adapted from the imperial kitchen are served.

The symbolic power of the Qing is not limited to entertainment and tourism. Mao Zedong clearly sought to expropriate the symbolic power of the Qing when he stood atop the **Gate of Heavenly Peace** on October 1, 1949 and declared the founding of the People's Republic of China. For decades China's top leaders have (in an explicitly symbolic move lost on no Chinese) lived in **Zhongnan Hai,** the former imperial gardens adjacent to the Forbidden City. Why does a country that has so fervently sought to sever itself from its pre-revolutionary past continue to celebrate its imperial roots?

The allure stems, in some part, from the sheer success of China's last dynasty, the Qing dynasty. In comparison to the long succession of dynasties that preceded it, the Qing stands out as one of China's most accomplished imperial dynasties. The Qing emperors ruled an empire of roughly 4.6 million square miles (larger than the modern People's Republic of China or the United States) that by the end of the Qing dynasty in the early nineteenth century contained nearly one-third of the world's population.

The Qing's rise to power was not without challenges. The Qing emperors were ethnically Manchu, not **Han Chinese.** The Manchus stormed into Chinese history as a powerful military presence out of the Northeastern Asian steppes in the late sixteenth and early seventeenth centuries. It was their ability to co-opt Chinese culture and attitudes—while retaining their ties and control of the Asian steppes—that helped to secure their rule over China.

The Qing dynasty also marked an era of increased contact between China and Europe. Western accounts of China have tended to exaggerate the insularity of late

LATE IMPERIAL CHINA—A period of Chinese history traditionally defined as beginning with the end of Mongol rule in 1368 and concluding with the fall of the Qing dynasty in 1911.

GATE OF HEAVENLY PEACE (TIANANMEN)—The main gate and entrance to the Forbidden Palace, erected during the Ming dynasty and rebuilt in 1651. Over one hundred feet tall, the gate has five arched portals through the base; the middle and largest reserved exclusively for the emperor.

ZHONGNAN HAI—A compound just west of the Forbidden City in the center of Beijing, which in the first decades of the PRC housed its top leaders and today serves as the headquarters of the party and top government officials.

HAN CHINESE—The term Han Chinese today refers to the ethnic majority of China's population. In imperial times "Han Chinese" often referred to individuals viewed as culturally Chinese regardless of their ethnicity.

imperial China and the Qing ruler's disdain for European ideas. Although most Chinese remained generally unaware of Europe, to suggest that this meant China had no interest in things non-Chinese over-simplifies the court's point of view. Documents in this chapter reveal that the Qing court had considerable contact with many Europeans including **Jesuit** priests, diplomatic envoys, and merchants. Still, Qing China remained quite selective in what they sought from Europe. China dominated much of Asia, politically, culturally and commercially. As a result, the Qing rulers focused, for the first century and a half of their rule, on consolidating and expanding their power over China and in Asia rather than worrying about the shifting global, political and military balances of power occurring in Europe at this time.

RISE OF QING: CONQUEST, CONSOLIDATION AND PRESERVATION

It is tempting when reading any history of China to accept the beginning and ending dates of an imperial dynasty as absolute. In the case of the Qing dynasty, 1644 marks the year the Qing dynasty was founded, but it would take several more decades of Qing military campaigns and conquests before China completely submitted to Manchu rule. Qing forces continued to battle Ming loyalists and other renegade forces for over forty years (1.3). Not surprisingly, most Chinese commoners did not immediately accept the new dynasty. As a result, the early Qing emperors expended considerable effort to sway and coerce the Chinese populace into accepting their new rulers (1.1 and 1.2). At the same time, the Manchu elite agonized over how best to preserve their own Manchu identity (1.4).

1.1 SHUNZHI'S HEAD-SHAVING DECREE (1644)

In 1644 the Manchu armies surged out of northeast Asia, captured Beijing and founded China's last imperial dynasty (1644–1911). Large swathes of China continued to oppose Qing rule giving the Manchu leaders the awkward task of separating those Chinese who supported them from those who did not. To clarify this process, the Shunzhi emperor (r. 1644–1661) issued a decree requiring all Chinese males to shave their forehead and wear a queue in the Manchu style. This decree was especially loathsome to most Chinese because Confucian beliefs dictated that "one's body, hair and skin are inherited from one's parents, one should not dare to mutilate them." The stark choice faced by most Chinese is caught in a popular saying of the day "lose your hair and keep your head, or keep your hair and lose your head" (*liutou bu liufa, liufa bu liutou*).

Questions

1. How did the typical Chinese male receive Shunzhi's decree?
2. Why might Qing officials be reluctant to enforce such a decree?

JESUITS (SOCIETY OF JESUS) — A Christian religious order of the Roman Catholic Church that first established Chinese missions in the sixteenth and seventeenth centuries. Successfully operating in the Ming and early Qing era, the Jesuits actively transmitted European knowledge to China and Chinese learning to Europe. Their influence ended when Pope Clement XI decided that Chinese Confucian practices and offerings to the emperor constituted idolatry.

The various decrees relating to head shaving have been purposefully inconsistent in some respects in order to meet a variety of situations that might arise. There has never been any doubt that once all of China is pacified, a decree will be issued to end all the inconsistencies. Now that all of China has become one family, it is mandatory that the emperor and his subjects be united as one, as a subject's disloyalty to his emperor can no more be tolerated than that of a son to his own father. To be otherwise is to regard the emperor and his subjects as strangers to each other—an absurdity so obvious that you must know it fully well without any of my elaborations.

It is therefore decreed that within ten days after this public announcement all the men in the capital and its adjacent areas must shave their heads and that all the men in the provinces must shave their heads within ten days after the arrival of this announcement in their respective provinces. Only those who shave their heads are to be considered loyal subjects of this empire; those who hesitate or refuse to do it are to be regarded as traitors and will be punished severely. No excuses for evasion, however cunning or clever, are to be tolerated.

It is further decreed that all the local officials, civilian as well as military, must see to it that the above order relating to head shaving is to be implemented without fail and that any official who is impudent enough to petition the government to delay or relax the enforcement of this order will be condemned to death without mercy. The same penalty will also be imposed upon those officials who are impudent enough to petition the government for the maintenance of those Ming customs that are at variance with those of the present dynasty. However, a reasonable length of time will be allowed for people to change from their old Ming attire to that of the present dynasty. From now on all people in China must obey the laws of this dynasty, and defiance in whatever form is not to be tolerated.

The Board of Rites is hereby ordered to proclaim this decree in all the provinces, districts, and other administrative units, as well as the capital and its adjacent areas, to assure its observance by all officials, civilian as well as military, teachers and students, and all other people in the empire.

1.2 SACRED EDICT OF THE KANGXI EMPEROR (1670)

Cognizant of their distinct ethnic and cultural background, the Qing emperors sought to portray themselves as overseers of Confucian values. Kangxi's **Sacred Edict** (later amended and expanded by his son, Yongzheng) is a recapitulation of imperial precepts from earlier dynasties. The edict presents the Qing rulers as concerned about the moral health of their subjects and thus promotes them as ideal Confucian rulers. The Confucian tenets included by **Kangxi** reflect his own concern with the stability, legitimacy and morality of his rule. The edict sought to spell out the moral underpinnings of the empire for its subjects. To this end, the Sacred Edict was often posted or read by local officials to foster the Confucian ideal of each individual serving their own role in society.

Questions

1. **In an era well before newspapers, television or the internet were common, what purpose do you believe the Sacred Edict served in Qing society?**
2. **Why do you imagine the emperor would order his officials to read the Sacred Edict in places where disturbances had occurred?**

SACRED EDICT—A list of Confucian rules of moral conduct and social relations compiled by the Kangxi emperor in 1670.

KANGXI (1654–1722)—The second emperor of the Qing dynasty. His 61-year-long reign oversaw the consolidation of Qing rule over China, including defeating the renegade General Wu Sangui, and other rebel generals of the Three Feudatories.

1. Uphold one's filial duties as a son and a brother, so as to strengthen familial relations.
2. Revere kinship structure and ties, so as to demonstrate harmony.
3. Strive to create good relations within local communities, so as to prevent disputes and litigation.
4. Focus on agriculture and silk production, so as to ensure an ample supply of food and clothing.
5. Adhere to a frugal lifestyle, so as to prevent lavish waste.
6. Foster and support education, so as to cultivate scholarly habits.
7. Eliminate heterodoxy so as to promote orthodoxy.
8. Extol the law, so as to warn the stupid and stubbornly wrong-headed.
9. Demonstrate courteousness so as to strengthen proper traditions
10. Devote oneself to one's proper vocation, so as to satisfy one's ambition.
11. Guide the younger generations, so as to prevent wrong-doing.
12. Prevent wrongful accusations, so as to protect the innocent.
13. Abstain from sheltering criminals, so as to avoid being implicated as an accomplice.
14. Promptly and fully pay taxes, so as to avoid being penalized for late payment.
15. Uphold the neighborhood mutual security system [*baojia*], so as to thwart theft and robbery.
16. Resolve hatred and animosities, so as to value life.

1.3   KANGXI'S EDICT REGARDING WU SANGUI (SEPTEMBER 2, 1674)

In 1644, General **Wu Sangui** allowed Manchu forces to pass unmolested through the Shanhaiguan Pass, a pivotal gateway in the Great Wall northeast of Beijing. This deed has forever since marked Wu Sangui as one of China's greatest traitors. Having proven his allegiance to the Qing court, he joined the Qing in a series of military campaigns against Ming loyalists and rebel armies. In return, the Qing rewarded Wu Sangui with numerous high titles, monetary payments, and ultimately a command over the southwestern provinces of Yunnan and Guizhou as one of the **Three Feudatories.** While there, his growing dissatisfaction with the central court led to his slow appropriation of power. The young Kangxi emperor was skeptical of Wu Sangui's loyalty, but there were few officials willing to step into the breach and challenge Wu. Few people were surprised then, when Wu Sangui, in 1674, dropped all pretense and openly revolted against the Qing. The following edict reflects the Kangxi emperor's resolve to swiftly and completely overwhelm Wu Sangui's kingdom. Before the Qing armies could defeat him, however, Wu Sangui died a painful death from dysentery. Soon thereafter, the Qing armies defeated the last of the rebel armies and finally incorporated southwest China into the Qing empire—nearly four decades after its founding.

Questions

1. **What does the emperor suggest motivated Wu Sangui to rebel?**
2. **How does the edict seek to show the strength of the Qing (and conversely the weakness of Wu Sangui)?**

THREE FEUDATORIES—Areas granted by the early Manchu emperors in southern China to three Chinese generals – Wu Sangui, Geng Jingzhong and Shang Zhixin – who aided in the Manchu's early conquest of China. All three later rebelled against the Qing rulers with the last rebel forces defeated in 1683.

WU SANGUI (1612–1678)—A Ming general who allowed the Manchu army to pass through the Great Wall and capture Beijing. He later revolted against the Qing and declared himself emperor of the new Zhou dynasty. He died of dysentery in 1678.

To the civil and military officials, residents, indigenous chieftains, and ethnic peoples of Sichuan, Yunnan, and Guizhou:

Rebel Wu Sangui initially surrendered to us due to his father's unnatural death. The late emperor rewarded his military service by bestowing a noble title for him and his decedents. What an honor. I bestowed upon him the title of prince due to his military successes in Yunnan. Such a promotion and imperial reward was rare in history.

Unfortunately, Wu Sangui was sly and untrustworthy. Such imperial honors and favors gave rise to total arrogance and betrayal. In the seventh month of Kangxi's twelfth year [September 1673], he asked to retire. Accepting his request at face value, and considering he was old and had fought long and over great distances, I allowed his retirement. I ordered offices to prepare the proper transfer of power while specifically sending officials to carry out my orders. I treated Wu Sangui considerately and honorably. But Wu Sangui rebelled and readily turned his back on the court's gracious treatment establishing an independent center of power. He collaborated with the Zheng Jiaolin to rebel together, disturbing people lives, which angered gods and people.

As a result, I have now stripped him of his noble titles and dispatched generals and armies to wipe him out. If Wu Sangui attempts to flee, Mongolian soldiers will be sent to capture and return him. I am now ordering the Dalai Lama to send soldiers into border areas in Sichuan. When the soldiers arrive, local officials and people ought to surrender and shave their foreheads [in submission], and quickly prepare supplies for the soldiers. Those who voluntarily lay down their arms and surrender their cities should be reported to military leader Dalai Batulu Taiji who will record and compensate them for their actions. Those who refuse to surrender or to offer supplies will be vanquished. When the [Qing] generals arrive, the [Dalai Lama's] military accomplishments should be clearly recorded and rewarded before returning home.

I am dispatching this edict to clearly inform my loyal subjects that even those who might have previously been forced into rebelling will be pardoned without fear of further prosecution as long as they show remorse for their crimes and wholeheartedly surrender. The Dalai Lama's military forces must implement strict discipline and prevent any disturbance. You all should remain law-abiding and your actions not raise any suspicions and cause regrettable behavior.

Announce and follow my orders!

Imperial decree

3rd day, 8th month, 13th year of the Kangxi reign.

1.4 QING RULERS PROMOTING AND PRESERVING MANCHU IDENTITY (1635–1850)

The Manchu rulers faced a complex set of issues as they conquered China and established the Qing dynasty. On the one hand, they sought to adopt Chinese methods of imperial rule. On the other, they simultaneously sought to retain their distinctive cultural identity. Beginning with Hongtaiji (1592–1643), the founder of the Qing dynasty, Manchu rulers aggressively sought to maintain their own ethnic identity while preventing the assimilation of Han Chinese cultural practices. With frequent threats and harsh enforcement, the Manchu leadership aggressively promoted their distinctive language, dress, and martial skills among the Manchus. As part of their Manchu identity, they cultivated the notion that they shared an affinity with Mongol and Tibetan peoples and actively promoted themselves as patrons of Mongol and Tibetan culture. These measures helped to preserve Manchu unity while advancing the Manchu's desire to create a multiethnic and cosmopolitan empire.

Questions

1. Why did the Qing emperors place such a premium on Manchu identity? What elements did they most cherish?
2. Do the pro-Manchu sentiments expressed below reveal anti-Han Chinese attitudes?

Hongtaiji on the Adoption of the Term Manchu (1635)

Our *gurun* (tribe, state) originally had the names Manju, Hada, Ula, Yehe, and Hoifa. Formerly ignorant persons have frequently called [us] *jušen*. The term *jušen* refers to the Sibo and Chaomergen barbarians and has nothing to do with our *gurun*. Our *gurun* establishes the name Manju. Its rule will be long and transmitted over many generations. Henceforth persons should call our *gurun* its original name, Manju, and not use the previous demeaning name. (*Taizong shilu*)

Hongtaiji on Maintaining Manchu Traditions (1636)

Nowadays sons are only acquainted with roaming the streets and planning plays and music. In the old days when everyone was poor, we were happy if a hunt was announced. Very few had servants; everyone looked over their horses, cooked food, and saddled up to go. Even with hardship everyone still unceasingly put forth their best effort. … Nowadays when there is a hunt, many youngsters say, "My wife or son is sick," or "I'm busy with affairs at home." If they're clinging to wife and babies and don't know how to exert themselves, how can the nation not be weakened? (Reported in *Gugong Bowuyuan yuankan*)

Qianlong on Manchu Women Adopting Chinese-Style Clothing (1759)

When I inspected the *xiunü* [marriage draft] this time, there were girls who emulated Han Chinese clothing and jewelry. This is truly not the Manchu custom. If they do this before me, what is willfully worn at home? … Although this is a small matter, if we do not speak to correct it, there must gradually be a change in our customs, which are greatly tied to our old Manchu ways. Take this and have the banner high officials proclaim it to the **bannermen.**

Qianlong on Manchus Adopting Chinese Names (1767)

Recently the Board of Rites nominated Manjishan, the son of Mamboo. The name Manjishan is really using 'man' as a surname. I have changed Manjishan's name to Jishan. Jishan is a *juelo,* which is very prestigious. But Jishan doesn't honor this, instead he takes 'man' as a surname, like Han people. Where's the principle in this? The Imperial Clan Court ought to pay attention to prevent this kind of thing. (*Da Qing huidian shili*)

A Reminiscence by Yihuan (Prince Chun) on the Royal Family's Skill at Archery (c. early 1850s)

During the Xianfeng reign [1851–1861], I accompanied eighth brother … and ninth brother … to reside in the **Agesuo.** We would be summoned to test our literary and martial skills for glory or shame. One day the emperor ordered me, followed by fourth elder sister … to compete in archery. Eighth brother put four arrows into the cloth target, ninth brother thirteen arrows, and the emperor gave each of them a jade piece. I hit the target three times, but I was not rewarded. Instead, he ordered a tiny pigeon five *cun* [inches] in size to be hung and said to me, "if you hit this pigeon, you'll get a reward." At this point fourth sister bent her bow and took her first shot, hitting the target. I then shot and with my second arrow I hit it. I was summoned in front of the emperor and he personally handed me a jade lion. (Reported in *Qinggong shuwen*)

XIUNÜ—A selection process used by the imperial household to select Manchu women as partners for the Qing emperors and princes.

BANNERMEN (QIREN)—"Banners" were large civil-military units, organized along ethnic (Manchu, Mongol or Han) and hereditary lines, though during the Qing the term "bannermen" became synonymous with being Manchu.

JUELO (GIORO)—Imperial kinsmen who, because of their relationship to the imperial line, received special treatment and titles.

AGESUO (NANSANSUO)—The residences of the Qing princes located near the Donghua Gate within the Forbidden Palace.

1.5 QING'S 29 REGULATIONS FOR REORGANIZING TIBET (1792)

By the mid-seventeenth century the Qing extended their political and military influence over Tibet. The depth, nature and precise extent of Chinese control in Tibet waxed and waned over time, but there was almost continuous military and political presence in many areas of Tibet. The following document denotes the high-water mark of Chinese imperial influence (and aspirations). The document was drafted by Fukang'an (a Manchu general), Lama Kyiron Hutuktu (representing the **Dalai Lama**), and a representative of the **Panchen Lama.** The document reveals both the frustration of the Qing court with Tibet and the court's efforts to standardize Tibetan practices through the offices of the Qing **Amban** (sometimes known as the Resident Official).

Questions

1. What reforms does Fukang'an seek to implement through the 29 Regulations for Better Government?
2. Is there any indication that the Qing imperial government has direct rule over any Tibetans? Why or why not?

1. *Tulkus* [reincarnated lamas] and Hutuktus [reincarnated senior lamas] are customarily determined by divinations of the Four Guardians of Dharma. Such a practice may be open to misuse, so to show the throne's favor of the **Gelugpa,** the emperor presented them with a Golden Urn. In the future, when selecting from among the identified *tulku* candidates, … the *tulku* candidates' names and dates of birth will be written in Manchu, Han, and Tibetan languages on metal slips and then placed in the Golden Urn. Following this procedure, a seven-day prayer session conducted by learned lamas. Then, the reincarnation will be officially confirmed before the statue of Sakyamuni in the Jokhang Temple by the Hutuktus and the Ambans in Tibet. When there is only one *tulku* candidate, a blank metal slip will be placed in the urn in addition to one with the *tulku* candidate's name. If the blank slip is drawn, that *tulku* will not be recognized as the reincarnation, and a new one shall be sought. The reincarnations of the Dalai Lama and Panchen Lama, who have a close relationship, will be confirmed in the same manner with *tulkus* candidate names and dates of birth written in Manchu, Han and Tibetan languages on metal slips. This new procedure is intended by the emperor to promote the Gelugpa and to prevent deception by the Guardians of Dharma. The Golden Urn should be kept clean and placed in front of **Tsongkhapa's** statue at all times.

[. . . .]

DALAI LAMA—Conventionally viewed as one of the two highest reincarnated lamas of Tibet's main Buddhist order (Gelugpa). Since the seventeenth century, the Dalai Lama has been the head of the Tibetan government based in Lhasa. In 1959, the Fourteenth Dalai Lama fled China and established a government in exile in neighboring India.

PANCHEN LAMA—A reincarnated Tibetan Buddhist religious leader in Tibet's Gelugpa Buddhist order, second only to the Dalai Lama. The Panchen Lama is traditionally based at the Tashilhunpo Monastery near Shigatse.

TULKU—A designation (in Tibetan *sprul sku*) meaning reincarnated (reborn) soul of former incarnate lama (Living Buddha) with the most famous example being the Dalai Lama.

GELUGPA—The dominant school of the four main branches of Tibetan Buddhism in Tibet often imprecisely referred to as the "Yellow Hats" headed by the Dalai Lama.

AMBAN—A Manchu term generically meaning high official but in the Tibetan context referring to the Qing imperial residents first assigned to Lhasa in 1727. Typically, two Ambans were assigned to Tibet to guide and supervise the political situation of the region.

TSONGKHAPA (1357–1419)—Founder of the Gelugpa branch of Tibetan Buddhism. The Gelugpa branch is also sometimes referred to as the "Yellow Hat" branch of Buddhism.

3. The Tibetan *thanka* currency is known to contain many impurities. Hereafter, the government shall use pure Han silver containing no impurities to mint coins. ... The new Tibetan coin will be imprinted with the words Qianlong Baozang [Emperor Qianlong's Treasury] on the front, with the year around its rim; the reverse side will be imprinted in Tibetan....

4. There has never been a standing army in Ü-Tsang and soldiers have been drafted only when Tibet has been threatened. Improperly trained, these soldiers have become a nuisance, harming the Tibetan people instead of protecting them. With the approval of the emperor, a standing army of three thousand men will be mobilized, with one thousand soldiers to be stationed in Ü [central Tibet], one thousand soldiers in Tsang [western Tibet], five hundred soldiers in Gyantse [a town in central Tibet], and another five hundred in Dingri [near the Nepal border].

[....]

8. Previously, the finances of the Dalai Lama and the Panchen Lama have not been overseen by the Amban. Since the Dalai Lama and Panchen Lama are wholly engaged with their religious duties, they tend to leave the detailed financial matters largely in the hands of relatives and attendants making it difficult to prevent abuses. Thus, the emperor instructed the Amban to audit their budgets and send a report twice annually in the spring and fall. Any misappropriation of funds will be subject to immediate punishment.

[....]

10. The Amban shall have the same level of power and authority as the Dalai Lama and the Panchen Lama in Tibetan administrative affairs. All officials under the *kaloons* [council ministers], including the *tulkus*, shall be subordinate to the Amban regardless of their position or rank. While the Panchen Lama is still under-aged, the *sopon khenpo* [Master of Religious Ceremonies] is responsible for the affairs of **Tashilhunpo.** To prevent favoritism, any significant decisions shall be reported to the Amban in advance so that he can offer his verdicts during his formal visits to Tashilhunpo.

[....]

22. All *tulkus* and lamas living in monasteries under the jurisdiction of the Dalail shall be registered with the list being given to both the Amban and the Dalai Lama. A second list is to be prepared by the *kaloons*, registering the village residents living under each *hutuktus* throughout Tibet. The *khenpos* [heads of monasteries] and *dzasas* [lower rank officials] shall be punished if the lamas in their charge are caught traveling without permits.

[....]

29. In Tibet, each village is required to pay taxes, land rent and tribute. In villages that lie close to the monasteries these payments are collected by monastic officials. In more distant villages secular officials are sent to collect it. Recently, it has been discovered cases in which a handful of dishonest monastic and secular officials ... have been caught stealing tax money and land rents which have resulted government tax revenues going astray and resulting in numerous instances of tax arrears. These investigations have also uncovered the practice of taxing a year or more in advance. As well, unpaid taxes owed by absentee laborers were arbitrarily transferred to those bound to their land. Such excessive taxes and practices made the people's life extremely onerous. In the future, all tax collectors will be appointed by *chanzods* [high officials] and shall abide to the designated taxable period. Monastic and secular officials, and *zhongpons* shall collect only the taxes and rents due that year; collecting one year in advance shall be prohibited. The taxation of runaway households shall be exempted until their return.

QING CHINA AND RELATIONS WITH EUROPE

China's interactions with Europeans and other Westerners in the centuries prior to the Qing dynasty were sporadic. In the last decades of the Ming dynasty, Jesuit missionaries had made considerable inroads with the ruling elite. After the Qing dynasty

TASHILHUNPO—One of Tibetan Buddhism's four great monasteries of the Gelugpa schools located in the central Tibetan city of Shigatse. It was founded in 1447 by the First Dalai Lama and is traditionally the seat of the Panchen Lama.

wrested power away from the Ming, the Jesuits continued to play a prominent role in the newly established imperial court. Their influence can be measured to some extent by Kangxi's edict officially permitting the practice of Christianity in China (1.6). Soon merchants and envoys began to arrive from European countries seeking to formalize ties with China. One of the most famous of these diplomatic efforts was the Macartney Embassy of 1793. Although the embassy did not obtain many of the goals desired by Lord George Macartney, it did mark the beginning of increased contact between China and the West (1.7, 1.8, 1.9).

1.6 KANGXI'S EDICT OF TOLERATION (MARCH 20, 1692)

The notion that China remained hostile to outside influences prior to the nineteenth century is a common one. However, the Qing court often welcomed foreign visitors and actively pursued non-Chinese knowledge. Jesuit missionaries arrived in China several decades prior to the founding of the Qing and remained well into the mid-Qing era serving at the highest levels of the Qing court. The Jesuits' introduction of western technology and manufacturing would later temper the court's "astonishment" over gifts presented by European embassies. The Jesuit presence and deft explanation of Christianity helped it be tolerated by Kangxi.

Questions

1. What value does Kangxi see in allowing Christianity to be practiced?
2. Does Kangxi's characterization seem to view Christianity as different than Chinese religions?

Following the emperor's instructions, a group of ministers met to discuss and report [on the status of Christianity in China]: Admiring our civilization, the Europeans (*xiyang ren*) sailed several tens of thousand *li* to come [to China]. Currently they oversee the calibration of the calendar. In times of war, they have manufactured weapons and cannons. When we sent a mission to Russia they joined the delegation, proving their allegiance [to China] and their support produced considerable achievements. The Europeans living in the provinces have perpetrated no evil behaviors, nor fomented any unrest. They have not deceptively enticed the common people with heretical ideas. Since we allow people to pray and burn incense in Tibetan, Buddhist and Daoist temples, and since the Europeans have violated no laws, it seems unreasonable to prohibit their religion.

We should order that Catholic churches throughout the empire be preserved as before. All believers should be permitted to carry out their religious practices as usual. With your Majesty's approval and order, this pronouncement is to be sent to Zhili and every province.

Kangxi 31st year, 2nd month, 3rd day. [1692.3.20] reported. On the 5th day of the month, emperor's approval was received and followed.

1.7 A LETTER FROM KING GEORGE III TO THE EMPEROR OF CHINA (1792)

King George III (r.1760–1810) and the Qianlong emperor (r.1735–1796) were two of the eighteenth century's longest reigning and most powerful monarchs in the world.

LI—A unit of measure equivalent in distance to about 1/3 mile or half a kilometer.

Although the impetus for the British mission, led by **George Macartney** in 1793, is often cast in largely economic and diplomatic terms, the embassy reveals the divergent cultural frameworks guiding each empire's actions. Unable to speak Chinese, Macartney relied on Jesuit priests and other court translators to put the carefully crafted letter of King George III (with considerable input from Macartney himself) into Chinese. Unbeknownst to Macartney, the Chinese version of the letter viewed by Qianlong adopted a much more deferential tone quite different from the English version included below.

Questions

1. **What goals did King George set out in this letter to Qianlong?**
2. **Does King George III's letter exhibit an understanding of China and Chinese diplomatic practices?**

His Most Sacred Majesty George the Third, by the Grace of God King of Great Britain, France and Ireland, Sovereign of the Seas, Defender of the Faith and so forth, To the Supreme Emperor of China Qianlong worthy to live tens of thousands and tens of thousands thousand Years, sendeth Greeting.

The natural disposition of a great and benevolent Sovereign, such as is Your Imperial Majesty, whom Providence has seated upon a Throne for the good of Mankind, is, to watch over the peace and security of his dominions, and to take pains for disseminating happiness, virtue and knowledge among his subjects, extending also the same beneficence with all the peaceful arts, as far as he is able, to the whole human race.

We have been still more anxious to enquire into the arts and manners of Countries where civilization has been perfected by the wise ordinances and virtuous examples of their Sovereigns through a long series of ages; and, above all, Our ardent wish had been to become acquainted with those celebrated institutions of Your Majesty's populous and extensive Empire which have carried its prosperity to such a height as to be the admiration of all surrounding Nations – And now that We have by prudence and justice avoided the calamities of War into which discord and ambition have plunged most of the other Kingdoms of Europe, and that by engaging Our Allies in Hindostan [India] to put an end to hostilities occasioned by the attack of an ambitious Neighbor, even when it was in Our power to destroy him, We have the happiness of being at peace with all the World, no time can be go as propitious for extending the bounds of friendship and benevolence, and for proposing to communicate and receive those benefits which must result from an unreserved and amicable intercourse, between such great and civilized Nations as China and Great Britain.

Many of Our subjects have also frequented for a long time past a remote part of Your Majesty's dominions for the purpose of Trade. No doubt the interchange of commodities between Nations distantly situated tends to their mutual convenience, industry and wealth, as the blessings which the Great God of Heaven has conferred upon various soils and climates are thus distributed among his Creatures scattered over the surface of the Earth. But such an intercourse requires to be properly conducted, so as that the newcomers may not infringe the laws and custom's of the Country they visit, and that on the other hand they may be received on terms of hospitality and meet the Justice and protection due to Strangers. We are indeed equally desirous to restrain Our Subjects from doing evil or even of showing ill example in any foreign Country, as We are that [they] should receive no injury in it. There is no method of effecting so good a purpose, but by the residence of a proper Person authorized by Us to regulate their conduct and to receive complaints against them whenever they should give occasion for any to be made against them, as well as any they might consider as having just cause to make of ill treatment towards them.

MACARTNEY, GEORGE (1737–1806)—Served as the British envoy to China in 1793 where he met with Emperor Qianlong and controversially refused to kowtow before him. The mission failed to achieve a permanent embassy in Beijing or a reduction of restrictions on British trade with China.

By such means every misunderstanding may be prevented, every inconvenience removed, a firm and lasting friendship cemented and a return of mutual good offices secured between our respective Empires.

We rely on Your Imperial Majesty's wisdom and justice and general benevolence to Mankind so conspicuous in Your long and happy reign that You will please allow Our Ambassador and Representative at Your Court to have the opportunity of contemplating the example of Your virtues and to obtain such information of Your celebrated institutions as will enable him to enlighten Our People on his return; He, on Our part being directed to give, as far as Your Majesty shall please to desire it, a full and free communication of any art, science, or observation, either of use or curiosity, which the industry ingenuity and experience of Europeans may have enabled them to acquire: And also that You will be pleased to allow to any of Our Subjects frequenting the Coasts of Your dominions, and conducting themselves with propriety a secure residence there and a fair access to Your Markets, under such laws and regulations, as Your Majesty shall think right, and that their lives and properties shall be safe under Your Imperial protection: that one Man shall not suffer for the crime of another, in which he did not participate, and whose evasion from justice he did not assist, but that every measure shall be taken on the part of Your Government as Our Ambassador is instructed strictly to direct to be taken on the part of Our People to seize and bring to condign Punishment, any of Our Subjects transgressing the laws or good order of Your Empire, or disturbing the Peace and friendship subsisting between Us.

We have particularly instructed Our Ambassador to take every method in his Power to mark Our regard and friendly disposition to Your Imperial Majesty, and it will give Us the utmost satisfaction to learn that Our wishes in that respect have been amply complied with and that as We are Brethren in Sovereignty, so may a Brotherly affection ever subsist between Us.

May the Almighty have you in his holy protection!

Given at Our Court at St. James's in London the and in the 32nd Year of Our Reign. Imperator Augustissime Vester bonus frater et Amicus GEORGIUS R

Augustissimo Principi
Qianlong
Sinarum Supremo Imperatori

1.8   JOURNAL ENTRIES OF LORD MACARTNEY DURING HIS JOURNEY TO CHINA (1793–1794)

Lord George Macartney (1737–1806) was appointed as the first British envoy to China in 1793. He kept an extensive record of his visit to China including a personal journal (which he likely hoped would be published upon his return, as it was). Most accounts of the embassy's time in China focus on Macartney's insistence on an audience with the emperor and his refusal to **kowtow** in the presence of the emperor. His journal offers a fuller view of his travels and thoughts on China. Specifically, Macartney writes that he was impressed with many things in China even as he sensed there were few British goods that might trade with China. It is equally clear that Macartney was bothered by Chinese efforts to make him conform to Chinese etiquette, though less bothered by the consequences such refusals may have on his negotiations. Macartney, it should be noted, was far more concerned than the Dutch and Portuguese envoys who proceeded him who willingly kowtowed before the emperor as requested.

Questions

1. **What about China surprised Macartney? What intrigued him?**
2. **To what degree might have cultural or language barriers hindered Macartney's mission?**

KOWTOW—From the Chinese term ketou or koutou, meaning to ritually prostrate and knock one's forehead to the ground. A gesture of respect and deference used in China before the Emperor, one's elders, or when worshipping.

Tuesday, September 10 – This day the Legate [Zhengrui], Wang [Wenxiong] and Qiao [Renjie] renewed the conversation of yesterday relative to the ceremony, in the course of which I told them it was not natural to expect that an Ambassador should pay greater homage to a foreign prince than to his own Sovereign, unless a return were made to him that might warrant him to do more. Upon which they asked me what was the ceremony of presentation to the King of England. I told them it was performed by kneeling upon one knee and kissing His Majesty's hand. 'Why then,' cried they, 'can't you do so to the Emperor?' 'Most readily,' said I; 'the same ceremony I perform to my own King I am willing to go through for your Emperor, and I think it a greater compliment than any other I can pay him.' ... Soon after the Legate arrived, and declared that it was finally determined to adopt the English ceremony, only that, as it was not the custom in China to kiss the Emperor's hand, he proposed I should kneel upon both knees instead of it. I told him I had already given my answer, which was to kneel upon one knee only on those occasions when it was usual for the Chinese to prostrate themselves. 'Well, then,' said they, 'the ceremony of kissing the Emperor's hand must be omitted.' To this I assented, saying, 'As you please, but remember it is your doing, and, according to your proposal, it is but half the ceremony, and you see I am willing to perform the whole one.' And thus ended this anxious negotiation, which has given me a tolerable insight into the character of this Court, and that political address upon which they so much value themselves.

Saturday, September 14 – This morning at four o'clock a.m. we set out for the Court under the convoy of Wang and Qiao, and reached it in little more than an hour, the distance being about three miles from our hotel. I proceeded in great state with all my train of music, guards, etc. Sir George Staunton and I went in **palanquins** and the officers and gentlemen of the Embassy on horseback. Over a rich embroidered velvet I wore the mantle of the Order of the Bath, with the collar, a diamond badge and a diamond star. Sir George Staunton was dressed in a rich embroidered velvet also, and, being a Doctor of Laws in the University of Oxford, wore the habit of his degree, which is of scarlet silk, full and flowing. I mention these little particulars to show the attention I always paid, where a proper opportunity offered, to oriental customs and ideas. ... We alighted at the park gate, from whence we walked to the Imperial encampment, and were conducted to a large, handsome tent prepared for us on one side of the Emperor's. After waiting there about an hour his approach was announced with drums and music, on which we quitted our tent and came forward upon the green carpet.

[The emperor] was seated in an open palanquin, carried by sixteen bearers, attended by numbers of officers bearing flags, standards, and umbrellas, and as he passed we paid him our compliments by kneeling on one knee, whilst all the Chinese made their usual prostrations. As soon as he had ascended his throne I came to the entrance of the tent, and, holding in both my hands a large gold box enriched with diamonds in which was enclosed the King's letter, I walked deliberately up, and, ascending the side-steps of the throne, delivered it into the Emperor's own hands, who, having received it, passed it to the Minister, by whom it was placed on the cushion. He then gave me as the first present from him to His Majesty the ***ruyi*** as the symbol of peace and prosperity, and expressed his hopes that my Sovereign and he should always live in good correspondence and amity. It is a whitish, agate-looking stone about a foot and a half long, curiously carved, and highly prized by the Chinese, but to me it does not appear in itself to be of any great value. ...

Sunday, September 15 – The Emperor, having been informed that, in the course of our travels in China, we had shown a strong desire of seeing everything curious and interesting, was pleased to give directions to the first Minister to show us his park or garden at Rehe. It is called in Chinese Wanshou Yuan, which signifies the paradise of innumerable trees. [...] Where any things particularly interesting were to be seen we disembarked [from the palanquins], from time to time, to visit them, and I dare say that in the course of our voyage we stopped at forty or fifty different palaces or pavilions. These are all furnished in the richest manner, with pictures of the Emperor's huntings and progresses; with stupendous vases of jasper and agate; with the finest

---

MACARTNEY'S ESCORT — Of these three officials only Zhengrui was a high official (and a Manchu). The other two, Wang Wenxiong and Qiao Renjie were local officials (military and civil respectively) assigned to accompany Macartney while traveling overland to their audience with the Emperor.

PALANQUIN — A chair for conveying one person. Often enclosed by a curtain, it is fastened to two horizontal poles projecting outward on either side and carried by two, four, or sometimes six men.

RUYI — A Chinese scepter made of jade, or other precious material, given as a sign of respect. Traditionally, it has a stylized head of a cloud and a long curved handle.

porcelain and japan, and with every kind of European toys and sing-songs; with spheres, orreries [model of the solar system], clocks, and musical automatons of such exquisite workmanship, and in such profusion, that our presents must shrink from the comparison and 'hide their diminished heads'. And yet I am told that the fine things we have seen are far exceeded by others of the same kind in the apartments of the ladies and in the European repository at Yuanming Yuan.

Thursday October 3 – [. . . .] It is now beyond a doubt, although nothing was said upon the subject, that the Court wishes us to be gone, and if we don't take the hints already given, they may possibly be imparted to us in a broader and coarser manner, which would be equally unpleasant to the dignity of the Embassy and the success of its objects.

That no time might be lost, or advantage taken, I have dispatched to the Minister the note which he desired me this morning to send to him. It consists of six principal articles extracted from my instructions, and compressed into as narrow a compass as possible.

The first is a request to allow the English merchants to trade to Zhoushan Island, Ningbo, and Tianjin. Second, to allow them to have a warehouse at Beijing for the sale of their goods, as the Russians had formerly. Third, to allow them some small, detached, unfortified island in the neighborhood of Zhoushan as a magazine for their unsold goods, and as a residence for their people to take care of them. Fourth, to allow them a similar privilege near Guangzhou, and some other trifling indulgences. Fifth, to abolish the transit duties between Macau and Guangzhou or at least to reduce them to the standard of 1782. Sixth, to prohibit the exaction of any duties from the English merchants, over and above those settled by the Emperor's diploma, a copy of which is required to be given to them (as they have never yet been able to see it) for their unequivocal direction.

Friday, October 4 – [**Father Amiot**] is of opinion that the Chinese consider embassies as mere temporary ceremonies, sent on particular occasion only, none of those from Europe having been of any considerable duration, and the last from Portugal, though very well received, of less than six weeks; that they have as yet no favorable ideas of treaties with distant powers, but that they might be rendered sensible of them if applied to and solicited without precipitation, and managed with caution and adroitness, for nothing was to be expected as attainable on the sudden.

[. . . .]

From living half a century in this country, possibly from well-grounded knowledge and experience, [Father Amiot] is become a very warm admirer of the Chinese nation, and has taken much pains, and in some instances, not without success, to remove several false ideas entertained in Europe of their character, customs, and policy. I have been but so short a time in the country, and he has been so long in it; I have seen so little of it, and he has seen so much; he is, besides, a man of such probity and universal charity that his opinion is entitled to considerable respect from me. Nevertheless, from the great deference and veneration which the Chinese have long paid to his acknowledged virtue and abilities, he may have insensibly contracted too great partiality for them, and may view their Government through a flattering medium. His apostolic zeal, too which is a predominant feature in his character, may tend to tender him sanguine.

1.9 QIANLONG'S EDICT TO KING GEORGE III OF ENGLAND (SEPTEMBER 23, 1793)

Many Western observers have taken Qianlong's response to the Macartney Embassy as evidence of a deluded and isolated empire intent on remaining closed to outsiders. It is more likely that the Qianlong emperor saw little benefit for his empire in granting Macartney his demands. Qianlong's judgment was guided primarily by China's desire to control and limit access to outsiders. The court had explicit (and functional) guidelines in place and the emperor saw little advantage in China in breaking with the practice of allowing British embassies permanent residence in Beijing. It is significant that the original letter was written in Manchu, Chinese and Latin but not English. The following English translation was made many years later.

FATHER MARIA AMIOT (1718–1793) – A Jesuit missionary born in France and sent to China in 1740, he quickly won the trust of the young Qianlong emperor and learned to speak Manchu and Chinese fluently.

Questions

1. **What reasons does the emperor give for rejecting Macartney's proposals?**
2. **Is the edict a rejection of any exchange with European countries or empires?**

We by the Grace of Heaven, Emperor, instruct the King of England to take note of our charge. Although your country, O King, lies in the far oceans, yet inclining your heart towards civilization you have specially sent an envoy respectfully to present a state message, and sailing the seas he has come to our Court to kotow and to present congratulations for the Imperial birthday, and also to present local products, thereby showing your sincerity.

We have perused the text of your state message and the wording expresses your earnestness. From it your sincere humility and obedience can clearly be seen. It is admirable and we fully approve. As regards the chief and assistant envoys who have brought the state message and tribute articles, we are mindful that they have been sent from afar across the sea, and we have extended our favor and courtesy to them, and have ordered our ministers to bring them to an Imperial audience. We have given them a banquet and have repeatedly bestowed gifts on them in order to show our kindness. Although the officers, servants and others, in charge of the ships more than six hundred in number, returned to Zhoushan and did not come to the capital, yet we have also bestowed gifts on them generally so that all should receive favors equally.

As to what you have requested in your message, O King, namely to be allowed to send one of your subjects to reside in the Celestial Empire to look after your country's trade, this does not conform to the Celestial Empire's ceremonial system, and definitely cannot be done. Hitherto, whenever men from the various Western Ocean countries have desired to come to the Celestial Empire and to enter the Imperial service we have allowed them to come to the capital. But once having come, they were obliged to adopt the costume of the Celestial Empire, they were confined within the Halls, and were never allowed to return home. These are the fixed regulations of the Celestial Empire, and presumably you also know them, O King. Now, however, you want to send one of your subjects to reside at the capital. But he could neither behave like a Western[er] … who comes to the capital to enter our service, remaining at the capital and not returning to his native country, nor could he be allowed to go in and out, and to have regular correspondence. So it would really serve no purpose.

Moreover, the territories ruled by the Celestial Empire are vast, and for all the envoys of vassal states coming to the capital there are definite regulations regarding the provision of quarters and supplies to them and regarding their movements. There never has been any precedent for allowing them to suit their own convenience. Now, if your country retains someone at the capital his speech will not be understood and his dress will be different in style, and we have nowhere to house him. If he is to resemble those Western Ocean men who come to the capital to enter the Imperial service we must order him, without exception, to change his dress to that of the Celestial Empire. However we have never wished to force on others what is difficult. Besides, if the Celestial Empire desired to send someone permanently to reside in your country surely you would not be able to agree to it? Furthermore, there are a great many Western Ocean countries altogether, and not merely your one country. If, like you, O King, they all beg to send someone to reside at the capital how could we grant their request in every case? It would be absolutely impossible for us to do so. How can we go as far as to change the regulations of the Celestial Empire, which are over a hundred years old, because of the request of one man—of You, O King?

'If it is said that your object, O King, is to take care of trade, men from your country have been trading at Macau for some time and have always been treated favorably. For instance, in the past Portugal and Italy and other countries have several times sent envoys to the Celestial Empire with requests to look after their trade and the Celestial Empire, bearing in mind their loyalty, treated them with great kindness. Whenever any matter concerning trade has arisen which affected those countries it has always been fully taken care of. When the Guangzhou merchant Wu Zhaoping owed money to foreign ships we ordered the Governor-General to advance the money out of the Treasury and to pay his debts for him at the public expense, and to have the debtor-merchant severely punished. Presumably your country has also heard about this. Why, then, do foreign countries need to send someone to remain at the capital? This is a request for which there is no precedent and it definitely cannot be granted. Moreover, the distance between Macau, the place where the trade is conducted, and the capital is nearly ten thousand *li*, and if he were to remain at the capital how could he look after it?

If it is said that because you look up with admiration to the Celestial Empire you desire him to study our culture, yet the Celestial Empire has its own codes of ritual which are different from your country's in each case. Even if the person from your country who remained here was able to learn them it would be of no use since your country has its own customs and regulations, and you would certainly not copy Chinese ones.

The Celestial Empire, ruling all within the four seas, simply concentrates on carrying out the affairs of Government properly, and does not value rare and precious things. Now you, O King, have presented various objects to the throne, and mindful of your loyalty in presenting offerings from afar, we have specially ordered the **Yamen** to receive them. In fact, the virtue and power of the celestial Dynasty has penetrated afar to the myriad kingdoms, which have come to render homage, and so all kinds of precious things from "over mountain and sea" have been collected here, things which your chief envoy and others have seen for themselves. Nevertheless we have never valued ingenious articles, nor do we have the slightest need of your country's manufactures. Therefore, O King, as regards your request to send someone to remain at the capital, while it is not in harmony with

the regulations of the Celestial Empire we also feel very much that it is of no advantage to your country. Hence we have issued these detailed instructions and have commanded your tribute envoys to return safely home. You, O King, should simply act in conformity with our wishes by strengthening your loyalty and swearing perpetual obedience so as to ensure that your country may share the blessings of peace.

Besides giving both the customary and extra gifts, as listed separately, to the chief and assistant envoys, and to the various officials under them as well as to the interpreters, soldiers and servants, now, because your envoy is returning home we have issued this special edict, and confer presents on you, O King, elaborate and valuable things all, in accordance with the usual etiquette. In addition, we have bestowed brocades, gauzes, and elaborate curios; all precious things. These are listed separately.

Let the King reverently receive them and know our kind regard for him.

'This is a special edict.'

[Qianlong promulgated September 23, 1793 and Latin translation delivered on October 3, 1793]

CASES OF JUSTICE AND TRANSGRESSION IN EIGHTEENTH-CENTURY QING

The reign of the Qianlong emperor officially lasted 60 years from 1735–1795, but he continued to exert considerable influence until his death in 1799. Many historians describe his reign as the Qing dynasty's golden era, but during the latter half of his reign corruption, fiscal deficits and internal uprisings began to plague the empire. One of the best known dimensions of this slow decline, is Qianlong's appointment of a young Manchu imperial guard, Heshen, to a series of high positions. Immediately after Qianlong's death, Chinese society was shocked when his son, the Jiaqing emperor, immediately pressed charges against Heshen (1.10). It was the contrast between Heshen's upright public image and his profligate private life that is sometimes said to serve as a fitting metaphor for Qianlong's reign. The tales spread about Heshen's immoral lifestyle reflect a common Chinese belief about retribution for one's actions that is also seen in the stories of Yuan Mei (1.11).

1.10   HESHEN'S TWENTY CRIMES (1799)

Although the Qianlong emperor is remembered in China today as one of the greatest emperors to ever rule China, the end of his reign was marred by considerable corruption and graft. A central figure in this era is **Heshen,** a courtier who came to Qianlong's

---

YAMEN—Yamen refers to the compound that houses the local administrative office of the magistrate, his judicial court and his official residence. It also less frequently refers to the magistrate himself.

HESHEN (1750–1799)—A high Manchu official and favorite of the Qianlong emperor later accused of numerous crimes, including corruption, extortion and the violation of imperial protocol, and he was sentenced to death.

attention in the 1760s (some say because Heshen reminded him of a former lover) and swiftly rose through the ranks eventually to serve as one of the most powerful ministers in the Qing court. Upon Qianlong's death, the Jiaqing emperor singled Heshen out as a deliberate statement against what many saw as the rising corruption. Heshen was swiftly arrested though he was allowed the "honor" to commit suicide by strangulation. While some suggest that he was not the most corrupt in the court, the favoritism displayed by the emperor towards him and the extent of his illegal earnings (estimated by the Jiaqing emperor to be larger than the state's annual income) made him an obvious and convenient target. His residence in central Beijing remains a popular tourist spot among Chinese sightseers today.

Questions

1. **How would you characterize the Jiaqing emperor's indictments against Heshen?**
2. **Do you find the accusations against Heshen worthy of a death sentence?**

1. On the third day of the ninth month in the sixtieth year of the Qianlong reign [October 15, 1795], the late emperor formally designated me as the crown prince. However, one day earlier on October 14th before the emperor had made the announcement public, Heshen leaked the information before me so as to curry favor with me. This was his first crime.

2. In February of last year, the Qianlong emperor summoned Heshen for an audience at the **Yuanming Yuan.** Heshen rode his horse through the left gate, passed the Hall of Justice and Honor up to the Hill of Longevity never bothering to dismount. His breech of etiquette displayed a deep disrespect to the late Emperor. This was his second crime.

3. Professing he could not walk due to a leg ailment, Heshen had himself carried in a sedan chair in and out of the Palace through the Shenwu Gate. Many witnessed his improper behavior, yet he showed no sense of concern. This was his third crime.

4. He shamelessly took courtesans released from their palace duties within the Forbidden City as his concubines. This was his fourth crime.

5. During the suppression campaigns against seditious rebels, the emperor conscientiously awaited the latest military reports from his field commanders. Heshen, however, willfully delayed presenting such reports and persistently distorted the information presented to the emperor needlessly extending the length of the military campaigns. This was his fifth crime.

6. When the late emperor's health declined and became seriously ill Heshen showed no signs of distress. In fact, after each visit he would laugh and talk with others as if nothing was wrong. This was his sixth crime.

7. Last winter, the emperor became quite weak due to his illness but still attempted to write comments on memorials, paintings and calligraphy as he had done in the past. Occasionally, when the emperor's abilities failed him, Heshen dared to suggest that it would be better to toss the emperor's comments out and let Heshen write up the remarks [without the emperor's knowledge]. This was his seventh crime.

8. The emperor ordered Heshen to head the Board of Personnel and Board of Punishment. Because of his experience with military supply budgets, Heshen was also ordered to oversee expenditures in the Board of Revenue. Instead, he interfered in the affairs of the entire Board of Revenue changing rules and regulations and then obstructed the other Board officials from intervening. This was his eighth crime.

9. At the end of last year, General Kuishu reported that over one thousand bandits ravaged the Qinghai districts of Shunhua and Guide killing two people and rustling cattle from merchants of the Dalai Lama. Heshen concealed the details of the case without taking any further action, simply dismissing the importance of border issues. This was his ninth crime.

10. After the death of the late emperor, I ordered that only Mongol princes who had previously

YUANMING YUAN—An immense garden with massive lakes, islands, and sprawling palaces begun in 1709 and expanded over several decades. The Jesuit priests serving in the Qing court helped design one section that had elaborate fountains and Baroque palaces. Sometimes referred to as the "Old Summer Palace."

had **smallpox** come to Beijing [so as not need-lessly endanger themselves to the disease while in Beijing]. Heshen disregarded my imperial order and instead excused all Mongol princes from coming to the capital to pay their last respects upon the death of the Qianlong emperor. With clearly evil intentions, he neglected the significant function that these visits played in pacifying the imperial borderlands. This was his tenth crime.

11. Although Grand Secretary Suling'a was elderly, weak and deaf in both ears, Heshen shielded his declining abilities from the emperor since he was related to Heshen's younger brother. At the same time, Heshen appointed Vice Ministers Wu Shenglan, Li Huang, and Imperial Councilor Li Guangyun to the level of minister and serve as Provincial Commissioners of Education simply because they had served as tutors for his children. This was his eleventh crime.

12. Among his numerous transgressions, Heshen appointed and dismissed personnel from the Grand Council according to his own whim and intentions. This was his twelfth crime.

13. Yesterday a search of Heshen's home revealed that his house was illegally built from cedar [reserved for the emperor's use], his Duobao Pavilion was constructed in the same style as the imperial Ningshou Palace, and that his garden was modeled on that of the imperial Summer Palace. What could have been the intention of luxuries that flaunt both imperial laws and customs! This was his thirteenth crime.

14. Heshen built a large tomb complete with inter-linking underground tunnels for his ancestors at Jizhou [Hebei]. Locals referred to it as the 'Imperial He Mausoleum.' This was his fourteenth crime

15. A search of Heshen's home found more than two hundred pearl bracelets, a number exceeding those of the imperial family. Some of the pearls were larger than even those on the imperial crowns. This is his fifteenth crime.

16. Heshen also possessed several dozen pieces of valuable jewelry containing numerous large diamonds of a perfect cut exceeding those owned by the imperial family. This was his sixteenth crime.

17. Silver, clothing and other valuables worth more than ten million *liang* were found in his home. This was his seventeenth crime.

18. Further investigation revealed twenty-six thousand *liang* of gold hidden in secret walls, six thousand *liang* of gold hidden in a covert cache, and over two million *liang* of silver buried in his storeroom. This was his eighteenth crime.

19. Heshen owned pawnshops and banks in Tongzhou and Jizhou valued at more than one hundred thousand *liang* of silver. In this unseemly manner, an official of the highest rank sought to vie with common people for profits. This was his nineteenth crime.

20. Heshen's servant, Liu Quan, was arrested having in his possession silver items, pearl bracelets, and large individual pearls worth more than two hundred *liang*. If Heshen had not tolerated and encouraged such misconduct, how could he become so wealthy? This was his twentieth crime.

1.11   TWO SHORT STORIES BY YUAN MEI (c.1788)

Yuan Mei (1716–1797) was one of China's most popular eighteenth-century authors. His tales (*chuanqi*) offer a rare glimpse into late imperial society. Yuan Mei's fiction illustrates, in ways that official documents often cannot, the role of officials, women, and gods in daily life. His stories also seek to show the false justice meted out by overly moralistic officials. Perhaps the most surprising elements are Yuan Mei's frank depiction of love and sex, as well as the commonly held belief that beings in the "after-life" and "this life" often interacted in meaningful (if often revengeful) ways.

SMALLPOX IN CHINA—Smallpox outbreaks remained quite common during the Qing. This was a particular concern to the Manchus, Mongols and Tibetans who had little natural exposure (and thus resistance) to the disease. As a result, the emperor often excluded those who had not had the disease from the requisite court appearance.

LIANG—A unit of weight generally said to be equal to one ounce and often referred to as a tael in western sources. However, it should be noted that there were local variations and the official weight fluctuated over the eighteenth, nineteenth, and twentieth centuries.

Questions

1. **What type of justice is displayed in these stories?**
2. **What role did women tend to play in these stories?**

Scholar Qiu

One summer's day a Nanchang scholar by the name of Qiu took a nap in the cool of the local earth god's temple. After returning home he became extremely ill. Qiu's wife decided that he must have offended the earth god, and she prepared offerings and burnt incense to placate the spirit. Surely enough, Qiu then regained his health.

His wife advised him to return to the temple to show his gratitude to the god. But Qiu was furious and instead filed a letter of complaint against the earth god, accusing him of using his powers to squeeze food and wine from the people. He sent this complaint to the city god by burning the letter. However, after ten days nothing had happened.

Qiu became even more furious and burned a second letter of complaint. This letter included an additional reference to the city god's own behavior, suggesting that by being lax with corrupt subordinates he was himself undeserving of any offerings.

That night he dreamed that a notice had been posted on the wall of the city god's temple. It read: "The local earth god is extorting food and drink from the people and has thereby abused his office. He is setting a bad example and as a consequence should lose his position. This man Qiu does not respect ghosts and spirits and pokes his nose into the affairs of others. He should be sent to Xinjian and be given twenty strokes."

After waking, Qiu remained convinced that the dream signified nothing. After all, he was a Nanchang resident, so even if he were to be punished, it would not be in Xinjian.

Not long after, there was a huge storm during which the earth god's temple was struck by lightning. Qiu became a bit worried and decided it would be safer to stay inside for a while. After a few weeks had passed without event he relaxed his guard.

One day, not long after this, the inspector of Jiangxi came to a nearby temple to pray. While praying he happened to be struck on the forehead by an axe. This event caused great consternation among the local officials, and they assembled at the scene to determine who should take responsibility. Scholar Qiu got wind of the spectacle and hurried over to watch.

One of the officials, the magistrate of Xinjian, thought Qiu's behavior rather odd. Suspecting him of being the culprit, he demanded that Qiu identify himself. Poor Qiu was terrified and could only stammer incoherently. From the clothing Qiu wore, the magistrate deduced that he was unlikely to be anyone of consequence, and in a fit of fury at Qiu's insolence he ordered that Qiu receive twenty strokes.

It was only after these strokes had been administered that Qiu regained his power of speech. "I am Scholar Qiu of the Qiu Sinong household," he said.

Hearing that his criminal was actually a scholar, the magistrate regretted his hasty verdict. To compensate Qiu for his suffering, the magistrate employed him as head teacher at Fengcheng.

Revenge of the Wronged Wife

In Hangzhou a coppersmith by the name of Xu Songnian opened a store in the wealthy suburb of Xianlin Bridge. When he was only thirty-two years old he suddenly became extremely ill. His sickness grew worse and worse and everyone fully expected him to die.

His wife cried and cried, saying, "We have two young sons. How will I manage if you die? I'm going to pray to the gods to exchange my life for yours.

"You would then be able to raise our sons to be good husbands and fathers themselves. The family line will thus continue without your having to remarry."

Xu agreed to her plan and so the wife went to the city god's temple to say her prayer. Then she returned home to pray to her husband's ancestors, so that they would be aware of the exchange she hoped would occur.

Surely enough, she grew sicker and sicker as her husband grew stronger and stronger. Within the year she had died. It wasn't long after her death that Songnian remarried, having forgotten his promise.

On their wedding night Songnian and his new wife, Mistress Cao, found themselves unable to consummate their union, a cold body lay on the bed between them. The bride leaped up in terror and in the light of the candle they saw lying on the bed the maid of Xu's former wife. Clearly possessed, her mouth moving mechanically, she heaped a torrent of abuse upon them.

The newlyweds slept like this for four or five months, having failed to placate the ghost with prayers and offerings. Xu Songnian died soon after this.

CHAPTER 2
THE OPIUM WAR

VISUAL SOURCE
Guangzhou Factories

GUANGZHOU (CANTON): The thirteen factories were located just outside the city walls of Guangzhou, the capital of Guangdong province. The older English designation for the city, "Canton" is likely a Portuguese corruption of the term Guangdong.

CHINESE HANG MERCHANTS: Each "factory" (hang) was run by a Chinese family. Westerners tended to identify each factory by the founding patriarch to which they added an honorific term (guan, or "qua" in Cantonese). These merchants were hardly minions of the state, rather some, like Wu Bingjian (Houqua) was reported to have a personal worth of more than $26,000,000 in the early 1830s.

LOCATION: Guangzhou's Thirteen Factories (gonghang) were located just south of the city walls. The factories functioned as the warehouse, administrative offices and residence all rolled into one. The term "factory" came from the fact that the European factors (or merchants) occupied the business premises. While the traders typically only occupied the buildings during winter months every year, after repeated seasons of usage each factory became associated with a particular nationality.

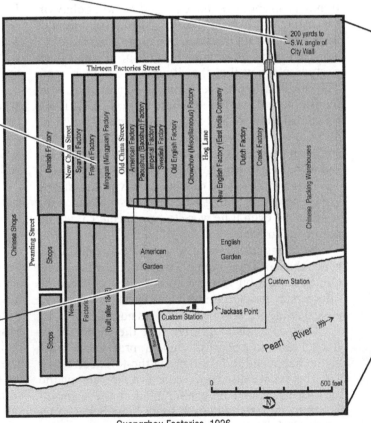

Guangzhou Factories, 1926.

Chinese map of the foreign ware houses at Guangzhou as viewed from the Pearl River

CHINESE TERMINOLOGY: From right to left, the Chinese labels along the top of the print are: Thirteen Foreign Guilds (*shisan yanghang*), Foreign warehouses (*yanghuo dian*), and the council hall (*yiguan*) where the Hang merchants would meet.

EUROPEAN FACADES: Aside from the neo-classical European facades, the factories differed little in layout or building materials from the surrounding Chinese buildings. The British East India Company's factory was constructed by the British East India Company after a fire in 1822. It was by far the most ornate and lavishly decorated of all the thirteen factories.

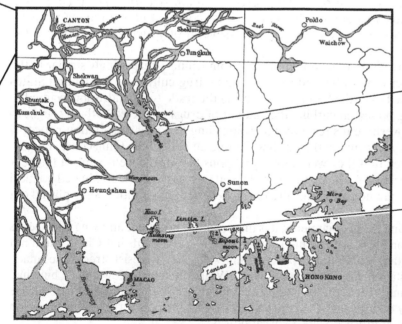

Pearl River Delta, 1926.

BOCA TIGRIS: The mouth of the Pearl River was traditionally referred to by the local Chinese as "Tiger's Mouth" (from the Chinese "Tiger Gate" [humen]). The Portuguese, translated the term literally into Portuguese as "Boca Tigris which was in turn shortened by the English corruption of the term, to "the Bogue". It was the site of several Chinese forts and the location where Lin Zexu chose to destroy the confiscated opium 1839 in two massive trenches filled with lime and seawater.

MACAU: A Portuguese enclave first leased from China in 1557. Macau remained a significant port of call for all European traders (and where many Europeans would stay when not in Guangzhou) until China ceded Hong Kong to Great Britain in 1847. Geographically, about one-sixth the size of Washington, D.C. Macau returned to Chinese control in 1999, and today earns more from gambling than even Las Vegas.

In June of 1997, prominent Chinese director Xie Jin premiered his film, *The Opium War,* in the Great Hall of the People in Beijing. Costing over $10 million dollars to make and employing more than 50,000 extras (3,000 of them Westerners), the film marked the latest Chinese motion picture to depict China's nineteenth-century confrontation with Great Britain. The opening night gala with Beijing's glitterati (and top political leaders) was timed to highlight Britain's actions in the Opium War just days before the return of **Hong Kong** from Great Britain to China.

The scope, scale and cost of Xie's *The Opium War* highlight just how potent a symbol the war remains in modern perceptions of China's past. In most mainstream Chinese history books published in China, the Opium War is cast as the demarcation between the pre-modern and modern eras. Chinese school children learn about arrogant Westerners and brave Chinese peasants from book-length comic books on the war that engender nationalistic feelings of humiliation at the hands of Western imperialism. As well, more than five books on the Opium Wars have been published in English in the last decade or so. The majority of these recent books were written for a popular, non-scholarly audience with an emphasis on telling (and re-telling) the story from the British perspective.

Despite this extended scrutiny of the war by both Chinese and Westerners, it is surprising how rarely a full picture of the opium debate is heard within either Western or Chinese societies. Only recently have scholars begun asking in earnest how Britain could possibly have justified peddling a highly addictive drug at gunpoint to China for well over a century. When one ponders the sheer volume of opium imported by the British to China—amounting to 5,610,000 pounds in 1839 alone—it boggles the mind.

The logic behind the opium trade, while not terribly complex, did reflect Western biases against the Chinese. A typical expression of this is given by John Crawfurd, a prominent British official, who characterized the Chinese as "a jealous and unsocial people" because they retain "their antipathy to strangers" thus failing "to perceive the benefits of a foreign commerce." (*Indian Archipelago,* 1820, p.169). Another motivation was making Britain's largest colony, India, a paying proposition. There were, however, voices of dissent—several of which are included in the documents below.

The debate surrounding the opium trade within China—surprisingly similar to the recent debates over how to best address a surging drug culture in the United States today—were divided over the best means to bring the trade to its end. Some wanted to focus the anti-drug policy on curbing the amount of drugs imported. Others sought to concentrate the government's resources on controlling the drug distribution networks and opium addicts. Adhering to their strong Confucian beliefs, the Qing court and government officials felt that they were morally responsible for the well-being of the people under their supervision. The opium problem and how to handle it dominated political discussions of the era and fueled the already heated factional politics being played out in the Qing court.

When examining these documents, it is important to note that allowing Europeans open access to China was not in China's best interest if it meant that China could not prevent the importation of opium. Nor was China's decision to resist "free trade" made without an understanding of the broader world. While the exact knowledge China had about Britain's control of India or about the Dutch and Spanish in Southeast Asia is unclear, it is fairly certain that the court understood Europe's territorial interests in Asia, and thus it treated Europeans very cautiously.

HONG KONG—An island south of Guangzhou, ceded to Great Britain in 1842 after the Opium War as part of the Treaty of Nanjing and returned to China in 1997.

TRADE IN EARLY NINETEENTH-CENTURY GUANGZHOU

Attitudes towards maritime exploration and expansion by Europeans and by the Chinese were dissimilar. While it is tempting to select one or the other as more "modern," it is risky to over-generalize the deeper meaning of Britain's ability to enforce its opium trade with China as being representative of Europe's superiority over Asia. A more constructive way to make sense of China's relations with Europe is to consider the different realities, needs, and ambitions shaping the actions of each empire.

By the mid-1700s, the majority of European maritime ventures were monopolies (such as the Dutch East India Company or the British East India Company), heavily underwritten by their respective governments. These companies were given exclusive rights to the trade within specific regions and for specific goods (and thus were far from being natural extensions of "free trade" as many Europeans would later suggest). Qing China had little interest in pursuing similar trading activities because of the colonial and military expenditures such ventures demanded. A significant reason for this difference is based on the simple fact that more than 90 percent of the "everyday luxuries" the European companies were pursuing in Asia (sugar, silk, and tea) were goods China markets could secure from domestic sources.

This is not to say that the Qing court was heedless of the fact that large numbers of Chinese living along the south China coast relied on overseas trade with Southeast Asia, Japan, and India. The court wished that external trade to continue, so long as it did not threaten China's security. Unlike Europe, when China's security was threatened by such trade there were few military, colonial, and mercantile interests able to contest a restriction of overseas activity. As a result, the Qing court could, and as the following documents illustrate, and would quickly restrict Chinese trade in ways that protected Chinese security, experiencing little or no effective opposition. The following documents relate the ways in which the Qing court's notions of security were inextricably tied to perceived or real threats to China's domestic, social and political stability.

2.1   DESCRIPTION OF EUROPEAN FACTORIES IN GUANGZHOU (1825–1844)

For the modern reader one of the most confusing aspects of the interaction of Westerners with Chinese in the late eighteenth and early nineteenth century is the vocabulary. Some words (like "chop-chop" from *kuai kuai* to mean "faster") are of indeterminate origin and were likely borrowed from Chinese or perhaps Cantonese, the dialect spoken by most of local population in the southern port city of Guangzhou. Other words were frequently borrowed from European languages. In the case of the factories at Guangzhou many of the terms have their origins from the Portuguese who had an extended and early contact with China from their enclave in Macau (south of Guangzhou). A useful example of this is the title "compradore" given to a native born agent in China. This term originated from the Portuguese *compra* ("to buy"). However, it is the term "factory" that most often confuses modern readers. A factory in this historical context referred to the warehouses and living quarters assigned to the foreign traders. The author of the following piece, William Hunter, arrived in China in 1824 and remained there through the Opium War.

Questions

1. **What is the function of the factory for foreign merchants?**
2. **What benefits does China gain by limiting foreigners to the factories?**

The word "Factory" was an importation from India, where the commercial establishments of the East India Company were so designated, and synonymous with "agency." It is well to explain this, as it is now being confounded with "manufactory."

The space occupied by the foreign community at Canton was about 300 feet from the banks of the Pearl River, eighty miles from Macau, sixty miles from Lingding [Island], forty miles from the Humen Forts, and ten miles from the **Huangpu** anchorage. In breadth from east to west it was about 1,000 feet. On it stood the Factories, which comprised the dwellings and places of business of each nation originally under one roof. The line of frontage was uniform, all looking due south. The distinction of *new* given to *one* of the two buildings occupied by the "**[East India] Company**" applied to that one which was rebuilt after the great fire of 1822, which destroyed all the others, with a few exceptions, as well as, according to official accounts, 12,000 Chinese houses, shops, and temples in the western suburb. Each Factory consisted of a succession of buildings, behind one another, separated by narrow spaces or courts, and running north. The front ones were numbered 1, those back of them, nearly all of three stories, No. 2, 3, and so on. The least numerous Factories were then in the American Hang, the greatest number were in the Danish and Dutch Hangs, which contained seven and eight respectively.

[. . . .]

The Factories were the individual property of the Hang merchants, and were hired of them. . . . . Entrance to the rear Factories was by arched passages running through those in front. The lower floors were occupied by counting-rooms, go-downs, and store-rooms, by the rooms of the **Compradore,** his assistants, servants and coolies, as well as by a massively built treasury of granite, with iron doors, an essential feature, there being no banks in existence. In front of each treasury was a well-paved open space, with table for scales and weights, the indispensable adjuncts of all money transactions, as receipts and payments were made by weight only, except in some peculiar case. The second floor was devoted to dining and sitting rooms, the third to bedrooms. As almost all were provided with broad verandahs and the buildings put up with care, they were quite comfortable, although in every respect devoid of ornamental work. In front of the middle Factories between Old China Street and Hog Lane ran a broad stone pavement, and this bordered an open space running down to the banks of the river, a distance of about three hundred feet. On the east side it was bounded by the wall of the East India Company's landing place and enclosure, and on the west by the wall in front of the landing and enclosure.

2.2 DEQING'S MEMORIAL ON THE RESPONSIBILITIES OF THE GONGHANG (MARCH 23, 1813)

In 1759, seeking to better control the increasing number of Western merchants initiating trade all along the coast of China, the Qing court mandated that Guangzhou would be the only port open for European (and American) traders. The government established a group of Chinese merchant families and empowered them to organize and act as the intermediaries between the foreign traders and Chinese merchants. Each family acted as a separate "company" within the larger guild. This merchant guild, or *gonghang,* was the venue for Western merchants to legally carry out trade with China. The merchant guild was in fact divided into two, the Yanghang which dealt primarily with

HUANGPU (WHAMPOA)—A deep water anchorage 12 miles downstream from Guangzhou serving as the primary port for sailing vessels involved in the China trade during the nineteenth century.

BRITISH EAST INDIA COMPANY—Founded in 1600, the East India Company was granted a monopoly on all British trade from western India to eastern China. The company lost its exclusive monopoly on Asian trade in 1813 and was dissolved in 1874.

COMPRADORE—The top Chinese agent serving in the factories in Guangzhou. The term was also used to apply to Chinese representatives on foreign sailing vessels.

GONGHANG (COHONG)—A merchant guild authorized in 1720 by the central government as the only organization through which western merchants were allowed to trade with China and designated to collect duties on Western trade. It was abolished by the Treaty of Nanjing in 1842.

Westerners and another branch which was responsible for trade with Southeast Asia. The gonghang merchants were overseen by a superintendent of maritime customs and duties (appointed by the **Board of Revenue**). The various financial exigencies required to succeed as a Yanghang merchant (enormous amounts of capital, good political ties and good business sense) made the appointment as one of the official thirteen merchants a dicey commercial venture. Throughout its history the efficacy of the entire merchant guild (gonghang) system described below was of key concern to the court and its officials.

Questions

1. **What concerns prompted Deqing to restructure the guild merchant system?**
2. **Deqing suggests that it is "better not to focus our energies on replacing merchants but instead to focus on bad practices early in order to prevent deeper problems later on." Do you think the emperor would agree?**

Report by Superintendent of Yue (Guangdong) Customs on Investigation of Custom Affairs and Request to Establish Gonghang General Office, Jiaqing 18th year, 2nd month, 21st day [March 23, 1813]

I, Deqing, deferentially submit my investigation on custom affairs, and request your guidance. Foreign traders coming by ship [to China] rely on the Yanghang guild merchants to supervise and assist their commercial dealings. Through these semi-officially recognized merchants, the foreign traders can successfully carry out trade and at the same time are exposed to a more civilized culture than their own barbarian culture. Since I was granted this position, I have followed the imperial regulations at all times and encountered no matters needing investigation. Only when I reviewed old files, did I discover that legal cases involving unpaid debt to foreigners were transferred to the offices of the Governor and Governor-General. The indebted merchant's assets would be confiscated to pay off the balance. If their assets were insufficient, the merchant who then took control of that business would be ordered to pay off the difference. If the company attracted no buyers, all the other guild-merchants would have to make

contributions to pay off the debt. If none of these measures cleared the debt owed to the foreigners, then [the superintendent] would meet with the governor-general and governor to submit a special memorial asking for severe punishment. This has been the procedure in the past.

[. . . .]

Humbly I propose to you my thoughts on this matter. The Yanghang merchants oversee an exchange of foreign goods that often exceeds hundreds of thousands **taels** (of silver). As a result they must pay tens of thousands of taels in duties. In reality, only but the most wealthy and reliable merchants have the financial means to bear such a financial burden. Yet, to become a Yanghang merchant is relatively easy, only needing to have one or two senior merchants pledge on one's behalf, and no further details are given to the Board. Such a procedure is simply not adequate. Every time a merchant fails, the other Yanghang merchants also suffer. In addition, when foreign ships arrive at port, deceitful Yanghang merchants secretly sell their goods too cheaply to the foreigners while buying the foreign goods at too high a price. These immoral

HUBU (HOPPO)—Nineteenth-century Western accounts of trade in Guangzhou refer to any customs officer (and sometimes the Superintendent of Maritime Customs) as the "hoppo." The term is a corruption of the Chinese designation for the Board of Revenue (hubu) to which all revenue from maritime customs was remitted.

TAEL—Technically, a Chinese ounce of silver, but in reality there were numerous different forms of taels, of unequal values. In international treaties the most commonly used tael was the "customs tael" (haiguan tael) equivalent to 37.68 grams of silver. The other commonly used tael was the "kuping tael" or "treasury tael" equivalent to 37 grams.

merchants simply want to buy the lion's share of foreign goods so as to corner the trade in foreign goods. Those who adopt this strategy rarely take into consideration the mounting debts they incur as a result. In the end, unable to pay off their debt and with taxes mounting they go bankrupt. All of this happens, simply because their actions are not regulated. Unhealthy practices proliferated when other merchants had to follow the other's example to obtain more [foreign] goods.

[. . . .]

Now, with regards to how to straighten out foreign trade, it is necessary to alter the procedures while clarifying the responsibilities of the merchants. We have to find one or two wealthy and morally upright local merchants in each guild, order them to take charge of the Yanghang merchants and to represent the guild's interests in negotiations with foreign merchants. They must not arbitrarily raise or lower prices, rather they ought to adhere to the going market price, conduct trade with fairness. If anyone secretly disobeys these rules, the head merchants must report them for prosecution.

I frequently encourage the merchants to live simple instead of lavish lives, to protect their reputation, and to eliminate evil customs. Only in this way will the merchant guilds become robust. In the future, when a new merchant is to be selected, the Head Yanghang merchant should notify all the wealthy and honest Yanghang merchants who should in turn jointly recommend a qualified candidate. Such pledge will be reported to and registered at the Board [of Revenue]. If the recommendation is deliberately false and they fall into debt, the debt will be the responsibility of those who recommended him. Similarly, when merchants retire from business for various reasons, a report must be sent to the Board of Revenue immediately to terminate their membership of the guild. At the end of each year, the list of registered Yanghang merchants will be reported to the Board of Revenue.

Should such a regulation be approved and incorporated, trade will improve quickly and the likelihood of employing unsuitable merchants into the Yanghang guild can be diminished and foreign trade will be improved.

Your slave's foolish proposal may be completely inappropriate; it is merely stating the situation. With my forehead on the floor, [I] report this memorial, to Your Majesty, for his judgment.

2.3 RULES REGULATING FOREIGN TRADING IN GUANGZHOU (1832–1835)

Concerned about Westerners attempting to settle permanently in China, foreigners in Guangzhou were obliged to adhere to a list of eight rules that defined where they went, what guests they could bring, even how many servants they could have. The list of regulations was first handed down in 1760 by the Qianlong emperor, revised by his son the Jiaqing emperor in 1810, and confirmed again by edict in 1819. These rules were not idle threats. In 1829, one Yanghang served as guarantor for a boat that clandestinely brought the wife of a powerful British merchant to the factories. When the governor-general learned of this transgression, the head merchant was sent to prison and the guild fined so severely that it was sent to the brink of bankruptcy.

Questions

1. **Why would the Qing emperor be concerned with regulating the lives of the European traders and sailors?**
2. **Do the rules appear intent on keeping the foreign merchants away from local Chinese or the reverse?**

Regulation 1   All vessels of war are prohibited from entering the **Humen.** Vessels of war acting as convoy to merchantmen must anchor outside at sea till their merchant-ships are ready to depart, and then sail away with them.

Regulation 2   Neither women, guns, spears, nor arms of any kind can be brought to the Factories.

Regulation 3   All river-pilots and ships' Compradores must be registered at the office of the assistant magistrate at Macau. That officer will also furnish each one of them with a license, or badge, which must be worn around the waist. He must produce it whenever called for. All other boatmen and people must not have communication with foreigners, unless under the immediate control of the ships' Compradores; and should smuggling take place, the Compradore of the ship engaged in it will be punished.

Regulation 4   Each Factory is restricted for its service to eight Chinese (irrespective of the number of its occupants), say two porters, four water-carriers, one person to take care of goods, and one shop merchant who originally performed all the duties of the 'House Compradore,' as he is styled today.

Regulation 5   Foreigners are prohibited from rowing about the river in their own boats for pleasure. On the 8th, 18th, and 28th days of the lunar month 'they may take the air,' as fixed by the government in the 21st year of Jiaqing (1819). All ships' boats passing the Custom-houses on the river must be detained and examined, to guard against guns, swords or firearms being furtively carried in them. On the 8th, 18th and 28th days of the lunar month these foreigners may visit the Flower Gardens and Buddhist Temple on Henan Island, but not in groups of over ten at a time. When they are 'refreshed' they must return to the Factories, not be allowed to pass the night 'out,' or collect together to carouse. Should they do so, then, when the next 'holiday' comes, they shall not be permitted to go. If they should presume to enter villages, public places, or bazaars, punishment will be inflicted upon the linguist who accompanies them.

Regulation 6   Foreigners are not allowed to present petitions [to the emperor]. If they have anything to represent, it must be done through the Hang merchants.

Regulation 7   Hang merchants are not to owe debts to foreigners. Smuggling goods to and from the city is prohibited.

Regulation 8   Foreign ships arriving with merchandise must not loiter about outside the river; they must come directly to Huangpu]. They must not rove about the bays at pleasure and sell to rascally natives goods subject to duty, that these may smuggle them, and thereby defraud His Celestial Majesty's revenue.

OPIUM IN EARLY NINETEENTH-CENTURY GUANGZHOU

Given the attention lavished on this historical period, it is perhaps surprising to learn that for the first several decades of intensive British and Chinese contact, both empires' relationship revolved around tea, not opium. To the Qing court this seemed perfectly natural. Tea was of central concern in the court's management of both maritime and overland trade. But with the emergence of Britain's massive demand for tea in the

---

HUMEN—The mouth of the Pearl River, known in Chinese as "Humen" or literally "Tiger's Gate." Early European sailors labeled it "Bocca Tigris" or "Mouth of the Tiger" which was later called the "Bogue" by British sailors.

late 1700s—from 6.8 million pounds per year in the 1770s to 19.7 million pounds in the 1790s—the relationship between the two empires changed dramatically. The steady growth of the tea trade caused the Chinese to redouble their efforts to regulate the maritime trade. In Great Britain, the British mania for tea, and the imbalance in trade that resulted, precipitated a frantic search for a corresponding habit for the Chinese.

Opium, while not unknown within China prior to the eighteenth century, had been used primarily as a quasi-medicinal product often mixed with tobacco and eaten rather than smoked. In the early eighteenth century, this began to change. The British discovery of new methods for refining opium greatly heightened its addictiveness while facilitating its transportability. As the documents below indicate, by the 1830s tea was no longer the primary concern of either government. Great Britain had become addicted to the profits gained by the opium trade to such an extent that at least one scholar has suggested that Britain's global supremacy in the nineteenth century was directly tied to its ability to continue selling opium to China. For the Qing government, however, the opium problem became, as the usage and cultivation spread to many parts of the China, a problem affecting the entire empire.

2.4 OPIUM AND TEA TRADE WITH CHINA

In 1668, the British East India Company ordered one hundred pounds of "goode tey" to be sent to Great Britain. By 1793, imports had risen roughly 40,000 percent. The burgeoning trade deficit forced the British government to seek a product they could sell to China. Although the British were producing numerous textiles and woolen goods, such products did not fit the needs or desires of the Chinese market. In the early 1700s, the British East India Company began exporting small amounts of opium from India. By 1839, enough Indian opium entered China to supply ten million addicts, and more importantly, enough silver flowed out to turn the trade deficit back to Britain's favor. As the charts below indicate, the opium trade only soared *after* the Opium War and played no small part in allowing Britain to maintain its position as a global powerhouse.

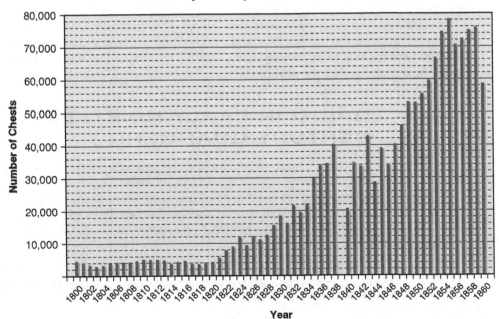

British Opium Imported to China (1800–1860)

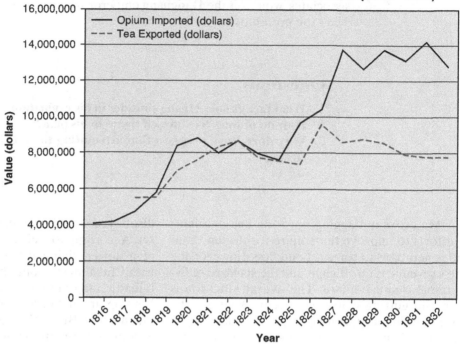

**Comparison between British Opium Imported to China
and Tea Exported from China to Britain (1816–1833)**

--- Opium Imported (dollars)
--- Tea Exported (dollars)

Value (dollars)

Year

Questions

1. Does Chart 1 support the claim made by many of Great Britain's officials, politicians, and merchants that if China had granted Britain the free trade they demanded, they could have avoided the forced importation of opium?
2. Supply and demand are only part of the equation in the opium trade. What other factors influenced the rising trade of opium into China?

2.5   HUANG JUEZI ON THE EVIL OF OPIUM (JUNE 2, 1838)

By the early nineteenth century, the Qing financial affairs were in dire straits. After a century of budget surpluses, internal spending had risen precipitously and the outflow of silver to pay for the importation of opium rocketed upward. As is often the case in economic recessions, while the immediate cause of inflation is relatively clear, discovering a solution to reverse such a trend is far less simple. In addition, Qing officials felt morally obliged to improve the situation for the common people. Qing officials tended to gravitate towards two basic positions. The first group advocated legalization to produce revenue and avoid war with Great Britain. The second group, headed by

Minister of Rites, **Huang Juezi,** advocated prohibition of opium and capital punishment for all opium users. The memorial below, written by Huang Juezi and other unnamed associates, won over the **Daoguang** emperor who within days appointed Lin Zexu to head the prohibition efforts in Guangzhou.

Questions

1. **What factors does Huang consider in his evaluation of the opium problem? How do officials like himself figure in his plan?**
2. **Why does Huang suggest that attempting to curb foreign trade is a bad strategy?**

Your Majesty's unflagging devotion and unrelenting efforts to improve the empire for the ten thousand generations to come is boundless. However, the state's revenue is insufficient and the standard of living remains substandard. The overall situation is bleak and getting worse each year. What are the causes? During the Qianlong reign, the empire's revenue more than covered the massive financial outlay on border defense, imperial inspection tours, and construction projects. That era can surely be considered one of the most wealthy and prosperous. Even during the Jiaqing period [1796–1819], the economy was healthy enough that gentry families and wealthy merchants still enjoyed a luxurious lifestyle—a lifestyle quite distant from which they lead today. It seems that they believed the wealthy could become wealthier by spending more even as the poor become poorer by being thrifty! Your humble servant noticed that recently the price of silver has steadily increased. A single *liang* of silver is now more than 1600 copper coins. This rise in the cost of silver is not a result of domestic consumption. Rather, it is primarily a result of the steady outflow of silver to foreign barbarians.

Since opium first began to arrive in China, the Jiaqing emperor understood the harm it could cause China and expressly forbid it. However, officials at that time did not fully realize the detrimental impact of opium on the empire. If they had, strict laws with severe consequences for those who

disobeyed would have been enacted from the outset. According to well-established regulations, foreign ships arriving at Guangdong wishing to trade with China must obtain the proper permit from the [Head] Hang merchant. He must guarantee there is no opium on board before they enter the port of Guangzhou. But such regulations are often treated as a mere formality with foreign ships continuing to import opium. As a result, by 1823, the annual outflow of silver exceeded several millions *liang*. At the beginning, opium consumption was limited to the wealthy and noble families who smoked it simply as part of their immoderate but lavish lifestyle still displaying a degree of self-control. Later, people of all backgrounds, including government officials, gentry, merchants, servants, women, Buddhist monks and nuns, Daoist priests, took up the opium habit and smoking opium publicly and purchased smoking equipment. Recently the opium smoking fad has reached even Beijing, the political center of the empire!

[....]

By now everybody has begun to recognize a central cause of the empire's economic downturn is the outflow of silver caused by the demand for opium. Different people have put forward a wide array of solutions for this problem. Some people suggest a system of strict inspections at the port-of-entry as a dual deterrent: to stop both the influx of opium and the outflow of silver. On the surface this makes sense,

HUANG JUEZI (1793–1853)—A powerful Qing official and leader of a prohibition faction that promoted the outlawing of opium enforced by harsh penalties instead of the legalization sought by other officials.

DAOGUANG (1782–1850)—Sixth emperor of the Qing dynasty, ruling from 1821 to 1850 during a period of tremendous internal turmoil and external threats to the empire.

however, who will guarantee that every inspector is honest? Annual trade today has reached a level that exceeds several tens of millions *liang*. Even a modest cut in trade would result in a reduction of several millions *liang* of silver. With such huge potential profits, which inspector would seriously implement the regulations? Even if occasionally a few smugglers could be detained, [China's] coastline is over ten thousand *li* long, which would allow smugglers an almost endless number of harbors to enter or leave, easily evading any efforts to deter them. That's the first reason of why the outflow of silver cannot be stopped.

Some people have suggested we should attack the source of the problem by simply eliminating all foreign trade. This too seems to make sense on the surface, but individuals who suggest this overlook the fact that the legitimate portion of foreign trade consists primarily of woolens, clocks and watches in exchange for tea, rhubarb, and silk and accounts for no more than ten million *liang* with a profit for those involved of only several million *liang*. Thus, lawful trading contributes only 2 to 3 percent of the profit made from the opium trade. Even if we set aside the tariff revenues collected by Guangzhou's maritime customs by banning foreign trade, opium ships could instead choose to anchor off the coasts while the price and demand for opium would undoubtedly rise. As demand from the inland opium smokers increases, miscreants will realize the profits to be made and will willingly engage in smuggling. Thus the second reason for stemming the outflow of silver is that it is harder to control deceitful opium smokers than foreigners.

Some people suggest harsh action against dealers through the enforcement of strict prohibition of opium dens. Though such steps would not cure the root of the problem, it could reduce its traffic. Those who propose such an idea seem to be unaware that rules and regulations already exist. Convicted opium dealers can be punished with exile to the distant border frontiers. If it can be proved that the

opium den owners coaxed innocent young people to smoke, the penalty is death by hanging. Yet while both the numbers of opium dealers and dens are countless, very few officials are able to handle the cases. The major Guangdong opium dealers have established extensive networks with contacts in every province along their supply routes guaranteeing safe delivery anywhere they wish. Officers responsible for land and water passes tolerate and assist the smugglers' trafficking. Instead, under the guise of carrying out opium inspections, officials often harass lawful merchants forcing them to pay bribes. [....] This is the third reason that outflow of silver cannot be stopped.

Some suggest stopping the ban on opium and legalizing domestic production so that local opium would curb the need of foreign import. Gradually, the outflow of silver would be controlled. They are unaware of the fact that domestic opium is not strong enough for domestic addicts. Smugglers only use it to mix with foreign opium to raise their profits. Therefore, legalizing domestic opium will not stop the outflow of silver. This is the fourth reason.

[....]

If foreign barbarians can resist and prohibit the use of opium through legal statutes, Your Majesty's authority can certainly allow us to do the same. ... When the imperial edict is first issued, it has to be strict. Only when the imperial edict is strict, will the officials implement it seriously; only when the officials are serious will the people not violate the law. Within a year of the law being enacted 80 or 90 percent of the smokers will end their addiction before any penalty is imposed upon them. In this way the law, will not only cause smokers to end their addiction and live out the rest of their lives in peace, but since nonsmokers will never be enticed to take up the habit they will live healthy normal lives. Exercising your Majesty's supreme power in this way is virtuous. I beg for your edict to order governor-generals and governors of all provinces to publicize the regulations and proscription on smoking opium.

2.6 THE OPIUM QUESTION AMONG WESTERNERS IN CHINA (1836–1837)

In 1836 *The Chinese Repository*—one of the most influential and widely circulated English-language periodicals on China—published an anti-Opium pamphlet with a preface written by Thomas Dealtry. Dealtry served as the Anglican Archdeacon of Calcutta, India and chaplain to the East India Company. The pamphlet (only the conclusion is included below) posed two basic questions: 1) Is a healthy person justified in using opium? 2) How far can such a person, if not justified in using it himself, be justified in encouraging its use by others? The document below offers a small indication of the broad range of opinions the article elicited among its European readers.

Questions

1. **From the perspectives given below was the opium trade a moral or economic activity?**
2. **How would you counter the arguments raised by "a Reader"?**

Conclusion of a Pamphlet Entitled "Remarks on the Opium Trade with China" (c. 1836)

I leave the question here. I wish I could utter one warning whisper that could be attended to. I wish that ministers of the gospel especially those at the seat of government, would work the problem out for themselves, and having brought it to a point, would step forward with the boldness that becomes them, and drag down this hideous national sin from the place where she sits in state; expose her more than **Duessa**-like foulness and deformity and warn all, high and low, of the guilt that attaches to every individual who knows the law, "as he hath opportunity to do good unto all men," and yet directly disobeys that command by countenancing a trade which has been more instrumental in killing souls and bodies than any curse ever inflicted on a people. [....] Our sin in growing, and encouraging the trade in opium is, indeed, one of the darkest that ever invoked the wrath of the most high God upon a people. Where are the preachers of the gospel, where is the spirit of the common humanity fled, that this sin should till this moment exist unrebuked? Oh what a wail of misery would awaken your remorse and compassion, could the dying agonies of one poor opium-victim reach your soul! Think then of THE MILLIONS who have already thus perished, and then ask yourself how long is this to continue and no man in a Christian land regard it? How long is a British government to be seen drawing revenue from this source, admitting the misery, and excusing itself for abetting, by a fallacy the most contemptible and insulting even to common sense? How long is a whole community of British merchants to be content with earning the price of blood, because if they do not, others will in their stead?

A Letter to the Editor of the Chinese Repository in Response to Archdeacon Dealtry

Sir,

An article appeared in your last number condemnatory of those engaged in the culture of opium, and of those supplying the Chinese with this luxury. The attack of archdeacon Dealtry on the produce of India which provides the government (perhaps in the least oppressive way to the subject) with means to pay his, and such like salaries as his, is beyond doubt, not a selfish argument. How far it is expedient, or necessary, for morals to put down opium will be the subject of this letter. The attack might have come at a fitter moment than when the emperor of China was fulminating his edicts on this subject against individuals, and to which his celestial majesty and his viceroys have been pleased to shut their eyes for the last twenty years as entirely on this side of Asia, as the Church of England has on the other side of Asia: still, if it is true that opium is solely a hateful poison, and those who deal in it are poisoners, truth will prevail, and it will be put down.

DUESSA—A character in Edmund Spenser's sixteenth-century poem *Faerie Queene* who appears beautiful but whose evil intentions lead upright individuals astray.

If on the other hand—and this is the opinion here argued for—opium is a useful soother, a harmless luxury, and a precious medicine, except to those who abuse it, then opium will increase and its merchants be freed from an unjust prejudice, and truth prevail! ...

The archdeacon in his crusade against opium, forgets a principle, which, however lost sight of by him, has been acknowledged and acted on by the two most civilized governments of Europe—France and England; and it is this, that in administration of any article likely to stimulate the passions to crime, the dealers in it should be kept not only as much as possible respectable, but even under the power of the police by license: so in France, as to gaming houses: so in England, as to wine houses and gin palaces: yet seeing this clear before him, the archdeacon without the shadow of a chance of stopping the trade in opium whether he is wrong or right in his tirade against it, is for holding the present dealers in it, up to odium and infamy; thus throwing its supply into hands of desperadoes, pirates, and marauders, instead of a body of capitalists, not participating certainly in what they carry, but in fact supplying an important branch of the Indian revenue safely and peaceably.

I leave the matter to the judgment of your distant readers, and I do so confidently. Were the appeal to be made to those here, as many participate in the profits, it might be considered a partial one. The safe test of experience has show that sovereigns and moralists are powerless against a pervading taste of a whole people. The proclamations of Elizabeth of England did not put down hops. The blast and counter blasts, are only to be found in the library of the curious collector of books, but tobacco is cultivated and used all the world more extensively than any other luxury. Muhammad by prohibiting wine only forced drunkards to use *rakee,* and opium: he was powerless to stop intoxication. What Temperance Societies may yet accomplish remains to be seen.

Very Faithfully,

A Reader

Canton 10th December 1836

A Letter to the Editor of the Chinese Repository in Response to "A Reader"

Sir,

Being a well-wisher to all free discussion, and convinced that a patient hearing of both sides of a cause is the best way to arrive at a fair conclusion, I have been glad to see that you have commenced a discussion as to the merits of the opium trade.... I have looked in vain throughout the letter of your Correspondent, "A Reader," for any more cogent argument than that of the hired bravo, "I do not see that I am doing any harm: if I did take the profit, some one else, not so thin skinned, would"—which may be broadly pronounced the most mischievous, false and dangerous principle to morality that has ever been invented....

Suppose, by any chance, that Chinese junks were to import into England, as a foreign and fashionable luxury, so harmless a thing as arsenic, or corrosive sublimate—that, after a few years, it became a rage—that thousands—that hundreds of thousands used it—and that its use was, in consequence of its bad effects, prohibited. Suppose that, in opposition to the prohibition, junks were stationed in the St. George's channel, with a constant supply, taking occasional trips to the Isle of Wight, and the mouth of the Thames, when the governmental officials were sufficiently attentive to their duty, at the former station, to prevent its introduction there. Suppose the consumption to increase annually, and to arouse the attention of government, and of those sound thinking men who foresaw misery and destruction from the rapid spread of an insidious, unprofitable and dangerous habit....

If the purveyors of opium said nothing, or did they only defend the practice on the ground that it gave a profit, which they coveted, not much need be said; but sophistication is a bad substitute for truth. The trade may be a profitable one—it may be of importance to the Indian government, and to individuals—but to attempt a defense on the ground of its not having a dangerous and pernicious influence on health and morals, is to say what cannot be borne out, by fact or argument; and what I, who reason on the subject, cannot but feel to be an important attempt to defend what is, in itself, manifestly indispensable.

I am, sir, your humble servant,

Another Reader

RAKEE (RAKI)—An anise or licorice flavored liquor prevalent in the eastern Mediterranean.

COMMISSIONER LIN ZEXU AND THE OPIUM WAR

Virtually every historical overview of nineteenth-century China mentions one man: **Lin Zexu.** Following the emperor's decision to implement Huang Juezi's recommendations, few officials were surprised by Lin's appointment as special commissioner to Guangzhou. Many westerners, however, were caught flat-footed. While they had been following the debates closely, they had wrongly speculated that the legalize opium faction was ascendant. In anticipation, the European traders had been building up stockpiles of opium in the Guangzhou factories. Thus, the merchants were doubly shocked when Lin Zexu, upon his arrival in Guangzhou, demanded their entire stock of opium be surrendered to Chinese authorities.

When reading the following documents, pay particular attention to the different ways in which the Chinese and British viewed their actions. The Chinese tended to limit the scope of their actions specifically to the opium trade while the British preferred to speak of defending their commercial and diplomatic rights by "opening China" to "international" trade guidelines. In an age when **Adam Smith's** economic policies prevailed, many British felt their economic superiority simply reflected a "natural" economic outcome. Of course, Adam Smith's economic policies did not factor in Britain's tendency to intervene with their not so invisible military when commercially advantageous.

2.7 EDICT FROM IMPERIAL COMMISSIONER LIN ZEXU TO THE FOREIGNERS (MARCH 18, 1839)

Lin Zexu's pronouncement to the foreign merchants trading in Guangzhou is traditional in tone and form. While it may seem at times patronizing, Chinese officials (and the emperor) sought to give all non-Chinese the benefit of the doubt regarding any transgressions of etiquette, customs, or laws. Equally characteristic was the fact that Lin publicly posted and delivered the edict to the offending parties. Lin's confidence that the top merchants would assist him in enforcing the laws is also quite typical (if misplaced). All of these actions reflect Lin's efforts to appear outwardly magnanimous and merciful. In other words, his edict to the foreigners demonstrates Lin's decision to employ tried-and-true Chinese methods in his initial step to stem the flow of opium. Initially, Lin Zexu's measures appeared successful when the British merchants reluctantly handed over their stocks of opium. Lin scored a second publicity coup when he publicly destroyed these stocks by placing them in two massive trenches that were then filled with lime and seawater.

LIN ZEXU (1785–1850) — A scholar-official who passed the highest (jinshi) civil exam at age 26, he was a favorite of the young Daoguang emperor (r. 1821–1850) and a member of Huang Juezi's "prohibition faction." In 1838 he headed the empire's anti-opium efforts, until he was banished to Xinjiang after failing to resolve China's confrontation with Britain.

ADAM SMITH (1723–1790) — A prominent eighteenth-century moral philosopher and political economist who published the influential book *An Inquiry into the Nature and Causes of the Wealth of Nations* in 1776. His written works promoted the idea that a free market and an "invisible hand" of supply and demand naturally shape market forces.

Questions

1. **Do you think that Lin Zexu displays a clear understanding of international relations and the regulations that govern such relationships?**
2. **How would you characterize Lin's approach? Do you find his demands reasonable?**

Edict to notify all foreigners:

Foreign ships that have come to Guangdong for trade have profited heavily. No matter what merchandise was imported, it all sold. No matter what merchandise was desired, it was procured. For this reason, the number of ships arriving annually has steadily increased from several dozen ships initially to several hundred of ships today. Our Great Emperor treats everyone equally, permitting all to trade and make a profit. If we were to close the port, how would that benefit your countries? How can you do without items such as tea and rhubarb which are necessities for foreigners' livelihood. Allowing you to trade them every year without tight control is a grace upon you. To show your gratitude you should respect our laws.

You should not harm others simply to benefit yourself. How come in your own country, smoking opium is forbidden, but you bring it to China, imposing it on people for money and harming their lives. You have seduced Chinese people with opium for several tens of years, making a shameful profit. Such behavior has caused common resentment, and cannot be tolerated by justice. Previously, the Imperial Kingdom's regulations have been generous and not overly strict but many ports had leaks [to allow smuggling]. Having learned about these transgressions, the Great Emperor is angered and determined to eliminate [opium] once and for all. All Chinese who sell or operate a smoking den are to be judged, sentenced to death, and immediately executed while smokers are also sentenced to death. Coming to our Imperial Kingdom, you ought to abide by our laws in the same manner as the local people do. I, the specially appointed commissioner, am from the coast of Fujian and familiar with all the tricks employed by foreigners. Therefore I have been repeatedly credited for the successful handling of frontier issues and was appointed by the Great Emperor to investigate the matters. If we were to prosecute the crimes [of smuggling opium]

committed by foreigners, it would be hard to avoid punishment. In the past, [we] would have take into consideration that you came from afar and were unaware of the strict restrictions. But now we have sought to clarify the laws and regulations so that there is no confusion. We do not wish to harm you without proper warning.

[. . . .]

Now I publicly declare the following edict and all foreign merchants should, upon receiving the edict, abide by its instructions without delay and to surrender to the imperial officials all the opium on your ships. The Hang merchants are responsible for inventorying how many cases are confiscated, examined, registered and destroyed. Eliminate the harmful substance with absolutely no exception. In the intervening time, an agreement declaring that [foreign] ships will never carry any opium again will be written up in both Chinese and Western languages. If anyone is found to be importing opium, their merchandise will be confiscated and the guilty individuals executed.

[. . . .]

If you continue to pursue the wrong course—continuously indulging in smuggling; having sailors smuggle it in, falsely claiming it is not yours; pretending to take [opium] back to your own country to be destroyed in sea [but actually smuggling it]; seeking opportunities to sell in other provinces; or try to play for time by turning in only 10–20 percent of your opium—all such behavior will be considered a deliberate violation and no leniency shown. Even though our empire has been kind to people from afar, but we cannot allow you to continue to flaunt our laws. New regulations must be implemented so as to punish the guilty.

I went to the capital myself in order to receive the imperial edict. As the imperial commissioner I bear the responsibility of coastal affairs and I will fully investigate this matter. I will not depart until the day the opium problem is fully resolved. I swear I will pursue it to the end and not accept half measures.

I have also discovered that the local populace is indignant over those foreigners who feel no regret and who only pursue their profit. We have powerful military forces on land and in the sea. But by simply calling upon the common people I could gather more than enough people to put a stop to those [illicit] traders. Also, if need be, we could close the ports indefinitely. How hard it would be to stop the [opium] traffic then! Our great empire spans ten thousand *li* with abundant resources. We do not depend on foreign products to survive. I am afraid it will be the livelihood of your countries that will be in trouble. [. . . .]

As for the wicked foreigners among you who have persistently smuggled opium, I, the commissioner, have made a list of your names. We will ensure those foreigners who do not trade opium are clearly acquitted. Anyone who can first identify the dishonest foreigners and then convince them to surrender their opium and agree to sign an agreement [to not sell opium in the future] will be considered good foreigners. I, the commissioners, will reward them. It is up to you to choose whether to honor or disgrace yourselves. Now I order the chief *yanghang* merchant Wu Shaorong and others to report back to me with the signed agreement in hand within three days. Then I will hold a meeting with governor-general and governor to settle a date on which all opium will be confiscated. Do not indulge in idle expectations or seek to postpone matters that will only result in further regret.

2.8 CHARLES ELLIOT'S PUBLIC NOTICE TO BRITISH SUBJECTS (MARCH 27, 1839)

Ten days after receiving Lin Zexu's declaration, Chief Superintendent of Trade **Charles Elliot** posted the following response. With communication to Britain (or even India) taking months rather than weeks, Elliot had no hope for an expedient response (or intervention). Consequently, he had little choice but to turn over the opium. This document reflects his strategy to placate the Chinese, as well as his fellow traders, by offering to compensate all losses while claiming Lin's acts as unlawful. Despite his assertion of unjust treatment at the hands of the Chinese, he never acknowledges his own transgressions. Instead, adopting a tactic that British officials would employ for several decades, Elliot avoids the entire issue of Britain continuing trade in an illegal substance. Instead, he seeks to shift the dispute to Lin's forced acquisition of the opium and to suggest that this action flouts the more universal rules of 'free trade.'

Questions

1. **What charges does Elliot level against the Chinese?**
2. **How does Elliot seek to placate both the merchant's interests and the Chinese demands?**

I, Charles Elliot, chief superintendent of the trade of British subjects in China, presently forcibly detained by the provincial government, together with all the merchants of my own and the other foreign nations settled here, without supplies of food, deprived of our servants, and cut off from all intercourse with our respective countries, (notwithstanding my own official demand to be set at liberty so that I might act without restraint,) have now received the commands of the high commissioner, issued directly to me under the seals of the honorable officers, to deliver into his hand all the opium held by the people of my country. Now I, the said chief

CHARLES ELLIOT (1801–1875) — A British diplomat serving as Chief Superintendent of Trade and British Minister to China from 1835 until 1841, when recalled from his position for not extracting harsh enough concessions in the Convention of Chuanbi (1841).

superintendent, thus constrained by paramount motives affecting the safety of the lives and liberty of all the foreigners here present in Guangzhou, and by other very weighty causes, do hereby, in the name and on the behalf of her Britannic majesty's government enjoin and require all her majesty's subjects now present in Guangzhou forthwith to make a surrender to me for the service of her said majesty's government, to be delivered over to the government of China, of all the opium under their respective control: and to hold the British ships and vessels engaged in the trade of opium subject to my immediate direction: and to forward to me without delay a sealed list of all the British owned opium in their respective possession. And I, the said chief superintendent, do now, in the most full and unreserved manner, hold myself responsible for, and on the behalf of her Britannic majesty's government, to all and each of her majesty's subjects surrendering the said British owned opium into my hands, to be delivered over to the Chinese government. And I, the said chief superintendent, do further specially caution all Her Majesty's subjects here present in Guangzhou, owners of or charged with the management of opium, the property of British subjects, that failing the surrender of the said opium into my hands at or before six o'clock this day, I, the said chief superintendent, hereby declare Her Majesty's government wholly free of all manner of responsibility in respect of the said British-owned opium.

And it is specially to be understood that proof of British property and value of all British opium surrendered to me agreeably to this notice shall be determined upon principles and in a manner hereafter to be defined by Her Majesty's government.

Given under my hand and seal of office at Guangzhou in China, this twenty-seventh day off March, one-thousand-eight-hundred-and-thirty-nine, at six of the clock in the morning.

[L.S]   (Signed)   Charles Elliot,

Chief superintendent of the trade of British subjects in China.

2.9   A LETTER FROM LIN ZEXU TO QUEEN VICTORIA (JULY 19, 1839)

Perhaps the most famous of all the extant Opium War documents, Lin Zexu's letter likely never reached its intended audience, Queen Victoria. Copied and given to the captain of the "Thomas Coutts" in February 1840, Lin sought to evade the obstinate British officials on the scene and appeal directly to the Queen. On many levels, Lin is reiterating many of the same points he made in 2.7, but the letter displays a more developed internal logic and a fuller awareness of the international economic and political situation. It has been suggested many times among western commentators that this letter was never viewed by Queen Victoria—and it may be true that she never viewed the actual letter Lin Zexu addressed to her—but only the most willfully unapprised could have missed its publication in the London Times on June 11, 1840.

Questions

1. It is often suggested by Western historians that China needed to be opened because it did not follow proper diplomatic procedures. How does the following document support or contradict such a perspective?
2. What do you think Lin Zexu hoped to achieve by writing directly to Queen Victoria?

Letter to Queen Victoria from Lin Zexu, Deng Tingzhen and Qialiang
   [....]
The rule of your distinguished country has been passed down for generations, each ruler has been known for their respectfulness, with their tributes [to China] accompanied by declarations such as, "When my countrymen went to conduct trade in China, they received blessed and fair treatment from your Great Emperor." We are delighted that rulers from your distinguished country understood the great principals of right and are grateful for our Emperor's kindness.

Therefore, our imperial dynasty cherishes even more [this relationship], redoubled its kindness towards you by allowing profitable trade, extended to you over the past two hundred years. This is the reason your country has become known for its wealth.

During this long period of trade, there were good and bad foreigners, some of them brought in opium to seduce Chinese people and disseminated vice to every province. They only focused on their own profits and cared nothing of the damage caused. The laws of heaven and the feelings of the people cannot tolerate such behavior. The Great Emperor, upon hearing of this, was filled with rage, and has specifically sent me, his commissioner, to Guangdong. There he has charged me together with the governor-general and governor, to investigate and settle this matter.

Any Chinese subject who is convicted of selling or smoking opium is punished to death. If we charge the foreigners for the years of their involvement in selling opium, and the deep harm they have caused in their pursuit of colossal profits, they would have been punished with death penalty as well. Nevertheless, we took into consideration the fact that many foreigners regret their crimes, have asked for forgiveness, and relinquished the opium from their ships in an amount of 20,283 chests to your representative Elliot; which has been confiscated and destroyed. I, [along with] the Governor-General, and the Governor, in a memorial to the Emperor have faithfully reported this information. The Emperor was exceptionally kind and pardoned the foreigners as a result of their cooperation. But if anyone repeats the crime, it will be hard to avoid punishment. With new regulations established, we presume the ruler of your distinguished country who favored our civilized culture, will instruct all foreigners to observe these new laws with care. The benefits and punishments of our imperial laws must be explained to all [who travel to China] and they must understand that under no circumstances will opium be allowed to cross our borders.

Having investigated the matter, we have determined that your country is sixty to seventy thousand *li* away from China, and that foreign ships compete for our lucrative trade. The foreigners have all profited from the wealth of China. Put another way, the large profits made by the foreigners are achieved only by the people of China seeking to share it with them. In return how could the foreigners use the poisonous drug to harm the Chinese people? Even though the foreigners may not necessarily intend to do any harm, in order to maximize their profit, they disregard the damages they impose on people. May I ask where is your conscience? We have heard that the smoking of opium is strictly forbidden in your country because the harm caused by opium is clearly understood. If you country does not wish such harm upon your own country, you should not impose it upon others, especially not China. Every single article exported from China whether it is to be eaten, used or resold, is for the good of foreign countries. Is there anything that China has done to harm foreign countries? This is not even mentioning the daily necessities, such as tea and rhubarb, that China provides to foreign countries.

[. . . .]

The goods imported to your country from China are not only consumed by your own people, but also sold to other countries, which triple your profits. You can earn these threefold-profits without selling opium. Yet, you still engage in a trade that is based on selling harmful products to others simply to fulfill your greedy desire? What if people from other countries sold opium to England, enticing your people to purchase and smoke opium? Certainly a ruler of your distinguished stature must despise and forbid it.

We have always heard that the ruler of your distinguished country is kind and benevolent. Naturally you would not wish to do unto others what you yourself do not want. We have also heard that the ships coming to Guangdong have all been given regulations and orders clearly outlining the forbidden goods are not permitted to ship to China. This indicates that the administrative orders by the ruler of your distinguished country are strict and clear. Only because the trading ships are numerous, heretofore perhaps they have not been examined with care. Now with this communication and a clear understanding of the strict laws by the imperial kingdom, certainly you will not let your subjects to violate the law again.

[. . . .]

The current penalty for Chinese who sell or smoke opium is death. Clearly, if foreigners do not bring opium in, then Chinese could not sell and smoke opium. It is really the wicked foreigners who cause the death of those Chinese. Why should opium smugglers be allowed to live? Anyone who takes a life has to pay with one's own life. Opium's harm is much beyond one life. Therefore the new law states foreigners who bring opium to China must be punished by decapitation or hanging. This is to eliminate the evils of the world.

Upon further investigation, we discovered in the second month of this year [April 9, 1839], Elliot, your consul, petitioned for an extension due to the stringent law. He requested an extension of five months for Indian merchants and ten months for England proper, after which new regulations will be enacted. Now we, the commissioners and officials, have memorialized to the Great Emperor and have received the extraordinary mercy from His Majesty, who has granted Elliot's petition with extraordinary consideration and compassion. Within a year [England proper] and six months [Indian areas], anyone who mistakenly brings in opium, but voluntarily surrenders themselves and all opium will be pardoned. After the deadline, anyone who violates the law does so deliberately and will be executed with no clemency. This truly demonstrates the height of kindness and the perfection of justice.

Our imperial dynasty rules over and supervises numerous states, and possesses unforeseen divine power. But we cannot bear to put people to death without giving them instructional guidance. Therefore, we specifically announce regulations clearly. If foreigners from your country are looking for long-term trade relationship, they must obey our statue, to permanently stop the source of opium. By no means should they test law with their lives.

May you, the Ruler, apprehend wicked people to guarantee the peace of your nation, to demonstrate further the sincerity of your submissiveness and enjoy the blessings of peace. How fortunate, how fortunate indeed! Upon receiving this letter will you give us a prompt reply regarding the details and circumstances of your opium ban. Please do not delay. The above is what has to be communicated.

Attached is the new law: If foreigners bring opium to sell in China, the leader will be executed by decapitation immediately; the followers are to be executed by hanging immediately. All merchandise is to be confiscated. Within the one year and six months granted clemency period, those who surrender all opium will be pardoned.

Daoguang 19th year, 6th month, 9th day [July 19, 1839]. Since the edict arrived belatedly, the clemency period ends on Daoguang 20th year, 12th month and 9th day. [March 12, 1840]

POPULAR RESPONSES AND DIPLOMATIC RESOLUTIONS TO THE OPIUM WAR

The Opium War (1839–42) was far from a popular war among either the Chinese or the British. There exist numerous instances in both countries of popular discontent over the manner in which the war was entered into and carried out. While the British lower classes were inevitably less aware of the war than their Chinese counterparts, several of the documents included below reveal that the greatest opposition to the war amongst the lower classes in both countries lay in moral objections to the opium trade. Such reactions are almost entirely forgotten in many histories of the war today. Instead many Western accounts seek to suggest that Britain's actions were entirely instigated by Chinese attacks on British goods. One wonders what Britain's options might have been without such an overwhelming military force to back up their commercial interests?

2.10 GUANGDONG RESIDENTS' DENUNCIATION OF THE BRITISH (1841)

The following anonymous document was almost certainly written by a local gentry member living in or near Guangzhou. The condemnation was likely hand-written, copied and then posted in several locations where the author(s) felt it would have the greatest impact. The language is idiomatic and employs crass vocabulary prevalent among the common classes. The document picks up the common themes (like the benevolence of the emperor, reliance on China for specific goods, etc. all employed in earlier documents) but turns them on their head to insult the British. The inclusion of rhubarb (here and by Lin in Document 2.7) reflects the mistaken belief that the British relied on the vegetable to prevent constipation. The defense of the emperor and attack on Qishan (Lin's replacement) is also quite typical, since it was often assumed that the emperor was at the mercy of his officials.

Questions

1. How do the popular sentiments expressed below diverge from that of the emperor and Lin Zexu?
2. Do you think the language employed is more reflective of the lower classes (and thus an attempt to curry favor among them) or intentionally provocative to anger the British?

Public announcement from all loyal and patriotic people of Guangdong to you, the barbarian dogs and sheep.

We have noted that you English barbarians are practiced in the plundering actions of animals, such as, hyenas and wolves, similar to the Japanese pirates and bandits during Ming Dynasty. Our imperial kingdom has previously defeated the likes of you. Because other overseas countries ask our Emperor to permit them to trade, our Emperor has benevolently tolerated trade between your dog-country and our own. You simply come for profit, what expertise do you have! Your greed for profit is just like an animal's pursuit of food. You have no knowledge of law and rites. Look at yourselves in the mirror! What is the difference between you and an animal? You are simply an animal who can talk. How can you understand loyalty, filial piety, and etiquette? How can you understand ritual manners and shame?

Although you have feather [down] and woolen goods, without our raw silk, how could you weave? Although you have your tricks, without our silver and white lead, how could you make your currency? Everything else was also following our imperial dynasty's rules. Your dog-country depends on our empire's tea, rhubarb and other medicine to survive. If our empire refuses to supply these goods, how are you going to live? Instead of having a sense of gratitude for the great favor of our empire, you repay us by harmful acts. You use opium to injure our people and cheat us of our silver. Your animal-country does not consume such products, so why poison our empire with them?

Enraged by what he learned [about your actions], our Emperor sent Commissioner Lin to eliminate the harmful opium. Initially, he announced that you would be pardoned if you surrendered your opium. As an animal, you understood enough to be afraid and surrender the opium. It was reported to the Emperor, who gave you rhubarb and tea as a reward. But you animals were not grateful. You refused to accept and sign the agreement. You have claimed to be powerful, why did you dare not to attack Guangdong where Commissioner Lin was posted? Instead, you snuck up the coast to Zhejiang, massacred civilians in Dinghai, and then went to Tianjin, attempting to present a petition to the emperor. If you were really wronged, why not present your petition earlier, why first attack Dinghai and only then go to Tianjin? It was obvious you understood your crimes were much too great to be forgiven, so you came up with another plan to deceive our officials. The corrupted minister Qishan was fooled by you, and passed the petition to the emperor for you. The Great Emperor was benevolent, and believed in it. [He] ordered the withdrawal of provincial military forces, pardoned your dog-lives, and ordered his soldiers not to open fire. If you were truly obedient, why did you not give up Dinghai, and return to Guangdong to await an investigation? Instead you continue to disrupt towns in the Guangdong area, and roam the seas. You duped Qishan, the corrupt minister, who withdrew soldiers from Shajiao and Hengdang [along the Pearl River]. He ordered soldiers not to fire their weapons, which encouraged you to go further inland. You colluded with the collaborators who had no respect for their Emperor or their fathers, and you paid them to create a disturbance. What kind of strength was that? You claim to be exceptional fighters, why not just use your English barbarians to fight. To use Chinese collaborators does not show your full talents, you English-dogs.

[. . . .]

Our hatred towards your brutal behavior is so fanatical, that if we do not exterminate you pigs and dogs completely, we cannot consider ourselves true men who support the weight of the sky on earth. We have made our pronouncement and we will not take it back. We are determined to kill you, cut off your head, and burn you to a crisp. Even if you implore people to stop us, nothing will cause us to change our minds. We will peel off your skins and eat your flesh. Only then will you understand just how tough we are. We are the first to announce to your Yilü [Elliot], Malixun, Diandi, and Danju, and the other Chinese collaborators who show no respect to their fathers and the emperor. We should have written in a more delicate style, but animals do not understand written words, therefore we have used vulgar language for you animals to understand in the simplest terms possible, to quickly confess your crime, surrender yourself and beg [for forgiveness]. Differentiate between the leaders and followers, as we are too kind to kill you all. If there is any delay, there will be no time for regret. Special announcement!

2.11 BRITISH PARLIAMENTARY DISCUSSION OF RESOLUTION ON THE "SUPPRESSION OF THE OPIUM TRADE" (APRIL 4, 1843)

Similar to the debate that raged within the pages of *The Chinese Repository* (2.6), many British were unconvinced by the rationale given for an expensive war halfway around the world against the Chinese over the importation of a highly addictive drug. Lord Ashley delivered an impassioned anti-war speech before the British Parliament that lasted for several hours and when transcribed was more than sixty pages long. Even when several members of Parliament attempted to stop discussion due to the late hour (after midnight) debate continued until after 2 a.m. The motion was ultimately withdrawn by Lord Ashley so as not to prejudice the diplomatic negotiations going on between China and Great Britain.

Questions

1. How does Ashley's line of reasoning parallel that employed by Dealtry (in 2.6)?
2. Why does Sir Robert Stanton claim "we did not subvert the complicated and ancient fabric of the Chinese government"? On what grounds does he make such a claim?

Sir, although I may be animadverted upon and perhaps rebuked for having presumed to handle so important a matter, I shall ever be thankful that I have acted as an instrument to lay this abominable evil before the eye of the public. I shall deeply regret to have given offence to this House, or to any individual; nevertheless, I shall rejoice in the disclosure and the possible removal of the mischief. Sir, the condition of this empire does demand a most deep and solemn consideration; within and without, we are hollow and insecure. True, it is that we wear a certain appearance of power and majesty, but, with one arm resting on the east, and the other on the west, we are in too many instances trampling under foot every moral and religious obligation. I confess I speak most sincerely, though few, perhaps, will agree with me; but I do say—it is in my heart and I will bring it out—if this is to be the course of our future policy; if thus we are to exercise our arts and arms, our science and our superiority of knowledge over the world—if all these are to be turned to our advantage of mankind, I should much prefer that we shrink within the proportions of our public virtue, and descend to the level of a third-rate power. But a great and a noble opportunity is now offered to us, of being just and generous in the height of victory. In such a spirit, and with such an aim, there is hope that we may yet be spared to run a blessed, a useful, and a glorious career; directing all our energies and all our vows—all that we have and all that we shall receive—to that one great end of human existence, "Glory to God in the highest; on earth peace, good-will towards men." The noble Lord [Ashley] concluded by moving—

> That it is the opinion of this House, that the continuance of the trade in opium and the monopoly of its growth in the territories of British India, is destructive of all relations of amity between England and China, injurious to the manufacturing interests of the country by the very serious diminution of the legitimate commerce, and utterly inconsistent with the honor and duties of a Christian kingdom; and that steps be taken as soon as possible, with due regard to the rights of Government and individuals, to abolish the evil."

RESPONSE: **Sir George Stanton:** However pernicious and impolitic the traffic in opium may be, and whatever opinion this House may pronounce tonight against its further continuance, we ought to recollect that these persons engaged in this traffic under the full sanction and indeed encouragement, both of the Indian and the home Government; and that they were deprived of their property by an act of violent and unjustifiable outrage on the part of the Chinese authorities. . . . The House has heard a good deal about the revenue which is hazarded by the adoption of my noble Friend's motion; it should also hear something of the nature and extent of those great interests which the adoption of his motion will tend to maintain and preserve. I trust I shall not say much regarding the advantages we derived from our position in China previous to the war. It is well known that we had long derived from China exclusively, our supply of the article of tea; that the China trade had yielded an annual revenue to the Exchequer of nearly four millions sterling, and that, even under the much reprobated monopoly of the East India Company, it was the medium by which the disposal was effected above a million sterling in value of the manufactures and productions of this country. [. . . .]

Our present great commercial advantages in China, which I have perhaps, detailed at too much length, have been obtained by the vigorous employment of our united sea and land forces in the proper quarter, and with the advantage, I must say, of considerable good fortune; for a single untoward casualty, either on land, or in that unexplored navigation, might have marred the whole campaign. We were also fortunate, not only in what we accomplished, but in what we did not accomplish; we did not subvert the complicated and ancient fabric of the Chinese government; we did not spread anarchy and confusion over its fine provinces. We subdued the government to that extent only which was requisite to dispose it to make the necessary reparation for the injuries which we had received, and to grant to us those commercial concessions which, I doubt not, will prove as beneficial to them as to ourselves.

2.12 TREATY OF NANJING (1842)

The **Treaty of Nanjing** is a representative (if unjust) coda to the Opium War. Defeated by the most powerful navy in the world at the time, China was forced to accept the continued importation of opium, pay a massive indemnity, and cede the island of Hong Kong "in perpetuity" to Great Britain. Symptomatic of the manner in which Britain treated the affair from the beginning, the treaty mentions opium only obliquely in reference to China's large indemnity. The treaty speaks of free trade and "opening" China, thereby suggesting that opium was incidental to the larger issues at hand. Despite Great Britain's insistence that the treaty marks China's entrance into "western-style diplomacy," it is highly unlikely the Qing court thought that much would change as a result of it. Hong Kong was a barren island, undesirable to most Chinese. Opening designated places for trade had long been a concession given to appease aggressive neighbors along China's inland borders. And the court had long questioned the effectiveness of the Yanghang guild system, so was not likely troubled by its demise. What Qing officials were most aggrieved by was the fact that they could not stop the only component of their relationship with Great Britain that mattered, opium.

Questions

1. **In what ways is the Treaty of Nanjing more a continuation of Britain's efforts begun in the Macartney Mission (1792–3) than a reaction to China's efforts to terminate the opium trade?**
2. **Aside from the heavy indemnity what aspects do you think most affected China?**

Peace Treaty between the Queen of Great Britain and the Emperor of China. HER MAJESTY the Queen of the United Kingdom of Great Britain and Ireland, and His Majesty the Emperor of China, being desirous of putting an end to the misunderstandings and consequent hostilities which have arisen between the two countries, have resolved to conclude a Treaty for that purpose [. . . .] and found them to be in good and due form, have agreed upon and concluded the following [selected] Articles:

  I. There shall henceforward be Peace and Friendship between Her Majesty the Queen of the

TREATY OF NANJING (1842) — Treaty ending the Opium War between China and Great Britain. It opened five treaty ports, ceded the island of Hong Kong, and imposed a 21 million taels indemnity.

United Kingdom of Great Britain and Ireland and His Majesty the Emperor of China, and between their respective Subjects, who shall enjoy full security and protection for their persons and property within the Dominions of the other.

II. His Majesty the Emperor of China agrees, that British Subjects, with their families and establishments, shall be allowed to reside, for the purposes of carrying on their Mercantile pursuits, without molestation or restraint, at the Cities and Towns of Guangzhou, Xiamen, Fuzhou, Ningbo, and Shanghai; and Her Majesty the Queen of Great Britain, etc., will appoint Superintendents, or Consular Officers, to reside at each of the above-named Cities or Towns, to be the medium of communication between the Chinese Authorities and the said Merchants, and to see that the just Duties and other Dues of the Chinese Government, as hereafter provided for, are duly discharged by Her Britannic Majesty's Subjects.

III. It being obviously necessary and desirable that British Subjects should have some Port where at they may careen and refit their ships when required, and keep stores for that purpose, His Majesty the Emperor of China cedes to Her Majesty the Queen of Great Britain, etc., the Island of Hong Kong, to be possessed in perpetuity by Her Britannic Majesty, her heirs and successors, and to be governed by such laws and regulations as Her Majesty the Queen of Great Britain, etc., shall see fit to direct.

IV. The Emperor of China agrees to pay the sum of Six Millions of Dollars, as the value of the opium which was delivered up at Guangzhou in the month of March, 1839, as a ransom for the lives of Her Britannic Majesty's Superintendent and subjects, who had been imprisoned and threatened with death by the Chinese High Officers.

V. The Government of China having compelled the British Merchants trading at Guangzhou to deal exclusively with certain Chinese Merchants, called Hang merchants (or gonghang), who had been licensed by the Chinese Government for that purpose, the Emperor of China agrees to abolish that practice in future at all **ports** where British Merchants may reside, and to permit them to carry on their mercantile transactions with whatever persons they please; and His Imperial Majesty further agrees to pay to the British Government the sum of Three Millions of **dollars,** on account of debts due to British subjects by some of the said Hang merchants (or gonghang), who have become insolvent, and who owe very large sums of money to Subjects of Her Britannic Majesty.

VI. The Government of Her Britannic Majesty having been obliged to send out an expedition to demand and obtain redress for the violent and unjust proceedings of the Chinese High Authorities towards Her Britannic Majesty's Officer and subjects, the Emperor of China agrees to pay the sum of Twelve Millions of Dollars, on account of the expenses incurred; and Her Britannic Majesty's Plenipotentiary voluntarily agrees, on behalf of Her Majesty, to deduct from the said amount of Twelve Millions of Dollars on account of the Expenses incurred, and Her Britannic Majesty's plenipotentiary voluntarily agrees, on behalf of Her Majesty, to deduct from the said amount of twelve millions of dollars, any sums which may have been received by Her Majesty's combined Forces as Ransom for Cities and Towns in China, subsequent to the 1st day of August, 1841.

[. . . .]

XIII. The ratification of this Treaty by Her Majesty the Queen of Great Britain, etc., and His Majesty the Emperor of China, shall be exchanged as soon as the great distance which separates England from China will admit; but in the meantime, counterpart copies of it, signed and sealed by the. Plenipotentiaries on behalf of their respective Sovereigns, shall be mutually delivered, and all its provisions and arrangements shall take effect.

Done at Nanjing, and Signed and Sealed by the Plenipotentiaries on board Her Britannic Majesty's ship *Cornwallis,* this 29th day of August, 1842, corresponding with the Chinese date, twenty-fourth day of the seventh month in the twenty-second Year of Daoguang.

(L.S.) HENRY POTTINGER.

[SIGNATURES OF THE THREE CHINESE PLENIPOTENTIARIES]

TREATY PORTS—Any city in which foreigners were to be allowed to trade and conduct business within China. In addition to treaty ports, foreign settlements and foreign concessions were carved out of existing Chinese cities. These were under the direct control and rule of resident foreign consuls.

MEXICAN DOLLAR—A silver coin minted in the Spanish Empire (later in Mexican mints) and the source of nearly all silver on the global markets during the sixteenth, seventeenth, and eighteenth centuries. The Mexican dollar (also referred to as the Spanish dollar or "pieces of eight") was the preferred international currency external to European commerce. Most treaties that indicate "dollars" referred to this currency.

CHAPTER 3
MID-NINETEENTH-CENTURY REBELLIONS AND QING RESPONSES

❧

VISUAL SOURCE
TAIPING SEAL

HEAVENLY KING STATE SEAL (yuxi): Made in 1860 or 1861, the largest characters on this seal identify it as the official seal of the Heavenly King. In Chinese society (even today) a seal serves as a crucial confirmation of any documents authenticity. In this case it not only would certify that any document bearing this mark was indeed from the Taiping government. All Chinese would have understood that the Taiping seal explicitly indicated the Taipings no longer perceived themselves to be subject to Qing rule.

EIGHT KINGS or EIGHT DIRECTIONS (bawei): How do you interpret a historical terminology when the authors of the text left no precise explanation? Some historians suggest that the seventh line of the seal refers to the top kings in the Taiping hierarchy along with Heaven, the Holy Spirit and Jesus Christ, while still others simply propose it is an allegorical reference to the Taiping Kingdom by indicating the cardinal directions. It remains a mystery.

HEAVEN (Tian): Heaven is one of the most fundamental concepts within Chinese ideas about death and the afterlife (whether it be Confucian, Daoist or Buddhist). Chinese emperors portrayed themselves as the Son of Heaven and ruling with the Mandate of Heaven (that is to say Heaven had given them the right to rule). The Taiping leader, Hong Xiuquan, was not the Son of Heaven, rather he was receiving orders from Heaven.

HOW TO READ: Scholars have long disputed the correct way to read this seal. The general consensus suggests that one should begin with the larger characters in the top-center (read from top-to-bottom), followed by reading the bottom rows alternating vertical lines of four characters (again, top-to-bottom) outward from the middle. One should then return to the lower section of the top half reading the larger outer characters (right side first, then the left), and finally concluding with the two remaining characters just inside the larger characters.

PHYSICAL DESCRIPTION: The jade seal measures 8 inches along each side and is 1 inch high. The handle rises nearly three inches above the top. The seal handle, top and underside are each adorned with carvings of two phoenixes facing a sun, dragons, and stylized clouds. These symbols are also carried over to the imprint visible here to which is also added stylized water. Note the almost utter absence of any traditionally "Christian" symbols.

TRANSLATION OF THE HEAVENLY KING SEAL:
(numbering refers to the KEY in the lower right corner)

1 - God the Father
2 - Heavenly Elder Brother Jesus Christ
3 - Heavenly King, Hong [Xiuquan], the Sun
4 - Ruler of the Bountiful Earth
5 - Savior and Young Monarch
6 - True King, Guifu [the Crown Prince]
7 - Long live the Eight Kings
8 - Eternally granting Heaven's favor
9 - Eternally maintaining Heaven and earth
10 - In gracious harmony
11 - [and] convivial peace
12 & 13 - Peace (taiping). The two characters form the term from which the movement takes its name "Taiping"

Students of American history are often surprised when they learn that the war in which the greatest number of Americans died was not World War Two or World War One, but the American Civil War (1861–1865) in which more than 600,000 people perished. In China, the mid-nineteenth century cast a similar shadow of loss across its history, but on a much larger scale. Between 1851 and 1864, conservative estimates suggest that 20 million Chinese lives were lost as a result of the Taiping Rebellion. Its destruction cut a swath across the wealthiest and most prosperous areas of southern and central China from Guangxi province in the south to Shanghai on the eastern seaboard. The Taipings' charismatic leader, **Hong Xiuquan,** challenged the imperial court with a movement based on Christian teachings. His ideology was shaped by visions in which he claimed to have visited heaven. In this heavenly visit he learned he was the younger brother of Jesus Christ and told by God to rid the earth of "demons." Hong's message quickly garnered acceptance in the ethnically diverse province of Guangxi (to the west of Guangdong) where many **Hakka** lived. Simultaneously, it attracted the less desirable attention of the Qing government which sought to squelch Hong's heterodox teachings. Extraordinarily, the Taipings strung together several victories against government troops, which prompted Hong Xiuquan in January 1851 to announce the founding of the Heavenly Kingdom of Great Peace (*Taiping Tianguo)* and to declare himself the Heavenly King.

The ideological teachings of the Taipings stimulated political and social changes unrivaled in China's two thousand year imperial history. Many historians suggest the Taiping movement, with its emphasis on land redistribution and gender equality, foreshadowed the cataclysmic Communist revolution a century later. Despite its name, in many ways the Taiping Rebellion was just as much a civil war as the American "War between the States." Many contemporary Western eyewitnesses referred to it as the "Chinese Civil War," pitting the Qing imperialists (and their primarily northern supporters) against the Taipings (and their southern core of support). Other historians suggest that, given the radical social, religious, and political changes advocated by the Taipings, it is far closer to a "revolution" than a civil war. The Taiping movement, as seen in the documents below, proposed a radically different vision of society and of the world in which they lived.

Despite the massive scale of the Taiping Rebellion and its radical theology, Hong Xiuquan's Heavenly Kingdom was not alone in its attempt to topple the Qing dynasty. The Qing court faced five other fullscale rebellions in virtually every corner of the empire between 1851 and 1877. There was the Miao Rebellion (1854–1873) in southwestern province of Guizhou, the Panthay Rebellion (1856–1873) in the neighboring province of Yunnan, the Yakub Beg Rebellion (1864–1877) in the northwestern province of Xinjiang, the Hui Rebellion in the bordering provinces of Gansu and Shaanxi (1862–73) and the Nian Rebellion (1853–1868) in the eastern province of Shandong. To continue the analogy with the American Civil War, it would be as if President Lincoln in 1861 faced not only a secessionist government of the southern states lasting for over a decade, but also had to cope with full scale uprisings (with functioning rebel regimes) in California and Arizona, another in Washington and Oregon, as well as a pesky revolt somewhere in Maryland. Such a comparison is imperfect since many of the Chinese rebellions were in remote regions along China's distant frontiers. In these regions large numbers of indigenous peoples had strong transnational relations, especially the ties between Muslim groups in northwestern China with their Islamic Central Asian neighbors.

HONG XIUQUAN (1814–1864)—Leader of the Taiping Rebellion (1851–1864). Born in the southern Chinese province of Guangdong of Hakka ethnicity. Failed to pass the civil service exam in four attempts, before he formed the Society of God Worshippers in Guangxi. He proclaimed himself the Heavenly King of the "Heavenly Kingdom of Great Peace" leading his followers in a failed rebellion against the Qing. Died, likely from suicide, on June 1, 1864.

HAKKA (KEJIA)—An ethnic minority prominent in southern China. Many of China's most prominent leaders were Hakka, including Taiping leader Hong Xiuquan, the Song family, and Deng Xiaoping.

Nonetheless, the ultimate Qing military victories over all these rebellions reveal the enduring effectiveness of the Qing court. The six mid-nineteenth-century Chinese rebellions at their peak controlled broad areas of China challenging Qing rule in the northwest, southwest, and the Yangzi valley. Only the extreme southern and northern parts of the empire escaped severe loss of life and property.

Needless to say, such a pervasive wave of rebellion pushed the Qing government to its fiscal, military and operational limits. Yet it also compelled the Qing government to innovate by instituting non-traditional solutions to the widespread agitation in what has come to be referred to as the "**Self-Strengthening Movement.**"

TAIPING REBELLION

Making sense of a foreign society, culture and religion is difficult under any circumstances. Deciphering meaning from events that occurred over a century and a half ago in the volatile circumstances present in nineteenth-century China is especially arduous. The **Taiping Rebellion** adds yet another layer of complexity to this task since many of the Taiping doctrines were adapted from Christianity yet retained a distinctly Chinese character. The fusion of these two make it easy to dismiss Hong Xiuquan's revelations as the confused ramblings of a delusional madman who misinterpreted fundamental Christian teachings. Yet his writings offer important insights into the Taiping movement's success within a Chinese context. For example, we might be tempted to view the poems that follow each of the Taiping's Ten Commandment (3.3.) as a superfluous departure from the Commandments of the Old Testament. But to do so would miss their interpretative function, a function that enabled Taiping adherents to make sense of this radically different set of ethical beliefs. To use his reading of the Bible—one that challenges traditional Western interpretations—as a litmus test for the validity of the Taiping Rebellion as a whole, would be deeply flawed. This is particularly the case since Hong Xiuquan's quasi-Christian views were only one part of the Taiping's appeal. The Taiping leadership deftly tapped into the deep (and widespread) ethnic prejudice against the Manchu Qing court, as is seen in their strong anti-Manchu stance (3.1). They also drew on a profound desire for social change in their land and social policies (3.2, 3.4). However, there is no doubt that the trajectory of the Taiping movement followed that of many other utopian political movements. Extravagance and infighting among the leadership quickly followed its early success and lead ultimately to its downfall.

3.1 TAIPING ANTI-MANCHU PROCLAMATION (1852)

The non-Chinese origins of the Manchu Qing dynasty remained a common rallying cry among many Chinese rebels. This attitude resulted from the pervasive animosity among the Han Chinese towards the Manchu ruling class. In the following document, two of Hong Xiuquan's deputy kings, Yang Xiuqing and Xiao Chaogui appeal to the strong anti-Manchu sentiments of the Chinese populace with a level of vitriol typical of the

SELF-STRENGTHENING MOVEMENT (c. 1861–1894)—A movement beginning in 1861 largely stemming from the urgent need to counter the mid-nineteenth-century Chinese rebellions. Initially, the campaign consisted of military reforms adopted by Zeng Guofan and later broadened to adopt western methods in education, industry and diplomacy.

TAIPING REBELLION (1851–1864)—The largest of China's mid-nineteenth-century rebellions, it was led by Hong Xiuquan which at its height ruled over 30 million people and lasted thirteen years before finally being suppressed by Qing military force.

era. In the original document they employ a highly derogatory, centuries-old term of "foxes" (hu) when referring to the Manchus. In accordance with Hong's vision, Yang Xiuqing and Xiao Chaogui refer to the Manchus as demons who need to be expunged from the earth. Aside from the unrelenting insults heaped on the Manchus, the two deputy kings cleverly employ well-known historical precedents, familiar even to their likely illiterate audience, to bolster their claims of the Taiping's righteous actions.

Questions

1. **What acts are the Manchus charged with committing?**
2. **How might a Chinese audience receive such a pronouncement? Why?**

Oh people, listen to our words! It is our belief that the empire is God's empire, not the Manchu's empire; that food and clothing are God's food and clothing, not the Manchu's food and clothing; sons, daughters, and commoners are God's sons, daughters, and commoners, not the Manchu barbarians' sons, daughters, and commoners.

The Manchus crept in and threw China into turmoil. China, with its vast territory and immense population, shamefully tolerated the Manchus' barbarous actions, without considering them improper. Can the Chinese still consider themselves human? Ever since the Manchus spread their poisonous influences throughout China, the flames of oppression have risen up to heaven, the vapors of corruption have defiled the celestial throne, the filthy odors have spread over the four seas, and their devilishness exceeds that of the five barbaric tribes of old. Yet the Chinese dejectedly lowered their heads and willingly became their servants. Is China devoid of people [prepared to stand up]?

China is the head and **Manchuria** is the feet; China is the land of spirits and Manchuria the land of demons. Why is China called the land of spirits? Because the Heavenly Father, the majestic God, is the true Spirit; heaven and earth, mountains and seas are his creations, therefore from time immemorial the land of spirits has been called China. Why are the Manchus considered demons? Because the demonic serpent—the demon of Hell—is a wicked demon and the Manchu demons worship only him. Thus, we should from now on treat the Manchus as if they are demons.

But so how have the feet assumed the place of the head? How did the demons steal the land of spirit; driving Chinese to turn into demons? Using all the bamboo from the South Mountain cannot completely record all of the Manchus' wickedness; and using all the waves of Eastern Sea cannot wash off their vast sins.

We shall enumerate the facts, which are known to all, and discuss them briefly:

The Chinese have Chinese characteristics; but now the Manchus have ordered them all to shave their hair, leaving a long tail in the back, thus making the Chinese appear like animals. The Chinese have Chinese dress and hats; but now the Manchus have ordered us to wear different style barbarian clothes and monkey caps, abandoning the robes and headdresses of ancestors. All with the purpose to make Chinese forget their roots.

The Chinese have Chinese family relationships. A previous false demon, Kangxi, secretly ordered each Manchu to take control of ten families and rape the Chinese women hoping that the Chinese would all become Manchu barbarians. The Chinese have Chinese wives, but now the Manchu demons have accosted all the beautiful girls of China to be their concubines and slaves. The Manchu dogs have tarnished three thousand beautiful women; one million beautiful young women have been forced to sleep with the stinking foxes. Thinking of it hurts our hearts; speaking of it pollutes our tongue. The reputation of all Chinese women has been put into question.

[. . . .]

The Manchu barbarians are like dogs and pigs. There are those of you who are educated and know your history, yet you do not feel the slightest shame. There was a time when Wen Tianxiang and Xie Fangde

MANCHURIA—An area roughly coterminous with northeastern China and the ancestral lands of the Manchu peoples that established the Qing dynasty. Japan occupied the territory in the 1930s and established the puppet state of Manchukuo.

preferred to die than serve the [Mongol] Yuan dynasty; Shi Kefa and Qu Shisi would rather die than to serve the [Manchu] Qing. You, our esteemed listeners, are all well aware of these precedents. We estimate that Manchu's population is no more than a hundred and thirty or forty thousand, while we Chinese number no fewer than fifty million. How humiliating it is for some fifty million to come under the oppression of one hundred thousand.

Fortunately divine virtue has now returned and China has revived its senses. As men's hearts lean towards order, there are signs that the Manchu barbarians are surely to be soon destroyed. The demon's preordained two-hundred-and-ten-year long rule has come to an end, and the rightful sovereign has already appeared. The Manchu's crimes have reached their just end.

[. . . .]

The beneficent God has bestowed a great favor on the Chinese empire and ordered our Supreme ruler, the Heavenly King, to reign. How could the Manchus be allowed to occupy and misrule China for any longer? You, our esteemed listeners, have lived in China for generations; who is not God's child? If you can follow Heaven's order in destroying the demons,

rise up and avoid **Fang Feng's** mistake of belatedly rallying to the cause. An official in this life, you will be a hero beyond compare; in Heaven you will enjoy eternal glory. If you are stubborn and refuse to change [your allegiances]; if you defend that which is false and reject that which is true, in life you will be a Manchu demon and in death a Manchu ghost. The line between right and wrong is clear; Chinese and barbarians are each clearly distinguished and have their distinct reputation. One and all should follow Heaven's destiny and emancipate themselves from the demons so you can once again be human.

You, our esteemed listeners, have long suffered from the Manchu calamity; if you are still unable to make up your mind to unite and sweep away the Manchu, how will you face God high above in Heaven? We have begun the righteous fight. For Heaven, we wreak vengeance [on the Manchus] in God's name. For those on earth, we liberate China's sufferings. We must clear away the Manchus entirely to enjoy the happiness of peace [Taiping – pun on the meaning of peace and the label of their movement]. Those who obey Heaven's order will be abundantly rewarded. Those who disobey Heaven will be executed. Make this proclamation known throughout the empire – let all hear and obey it.

3.2   THE DAYS WHEN THE TAIPINGS ARRIVED AT NANJING (1853–1854)

Zhang Runan, a pro-Qing scholar official, wrote the following eyewitness account of the Taiping capture of Nanjing. He remained in the city for over a year until the autumn of 1854 and published his observations three years later to considerable public interest. His description is unique for the amount of detail it gives about the Taiping's early reforms, such as segregation of the men and women, communal dining halls, and daily prayers. While Zhang paints these in a rather negative light, many Chinese commoners, who prior to the Taiping's rise to power could not expect a daily meal, were less critical.

Questions

1. **How do you think the Taipings were received after taking control of Nanjing?**
2. **What elements of Zhang's report would have most shocked the Qing scholar officials who read it?**

The moment they entered the city [Nanjing], the bandits [the Taiping rebels] went up and down the streets, shouting aloud that all residents must close their

front doors and that anyone who dared to venture into the streets would be immediately killed. They also issued an order that a piece of paper with the

FANG FENG (c. 2150 BCE) — A local ruler summoned by Emperor Yu of the Xia dynasty. Vexed at his late arrival (perhaps seeing it as an indication of Fang's tepid support) the emperor had Fang Feng executed.

word OBEDIENCE on it must be pasted on each front door, that an altar with three cups of tea on it must be set up inside each house, and that all residents, men and women must not wear any hats. Full of apprehension, all the people in the city obeyed the order without asking any questions.

Moments later, the bandits gathered their forces and surrounded the Manchu portion of the city. The roaring of cannons and the firing of rifles, intermingled with cries of "Kill," could be heard several *li* away. The Manchu City, called the Inner City during the Ming Dynasty, was high and well-fortified. All of its residents rallied to defend the city wall, including the Manchu women who, like their men, were proficient in the handling of weapons. The bandits attacked the city in large numbers and suffered heavy casualties. As dead bodies were piled up higher and higher outside the wall, the attackers were also able to climb higher and higher to assault the city. The moment eventually arrived when the defenders were simply overwhelmed by heavy waves of attacks from all sides. Upon the fall of the Manchu City it was learned that all Manchu generals and commanders, including Gushan, had died in action. The Manchu soldiers who managed to escape by fighting their way through layer after layer of besiegers numbered no more than four hundred. Even women and children fought as best as they could; though they killed many of their enemies, their own casualties were also extremely heavy. The Manchu men who survived the battle numbered no more than a few thousand; later, after being chased out from the Chaoyang Gate, they were completely surrounded and then slaughtered one by one. Between 8 and 12 A.M., when the Manchu City fell, even the sun looked melancholy and dispirited, and the spirit of death could be felt miles away. As the battle raged on, all the people outside the city were tormented by agony and frozen with fear: how helpless they must have felt! After the fall of the Manchu City and for the rest of the day, Nanjing was as still and motionless as in the middle of the night.

The next day, the twelfth of the second month [March 21, 1853], the bandits in small groups of three or four each once again emerged in the streets. They knocked at people's doors, announcing that they were searching for "demons," by which they meant government officials, soldiers, or Manchus. If they found inside a house such things as official hats, boots, or clothing, or governmental seals and documents that had been carefully hidden, the head of the household would be immediately put under arrest and sped away.

Before entering a house, they parked their rifles outside the door and carried with them only short knives. "Are you a demon?" they would ask. Upon receiving a negative answer, they would ask again "Do you hide any demons inside your house?" If the response was again negative, they would not ask any more questions. Then they would order the residents to open their chests and drawers and, whenever they saw something particularly valuable, such as silk, velvet, gold, or curios, they would take it away as if it had always belonged to them. It may be added, however, that some of the bandits never asked people to open their chests or drawers.

[. . . .]

Shortly after it took over Nanjing, the bandit government issued an order saying that men and women should be segregated and should in fact live in separate dormitories. Understandably the people did not take kindly to this order, and force was therefore used to carry it out. (Whenever a bandit saw a child he liked, he would compel its parents to let him adopt it. The child would be from then on called a *daizai*.) This order for sexual segregation separated husband from wife, parents from children and brothers from sisters, and in short, broke up the whole family. Sometimes a family would request the bandit authorities to postpone the enforcement of their segregation order for one day. Then, in the middle of the night, all of its members would commit suicide: they either hanged themselves, jumped into a nearby river, or set their own house on fire and burned themselves to death. Previously the bandits had forced local residents to serve as night watchmen the moment they entered the city. Now, seeing houses catching fire at night, they sent these watchmen to fight the fire. They were afraid that some of the government soldiers, who still hid inside the city, might use the fire as a smokescreen to launch a counter attack.

The next day [March 23, 1853] the order to segregate the sexes was even more strictly enforced. Among those who had been living in the segregated quarters some managed to sneak out at night and committed suicide at home. As this situation continued, strong measures were introduced to prevent its repetition. Each female dormitory housed approximately twenty residents, all of whom were required to address each other as "new sisters," regardless of their age differences. At the head of the twenty "new sisters" was an "old sister," their "squad leader" who, more often than not, was a Guangxi woman. Most of the female dormitories were located near the Xihua Gate, collectively, they were called the "women's battalion." The women's battalion was divided into five armies: the front, the rear, the left, the right, and the center, and each army was jointly commanded by a female commander, usually a Guangxi woman, and a male inspector. Husbands were not allowed to go inside a female dormitory to visit their wives; nor were sons allowed to go inside to see their mother. Whenever a visit took place, the visitor and the visited could only speak to each other across a fence and at a considerable distance. The bandits were very strict with adultery: once an act of adultery was discovered, both the adulterer and the adulteress would be immediately put to death on the grounds that they had violated a heavenly commandment. Even the old bandits from Guangxi were not exempted from this rule.

[. . . .]

Once every ten days each dormitory sent a man to the "Heavenly Granary" to receive its share of rice. Before each meal, a gong was sounded to summon all residents of the dormitory to a room. In the center of the room was a table on which were placed three cups of tea, three bowls of rice, and well-lit lamps; there were no incense burners. The meal-takers were then seated on both sides of the table, closed their eyes, and began to chant, much as a Buddhist monk chants in the presence of Buddha. The hymn was composed by the bandit chieftain Hong Xiuquan and read as follows:

Glory to God who is our Heavenly Father;
Glory to Jesus who is the Savior of the World;
Glory to the Holy Ghost who is the Divine Spirit;
Glory to all the Three who are unified as
One—the true, only God.
The Way of Heaven is the same as the
    Way of Man;
Those who save man will enjoy eternal bliss.
Wise man, come quickly and receive Him—
That thou mayst share His Blessing.
Ignorant man, wake up—
That to thee the road to Heaven may
    also be open.
God's grace is unlimited and abounding.
He sent to earth His only begotten Son
Who sacrificed His life to redeem us
    from our sins.
Repent, lest thou go not to Paradise!

After the chanting was over, all knelt down, facing outside. The scribe of the dormitory would then pray, in a barely audible voice, as follows: "This humble son (in the female dormitory, "daughter") of Yours entreats You, Heavenly Father, to bestow upon us all Your infinite blessing," etc. Towards the end of the prayer and before he stood up, he would suddenly raise his voice and shout aloud: "Kill off all the devils and demons!" Only after all these rituals were over could the diners sit down and take their meal. The same rituals were observed in the Inner Court as well as among the military ranks.

3.3   TAIPING TEN COMMANDMENTS (1852)

It is difficult not to contrast the Taiping Ten Commandments with their Old Testament counterpart. Though undeniably similar, the Taiping version serves the broader purpose of introducing the Taiping followers to Hong Xiuquan's version of Christianity. The following translation of the Taiping Commandments has deliberately attempted to avoid a falsely "biblical" sounding translation. Rather it is rendered in the manner a Chinese, unfamiliar with the Bible, might have understood it. A reader of the Taiping Commandments must pay special attention to the explanations and poems that offer insight into how the Taiping leaders hoped to have the Commandments understood by their Taiping followers. These provide essential clues to the Taiping leadership's concern over how a deeply Confucian and Buddhist populace should adopt the new teachings.

Questions

1. **What commandments do you sense the Taipings placed more stress upon?**
2. **Given that Chinese society has a deep tradition of polytheism, how might Chinese who came under Taiping rule react to the following commandments?**

The Ten Heavenly Commandments, as Created by the God, Are to be Observed at all Times:

FIRST HEAVENLY COMMANDMENT: YOU SHALL HONOR AND WORSHIP GOD.

Explanation

God is the Father of all people; every life is given and nurtured by Him; everyone is blessed by Him; every morning and night each person shall pray and be grateful for His grace. As a common proverb states: "Created by Heaven, nourished by Heaven and protected by Heaven." As another common saying goes: "Provided with food, we must not deceive Heaven." Therefore, all who do not worship God violate the Heavenly commandment.

The God is the true God,
Worship Him morning and night so as to be forgiven.
The Ten Heavenly Commandments must be
    followed,
You must not let demons mislead and confuse your
    true nature.

SECOND HEAVENLY COMMANDMENT: YOU SHALL NOT WORSHIP FALSE GODS.

Explanation

God says: "There are no other gods besides me." Therefore except God, all others are demons that confuse and harm people and must not be worshipped; whoever worships such gods violates the Heavenly Commandment.

People are easily deluded by demons,
To misguidedly have faith in them will eventually
    lead you to Hell,
We urge you valiant ones to awaken yourselves,
The Heavenly Father is urgently waiting to be
    close to you.

THIRD HEAVENLY COMMANDMENT: YOU SHALL NOT TAKE THE NAME OF THE GOD IN VAIN.

Explanation

The name of God is Jehovah which must not be taken in vain. Whoever uses His name as a curse is violating the Heavenly Commandment.

The Heavenly Father is infinitely respected,
Those who offend His name will eventually be led
    to a bad end.
If you are not on the right Way, you must rouse
    yourself.
Those who wantonly behave irreverently are
    conducting colossal crimes.

FOURTH HEAVENLY COMMANDMENT: ON THE SEVENTH DAY, THE DAY OF WORSHIP, YOU SHALL PRAISE THE GOD FOR HIS GRACE AND VIRTUE.

Explanation

At the beginning, the God created heaven and the earth, the mountains and the seas, humankind and things, all in six days. On the seventh day, it was done and it is called the day of rest. Everyone benefits from the God's grace, and therefore, everyone who benefits should on the seventh day praise him for his goodness.

All happiness enjoyed on earth comes from the
    Heaven,
It is only appropriate then to praise His virtue
    and sing His merits.
Every morning and evening meal, one should give
    thanks,
On the seventh day you shall pray with special
    devotion.

FIFTH HEAVENLY COMMANDMENT: YOU SHALL HONOR YOUR FATHER AND MOTHER.

Explanation

God says: "Be filial and honor your parents, then the days will be prolonged." Any disobedience to one's parent is violating the Heavenly Commandment.

It is recorded that **Youyu** dutifully cared for his parents,
Bringing both his parents the greatest happiness.
As Heaven is boundless, you should?care for them.
Meet the expectation that you are worthy of being
    full person.

SIXTH HEAVENLY COMMANDMENT: YOU SHALL NOT KILL OR HARM PEOPLE.

Explanation

To kill others is the same as killing oneself; to harm others is the same as harming oneself. Anyone who kills or harms people is violating the Heavenly Commandment.

YOUYU—The fifth of China's so-called Five Mythical Emperors (*sanhuang wudi*) who was said to have established and shaped Chinese culture, society and the beginnings of the Chinese state. Also known as "Shun."

The world is one family and all are brothers,
How can killing and harming one another be
    tolerated!
One's outer physical form and inner nature are
    Heaven-given,
Let all live and enjoy a peaceful life.

SEVENTH HEAVENLY COMMANDMENT: YOU SHALL NOT COMMIT ADULTERY OR BE LICENTIOUS.

Explanation

There are many men on earth, all are brothers; there
are many women on earth, all are sisters. For sons and
daughters under Heaven, men have their place; and
women have their place; they shall not be allowed to
intermix. Men and women who conduct adultery or
licentious acts are demons. Such acts are the greatest
violation of the Heavenly Commandment. Flirting
with enticing glances, thinking lustful thoughts, smoking opium and singing provocative songs all violate
the Heavenly Commandment.

Adultery is the biggest source of every evil,
The offenders become pathetic demons and monsters.
To enjoy the true happiness of Heaven,
You must begin with restraining and cultivating
    yourself.

EIGHTH HEAVENLY COMMANDMENT: YOU SHALL NOT STEAL OR LOOT.

Explanation

Poverty and fortune are both given by the grace of
God. Whomever steals or robs others violates the
Heavenly Commandment.

One shall be satisfied with poverty and your status,
    and not steal.
Theft and violence represents the basest behavior.
Harming others can only harm yourself.
Those who are truly daring, why not turn yourself
    around now!

NINTH HEAVENLY COMMANDMENT: YOU SHALL NOT LIE.

Explanation

All who speak wild, monstrous, cunning words, and
those who use coarse and loathsome language, are all
in violation of the Heavenly Commandment.

Lies and groundless talk must be forsaken,
Treachery and perversity are crimes against Heaven.
Too much sinful chatter will only result in harming
    yourself.
It is better to be cautious and focus your thoughts.

TENTH HEAVENLY COMMANDMENT: YOU SHALL NOT BE GREEDY.

Explanation

Those who yearn for someone else's wives or daughters;
or who crave someone else's possessions; or who gamble or buy lottery tickets are all in violation of the
Heavenly Commandment.

One must not be greedy,
To get caught up in the sea of lust can only end in
    disaster.
These Commands are issued before Mt. Sinai,
Every Heavenly Commandment is in force to
    this day.

Repent and be loyal to our Heavenly Father,
    and God will obtain happiness;
Disobey or act against our Heavenly Father,
    and God will surely make you weep.
Obey the Heavenly Commandments and worship a
    true god, and when it is time to depart you will
    easily ascend to Heaven;
Engage in worldly desires and continue to believe in
    demons, and when it comes to an end you will
    have a hard time escaping hell.
Those who continue to believe in demons will turn
    them into demon's slaves,
Those who are involved with ghosts while living,
    will be taken by ghosts when they die.
Those who worship God are the sons and daughters
    of God; since you came from Heaven, you will
    ascend to Heaven.

God has His plan and you need not worry;
Devote all your heart to him and you will go to
    Heaven.
Truly respect God and do not believe other's words,
Abandon all worldly attachments and you will
    go to Heaven.

Up in Heaven there is one true spirit, God,
Mortal people often behave immorally and are
    ignorant;
You prostrate before molded clay, wood, and stone
    [statues]
I ask you, when was it that you lost your
    heart and soul,
To follow Heaven, it is wrongfully said, is
    to follow barbarians,
Truly mortal people are stupid and stubborn.
Since ancient times rulers and people believed
    in God,

Valiant individuals swiftly overpowered the demon's gate.

Follow Heaven and achieve happiness, defy Heaven and you will perish.

Why do mortal people discuss the arguments for and against [God]?

Looking at you, none of you appear to be Buddha's children,

Why do you not want to turn towards the Heaven?

3.4 THE TAIPING PLAN FOR REORGANIZING CHINESE SOCIETY (1853)

The Taiping plan for reorganization sought to regulate, systematize, and classify Chinese society in fundamentally new ways. The plan contained both incentives (especially for the lower classes) for adhering to the new Taiping principles as well as disincentives for those who did not. Deliberately shunning the easier path of retaining or only minimally altering the Qing administrative structure, the Taiping plan reveals sweeping changes and an attempt to establish an intricate bureaucracy to oversee their reforms. The plan demonstrates a desire to completely displace the traditional regime of landed wealth with an uncompromising devotion to Taiping-style Christian faith. The Taiping plan, however, should not be mistaken for a portrait of Taiping society. The Taiping kingdom experienced few periods of outright peace leaving little time for the plan to be fully implemented.

Questions

1. **Based on your reading of the earlier documents, what aspects of the plan do you think would have been implemented first?**
2. **In the Taiping Plan, why do you think there is such an emphasis on precise detail of hierarchy and the chains of command?**

Throughout the empire, the mulberry tree is to be planted close to every wall, so that all women may engage in rearing silkworms, spinning the silk, and making garments. Throughout the empire every family should keep five hens and two sows, which must not be allowed to miss their proper season. At the time of harvest, every sergeant shall direct the corporals to see to it that of the twenty-five families under his charge each individual has a sufficient supply of food, and aside from the new grain each may receive, the remainder must be deposited in the public granary. Of wheat, lentils, hemp, flax, cloth, silk, fowls, dogs, etc., and money, the same is true; for the whole empire is the universal family of our Heavenly Father, the Supreme Lord and Great God. When all the people in the empire will not take anything as their own but submit all things to the Supreme Lord, then the Lord will make use of them, and in the universal family of the empire, every place will be equal and every individual well fed and clothed. This is the intent of our Heavenly Father, the Supreme Lord and Great God, in specially commanding the true Sovereign of Taiping to save the world.

However, the sergeant must keep an account of money and grain figures in a record book, which he must present to those in charge of money and grain, and those in charge of receipts and disbursements. For every twenty-five families there must be established one public granary, and one church where the sergeant must reside. Whenever there are marriages, or births, or funerals, all may go to the public granary; but a limit must be observed, and not a cash be used beyond what is necessary. Thus, every family which celebrates a marriage or a birth will be given one thousand cash and a hundred **catties** of grain. This one rule is applicable throughout the empire. In the use of all things let there be economy, to provide against war and famine. As for marriages in the empire, wealth should not be a consideration.

JIN (CATTIE)—A unit of weight (often translated as "catty") typically equal to 1.3 pounds or 0.5 kilograms with considerable local variation.

In every circle of twenty-five families, the work of the potter, the blacksmith, the carpenter, the mason, and other artisans must all be performed by the corporal and privates; when free from husbandry they are to attend to these matters. Every sergeant, in superintending marriages and funeral events in the twenty-five families, should in every case offer a eucharist to our Heavenly Father, the Supreme Lord and Great God; all corrupt ceremonies of former times are abolished.

In every circle of twenty-five families, all young boys must go to church every day, where the sergeant is to teach them to read the Old Testament and the New Testament, as well as the book of proclamations of the true ordained Sovereign. Every Sabbath the corporals must lead the men and women to the church, where the males and females are to sit in separate rows. There they will listen to sermons, sing praises, and offer sacrifice to our Heavenly Father, the Supreme Lord and Great God.

In every circle of twenty-five families, the diligent husbandmen will be rewarded and the idle husbandmen punished; should disputes arise among the families, both parties must go to the sergeant. The sergeant will hear the case; if it is not settled, the sergeant must bring both parties before the lieutenant. The lieutenant will hear the case; if it is not settled, the lieutenant will report the case successively to the captain, the colonel, the provost marshal, and the corps general. The corps general, in consultation with the provost marshal, must try to decide the case. Having come to a decision, the corps superintendent must next report it to the corps commandant, the general, the imperial guard, the commander, the senior secretary, and the chancellor. The chancellor must report to the chief of staff, and the chief of staff must memorialize the *Tian Wang* [Heavenly King]. The *Tian Wang* [Heavenly King] will then issue an edict instructing the chief of staff, the chancellor, the senior secretary, the provost marshal, and others, to examine the case carefully; and if there is no discrepancy, then the chief of staff, the chancellor, the senior secretary, the provost marshal, and others shall report the case directly to the *Tian Wang* [Heavenly King] for his final decision. The *Tian Wang* [Heavenly King] will then issue an edict giving his verdict; and whether it be for life or for death, for giving or for taking, the chief of staff shall, in obedience to the edict, carry out the judgment.

Among all officials and subjects throughout the empire, those who universally keep and obey the Ten Heavenly Commandments and who obey orders and faithfully serve the state shall thus be considered loyal subjects, and shall be raised from a low to a high station, their descendants inheriting their official title. Those officials who break the Ten Commandments of Heaven, disobey orders, receive bribes, or engage in corrupt practices shall thus be considered traitors, and shall be degraded from a high to a low station and reduced to mere husbandry. Those subjects who obey the commandments and orders and exert themselves in husbandry shall be considered honest and faithful, and either elevated or rewarded; but those subjects who disobey the Commandments and orders and neglect the duties of husbandry shall be considered as evil and vicious, to be either put to death or punished.

[. . . .]

In the creation of an army, for each 13,156 families there must first be a corps general; next there must be five colonels under the command of the corps general; next there must be five captains under the command of each colonel, altogether twenty-five captains; next each of the twenty-five captains must have under his command five lieutenants, altogether 125 lieutenants; next each of the 125 lieutenants must have under his command four sergeants, altogether 500 sergeants; next each of the 500 sergeants must have under his command five corporals, altogether 2,500 corporals; next each of the 2,500 corporals must have under his command four privates, altogether 10,000 privates, the entire army numbering altogether 13,156 men.

After the creation of an army, should the number of families increase, with the increase of five families there shall be an additional corporal; with the increase of twenty-six families there shall be an additional sergeant, with the increase of 105 families there shall be an additional lieutenant; with the increase of 526 families there shall be an additional captain; with the increase of 2631 families there shall be an additional colonel, with the total increase of 13,156 families there shall be an additional corps general. Before a new corps general is appointed the colonel and subordinate officers shall remain under the command of the old corps general; with the appointment of a corps general they must be handed over to the command of the new corps general.

Within [the court] and without, all the various officials and people must go every Sabbath to hear the expounding of the Holy Bible, reverently offer their sacrifices, and worship and praise the Heavenly Father, the Supreme Lord and Great God. On every seventh seven, the forty-ninth day, the Sabbath, the colonel, captains, and lieutenants shall go in turn to the churches in which reside the sergeants under their command and expound the Holy books, instruct the people, examine whether they obey the Commandments and orders or disobey the Commandments and orders, and whether they are diligent or slothful. On the first seventh seven, the forty-ninth day, the Sabbath, the colonel shall to a certain sergeant's church, on the second seventh seven, the forty-ninth day, the Sabbath, the colonel shall then to another sergeant's church, visiting them all in order, and after having gone the round he must begin again. The captains and lieutenants shall do the same.

Each man throughout the empire who has a wife, sons, and daughters amounting to three or four mouths, or five, six, seven, eight, or nine mouths, must give up one to be a soldier. With regard to the others, the widowers, widows, orphaned, and childless, the disabled and sick, they shall all be exempted from military service and issued provisions from the public granaries for their sustenance.

Throughout the empire all officials must every Sabbath, according to rank and position reverently present sacrificial animals and offerings, sacrifice and worship, and praise the Heavenly Father, the Supreme Lord and Great God. They must also expound the Holy books; should any dare to neglect this duty, they shall be reduced to husbandmen. Respect this.

MUSLIM REBELLIONS

After the Taiping Rebellion struck at the heart of the Qing empire, several other uprisings broke out in quick succession. This was, in no small part, a result of the Qing's attention being diverted from its border regions in order to fend off the fierce Taiping assault. The longest, most organized and—from the Qing perspective—most menacing of these were the Muslim rebellions that occurred in the southwestern and northwestern corners of the empire. The Panthay Rebellion (1856–1872) took place in the multi-ethnic southwestern province of Yunnan. This rebellion followed a series of officially condoned massacres in which over 10,000 Muslim men, women and children were slaughtered. Although the catalyst for the rebellion was the anti-Muslim sentiment of the Han Chinese, the rebellion also reflected the multi-ethnic context in which it took place. Similarly, the Yakub Beg Rebellion of the newly annexed Xinjiang region in northwestern corner of China underscored the Qing's tenuous hold on a decidedly un-Chinese and transregionally positioned territory. This rebellion, unlike the Panthay Rebellion, reflected the lingering and complex transregional religious and ethnic ties that many of its new subjects shared with China's Central Asian neighbors. Both rebellions, like the Taiping Rebellion, were notable in that effective and independent governments were created that ruled over large areas of territory for more than a decade.

3.5 PANTHAY REBELLION SUMMONS TO ARMS (1868)

Written at the height of the rebel regime's powers, the following document sought to bolster the already popular rebel government's efforts to wrest control of the provincial capital from the last remnants of Qing rule. The **Hui** (Muslim Chinese), although not indigenous to Yunnan, had first settled in large numbers during the thirteenth century. The Hui comprised a large part of Kublai Khan's Mongol army and provided many of its subsequent civil officials. By the nineteenth century the Hui had become highly acculturated, spoke Chinese and often dressed in a manner that was indistinguishable from their Han Chinese counterparts. The author of the following document, Du Wenxiu

HUI—A Chinese ethnic group largely defined by their practice of Islam and often referred to as 'Chinese Muslims' though the label does not include other Muslim groups within China such as the Uigur, Kazakhs, or Kyrgyz peoples.

(1823–1872), was the leader and strategist of the multi-ethnic rebel government. From the inception of the rebellion he sought to be inclusive of all ethnic groups including the Han Chinese. By 1868, he had fashioned a tolerant and effective government that tapped into the potent non-Chinese desire for a government that permitted greater local autonomy. In structuring this government, he did not abandon his Hui and Islamic identity. His state seal (like that of Hong Xiuquan's pictured at the beginning of this chapter) included his titles in Chinese. But Du Wenxiu's also included his Arabic titles.

Questions

1. **Does Du Wenxiu seek to promote Islamic culture and Muslims over the Chinese culture and the Han?**
2. **What similarities exist between Du's grievances against the Manchu Qing regime and those leveled by the Taipings (3.1)?**

Wuchen year 7th month 5th day [August 22, 1868]

General **Du Wenxiu** is leading an expedition along five fronts to recover the whole realm of Yunnan to expel cruelty and to improve the fortunes of the good and lawful:

Ponder for a moment the fact that the three peoples of Yunnan–Hui, Han and the indigenous peoples–have lived peacefully together for thousands of years. Friendly towards each other and helping one another in times of need, how could there be profound divisions amongst us? But since the Manchus usurped the throne for more than two hundred years, we have been mistreated. Evil officials carrying out unfair policies caused the **Shiyang Mine massacre** and triggered suffering amongst us all. Those who were strong turned more violent and oppressive. Those who were weak and vulnerable had nowhere to hide. At that time, people were in such danger, but the evil Qing officials still insisted nothing was wrong, expressing no concern for the lives of the common people. What was worse, when the Han Chinese were strong they assisted the Han to kill the Hui; and then when the Hui were powerful helped the Hui to kill Han. Facing such misfortune the people's thoughts were unsettled.

Witnessing such hardships and caring for the people, I cannot tolerate innocent Hui being killed by Han.

I am even less tolerant of innocent Han being mistreated by Hui. I began the rebellion in order to eliminate the Manchu demons. My goal is to save people, and resolve the strife between the Hui and Han. When the mission is accomplished, I will obey Heaven's orders.

Incompetent Qing officials, using every ploy in their bag of tricks, made policies up as they went. ... Now employing a new strategy, we already achieved reports of three victories within a month; mobilizing half of the military force [we] gained control over quite a few towns. But we have yet to rid ourselves of the demon officials and so the root of the disaster remains. Millions of people cannot live peacefully if we do not take full control of Yunnan. How can we allow others to sleep right next to our bed!

We have mobilized our entire military force, maintaining a steady flow of supplies with millions spent on expenditures. Opening five offensive fronts, each with the guns and cannons in front, followed by bow and arrows, and then long swords and short knives, all are eager to fight for the people. Swords drawn and in high spirits, our flags stretch for over a thousand *li* and the sounds of our shouts and drums reach the heavens. Equipped in this way, what enemy can withstand our attack? What goals can we not achieve?

DU WENXIU (1823–1872)—Hui leader of the Yunnan Panthay Rebellion from 1856–1872. Born in western Yunnan, he passed the civil exam at age sixteen. In 1856, after helping capture the western Yunnan city of Dali he was selected to rule the new rebel regime. He died in 1872 after surrendering to Qing troops.

SHIYANG MINE MASSACRE (1854)—One of several instances of Han-Hui violence occurring in the years leading up to the Panthay Rebellion in the southwestern province of Yunnan.

3.6 ROCHER'S DESCRIPTION ON THE GREAT MUSLIM REBELLION OF YUNNAN (1873)

Serving as a foreign technical advisor to the Qing forces, Emile Rocher offers one of the few non-Chinese perspectives on the Panthay Rebellion. Dali, the capital of the Panthay regime, was one of the first cities to fall to the rebels, and was one of the last cities to succumb to Qing forces at the end of the rebellion. According to most accounts, life under the rebels was far more tranquil than in neighboring areas under Qing rule, which remained chaotic and without a stable rule of law. Yunnan Governor Cen Yuying became a principal actor in the Qing's suppression of the rebellion in Yunnan and was rewarded with one of the longest tenures as Yunnan-Guizhou Governor-General.

Questions

1. **Why would government forces feel it necessary to pursue a policy of extermination after the city was effectively under their control?**
2. **How do you think Du Wenxiu is remembered today? Do you think he is remembered similarly among all ethnic groups?**

Early in 1872, [military commander] Yang Yuke had reduced the last fortress along the road and reached the immediate neighborhood of Dali. Here his onward course was again checked for a considerable time. Dali occupies a position of immense military strength. It is situated on an oval or crescent-shaped plain on the western shore of a large lake. In the rear runs a range of lofty mountains, capped with snow and perfectly impassable for troops. At either end of the plain the mountains approach the lake leaving only a narrow pass, occupied by a strongly fortified town. ... Yang Yuke having reached this point, recognized the impossibility of forcing an entrance. He therefore quietly encamped his army on the shores of the lake, beyond the reach of the defender's fire, and waited till an opportunity for action should present itself.

[....]

Inside Dali the question of capitulation was discussed with much vehemence. One party urged the impossibility of resistance, the other the hopelessness of expecting good faith on the part of their enemies. At length the advocates of peace prevailed, and the leading men on their side were deputed to conduct the negotiations. A flag of truce was displayed from the walls, under the protection of which the delegates sought an interview with Yang Yuke. The Chinese general received them kindly. He must refer the matter, he said, to Cen Yuying, who, as Governor of the province was his superior. But the terms would be comparatively light, though the lives of some of the leading men would

have to be sacrificed. Next day the delegates came again. They were told that the Governor would be content with one life, that of Du Wenxiu, but the city must pay a considerable indemnity towards the expenses of the war. The delegates themselves were promised appointments in the emperor's service, if they brought the negotiations to a successful issue. On their return to the city a stormy discussion commenced anew. Du Wenxiu, weary and despairing, was quite willing to lay down his life on behalf of his subjects; and the partisans of peace carried the day. The Great Seal of Dali was sent to Yang Yuke as a sign that the terms were accepted; and it was intimated to him that Du Wenxiu would shortly surrender himself.

On the [December 26, 1872] Du Wenxiu dressed himself in his robes of state. The previous night all his articles of value had been destroyed or thrown into the lake. ... When the appointed moment came he passed from his private apartments into the Audience Hall, where he was received by the delegates who had made arrangements for his departure. Mounting his state chair, he was borne out of the palace, which was his no longer. Slowly and with difficulty he proceeded through the streets. For they were crowded with thousands of subjects, weeping bitterly and desirous to prostrate themselves before their prince for the last time. In this supreme moment his previous shortcomings were forgotten, his many merits alone remembered. The hearts of all were ready to break, as they thought of the sad and solemn circumstances under which he went out from among them for the last time. Reaching the city gates he halted his chair, from which he descended for an instant to thank the people for their demonstrations of affection and to bid them a final farewell. Remounting, he was carried rapidly to the headquarters of Yang Yuke. Here he was received with becoming respect. A few questions were put to him, but he appeared too confused to reply. It was then discovered that he had taken poison before leaving the palace. Indeed he was able to do no more than to proffer a brief request that the victors would "spare the people." These noble words were the last he uttered. He was placed once more in his chair and dispatched to the quarters of Cen Yuying, some miles to the rear. When he arrived there, he was already senseless, and in a few minutes breathed his last. The next morning his head was struck from his corpse and sent by a special messenger to [Kunming]. There it was enclosed in a jar of honey and forwarded triumphantly to Beijing.

[....]

On the eleventh day after the occupation, Cen Yuying who had also entered the city, gave a feast to celebrate the capture of the town. Among those bidden were the principal Muslim [officials], seventeen in number. Those of them who had opposed the surrender came unwillingly, dreading a snare, but still more afraid of giving offence by staying away. Those who had acted as delegates, on the contrary, had nothing to fear and appeared proudly dressed in their new official uniforms. When the guests were all assembled and were on the point of entering the banqueting hall, the host gave his sign. His guards rushed in and seized the Muslims; and seventeen heads rolled on the ground at once. The men whose influence caused the acceptance of the capitulation were slaughtered with the rest. They had gained nothing in the end by their cowardice and selfish abandonment of their [ruler]. At the same instant the startled inhabitants heard the roar of six cannon fired in quick succession. Almost before they had time to wonder, they learned the meaning of the sound. It was the signal for a general massacre. The soldiers rushed upon the people, butchering them without mercy. Cen [Yuying] showed a fiendish cleverness in the way in which he carried out his fearful scheme. Ten days having been allowed to elapse since the commencement of the occupation, the inhabitants had thrown aside their suspicions and had resumed their daily business once more, without a thought of protecting themselves. Under such conditions successful resistance was an impossibility. One body of men, perhaps five hundred in number, one report said five thousand, was charged by a superior force and driven fighting into the lake, where all were engulfed together. The carnage continued till darkness brought a temporary relief. ... Meanwhile, [the next day] the massacre continued in the suburbs set fire to the houses and shot down by the inmates as they attempted to run. By the end of the third day, out of fifty thousand inhabitants, thirty thousand were lying dead, and the rest driven from their homes. The fall of Dali was the real end of the war.

3.7 RUMORS OF A TUNGAN MASSACRE (1864)

Throughout history we encounter the power of rumors. Rumors are for the historian extremely difficult to verify or even quantify. Yet, key historical junctures are often rife with rumors that shape people's actions. As the following document indicates, the rumor of a massacre was the likely catalyst for the inception of the Yakub Beg Rebellion (1864–1877). In this instance, we know from the Qing emperor himself, that rumors of a massacre did circulate. What we cannot discern is if it was more than a rumor. The essential element of this rumor is the mutual distrust felt towards the **Tungans** by both the Central Asian peoples living in Xinjiang (who felt the Tungans were overly Chinese) and the Chinese (who felt the Tungans were overly Islamic). The author of this document, historian Mulla Musa Sayrami (1836–1917) wrote his *History of Kashgar Rulers* around the turn of the century offering one of the few indigenous perspectives of the uprising.

TUNGAN (DONGGAN)—An ethnic label for Muslim Chinese employed only in northwestern China. Also referred to in late imperial documents as Han-Hui.

Questions

1. **How do we assess the responsibility for a rebellion largely incited by false rumors?**
2. **What exactly are the Tungans accused of doing? According to the rumor, who is afraid of them?**

At the time English Christians overpowered the country of Chinese emperor and conquered seventy-two large cities in the region called Burma. They even destroyed some of them. At this juncture, a group of people called *Usūnggū Chanmūzā* [i.e., Taipings] arose contending sovereignty on the one hand, and the Tungans caused troubles on the other. In the end when the Great Khan (*Ulūgh Khān*) [meaning Chinese emperor] heard the news that Tungans, not being able to stay at *Chingchūfū* [i.e., Jinjibao], consulted with each other and moved to the west in order to take the nearby areas, he sent the following edict to the chiefs of the provinces in this direction. "Several Tungans defied the submission, so we gave them advice and promise. However, because they were worried and afraid of their crime and unruly behavior, they could not stay and went to the west. If they go to that region, it is possible that the Tungans in that area will become friendly with them and the common people will become disorderly. As soon as you read this edict, exterminate the Tungans in [the] city and, then, report the result to me, the Great Khan! In this way, he sent the edict to the General of Ili. The General was also startled at this and, after consultations, said, "Tungans are the people of a large number, and their nature and behavior are different [from us]. If they got a scent of [our weakness], we would become like evening and they would become like morning. There is still a long distance for the Tungans to come from the inland (*ichkiri*), so if we invite the Tungans living here and, giving them advice with friendly words, conclude an agreement, then would they not be calmed down and devote themselves to their own livelihood?" … However, they did not become calm. Every night they did not go to sleep, spending nights in holy tombs (*mazār*) [to show their religious fervor]. They vowed and vowed, and even those who had not performed an ablution once a month now did it several times a day. Their sorrow and anxiety grew deeper day by day. The [Ili]General, having found out such activities of these Tungans, became very anxious. Then he ignored the agreement and, executing the emperor (*khān*)'s edict, sent letters to ambans in every city: "On such and such time of such and such day, massacre the Tungan people!"

NOTE: The original Turkic terms are retained to highlight the fact that the rumor (and document) was not Chinese. Typical of rumors, many elements are distorted in its transmission. Also one should be attentive to the fact that the "Great Khan" referred to above is the Chinese emperor.

3.8 ROBERT SHAW'S VISIT TO YARKAND AND KASHGAR (MARCH 3, 1870)

A common aspect of the mid-nineteenth-century rebellions was the attempt by virtually all of the rebel regimes to garner European support for their conflict with the Qing. Although Western powers often considered supporting the rebel regimes, in most instances they decided it was more advantageous to have a weakened Qing imperial government rather than a fractured and warring China. For the British, Yakub Beg's regime proved especially tempting, given the emergent Russian interest in Central Asia. The British believed that a Russian presence in Central Asia might threaten their India colonies. Yakub Beg (1820–1877) proved as equally adept as the Europeans in political intrigue, negotiating with and gaining some degree of support from Russia, Britain, and the Ottoman Empire. In the end, however, Yakub Beg's unstable multi-ethnic alliance proved untenable, and the Chinese imperial army too powerful. Yakub Beg would die in 1877 and his independent kingdom collapsed very soon after. The following article was printed in the London Times reporting on a paper delivered by Robert B. Shaw who had recently returned from meeting with Yakub Beg in 1869.

Questions

1. Why would Robert Shaw be interested in painting a particularly rosy picture of Yakub Beg's rule to his British audience?
2. Why would the Qing court be so interested in bring the area ruled by Yakub Beg back under imperial control? Why would Yakub Beg and the people of western Xinjiang be so reluctant to return to Qing rule?

Mr. Robert B. Shaw, lately arrived in England after his adventurous journey in Chinese **Tartary**... said that the common idea of Tartary was that of a succession of vast plains, over which hordes of barbarians wandered at will with their cattle and tents. He had found the reality widely different. It is a well-cultivated country, containing flourishing cities of more than 100,000 inhabitants, where many of the arts of civilization are carried on. Security of life and property exists; commerce is protected; the roads are full of life and movement, and markets are held on a fixed day of the week, even in the smallest villages. In the towns extensive bazaars, covered in against the rage of the sun, contain rows of shops, where goods of every kind and from every country are exhibited. In **Yarkand** alone there are 60 colleges, with endowments in land, for the education of students of Muslim law and divinity, while every street contains a primary school attached to the mosque, where turbaned rows of boys may be seen daily at their first lessons in reading and writing. There are special streets for the various trades. In one street will be found spread out the silks of China, in another the cotton goods and prints of Russia, while a third will contain robes made of both materials, three or four of which make up the ordinary dress of the Turkic inhabitants. In some streets all kinds of groceries are sold; others are set apart for the butchers, who offer a choice of horseflesh, camel, beef, or mutton; the first is rather a luxury, but the last two are most abundant, selling at about one penny a pound. The bakers make most excellent light loaves by a process of steaming the bread. The greengrocers present abundant supplies of vegetables in great variety, besides cream nearly as thick as that of Devonshire, and delicious cream cheeses. Everywhere sherbet made of fruit is sold, which you can get cooled at any street corner where there are stalls for the sale of ice. There are tea-shops, where the great urns are ever steaming and the eating-houses in abundance. Such is the manifold life of this little-known nation, living a life of its own, making history very fast and looking upon European politics with the same indifference with which its' own have been regarded by us.

The author, who is well known, made his journey with the view of opening the way for trade, especially in tea, between India and Eastern Turkistan, described the manner of his reception by the Governor of Yarkand and by the *Ataliq ghazi,* the ruler of the country, who was then resident in Kashgar. The *Ataliq,* under his former title, Yakub Beg, wrested this flourishing country from the Chinese five or six years ago, but the blow to Chinese domination was struck by the Tooras, a family claiming descent from Genghis Khan, who had formerly been disposed by the Chinese. These, assisted by a force of Andijanis from **Kokand,** who were led by Yakub Beg, expelled or destroyed the Chinese garrisons in 1864; but the fruits of victory were gathered by Yakub Beg, who now seems firmly established as King over a productive region containing a population variously estimated at from 20 to 60 millions. The Andijanis now occupy the chief places in the Administration and form the strength of the army; but their attitude towards the

TARTARY—A European term for Central Asia. Europeans also referred to the nomadic peoples of the steppes (e.g. Mongol, Turkic, Manchu) as "Tartars."

YARKAND (YARKENT)—Located in the modern autonomous region of Xinjiang in western China, Yarkand was an important trading city populated predominantly by Uigurs.

KOKAND—Located in the Central Asian Republic of Uzbekistan, Kokand was positioned at the juncture of two of Central Asia's main trade routes, one into the fertile Ferghana Valley and the other to Tashkent.

native Yarkandis is very conciliatory, and they are looked upon not as conquerors but as brothers in faith and blood, who have delivered them from the yoke of unbelievers and idolators. The Yarkandis are naturally addicted to commerce and the arts of peace, while the Uzbeks of **Andijan** find their most congenial occupation in the administration and arms. Both peoples speak the same language, which is essential that of the Turks of Istanbul. Yakub Beg impressed Mr. Shaw as a man of remarkable intelligence and energy. After the expulsion of the Chinese he overawed the unruly population of Turkistan by acts of severity and cruelty, but secured by these means perfect order and security, without alienating the mass of his subjects. He sits every day in the gateway of **Kashgar** for two or three hours to hear complaints and administer justice. Mr. Shaw's first presentation to him was an effective scene.... At an inner quadrangle he was left to proceed alone to the inner chamber with one official and he there saw the King sitting in expectation at the farther end. When he approached he put out his hands to greet his guest, smiling pleasantly and invited him to sit down on a cushion opposite to him. Mr. Shaw found him to be a man of about 45 years of age, short and stoutly built, with a very broad forehead. He bid him welcome as the first Englishman that had ever been in his country, and said God put it into his heart to accept this arrival as a favorable omen to himself. In subsequent interviews Yakub expressed his great desire to be friendly with the English. He said often, "Your Queen is like the sun which warms everything it shines upon; I am in the cold and desire that some of its rays should fall upon me. I am very small (showing the tip of his finger), a man of yesterday; in these few years God has given me this great country. Whatever services I can render you here you may command, and you must do the same for me."

SELF-STRENGTHENING MOVEMENT

In the years following the Treaty of Nanjing (1842), China obtained only a temporary respite from the demands of Western imperialist powers who wanted ever-increasing commercial, diplomatic and religious privileges. As these calls reached a fever pitch in the 1850s, the Qing court was simultaneously faced with widespread internal rebellions which required the expenditure of considerable military, political, and fiscal resources. Lacking the means to combat both challenges to its authority, the Qing court acquiesced to a series of "unequal treaties" so as to more ably confront the internal threats to their rule. Even as Western military technology began to be used to suppress the Taiping and other rebellions, a small group of Chinese literati began to suggest that Western learning might be employed to address China's domestic problems. The advocates of this "self-strengthening" were *not* wholesale advocates of Western ideas and technology, rather many of them believed they could graft the "substance" (*ti*) of Confucian culture to the "utility" (*yong*) of Western technology. Regardless, the root of Qing reform efforts emerged from the dynasty's efforts to suppress the numerous mid-nineteenth-century rebellions.

3.9   FENG GUIFEN ON THE ADOPTION OF WESTERN LEARNING (1860)

An immensely talented scholar, **Feng Guifen** fled his hometown of Suzhou in the face of the Taiping Army and sought refuge in Shanghai. By this time Shanghai had become the metropolitan base for Western interests in China. Although he remained there for

ANDIJAN—Located in the Central Asian Republic of Uzbekistan, roughly half way between Kashgar and Kokand.

KASHGAR—Located in the modern autonomous region of Xinjiang in western China, Kashgar was the meeting point between two trading routes around the Taklamakan Desert. Today, it remains populated by Uigur, Kazak and Uzbek peoples.

FENG GUIFEN (1809–1874)—A precociously bright scholar, he achieved his jinshi degree at the age of 32 and was immediately appointed to the prestigious Hanlin Academy. A reformer who advocated using Western methods within a Chinese context, he is best known for championing a school to teach Western languages and sciences.

less than a year, Feng became familiar with Western political theory and began to contemplate how such theories might be adapted to aid China in suppressing the domestic threats it faced. The following document is part of Feng's forty *Essays of Protest* initially written during his time in Shanghai and then circulated among influential scholar-officials of the day. They delineate specific reforms he felt the Qing dynasty should implement in order to gain greater internal control and international stature.

Questions

1. **Why would Feng Guifen's proposals seem radical to the more conventional minds of mid-nineteenth-century China?**
2. **What areas of China's domestic political scene does Feng hope to improve with his proposal?**

Currently those who are aware of Western affairs are called *tongshi* [translator]. All are people who engage in trivial affairs, and are not valued by the community. Simply looking for a way to feed and clothe themselves they begin to work for Westerners. Their character is rough and shallow, their intentions despicable. All they lust for is profit. In addition their knowledge of Western languages is limited mostly to merchandise, commerce and slang. How could they be expected to pay attention to scholarly topics? Since there was a need, we established special schools to enroll children from poor families to study both Chinese and Western languages. However, most of those village children are misbehaved and not very intelligent (for several decades I have even tried to find smart students from my own villages and found none). Even worse, they slowly adopted the bad habits of Westerners. What we achieved is no better than previous ones.

If we want to use Western learning, it is necessary to create translation academies at Guangdong and Shanghai. We should select gifted children younger than fifteen-years-old from the nearby areas and offer them a small living allowance along with room and board. Westerners from a variety of countries should be hired to teach their spoken and written languages. Famous scholars from within China should be hired to teach the classics, history, and other subjects. The students should at the same time be taught mathematics. (All Western learning derives from mathematics).

[. . . .]

After three years, all those students who can smoothly read and recite foreign books should be

licensed. The especially gifted students who practically apply their learning should be recommended by the Minister of Trade to receive the *juren* degree as a reward. As I previously indicated, China has many talented minds. Certainly, there are those who having learned from Westerners can surpass them. One of the main responsibilities of government is education.

[. . . .]

Since the expansion of trade over the past 20 years, many foreigners have learned our language and studied our literature. Some of them can even read our classics and history, recognize our statutes and administration, and know our geography and customs. Our officials under the rank of Military Commander (*duhu*) level know nothing about other countries. By comparison should we not be ashamed? As a result, we have to rely on dull-witted translators to communicate. The tone and basic meaning were transmitted, much of the original significance is lacking—and many small inaccuracies have caused big disputes. I lament the fact that our foreign affairs, the key concern for our government, are dependent upon such people. No wonder, we do not understand each other thoroughly, and cannot distinguish the truth from lies. Negotiations for peace or war are carried out without fully understanding the matters at hand. These unresolved issues are our country's unseen peril. If this proposal is implemented, if many more people study foreign languages surely many more people with high standards and character will appear among them. Afterwards, we will understand the crucial elements of our foreign policy and manage them more appropriately.

3.10 ZENG GUOFAN ON FOUNDING THE SHANGHAI ARSENAL (1868)

The primary architect of the "Self-Strengthening Movement," **Zeng Guofan** (1811–1872) combined a strong adherence to traditional Confucian beliefs with an openness to Western methods. His rise coincided with the court's willingness to allow more candid discussion amongst Chinese literati about Western techniques as the empire searched for solutions to its deepening crises. Initially, Zeng Guofan focused on the immediate Taiping threat by advocating a combination of military and fiscal reforms. Turning away from the traditional centralized mechanisms, he created a provincially-based and funded army known as the Hunan (Xiang) Army. In 1865 Zeng Guofan established China's first western-style arsenal. The following memorial was written to provide a brief account of the arsenal's evolution and as a deliberate prod to the Qing court to implement further reforms.

Questions

1. **Why does Zeng Guofan differentiate between using western methods and using foreign products, tradesmen, and teachers?**
2. **What is the primary motivation for Zeng Guofan's reforms? What outcomes are foremost in his mind?**

Zeng Guofan's chief effort at Westernization was the Jiangnan Arsenal established by himself and Li Hongzhang at Shanghai in 1865. Shortly after his transfer to the governor-generalship of Zhili in 1868, Zeng wrote a memorial to present a retrospective account of its founding. He first recalled that his memorial of August 14th, 1861, had urged the building of steamships, and then continued:

In 1862–63, when I was encamped at Anqing [Anhui], where I established a factory to try to make foreign weapons, I used Chinese exclusively and did not employ any foreign mechanics. Although a small steamboat was built, its speed was very slow. The knack of building it was not completely acquired. In the winter of 1863 I sent the expectant sub-prefect **Rong Hong** abroad to purchase machinery, since I intended to make a gradual expansion. Your minister, Li Hongzhang, now Governor-General of Huguang, had paid attention to foreign weapons since the beginning of his tenure or the governorship of Jiangsu [1862]. At the time Ding Richang was the *daotai* of Shanghai. Both he and Li discussed the strategy of resisting foreign aggression and the method of manufacturing weapons. In the fifth month [May 25–June 22] of 1865, I purchased a set of machines in Shanghai and sent the prefects, Feng Junguang, Shen Baojing, and others to open a machine shop [lit., *tiechang,* iron factory]. At this juncture the machines bought by Rong Hong, having also arrived at Shanghai, were combined with the others into one arsenal. At first, because it was at the height of the attack on and suppression of the Taipings, guns and cannon were made. Also, on account of the shortage of funds, it was difficult to start shipbuilding until the fourth [lunar] month of 1867, when your minister memorialized and requested the assignment of twenty per cent from the foreign customs revenue, using ten per cent particularly for the expense of building steamships. Fortunately we are indebted to the Sacred Empress [Cixi] for her acceding to the request. Thereupon both the funds appropriated and the materials purchased gradually became more abundant.

[. . . .]

ZENG GUOFAN (1811–1872) — A strict Confucian who nonetheless championed progressive fiscal and military reforms in the early 1860s helping the Qing to suppress the Taiping Rebellion.

RONG HONG (1828–1912) — More familiar to Western readers as Yung Wing, Rong Hong traveled to the US in 1847, became a US citizen in 1852, graduated from Yale in 1854 and served as an early emissary between China and the United States.

DAOTAI — A sub-provincial level civil official, often translated as 'intendant', he oversaw various sections (or 'circuits') of a province or particular waterways, monopolies, and transportation networks.

It has been learned that in building steamships the boiler, the engine, and the hull are the three most important parts. Formerly when the steamship was built by ourselves in the foreign factory at Shanghai the boiler and engine were both bought from foreign countries and brought to China to be fitted into the hull. There has never been a case where we ourselves designed the blueprint and made the whole set of heavy engine and boiler. This time, when we began construction, we employed our own ingenuity in the study of the blueprint... During the first ten days of the seventh month [August 18–27, 1868], the building of the first ship was completed. Your minister named her the S.S. Tianji [Lit., peaceful and auspicious], meaning that she will be in calm waves within the four seas, and the factory business will be secure and prosperous. Two parts, the boiler and the hull, were both made by ourselves in the factory, but the engine was an old one which was purchased and repaired ...

The said arsenal was formerly at Hongkou, Shanghai, where a foreign workshop was temporarily rented, located in the midst of Chinese and foreigners. This caused much inconvenience. Moreover, the number of machines had daily increased, so that the factory became too small to contain them. During the summer of 1867, we began to build a new arsenal south of the city of Shanghai [....]

In addition a school should be established in which to learn translation, because translation is the foundation for manufactures. Foreign manufacturing is derived from mathematics, all the profound mysteries of which can be discovered through diagrams and explanations. It is simply because the languages are mutually incomprehensible that, even though every day we practice on their machines, after all we do not understand the principles underlying their manufacture and operation. This year the commissioners in the arsenal have paid great attention to translation. At different times we have invited three persons, Wei-lie-ya-li [Alexander Wylie] of England, Fu-lan-ya [John Fryer] and Ma-gao-wen [John MacCowan] of America, who have devoted their energies to selecting and carefully translating books which would be beneficial to manufacturing.

3.11 LI HONGZHANG'S MEMORIAL ADVOCATING FOREIGN LANGUAGE TRAINING (1863)

Grand statesman of the late Qing period, **Li Hongzhang** (1823–1901) came to prominence under Zeng Guofan as a commanding officer in the Hunan Army. Shortly thereafter he organized a separate Huai Army utilizing the same model of organization in the neighboring Anhui province to combat the Nian and Taiping rebel forces in the region. During the 1860s he came into substantial contact with Western military advisors (notably, **Charles "Chinese" Gordon**) As a result of these associations, Li Hongzhang became increasingly convinced of China's need to adopt Western technology. A major force in the Self-Strengthening movement, Li oversaw the building of military academies and naval bases and was an important proponent of other progressive reforms. In the following proposal to the emperor, Li Hongzhang discusses his efforts to build up a body of able translators through a network of translator schools similar to those proposed by Feng Guifen several years earlier.

Questions

1. What rationale does Li Hongzhang offer for the creation of the Tongwen Guan?
2. Does Li Hongzhang envision the students of the Tongwen Guan being different from those who are taking the imperial civil service exams?

LI HONGZHANG (1823-1901) — A major figure in the Self-Strengthening Movement, Li Hongzhang rose to prominence under the tutelage of Zeng Guofan and commanded the Anhui (Huai) Army. In the 1870s he promoted the adoption of Western technology such as railways and arsenals as well as Western-style education. In the last decades of his life Li Hongzhang became the Qing empire's preeminent (if underappreciated) diplomat.

CHARLES "CHINESE" GORDON (1835–1885) — A British officer serving in China during the Taiping Rebellion. He initially fought with British forces, then was appointed to head a joint force of Europeans and Asians known as the "Ever Victorious Army."

In China's contacts with foreigners, we must first of all comprehend their ambitions, be aware of their desires, and have a thorough knowledge of their strengths and weaknesses, of where they are sincere and where they dissemble, before we can expect to be treated equitably. During the past twenty years of trade relations, quite a few of their leaders have learned our language, ... but among our officials and gentry only a very small number understand foreign languages. All the foreign countries have one of two interpreters at Shanghai, and whenever there are discussions between Chinese and foreign high officials, we depend on these foreign interpreters to transmit the discussions. It is difficult to guarantee that there are no biases or misinterpretations

[....]

Your minister requests that, following the example of the Tongwen Guan, we establish an additional foreign language school at Shanghai, select bright, upright, and quiet youngsters fourteen years of age or under from the vicinity, invite Westerners to teach them [foreign languages] and *juren* [civil degree holders] and licentiates of superior character and learning to teach them the classics, history, and literature. After completing their studies, they should be sent to the Governor-General and Governor of their home provinces and examined to be made supplementary district licentiates. ... In three to five years, after we have these educated men skilled in foreign languages, an interpreter should be added to the yamens of all Governors and Governors-General who deal with foreign trade and to the Superintendent of Maritime Customs to handle foreign affairs.... Chinese wisdom and intelligence are hardly inferior to those of the Westerners. If we attain mastery of Western languages, and then teach them to one another, a thorough understanding of all their clever techniques of steamships and firearms can gradually be attained in China.

3.12 WOREN'S MEMORIAL OBJECTING TO WESTERN LEARNING (1867)

In 1862, the Qing court founded the Tongwen Guan (Foreign Languages College), the first imperially sponsored institution of Western learning. Originally designed to teach Western languages as subjects, the school quickly added courses in geometry, chemistry, law, physics, economics, and astronomy to their multi-year program. It quickly became a flashpoint between conservative and liberal officials. The conservatives, led by Woren, the powerful head of the Grand Secretary, vigorously opposed such a Westernized focus. The following document is significant as a reminder that while the mid-nineteenth century marked a period of reform, traditionalists remained hostile to Western subjects, believing they undermined the classical teachings that formed the basis of imperial China's culture and society.

Questions

1. **Is Woren objecting to the subjects taught or is he objecting that they are from the West?**
2. **Is Woren's primary point, that Westerners in China have done more harm than good, a valid one in the 1867 context?**

TONGWEN GUAN (Foreign Languages College)—Founded in 1862 to systematically begin foreign language instruction under government oversight, the college taught English, French, German, Russian and Japanese as well as courses in science, philosophy and international law. In 1902 it was consolidated into the Imperial University (which later became Beijing University).

WOREN (1804–1871)—A powerful Qing official who served as head of the influential Hanlin Academy. Woren espoused strong Neo-Confucian views and vigorously opposed the westernized curriculum advocated by the Self-Strengthening Movement.

In his petition Censor Zhang Shengzao maintains that the government has no need whatever to recruit successful candidates in the civil service examinations to learn about mathematics and astronomy. However, in a decree issued by Your Majesty it is stated that the government-operated Tongwen Guan should in fact recruit these candidates to study these two subjects on the grounds that the subjects are more than technical in nature and are thus not entirely beneath a gentleman's serious concern and that in the pursuit of knowledge a Confucian scholar should not concentrate on one field to the exclusion of all others.

Your Majesty is certainly correct when you say that mathematics, being one of the Six Arts, is a legitimate field of study and should by no means be confused with heretical or unorthodox learning. However, as your humble servant sees it, whatever small advantage can be derived from studying mathematics and astronomy is more than offset by the great harm that would certainly come about when we have to employ Westerners to teach them. In the opinion of your humble servant, we should certainly study this project more carefully before carrying it out. Let me elaborate on this point.

Your humble servant has heard that the foundation of a nation lies in the virtues (such as righteousness and propriety) she possesses rather than in transient advantages she may have or fanciful expedients she can devise. Her true strength is derived from the collective mind of her citizens rather than some unusual skills she happens to possess. Now we are asked not only to pursue a small, an insignificant skill but also honor foreigners as teachers. Since foreigners are known for their treachery, it is extremely doubtful if they will reveal to us all of their secrets. Even if they did, their contribution would amount to no more than the training of technicians. Throughout history no country has ever become strong by relying on achievement in technology.

Being so large, China has many talented men within her national boundaries. If, say, such subjects as mathematics and astronomy are really important enough to be taught, we can certainly find, if our search is wide and intense enough, Chinese experts to teach them. Why do we have to employ foreigners? Why do we have to honor them as our teachers?

Moreover, foreigners have always been our enemies. In the tenth year of Xianfeng (1860), they launched a vicious attack against China without any provocation. They ravaged our capital, thus shaking the nation to its very foundation. They not only set fire to the [Yuanming Yuan] and destroyed it but also indiscriminately murdered civilians and officials alike. This humiliation was unprecedented in the 200-year history of our dynasty and has been deeply resented by both scholars and officials. Though the government was then forced to negotiate peace with these foreigners, how can it ever forget the unavenged shame? Since the conclusion of the peace treaty, Christianity has spread far and wide and with great cunning has beguiled and entrapped many innocent but ignorant citizens. In these critical times the only thing the nation can rely on for its survival is the rectitude of its intelligentsia, who, we hope, can continue to maintain people's integrity by pointing out to them the correct path to follow. Now that we are asked to transform our most talented young men, upon whom the future of our nation relies, into the followers of foreign ways, not only will the best of our tradition suffer regression, but the unorthodox, alien spirit will continue to spread. If this situation continues, I am afraid that in a few years all of us will become foreigners instead of remaining Chinese.

Your humble servant has had the occasion of reading the collected works of the late Emperor Shengzu Ren [Kangxi]. In a decree issued to the Grand Chancellor and the Nine Ministers, he said that China would suffer at the hands of Western powers for several hundred years. How farsighted he was! Though he adopted foreign ways for his own purpose, deep in his heart he never trusted foreigners. In view of the fact that China has suffered greatly at the hands of foreigners for such a long time, why should we insist on spreading their evil ideas? I have heard that foreign missionaries often resent the fact that Chinese intellectuals do not wish to learn about their religion. If we allow successful examination candidates to learn from these people, they will be deluded and led astray by this alien religion before they can learn anything really useful. This is a trap the foreigners have carefully set up: by no means should we fall into it!

It is the hope of your humble servant that Your Majesty, by invoking the power you alone possess, will immediately put an end to the proposal in question, so that the hidden danger contained in it will be eliminated before it can emerge and the future of the nation will remain orthodox and safe. This action on your part will bring great benefit to the nation as a whole.

CHAPTER 4
THE DEEPENING CRISIS
OF IMPERIALISM IN CHINA
(1856–1890)

VISUAL SOURCE
Maps of Treaty Ports

WHAT IS A TREATY PORT? The original impetus for the treaty ports came very much out of the frustrations experienced by foreign merchants in Guangzhou. Thus the original five Chinese treaty ports sought to resolve their key concerns: 1) extend the number of ports where foreign traders could carry out their business 2) allow for year-round residency and 3) provide extraterritorial rights (that is to say only subject to their own consular jurisdiction). Often the term was used more broadly to mean any foreign concession, settlements, or military bases, though technically speaking a treaty port was simply a city open to foreign trade.

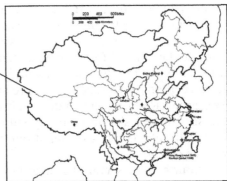
Treaty Ports in China up to 1844

LIFE IN A TREATY PORT: Westerners living in the treaty ports often had a lifestyle that far surpassed that which they could have experienced in their home country. Large homes, servants, social clubs, and a sense of privilege often lead to what many called the "Shanghai mind." Many western residents felt socially, culturally, and racially superior to the Chinese. Few foreigners were interested in China and learning Chinese was seen as something only done by missionaries, consuls, or lower class Westerners who depended upon their daily interaction with Chinese for their livelihood.

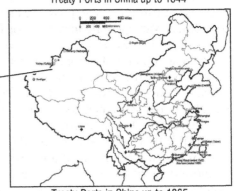
Treaty Ports in China up to 1865

TREATY PORTS: From 1757 until 1842, all Western merchants were restricted to Guangzhou, but with the Treaty of Nanjing (1842), foreign trade was opened at five ports: Guangzhou, Xiamen, Fuzhou, Ningbo, and Shanghai. The Treaty of Tianjin (1860) opened up eleven more ports, and by the turn of the century the number (some of them thousands of miles inland) had risen to nearly 50.

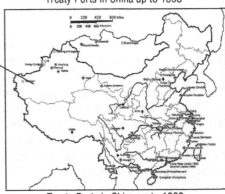
Treaty Ports in China up to 1900

SPHERES OF INTEREST: In the wake of the Sino-Japanese War (1894–95), many of the Western imperialist powers in China perceived their political, commercial, and even religious activities within specific regions, or "spheres." In large part these spheres were shaped by geographical proximity with France most interested in southwestern China (which bordered on French Indochina), Russia directing their resources all along China's northern border, the British primarily focused from Shanghai up the Yangzi river, Germany on the Shandong peninsula, and Japan in northeast China.

ONE PLACE, MULTIPLE NAMES: During the 19th and early 20th century, there existed no commonly agreed upon manner in which to romanize Chinese city names. The variety of languages spoken by the Western imperialist powers further complicated this problem. As a result, there often were large variances in spelling or even the name given to a single city or town. For example, the Shandong port of Qingdao (青岛) was known variously as Ch'ing-tao, Tsingtau, or Tsingtao (a spelling which remains on the popular beer produced in the city).

SHANGHAI: While already a burgeoning river town during the Qing dynasty, its designation as a treaty port in 1842 propelled Shanghai as the preferred meeting points for Western and Chinese merchants. Numerous foreign banks and corporations set up branch offices along the banks of the Huangpu River, in an area known then (as today) as the Bund.

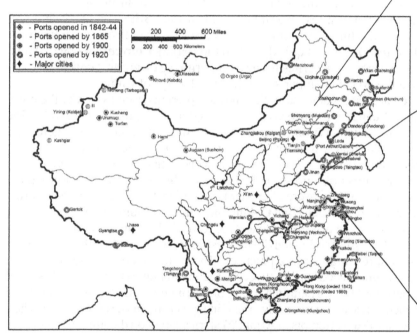

Treaty Ports in China up to 1920

For many years in the 1990s, a large billboard on the road to the **Imperial Summer Palace** on the outskirts of Beijing read, "Do not forget the national shame; rebuild the Chinese nation." The sign marked the entrance to the ruins of a former imperial garden, the Yuanming Yuan. The meaning of the sign was probably lost on most Western tourists, if any even noticed it. Its message, though, would have been immediately apparent to most Chinese. In 1860 the Yuanming Yuan was deliberately looted and then systematically burned to the ground by an Anglo-French military force.

Begun in 1709 as a garden for the Kangxi emperor by his fourth son (and future Yongzheng emperor), it was extended, developed and embellished so that when completed in the 1740s it was a massive imperial retreat. The garden's construction coincided with the period of greatest Jesuit influence within the court. A section of the garden contained buildings and fountains based on Western architectural designs and engineering. Part park, part garden, and part imperial retreat, the Yuanming Yuan at its height covered nearly 900 acres of lakes, islands and palaces. (By comparison the famous Versailles gardens of Louis XIV covered 250 acres). Those who witnessed its splendor found it awe-inspiring.

As the documents below attest in graphic detail, in 1860 British and French forces methodically pillaged the Imperial grounds, then set fire to the entire area. In the wake of such destruction, the Qing court quickly signed the **Beijing Convention** (1860). Western papers hailed the treaty as ushering in a new era, writing glowing accounts of the "civilized" methods of the West in comparison to the "barbarity" of China.

While such acts are hardly defensible, the question presents itself as to why the burning of the Yuanming Yuan remains a focus of "national shame" for the Chinese today. The answer lies in a rigorous exploration of the path of Western imperialism in nineteenth-century China. Many Western textbooks on the topic have, until recently, focused on the diplomatic process, rather than the mechanisms, often violent, that allowed Western powers to elicit an ever-rising number of concessions from China. Chinese historians who see these mechanisms for the coercion they were often label the conflict that lead up to the destruction of the Yuanming Yuan as the **Second Opium War** (though opium was not the focus of the war for either side). It was a process that one American scholar scathingly, and with deliberate irony, described as "English Lessons." The Western powers justified their actions by suggesting they were spreading "civilized practices." They simultaneously made free use of violent and distinctly "uncivilized" tactics to secure their demands. When reading firsthand accounts of the burning of the Yuanming Yuan, one wonders what "lesson" was being taught. The documents below do not absolve the Qing government of responsibility. Their reactive and often ham-fisted attempts to stymie Western aggression did little to resolve the diplomatic situations that were presenting themselves. These reports do reveal a pattern among the Western imperialist powers of repeatedly looking for, creating, or concocting incidents by which they could leverage greater concessions from the Chinese.

The last decades of Qing rule are a disheartening tale. A quarter century of internal rebellions, along with the predatory practices of the West, impeded China's reform efforts. The Qing empire's reduced status within East Asia and in world trade became more evident. China's downward trajectory was humiliatingly clear when Japan defeated

SUMMER PALACE (YIHE YUAN)—An imperial garden constructed in 1888 for the Dowager Empress Cixi. In some English language sources, the Yuanming Yuan is also referred to as the "Old Summer Palace."

BEIJING CONVENTION (1860)—A set of three separate treaties signed by China with Great Britain, France and Russia after the Second Opium War.

SECOND OPIUM WAR (1856–1860)—Known by a variety of names, including the Arrow War, the Second Anglo-Chinese War, as well as the Second Opium War, the war is traditionally understood as taking place in two parts: the first began with the Arrow Incident in 1856 and ended with the signing of the Treaty of Tianjin in 1858. The second part began with the attack on Tianjin and Beijing and ended when the Qing acquiesced and signed the Conventions of Beijing in 1860.

China in the Sino-Chinese War (1894–1895). With that devastating defeat, the last vestiges of Qing China's claim to be an imperial power were lost. The Western powers (along with Japan) began to think of how to divide China's riches (if not the actual country [4.13]).

On many levels the Qing dynasty's decline and China's global humiliation can be traced to the burning of the Yuanming Yuan. Today when Chinese hear the words "Yuanming Yuan," it is the destructiveness of Western imperialism that immediately comes to mind. The havoc wreaked on the Yuanming Yuan by Westerners not only obliterated a stunning element of their past but also ushered in one of the darkest eras of China's history. Today, as European and American chain stores proliferate across China, the Chinese still wonder aloud if the burning of the Yuanming Yuan is indicative of the dangers posed by unbridled Western influence in China today.

THE SECOND OPIUM WAR, THE TREATY OF TIANJIN, AND THE BURNING OF YUANMING YUAN

How does an incident that seems of little consequence at the time evolve into a war between two massive empires? This is the question that arises when trying to pinpoint the events leading to the sack of the Yuanming Yuan and all that came after. The answer lies in paying attention not only to the broader picture but also to how a sequence of small choices, decisions and biases can propel a succession of events to a conclusion completely out of proportion to the original actions. On October 8, 1856 the sequence began when Chinese authorities, following a tip, seized the *Arrow,* a Chinese vessel, and her crew in the waters off of Guangzhou. The *Arrow* was built in China, sailed by a Chinese crew, owned by a Chinese subject, and **sailed under** an expired colonial certificate of registry. The *Arrow*'s captain, a British citizen, was on an outlying vessel having breakfast at the time of the crew's arrest. The captain claimed to have witnessed the seizure when he later notified British authorities. When he heard of the incident, Guangzhou British Consul Harry Parkes insisted the vessel was flying the British flag at the time of seizure and was thus under British jurisdiction (4.1). Over the next months, with the firm belief, and virtually no evidence, that national honor and trade depended on retaliation, British officials attacked Chinese naval defenses, then bombarded, looted and occupied Guangzhou. The British eventually established an allied "provisional government" to rule over the provincial capital. In response to the bombardment, Chinese mobs attacked the old factory area of the city, burning the entire factory district to the ground and destroying both buildings and warehoused trade goods. The British deemed these mob attacks worthy of a military response. In quick order the British Prime Minister sent Lord Elgin as head of an expeditionary force to China. Upon his arrival Lord Elgin immediately diverged from his government's clearly delimited instructions by doggedly pursuing the appointment of a British representative (ambassador) in Beijing (4.2). In 1858 Qing officials balked at ratifying the treaty that **Lord Elgin** had presented. This led to China's second military engagement with Britain, and eventually to the burning of the Yuanming Yuan.

SAILING UNDER A FOREIGN FLAG—In a tactic common in the mid-nineteenth century, Chinese smugglers would hire Europeans to serve as the ostensible captains of their vessels. Often unable to speak Chinese and unfamiliar with the waters in which the ship sailed, these "captains" were little more than a maneuver to secure the protection of the British flag.

LORD JAMES ELGIN (1811–1863)—Britain's High Commissioner and Plenipotentiary to China accompanied by an expeditionary force of 5000 men during the Second Opium War and ordered the destruction of the Yuanming Yuan.

4.1 HARRY PARKES' LETTER TO COMMISSIONER YE MINGCHEN (OCTOBER 8, 1856)

The following letter was written only hours after Harry Parkes learned of the arrest of the *Arrow* crew and was immediately followed by a similar letter to his superiors in Hong Kong. It is unclear whether at the time Parkes wrote the letter he was simply misinformed or deliberately untruthful. First, the English captain was not on the boat at the time of the arrest. Second, as attested to by British witnesses, when ships were at anchor they did not fly their national flag, so it was difficult to see how the Chinese "dishonored the flag." Third, given that Parkes had not proven either of the first two points, the Chinese authorities were completely within their rights not to hand over the prisoners (the Chinese crew). Yet even when Commissioner Ye Mingchen did attempt to hand over the crew, stating, "this is a trivial affair not worthy to be disputed," Parkes refused to receive them, taking it as an insult that Ye Mingchen did not personally escort them.

Questions

1. What crimes does Parkes suggest have occurred? What is his primary intention in pursuing the case?
2. What precisely does Parkes want Commissioner Ye Mingchen to do in order to resolve the matter?

No. 69. British Consulate, Canton,

October 8, 1856

Sir,

I hasten to bring to your Excellency's notice an insult of a very grave character, which calls for immediate reparation.

This morning shortly after eight o'clock a Chinese war boat boarded an English **lorcha,** the *Arrow,* lying at anchor in the river near the *Dutch Folly,* and regardless of the remonstrances of her master, an Englishman, seized, bound and carried off twelve of her Chinese crew, and hauled down the English colors which were then flying.

Hesitating to rely solely on the master's account of so gross an outrage, I at once dispatched people to make enquiries and found that the facts were as he had stated, and that the war boat, said to be under the command of Liang Guoding, a captain in the imperial service, after leaving the lorcha, had dropped down the river, and was lying off the Yongqing gate, with the crew of the lorcha still on board as prisoners.

On receiving this intelligence, I proceeded in person to the war boat accompanied by Her Majesty's Vice-Counsel, and explained to the officer whom I found in charge called Li Yongxing the gravity of the error committed by the said war boat in boarding and carrying off by force of arms the crew of an English vessel and the gross indignity offered to the national flag by hauling down the lorcha's ensign. I also required him to bring his prisoners to the British Consulate, there to await examination; but this he refused to do, and upon my claiming them and insisting upon their being delivered to me, he made a display of force, and threatened me with violence if I attempted to take them with me.

I hasten therefore to lay the case before your Excellency, confident that your superior judgment will lead you at once to admit that an insult so publicly committed must be equally publicly atoned. I therefore request your Excellency to direct that the men who have been carried away from the *Arrow* be returned by the Captain Liang Guoding to that vessel in my presence; and if accused of any crime, they may be conveyed to the British Consulate, where in conjunction

LORCHA—A sailing vessel of about 100 tons, with a European built hull and Chinese masts and sails.

with proper officers deputed by your Excellency for the purpose, I shall be prepared to investigate the case.

At the same time that I address your Excellency on this subject, I am submitting both to Her Majesty's Plenipotentiary and Commodore in command of H.M. naval force in this river, a report of what has occurred, and I should add that the said lorcha being at present detained here, in consequence of the seizure of her crew, has a claim upon your Excellency's Government for the expenses which this delay occasions her.

I have &c.

[signed] H.S. Parkes, Consul.

4.2   REFLECTIONS OF LORD ELGIN ON THE TREATY OF TIANJIN (JUNE 29, 1858)

Lord Elgin arrived in Hong Kong in 1857 as Britain's High Commissioner and **Plenipotentiary** accompanied by an expeditionary force of 5000 men. While not wholly in agreement with Parkes' decision regarding the *Arrow,* Elgin and the other British officials on the scene decided to press the matter on principle. On December 24th, the British delivered an ultimatum, giving the ranking official, Commissioner Ye Mingchen, forty-eight hours to begin to respond to their demands. The ultimatum insisted that the Chinese agree to face-to-face negotiations, repair the destroyed factories, re-establish trade, allow foreigners to enter the city, and pay six million taels in compensation. When they received no response, they attacked the city's forts, then bombarded and captured the city. Commissioner Ye Mingchen, who sought to avoid a military conflict in a futile attempt to save the city, was arrested and eventually transported on a British vessel to India. He departed from Guangzhou on February 23, 1858 and died the following spring in a Calcutta prison. When the occupation of Guangzhou still did not move the Qing court to action, Elgin sailed north up the coast of China and threatened the Dagu forts outside of Tianjin. Finally, in May 1858, imperial officials drew up terms for the **Treaty of Tianjin.** It is the end of this negotiation process that Elgin refers to in the following document.

Questions

1. **What is Lord Elgin's opinion of the Chinese officials with whom he is negotiating?**
2. **Why is he disturbed with the attitude of the French and American ministers?**

Lord Elgin's diary.

June 29th—I have not written for some days, but they have been busy ones.... We went on fighting and bullying, and getting the poor commissioners to concede one point after another, till Friday the 25th, when we had reason to believe that all was settled, and that the signature was to take place the following day.... On Friday afternoon, however, Baron Gros came to me with a message from the Russian and American ministers to induce me to recede from two of my demands—1) a

PLENIPOTENTIARY—A person, especially a diplomatic agent, vested with full power to transact any business, such as negotiating a treaty with a foreign power

TREATY OF TIANJIN (1858)—Treaty ending the first phase of the Second Opium (Arrow) War. Its terms forced the Qing court to accept a British ambassador in Beijing, as well as the addition of ten cities as treaty ports, and the opening all of interior China to travel, trade and Christian proselytizing. The treaty was ratified in the Beijing Convention by the emperor in 1860, only after British and French forces looted and burned the Yuanming Yuan.

resident minister at Beijing, and 2) permission to our people to trade in the interior of China; because, as they said, the Chinese plenipotentiaries had told them that they had received a decree from the Emperor stating that they should infallibly lose their heads if they gave way on these points.... The resident minister at Beijing I consider far the most important matter gained by the treaty; the power to trade in the interior hardly less so.... I had at stake not only these important points in my treaty, for which I had fought so hard, but I know not what behind. For the Chinese are such fools that it was impossible to tell, if we gave way on one point, whether they would not raise difficulties on every other. I sent for the admiral; gave him a hint that there was a great opportunity for England; that all the powers were deserting me on a point which they had *all,* in their original applications to Beijing, demanded, and which they all intended to claim if I got it; that, therefore, we had it in our power to claim our place of priority in the East by obtaining this when others would not insist on it. Would he back

me?...This was a forenoon of Saturday, 26th, and the treaty was to be signed in the evening. I may mention, as a proof of the state of people's minds, that Admiral Seymour told me that the French admiral had urged him to dine with him, assuring him that no treaty would be signed that day! I sent Frederick to the imperial commissioners to tell them that I was indignant beyond all expression at their having attempted to communicate with me through third parties; that I was ready to sign at once the treaty as it stood; but that if they delayed or retreated, I should consider negotiations at an end, go to Beijing and demand a great deal more, etc.... Frederick executed this most difficult task admirably, and at six p.m. I signed the Treaty of Tianjin.... I am now anxiously awaiting some communication from Beijing. Till the Emperor accepts the treaty I shall hardly feel safe. Please God he may ratify without delay! I am sure that I express the wish just as much in the interest of China as our own. Though I have been forced to act almost brutally, I am China's friend in all this.

4.3 TREATY OF TIANJIN (JUNE 26, 1858)

One of Lord Elgin's primary goals in negotiating the 1858 Treaty of Tianjin was to gain the right to post a consular representative to Beijing. Britain had pursued this diplomatic goal since Lord Macartney first traveled to China three-quarters of a century earlier (1.8). The treaty also addressed several of Britain and France's outstanding and unresolved issues, namely to further open China religiously and commercially. The treaty also established the central legal concept of **"extraterritoriality"** that would shape interactions between China and Westerners for the next fifty years. In practice extraterritoriality meant that those Westerners who committed a crime in China would be judged not by local Chinese officials but by the laws and officials of their own country (usually the consular officials posted in the nearest treaty port). Although initially signed by representatives from each country in 1858, China refused to ratify it. This led to further hostilities against China in 1860.

Questions

1. In what way(s) does the Treaty of Tianjin differ from that of the Treaty of Nanjing which it is seeking to replace?
2. Why do you think the British (and other Western powers) sought to include Article LI which prohibited the use of a specific Chinese term in reference to them?

EXTRATERRITORIALITY—A legal practice that gives individuals from foreign countries immunity from local laws. In theory, an individual's home country would try the person for a crime under their country's laws, but in practice this rarely occurred.

[Ramifications exchanged at Beijing, October 24, 1860.]

Her Majesty the Queen of the United Kingdom of Great Britain and Ireland, and his Majesty the Emperor of China, being desirous to put an end to the existing misunderstanding between the two countries, and to place their relations on a more satisfactory footing in future, have resolved to proceed to a revision and improvement of the treaties existing between them; and, for that purpose, have named as their plenipotentiaries, that is to say:

Her Majesty the Queen of Great Britain and Ireland, the right honourable the Earl of Elgin and Kincardine, a peer of the United Kingdom, and knight of the most Ancient and most noble Order of the Thistle;

And his Majesty the Emperor of China, the High Commissioner Guiliang, a senior Chief Secretary of State, styled of the East Cabinet, Captain-General of the Plain White Banner of the Manchu banner force, Superintendent-General of the administration of criminal law; and Huashana, one of his imperial Majesty's Expositors of the Classics, Manchu President of the Office for the regulation of the Civil Establishment, Captain-General of the Bordered Blue Banner of the Chinese Banner Force, and Visitor of the Office of Interpretations;

Who, after having communicated to each other their respective full powers, and found them to be in good and due form, have agreed upon and concluded the following articles:—

ARTICLE I

The Treaty of peace and amity between the two nations signed at Nanjing (1842)... is hereby renewed and confirmed.

[....]

ARTICLE III

His Majesty the Emperor of China hereby agrees, that the ambassador, minister, or other diplomatic agent, so appointed by her Majesty the Queen of Great Britain, may reside, with his family and establishment, permanently at the Capital, or may visit it occasionally, at the option of British Government. He shall not be called upon to perform any ceremony derogatory to him as representing the sovereign of an independent nation, on a footing of equality with that of China. On the other hand, he shall use the same forms of ceremony and respect to his Majesty the Emperor as are employed by the ambassadors, ministers, or diplomatic agents of her Majesty towards the sovereigns of independent and equal European nations.

It is further agreed that her Majesty's Government may acquire at Beijing a site for building, or may hire Houses for the accommodation of her Majesty's mission, and that the Chinese Government will assist it in so doing.

Her Majesty's Representative shall be at liberty to choose his own servants and attendants, who shall not be subjected to any kind of molestation whatever.

Any person guilty of disrespect or violence to her Majesty's representative, or to any member of his family or establishment, in deed or word, shall be severely punished.

[....]

ARTICLE VIII

The Christian religion, as professed by Protestants or Roman Catholics, inculcates the practice of virtue and teaches man to do as he would be done by. Persons teaching or professing it, therefore, shall alike be entitled to the protection of the Chinese authorities, nor shall any such, peaceably pursuing their calling, and not offending against the law, be persecuted or interfered with.

ARTICLE IX

British subjects are hereby authorized to travel for their pleasure or for purposes of trade, to all parts of the Interior, under passports which will be issued by their consuls, and countersigned by the local authorities. These passports, if demanded, must be produced for examination in the localities passed through. If the passport be not irregular, the bearer will be allowed to proceed, and no opposition shall be offered to his hiring persons or hiring vessels for the carriage of his baggage or merchandise. If he be without a passport, or if he commit any offence against the law, he shall be handed over to the nearest consul for punishment, but he must not be subjected to any ill-usage in excess of necessary restraint. No passport need be applied for by persons going on excursions from the ports open to trade to a distance not exceeding one hundred *li,* and for a period not exceeding five days.

The provisions of this article do not apply to crews of ships, for the due restraint of whom regulations will be drawn up by the consul and the local authorities....

ARTICLE X

British merchant-ships shall have authority to trade upon the Great River (Yangzi). The upper and lower valley being, however, disturbed by outlaws, no port shall be for the present opened to trade, with the exception of Zhenjiang, which shall be opened in a year from the date of the signing of this Treaty.

ARTICLE XI

In addition to the Cities and Towns of Guangzhou, Xiamen, Fuzhou, Ningbo and Shanghai, opened by the Treaty of Nanjing, it is agreed that British subjects may frequent the Cities and Ports of Niuzhuang, Dengzhou, Taiwan, Chaozhou and Qiongzhou....

ARTICLE XII

British subjects, whether at the ports or at other places, desiring to build or open houses, warehouses, churches, hospitals, or burial-grounds, shall make their agreement for the land or building they require, at the rates prevailing among the people, equitably, and without exactions on either side.

ARTICLE XIII

The Chinese Government will place no restrictions whatever upon the employment, by British subjects, of Chinese subjects in any lawful capacity.

ARTICLE XIV

British subjects may hire whatever boats they please for the transport of goods or passengers, and the sum to be paid for such boats shall be settled between the parties themselves without the interference of the Chinese Government....

ARTICLE XV

All questions in regard to rights, whether of property or person, arising between British subjects, shall be subject to the jurisdiction of the British authorities.

ARTICLE XVI

Chinese subjects who may be guilty of any criminal act towards British subjects shall be arrested and punished by the Chinese authorities according to the Laws of China.

British subjects who may commit any crime in China shall be tried and punished by the consul or other public Functionary authorized thereto, according to the Laws of Great Britain.

Justice shall be equitably and impartially administered on both sides.

[....]

ARTICLE L

All official communications, addressed by the diplomatic and consular agents of her majesty the Queen to the Chinese authorities, shall, henceforth, be written in English. They will for the present be accompanied by a Chinese version, but it is understood that, in the event of there being any difference of meaning between the English and Chinese text, the English Government will hold the sense as expressed in the English text to be the correct sense. The provision is to apply to the treaty now negotiated, the Chinese text of which has been carefully corrected by the English original.

ARTICLE LI

It is agreed that, henceforward, the Character "yi" 夷 (barbarian), shall not be applied to the Government or subjects of her Britannic Majesty, in any Chinese official document issued by the Chinese Authorities either in the capital or in the provinces.

ARTICLE LII

British ships of War, coming for no hostile purpose of being engaged in the pursuit of Pirates, shall be at liberty to visit all Ports within the Dominions of the Emperor of China, and shall receive every facility for the purchase of provisions, procuring water, and, if occasion require, for the making of repairs. The commanders of such ships shall hold intercourse with the Chinese authorities, on terms of equality and courtesy.

Done at Tianjin, this twenty-sixth day of June, in the year of our Lord one Thousand eight hundred and fifty-eight; corresponding with the Chinese date, the sixteenth day, fifth month, of the eighth year of Xianfeng.

(L.S.)   Elgin and Kincardine.

Signatures and Seal of Chinese Plenipotentiaries

Separate article annexed to the Treaty concluded between Great Britain and China, on the twenty-sixth day of June, in the year one thousand eight hundred and fifty-eight.

It is hereby agreed that a sum of two millions of taels on account of the losses sustained by British subjects, through the misconduct of the Chinese authorities at Guangdong, and a further sum of two millions of taels on account of the military expenses of the expedition which her Majesty the Queen has been compelled to send out for the purpose of obtaining redress, and of enforcing the due observance of Treaty provisions, shall be paid to her Majesty's representative in China by the authorities of the Guangdong province.

The necessary arrangements with respect to the time and mode of effecting these payments, shall be determined by her Majesty's representative, in concert with the Chinese authorities of Guangdong.

When the above amounts shall have been discharged in full, the British forces will be withdrawn from the city of Guangzhou.

Done at Tianjin, this twenty-sixth day of June, in the year of our Lord one Thousand eight hundred and fifty-eight; corresponding with the Chinese date, the sixteenth day, fifth month, of the eighth year of Xianfeng.

(L.S.)   [Earl of] Elgin and Kincardine.

Signatures and Seal of Chinese Plenipotentiaries

4.4   A NARRATIVE ON THE BURNING OF THE YUANMING YUAN (OCTOBER 18, 1860)

In 1860, Lord Elgin returned to China as the leader of a second expeditionary force to demand the ratification of the Treaty of Tianjin. After a successful attack on the Dagu fort near Tianjin, the armies marched inland to Hexiwu, a small town about halfway between Tianjin and Beijing. Elgin then sent a small contingent lead by Thomas Wade, Harry Parkes and Henry Loch to negotiate with the Qing. At the same time the Qing court learned the British had detained a Tianjin official. Prince Yixin (the emperor's brother), likely remembering the treatment of Commissioner Ye Mingchen by the British, ordered the British arrested—including Parkes and Loch. The prisoners were quickly divided into several groups of four or five men and whisked away to separate locations. After the looting of the Yuanming Yuan, on October 13th, Britain and French delivered an ultimatum that demanded the release of the prisoners. The next day Parkes and Loch were released. As the prisoners' deplorable treatment became known (nineteen of the thirty-six prisoners died, largely from neglect, exposure, and starvation), outrage soon shaped Western actions. The Reverend M'Ghee, chaplain to the British forces, wrote the following description.

Questions

1. **What objective does M'Ghee suggest the burning of the Yuanming Yuan will achieve?**
2. **What sentiments does M'Ghee express about the destruction of the Yuanming Yuan? Do you agree with his conclusions?**

My duties did not permit me to be present on the first day when this work of destruction was begun; the troops were spread over the country[side] by one and two companies, and fired every building in four palatial "gardens," as they are called, beginning with the Yuanming Yuan; next, and to the west, the Wanshou Yuan; then the Jinming Yuan; and last the Xiangshan, which mean respectively the "enclosed and beautiful garden," "the birthday garden," "the golden and brilliant garden," and the "fragrant hills."

On the second day I arrived at about eight o'clock in the morning, at the Yuanming Yuan... We marched through scenery of the most enchanting beauty, planted hills, lakes, temples, with villages interspersed, which were the abodes of the Imperial troops; many a matchlock was to be seen in their houses, but they thought only of conciliating us by **"chin-chining,"** "kow-towing," and offerings of hot tea and cold water. I never experienced more mingled feelings than upon this occasion. As I rode along through scenes which

CHIN-CHIN—A type of "pigeon English" phrase used in Chinese ports as a greeting or salute. It is likely a corruption of the Chinese phrase qing-qing, a response akin to "salutation," or "with regards."

(if anything can compensate for the absence of those "looks that we love," as Moore calls them) it was worthwhile coming all the way from home to see; I could not help giving to them all the admiration of my heart which their beauty demanded. A tribute so due that you must perforce pay it.

I turned the corner of a high wall round which the paved road led, and before me was a dense mass of smoke, and the fierce blaze of the raging fire towering above it, and far above the trees. A temple, which means not one building, but a whole cluster of separate edifices, circling round one great shrine, was in flames, and communicating destruction to the noble trees, in and around it, which had shed their grateful shade over it for many a generation: its gilded beams and porcelain roof of many colors, in which of course the Imperial yellow claimed the superiority—all, all, a prey to the devouring element. You could not but feel that although devoid of sympathy for its deity, there was a sacrilege in devoting to destruction structures which had been reared many, many hundred years ago; nor was it the buildings only, adorning as they did the scenery which claimed your sympathy, but every building was a repository of ancient and curious art, enamels made before the present dynasty of China, books to no end, engravings of all sorts of scenes, historical, illustrating the wars of the Chinese and Manchus, some the production of purely native talent, and others by Jesuit missionaries, and drawn in the Chinese style. These missionaries are generally learned in something else besides religion, and thus they beat ours [British] out of the field altogether. Embroidered hangings of enormous value, altar furniture plated with gold, things, which apart altogether from their value, were full of interest from their beauty and rarity, all devoted to destruction; some few were saved by officers, but as carriage was difficult, but few.

[. . . .]

Soon the wreath becomes a volume, a great black mass, out burst a hundred flames, the smoke obscures the sun, and temple, palace, buildings and all hallowed by age, if age can hallow, and by beauty, if it can make sacred, are swept to destruction, with all their contents, monuments of imperial taste and luxury. A pang of sorrow seizes upon you, you cannot help it, no eye will ever again gaze upon those buildings which have been doubtless the admiration of ages, records of by-gone skill and taste, of which the world contains not the like. You have seen them once and forever, they are dead and gone, man cannot reproduce them. You turn away from the sight; but before you arises the vision of a sad, solemn, slow procession. Mark that most touching sight, the dashing charger led, not ridden; the saddle is empty, the book is in the stirrup, but it is empty also; the limb that filled it forms now a part of the skeleton that lies in the coffin on that gun-carriage. You saw that sight two days ago, you see a vision of it now; you turn back and gaze with satisfaction on the ruin from which you had hidden your face and say, "Yes, thank God, we can make them feel something of the measure of their guilt;" and if there were another building left to burn, you would carry the brand to it yourself.

[. . . .]

Yes, a good work, I repeat it, though I write it with regret, with sorrow; stern and dire was the need that a blow should be struck which should be felt at the very heart's core of the Government of China and it was done. It was a sacrifice of all that was most ancient and most beautiful, but it was offered to the manes of the true, the honest, and the valiant, and it was not too costly, oh no! one of such lives was worth it all. It is gone, but I do not know how to tear myself away from it. I love to linger over the recollection and picture it to myself, but I cannot make you see it. A man must be a poet, a painter, an historian, a virtuoso, a Chinese scholar, and I don't know how many other things besides, to give you even an idea of it, and I am not an approach to any of them. But whenever I think of beauty and taste, of skill and antiquity, while I live, I shall see before my mind's eye some scene from those grounds, those palaces, and ever regret the stern but just necessity which laid them in ashes.

4.5 A NARRATIVE ON THE LOOTING AND PRIZE MONEY AT THE YUANMING YUAN (OCTOBER 7, 1860)

The Allied forces of France and Britain marched to the Chinese capital in early October of 1860. However, neither army occupied Beijing. Instead they marched to the Yuanming Yuan, twelve miles north of the city. While French accounts accuse the British of starting the looting and British reports blame the French, there is absolutely no doubt that both armies were heavily involved in pillaging the imperial garden. What is often misunderstood or overlooked is how the two armies organized and carried out the collection and distribution of plundered goods. The items seized by the British were collected, cataloged, and auctioned off. Each British soldier received a share of the total public sale proceeds. Within a year, British auction houses were offering "the emperor of China's Great Seal of State" and other items clearly listed as having originated from the Yuanming Yuan. Garnet Wolseley, who served as a quartermaster-general in the British armed forces, offered the following account.

Questions

1. **Why do you think the two European armies chose the imperial garden as their target of their military operation?**
2. **What attitudes does Wolseley express with regards to the looting?**

[At the Yuanming Yuan palace gates] about twenty badly-armed eunuchs made some pretence at resistance but were quickly disposed of, and the doors burst open, disclosing the sacred precincts of his Majesty's residence, to what a Chinaman would call the sacrilegious gaze of the barbarians. A mine of wealth and of everything curious in the empire lay as a prey before our French allies. Rooms filled with articles of vertu [fine art] both native and European, halls containing vases and jars of immense value, and houses stored with silks, satins, and embroidery, were open to them. Indiscriminate plunder and wanton destruction of all articles too heavy for removal commenced at once. Guards were placed about in various directions; but to no purpose. When looting is once commenced by an army it is no easy matter to stop it. At such times human nature breaks down the ordinary trammels which discipline imposes, and the consequences are most demoralizing to the very best constituted army. Soldiers are nothing more than grown-up schoolboys. The wild moments of enjoyment passed in the pillage of a place live long in a soldier's memory.... Officers and men seemed to have been seized with a temporary insanity; in body and soul they were absorbed in one pursuit, which was plunder, plunder. I stood by whilst one of the regiments was supposed to be parading; but although their fall in was sounded over and over again, I do not believe there was an average of ten men a company present. Plundering in this way bears its most evil fruit in an army; for if when it is once commenced an effort is made to stop it, the good men only obey; the bad soldiers continue to plunder, and become rich by their disobedience, whilst the good ones see the immediate effect of their steadiness is to keep them poor.

[....]

Our allies were so busy in the collection of their plunder that they did not move upon Beijing until the 9th October. Numbers of our officers had consequently an opportunity of visiting the palaces and securing valuables; but our men were carefully prevented from leaving camp. Those officers who were fortunate enough to have carts and time for amusement, brought into camp large collections of valuables. It was naturally most riling to our soldiers to see their allies rolling in wealth, and even their own officers all more or less provided with curiosities whilst they themselves got nothing. It would have been very easy for the Commander-in-Chief to have allowed our regiments to go out there one by one; but the state in which the French army was then in, and the recollection of what ours had been after the capture of Dehli were cogent reasons for avoiding such an arrangement. Subsequent to Sir Hope Grant's visit to the palaces upon the 7th October, a room of treasure was discovered there, a small share of which was secured for our army by the active exertions of Major Anson, A.D.C., who had been appointed one of our prize agents. The treasure chiefly consisted of golden ingots, the portion falling to our lot amounting about eight or nine thousand pounds sterling. To have permitted our officers to retain what they had personally taken from the palaces, whilst the private soldier received nothing, would have been very hard upon the latter. The Commander-in-Chief therefore issued an order directing all officers to send in everything they had taken to the prize agents, who had been nominated to receive all such property, for the purpose of having it sold by public auction upon the spot and the proceeds distributed immediately amongst the army.

The sale took place in front of the large **joss**-house at headquarters, realizing 123,000 dollars, which enabled

---

JOSS—A term used by Europeans to mean a religious icon or statue. Likely a Chinese corruption of the Portuguese Deos, "God," the term was re-adopted by Europeans who thought it was a Chinese word. A "joss house" was any Chinese temple whether Buddhist, Confucian or Daoist.

the prize agents to issue seventeen dollars (nearly four pounds sterling) to every private belonging to our army. The officers were divided into three classes and received in the same proportion. The Commander-in-Chief whose share would have been considerable, renounced his claims; the Major-Generals, Sir John Michel, K.C.B. and Sir Robert Napier, K.C.B., following his example. One third went to the officers, two-thirds to the non-commissioned officers and men.

Prize money is a subject well understood but seldom received by our soldiers. [. . . .] Any who have ever been present at the assault of a town will, I am sure, agree with me in thinking that no price is too high which we can pay for the prevention of those dreadful scenes of riot and consequent insubordination which have upon several occasions followed

such an event. Discipline once relaxed as it must be when plunder is permitted, its entire fabric of regulations break down in one moment, which it takes many months of subsequent reorganization to reassert. If Sir Hope Grant had contented himself with promising that the question of prize money should be referred to the Home Government, after their recent Indian experience, our men would have been very dissatisfied, seeing every French soldier going about with his pockets filled with dollars and **Sycee** silver. Indeed, I fear that the temptation would have been too great for many of our men who knew that the Yuanming Yuan was only a few miles off. The plan which he adopted, although novel, was thoroughly successful, and all were pleased with its results.

MARGARY AFFAIR AND EFFECTS OF IMPERIALISM ON CHINA

In 1874 a young British translator, Augustus R. Margary, was dispatched from Beijing to the southwestern province of Yunnan to escort a group of British officials from Burma back to Beijing. He did not live to see Beijing again, for he was killed only days after meeting with the Burmese delegation near the Yunnan-Burma border.

The highest Qing official in the region, Yunnan-Guizhou Governor-General **Cen Yuying,** a year earlier had extinguished the final remnants of the Panthay Rebellion (3.6). Promoted, rewarded with several honorary titles, and given considerable latitude in bringing Yunnan back under imperial control, Cen Yuying was highly regarded by the emperor for imposing order and normalcy on a distant and unsettled province. Yet as the documents in this section suggest, an official who had helped quell a grave threat to Qing imperial control was not necessarily equipped to handle crises involving Westerners.

By the 1870s, Westerners were increasingly insistent on making inroads into internal China with its larger markets. As is described in the following documents, Chinese officials faced a double-edged danger from the increased presence of Westerners. Any warning against entering China or traveling to specific cities would be grounds for Westerners to accuse the Chinese of failing to meet their agreements in existing treaties. And any crime that was perpetrated against Westerners would be portrayed as evidence that the government harbored anti-foreign sentiments. As the following three documents (4.6, 4.8, 4.9) underscore, the Western powers began to adopt a more aggressive style of diplomacy and to bombard the **Zongli Yamen** with queries and

SYCEE—A term employed by Europeans in China to refer to silver ingots.

CEN YUYING (1829–1889)—A native of Guangxi, he rose rapidly through official ranks in Yunnan province during the Panthay Rebellion by pursuing an anti-Hui policy, later becoming Governor-General of Yunnan and Guizhou for much of the 1870s and 1880s.

ZONGLI YAMEN—Established in 1861 following the Convention of Beijing, its primary goal was to handle China's foreign relations in a more systematic manner. Often simply called the "Foreign Office," the office's full title Zongli Geguo Shiwu Yamen translates as "Office for the Management of the Affairs of All Foreign Countries."

demands. These expanded initiatives included protests over a host of minor infractions—all in an effort to leverage further concessions from the faltering Qing court. The Margary Incident is perhaps the most straightforward of many such cases and illustrates the growing prevalence of such tactics. The case as detailed below points out that the burden of proof lay almost exclusively with the Chinese, and that in most cases no amount of evidence was sufficient to allay the West's suspicions.

4.6 THOMAS WADE'S DESCRIPTION AND PROTEST OF MARGARY MURDER (MARCH 19, 1875)

In 1875, British Minister to China **Thomas Wade** took up the case of Augustus Margary's murder. Despite Wade's bombast, there is no doubt that Margary's orders to travel through Yunnan Province had placed him in danger. It was a reckless venture in the best of times and sheer folly in 1875. The road Margary traveled took him through extremely remote areas, many of which were still under the rule of indigenous native chieftains (*tusi*) and far from the long arm of the state. While native chieftains were ostensibly part of the imperial government, they were notoriously unreliable. Furthermore, given that the Panthay Rebellion had been suppressed just a few months earlier, the border area remained unstable. Substantial remnants of rebel forces had fled into the mountains on the Yunnan-Burma border to escape Qing persecution. Wade's harangue against the Qing, however, is typical of the tactics adopted by the Western powers. In this exchange he suggests that by issuing a passport to a Westerner China was responsible for the outcome and should have protected Margary from all eventualities, no matter the context.

Questions

1. **How does Wade assert Margary's death is the responsibility of the Chinese government?**
2. **What response does Wade seem to desire from the Chinese?**

A party of British officers and others, to whom passports under the seal of the Zongli Yamen were issued last July, authorizing them to pass from Burma into Yunnan, and to travel in China, were attacked on the 22nd February by a Chinese force in the sub-prefecture of Tengyue, otherwise known as Momein [near the Burmese border].

[. . . .]

From an observation made by one of the Ministers who called at the Legation on the 19th instant, it is evident that the Chinese Government is unacquainted with the relations between Burma and England; it is unaware that a large portion of Burma is a British province, and that, with the consent of the King of Burma, British officers of the Indian Government are stationed permanently at different points in his dominions for the surveillance of British interests. They are well acquainted with the language and people of the country, and their information is excellent.

In the telegram of the 2nd instant the Chief Commissioner in Burma states that the body who

WADE, THOMAS F. (1818–1895)—A British diplomat and talented linguist who was first posted to China during the Opium War in 1841 and rapidly promoted to higher positions eventually becoming Britain's representative to China. Upon his retirement from the diplomatic service, he became the first professor of Chinese at Cambridge where he taught until his death in 1895.

attacked the British party was but the advanced guard of a force of 3000 men sent down by the Tengyue authorities to annihilate the British expedition. Of this, adds the Commissioner, there is not any doubt. He goes on to say that Mr. Margary was killed with his Chinese servants at a town called Manyun... and that his head and the heads of his servants were exposed on the walls of the town.

Mr. Margary, as your Imperial Highness is aware, was sent by me to meet this mission. Being thoroughly alive to the importance of having some one with the mission, who, besides being acquainted with the Chinese language, was in other respects a competent agent, I specially selected Mr. Margary, a young man of great promise, for the service.

Since the arrival of the Viceroy's telegram announcing his murder, I have received, by way of Rangoon, a note written to me by Mr. Margary from Bhamo, dated the 18th January.

From this it appears that on reaching Momein he had found letters waiting for him from the Political Agent of the Indian Government stationed at Bhamo in Burma, informing him that the expedition would not be able to move forward quite so early as had been expected, and leaving it to him to wait for it at Momein or to come on as he thought best.

After some reflection Mr. Margary pushed on to Nantian and thence to Manyun, at which place he found Li Sidai (Sitai) engaged in an attempt to establish regulations for the trade of the tribes in the neighborhood. From Manyun he sent on his Chinese messenger Liu to Bhamo for instructions. Several days passed before Liu returned. During the whole of that time Mr. Margary remained at Manyun, where he reports that Li Sidai treated him with the greatest civility.

I draw particular attention to the fact of his friendly reception by Li Sidai, and of his prolonged residence at Manyun; because, according to the Chief Commissioner's telegram, it was by Li Sidai's nephew that the attacking party was commanded on the 22nd February, and it is in or near Manyun that Mr. Margary and his Chinese attendants were barbarously murdered.

I most distinctly protest, therefore, before any inequity takes place, against all explanations attributing what has happened to misconception of the nature of the mission that has been repulsed. It consisted of a military officer, a medical man, an interpreter, and a civilian tourist without any official character—the four persons, in short, for whom the passports of July last were obtained. The Government of Yunnan was advised by the letter from Yamen, which Mr. Margary carried with him, of the approach of the mission, and the direction it would probably take. The Governor of Yunnan sent officers with him as far as Yongchang. Mr. Margary passed a number of days at Manyun in friendly intercourse with Li Sidai, and the telegram announcing his arrival at Bhamo on the 17th January, which called for my letter of acknowledgements addressed to your Imperial Highness on the 3rd March, assured me (of course on the testimony of Mr. Margary), that the Chinese officials in Yunnan were anxiously awaiting the mission.

4.7 MEMORIAL FROM YUN-GUI GOVERNOR-GENERAL CEN YUYING RECOUNTING MARGARY'S MURDER (APRIL TO JULY OF 1875)

After Margary's murder, Cen Yuying exchanged correspondence almost daily with the central court attempting to keep them abreast of developments. The following memorial exhibiting Cen's frustration is typical of provincial officials caught between the anxieties of the central government and the demands of the Western governments. Like all administrators, Cen's power at the local level was entirely dependent on the skills of his local officials. The location of the attack was several weeks' travel away from Kunming, the provincial capital, making an investigation particularly laborious. The biggest barrier for everyone involved was assessing the role of the indigenous *Yeren*—an ethnic group who remained largely autonomous of Chinese imperial control—who were commonly known for carrying out raids on vulnerable travelers. For Cen Yuying the most problematic barrier remained discharging his responsibilities to the satisfaction of Thomas Wade, knowing that the British government would only accept full admission of guilt as a final verdict.

Questions

1. **What does Cen Yuying suggest occurred to Margary?**
2. **What has Cen Yuying done to discover Margary's murderer? Why would this be unsatisfactory to Wade?**

Guangxu 1st year, 3rd month, 9th day **[April 4, 1875]**

On the April 10, 1875 I received a dispatch from the Foreign Office (Zongli Yamen) relaying to me the British ambassador's claim that "Mr. Margary, a British translator, had been ordered to travel to Burma via Yunnan. All along his route he was properly received by local officials and safely arrived at the Burmese town of Bhamo. Only on March 11th, did I receive a telegram from an official in India, indicating to me that:

"On February 22nd, the officials who had been sent to Yunnan, upon arriving at a village.... they were suddenly attacked by Tengyue Chinese and local militia. Margary and his Chinese escort were killed and their belongings were looted. The remaining survivors returned [across the border] to Bhamo."

[....]

Yunnan is a province located on the Chinese border, with the treacherous roads, inaccessible by any river, and has no open foreign treaty ports. Indeed, early last year when we heard that the military situation in Vietnam had deteriorated, my first thoughts were that there might be foreign bandits, posing as French, attempting to carry out disturbances in Yunnan. Conversely, I also worried that bandits might attempt to pose as Yunnanese soldiers as a ruse to rob people along the road. I worried they might even harm any French travelers passing through the province. Therefore I immediately requested that the Foreign Office notify the French embassy to suspend all French travel to Yunnan.

In November 1874, Margary, the British translator, arrived in Yunnan having traveled from Beijing carrying documentation from the Foreign Office and his passport. I immediately told the Western Intendant (*daotai*) to arrange for civil and military escorts with him until he safely crossed the border. Along his route, local officials were alerted to ensure his safety. Soon thereafter we heard that Margary had safely arrived at the Burmese town of Xinjie.

However when Margary decided to return from Burma into Yunnan, he did not properly notify Yunnan officials and so was not met by any officials.

Instead, he unadvisedly crossed the border alone without an escort. The events, which subsequently occurred along the road, were not properly reported to us in a timely manner either. When the translator traveled through Yunnan to Tengyue [on his way to Burma], he was properly received by both civil and military officers, without the slightest problem. Why would [Chinese officials] take hostile action against him [upon his return]? I was terribly puzzled to receive this document.

[....]

Guangxu 1st year, 7th month, 5th day **[August 5, 1875]**

The [Margary] case occurred in a very remote border area quite distant from the provincial capital in an area under the supervision of native chieftains. Previously I reported that I sent the provincial military commander (*tidu*), Yang Yuke, the western intendant, Chen Xizhen, and the prefect Xu Chengxun to investigate.... What they reported had already been discovered by my earlier enquiries.... The fact is that the foreigner's relentless suspicions regarding Margary's death at the hands of the *Yeren* hill tribes makes it impossible for the civil and military officers to carry out their routine duties. I have reported the facts when and as soon as they became known to me. At the same time, I ordered Yang Yuke, Chen Xizhen and the Tengyue sub-prefectural Head, Wu Qiliang, to capture the criminals and bring them to provincial capital for trial. I have tolerated no excuses or delays in the investigation.... Once the criminals are captured, the criminals will be brought to provincial capital to be tried by Li Hanzhang the Hunan-Hubei Governor-General who has been imperially commissioned to oversee the case. We expect to have an accurate confession and evidence and will carefully handle the case in order to pacify the foreigners' feelings. We dare not to leave any doubts.

[....]

Now local areas are as peaceful as usual. I submit this report. On my knees I beg for instructions. Report this!

4.8   ZHIFU (YANTAI) CONVENTION (SEPTEMBER 13, 1876)

With dogged determination Thomas Wade pursued Margary's murder to the greatest extent of his diplomatic powers. In the end, the Qing government had no choice but to accept responsibility. The **Zhifu Convention** reflects the level to which such negotiations had evolved (or devolved). The British took a tone closer to that of a parent to a naughty child (e.g., "a letter will be written expressing regret for what occurred in Yunnan") than between two of the world's largest empires. More significant was the fact that the Margary case provided the thin end of a diplomatic wedge for demanding other concessions (Parts II and III in the convention), including the opening of four more treaty ports. One can only imagine the growing frustration of the Qing at their inability to withstand such patently mistaken and frivolous diplomatic maneuvering by the British and other Western countries.

Questions

1. How does the Zhifu Convention strengthen the extraterritoriality rights of Westerners' in China?
2. What relationship is there between the manner of Margary's death and the resolutions outlined in Section I of the convention?

Section I. Settlement of the Yunnan Case

A Memorial is to be presented to the Throne, whether by the Zongli Yamen or by the Grand Secretary is immaterial, in the sense of the Memorandum prepared by Sir Thomas Wade. Before presentation the Chinese text of the Memorial is to be shown to Sir Thomas Wade.

The Memorial having been presented to the Throne, and the Imperial Decree in reply received, the Zongli Yamen will communicate copies of the Memorial and Imperial Decree to Sir Thomas Wade, together with copy of a letter from the Zongli Yamen to the Provincial Governments, instructing them to issue a proclamation that shall embody at length the above Memorial and Decree. Sir Thomas Wade will thereon reply to the effect that for two years to come officers will be sent by the British Minister to different places in the provinces to see that the proclamation is posted. On application from the British Minister, or the Consul of any port instructed by him to make application, the high officers of the provinces will depute competent officers to accompany those so sent to the places which they go to observe.

[....]

The British Government will be free for five years, from the 1st of January next, being the 17th day of the 11th month of the 2nd year of Guangxu, to station officers at Dali Fu, or at some other suitable place in Yunnan, to observe the conditions of trade; to the end that they may have information upon which to base the regulations of trade when these have to be discussed. For the consideration and adjustment of any matter affecting British Officers or Subject, these Officers will be free to address themselves to the Authorities of the province. The opening of the trade may be proposed by the British Government, as it may find best, at any time within the term of five years, or upon expiry of the term of five years.

[....]

The amount of indemnity to be paid on account of the families of the officers and others killed in Yunnan; on account of the expenses which the Yunnan case has occasioned; and on account of claims of British Merchants arising out of the action of officers of the Chinese Government, up to the commencement of the present year, Sir Thomas Wade takes upon himself to fix at two hundred thousand taels payable on demand.

ZHIFU (YANTAI) CONVENTION 1876—A treaty (sometimes referred to as Chefoo Convention) between China and Great Britain imposed largely because of the Qing government's ostensible complicity in the murder of British translator Augustus Margary.

When the case is closed an Imperial Letter will be written expressing regret for what has occurred in Yunnan. The Mission bearing the Imperial Letter will proceed to England immediately. Sir Thomas Wade is to be informed of the constitution of this Mission for the information of his Government. The text of the Imperial Letter is also to be communicated to Sir Thomas Wade by the Zongli Yamen.

[....]

Section III. — Trade

With reference to the area within which, according to the Treaties in force, *lijin* ought not to be collected on foreign goods at the open ports? Sir Thomas Wade agrees to move his Government to allow the ground rented by foreigners (the so-called concessions) at the different [treaty] ports to be regarded as the area of exemption from *lijin;* and the government of China will thereupon allow Yichang in the Province of Hubei, Wuhu in Anhui, Wenzhou in Zhejiang and Beihai in Guangdong, to be added to the number of ports open to trade, and to become Consular stations. The British Government will farther be free to send officers to reside at Chongqing, to watch the conditions of British trade in Sichuan. British merchants will not be allowed to reside at Chongqing or to open establishments or warehouses there, so long as no steamers have access to the port. When steamers have succeeded in ascending the river so far, further arrangements can be taken into consideration.

[....]

Done at Zhifu [Yantai], in the Province of Shandong, this thirteenth day of September in the year of Our Lord one thousand eight hundred and seventy-six.

(L.S.) (Signed)　　　THOMAS FRANCIS WADE

(L.S.) (Signed)　　　CHINESE PLENIPOTENTIARY.

4.9　ZONGLI YAMEN CIRCULAR ON UNEQUAL TREATIES (1878)

In 1878, the following Zongli Yamen document circulated among top Qing officials in an attempt to establish a common set of foreign policy objectives. This document, translated below, distills with rare clarity, the three central challenges to China's legal sovereignty: extraterritoriality, missionary conflicts, and the "most favored nation" clause. Of the three, the **"most favored nation"** clause was the most insidious since it accelerated the speed with which Western powers gained concessions in China. Given the vast number of treaties and conventions in the post-Taiping era, China could not withstand such united opposition to their own internal autonomy. Furthermore, it was difficult, at the local enforcement level, for Chinese officials to differentiate the citizen of one European country from another. As a result, each treaty China signed was, in effect, unilaterally granting concessions to the entire Western world.

Questions

1. **Of the issues raised below which do you think most troubled officials in the Zongli Yamen?**
2. **How did extraterritoriality undermine China's own efforts to maintain law and order?**

LIJIN—A form of local taxation first introduced by Zeng Guofan to fund his Hunan (Xiang) Army. The tax was levied on goods in transit, on shops, and was a tax many foreigners believed a barrier to import goods.

MOST FAVORED NATION STATUS—Under terms first granted by China to Britain in the 1842 Treaty of Nanjing, and in 1844 extended to all the foreign powers present in China, the Most Favored Nation status stipulated that any concessions given to one Western country would automatically entitle other Western countries to seek (and likely be granted) the same concessions.

1. Since the Treaties of Tianjin were ratified, China's relations with foreign Powers have invariably been conducted in accordance with their stipulations. Whatever complaints there may have been on the part of foreign Governments on this head have in the main been occasioned by accidents to individuals and the incidence of taxation. As regards the first class of complaints, it must be remembered that such things may occur in any country, and that no amount of foresight can effectually guard against them; while as to taxation it is where there are no Treaty provisions, or where Treaty provisions are read two ways, that differences occur.

2. Treaties may be revised once in every ten years, and such additions, abrogation, or modifications as are introduced depend of course on the voluntary assent of the contracting Powers. The first revision of the British Treaty was concluded by the Yamen and British Minister in 1869; but notwithstanding that friendly negotiations had extended over as much as two years, the British Government refused to ratify the arrangements of its representative, and the Revised Treaty has never been in force. For a year past the revision of the German Treaty has been going on; and among the proposals of the German Minister there are some to which it is impossible for China to assent; so, although there has been much discussion, no settlement has been yet arrived at. In this matter of Treaty revision, a mutual interchange of views is a preliminary of much importance and it appears to us that there are four cardinal points regarding which it would seem that we have up to the present failed to make the Chinese view understood. They are: (1) Transit; (2) *Lijin* Taxation; (3) Extraterritoriality; (4) The "Most Favored Nation" clause. We propose to state our views in connection with them for Your Excellency's information.
   [. . . .]

7. As regards *jurisdiction,* i.e. *Extraterritoriality.* By the terms of the Treaties foreigners in China are not amenable to the jurisdiction of the Chinese authorities, *i.e.* they are exterritorialized. If they have disputes among themselves, their own authorities are to settle them; if they commit an offence, their own authorities are to punish them according to their own national laws. But foreigners claim much more than this: they interpret the extraterritorial privilege as meaning, not only that Chinese officials are not to control them, but that they may disregard and violate Chinese regulations with impunity. To this we cannot assent. China has not by any treaty given foreigners permission to disregard or violate the laws of China: while residing in China they are as much bound to observe them as Chinese are; what has been conceded in the Treaties in this connection is merely that offenders shall be punished by their own national officials in accordance with their own national laws. For example, if Chinese law prohibits Chinese subjects from going through a certain passage, foreigners cannot claim to go through that forbidden passage in virtue of extraterritoriality. If they go through it and thereby break a Chinese law, their own national officials are to punish them in accordance with such laws as provide for analogous cases in their own country. In a word, the true meaning of the extraterritoriality clause is not that a foreigner is at liberty to break Chinese laws, but that if he offends he shall be punished by his own national officials. Again, seeing that China has agreed that these judicial powers shall be exercised by foreign consuls within Chinese territory, foreign governments should on their side take care that none but good and reliable men are appointed to these posts. Several states, however, appoint merchant consuls. Now, in so far as concerns that part of a consul's duty which comprises the reporting and clearing of ships and the shipping and discharging of sailors, China does not object to its being discharged to merchant consuls. But in China a consul's duties comprise judicial functions as well, and the importance of such functions is such as to seem to demand the appointment of *bona fide* officials to consular posts; moreover, where cases requiring joint investigation occur, it is neither convenient nor dignified for a Chinese official to sit on the bench with a merchant consul, who may have been fined for smuggling the day before, or who, in his mercantile capacity, may perhaps be personally interested in the case at issue.

8. The "*most favored Nation*" clause is found in all the Treaties, and it is well that it should be so, for it is difficult for China to distinguish between foreigners or say which belongs to

which nationality; and so much is this so, that even non-Treaty Power foreigners are treated like the others. The object of the foreign negotiator in introducing this clause was to prevent his own nationals from being placed at a disadvantage as compared with others, and to secure that all should be equally favored. Now this is precisely what China desires. But foreign governments, although their objects in negotiating for the "most favored nation" clause were similar to those of China, are not always fair in their interpretation of it. For example, if China *for a consideration* grants a certain country a few privileges on such and such conditions, this would be of the nature of a special concession for a special consideration. Should other countries come forward and in virtue of the "most favored nation" clause claim to participate in the new privileges, although China need not necessarily exact a similar consideration in return, yet it would be only just to expect that in enjoying the privileges they would consent to observe the conditions accepted by the power to which it was originally granted. But, far from this being the case, there are some who, while demanding the privilege, refuse to be bound by the conditions attached to it. This is the unfair interpretation to which China objects. In a word, as regards this "most favored nation" clause, we hold that if one country desires to participate in the privileges conceded to another country, it must consent to be bound by the conditions attached to them and accepted by that other.

9. Over and above the four points commented on there is the *Missionary question.* China, recognizing that the object of all religious systems is to teach men to do good, has by treaty assented to missionaries coming to teach their doctrines in China, and has also guaranteed protection to them and to their converts. But among the missionaries are some who, exalting the importance of their office, arrogate to themselves an official status, and interfere so far as to transact business that ought properly to be dealt with by the Chinese local authorities; while among their converts are some who look upon their being Christians as protecting them from the consequences of breaking the laws of their own country, and refuse to observe the rules which are binding on their neighbors. This state of things China cannot tolerate or submit to. Under the extraterritoriality clause foreigners are to be dealt with by their own national authorities, but as regards Chinese subjects on Chinese soil, it is only the Chinese authorities who can deal with them, and Chinese subjects, whether Christians or not, to be accounted good subjects, must render an exact obedience to the laws of China; if any offend against those laws, they must one and all, Christians alike, submit to be dealt with by their own native authorities, and the foreign missionary cannot be permitted to usurp the right of shielding them from the consequences of their acts.

10. In order that negotiations for Treaty revision may be facilitated, what is required is reciprocal consideration and mutual forbearance. We accordingly address to Your Excellency this communication.

SINO-JAPANESE WAR

Despite China's many military encounters in the nineteenth century, no military loss affected the Qing court and Chinese populace quite as much as their defeat at the hands of the Japanese in the Sino-Japanese War (1894–95). For centuries China had sat at the center of a vast tributary network, with neighboring countries acknowledging China's dominant military, political and commercial importance. These neighbors demonstrated their fealty by sending periodic tribute missions to China's court. China, and most European observers, continued to give strong credence to China's traditional position as the East Asian powerhouse. Contemporary observers all assumed Japan would be defeated quickly. It was a horrible shock to China when Japan not only routed the Chinese troops dispatched to Korea, but with devastating precision demolished China's navy. These defeats dealt a savage blow to China's national pride and were a shock to many Western observers.

If the war eroded China's confidence, the peace was excruciating. With the Treaty of Shimonoseki (4.12) Japan proved itself fully as capable as its European counterparts at extracting concessions, indemnities, and territories. The Chinese public, who had been sheltered from the Qing military's lack of modernization, were whipped into a frenzy over the defeats and were further enraged at what they perceived as Li Hongzhang's submissive acceptance of Japan's peace terms. While the Qing dynasty survived for another fifteen years, it would never recover psychologically from the humiliation it received at the hands of the Japanese. This truly marks the beginning of the end for the Qing dynasty.

4.10 CHINA'S DECLARATION OF WAR (JULY 31, 1894)

China's Declaration of War on Japan is the first formal declaration of war ever made by the Qing. Oddly casual while courteous in tone, China's Declaration of War underscores its discomfort over treating Japan as either an equal or as a tributary. Despite its succinctness, one can sense the Zongli Yamen's confidence that Japan will regret their action. Perceiving Korea's request for military assistance as conforming to the centuries-long tributary relationship, and having already agreed to terms with Japan regarding Korea's special rapport, China was stunned by Japan's forceful response.

Questions

1. **Why do you think that China chose to go to war with Japan rather than seeking a more diplomatic resolution?**

The Prince Gong and the ministers of the Zongli Yamen issued a communication to Mr. Komura Japanese *charge d'affaires* at Beijing:

We had long hoped to settle by negotiation, without a rupture of our friendship, the disagreements that existed between China and your country with reference to the affairs of Korea. On the 25th of July, however, at the seaport of Yashan in Korea, your forces made an attack upon our ships. Hostilities have therefore now begun, the treaties between our countries are henceforth void and this Yamen, to its great regret, will in future treat of no matters with you. Mr. Komura,

Chargê d'affaires of Japan

The 29th year of Guangxu, 6th month, 29th day (July 31, 1894).

4.11 JAPAN'S DECLARATION OF WAR (AUGUST 1, 1894)

Japan's desire to bring Korea within a more formal sphere of influence had long been known to the Chinese. The speed with which Japan took the offensive after Korea's request for Chinese troops to defend their capital from a rebel attack shocked many nations (not just China). Prior to the military engagements, most European observers quietly assumed that China would make quick work of the Japanese. Take special note of Japan's awareness of the language of international law, and how they lay the groundwork, prior to the war, for a post-war settlement.

Questions

1. **How does the Japanese declaration differ from that of China's?**
2. **What points does Japan's declaration seek to delineate regarding Korea and Japan's positions vis-à-vis China?**

We, by the grace of Heaven, Emperor of Japan, seated on a Throne occupied by the same dynasty from time immemorial, do hereby make proclamation to all our loyal and brave subjects, as follows:—

We hereby declare war against China, and we command each and all our competent authorities, in obedience to our wish and with a view to the attainment of the national aim, to carry on hostilities by sea and by land against China, with all the means at their disposal consistently with the Law of Nations.

During the past three decades of our reign our constant aim has been to further the peaceful progress of the country in civilization, and, being sensible of the evils inseparable from complications with foreign states, it has always been our pleasure to instruct our Minister of State to labor for the promotion of friendly relations with our Treaty Powers. We are gratified to know that the relations of our Empire with those Powers have yearly increased in goodwill and in friendship. Under the circumstances, we were unprepared for such a conspicuous want of amity and of good faith as has been manifested by China in her conduct towards this country in connection with the Korean affair.

Korea is an independent State. She was first introduced into the family of nations by the advice and guidance of Japan. It has, however, been China's habit to designate Korea as her dependency, and both openly and secretly to interfere with her domestic affairs. At the time of the recent insurrection in Korea, China dispatched troops thither, alleging that her purpose was to afford a succor to her dependent State. We, in virtue of the treaty concluded with Korea in 1882, and looking to possible emergencies, caused a military force to be sent to that country.

Wishing to procure for Korea freedom from the calamity of perpetual disturbance, and thereby to maintain the peace of the East in general, Japan invited China's co-operation for the accomplishment of the object. But China, advancing various pretexts, declined Japan's proposal. Thereupon Japan advised Korea to reform her administration so that order and tranquility might be preserved at home, and so that the country might be able to discharge the responsibilities and duties of an independent State abroad. Korea has already consented to undertake the task. But China has secretly and insidiously endeavored to circumvent and to thwart Japan's purpose. She has further procrastinated and endeavored to make warlike preparations both on land and at sea. When those preparations were completed she not only sent large reinforcements to Korea, with a view to the forcible attainment of her ambitious designs, but even carried her arbitrariness and insolence to the extent of opening fire upon our ships in Korean waters. China's plain object is to make it uncertain where the responsibility resides of preserving peace and order in Korea, and not only to weaken the position of that state in the family of nations—a position obtained for Korea through Japan's efforts—but also to obscure the significance of the treaties recognizing and confirming that position. Such conduct on the part of China is not only a direct injury to the rights and interests of this Empire, but also a menace to the permanent peace and tranquility of the Orient. Judging from her actions it must be concluded that China from the beginning has been bent upon sacrificing peace to the attainment of her sinister object. In this situation, ardent as our wish is to promote the prestige of the country abroad by strictly peaceful methods, we find it impossible to avoid a formal declaration of war against China. It is our earnest wish that, by the loyalty and valor of our faithful subjects, peace may soon be permanently restored and the glory of the Empire be augmented and completed.

Given this 1st day of the eighth month of the 27th year of Meiji.

(His Imperial Majesty's Sign-manual)

Counter-Signatures of the Minister President of State of the other Ministers of State.

4.12   THE TREATY OF SHIMONOSEKI (APRIL 17, 1895)

Surprising even the Western powers, it was Japan's demands for territorial acquisitions and a sizable indemnity in the Treaty of Shimonoseki that pushed Japan's imperialist aspirations to new heights and achieved a new low for Qing China. With a vision far more strategic than any of the previous treaties with European or American governments, Japan aggressively staked out a sphere of control that stretched from the Qing

Manchurian homelands in northeast China to the southeastern Chinese province of Taiwan. This territorial conquest, combined with the implicit acknowledgement that Korea would fall under Japan's influence, meant that with one treaty Japan had moved from a seemingly peripheral power to one that became a major threat to China's autonomy. Several of the European powers would, in what is referred to as the **Triple Intervention,** force Japan to return much of the northeastern Chinese territory (Fengtian).

Questions

1. **In what ways does the Treaty of Shimonoseki mirror the earlier treaties China signed with the Western powers? In what ways does it differ?**
2. **Looking at a map, how do Japan's territorial demands strengthen Japan's presence in East Asia?**

ARTICLE I

China recognizes definitively the full and complete independence and autonomy of Korea, and, in consequences, the payment of tribute and the performance of ceremonies and formalities by Korea to China, in derogation of such independence and autonomy, shall wholly cease for the future.

ARTICLE II

China cedes to Japan in perpetuity and full sovereignty the following territories, together with all fortifications thereon:

The southern portion of the province of Fengtian within the following boundaries:

The line of demarcation begins at the mouth of the River Yalu and ascends that stream to the mouth of the River Anping, from thence the line runs to Fenghuang, from thence to Haicheng, from thence to Yingkou, forming a line which describes the southern portion of the territory. The places above named are included in the ceded territory. When the line reaches the River Liao at Yingkou, it follows the course of that stream to its mouth, where it terminates. The mid-channel of the River Liao shall be taken as line of demarcation.

This cession also includes all islands appertaining or belonging to the province of Fengtian situated in the eastern portion of the Bay of Liaodong and in the northern part of the Yellow Sea.

The island of Formosa [Taiwan], together with all islands appertaining or belonging to the said island of Formosa.

The Pescadores Group, that is to say, all islands lying between the 119th and 120th degrees of longitude east of Greenwich and the 23rd and 24th degrees of north latitude.

[…]

ARTICLE IV

China agrees to pay to Japan as a war indemnity the sum of 200,000,000 *Kuping Taels* [Treasury taels]; the said sum to be paid in eight installments. . . .

ARTICLE V

The inhabitants of the territory ceded to Japan, who wish to take up their residence outside of the ceded districts, shall be at liberty to sell their real property and retire.

For this purpose a period of two years from the date of exchange of the ratifications of the present act shall be granted. At the expiration of that period those of the inhabitants who shall not have left said territories shall, at the option of Japan, be deemed Japanese subjects.

TRIPLE INTERVENTION—Germany, France and Russia, ostensibly seeking to help the Qing empire but acting more in self-interest, forced Japan to return territory in northeastern China in exchange for an additional payment to Japan of 30 million taels. Quickly thereafter, Russia, Germany and France each demanded a territorial concession in exchange for their role in the intervention.

Each of the two Governments shall immediately upon the exchange of the ratifications of the present act send one or more commissioners to Taiwan to effect a final transfer of that province, and within the space of two months after the exchange of the ratification of this act such transfer shall be completed.

ARTICLE VI

All treaties between China and Japan having come to an end, in consequences of war, China engages immediately upon the exchange of the ratifications of this act, to appoint plenipotentiaries to conclude with the Japanese Plenipotentiaries, a treaty of commerce and navigation and convention to regulate frontier intercourse and trade.

The treaties, conventions, and regulations now subsisting between China and European powers shall serve as a basis for the said treaty and convention between China and Japan. From the date of the exchange of the ratification of this Act until the said treaty and convention are brought into actual operation, the Japanese Government, its officials, commerce, navigation, frontier intercourse and trade industries, ships, and subjects, shall in every respect be accorded by China most-favored-nation treatment.

China makes, in addition, the following concessions, to take effect six months after the date of the present Act: —

First. The following cities, towns, and ports, in addition to those already opened to the trade, residence, industries, and manufactures of Japanese subjects, under the same conditions and with the same privileges and facilities as exist at the present open cities, towns, and ports of China:

Shashi, in the province of Hubei.
Chongqing, in the province of Sichuan.
Suzhou, in the province of Jiangsu.
Hangzhou, in the province of Zhejiang.

The Japanese Government shall have the right to station consuls at any or all of the above-named places.

Second. Steam navigation for vessels under the Japanese flag, for the conveyance of passengers and cargo, shall be extended to the following places:

On the Upper Yangzi River, from Yichang to Chongqing.
On the Wusong River and the canal, from Shanghai to Suzhou and Hangzhou.

[. . . .]

In witness whereof the respective Plenipotentiaries have signed the same and affixed thereto the seal of their arms.

Done at Shimonoseki, in duplicate, this 23rd day of the 3rd month of the 21st year of Guangxu, corresponding to the 17th day of the 4th month of the 28th year of Meiji.

Li Hongzhang,[L.S.]
Plenipotentiary of His Majesty the Emperor of China
Senior Tutor to the Heir Apparent
Senior Grand Secretary of State
Minister Superintendent of Trade for the Northern Ports of China
Viceroy of the Province of Zhili
Earl of the First Rank
Count Ito Hirobumi, [L.S.]
Junii, Grand Cross of the Imperial Order of Paullownia
Minister President of State
Plenipotentiary of His Majesty the Emperor of Japan

Viscount Mutsu Munemitsu
Junji, First Class of the Imperial Order of the Sacred Treasure
Minister of State for Foreign Affairs
Plenipotentiary of His Majesty the Emperor of Japan.

4.13 JOHN HAY'S OPEN DOOR NOTE (SEPTEMBER 6, 1899)

In the wake of the Sino-Japanese War and the ensuing Triple Intervention of Germany, France and Russia (into the settlement of the war), there was a growing sense that China could be divided up into **"spheres of interest."** In 1899, John Hay, the United

SPHERES OF INTEREST (SPHERES OF INFLUENCE)—Areas of China in which a specific Western power was said to hold particular interest, but no specific powers during the late nineteenth century.

States Secretary of State, worried that the United States would be denied commercial access to China, sought to forge an agreement among the Western powers present in China. Hay's agreement would allow an "open door" to all countries in all areas. Quite indicative of the period, China was not consulted, much to the chagrin of the increasingly impotent Chinese diplomatic corps. Far from exhibiting an anti-imperialistic tone, as is often asserted, the agreement simply suggested the empire should remain open to all foreign nations on an equal basis.

Questions

1. What are the key elements of the Open Door Note?
2. Why do you think the granting of Germany's holdings at Jiaozhou (Qingdao) was the catalyst for such an agreement?

John Hay, U.S. Secretary of State to Andrew D. White, US Ambassador to Germany

Washington, September 6, 1899

Sir:

At the time when the Government of the United States was informed by that of Germany that it had leased from His Majesty the Emperor of China the port of Jiaozhou [Qingdao] and the adjacent territory in the province of Shandong, assurances were given to the ambassador of the United States at Berlin by the Imperial German minister for foreign affairs that the rights and privileges insured by treaties with China to citizens of the United States would not thereby suffer or be in anywise impaired within the area over which Germany had thus obtained control.

More recently, however, the British Government recognized by a formal agreement with Germany the exclusive right of the latter country to enjoy in said leased area and the contiguous "sphere of influence or interest" certain privileges, more especially those relating to railroads and mining enterprises; but as the exact nature and extent of the rights thus recognized have not been clearly defined, it is possible that serious conflicts of interest may at any time arise not only between British and German subjects within said area, but that the interests of our citizens may also be jeopardized thereby.

Earnestly desirous to remove any cause of irritation and to insure at the same time to the commerce of all nations in China the undoubted benefits which should accrue from a formal recognition by the various powers claiming "spheres of interest" that they shall enjoy perfect equality of treatment for their commerce and navigation within such "spheres," the Government of the United States would be pleased to see His German Majesty's Government give formal assurances, and lend its cooperation in securing like assurances from the other interested powers, that each, within its respective sphere of whatever influence —

First. Will in no way interfere with any treaty port or any vested interest within any so-called "sphere of interest" or leased territory it may have in China.

Second. That the Chinese treaty tariff of the time being shall apply to all merchandise landed or shipped to all such ports as are within said "sphere of interest" (unless they be "free ports"), no matter to what nationality it may belong, and that duties so leviable shall be collected by the Chinese Government.

Third. That it will levy no higher harbor dues on vessels of another nationality frequenting any port in such "sphere" than shall be levied on vessels of its own nationality, and no higher railroad charges over lines built, controlled, or operated within its "sphere" on merchandise belonging to citizens or subjects of other nationalities transported through such "sphere" than shall be levied on similar merchandise belonging to its own nationals transported over equal distances.

[. . . .]

In view of the present favorable conditions, you are instructed to submit the above considerations to His Imperial Germany Majesty's Minister for Foreign Affairs, and to request his early consideration of the subject.

Copy of this instruction is sent to our ambassadors at London and at St. Petersburg for their information.

I have, etc.

JOHN HAY.

CHAPTER 5
SEEKING TO SOLVE CHINA'S ILLS

VISUAL SOURCE
Picturing the Boxers

WHO WERE THE BOXERS? Boxers were typically young and male. Many were around 19 or 20 years of age but some as young as 12 or over 40. The majority of the Boxers were poor peasants though many landowners also joined. The term "Boxer" was used by Westerners at the time to describe any anti-foreign violence. The Chinese term for the movement itself was "Boxers United in Righteousness" (Yihetuan) and delimited to uprisings confined to northern China.

BOXER MAGIC: Boxer magic was a unique blend of ritual and theater based on mass spirit possession. The Boxers believed that with a specific combination of spells and series of specific gestures spirit deities ould possess their bodies. Boxer spirit masters also plied a variety of other spells, amulets and incantations to provide them with extra strength, speed even the ability to fly.

NORTH CHINA PLAIN: The Boxers emerged largely out of the North China Plain though anti-foreign massacres occurred in many other areas of China. North China in the years leading up to the Boxer Uprising experienced several years of repeated droughts, crop failures, and general hardship. This coincided with a surge in the presence of western missionaries, the extension of railroads and telegraphs, and new foreign concessions. Both pictures were likely taken in 1900 in the North Chinese cities of Beijing and Tianjin.

BOXER WEAPONS: While there are some instances of Boxers using matchlock style rifles, most Boxers shunned the use of guns perceiving them as foreign. Instead, most Boxers were armed with spears, swords, and, they believed, magical powers.

BOXER BANNER: The Boxer's banner in the photo reads (beginning with the small characters in the upper right) "Imperially ordered Boxers United in Righteousness; and finally Grain Unit."

BOXER CLOTHING: The typical Boxers wore headscarves, a sash around their waist, and leggings. Across their chest they would wear a chest covering with magical protective qualities. If more affluent the Boxer might wear more ornate clothing. The Boxer pictured here represents a small minority of Boxers that could afford to dress in bright colored clothing complete with ornate flags.

BOXER ANTIFOREIGNISM: Boxers renounced all foreign things and classified all Chinese who interacted with foreigners and used foreign items into three categories:
1) "Hairy ones" (maozi) referred to the foreigners themselves 2) "Secondary Hairy ones (er maozi) were Chinese Christian converts" and Chinese who worked for foreigners and 3) "Tertiary Hairy ones" (san maozi) those Chinese who sold or used foreign books, fountain pens, matches, or foreign style umbrellas. Boxers renounced all foreign things and all Chinese who interacted with foreigners and used foreign items.

On November 14, 1908, the Guangxu emperor died at the age of thirty-seven. His life ended in much the same way as it had been lived, in the shadow of his aunt, the **Dowager Empress** Cixi (1834–1908). She would die within hours of his death. From her deathbed, she orchestrated the third successive installation of a child emperor on China's imperial throne. For forty-eight years her decisions had, for better or worse, defined Chinese domestic and external policies. There remains today an image both shadowy and sinister of this woman who reigned from **behind the curtain** (*chuilian tingzheng*). Such a characterization simultaneously exaggerates her sinister powers and diminishes her productive accomplishments in China's history. While Chinese imperial customs stipulated that only male heirs could sit on the throne, there were historic precedents for a woman to take the reins of power when exigency, expediency and personal ambition converged. In 1861, with the Taiping Rebellion raging, Western imperialism at its height, and a budding reform movement taking shape in China, the ambitious mother of the new emperor found her moment in history.

Born in 1834 to Manchu parents, Cixi entered the Forbidden City at the age of sixteen as an imperial courtesan. She caught the attention of the Xianfeng emperor (1851–1861) and soon gave birth to his only son, elevating her status to imperial consort and secondary wife. In 1861, after the emperor's sudden illness and demise, her 6-year old son ascended the throne as the Tongzhi emperor (1856–1875). Too young to rule on his own, Cixi, with the Xianfeng emperor's widow Ci'an and **Prince Yixin** became the young emperor's regents and prevented other challengers to the throne. When the Tongzhi emperor died fourteen years later (some say as the result of syphilis, others smallpox), she engineered the selection of her four-year-old nephew as the Guangxu emperor (1871–1908) assuring her continued role as regent.

Despite many popular claims to the contrary, Cixi did very little that many men had not already done before her. Why is it then that Cixi is portrayed to this day as the epitome of the Chinese "dragon lady" within both Chinese and Western historiographic traditions? The answer lies in the complex politics of the period and diverse challenges facing the Qing court.

The Forbidden City—the heart of China's imperial bureaucracy—even in the best of times was a secretive, guarded and conservative entity run by an all-male bureaucracy. Opponents of her vision could (and did) offer equally viable all-male alternatives to her proposals. Her path to power was not only difficult, but also singular, with no precedent to it. She entered the Forbidden City as one of many young women selected to serve as low-level concubines, and within a few years she had secured herself a preeminent position by giving birth to the future heir to the throne. She also became highly educated and mastered the administrative intricacies of the Qing civil service, which readily enabled her to parry the numerous conspiracies and intrigues against her.

There can be little doubt that her success was the source of unending fascination, slander and scorn by both Chinese and Western observers. The speculation surrounding her exploits runs the gamut from perverse to outrageous. If we are to believe all that has

---

DOWAGER EMPRESS—Dowager indicates the empress is widowed. In Cixi's case the term is an oversimplification since she was the widowed mother of the Tongzhi emperor, the aunt of the Guangxu emperor and the great-aunt of the Xuantong emperor (better known as Puyi, the last emperor).

BEHIND THE CURTAIN (*CHULIAN TINGZHENG*)—During both of Cixi's regencies, the Tongzhi and Guangxu emperors, when the young emperor sat on the throne for any audience with his officials, the empress would sit behind a silk curtain (or by some accounts a decorative screen) where she could hear everything said to and by the emperor as well as issue instructions.

YIXIN (1833–1898)—The sixth son of the Daoguang emperor often referred to as Prince Gong. He served as regent for the young Tongzhi emperor and became a strong proponent of the Self-Strengthening Movement and the establishment of the Zongli Yamen.

been written about her, the misdeeds include terminating the lives of two emperors, one consort, and numerous officials. It is also said she encouraged her son's early initiation into Beijing's brothels and diverted the entire Navy's budget to build the Summer Palace (Yihe Yuan)—to list the most infamous hearsay attributed to her.

If the more lurid conjecture is set aside, however, it is apparent that Cixi's legacy is chiefly tarnished, not by rumors or palace intrigue, but by her actions in 1898 and 1900. As China emerged from its mid-century rebellions and fended off challenges from Western imperialists, many officials and advisors pressed for faster-paced reform. As calls for reform (and even revolution) mounted in the late 1890s, Cixi made two ill-advised decisions. In 1898, several of China's leading reformers began to persuade the **Guangxu** emperor of needed reforms (known as the Hundred Days of Reform). Cixi intervened and orchestrated a conservative counter-attack by removing the emperor from the decision-making process, reversing many of his reforms, and summarily executing six top reformers. Two years later Cixi made matters worse when she catastrophically sided with the anti-foreign Boxer (*Yihetuan*) Movement. She hoped that her support would thwart the deep inroads being made by foreign governments, religious groups and trading companies into Chinese affairs and culture. Her support of the Boxer Movement resulted in an invasion by an **eight-nation foreign expeditionary force,** the occupation of Beijing for over a year, and imposition of a massive $330 million indemnity.

Cixi, in the last decade of her life, did attempt to counter her earlier mistakes. Specifically, she became a forceful champion of the **"New Policies"** (*xinzheng*) focused on educational reform, constitutionalism, and institutional reorganization. While her patronage of the reforms is Cixi's finest legacy, her efforts did not keep pace with the "revolution of rising expectations." Many Chinese then (and today) felt that her actions in the late 1890s tipped the scales in favor of reactionary conservatism precisely when the empire desperately needed aggressive reform. The efforts in the last years of her life were too little and too late. As a result, the last emperor of China, **Puyi,** inherited a politically diminished and socially deeply traumatized empire.

HUNDRED-DAYS REFORM MOVEMENT

1898 was a tumultuous year in a chaotic era. In the wake of the Sino-Japanese War (1894–95), a group of liberal advisors and confidantes (the so-called "Emperor's clique" [*didang*]) wielded increasing influence over the young Guangxu emperor. Among this group, **Kang Youwei,** a pro-reformist scholar, became particularly influential. Seeking

GUANGXU (1871–1908)—The ninth emperor of China, selected at the age of four by his aunt Cixi. He initiated the Hundred Days' Reform of 1898, which was abruptly halted by Cixi who stripped him of all power, privileges and honors. He died on November 14, 1908, a day before Cixi.

EIGHT-NATION FOREIGN EXPEDITIONARY FORCE—An alliance of eight nations (Austria-Hungary, France, Germany, Italy, Japan, Russia, United Kingdom, and the United States) who came together to quell the Boxer Rebellion.

NEW POLICIES (1901–1910)—A series of political reforms set in motion by Cixi in an effort to erect a modern administrative bureaucracy.

PUYI (1905–1967)—More formally known as the Xuantong emperor, he was the tenth and last emperor of the Qing dynasty. He became emperor at the age of three, abdicated at the age of 7 in 1912, and was the titular head of Manchukuo, the Japanese puppet state in northeastern China at the age of 27 in 1932.

KANG YOUWEI (1858–1927)—A prominent late-Qing classically trained scholar who advocated modernization and reform within a Confucian framework. His influence peaked during the Hundred Days of Reform when the Guangxu emperor selected his proposals as the framework for reforms. He was forced to flee China when Dowager Empress Cixi abruptly seized power and executed Kang Youwei's younger brother and five other top reformers.

to capitalize on the growing popular discontent over the Treaty of Shimonoseki and on the rising resentment resulting from concessions given to the Western powers, Kang Youwei flooded the emperor and other high officials with calls for urgent reforms (5.1). In the period between June 11 and September 21,1898 (now known as the **"Hundred Days Reform Movement"**), the Guangxu emperor issued, in quick succession, a series of edicts that attempted to usher in an unparalleled era of reform. The response from the Dowager Empress Cixi and her more conservative allies was swift. Six officials were hastily executed, and Kang Youwei fled China to pursue his reformist ideals amongst the vast (and quite wealthy) Chinese overseas population.

5.1 KANG YOUWEI'S MEMORIAL ON INSTITUTIONAL REFORM (JANUARY 29, 1898)

The following document was Kang Youwei's sixth memorial to the emperor urging major institutional changes. Despite the influence he ultimately attained, Kang Youwei did not have an audience with the emperor for almost six months after writing this memorial, nor would his recommendations take the shape of an imperial edict until June 1898. Kang Youwei's intellectual make-up, though perhaps staid by modern standards, was typical for the scholar-official reformers of the day. His logic and reasoning (using past historical examples and Chinese classics to support his views) reflect the reformers' classical orientation. Despite the traditional veneer, Kang Youwei's reforms sought to alter the foundation of Chinese society. Kang Youwei should still be seen as a moderate pursing the middle ground. He championed reforms that fell between the conservative traditionalists who sought to preserve a traditional interpretation of the Confucian classics and the revolutionaries who advocated ending the examination system, modernization of the police and military, and creation of new institutions to modernize China.

Questions

1. **What reasons does Kang suggest hinder China's reform? How does he suggest the emperor resolve these problems?**
2. **Does Kang favor or resist "Western" reform?**

A survey of all states in the world will show that those states which undertook reforms became strong while those states which clung to the past perished. The consequences of clinging to the past and the effects of opening up new ways are thus obvious. If Your Majesty, with your discerning brilliance, observes the trends in other countries, you will see that if we can change, we can preserve ourselves; but if we cannot change, we shall perish. Indeed, if we can make a complete change, we shall become strong, but if we only make limited changes, we shall still perish. If Your Majesty and his ministers investigate the source of the disease, you will know that this is the right prescription.

Our present trouble lies in our clinging to old institutions without knowing how to change. In an age of competition between states, to put into effect methods appropriate to an era of universal unification and laissez-faire is like wearing heavy furs in summer or riding a high carriage across a river. This can only result in having a fever or getting oneself drowned.

HUNDRED DAYS REFORM MOVEMENT (1898)—A period that lasted from June 11 to September 21, 1898 when the Guangxu emperor, on advice from Kang Youwei and other top reformers, issued a series of decrees instituting far-reaching reforms. The reform movement ended when Cixi, Dowager Empress, staged a coup, executed several reformers, and effectively removed the emperor from power.

It is a principle of things that the new is strong but the old weak; that new things are fresh but old things rotten; that new things are active but old things static. If the institutions are old, defects will develop. Therefore there are no institutions that should remain unchanged for a hundred years. Moreover, our present institutions are but unworthy vestiges of the Han, Tang, Yuan, and Ming dynasties; they are not even the institutions of the [Manchu] ancestors. In fact, they are the products of the fancy writing and corrupt dealing of the petty officials rather than the original ideas of the ancestors. To say that they are the ancestral institutions is an insult to the ancestors. Furthermore, institutions are for the purpose of preserving one's territories. Now that the ancestral territory cannot be preserved, what good is it to maintain the ancestral institutions? ...

Although there is a desire for reform, yet if the national policy is not fixed and public opinion not united, it will be impossible for us to give up the old and adopt the new. The national policy is to the state just as the rudder is to the boat or the pointer is to the compass. It determines the direction of the state and shapes the public opinion of the country.

Nowadays the court has been undertaking some reforms, but the action of the emperor is obstructed by the ministers, and the recommendations of the able scholars are attacked by old-fashioned bureaucrats. If the charge is not "using barbarian ways to change China," then it is "upsetting the ancestral institutions." Rumors and scandals are rampant, and people fight each other like fire and water. A reform in this way is as ineffective as attempting a forward march by walking backward. It will inevitably result

in failure. Your Majesty knows that under the present circumstances reforms are imperative and old institutions must be abolished. I beg Your Majesty to make up your mind and to decide on the national policy. After the fundamental policy is determined, the methods of implementation must vary according to what is primary and what is secondary, what is important and what is insignificant, what is strong and what is weak, what is urgent and what can wait. ... If anything goes wrong, no success can be achieved.

After studying ancient and modern institutions, Chinese and foreign, I have found that the institutions of the sage-kings and Three Dynasties [of Xia, Shang, and Zhou] were excellent, but that ancient times were different from today. I hope Your Majesty will daily read Mencius and follow his example of loving the people. The development of the Han, Tang, Song, and Ming dynasties may be learned, but it should be remembered that the age of universal unification is different from that of sovereign nations. I wish Your Majesty would study Guan Zi and follow his idea of managing the country. As to the republican governments of the United States and France and the constitutional governments of Britain and Germany, these countries are far away and their customs are different from ours. Their changes occurred a long time ago and can no longer be traced. Consequently I beg Your Majesty to adopt the purpose of Peter the Great of Russia as our purpose and to take the Meiji Reform of Japan as the model of our reform. The time and place of Japan's reform are not remote and her religion and customs are somewhat similar to ours. Her success is manifest; her example can be followed.

5.2 EXAMINATION SYSTEM AS AN OBSTRUCTION TO REFORM (AUGUST 23, 1898)

No reform struck at the heart of traditional Chinese culture (let alone Qing bureaucracy) more than the attempt to overhaul China's examination system as the primary method of selecting its civil officials. It is difficult for us in the modern era to understand how these exams were intertwined with Chinese society. Officials were selected by it; the entire education system revolved around it; and many believed the culture's whole moral make-up was shaped by it. To reformers the exams became the cause of everything that kept China from modernizing. For conservatives the exam structure defined the very bonds that held Chinese society together. The exam topics themselves had been slowly modernized so that by the end of the nineteenth century, questions on issues of reform and modernization were included. However, many traditional elements such as the need to adhere to a strict rhyme scheme, rigid format, and calligraphy remained. The question of how to refine the exam system does, on many levels, reflect the tensions throughout Chinese society at the turn of the century.

Questions

1. **What negative attributes does the author see in the exam system?**
2. **What positive elements might a conservative official use to counter such an argument?**

The dynasty's examination system is extremely annoying and cumbersome. From the district examinations to the two Palace Examinations, there is not a single year without exams of some sort, and not one exam without a preliminary test, in order to prevent cheating and to stress recruiting men of talent. In the district and prefectural examinations there are at least four or five sessions, and as many as six or seven. And in addition, there are three or four sessions of examinations supervised by the Provincial Commissioner of Education. Students go through innumerable hardships before they can obtain the right to wear the robes designating them as officially authorized students. Hence, year after year they persist in their studies until their hair turns white. One half of each year is taken up with examinations, and the other half is burdened with wife, children, home and family. Any spare time is spent trying to master the eight-legged essay style. And yet, it still is very difficult to attain satisfactory competence in the eight-legged style, even though it is considered so vital, and pursued month after month and year after year. What then, if in addition, one wants to read useful books and study useful subjects?

The Palace Examinations rely solely upon ability in fine script [*xiaokai*], poetry, and rhyme-prose, not at all what the candidates are used to studying. [Even] members of the Hanlin Academy do not dare to discard the eight-legged style, poetry, rhyme-prose, and fine script before attaining the Third Rank, because they want to pass the test for Supervisor of Imperial Instruction. This is all because the difference between passing and failing the examinations depends on abilities in these areas. Hence, though after entering officialdom and becoming officials in the provinces for five or ten years scholars may gain some experience and some knowledge and understanding, it is easy to be infected by the heavy-laden atmosphere of officialdom, and the desire for personal gain is apt to affect the mind. As for Hanlin and other metropolitan officials, they are busily occupied with writing poetry, rhyme-prose, and fine script. And what is even more ridiculous, they spend their days going to the residences of fellow graduates of the same year, with a volume in hand, earnestly encouraging each other at their group study, just like in their *xiucai* days. Alas, are they this vulgar? Nevertheless, since those above recruit and select this way, those below respond accordingly. This is a circumstance about which aspiring scholars can do nothing. . . .

For the court to use poetry, rhyme-prose, and fine script as the criteria for passing or failing the examinations for men of ability is truly vulgar and ridiculous. Now, if peace reigned throughout the empire, and the court had no problems on its hands, then it would be proper for officials in the Hanlin Academy to serve His Majesty by lauding peace and plentitude through these means. But the multitude of problems on the coast has steadily weakened the nation. Poetry and rhyme-prose are not adequate to cope with this changing situation, and fine script is not adequate to withstand the enemy. How are we to devise a policy to bring peace and to emulate the wealth and power [of Western nations]? Every meaningless and extravagant custom should be reformed, one after another—the strings must be changed, and then tightened up. Only then will officials of the court and members of the Hanlin Academy, as well as scholars outside officialdom, be able to devote themselves to useful studies. Their ambitions will no longer be diverted by eight-legged essays, poetry, rhyme-prose, and fine script, nor will their minds be disturbed by all the various examinations. Who but a sagacious sovereign could thus respond to the times with the appropriate measures, and reform anachronistic laws? Nevertheless, scholars fortunate enough to have been born in an age when men of ability are sought out and rewarded, and incentives are given for practical leaning, but who still fail to exert themselves to be of use and to respond to the generous intentions of the court, should feel ashamed of themselves, should they not?

5.3 GUANGXU'S THREE SECRET DECREES (SEPTEMBER, 1898)

As the Guangxu's reform effort entered its third month, intense pressures began to build between the pro and anti-reform factions within the Forbidden City. The following secret imperial decrees sought to circumvent the conventional delivery system so as to avoid detection by Cixi and her allies. They offer a rare insight into the decision making process of the Guangxu emperor. They also underscore the limits of the emperor's authority over the entire empire. Note the types of relationships the emperor developed, and found necessary to implement his vision, given his isolated position within the imperial bureaucracy.

Questions

1. **What do the following secret imperial decrees reflect about the nature of the Hundred Days Reform movement?**
2. **What was the relationship between the Guangxu emperor and Dowager Empress Cixi?**

On the 27th of the 7th month in Year of Wuxu [Sept. 12, 1898], Emperor Guangxu issued a decree to Yang Rui, which reads:

Recently, I have been trying to understand the thoughts of Her Majesty, the Dowager Empress. Uninterested in pursuing reforms she does not want to dismiss elderly and incompetent ministers or bring in bold and enterprising young men. She opposes such measures fearing such a move would cost her the confidence of the people. I have issued numerous decrees to clarify the situation in an effort to persuade Her Majesty. But her mind remains unchanged and nothing more can be done. For example, the Dowager considered the decree of the 19th [September 4, 1898] too extreme and [forced] me to amend it. This is the challenging situation in which we presently find ourselves. How can I fail to recognize that China's deficiencies and instability are due to the actions of this [conservative] group of ministers? If you are asking me to issue immediate decrees to abolish the old laws and dismiss these incompetent officials, then I can only reply I truly do not possess such power. If we persist along these lines of action, then, my position as emperor will be in danger, not to mention everything else. Now I am asking you for any constructive proposals that would allow us to slowly revise the old statutes and gradually dismiss all the old and incompetent ministers. I am asking for proposals to attract spirited and sophisticated men to participate in the government and to steer China away from danger and toward stability; away from weakness and toward strength. All must be accomplished without violating Her Majesty's wishes. You must immediately confer with Lin Xu, Tan Sitong, Liu Guangdi and other associates to draw up an appropriate proposal, and deliver it to me in a sealed envelop via the Grand Council. The implementation will be conducted only after I have thoroughly considered the plan. I am extremely uneasy and anxiously await your proposal. Respect this.

YANG RUI (1857–1898)—One of the key reformers in the Guangxu emperor's inner circle during the Hundred Days Reform. He was one of six reformers arrested and executed by Dowager Empress Cixi upon her return to power.

On the same day, an imperial decree was issued to Kang Youwei which reads:

I feel that the situation is very precarious and that reform is the only way to save China; the only way to reform is to first dismiss those conservative and inept ministers, and replace them with knowledgeable and bold men. However, the Dowager Empress disagrees. I tried to engage her on this topic numerous times, which only enraged her. Now I am about to lose my position as the emperor. You along with Yang Rui, Lin Xu, Tan Sitong, and Liu Guangdi must immediately secretly discuss with to come up with a rescue plan. I am extremely worried and anxiously awaiting for your response. Respect this.

On the 2nd day of the 8th month [September 17, 1898], a decree was issued to Kang Youwei, which reads:

It is hard to explain in words how reluctant I was, but it seemed that I had no other choice but to appoint you to be in charge of the publication of the official newspapers. You must leave the country immediately without any delay. I am profoundly aware of your loyalty and devotion to the throne. Take good care of your health and yourself so that some day in the future we can attain this great accomplishment together. I have great hope in you. Respect this.

BOXER UPRISING

In the spring of 1900, an anti-foreign insurrection began among the largely rural populace of the North China Plain. The English appellation for this movement, "Boxers," is derived from the group's Chinese name, "Boxers United in Righteousness" (*yihequan*). The leaders claimed to have special rituals to bestow special powers—such as being impervious to bullets, flying, and extraordinary strength—on their followers. Tapping into the rising anti-foreign sentiments (particularly within Shandong province), the uprising was virulently xenophobic. The resentment against Christianity—particularly of missionaries and their converts—was based both on its foreign origins and that Christianity sought to displace many traditional Chinese beliefs and practices (5.5). Chinese converts to Christianity were commonly instructed to cease "worshiping" their ancestors and praying to the large pantheon of smaller gods that regulated everyday life in China.

Despite considerable ambivalance among many senior Qing officials, the success of the Boxer's anti-foreign movement emboldened the Dowager Empress Cixi who was in sympathy with their goals. In late mid-1900 she declared war on all the foreign powers present in China. The Qing court sought to follow up on the Boxer's initial victories against Western forces with several edicts supporting the Boxers' efforts to kill all foreigners as well as all Chinese Christians (5.7). The reaction by the imperialist powers was swift and devastating. An Eight-Nation Allied military marched inland from Tianjian in order to rescue the besieged foreign community. After gaining control of Beijing from the Boxers, the Allied leaders wrangled for nearly a year over the demands to be made of China. They finally presented China with the **Boxer Protocol** on September 7, 1901 (5.8), which imposed a devastating 450 million taels ($333 million dollars) indemnity on an already impoverished empire.

5.4 MALAN BOXER PROCLAMATIONS (1900)

As with many popular uprisings, it is difficult to pinpoint exactly where, when and how the Boxer revolt began. The following proclamation was posted in a village outside of Beijing. It is typical of placards that appeared in villages between Shandong and Beijing

BOXER PROTOCOL (1901)—An extremely harsh peace treaty imposed by the Eight-Nation Alliance upon the Qing government, including a 450 million taels ($333 million dollar) indemnity, almost twice the annual Qing budget of 250 taels, and with interest totaling nearly 1 billion taels over 33 years.

in the spring of 1900. The Boxers reflect one of the few popular Chinese movements of the nineteenth century that openly supported the Manchu Qing dynasty. The primary focus of their rage was the foreign presence, reflecting the deep animosity towards Western imperialism among a growing portion of the Chinese populace. The one central point of contention for virtually all Chinese was the extension of extraterritoriality to converts given by foreign missionaries and clergy that protected these converts from legal lawsuits. The following conforms to a somewhat traditional listing of grievances and appeals from a Confucian cultural outlook.

Questions

1. **Why, according to this notice, are foreigners the focus of the Boxer anger?**
2. **What are the main objectives of the Boxers?**

Public Notice of Malan Village the Kan Army (Wanping County in Beijing Suburb)

Since the Xianfeng reign [1851–1861], Catholics have been conspiring with foreigners; causing chaos in China; squandering the state's revenue; tearing down temples and monasteries; destroying Buddhist statues; and taking over people's graveyards. Such evil acts have aroused hatred far and wide. They have also caused swarms of locusts and droughts which harm the trees and plants. Our country is no longer harmonious and the Chinese people are no longer secure. This has angered Heaven.

Blessed by the great god in Heaven, all the spirits have descended to set up an altar. They will teach our young men how to support the Qing, eliminate the foreigners, and implement virtuous principles on behalf of Heaven. We want to contribute to the country so that it will be at peace; and to help the peasants so that the villages and neighborhoods are safe. In the end, misfortune will come to an end while prosperity returns. Yet, we worry that ignorant people and hooligans will use the support of the foreigners to mistreat the weak. All such behavior should be reported to the local leaders to be dealt with publicly and in accordance with the laws and regulations. It is forbidden to resolve the matter in a purely selfish manner. The eyes of the gods are as sharp as lightening and will see those who are pursuing the cases purely with selfish motives and will punish them accordingly.

The false methods perpetrated by the deluded foreign missionaries have angered Heaven who has ordered the spirits to descend to the divine altar in order to teach the youth. The meaning of Yihetuan (Boxer) is as follows: *yi* means benevolent and *he* means unified. Benevolence and unity keep villages and neighborhoods peaceful and harmonious. Virtue is the foundation of living. Agriculture is the means by which we make a living. Buddhism is the religion that we should follow. Public matters should not to be handled with selfish aims of revenge. It is not allowed to mistreat the poor and the weak. No one should mistake wrong for right.

5.5 SPIRIT BOXER POSSESSION (1900)

The Boxer's success spread primarily from the group's teachings that resonated with China's large peasant class. One distinguishing characteristic of the Boxer movement was that the Boxer teachings offered spells and incantations that permitted spirits to possess all the initiated. Such egalitarian spirit possession made the Boxers an extremely engaging movement. The spells typically gave the initiated some form of protection. The final poem or incantation of invulnerability at the end of the document is representative of many magic charms, amulets, and enchanted objects prevalent during the Boxer movement. There were many slight variations on the wording, and they were often written on paper that would be burned, the ashes mixed in water, and then drunk by the initiate.

The Spirit Boxers United in Righteousness arose in reaction to the foreign devils' invasion of China. They persuaded people to believe in their religion, in their God, to abandon [Chinese] gods, and ignore our ancestors and spirits. Their men are amoral and their women licentious, all the devil children are born from mothers and sons. If you do not trust this, look carefully at all foreigners, their eyes are blue. There is no rain coming from above and down below only drought, all because the churches are blocking the sky. Spirits are angry and the fairies are mad, together they come down the mountain to show us the correct way. [Our teaching] is not heretical, it is not the **White Lotus** Teachings. It is nothing but reciting spells and reading incantations; learning the true words, burning yellow prayer paper and burning incense; inviting spirits and fairies from all their caves. Fairies leave their caves, spirits come down from mountains, and possess one's body allowing them to perform the "boxing movements." All martial arts are wholly understood. Defeating the foreigners will not be difficult at all. We tear down the railways, rip up the electric poles, rush to destroy the steam ships. France is terribly scared; Britain, America, Germany and Russia will all disappear. All foreigners will be wiped out. The Great Qing will unite once more.

Incantation of Invulnerability:

United brothers will give it their all,
Each blade of grass and every tree become our
  warriors.
When ordinary bodies are possessed by magic,
All foreigners will surely be exterminated.

5.6 IMPERIAL EDICT TO "DECLARE WAR" (JUNE 21, 1900)

After several weeks of vacillation and indecision, the Qing court issued this declaration of war against all foreigners residing in China. As irrational as the Dowager Empress **Cixi's** support of the Boxers may seem, the edict captures the profound fear and loathing felt by many Chinese citizens for the imperious style of foreigners in China. Very few of the assertions made in this declaration are made without basis. It underscores the pent-up frustration over the imperial court's inability to develop ways to contain the foreign powers. The Dowager Empress and her advisors did not, however, have the complete support of Qing officials, many of who implored them not to offer another pretext for foreign aggression against China.

WHITE LOTUS SOCIETY—A secret society based on a mixture of Buddhist, Daoist and local spiritual beliefs prevalent since the seventeenth century. It was declared heretical and prohibited by the Qing government.

CIXI (1834–1908)—An imperial courtesan of the Xianfeng emperor, she gave birth to his only son, the Tongzhi emperor. After the Xianfeng emperor's death, she served as regent to the Tongzhi emperor and, after his death, to the Guangxu emperor. She remained a driving, if controversial, force within the Qing government until her death in 1908.

On the 25th day of 5th month, Guangxu 26th year. [June 21, 1900]

Ever since the foundation of the Dynasty over two hundred years ago, foreigners coming to China have been treated kindly. In the Daoguang (1821–1850) and Xianfeng (1851–1861) reigns, they were allowed to trade. They also asked to propagate their religion, a request that the Throne reluctantly granted. At first they were amenable to Chinese control, but for the past thirty years they have taken advantage of China's forbearance to encroach on China's territory, trample on the Chinese people and to demand China's wealth. Every concession made by China only heightened their reliance on violence. They oppressed peaceful citizens and insulted our gods and religious leaders. Their actions provoked a burning fury within the people, hence the burning of chapels and slaughter of converts by patriotic warriors. The Throne was anxious to avoid war, like previous protectors, we worried about harming our people. Therefore time and time again we issued edicts protecting the legations and defending the [Christian] converts. The earlier decrees stating that the Boxers and converts are all our children were issued with the hope of ending the feud between commoners and converts. Exceptional kindness was shown towards the 'people from afar' [e.g. foreigners]. But these people knew no gratitude and increased their pressure. A dispatch was yesterday sent by George Du Chaylard, calling us to turn over the Dagu Forts to them, otherwise they would be taken by force.

These threats only serve to reveal their aggressive intentions. In all matters relating to international intercourse, we have never been wanting in civility. But while styling themselves as 'civilized states' they continue to act with complete disregard to what is right, depending solely on their military force. I have now reigned for nearly 30 years and have treated the people as children, and the people in return have treated me as their divinity. In the midst of our reign we have been the recipients of the gracious favor of the Dowager Empress. Furthermore, our ancestors have come to our aid, the gods have answered our call, and never has there been so universal a manifestation of loyalty and patriotism. With tears have I announced war in the ancestral shrines. Better to enter the struggle and do our utmost than seek some measures of self-preservation involving eternal disgrace. All our officials, high and low, are of one mind, and there have assembled without official summons several hundred thousand patriotic soldiers ("Boxers"). Even children are carrying spears in the service of the State. Those others [foreigners] rely on devious schemes, our trust is in Heaven's justice. They depend on violence, we on humanity. Not to speak of the righteousness of our cause, our provinces number more than twenty, our people over 400,000,000. It will not be difficult to vindicate the dignity of our country.

We conclude this decree by promising heavy rewards to those who distinguish themselves in battle or subscribe funds, and threatening punishment to those who show cowardice or act treacherously.

5.7 IMPERIAL EDICT TO SLAY FOREIGNERS AND CONVERTS (JULY 1, 1900)

This edict was sent to top provincial officials throughout the empire in the summer of 1900. Any attempt to fathom the Dowager Empress Cixi's precise motives is difficult. Some have speculated that through this action she hoped to undermine foreign delegations' calls for the reins of power to be returned to the Guangxu emperor. Others suggest that the Dowager Empress Cixi hoped to roll back foreign influence, falsely believing that any backlash would not restore them to their pre-Boxer presence. With either interpretation it is apparent that she hoped to usher in an era of xenophobic renewal for China and the revitalization of her diminishing authority over her conservative faction. Both proved to be illusory goals with ruinous results.

Questions

1. **What does the Dowager Empress Cixi suggest is the problem between the Chinese Christian converts and non-converts?**
2. **Whose safety is the Dowager Empress Cixi more concerned about—that of the foreign missionaries or that of the Chinese converts?**

On the 5th day of 6th month, 26th year during Guangxu reign [July 1, 1900], an edict was issued to the Grand Secretariat (*neige*)

Since foreigners from all countries began to proselytize, there have been many instances of mutual animosity between the people and converts. All this is due to the flawed leadership of the local authorities leading to disputes and conflicts. The truth is that the converts are also the empire's children, and among them there are kind people. But they have been led astray by false doctrines and have relied on the missionaries for protection allowing them to commit misdeeds. They cling to the misconceptions and will not change. Thus irreconcilable enmity has grown up between the converts and the people. Now the Court is exhorting members of the Boxers (*Yihetuan*) to render loyal and patriotic services, and to take part against the enemies so that the entire population will be of one mind. Since the converts are also our subjects and common people, it seems infeasible they would truly seek to alienate themselves [from their country] and

bring about their own destruction. If they repent, they can still escape the net [of punishment] and be pardoned. The governors-general and governors of all provinces are hereby commanded to give all the local officials the following notification:

Converts who repent their former errors and give themselves up accordingly to the authorities shall be allowed to reform and their past misdeeds will be overlooked. The public shall also be notified that in all places where converts reside they shall be allowed to present their case to the appropriate local authority. Each case will be settled according to regulations that will be drawn up at a later date. As hostilities have now broken out between China and the foreign powers, the missionaries of every nationality must all be expelled at once and ordered to return to their own countries so as to avoid difficulties caused by continued presence. Measures should be taken to secure their safe departure. Provincial authorities are to make due investigation into the circumstances of all places in their jurisdiction, and speedily take the necessary steps. Let there be no carelessness. The above is to be circulated. Respect this!

5.8   BOXER PROTOCOL (SEPTEMBER 7, 1901)

From the moment the Eight-Nation Alliance decided upon the need for a multi-national force, disagreements between them emerged. Fearful of Japan's intentions in China, the European and American governments refused Japan's proposition to send 20–30,000 troops to relieve the siege of Beijing, effectively postponing the relief mission for six weeks until the other nations could transport their forces to China. The allied troops entered Tianjin in early July and reached Beijing in early August. Once the troops had occupied the city, they plundered and looted the Yihe Yuan in a grim repeat of the 1860 Anglo-French destruction of the Yuanming Yuan four decades earlier. It took nearly a year for the various governments to agree upon demands to impose on China. The final protocol required China to pay an indemnity of 450 million taels (or roughly $333 million US gold dollars at 1901 exchange rates). It was the largest indemnity in China's history and effectively bankrupted the imperial treasury, already in a state of financial crisis.

Questions

1. What goals does the protocol appear to be pursuing? How does an indemnity of 450 million taels help or hinder them?
2. What role does the fear of anti-foreignism in China play in the protocol (specifically Articles IIa, X, and XII)?

ARTICLE IA

By an Imperial Edict of the 9th of June last, Zaifeng, Prince of Chun, was appointed Ambassador of His Majesty the Emperor of China, and directed in that capacity to convey to His Majesty the German Emperor the expression of the regrets of His Majesty the Emperor of China and of the Chinese Government for the assassination of His Excellency the late Baron von Ketteler, German minister.

Prince Chun left Beijing the 12th of July last to carry out the orders which had been given him.

ARTICLE IB

The Chinese Government has stated that it will erect on the spot of the assassination of His Excellency the late Baron von **Ketteler** a commemorative monument, worthy of the rank of the deceased, and bearing an inscription in the Latin, German, and Chinese languages, which shall express the regrets of His Majesty the Emperor of China for the murder committed.

Their Excellencies the Chinese Plenipotentiaries have informed His Excellency the German Plenipotentiary, in a letter dated the 22nd of July last that an arch of the whole width of the street would be erected on the said spot, and that work on it was begun the 25th of June last.

ARTICLE IIA

Imperial Edicts of the 13th and 21st of February, 1901, inflicted the following punishments on the principal authors of the outrages and crimes committed against the foreign Governments and their nationals:

Zaiyi Prince Duan, and Zailan Duke Fuguo were sentenced to be brought before the autumnal court of assize for execution, and it was agreed that if the Emperor saw fit to grant them their lives, they should be exiled to Turkestan and there imprisoned for life, without the possibility of commutation of these punishments.

Zaixun Prince Zhuang, Ying Nian, President of the Court of censors, and Zhao Shuqiao, President of the Board of punishments, were condemned to commit suicide.

Yu Xian, Governor of Shanxi, Qixiu, President of the Board of rites, and Xu Chengyu, formerly senior vice-President of the Board of punishments were condemned to death.

[....]

ARTICLE IIB

Imperial Edict promulgated the 19th of August, 1901, ordered the suspension of official examinations for five years in all cities where foreigners were massacred or submitted to cruel treatment.

ARTICLE III

So as to make honorable reparation for the assassination of Mr. Sugiyama, chancellor of the Japanese legation, His Majesty the Emperor of China by an Imperial Edict of the 18th of June, 1901, appointed Natong, vice-President of the Board of revenue, to be his Envoy Extraordinary, and specially directed him to convey to His Majesty the Emperor of Japan the expression of the regrets of His Majesty the Emperor of China and of his Government at the assassination of the late Mr. Sugiyama.

[....]

ARTICLE VI

By an Imperial Edict dated the 29th of May, 1901, His Majesty the Emperor of China agreed to pay the Powers an indemnity of four hundred and fifty million of Haiguan taels. This sum represents the total amount of the indemnities for States, companies or societies, private individuals, and Chinese referred to in Article VI of the note of December 22nd, 1900.

a. These four hundred and fifty million taels constitute a gold debt calculated at the rate of the of the Haiguan tael to the gold currency of each country .... This sum in gold shall bear interest at 4 percent per annum, and the capital shall be reimbursed by China in thirty-nine years in the manner indicated in the annexed plan of amortization.

[....]

ARTICLE VIII

The Chinese government has consented to raze the forts of Dagu and those which might impede free communication between Beijing and the sea; steps have been taken for carrying this out.

ARTICLE IX

The Chinese Government has conceded the right to the powers in the protocol annexed to the letter of

KETTELER, KLEMENS von (1853–1900) — German ambassador to China killed by pro-Boxer soldiers. His death became a cause célèbre among the foreign powers.

the 16th of January, 1901, to occupy certain points, to be determined by an agreement between them, for the maintenance of open communication between the capital and the sea. The points occupied by the powers are: Huangcun, Langfang, Yangcun, Tianjin, Junliangcheng, Tanggu, Lutai, Tangshan, Luanzhou, Changli, Qinhuangdao, Shanhaiguan.

ARTICLE X

The Chinese Government has agreed to post and to have published during two years in all district cities the following Imperial Edicts:

   a. Edict of the 1st of February, prohibiting forever, under pain of death, membership in any antiforeign society.
   b. Edicts of the 13th and 21st February, 29th April, and 19th August, enumerating the punishments inflicted on the guilty.
   c. Edict of the 19th August, 1901, prohibiting examinations in all cities where foreigners were massacred or subjected to cruel treatment.
   d. Edict of the 1st of February, 1901, declaring all governors-general, governors, and provincial or local officials responsible for order in their respective districts, and that in case of new antiforeign troubles or other infractions of the treaties which shall not be immediately repressed and the authors of which shall not have been punished, these officials shall be immediately dismissed, without possibility of being given new functions or new honors.

The posting of these edicts is being carried on throughout the Empire.

ARTICLE XII

An Imperial Edict of the 24th of July, 1901, reformed the Office of Foreign Affairs (Zongli Yamen), on the lines indicated by the Powers, that is to say, transformed it into a Ministry of Foreign Affairs (Waiwu Bu), which takes precedence over the six other Ministries of State. The same edict appointed the principal members of this Ministry.

An agreement has also been reached concerning the modification of Court ceremonial as regards the reception of foreign Representatives and has been the subject of several notes from the Chinese Plenipotentiaries, the substance of which is embodied in a memorandum herewith annexed.

Finally, it is expressly understood that as regards the declarations specified above and the annexed documents originating with the foreign Plenipotentiaries, the French text only is authoritative.

The Chinese Government having thus complied to the satisfaction of the Powers with the conditions laid down in the above-mentioned note of December 22nd, 1900, the Powers have agreed to accede to the wish of China to terminate the situation created by the disorders of the summer of 1900. In consequence thereof the foreign Plenipotentiaries are authorized to declare in the names of their Governments that, with the exception of the legation guards mentioned in Article VII, the international troops will completely evacuate the city of Beijing on the 17th September, 1901, and, with the exception of the localities mentioned in Article IX, will withdraw from the province of Zhili on the 22nd of September.

The present final Protocol has been drawn up in twelve identical copies and signed by all the Plenipotentiaries of the Contracting Countries. One copy shall be given to each of the foreign Plenipotentiaries, and one copy shall be given to the Chinese Plenipotentiaries.

Beijing, 7th September, 1901.

A. V. Mumn [Germany]
M. Czikann [Austria-Hungary]
Joostens [Belgium]
B. J. de Cologan [Spain]
W. W. Rockhill [United States]
Paul Beau [France]
Ernest Satow [Great Britain]
Salvago Raggi [Italy]
Jutaro Komura [Japan]
F. M. Knobel [Netherlands]
M. de Giers [Russia]

Signatures and seals of Chinese plenipotentiaries

POST-BOXER REFORM AND THE PUSH FOR REVOLUTION

After the failure of the Boxers and China's ignominious military defeat, few Chinese denied that China needed to reform. The debate after 1900 shifted from one of whether to reform to one of what type of reform was most suitable. The majority of

Chinese reformers were split between two options for China's future: 1) a constitutional monarchy (as existed in England and Japan), or 2) a republic. The Dowager Empress Cixi, seemingly truly repentant for her role in the Boxer debacle, advocated incremental change and promised a timeline for establishing a constitutional government and reforming the examination system. There were numerous reformers advocating various permutations of these two options, but two of the most respected "radicals" seeking to push far beyond simple reform were Wang Jingwei and **Sun Zhongshan.** While the two men's specific visions for China differed, they agreed that a modern China needed a modern form of government. In their political treatises on the topic they actively adopted elements from foreign countries and earlier foreign revolutions to make their points (5.11 and 5.12). In recent years, more and more scholars of China's past have realized that the Qing dynasty's last decade was not politically moribund, nor was Chinese society stagnant as long assumed. The four documents below reveal the vigorous and spirited debates that inspired a growing segment of the population.

5.9 QING OFFICIALS' JOINT PROPOSALS FOR POST-BOXER REFORM (1901)

Official and public opinion in China shifted extensively in the years between 1895 and 1901. Prior to 1895, many conservative officials and large segments of the populace remained certain that only minor alterations to China's traditional structure were needed for China to remain a powerful Asian empire. With the loss of the Sino-Japanese War, Guangxu emperor's failed effort to implement reform, and the disastrous Boxer Uprising, all but the most ultra-conservative realized that fundamental changes needed to be implemented. The fact that the Emperor and the Dowager Empress remained in the western city of Xi'an where they had fled to from the International Allied Force offers a stark backdrop to the following memorial advocating change. Liu Kunyi and Zhang Zhidong were two prominent Qing reformers and among the earliest to frame and set the agenda for many of the New Policies (*xinzheng*) called for by the Guangxu emperor (and the Dowager Empress) earlier that year.

Questions

1. **What do Liu Kunyi and Zhang Zhidong identify as the areas within China's government most in need of reform?**
2. **Given the long list of problems (and their entrenched nature) which of their reforms would most quickly bring about institutional change?**

Your ministers have planned and proposed four items for developing education and nurturing ability, which have been jointly memorialized and are on record.... In general there are three important factors in building a good nation: good administration, wealth, and strength... The reorganization of the Chinese political system is to serve as an instrument for bringing about better administration. The adoption of Western methods is for the purpose of attaining wealth and strength. We have carefully considered those aspects of the

SUN ZHONGSHAN [SUN YAT-SEN] (1866–1925)—Often called the "Father of Modern China," Sun was a principal revolutionary leader during the last decades of the Qing Dynasty. He served as the provisional president of the Republic of China, but resigned in favor of Yuan Shikai. Over the next two decades he headed the Guomindang party until his death in 1925 from cancer.

Chinese system which ought to be reorganized and reformed, and make proposals under twelve heads: (1) to honor frugality, (2) to break down customary formalities [red tape], (3) to stop the contributions or payments for the official rank, (4) to examine the officials and increase their emoluments, (5) to remove the useless clerical staff, (6) to weed out the government servants and messengers, (7) to lighten punishments and imprisonments, (8) to reform the method of civil service examination, (9) to plan for the livelihood of the Manchu Bannermen, (10) to abolish the military colonies and garrisons, (11) to abolish the Army of the Green Standard (*lüying*) and (12) to simplify the documents and laws. These are reverently prepared for the Court's selection and adoption.

[....]

The above twelve items are concerned with the causes of China's chronic weakness, which makes her incapable of exerting herself. They are particularly the hooks on which foreign countries hang their criticisms and abuse of us. Of the plans proposed by your ministers, some are for cultivating the peoples' strength, some for cleansing official circles, and some for arousing the scholars' spirit. Many people had discussed these matters before. But because they had such mistaken notions as that among evils one should remove only the worst, and because they were afraid of being criticized for changing everything, all the statutes, orders, documents, and notices have remained mere paper documents. They may have achieved something but they have lacked long-term and far-reaching plans.

Now foreign aggression is becoming daily more serious. Those who like to follow tradition and devote themselves to cheating and glossing things over always say that the peoples' minds are solidly united. They do not know that popular feelings are not the same as thirty years ago. The people admire the wealth of foreign countries and despise the poverty of the Middle Kingdom. Seeing the strength of foreign soldiers, they are sick of the timidity of their own government's troops; delighted at the fair play of the Maritime Customs Service, they hate the *lijin* (transit tax) offices which purposely cause them trouble; praising the stern orderliness of the foreign concessions and settlements, they are tired of the disorder caused by our official clerks. Therefore our people believe in the foreign religion, merchants display foreign flags, and schools register in the names of foreign nationals. All has resulted in a disunited and disillusioned national morale. Insurgents are slowly emerging, and they take this opportunity to spread subversive doctrines. This concerns the very foundation of the nation. We cannot overcome our anxiety and apprehension. We must first entirely wipe out the various defects mentioned above before we may expect a permanent unification of the popular mind. Then we may speak of being affectionate to our superiors, dying for our elders, opposing humiliation and resisting aggression. We humbly beseech your sacred enlightenment to decide with discrimination and to put these proposals into practice, and use them as the foundation for self-strengthening

5.10   THE ABOLITION OF THE COMPETITIVE EXAMINATIONS IN CHINA (1905)

By 1905 the examination system reformers had gained increasing support since first proposing reforms in the late nineteenth century. The system was perceived as antiquated and perpetuating an outmoded style of learning ill-suited for China's modern needs. To many reformers its abolition seemed well overdue. The examination system depended on a largely ad-hoc system of private schools and tutors focused on rote memorization. The exams, while merit-based, required years of education that only a few children from the wealthiest families could afford. Although the topics covered in the exams had begun to include more modern topics, the structure of the examinations remained antiquated. The following memorial and edict attempt to provide an infrastructure for a broader-based education system. With an imperial system on its last legs and a population approaching a half-billion, the revisions presented to the throne sought to modernize a system that had shaped Chinese culture for well over a thousand years. The following is a memorial written by several senior Qing officials within the inner circle of the Dowager Empress.

Questions

1. **Why does the memorial advocate an immediate rather than gradual abolition of the examination system?**
2. **Reading through the memorial and the emperor's rescript, what factors do they fear the most in adopting a new style education system?**

MEMORIAL

A Joint Memorial by the Manchu General of Shenyang, Zhao Erxian; the Governor-General of Zhili, Yuan Shikai; the acting Governor-General of Liang-Jiang [Jiangxi, Jiangsu, and Anhui], Zhou Fu; the Governor-General of Hu-Guang [Hubei-Hunan], Zhang Zhidong; the acting Governor-General of Liang-Guang [Guangdong and Guangxi], Cen Chunxuan; the Governor of Hunan, Duanfang, respectfully presented for Imperial consideration, in which the urgent need of national preservation, due to the strenuous difficulties of the times, is pointed out and the proposal to abolish the system of examinations and to promote the establishment of schools is made, together with careful and safe plans for the carrying out of the scheme.

The defects of the system of examinations have been spoken of in detail by men of ancient and recent times, and your memorialists [Yuan] Shikai and [Zhang] Zhidong have also presented several memorials for Imperial consideration in which it was shown that this system was a hindrance to the establishment of schools. The arguments used in these memorials need not be repeated. Recently an Imperial Edict has been issued for the gradual abolition of the system of examinations extending over a period of three triennial examinations, so that after ten years all promotions should be made from schools. ... Such a system of examinations has long been considered a source of reproach by foreigners, but schools are considered to be the chief factor in a reformed government. As soon as conservative methods are boldly and rigorously abandoned and new methods adopted, those who see and hear what is being done will all use their best endeavors to treat with us on a basis of mutual respect, and the students from China who are pursuing their studies in foreign countries will also receive encouragement. Emphasizing the importance of schools will obviate the possibility of being carried away by gross superstition and idle rumors. The value of men of intelligence equipped with useful knowledge cannot be over-estimated. The establishment of schools is not solely for the training of learned men but for the general dissemination of knowledge among the people, so that all may receive the advantages and acquired powers of an elementary education. This will result in patriotic loyalty to the country and in increased ability to earn a livelihood. ...

Although the examination system may be abolished, there are several important matters to be attended to, and the first of these in importance is that due regard should be paid to classical learning. There are those who fear that when these examinations are abolished classical learning will be neglected. ... In the present system of education, which has received Imperial sanction, the study of the classics is emphasized. There will be no lessening of the study or explanation of the Classics either in the primary or secondary schools, the purpose being that pupils who have finished the courses of these schools shall have studied Ten Classics so as to understand them. In the colleges there will be a special department for classical study in which history, literature, and philosophy will be studied. It will thus be seen that all of the ancient learning will be included in the curricula of the schools and none of it will be lost. ...

A second important matter which needs attention is that emphasis should be placed upon personal character. Under the old system students were only examined as to the quality of their literary attainments, but no attention was paid to their character, with the result that there was often a feeling of shame as to the attainment of students in this respect. In the present regulations for schools, however, it is provided that in addition to their examination in literary subjects, they shall also be given marks for conduct. These marks will be given to students for six things, viz: good conversation, careful personal appearance, attention to etiquette, diligence, intercourse with friends, and conduct on the street. When students are examined in their studies an average will be made between these marks and those for daily conduct.

This matter should also form the subject of a special edict to governors-general and governors of the various provinces.

A third important matter is the immediate establishment of normal schools. The greatest cause of concern is not that there are no schools or no funds to establish them, but that there are no teachers. A special edict should also be issued commanding the provinces to send pupils who have finished their secondary studies to foreign countries to take courses in normal studies, some longer and some shorter. The selection of men who have already taken their first and second degrees would be still more advisable. If normal schools are established in all the provinces, teachers will be trained and the first step taken toward the advancement of schools....

Another important matter is that a way of preferment should be left open for scholars of the old school. To this end during the next nine years students who have already taken their degrees and who also show proficiency in any one of the following subjects, viz: Arithmetic, geography, science of government, political economy, military science, politics, railroads, mining, police work, or western governmental science, may be sent from the various provinces to Beijing for examination....

The above five suggestions are all practicable, and we respectfully beseech Your Majesties to command the Governors-General, Governors, and literary chancellors or the various provinces to put them into immediate execution....

Respectfully submitted for Imperial consideration.

IMPERIAL RESCRIPT
SEPTEMBER 2, 1905

We have received a Memorial from Yuan Shikai, Governor-General of Zhili Province, and other high officials advocating the summary abolition of the old style of literary examinations for the *juren* degree in order to allow the expansion of the modern modes of education. In this connection the said Governor-General has also handed up his scheme for the successful accomplishment of the new regime....

On a former occasion the Ministers of Education memorialized us, suggesting that the old style of literary examinations should be gradually abolished by extending by three times the period for them. Governor-General Yuan Shikai in his present memorial, however, asserts that unless these old-style examinations be abolished once for all, the people of this Empire will continue to show apathy and hesitate to join the modern schools of learning. Hence if we desire to see the spread of modern education by the establishment of a number of schools, we must first abolish the old styles of studying for the examinations. The said memorialist's arguments on the subjects show the result of experience and knowledge, and we, therefore, hereby command that, beginning from the Bingwu Cycle [1906], all competitive examinations for the literary degree of *juren* and *jinshi* after the old style shall be henceforth abolished, while the annual competitions in the cities of the various provinces for the *xiucai* or licentiate degree are also to be abolished at once.... We also approve of the other suggestions made by the said Governor-General in his Memorial on the above subject and command that they shall be put into force as proposed. In a word, the methods and aims of our modern schools of learning have the same force as the ancient form of selection of men for office from the schools, as mentioned above, and the methods of rewards in rank and degrees are the same as those hitherto obtained by the old style of literary competitions. The regulations and rules for the various modern schools of learning and their various branches of studies have for their aims the attainment of substantial and practical knowledge.... We hereby further command our Ministers of Education on receiving this our Imperial Decree, to lose no time in distributing at once to the various provinces the text-books for schools that have been prepared, so that we may have a uniform system of teaching in all our schools. We also command our governors-general and governors to insist that their subordinates, the prefects, sub-prefect, and district magistrates, shall make haste to establish primary schools in all the towns, hamlets, and villages within their respective jurisdictions, and that the utmost care be taken to select intelligent teachers for them, so that the minds of all our subjects be open for the reception of modern knowledge. Let all our officials be earnest and diligent in obeying these our commands and let there be no lagging and carelessness, so as to avoid faults and mistakes in the administration of these schools. Let no one fail in deserving the confidence we have placed in each.

5.11 THE THREE PEOPLE'S PRINCIPLES AND THE FUTURE OF THE CHINESE PEOPLE (1906)

Perhaps no single political ideology of early twentieth-century China is better known than Sun Zhongshan's "**Three People's Principles:** Nationalism, Democracy and Livelihood." The Three Principles themselves never changed, though, the manner in which Sun described them evolved over time (compare with 8.5). His description often depended on the audience being addressed. The explication he gives below captures the key concerns of the Chinese in the twilight of the Qing but before the Republic of China actually existed. Sun neatly encapsulates three main forces that will ultimately fuel the 1911 Revolution: the still lingering anti-Manchu sentiment, a desire for a democratic government, and China's need for economic viability in the modern world. His ideas also reflect a new generation of political leaders who unabashedly embraced Western political philosophy. His explanation, unlike many of his predecessors, avoids a defense of Western methods, while revealing that his listeners are quite familiar with competing modes of governance in place around the world. The following appeared in the official newspaper of the Tongmenghui (the leading revolutionary party of the period of which Sun Zhongshan was a central figure).

Questions

1. Why does Sun suggest the need for five separate branches of government instead of the three employed in the American constitution?
2. Sun's third People's Principle, "Livelihood" is often translated as "Socialism" because of its emphasis on redistribution of wealth. From Sun's description what do you think his main concern is?

... The first issue of *Minbao* dealt with three issues: first, the principle of Nationalism; second, the Principle of Democracy; and third, the Principle of the People's Livelihood.

It is not necessary to do research in order to know what nationalism is. A person always recognizes his parents and never confuses them with strangers. Nationalism is analogous to this. It has to do with human nature and applies to everyone. Today, more than 260 years have passed since the Manchus entered China proper, yet even as children we Han would certainly not mistake them for fellow Han. This is the root of nationalism. On the other hand, we should recognize that nationalism does not mean discriminating against people of a different nationality. It simply means not allowing such people to seize our political power, for only when we Han are in control politically do we have a nation. If that political control is in the hands of people of another nationality, then there is no Han nation.

Let us pause to consider for moment: where is the nation? Where is the political power? Actually, we are already a people without a nation! The population of the globe is only one billion, several hundred million; we Han, being 400 million, comprise one-fourth of that population. Our nation is the most populous, most ancient, and most civilized in the world, yet today we are a lost nation. Isn't that enormously bizarre? ... We Han are now swiftly being caught up in a tidal wave of nationalist revolution, yet the Manchus continue to discriminate against the Han. They boast that their forefathers conquered the

THREE PRINCIPLES OF THE PEOPLE (THREE PEOPLE'S PRINCIPLES)—A political philosophy developed by Sun Zhongshan grouped into the three guiding principles of Nationalism, Democracy and Livelihood.

Han because of their superior unity and military strength and that they intend to retain these qualities so as to dominate the Han forever....

On the other hand, I have heard claims that the nationalist revolution is aimed at exterminating the Manchus as a people. This is utterly mistaken. The reason for the nationalist revolution is our unwillingness to let the Manchu extinguish our nation and dominate us politically, and our determination to restore our nation by liquidating their regime. Thus, we do not hate the Manchus per se, but only those Manchus who are harming the Han. ... If the Manchus stubbornly continue to hold onto political power and keep the Han under their yoke, then as long as breath remains in the Han, the Han will refuse to accept it meekly. I presume you gentlemen will agree.

These are the basic ideas behind the nationalist revolution.

As for the Principle of Democracy, it is the foundation of the political revolution. In the future, to be sure, the vicious politics of today will be swept away after the nationalist revolution triumphs, but it will also be necessary to eradicate the roots of such politics. For several thousand years China has been a monarchical autocracy, a type of political system intolerable to those living in freedom and equality.... The study of what a political revolution entails is a very difficult undertaking. As to practice, a political revolution must proceed simultaneously with the nationalist revolution. When we overthrow the Manchu regime, we will achieve not only a nationalist revolution against the Manchus but also a political revolution against monarchy. They are not to be carried out at two different times. The aim of the political revolution is to create a constitutional, democratic political system. In the context of the current political situation in China, a revolution would be necessary even if the monarch were a Han. Neither the French Revolution nor the Russian Revolution involved racial issue; the issues were strictly political. A democratic political system has been achieved in France, and in Russia the Nihilist party will also ultimately reach this goal. After the revolution in China, this will be the most appropriate political system. This, too, everyone knows.

[....]

Now, let me begin by discussing the origins of the Principle of the People's Livelihood, a principle that began to flourish only in the latter part of the nineteenth century. Before that it did not flourish because civilization was not as highly developed. The more civilization developed, the more pressing its social problems became. The reasons are very difficult to explain, but we can use a simple analogy. As civilization advanced, people relied less on physical labor and more on natural forces, since electricity and steam could accomplish things a thousand times faster than human physical strength. ... In view of this, everyone in Europe and America should be living in a state of plenty and happiness undreamed of in antiquity. If we look around, however, we see that conditions in those countries are precisely the opposite. Statistically, Britain's wealth has increased more than several thousand-fold over the previous generation, yet the poverty of the people has also increased several thousand-fold over the previous generation. Moreover, the rich are extremely few, and the poor extremely numerous. ... The reason the Socialist party advocates the Principle of the People's Livelihood is precisely that it seeks to remedy the unequal distribution of wealth. As its advocates grew in number, the principle became a highly complex science that has given rise to numerous schools. Some of them advocate getting rid of the capitalists and replacing them with state ownership. Others want to distribute wealth evenly among the poor, while still others propose public ownership. There are many opinions, but every informed person knows that a social revolution is inevitable in Europe and America.

[....]

After all, at present it will be much easier to implement the Principle of the People's Livelihood in China than in Europe and America because social problems are caused by the advance of civilization and are correspondingly less serious where civilization is less advanced....

I have heard it said that the Principle of the People's Livelihood would entail killing half of our 400 million people and taking the land of the rich for ourselves. This irresponsible talk is based on ignorance, and we can ignore it. With respect to a solution, although the socialists have different opinions, the procedure I most favor is land valuation. For example, if a landlord has land worth 1,000 dollars, its price can be set at 1,000 or even 2,000 dollars. Perhaps in the future, after communications have been developed, the value of his land will rise to 10,000 dollars; the owner should receive 2,000, which entails a profit and no loss, and the 8,000 increment will go to the state. Such an arrangement will greatly benefit both the state and the people's livelihood. Naturally, it will also eliminate the shortcomings that have permitted a few rich people to monopolize wealth. This is the simplest, most convenient, and most feasible method....

In short the objective of our revolution is to promote the well-being of our people as a whole. Because we are unwilling to let a small number of Manchus enjoy all the privileges, we want a nationalist revolution. Because we do not want one man, the monarch, to enjoy all the privileges, we want a political revolution. And because we do not want a small number of rich people to enjoy all the privileges, we want a social revolution. Anything short of these three revolutions will not fulfill our original aims. When they have been accomplished, our nation of China will be a most perfect nation.

There remains another issue worth studying: the future constitution of the Republic of China. Recently, the word *constitution* has been on everyone's lips. Even the Manchu government has been shrewd enough to send lackeys abroad to inquire into the political situation there so that they can concoct some imperial edicts having to do with constitutionalism. They're only creating a disturbance for themselves.... As to the future constitution of the Republic of China, I propose that we introduce a new principle, that of the "five separate powers."

Under this system, there will be two other powers in addition to the three powers just discussed. One is the examination power. Citizens have the right to freedom and equality, and officials are public servants of the citizenry. American officials are either elected or appointed. Formerly there were no civil service examinations, which led to serious

shortcomings with respect to both elected and appointed officials.... Therefore, the future constitution of the Republic of China must provide for an independent branch expressly responsible for civil service examinations. Furthermore, all officials, however high their rank, must undergo examinations in order to determine their qualifications. Whether elected or appointed, officials must pass those examinations before assuming office. This procedure will eliminate such evils as blind obedience, electoral abuses, and favoritism. From the beginning, China selected its officials according to their qualifications, and those qualifications received great emphasis....

The other power is the supervisory power, responsible for monitoring matters involving impeachment. For reasons that should be evident to all, such a branch is indispensable to any nation. The future constitution of the Republic of China must provide for an independent branch....

With this added to the four powers already discussed, there will be five separate powers. As such a system is unknown among the nations of the world and has rarely been mentioned even in theory, it should be termed a political innovation. I have invented only the foundations of that system, leaving the details and the rest of the structure to the devoted efforts of all my comrades, who, by remedying my own inadequacies, will create the future constitution of the Republic of China. The constitution will form the basis of the sound government of a nation that belongs to its own race, to its own citizens, and to its own society. This will be the greatest good fortune for our 400 million Han people. I presume that you gentlemen are willing to undertake and complete this task. It is my greatest hope.

5.12 WANG JINGWEI ON WE WANT A REPUBLIC, NOT A CONSTITUTIONAL MONARCHY (APRIL 25, 1910)

Born in the southern province of Guangdong, Wang Jingwei as a young man traveled on a government scholarship to study in Japan. He returned to China in early 1910 intent on assassinating Regent Zaifeng (father of the young emperor also known as Prince Chun). On April 16, his plans were discovered and he was arrested. He and his collaborators were imprisoned on May 1. In prison and fully expecting to be executed, he composed the following defense of his political views, emphasizing the need to move beyond a constitutional monarchy. His commentary offers an eloquent rebuttal to the conservatives of the period who sought to retain key vestiges of the imperial system. Wang remained in prison until December 1911, a month after the Wuchang

Uprising, an uprising which triggered the Chinese revolution and ultimately the end of the Qing dynasty.

Questions

1. **Why does Wang Jingwei believe "neither will the situation in China improve nor can she be rejuvenated unless there is a basic change in political structure?"**
2. **How does Wang Jingwei suggest China's circumstances are different from those of France, England, Germany and Japan?**

Some people may ask: since China already has a constitution, why should we speak of revolution? Alas! People who ask this question must think that by having a constitution, China has laid the foundation of good government and everlasting peace and not realize that she is in serious danger at this very moment. From the point of view of us revolutionaries, the factors that contribute to our people's sufferings and insecurity have not been reduced by one iota during the past few years: in fact, they have become more numerous. The Constitutionalists say that once the constitution takes effect, there will be equality between the Manchus and the Chinese and all the people in China will enjoy the same political rights. Our goal of nationalism and democracy will then be achieved. In short, the establishment of a constitutional monarchy will lead to the establishment of a good government. But we revolutionaries emphatically do not share this optimism. Not only do we doubt the validity of the assumption that the constitution will create equality between the Manchus and the Chinese; we also firmly believe that the establishment of a constitutional monarchy will not serve the best interest of the people and will instead bring the greatest harm to it.

The Constitutionalists say that as long as the monarch is merely a symbol of the state whose power is clearly restricted by the constitution and as long as he does not have political responsibilities even though he is personally inviolable, constitutional monarchy will bring about good government. This statement, though it sounds like a legalist theory, does not, unfortunately, conform to the known facts. Without a single

exception, the countries that have a constitutional government, whether it be a constitutional monarchy or a constitutional republic, acquired their constitution by revolutionary methods. This is so because monarchal power, through custom and usage that may have lasted for a long, long time, becomes in the end synonymous with the state power; and unless the monarchal power is destroyed, there is no way of eliminating the existing state system and replacing it with something new. A constitutional monarchy was almost established during the reign of Louis XVI, and yet France could not forego her experience of having a great revolution. The inevitability of revolution as a means of establishing a constitutional government is not only true in a republic like France but also true in monarchies like England, Germany and Japan. While England is the oldest constitutional monarchy in the world, Germany and Japan are two of the strongest. People who speak of constitutional government often cite them as examples. Yet, have they taken time to trace the constitutional development of each of these three countries?

[. . . .]

If we measure the situation in China against the constitutional development of these three countries, we will find that China has nothing in common with any of them. She does not share England's experience of a slow, gradual constitutional development; nor does she have a system of local autonomy that characterized Germany before her unification. She certainly has not had a great revolution which Japan experienced in overthrowing the **shogunate.** For several thousand

---

WANG JINGWEI (1883–1944)—Born in Guangdong, he joined the Tongmeng Hui in 1905 and attempted to assassinate the last emperor's father Prince Chun. After his release, he worked closely with Sun Zhongshan and challenged Jiang Jieshi for leadership of the GMD. In 1940 he became the head of state for Japanese-occupied China.

NOTE: Wang Jingwei means that in 1910 the throne had agreed to a Constitutional Calendar.

SHOGUNATE—Japan's military government that ended with the Meiji Restoration of 1867 and ushered in a constitutional parliamentary system of government.

years China has practiced nothing but autocracy, an autocracy that reached the highest point or the most absolute stage during the past 260 years. The state power is vested with the monarch, and officials on all levels, central or local, are merely his servants or slaves whom he can order to do whatever he pleases. Suddenly enchanted with the good name of constitution, this autocratic China decided to promulgate one.

[. . . .]

Since no hope of establishing an honest constitutional government has existed or will exist, we revolutionaries believe that only by waging a life-and-death struggle can the goal of establishing a democracy be achieved in China. The Revolutionary Party made this decision a long time ago. It is our belief that only under a constitutional government established in the wake of a revolution can the principles of nationalism and democracy be carried out and can the disaster of a bloody war be avoided....

We have briefly described the domestic situation in China. Speaking of her relations with the outside world, we cannot but feel frightened and alarmed; she is so weak that her chance of survival, for all practical purposes, has become very slim indeed. Knowing her impending peril, how can any Chinese enjoy peace of mind even for the briefest moment? When China was invaded in 1900, people realized how deadly our foreign enemies could be. Today they are indifferent—how much we should lament this indifference! ...

The factor that prevents China from being partitioned at this moment is the fear on the part of England and France that Germany might not cooperate, and on the part of Japan that the United States might strike her from the rear. For several years there has been speculation about the inevitability of clashes between the United States and Japan, and several months ago there was even a rumor that these two countries would wage war against each other at any moment. Now suddenly there is talk about an alliance between England, Japan, and the United State. A Japanese newspaper recently commented that once this alliance is formed, it can quickly put an end to the old Chinese empire. How anxious the Japanese are to put an end of all of us!

[. . . .]

Meanwhile we continue to congratulate ourselves by saying that they have treated us well. Whenever by chance we recover some of our lost rights, we become jubilant or even ecstatic, and close our eyes to their joint efforts to bring us the greatest harm. This is like a swallow that tries to make a nest underneath the main beam without knowing that the whole house is about to collapse. Why? The reason is that with a constitutional government scheduled to be established, everyone believes that all of China's problems, foreign and domestic, will be automatically resolved. Like a man who has taken hallucinatory drugs, we are fascinated with appearance at the expense of reality. It will be eight years before the constitution takes effect; I can easily visualize how intolerable the situation will be at the end of this long, long period.

Neither will the situation in China improve nor can she be rejuvenated unless there is a basic change in political structure. The time for making this change is very late, but by no means too late. I hope that all those who die after I do will consider making this change their sacred responsibility.

CHAPTER 6
QING SOCIETY, CULTURE, AND PEOPLES

VISUAL SOURCE
How To Take an Exam in Qing China

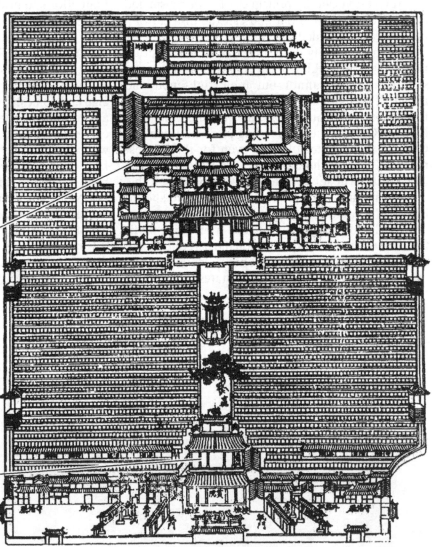

SHUNTIAN (BEIJING) EXAMINATION HALL: The Shuntian Examination Hall (first built in the early Ming dynasty [1368-1644]) had more than 50 rows of low buildings with over 17,000 examination cells. It was one of the largest in the whole of China (only Nanjing's was larger). The larger buildings in the center and upper portion of the compound were walled-off and separate from the rest of the compound and was where the administrative staff and officials (who graded the exams) resided.

EXAMINATION SYSTEM: Using exams to select imperial officials began in China as early as 165 BCE. A three-tier system with each tier conferring a more prestigious degree (and access to a higher office) began around 1370. The examination hall shown here held the provincial level (juren) exams. While the notion of an examination to select officials may sound quite conventional, the first record of any exams in European universities is in the early 18th century.

Birdseye view of Shuntian (Beijing) Examination Hall

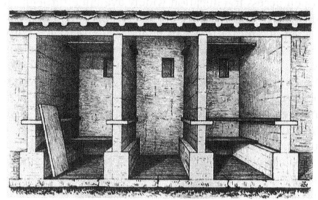

Individual examination cells

EXAMINATION CELLS: Each cell contained a bench, a table and a high shelf. The cell itself was a little over 3 feet wide and 4 feet deep. The provincial exam was typically held once every three years. Given the open nature of the cells, the exam experience was highly dependent upon the weather. With the stress and minimal amenities, it is no surprise that candidates (some were in their 60s and 70s) died during the exam. In such cases, their bodies were wrapped, labeled with their name and thrown over the wall for municipal authorities to collect and notify their next of kin.

Side-passages (with examination cells visible)

A TYPICAL DAY AT THE EXAMS: The question for the day would be received at 10 a.m. in the morning. The exam candidates would remain in their cells until dusk to writing a draft and then carefully copy out a final copy. The essay should be between six and seven hundred characters long. Simply copying the essay in the correct and elegant calligraphic style could, even for a rapid writer, take many hours. After handing their exam papers in they would then be provided with a meal and then attempt to get a night's rest in preparation for the next day's exam (the exam would usually have at least 3 days of exams).

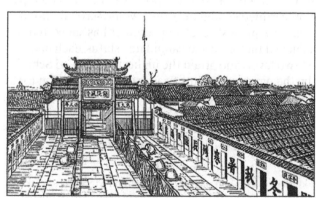

View down central passage

CHEATING: Exam candidates upon arriving at the examination hall had to provide proof of their identity and status (to prevent others from taking the exam in their place). As they passed through the central gate they then would be thoroughly searched for cheat sheets, and forbidden from leaving the examination hall during the entire exam. Those caught cheating would be dismissed and forbidden from taking the exam for the next two cycles.

In the United States today, 34 out of every 100 students will receive an associate's or bachelor's degree. Given the open access to education widely available throughout much of the modern world, it is difficult to imagine a society where only two people out of every 1000 achieved a similar level of education. Yet students of nineteenth-century China faced precisely these daunting odds. As different as the modern American and late imperial Chinese educational systems may seem on the surface, they are based on a similar mythos of education as the great equalizer. Both cultures promote education as offering advancement open to both rich and poor regardless of class background. But, if the American notion of education is a "pulling oneself up by one's boot straps" variety, that of imperial China was rooted in something quite different.

For three thousand years, examinations have been the mode by which the Chinese imperial governments selected its officials, insinuating itself into the very fiber of Chinese society. Over the centuries, the sacrifices made by young students and scholars in the pursuit of securing an official post evolved into elaborate narratives and moral tales. Parents and teachers would tell children about former scholars who repeatedly jabbed themselves in the leg with an awl to remain awake; or one who collected fireflies allowing him to read through the night. Such stories became as an integral a part of Chinese culture as those of a young Abe Lincoln walking miles to borrow books to be read by candlelight in his log cabin. Yet, these stories all had a grain of truth to them. The most viable means by which a family could acquire wealth, land, or influence was for one of its members to become an official.

The Chinese civil service examination system can best be understood as a three-tier system preceeded by an entrance (or qualifying) exam (*tongsheng*). After passing this qualifying exam, one could be admitted to the prefectural (*shengyuan*) exam typically offered twice every three years. If you happened to be among the privileged few to pass (**examination quotas** allowed only 50,000 every three years), you were then eligible to take the provincial level (*juren*) exam held in the provincial capital every three years. By the mid-nineteenth century only 1,500 scholars were selected every three years. Those *juren* could then attempt the pinnacle of the examination system by traveling to Beijing to take the Metropolitan Examination (*jinshi*) with only 550 individuals succeeding every three-year cycle.

In comparison to the highly rigid class-based European system where upward class movement was extremely rare, the Chinese examination system can better be understood as a meritocracy. A system through which, theoretically, even the poorest Chinese subject from the remotest corner of the empire could experience upward mobility by taking and passing the exam. Although the government did not formally institute restrictions on those who could take the exams, there did exist some very real obstacles. For any child to be able to master the necessary knowledge needed to pass the exams, a family would have to possess the means to pay for his education and be able to spare him from the home. But even if the children could be educated to the point where they could pass the certification exam (*tongsheng* or 'certified candidate'), they would have an infinitesimally small chance of moving upward to the next level. One scholar has suggested that of the 2 percent of Chinese who achieved the "certified candidate" status, each had only a 1-in-6,000 chance to pass the next two levels and attain the highest "Achieved Scholar" (*jinshi*) status. Thus there existed by the nineteenth century a certain self-delusion to the entire venture not unlike those who continue to buy lottery tickets fully realizing the long-odds of ever winning the jackpot. This comparison is flawed however, in that the examination system (and the scholar-officials that were selected by it) was perceived as a central pillar of the political, social and cultural framework of Chinese society.

EXAMINATION QUOTAS—Unlike modern university entrance or SAT exams on which the test taker is given an objective score, each sitting of the imperial exams had a specific quota of degrees to be offered that year with each province designated a pre-determined number of degrees to be issued to those candidates who scored highest on the examination.

The social, familial, and personal pressure to pass the examinations often pushed the candidates to find ways of "improving" their odds. Aside from the familiar "crib sheets," there was a thriving industry in printing minuscule copies of the key texts, and even producing undergarments with key passages inscribed on them. Some especially desperate (and rich) individuals hired someone to take the exam in their place. In still other cases the exam-takers (or their families) simply bribed the examination officials. Such practices, (admittedly highly honed by the nineteenth century), caused elaborate countermeasures to be instituted by the state. Before entering the examination hall, all examinees had to produce letters vouching for their identity. Then they would be meticulously searched for banned items. In some instances individuals would be stripped of their inner garments when it was learned some test takers were lining their garments with study aids. Throughout the entire examination period (lasting over a week at the provincial and metropolitan levels), guards were stationed throughout the entire compound. To prevent the examiners from recognizing handwriting (or other prearranged signals), scribes copied each essay before being read by the judges. None of these measures prevented periodic scandals, including a famous instance in 1858 when the chief examiner in Beijing was found guilty of improprieties and sentenced to death.

Given the years of learning and the numerous exams the average scholar took before passing—to achieve success at any level of the exams was worthy of considerable celebration. Villages and cities would erect monuments trumpeting their top scholars and the populations of entire provinces would take pride (and boast) of native sons who had achieved high imperial positions. It is perhaps no surprise that in an age when no higher respect could be achieved than to be an imperial official, so many spent their entire lives attempting to pass the imperial exams and become a coveted degree-holder. There was considerable truth in the Chinese proverb that "no one knows the ten-years of cold-windows, but once you succeed you are known by the world."

EDUCATION

Despite the centrality of the examinations to the Chinese government and the prestige that came with the **degree-holders,** instruction remained by and large in the private sphere. While the wealthiest families might hire a private tutor for their children, most Chinese students attended private village schools. The teachers, usually low or non-degree holders, charged rates according to their ability, reputation, and track record with producing successful examination candidates.

Typically, young boys would begin their education around the age of six or seven. Since they needed some means by which to learn to read the Chinese characters and yet also acquire the rudimentary precepts of classical Chinese necessary to read the Confucian classics, most students would begin their education with the ***Three Character Classic,*** before moving onto the *Thousand Character Treatise*. When the student had memorized these two tracts, they would have a vocabulary of approximately 2,000 characters, but even at this stage they were academically unprepared to begin the ***Four Books*** that formed the

EXAMINATION DEGREES—The three imperial exam degrees relate to the modern system as follows: the shengyuan (or "Budding Genius") is a bachelor's degree (BA), the juren (or "Promoted Gentleman") is a master's degree (MA), and the jinshi ("Achieved Scholar") is a doctorate (Ph.D). The average age for passing was 24 years old for the shengyuan degree, 31 for the juren, and 35 for the jinshi.

THREE CHARACTER CLASSIC—A Confucian primer, which served as an introduction to Confucian thought for most young children

FOUR BOOKS—The core of classical learning in late imperial China included: Confucius' Analects (*Lun Yu*), Mencius (*Mengzi*), The Doctrine of the Mean (*Zhong Yong*), and the Great Learning (*Da Xue*)

foundation of the Confucian classics (and the examinations themselves). Students studied a series of intermediate texts (often Zhu Xi's *Basic Learning* and others) which dealt with history and moral exhortation. Couplet-making and poetry (skills required for the exams) rounded out the curriculum.

While highly precocious students might contemplate taking exams in their early teens, most would be seventeen or eighteen when they could competently write the requisite eight-legged (6.1) essay to become "qualified candidates" (*tongsheng*). Until these individuals passed the provincial level, *juren,* exam they could not expect an official appointment and would remain part of the over-educated but under-employed sub-class of China's intellectual elite.

6.1 EIGHT-LEGGED ESSAY – CIVIL SERVICE EXAMINATION (1818)

Unlike the modern style civil service examinations composed of multiple choice, essays, and interviews the Qing imperial tests were based on specific texts of the Confucian classics. Moreover, your essay had to be written in a rigidly proscribed configuration known as an "eight-legged essay" (*bagu wen*). Highly formalized, limited to between six and seven hundred characters, the essay structure put severe structural limitations on how the author composed his essay. The eight-legged form consisted of an introductory analysis and amplification of the theme, immediately followed by an explanation. The body would be divided into eight paragraphs in two parallel parts (not necessarily of equal length). There existed a host of other rules that the examinees must keep in mind: avoiding "forbidden characters" (names of sages and emperors), writing only twenty-five characters per line, and not having more than a hundred errors/corrected characters (or be banned for the next three examinations, typically nine years).

Questions

1. How accurate a measure do you think the following essay is of this candidate's ability as an official?
2. What elements of this essay might have made it stand out and be ranked as the best of the examinations?

EXAM QUESTION: *When persons in high stations are sincere in the performance of relative and domestic duties, the people generally will be stimulated to the practice of virtue.*

EXAM CANDIDATE'S RESPONSE: When the upper classes are really virtuous, the common people will inevitably become so. For, though the sincere performance of relative duties by superiors does not originate in a wish to stimulate the people, yet the people do become virtuous, which is proof of the effect of sincerity. As benevolence is the radical principle of all good governments in the world, so also benevolence is the radical principle of relative duties amongst the people. Traced back to its source, benevolent feeling refers to a first progenitor; traced forwards, it branches out to a hundred generations yet to come. The source of personal existence is one's parents, the relations which originate from heaven are most intimate; and that in which natural feeling blends is felt most deeply. That which is given by heaven and by natural feeling to all, is done without any distinction between noble or ignoble. One feeling pervades all. My thoughts now refer to him who is placed in a station of eminence, and who may be called a good man. The good man who is placed in an eminent station, begins with his own relations, and performs his duties to them.

In the middle ages of antiquity, the minds of the people were not yet dissipated—how came it that they were not humble and observant of relative duties, when they were taught the principles of the five social relations? This having been the case, makes it evident that the enlightening of the people must depend entirely on the cordial performance of immediate relative duties. The person in an eminent station who may be called a good man, is he who appears at the head of all others in illustrating by his practice the relative duties. In ages nearer to our own, the manners of the people were not far removed from the dutiful, how came it that any were disobedient to parents, and without brotherly affection, and that it was yet necessary to restrain men by inflicting the eight forms of punishment? This having been the case, shows that in the various modes of obtaining promotion in the state, there is nothing regarded of more importance than filial and fraternal duties. The person in an eminent station who may be called a good man, is he who stands forth as an example of the performance of relative duties.

The difference between a person of a high station and one of the common people, consists in the department assigned them, not in their relation to heaven; it consists in a difference of rank, not in a difference of natural feeling; but the common people constantly observe the sincere performance of relative duties in people of high stations. In being at the head of a family and preserving order amongst the persons of which it is composed, there should be sincere attention to politeness and decorum. A good man placed in a high station says, "Who of all these are not related to me, and shall I receive them with mere external forms?" The elegant entertainment, the neatly arranged tables and the exhilarating song, some men esteem mere forms, but the good man esteems that which dictates them as a divinely instilled feeling, and attends to it with a truly benevolent heart. And who of the common people does not feel a share of the delight arising from fathers, and brothers, and kindred? Is this joy resigned entirely to princes and kings?

In favors conferred to display the benignity of a sovereign, there should be sincerity in the kindness done. The good man says, 'Are not all these persons whom I love, and shall I merely enrich them by largesse?' He gives a branch as the scepter of authority to a delicate younger brother, and to another he gives a kingdom with his best instructions. Some men deem this as merely extraordinary good fortune, but the good man esteems it the exercise of a virtue of the first order, and the effort of inexpressible benevolence. But have the common people no regard for the spring whence the water flows, nor for the root which gives life to the tree and its branches? Have they no regard for their kindred? It is necessary both to reprehend and to urge them to exercise these feelings. The good man in a high station is sincere in the performance of relative duties, because to do so is virtuous, and not on account of the common people. But the people, without knowing whence the impulse comes with joy and delight are influenced to act with zeal in this career of virtue; the moral distillation proceeds with rapidity, and a vast change is effected.

The rank of men is exceedingly different; some fill the imperial throne, but every one equally wishes to do his utmost to accomplish his duty; and success depends on every individual himself. The upper classes begin and pour the wine into the rich goblet; the poor man sows his grain to maintain his parents; the men in high stations grasp the silver bowl, the poor present a pigeon; the rouse each other to unwearied cheerful efforts, and the principles implanted by heaven are moved to action. Some things are difficult to be done, except by those who posses the glory of national rule; but the kind feeling is what I myself possess and may increase in an unlimited degree. The prince may write verses appropriate to his vine bower; the poor man can think of his gourd shelter: the prince may sing his classic odes on fraternal regards; the poor man can muse on his more simple allusions to the same subject, and asleep or awake indulge his recollections; for the feeling is instilled into his nature.

When the people are aroused to relative virtues, they will be sincere; for where are there any of the common people that do not desire to perform relative duties? But without the upper classes performing relative duties, this virtuous desire would have no point from which to originate, and there fore it is said, 'Good men in high stations, as a general at the head of the armies, will lead forward the world to the practice of social virtues.'

6.2 DESCRIPTION OF PROVINCIAL EXAMINATION (c.1845)

If the examination itself was not difficult enough, the conditions in which the examinations themselves were held must have been particularly nightmarish for the examinees. The provincial exams were held simultaneously across the empire in each of the provincial capitals once every three years. The test-taker composed a total of thirteen essays during three sessions. By the mid-nineteenth century the numbers of prospective candidates could surpass ten thousand candidates per examination flooding the provincial capitals with officials, examinees, as well as all sorts of merchants, hawkers and entertainers attracted by the massive crowds. The following is a description of a provincial examination by a visiting British observer who captures nicely the flavor of the whole affair.

Questions

1. **What aspect of these examination processes do you think the examinees found most difficult?**
2. **Do you think the manner in which the examinations occurred (held triennially, in provincial capital, thousands of candidates, etc.) increased or decreased the stature of examination system?**

The candidates for this degree are narrowly examined when they enter the hall, their pockets, shoes, wadded robes, and inkstones, all being searched, lest precomposed essays or other aids to composition be smuggled in. When they are all seated in the hall in their proper places, the wickets, doors, windows and other entrances are guarded by men, and pasted over with strips of paper. The room is filled with anxious competitors arranged in long seats, pencil in hand, and ready to begin. The theme is given out, and every one immediately writes off his essay, carefully noting how many characters he erases in composing it, and hands it up to the board of examiners; the whole day is allotted to the task, and a signal-gun announces the hour when the doors are thrown open and the students can disperse. The first two trials thin off the crowd amazingly, and the examiners easily reduce the number of hopeless competitors, so that not one-tenth of those who appear at the first struggle are seen at the third. A man is constantly liable to lose his acquired honor of *xiucai,* if at a subsequent inspection he is found to have discarded his studies, and he is therefore impelled to pursue them in order to escape disgrace, even if he does not reach the next degree.

[....]

This examination is held at the same time in all eighteen provincial capitals, on the 9th, 12th, and 15th days of the 8th moon [lunar month], or about the middle of September; while it is going on, the city appears exceedingly animated, in consequence of the great number of relatives and friends assembled with the students. The persons who preside at the examination, besides the imperial commissioners, are ten provincial officers ... who jointly form a board of examiners, and decide upon the merits of the essays. The number of

candidates who entered the lists at Guangzhou in the two years 1828 and 1831 was 4800; in 1832 there were 6000 which is nearer the usual number. In the largest provinces it reaches as many as 7,000, 8,000 and upwards. The examinations are held in *Gongyuan,* large and spacious building built expressly for this purpose, and which contains a great number of cloisters and halls, where the candidates can write their essays, and the examiners look at them. The hall at Guangzhou is capable of accommodating over ten thousand persons, and in some of the northern cities they are still larger, and generally filled with students, assistants and other persons connected with the examinations.

Before a candidate can enter the hall, he must give in an account of himself to the chancellor, stating all the particulars of his lineage, residence, birthplace, age, etc. and where he received his first degree. He enters the establishment the night before and is searched on entering, to see that no manuscript essay or miniature which can assist in the task he is to undertake. If anything of the sort is discovered, he is punished with the cangue, degraded from his first degree, and forbidden again to complete at the examination; his father and tutor are likewise punished. The practice is, however, quite common, notwithstanding the penalties, and one censor requested a law to be passed forbidding small editions to be printed, and booksellers shops to be searched for them.

The hall at Guangzhou contains 7500 cells, measuring four feet by three, and high enough to stand up in; the furniture consists of two boards, one for sitting, and the other contrived to serve both for an eating table and a writing-desk; all these things as well as the writing materials, cooking apparatus, and every officer, porter and menial about the establishment are carefully searched. The cells are arranged around a number of open courts, receiving all their light and air from the central area, and exposed to the observation of the soldiers who guard the place, and watch that no one has the least intercourse with the imprisoned students. Confinement in this cramped position, where it is impossible to lie down, is exceedingly irksome, and is said to cause the death of many old students, who are unable to go through the fatigue, but who still enter the arena in hopes of at last succeeding. Cases have occurred where father, son, and grandson, appeared at the same time to compete for the same prize. The unpleasantness of the [small] cell is much increased by the smoke arising from the cooking, which is all done in the court, and by the heat of the weather. Whenever a student dies in his cell, the body is pulled though a hole made in the wall, and left there for his friends to carry away. Whenever a candidate breaks any of the prescribed regulations of the contest, his name and offence are reported, and his name is "pasted out" by placarding it on the outer door of the hall, after which he is not allowed to enter until another examination comes around. More than a hundred persons are thus "pasted out" each season, but no heavy disgrace seems to attach to them in consequences.

[....]

Twenty-five days are allowed for the examining board to look over the essays, and few tasks can be instanced more irksome to a board of honest examiners than the perusal of between fifty and seventy-five thousand papers on a dozen subjects, through which the most monotonous uniformity must necessarily run, and out of which they have to choose the seventy or eighty best—for the number of successful candidates cannot vary far from this, according to the size of the province.... When the graduates are decided upon, their names are published by a crier at midnight, on or before the 10th of the 9th moon; he mounts the highest tower in the city, and, after a salute, announces them to the expectant city; the next morning lists of the lucky scholars are hawked about the streets, and rapidly sent to all parts of the province. The proclamation which contains their names is [posted ... with] a salute of three guns; his Excellency comes out and bows three times towards the names of the promoted men, and retires under another salute. The disappointed multitude must then rejoice in the success of the few, and solace themselves with the hope of better luck next time; while the successful ones are honored and feasted in a very distinguished manner, and are the objects of flattering attention from the whole city.

6.3   PU SONGLING'S "THREE GENII" (c.1679)

Ghosts (*gui*), spirits (*shen*) and other deities (*ling, yao, guai, mo* or *hunpo*) played an integral part of the living in Chinese society. Tales and stories of these supernatural creatures existed throughout China's rich literary history. Confucius himself is credited with saying "Respect the ghosts and spirits but keep them at a distance." The following story written (some say "collected") by Pu Songling in the early Qing was known to virtually all Chinese. It typifies a category of these stories in which the other-worldly creatures influence this world (in this instance in a positive manner). Quite characteristically, the story suggests that the spirits have similar interests and diversions (like writing test essays as a type of drinking game).

Questions

1. **Why do you think stories like this were popular among all classes of Chinese?**
2. **What does the fact that the three genii's exam topics were the same topics as those chosen for Suqian's exam suggest about the relationship between "this world" and the "other world?"**

THERE was a certain scholar who, passing through Suqian on his way to Nanjing, where he was going to try for his master's degree, happened to fall in with

three other gentlemen, all graduates like himself, and was so charmed with their unusual refinement that he purchased a quantity of wine, and begged them to join him in drinking it. While thus pleasantly employed, his three friends told him their names. One was Jie Qiuheng; the second, Chang Fenglin; and the other, Ma. They drank away and enjoyed themselves very much, until evening had crept upon them unperceived, when Jie said, "Here we, who ought to have been playing the host, have been feasting at a stranger's expense. This is not right. But, come, my house is close by; I will provide you with a bed." Chang and Ma got up, and, taking our hero by the arm, bade his servant come along with them. When they reached a hill to the north of the village, there before them was a house and grounds, with a stream of clear water in front of the door, all the apartments within being beautifully clean and nice. Jie then gave orders to light the lamps and see after his visitor's servant; whereupon Ma observed, "Of old it was customary to set intellectual refreshments before one's friends; let us not miss the opportunity of this lovely evening, but decide on four themes, one for each of us; and then, when we have finished our essays, we can set to work on the wine." To this the others readily agreed; and each wrote down a theme and threw it on the table. These were next divided amongst them as they sat, and before the **second watch** was over the essays were all completed and handed round for general inspection; and our scholar was so struck with the elegance and vigor of those by his three friends, that he [made] a copy of them and put it in his pocket. The host then produced some excellent **wine,** which was drunk by them in such bumpers that soon they were all tolerably tipsy. The other two now took their leave; but Jie led the scholar into another room, where, so overcome was he with wine, that he went to bed in his boots and clothes. The sun was high in the heavens when our hero awaked, and, looking round, he saw no house or grounds, only a dell on the hillside, in which he and his servant had been sleeping. In great alarm he called out to the servant, who also got up, and then they found a hole with a [small stream] of water trickling down before it. Much astonished at all this, he felt in his pocket, and there, sure enough, was the paper on which he had copied the three essays of his friends. On descending the hill and making inquiries, he found that he had been to the Grotto of the Three Genii—namely, Crab, Snake, and Frog, three very wonderful beings, who often came out for a stroll, and were occasionally visible to mortal eyes. Subsequently, when our hero entered the examination hall, lo! The three themes set were those of the Three Genii, and he came out at the top of the list.

GOVERNMENT, DAILY LIFE AND CULTURE

Historians of China typically place considerable emphasis on the significance of the imperial court, emperor, and China's interaction with the West in describing late imperial China. This is in large part due to the plethora of written documents available to the historian from (and about) these sources. Yet, such sources by definition tell us less about what life was like for the typical Chinese subject during the eighteenth and nineteenth centuries while projecting idealized concepts about the society as a whole. Although few non-elite (and usually non-literate) Chinese accounts survive, there remain several avenues to obtain insight into the lives of the common Chinese subject. (This is particularly important since the Chinese populace were overwhelmingly non-elites). China during the Qing dynasty was effectively a land-based economy and so the procurement (and maintenance) of land was of preeminent importance. The law code as well as individual aspiration often revolved around the buying, selling and controlling of land (6.6). Yet, perhaps the most maligned segment of Chinese society remained the soldiers who rarely left historical sources that allow insight to their outlook, concerns or worries in a Confucian based society that belittled the value of the military (6.5). Together such snapshots can offer a fuller (if still incomplete) portrait of Chinese society.

WINE PARTY—No Chinese wine-party is complete without some literary game. Writing verses, composing impromptu odes on persons or places, giving historical and mythological allusions, are among the ordinary diversions of this kind.

NIGHT WATCH—Traditionally the night watch lasted from 7 P.M. to 5 A.M., and was divided into five intervals of two hours each.

6.4 DESCRIPTION OF A CHINESE FAMILY'S LIFE (1883)

What does a typical nineteenth-century Chinese family look like? With statistics thin on the ground in late imperial China, first-person descriptions offer one of the few opportunities to get a better picture of Chinese society. The following life history recorded in the English-language periodical *China Review* is offered by an "expectant official" — one of tens of thousands who had passed the lowest rung of the examination and still attempting to pass the next level—from Hunan province in central China. While deceptively simple, the document contains a wealth of cultural and social norms that defined life in late imperial China.

Questions

1. If we take the following statement as representative what did the Chinese typical family look like? How many children, sisters, relatives, etc?
2. Would you think this man is well off, just getting by, or poor?

I am a Hunan man from the District of Baling, in the Yuezhou prefecture. Our family has been in Hunan since the Song Dynasty, when my ancestor from Jiangxi, who held office in Hunan, removed there. We have of course a genealogical register, but I know no more than that there have been from 20–30 generations of us since our immigration. We have lost all trace of our Jiangxi relatives, and of our tombs there. Our modern cemeteries are in several places, and not in one spot. My mother is still alive, aged 68, but my father died in the year of 1855, at the age of 41. I was then 20 years of age; and, being the eldest of three sons, left the management of our property to my mother. If my mother had married again it would not have been respectable, but under such circumstances, what can a son do? He cannot throw her over; for, whatever principle is involved, she is still his mother. My next younger brother died young. Then comes a sister, aged 40, with two sons and two daughters. Then another sister with two daughters. Then another brother, aged 35, with five sons: he has no particular occupation beyond looking after family interests. Then comes a brother aged 30, still studying: he has one son and one daughter. Lastly a sister, aged 28, with one son and two daughters. Of course the sisters no longer belong to our family. I myself have had four sons and five daughters. The two eldest children, girls, died at the ages of 20 and 7 respectively. My eldest son, now 20, was married last year. The next child is a girl, aged 17, unengaged. Then a girl, aged 14, engaged to an old playmate of hers. Then sons, aged 10 and 8; then a daughter; and lastly a son aged 4.

We have between us three brothers about 1000 *tiao*, of land, all paddy. In our country we do not count by the *mu*, but, as a matter of fact, four *tiao* would equal one *mu*. Four *tiao* pay once a year three quarts, of land-tax, which is commuted to three candareens of silver. In addition, each *tiao* pays one *ge* or gill, of grain-tax. I don't exactly know how the total is arrived at; but, what with extras, squeezes, &c., we pay 41 *tiao* [about 30 taels], of taxes a year. The collection is divided between the 5th and 11th moons, and we ourselves pay it in, not waiting for the runners to dun us. On the death of a brother, his share goes to his male children, but no division is necessarily made. Our mother, if she chooses, can exercise great influence in matters of property. In cases of difference of opinion, our mother's would probably prevail. My father had no occupation; neither had my grandfather. My great grandfather was an educational officer. Beyond his father (my paternal great great grandfather [*gaozu*]) I know nothing in detail. Wills are not in vogue where I come from; but adoptions, i.e. by uncles, are common. So also is it not uncommon for one man to serve as son to two brothers. If he is rich, he has two wives, the sons of each wife calling the other wife "elder brother's wife" (*bomu*) and "younger brother's wife" (*shenniang*) respectively, and, in matters of mourning, treating them as aunts, although wives of the same man, their father. If he is not rich, his eldest son will be grandson to his father, and the next to his uncle. With us concubines are not common, unless the wife has no children. My wife is now 44 years of age.

About 20 years ago I purchased a degree (*ligong*) for 200 taels, and since then I have been a sort of secretary or scribe, but not an official. Two years ago I purchased an Assistant District Magistrate (*xiancheng*) for 500 taels; and, as I have friends in the border province where I am serving, I hope to make money some time or other. At present there are 200 expectants of my class for 16 vacancies. Before the sale of office was abolished last year, I could have purchased a second-class sub-prefect (*tongpan*) for 300 taels or more, or a district (*xian*) for 2000 taels. Though the former ranks above the latter, he is only an auxiliary office (*zuoza*); hence the anomaly. I would gladly abandon officialdom and go home; but, during these years of expectancy, I have been borrowing right and left and must pay off my liabilities. If I get office, I must take with me a harpy called a "*daiduzi,*" who will watch my gains, and gradually obtain repayment of advance. I may either pay him 3 per cent a month interest, or pay off the principal. These fellows are very dangerous if you let them interfere in public business. We expectants are miserably off, many of us literally beggars of our food. With us in Hunan the head of the family (*zuzhang*), is not an institution. Each branch arranges its own affairs, or leaves them to the ablest relative.

6.5   WANG ZHUOTANG'S ADVICE TO THE TROOPS (OCTOBER 8, 1884)

In 1884–1885 China and France went to **war** over French Indochina's growing influence in Vietnam along China's southern border. While France's navy controlled the coastline and could attack with general impunity, French armies proved far less effective against the Chinese armies. Wang's call to his troops offers a rare look at a mid-ranking military official's attitude both towards the common soldier and the China's fight against Western imperialism.

Questions

1. **How does Wang bolster the soldiers for their upcoming encounter with the French?**
2. **What does he admonish the soldiers to avoid and why?**

Sit down and listen for a little while
To good advice in simple words, my men!
You're far from home on soldiers' service now
To toil for kith and kin and earn renown.
Think how in every province many posts
Are filled by those whose life commenced like
   yours.
Now China and the French are bent on war;
And by decree both North and South prepare,
But most Qiongzhou, so near to Haiphong,
Where you may have to fight at anytime.
We're told the Frenchmen's steel-clad ships are strong.
They dare to work their perverse will at sea.
Our ships are few and weak compared with theirs;
But, on land, why should we fear the French?
Precise they are, but we will hem them in
By overwhelming numbers speedily.

[We] must stand up for state and home.
Come, soldiers, one in will, be like a wall
Against the mighty foe, each lance in front.
By daily drill attain to perfect skill.
In musketry fail not to hit the mark;
Then when you fight each shot will wound a man.
In handling sword and spear be firm of foot;
To thrust or stand on guard be still prepared.
And gunners, first of all, be self-possessed.
The victory depends on cannon most.
With shot and powder in proportion due
And aim precise like magic strike the foe,
Shield-practice too and crouching must be learnt
To shun the balls and ward the falling blow.
Twice daily, morning and night, be prompt at drill.
Learn everything but sloth, which numbs the hands
   and feet.

SINO-FRENCH WAR (1884–1885) — A war between China and France for control of Vietnam which China continued to view as a tributary state but which France saw as part of its Indochinese colonial holdings.

The more you exercise the stronger you are.
Work makes of iron steel and glass of flint;
So I would have you wrought to perfectness.
For courage you of Wu and Yue are famed.
Be patient workers too, to dig and build.
Avoid, I pray you, sloven negligence,
The trenches must be deep and wide and firm,
Just as your courage must, to meet a foe.
As he who holds a house must keep its doors
With bolts and locks all fast to bar access,
So you must cover every passage well.
Stand firm as hills, as water nimbly move.
And first, I warn you – Smoke no Opium.
He cannot walk or run who smokes the drug.
But weeps away his days, a victim base.
Oh, well I know that weapon's deadly power!
The climate here is changeful and severe,
And temperance is the way to keep your health.
They says they ward fever off by smoke.
They lie, I vow. Avoid the tempting snare.
Again I warn you—Gamble not at all.
Believe me, if you do, you're sure to lose.
The rogues that keep the dice will fleece you clean.
They've ruined many good and honest men.
To leave your homes is hardship any way,
If even you hope to gain somewhat thereby;
But sadder far to bear all this for naught,
And waste your means on thankless vagabonds;
Even granting that your crime is not found out.
If it is, you're flogged, or else dismissed, to boot.
And further,—Keep from drinking and
   debauchery.
Each selfish lust, self-punishment will bring.
In brothels men may buy disease dear.
One thoughtless hour may sink you down to hell.
But virtuous women even more, I say,

Dare not to touch or rudely look upon.
Of deadly sins adultery is the worst;
And martial law counts rape the basest of crime.
Thus far you have eschewed this evil here;
And may you all eschew it evermore!
So keep the laws, and keep your manhood too.
Unless on duty, stray not from the camp.
And don't cut down the trees, or brawl or cheat.
You're nourished for the State and people's weel.
But, if you break the peace with those below,
They'll dread you as they dread bandits
Or savage **Li** whose hordes infest Hainan.
Our people oft have found our troops a scourge.
But you must treat them as your flesh and blood,
In friendly concert, paying as you go;
The more that now in this emergency
They all unite to drill as volunteers.
On me the double charge both devolves,
And my desire is for impartial ways.
Good-will to soldiers I have always shown,
And sympathized with sick and suffering men.
The death of one has caused me sleepless nights.
I would not punish wrongly for the world.
Hear then my words. Be faithful to yourselves.
If wrong, amend. If right, then persevere.
And may we soon be blest with news of peace!
Then you'll go home and feast on what you've saved.
But failing that, if fight we must, or fall,
You'll brave the worst, and leave a glorious name.
These counsels few, though rude and badly rhymed.
Lay to your hearts assured they come from mine.
Don't let them pass your ears like gusts of wind,
And thankless slight the best a friend can give.
Though toils and pains march onward to success.
Forever true's the word:—THE STOUT HEART
   WINS.

6.6 LEGAL CASE STUDY: FRAUDULENT SALE OF LAND (1889)

Land constituted for most Chinese the most valuable commodity obtainable. In addition, Confucian prejudice against commercial ventures predisposed many Chinese towards purchasing land as an investment to be handed down through the generations. Chinese law reflected this predisposition protecting landowners and inclined to protect the landowner rights over that of a renter, lessee, or even buyer. Government lands, especially those in the Manchu "homelands" of northeastern China were protected and afforded a special status. As the following cases point out, any attempt at land fraud was dealt with extremely harshly.

LI—The Li are an ethnic group that inhabited the mountains of Hainan Island and had a fierce reputation amongst the Chinese.

Questions

1. What role does intent play in the penalty/sentencing meted out by the imperial officials?
2. Why would land be of significant interest to the imperial state?

Sale of Land (Case #1)

Li Sheng, the proprietor of a coal mine in the Beijing district, being on account of illness unable to look after it himself, appointed Zhang Yongsheng to manage it for him. The latter asked for some written authority that he might produce, if called on to do so, and fraudulently induced Li to sign a document giving him the mine. He then inserted his own name in the contract with the workmen, who duly appended their signatures thereto.

As he had received instructions from Li to look after the mine and in addition had written authority to that effect, his offence is not quite so aggravated as that of wrongfully taking possession of the estate of others, and he was accordingly sentenced to a punishment one degree less severe than that for the latter crime, namely one hundred blows and banishment for three years.

Sale of Land (Case #2)

An Qisuo held, on lease from one of the Imperial Princesses, 99 *mu* of land, which had been allotted to her by Imperial Decree and was thus Government property, so to speak. He was repeatedly called upon by the Prefect to give up the land and pay the due rent and on being arrested made his escape. After a few years he returned and again took possession of the land, alleging it to be his own property and refusing to pay rent for it, at the same time inducing the other tenants to pursue a similar course. In accordance with the punishment due to all those who take possession of land in a Government settlement, if it be over 50 *mu* in extent, he was sentenced to transportation to the nearest frontier.

Sale of Land (Case #3)

Dong Wu, a small official in the Neiwufu [Qing imperial Household Agency], had a piece of ground which he gave up to the Government by whom it was entered on the Banner Roll as public property, and as such it could not of course be disposed of by private sale. It was lent to him shortly afterwards to build a house on, when he took the opportunity of selling, alleging it to be people's land (*mindi*). For this he was punished in accordance with the number of stripes allotted to all who fraudulently dispose of other people's property, increased by two degrees, as the property he had disposed of belonged to the Government.

Sale of Land (Case #4)

Huang Tianrong, a soldier who had been dismissed the service, although well aware that all uncultivated ground (the expression used is *tantang*) is Government property on which no trespassing is allowed, forcibly took possession of a piece of such land and let it out to a tenant, who paid him rent, as if it were his own. It appeared, however, that his late grandfather had been the first to cultivate the ground and raise a crop on it, so that he could hardly be punished to the full extent for his offence, and his punishment was reduced by one degree, but as he was an ex-soldier, this reduction was counterbalanced by the increase of one degree which falls to be inflicted on such individuals.

Sale of Land (Case #5)

Xian Yiyue took possession of land which had formed in the middle of a river and proceeded to sell the land. On the appearance, however, of a proclamation by the District Magistrate forbidding such practices, he discontinued the sales. As his case differed from that of those who fraudulently take permanent possession of Government and other people's property, his punishment is reduced by one degree.

Sale of Land (Case #6)

Xu Baozhou bought a piece of land from Hu Juewen, although at the time aware of the fact that his ground was part of a lot which had descended by inheritance to the whole of the Xu family, and which Juewen had no right to sell, notwithstanding his statement to the effect that it was "re-formed land" which had been duly entered on the register. There is no provision made in law regulating the punishment of those who buy land although aware of the fraudulent nature of the transaction; but in the law of mortgages it is laid down that if the mortgagee is aware that the mortgagor is raising a second mortgage on a piece of land and notwithstanding such knowledge closes the transaction, his guilt shall be held equal to that of the mortgagor, so in the present case Xu Baozhou's, the buyer's guilt, was held to be equal to that of Xu Juewen, the seller.

Sale of Land (Case #7)

Wang Chaozuo mortgaged a piece of land to Zhou Pingfu, reserving to himself the right of redemption. As the soil was extremely fertile, Zhou tried to get possession of it in the following way. He made an exact copy of the deed of mortgage, fraudulently however inserting the flowing clause: 'should the mortgagor through lack of funds be unable to redeem the land, the mortgagee is permitted to pay the land tax on it in his stead,' hoping that if his payment of the land tax had been officially sanctioned, he would be able to debar Wang from redeeming the property. In summing up the case, it was held that as he, as a matter of fact, had an interest in the land, his conduct was not so reprehensible as if he had taken possession by a fictitious agreement, without due pecuniary consideration, of the land of another, and his punishment was accordingly reduced by one degree.

6.7 PU SONGLING'S "THE BOATMEN OF LAOLONG" (c.1679)

The following story plays off of the popular belief that the world of spirits and demons had a bureaucracy that not only was similar to that of imperial China, but interacted with the officials of the Chinese administrative system. The "Municipal God" aids the governor-general solve a crime, but in other tales the corrupt or immoral officials are punished or exposed by the very same ghosts. As a result, the reader (or listener) of the following tale implicitly understood that the governor-general in this story must have been an upright official deserving of the Municipal God's assistance. Such tales were extremely common throughout China and, even today, are told and dramatized on television.

Questions

1. **What does this story suggest about the nature of crime solving in imperial China?**
2. **Why is the Municipal God's assistance given in the form of a riddle and not more direct form?**

When His Excellency Zhu was Governor-General of Guangdong, there were constant complaints from the traders of mysterious disappearances; sometimes as many as three or four of them disappearing at once and never being seen or heard of again. At length the number of such cases, filed of course against some person or persons unknown, multiplied to such an extent that they were simply put on record, and but little notice was further taken of them by the local officials.

Thus, when His Excellency entered upon his duties, he found more than a hundred plaints of the kind, besides innumerable cases in which the missing man's relatives lived at a distance and had not instituted proceedings. The mystery so preyed upon the new Governor-General's mind that he lost all appetite for food; and when, finally, all the inquiries he had [made] resulted in no clue to an elucidation of these strange disappearances, then His Excellency proceeded to wash and purify himself, and, having notified the **Municipal God,** he took to fasting and sleeping in his study alone. While he was [dreaming], lo! an official entered, holding a tablet in his hand, and said that he had come from the Municipal temple with the following instructions to the :—

Snow on the whiskers descending:
Live clouds falling from heaven:
Wood in water buoyed up:
In the wall an opening effected.

The official then retired, and the Governor-General waked up; but it was only after a night of tossing and turning that he hit upon what seemed to him the solution of the **enigma.** "The first line," argued he, "must signify old (*lao*); the second refers to the *dragon* (*long*); the third is clearly a boat; and the fourth a door (*men*)." Now, to the east of the province, not far from the pass by which traders from the north connect their line of trade with the southern seas, there was actually a ferry known as the Old Dragon (*Lao-long*); and thither the Governor-General immediately dispatched a force to arrest those employed in carrying people backwards and forwards. More than fifty men were caught, and they all confessed at once without the application of torture. In fact, they were bandits under the guise of boatmen; and after beguiling passengers on board, they would either drug them or burn stupefying incense until they were senseless, finally cutting them open and putting a large stone inside to make the body sink. Such was the horrible story, the discovery of which brought throngs to the Governor-General's door to serenade him in terms of gratitude and praise.

WOMEN

Western representations of Chinese women, whether in Hollywood movies, two-dimensional portrayals like those in Pearl S. Buck novels, or the recent book *Balzac's Seamstress,* reinforce the impression of Chinese women as uneducated, exotic, and repressed. Such portrayals are not so much outrageously inaccurate as they often perpetuate half-truths that do not give a full picture. Generally speaking, women in the Qing era rarely held public positions of power outside of the home. **Footbinding** remained common among the vast majority of Han Chinese women (the Manchu and other ethnic groups being prominent exceptions). However, significant trends regarding the education, treatment and opportunities for women did occur in the eighteenth and nineteenth centuries with an increasing number of essays and primers written specifically for women (6.8). Despite such substantial advances, the restricted legal status of women (6.9) in the law code, and footbinding remained a conspicious aspect of Chinese society. By the last decades of the Qing, the topic of women's rights moved to the forefront of discussions of the mainstream discussions of modernization and political reform occurring throughout the empire (6.11).

CITY GOD—Each city had a deity, said to serve the same purpose as his "earthly" counterpart but in the "other worldly" realm. This partnership between city gods and magistrates is one of the most common intersections between the spiritual world and the temporal world. The city god temple would be the first official visit any magistrate or official made upon taking up an official posting.

CHINESE RIDDLES—Double meanings, puns and brainteasers are common in Chinese popular culture. The deciphering of the poem relies on several common associations in Chinese—namely that clouds and dragons are frequently linked, and that the character for *door* in Chinese (*men*) has a lesser known meaning, that of *people*. Thus the first two lines offer the place name—"lao" and "long"—and the second two lines describe the occupation of the killers.

FOOTBINDING—By the nineteenth century footbinding for women had been practiced within China among the rich and the poor for many centuries. The foot was bound by breaking the bones in the foot's arch, then curling the outer toes underneath by wrapping long cloth bindings tightly around the foot. If done correctly, this produced feet 3 to 5 inches in length.

6.8 LAN DINGYUAN ON FEMALE EDUCATION (1712)

The Confucian underpinnings of Qing China were overwhelmingly patriarchal. Young boys were instructed from an early age through the memorization of Confucian texts that men were superior to women. The rise of women's education in China was not an abrupt break with this tradition, but rather an offshoot from the main tenets of Confucian. As a result, the dialogue surrounding women's education and literacy emphasized learning for moral refinement and nourishing a woman's virtue. The author of the following essay, Lan Dingyuan (also known by his sobriquet Lu Zhao) is careful not to contravene basic Confucian teachings, but he seeks to acknowledge the need for women's education even if it is only with the ultimate goal to better serve the men in her life.

Questions

1. In what ways does Lan suggest women differ from men?
2. What type of education does Lan indicate is appropriate for women?

The basis of the government of the empire lies in the habits of the people, and the surety that their usages will be correct is in the orderly management of families, which last depends chiefly upon the females. In the good old times of Zhou, the virtuous women set such an excellent example, that it influenced the customs of the empire—an influence that descended even to the times of the Zheng and Wei states. If the curtain of the inner apartment gets thin, or is hung awry [if the sexes are not kept apart], disorder will enter the family, and ultimately pervade the empire. Females are doubtless the sources of good manners; from ancient times to the present this has been the case. The inclination to virtue and vice in women differs exceedingly; their dispositions incline contrary ways, and if it is wished to form them alike, there is nothing like education. In ancient times, youth of both sexes were instructed. According to the Ritual of Zhou, 'the imperial wives regulated the law for educating females, in order to instruct the ladies of the palace in morals, conversation, manners, and work; and each led out their respective classes, at proper times, and arranged them for examination in the imperial presence.' But these treatises have not reached us, and it cannot be distinctly ascertained what was their plan of arrangement.

[. . . .]

The education of a woman and that of a man are very dissimilar. Thus, a man can study during his whole life; whether he is abroad or at home, he can always look into the classics and history, and become thoroughly acquainted with the whole range of authors. But a woman does not study more than ten years, when she takes upon her the management of a family, where a multiplicity of cares distract her attention, and having no leisure for undisturbed study, she cannot easily understand learned authors; not having obtained a thorough acquaintance with letters, she does not fully comprehend their principles; and like water that has flowed from its fountain, she cannot regulate her conduct by their guidance. How can it be said that a standard work on female education is not wanted! Every profession and trade has its appropriate master; and ought not those also who possess such an influence over manners [as females] be taught their duties and their proper limits? It is a matter of regret, that in these books no extracts have been made from the works of Confucius in order to make them introductory to the writings on polite literature; and it is also to be regretted that selections have not been made from the commentaries of Cheng, Zhu and the other scholars, who have explained his writings clearly, as also from the whole range of writers, gathering from them all that which was appropriate, and omitting the rest. These are circulated among mankind, together with such books as the *Juvenile Instructor;* yet if they are put into the hands of females, they cause them to become like a blind man without a guide, wandering hither and thither without knowing where he is going. There has been this great deficiency from very remote times until now.

Woman's influence is according to her moral character, therefore that point is largely explained. First, concerning their obedience to her husband and to his parents; then in regard to her complaisance to his brothers and sisters, and kindness to her sisters-in-law. If unmarried, she has duties towards her parents, and to the wives of her elder brothers; if a principal wife, a woman must have no jealous feelings; if in straitened circumstances, she must be contented with her lot; if rich and honorable, she must avoid extravagance and haughtiness. Then teach her, in times of trouble and in days of ease, how to maintain her purity, how to give importance to right principles, how to observe widowhood, and how to avenge the murder of a relative. Is she a mother, let her teach her children; is she a stepmother, let her love and cherish her husband's children; is her rank in life high, let her not be condescending to her inferiors; let her wholly discard all sorcerers, superstitious nuns, and witches; in a word let her adhere to propriety, and avoid vice.

In conversation, a female should not be forward and garrulous, but observe strictly what is correct, whether in suggesting advice to her husband, in remonstrating with him, or teaching her children; in maintaining etiquette, humbly imparting her experience, or in averting misfortune. The deportment of females should be strictly grave and sober, and yet adapted to the occasion; whether in waiting on her parents, receiving or reverencing her husband, rising up or sitting down, when pregnant, in times of mourning, or when fleeing in war, she should be perfectly decorous. Rearing the silkworm and working cloth are the most important of the employments of a female; preparing and serving up the food for the household, and setting in order the sacrifices, follow next; each of which must be attended to; after them, study and learning can fill up the time.

6.9 LEGAL CASE STUDY: MARRIAGE (1882)

It was expected that all young Chinese girls, aside from those prominent exceptions who chose to become a Buddhist nun, concubine, or courtesan, would to be married by their mid-to-late teens. According to the Confucian ideal, women should only marry one man, though after a mourning period (usually three years), women were permitted to remarry. Late imperial Chinese political culture esteemed those widows who remained chaste while educating her children. Memorial arches were erected for them, and biographies of them placed in local histories. As the legal cases below indicate however, life as a widow was rarely easy and it was often an economic burden on close relatives. The Qing legal code firmly sided on the moral, not the economic, interests of families.

Questions

1. From the legal cases below what benefits did women receive from the strict legal interpretations of Confucian model of widowhood?
2. How did the Qing government treat those who forced widows to remarry against their will?

Case #1: Remarriage of a Widow While in Mourning

A man named Yang Zhangchun belonging to Beijing had gone to Guangdong in the delegation of an official and there died. As the family were poor and as deceased had left no children it was arranged by the mother of the widow, in consultation with the mother of deceased, that the widow should return to her old home and be re-married. This was done and she was forthwith married to a man named Ren Dongxin. A brother of the deceased, who had never been satisfied as to the circumstances of the death, laid a plaint against the widow on the ground of the premature remarriage—and the Provincial Courts held that the marriage having taken place before the expiry of the legal period of mourning for the first husband, was contrary to law and void, and decreed that the parties should be separated. Against this decree the husband Ren Dongxin appealed. The Board reversed the decision on the ground that, though in accordance with the letter of the law, yet considering that this second marriage was arranged by the woman's mother, that the husband was in ignorance of the fact of her being a widow in mourning, and that there was no prior illicit intercourse between the parties, it would be doing violence to the woman's feelings if she were now compelled to change her condition a third time. Moreover it would be unreasonable to remove her from the husband's family who were innocent parties for the benefit of the family of her mother who was the person really to blame in the transaction. The Board further adds that in cases where a man had sold his wife through extreme poverty as wife to another man, they have upheld such unions under the particular circumstances, notwithstanding that they are forbidden in the code, and on the same principle Ren Dongxin may keep his wife.

Case #2: Marriage with a Woman Who Has Been Betrothed to One's Brother

Su Zongde betrothed his niece Su Dage with due formalities to one Liu Ba. Before the marriage was completed Liu Ba absconded and was never afterwards heard of again. After a lapse of 8 years Su Zongde, fearing his niece should lose her chance of matrimony, engaged her to a brother of the first intended—another brother Liu Mei acting as negotiator on his side. This engagement was afterwards carried out and the marriage completed. On the case coming before the authorities, it was held that the marriage was illegal, and that the parties must be separated. The negotiators on both sides were sentenced to banishment. This decision was upheld on reference to the Supreme Authorities at Beijing, on the principle that a formal betrothal was sufficient to constitute the relationship of man and wife between the parties, and inasmuch as no one can marry the widow or divorced wife of a brother or other relation within the degrees of mourning, so neither can he marry one who has legally put herself in the position of a wife. It would have been quite competent for Su Zongde, after application to the authorities, grounded on the undue absence of the intended husband, to have married his niece to a stranger, but under no circumstances could she have been married to one of that family. As the case was novel and there was no precedent to be found like it, it was directed to that a circular of instructions should be sent to all the provincial authorities enclosing a copy of the Decision for their guidance.

Case #3: Brother-in-Law Seeking Remarriage of Sister-in-Law to Procure Property

The prisoner Guo Shina was the [paternal cousin] of Guo Shilou who had died long ago leaving a widow and a son. He left also some nine *mu* of land and some houses which the widow was in possession of. Her young son and only child having died she, with the assent of her mother's family, got a nephew by the mother's side (a son of a her brother's) to come over and live with her—a young lad named Fu Geliang. Guo Shina being hard up and wishing to get possession of the property left by his brother, went one evening along with another relation of the family to visit the widow, and told her he wished her to remarry. She cried and swore and Guo Shina lost his temper and said "he would find a master and they would force her to marry," whereupon she cried and stormed all the more until the neighbors came in and persuaded the visitors to go away. After they had gone she said to her nephew with tears that having kept her widowhood for so long, she would rather die than remarry, and although she retired to rest pacified, that same night she put an end to her existence. The provincial court held that this case differed from that actually using violence to compel remarriage, inasmuch as the woman had only been frightened with empty words. The penalty for compelling a remarriage of a widow in the degree of relationship in which they stood to each other is strangulation after the usual term of imprisonment, and under the circumstances this was mitigated to banishment for life. This sentence, though at first queried by the Board, was afterwards upheld and confirmed.

6.10   SHEN FU'S "WEDDED BLISS" (1808)

Shen Fu's (1763–1825) *Six Chapters of a Floating Life* is considered by many Chinese to be a classic work of eighteenth-century society, culture and life. The following excerpts are from one chapter of that book that centers on his arranged marriage to his cousin

---

MU—A unit of measure for land equivalent to 0.16 acres.

Chen Yun. Neither their early engagement (as children) nor the fact that they were cousins was remarkable for the era (within traditional Chinese society, cousins on the mother's side were not seen as related—though one would have been forbidden to marry one's paternal cousin). His account offers a powerful corrective to the notion that Chinese arranged marriages were loveless and cold, though neither were they the open and equal marriages of the modern era. It also highlights the common practice of men of the upper classes having more than one wife (or mistress).

Questions

1. **How do you think the early engagement to his cousin affected Shen's feelings toward Chen Yun?**
2. **What aspects about Chen do you find most surprising? Do you think she found her marriage to Shen satisfying and happy? Why?**

I was born in 1763, under the reign of Qianlong, on the twenty-second day of the eleventh moon. The country was then in the heyday of peace and, moreover, I was born in a scholars' family, living by the side of the Canglang Pavilion in Suzhou. So altogether I may say the gods have been unusually kind to me. Su Dongpo said: "Life is like a spring dream which vanishes without a trace." I should be ungrateful to the gods if I did not try to put my life down on record.

[. . . .]

I was engaged in my childhood to one Miss Yu, of Jinsha, who died in her eighth year, and eventually I married a girl of the Chen clan. Her name was Yun and her literary name Suzhen. She was my cousin, being the daughter of my maternal uncle, Xinyu. Even in her childhood, she was a very clever girl, for while she was learning to speak, she was taught Bai Juyi's poem, the *Pipa Player,* and could at once repeat it. Her father died when she was four years old, and in the family there were only her mother (of the Jin clan) and her younger brother Kechang and herself, being then practically destitute. When Yun grew up and had learnt needlework, she was providing for the family of three, and contrived always to pay Kechang's tuition fees punctually. One day she picked up a copy of the poem the *Pipa Player* from a wastebasket, and from that, with the help of her memory of the lines, she learnt to read word by word. Between her needlework, she gradually learnt to write poetry. One of her poems contained the two lines:

Touched by autumn, one's figure grows slender,
Soaked in frost, the chrysanthemum blooms full.

When I was thirteen years old, I went with my mother to her maiden home and there we met. As we were two young innocent children, she allowed me to read her poems. I was quite struck by her talent, but feared that she was too clever to be happy. Still I could not help thinking of her all the time and once I told my mother, "If you were to choose a girl for me, I won't marry any one except Cousin Su." My mother also liked her being so gentle, and gave her gold ring as a token for the betrothal.

This was on the sixteenth of the seventh moon in the year 1775. In the winter of that year, one of my girl cousins, (the daughter of another maternal uncle of mine) was going to get married and I again accompanied my mother to her maiden home. Yun was the same age as myself, but ten months older, and as we had been accustomed to calling each other "elder sister" and "younger brother" from childhood, I continued to call her "Sister Su."

At this time the guests in the house all wore bright dresses, but Yun alone was clad in a dress of quiet color, and had on a new pair of shoes. I noticed that the embroidery on her shoes was very fine, and learnt that it was her own work, so that I began to realize that she was gifted at other things, too besides reading and writing.

Of a slender figure, she had drooping shoulders and a rather long neck, slim but not to the point of being skinny. Her eyebrows were arched and in her eyes there was a look of quick intelligence and soft refinement. The only defect was that her two front teeth were slightly inclined forward, which was not a mark of good omen. There was an air of tenderness about her which completely fascinated me.

[. . . .]

Our wedding took place on the twenty-second of the first moon in 1780. When she came to my home on that night, I found that she had the same slender figure as before. When her bridal veil was lifted, we looked at each other and smiled. After the drinking of the customary twin cups between bride and groom we sat down together at dinner and I secretly held her hand under the table, which was warm and small, and my heart was palpitating. I asked her to eat and learnt that she was in her vegetarian fast, which she had been keeping for several years already. I found that the time when she began her fast coincided with my smallpox illness, and said to her laughingly: "Now that my face is clean and smooth without pock-marks, my dear sister, will you break your fast?" Yun looked at me with a smile and nodded her head.

As a bride, Yun was very quiet at first. She was never sullen or displeased, and when people spoke to her, she merely smiled. She was respectful towards her superiors and kindly towards those under her. Whatever she did was done well, and it was difficult to find fault with her. When she saw the grey dawn shining in through the window she would get up and dress herself as if she had been commanded to do so. "Why?" I asked, . . she replied ". . . I am not afraid of people's talk; I only fear that our parents might think their daughter-in-law is lazy."

Although I wanted her to lie in bed longer, I could not help admiring her virtue, and so got up myself, too, at the same time with her. And so every day we rubbed shoulders together and clung to each other like an object and its shadow, and the love between us was something that surpassed the language of words.

[. . . .]

When I came back from East Guangdong in the seventh moon, 1794 there was a boy cousin-in-law of mine, by the name of Xu Xiufeng, who had brought home with him a concubine. He was crazy about her beauty and asked Yun to go and see her. After seeing her, Yun remarked to Xiufeng one day, "She has beauty but no charm." "Do you mean to say that when your husband takes a concubine, she must have both beauty and charm?" answered Xiufeng. Yun replied in the affirmative. So from that time on, she was quite bent on finding a concubine for me, but was short of cash. . . . On the fifth day of the eighth moon in the following year, my mother was going to see Huqiu with Yun, when [my friend, Zhang] Xianhan suddenly appeared and said: "I am going to Huqiu too. Will you come along with me

and see a beautiful courtesan?" I told my mother to go ahead and agreed to meet her at Bantang near Huqiu. My friend then dragged me to [courtesan] Lengxiang's place. I saw that Lengxiang was already in her middle-age, but she had a girl by the name of Hanyuan, who was a very sweet young maiden, still in her teens. Her eyes looked "like an autumn lake that cooled one by its cold splendor." After talking with her for a while, I learnt that she knew very well how to read and write. There was also a younger sister of hers, by the name of Wenyuan, who was still a mere child. I had then no thought of going about with a courtesan girl, fully realizing that as a poor scholar, I could not afford to take part in the feast in such a place. But since I was there already, I tried to get along as best I could.

"Are you trying to seduce me?" I said to Xianhan secretly? No," he replied, "someone had invited me today to a dinner in Hanyuan's place in return for a previous dinner. It happened that the host himself was invited by an important person and I am acting in his place. Don't you worry!"

I felt then quite relieved. Arriving at Bantang, we met my mother's boat, and I asked Hanyuan to go over to her boat and meet her. When Yun and Han met each other, they instinctively took to each other like old friends, and later they went hand-in-hand all over the famous places on the hill. Yun was especially fond of a place called "A Thousand Acres of Clouds" for its loftiness, and she remained there for a long time, lost in admiration of the scenery. We returned to the Waterside of Rural Fragrance where we tied up the boats and had a jolly drinking party together.

When we started on our way home, Yun said: "Will you please go over to the other boat with your friend, while I share this one with Han?" We did as she suggested, and I did not return to my boat until we had passed the Duting Bridge, where we parted from my friend and Hanyuan. It was midnight by the time we returned home.

"Now I have found a girl who has both beauty and charm," Yun said to me. "I have already asked Hanyuan to come and see us tomorrow, and I'll arrange it for you." I was taken by surprise.

"You know we are not a wealthy family. We can't afford to keep a girl like that, and we are so happily married. Why do you want to find somebody else?"

"But I love her," said Yun smilingly. "You just leave it to me."

[. . . .]

Yun came to me all smiles and said, "now that I have found a beauty for you, how are you going to reward the go-between?" I asked her for the details.

"I had to broach the topic delicately to her," she said "because I was afraid that she might have someone else in mind. Now I have learnt that there isn't anyone, and I asked her, 'Do you understand why we have this pledge today?' 'I should feel greatly honored if I could come to your home, but my mother is expecting a lot of me and I can't decide myself. We will watch and see,' she replied. As I was putting on the bracelet, I told her again, 'The jade is chosen for its hardness as a token of fidelity and the bracelet's roundness is a symbol of everlasting faithfulness. Meanwhile, please put it on as a token of our pledge.' She replied that everything depends on me. So it seems that she is willing herself. The only difficulty is her mother, Lengxiang. We will wait and see how it turns out."

"Are you going to enact the comedy *Lian Xiangban* of Li Liweng right in our home?

"Yes!" Yun replied.

From that time on, not a day passed without her mentioning Hanyuan's name. Eventually Hanyuan was married by force to some influential person, and our arrangements did not come off. And Yun actually died of grief on this account.

6.11 QIU JIN'S ADDRESS TO TWO HUNDRED MILLION FELLOW COUNTRYWOMEN (1904)

A famous poet and revolutionary, Qiu Jin (1875–1907), typified the earliest generation of revolutionary women. Born into a family of moderately wealthy means and liberal sentiments, her family made certain Qiu Jin received a modern education and socialized in progressive social circles. Leaving a short-lived marriage in 1903, she traveled to Japan which had pioneered women's education within Asia. Three years later she returned to China advocating Westernization and a democratic (non-monarchical) government. Her activities, illegal at the time, were discovered, and she was arrested and executed by decapitation on July 12, 1907. Today she remains a potent symbol of China's women's liberation movement. The following document is her most famous appeal for women's rights.

Questions

1. **Why would having daughters be considered undesirable in late imperial China?**
2. **Why do you think that Qiu Jin believes education is key for the liberation of women?**

Alas, the most unfairly treated things on this earth are the two hundred million who are born as Chinese women. We consider ourselves lucky to be born to a kind father. If we are unlucky, our father will be an ill-tempered and unreasonable person who repeatedly says, "How unlucky I am, yet another useless one," as if at any instant he could pick us up and throw us to our death. He will resent us and say things like "she's eventually going to someone else's family" and give us cold and contemptuous looks. When we grow a few years older, without bothering to ask us our thoughts, they will bind our tender, white and natural feet with a strip of cloth never loosening them even when we sleep. In the end, the flesh is mangled and the bones broken, all so that relatives, friends and neighbors can say, "the girl from so and so's family has tiny feet."

When the time comes [for the parents] to select a husband, everything is based on the promises of two shameless matchmakers. The daughter's parents will go along with any proposal as long as his family is rich

PITYING THE FRAGRANT COMPANION (*LIAN XIANGBAN*)—Li Liweng's play *Lian Xiangban* (Pitying the Fragrant Companion) is a story of a same-sex love affair between a wife and a girl whom the wife has convinced her husband to take on as a maid.

and powerful. Her parents do not bother to ask if the man's family is respectable, or inquire about the groom's temperament and level of education. On the wedding day, one will sit in the brightly decorated bridal sedan chair barely able to breathe. When we arrive at the new home, if the husband is found to be unambitious but even-tempered, her family will say we are blessed with good fortune from a previous life. If he is no good, her family will blame it "on our wrong conduct in a previous life," or simply "bad luck." If we dare complain, or otherwise try to counsel our husbands, then a scolding and beating will befall us. Others who hear of the abuse will say: "She is a woman of no virtue. She does not act as a wife should!" Can you believe such words! These aspersions are cast without the chance for an appeal? Further inequities will follow if the husband dies. The wife will have to wear a mourning dress for three years and will not be allowed to remarry. Yet, if the wife dies, the husband only needs to wear a blue [mourning] braid. Some men find even that unbecoming and do not bother to wear it at all. Even when the wife has only been dead for three days, he can go out and cavort and indulge himself. A new wife is allowed to enter the household even before the official seven weeks of mourning is over. In the beginning, Heaven created all people with no differences between men and women. Ask yourselves this, how could these people have been born without women? Why are things so unjust? Everyday these men say, "We ought to be equal and treat people kindly." Then why do they treat women so unfairly and unequally as if they were African slaves?

A woman has to learn not to depend on others, but to rely on herself instead. In the beginning, those rotten Confucianists said things like "men are superior while women are inferior," "a woman without talent is a woman with virtue," and "a wife should submit to her husband" and other such rubbish. If women have any ambition, we should call upon our comrades to oppose them. Chen Houzhu, the ruler of Chen Dynasty, started the practice of foot binding. If we, as women, feel any shame, then we should condemn the practice. It is not like our legs were tied while they bound our feet. Why can't we reject footbinding? Are they afraid of women being educated, knowledgeable, and perhaps surpassing them, men do not allow us to study. We must not simply go along with their decision without even challenging them. We cannot surrender our own responsibilities and be content with a lazy and undemanding life while men control the important matters.

If men call us useless, we become useless. So why are we are not bothered when we are called inept? Why do we not even question them when we are turned into slaves, all in exchange for our comfort? Are we to enjoy life while contributing nothing? Perhaps we are worried that our comforts may not last. As soon as we hear that men crave for 'small feet,' we rush to bind our feet to please them. For this sacrifice we earn the right to live a life in which we contribute nothing. And being forbidden to read and write, is precisely what we, as women, desire. Why do we disagree? Remember, there is no such fortune in the world that is just there for the taking! Power belongs to the learned and knowledgeable men who contribute to society, and we become their slaves. Since we are the slaves, how can we not be oppressed? We have brought this upon ourselves. How can we blame others? It is depressing to talk about this. We all have experienced this type of life, so there is no need for me to go further into details.

However, from now on I hope we can leave the past behind us and focus on our future. Assuming we have died in the past and are reincarnated into our next life the elders should not say "too old to be of any use." If you have a decent husband who wants to establish a school, do not stop him. If you have a fine son who wishes to study abroad, do not stop him. The middle-aged wife should not hinder her husband down causing him to have no ambition and achieve nothing. If you have a son, send him to school. Do the same for your daughter and never bind her feet. If you have a young girl, the best choice would be for her to attend school, but even if she is unable to attend schools, you should teach her to read and write at home. If you come from a family of officials that has money, you should persuade your husband to establish schools and factories and do good deeds that will help common people. If your family is poor, you should work hard to help your husband. Do not be lazy and do nothing. These are my hopes. All of you are aware that we are about to lose our country. Men can barely protect themselves. How can we rely on them? We must revitalize ourselves. Otherwise all will be too late when the country is lost. Everybody! Everybody! Please keep my hopes alive!

CHEN DYNASTY (557–589)—The last of the Southern dynasties during China's period of disunion just prior to the Sui dynasty.

USEFUL READINGS AND WEBSITES FOR PART ONE

Useful Websites

1. **RECORDING THE GRANDEUR OF THE QING:** http://www.learn.columbia.edu/nanxuntu/start.html – A visually stunning website organized around illustrated scrolls of the Kangxi and Qianlong emperors' Southern Inspection Tours of the empire. Includes a variety of interactive, graphic and textual features on numerous aspects of Qing society and governance including primary sources.
2. **A VISUAL SOURCEBOOK FOR CHINESE CIVILIZATION:** http://depts.washington.edu/chinaciv/index.htm – A website created by the well-known Chinese historian Patricia Ebrey. The site is devoted to Chinese civilization using visual images that focus on ten topics: geography, archaeology, religion, calligraphy, military technology, painting, homes, gardens, clothing, and the graphic arts.
3. **FORBIDDEN CITY:** http://www.forbiddencitychina.com – A sprawling website with audio introduction, over 500 pictures and a wealth of maps. Visually detailed with numerous ways to "explore" the Forbidden City.
4. **LIVING IN THE CHINESE COSMOS:** http://afe.easia.columbia.edu/cosmos/ – A remarkably useful website that introduces Confucianism, Buddhism, and Daoism in historical and cultural contexts. Includes sections on the Civil Service examinations, funeral customs and on religion as it is practiced in China today.
5. **TREATY PORTS & EXTRATERRITORIALITY IN CHINA :** http://www.geocities.com/treatyport01/TREATY01.html – A useful introduction to treaty ports and foreign settlements in general, the site is a good starting place for students interested in exploring the broader ramifications of the treaty ports in China from 1842–1920s.

Suggested Readings

1. **Evelyn Rawski, *The Last Emperors: A Social History of Qing Imperial Institutions* (Berkeley: University of California Press, 1998).** An in depth examination of the Qing court's customs, rituals and worldview. Includes details, vivid examples and accessible descriptions of the values, goals and material culture of China's ruling class.
2. **Mark C. Elliot, *The Manchu Way: The Eight Banners and Ethnic Identity in Late Imperial China* (Palo Alto: Stanford University Press, 2001).** A fascinating study of the way in which Manchu identity was cultivated, shaped, and maintained by the Qing court's Manchu heritage. Wonderfully written and intellectually engaging.
3. **Pamela Kyle Crossley, Helen F. Siu, and Donald S. Sutton, *Empire at the Margins: Culture, Ethnicity and Frontier in Early Modern China* (Berkeley and Los Angeles: University of California Press, 2006).** A volume of essays written by the top scholars in the field on China's ethnic groups and the border regions of late imperial China. The editors also provide a concise and approachable discussion of sinization in the late imperial context.
4. **Jonathan Spence, *God's Chinese Son: The Taiping Heavenly Kingdom of Hong Xiuquan* (New York: W.W. Norton, 1996).** A lively and fast paced account of the Taiping Rebellion by one of the field's foremost historians. His sophisticated analysis of the Taipings is especially powerful in explaining their interpretation of Christian beliefs and the reshaping of society under Taiping rule.

5. **James Hevia,** *English Lessons: The Pedagogy of Imperialism in Nineteenth-Century China* **(Durham: Duke University Press, 2003).** One of the most incisive critiques of Western imperialism in China written to date. Traces the rationale employed by Western (particularly British) nations to preserve the opium trade and other unequal economic and diplomatic advantages throughout the nineteenth century.

6. **Paul Cohen,** *History in Three Keys: The Boxers as Event, Experience and Myth* **(New York : Columbia University Press, 1997).** An elegantly written account of the Boxer Uprising that looks at the various ways in which the rebellion has been understood and how its' meaning has been appropriated for different means in the decades since the Boxer Uprising unfolded.

7. **Geremie R. Barmé,** *Forbidden City* **(Cambridge: Harvard University Press, 2008).** A detailed yet fascinating look at China's famed imperial palace from its construction to its conversion to a museum in the twentieth century. Richly textured and engagingly written with high quality illustrations.

PART TWO

REPUBLICAN CHINA
(1912–1949)

Timeline

World		China
	1912	Republic of China established
Gandhi returns to India	1914	
	1915	*New Youth* (Xin Qingnian) published
	1916	Yuan Shikai dies
Trans-Siberian Railway completed	1917	
	1919	May Fourth Demonstrations begin in Beijing
League of Nations founded	1920	
	1924	Huangpu (Whampoa) Academy established
	1925	Sun Zhongshan dies
	1926–28	Northern Expedition
	1927	Nanjing becomes capital of Guomindang government
	1928	Ding Ling's *Miss Sophie's Diary* published
All Quiet on the Western Front published	1929	
	1931	Mukden (Shenyang) Incident
	1932	Manchukuo formally established by Japan
Adolph Hitler appointed chancellor	1933	
	1934–35	Long March
	1936	Xi'an Incident
	1937	Lugouqiao (Marco Polo) Incident / Beginning of China's War of Resistance
Austria annexed by Hitler	1938	
	1940	Wang Jingwei collaborationist government established
First electron microscope demonstrated	1941	
First atomic bomb detonated in New Mexico	1945	Japan formally surrenders to China
	1946	Jiang Jieshi and the Guomindang formally re-establish capital in Nanjing
Gandhi assassinated	1948	
	1949	Beijing is captured by PLA troops

CHAPTER 7

REVOLUTION, WARLORDISM, AND INTELLECTUAL TRANSFORMATION

VISUAL SOURCE
The Making of a Movement:
1919 Demonstrations in Tiananmen

TIANANMEN GATE: Tiananmen Gate (often known in English as the "Gate of Heavenly Peace") was the formal entrance to the former imperial palace and Forbidden City. This space in front of the gate, much smaller than today's Tiananmen Square, had only been opened to the public several years prior to the May Fourth protests. Utilized in a manner never anticipated by the governments, the space in front of the Tiananmen Gate quickly became a focal point for most every major demonstration in 20th century China, including the May Fourth and December 1919 anti-Japanese protests following the Fuzhou Incident.

MAY FOURTH PLACARDS:
The demonstrators in the May Fourth photo (left) carried signs with a variety of slogans:

"Abolish the 21 Demands"
"Return Our Qingdao"
"Down with the Traitors"
"Internationally fight for our sovereign rights, domestically rid the country of traitors"
"Rebuff all efforts to sign the Peace Treaty"
"Cao Rulin should suffer death by the 10,000 cuts"

MAY FOURTH DEMONSTRATIONS:
On May 4, 1919 roughly 3,000 Beijing students and professors marched to the front of Tiananmen Gate to protest the news that the Allied Powers would grant Japan control over Germany's former holdings in Shandong province. Later the protestors marched to the diplomatic quarter intent on attacking the European embassies only to be turned away by police. Thirty-two students were arrested and one student died later as a result of clashes with the police.

May 4th Demonstrations in front of Tiananmen Gate (May 4, 1919)

Demonstrations and speeches in front of Tiananmen Gate (December 1919)

CLOTHING: The clothing worn by the students and professors reveal the changing social and political climate of the late 1910s. Most obviously, gone are the long queues common less than a decade earlier. On the far right, several participants are wearing western style hats intermingled with some participants wearing the traditional mandarin cap.' Others wear the long padded gowns with vest (changpao magua) which would remain popular into the 1940s.

MAY FOURTH GENERATION: The original demonstrators in the May Fourth demonstrations were almost entirely students and professors from Beijing's thirteen universities and colleges. By the December demonstrations seven months later, the participation included a far broader swath of Chinese including merchants, businessmen, workers, and laborers. As the movement grew it would take on broader dimensions and meanings that shape an entire generation of Chinese.

DECEMBER 1919: The December 1919 demonstrations took on a much larger and different flavor than the earlier May Fourth demonstration. More organized now (with food vendors visible in the foreground), many participants prepared speeches and pamphlets to hand out (in center). The number and variety of participants increased as the Chinese populace became increasingly politicized and similar demostrations occurred throughout China.

On the morning of October 11, 1911, the Chinese revolutionary leader and head of the **Revolutionary Alliance,** Sun Zhongshan walked downstairs from his Denver hotel room to eat breakfast in the grand dining room. A wanted man in China with a price on his head, Sun was on a fundraising tour of the United States seeking financial support for China's revolutionary cause. The Qing government had put considerable pressure on foreign governments to hand Sun over, as they had with many other top revolutionary leaders who had fled the country. As he waited for his breakfast that morning, he opened the local newspaper to see the headline: "Chinese Revolt is Menace to Manchu Dynasty" (the headline in Denver's other paper more typically reflected the concerns of the era: "Foreigners Throughout Empire in Deadly Peril"). Sun scanned the article and quickly confirmed that a group of young revolutionaries and sympathetic army units had taken Wuchang, one of three cities in the tri-city metropolis of **Wuhan.** The uprising had been in the planning stage for some months. After more than ten abortive attempts, the long awaited revolution to topple the Qing government had begun, and not a single major revolutionary leader was anywhere near Wuhan.

The revolt was ignited prematurely, quite literally, on October 9, 1911. A young activist's cigarette got too close to a bomb that a group of revolutionaries was making and set the entire building ablaze. The ensuing explosion attracted the attention of the Qing authorities. In their investigation they discovered, among other things, a list of pro-revolutionaries, including supportive individuals within the Qing army. Faced with the choice of waiting to be arrested or of going forward with their revolutionary plans, renegade army units seized the government munitions depot on **October 10, 1911.** The Qing governor and governor-general hastily fled, allowing the revolutionaries to gain control of the city. Their success in turn triggered provincial declarations of independence across the empire and crippled Qing authority.

Back in Denver, Sun faced a dilemma. At that precise moment, as he waited for his breakfast, Sun sat 6,000 miles and nearly two-weeks travel time away from China. While the unexpected timing of the revolt may have caught Sun unaware, his absence from the center of the Wuhan revolt was not unanticipated. The price on his head and the revolution's need for funds had made it imperative that he seek support abroad. Sun immediately checked out of his Denver hotel and headed east. He made several stops in the United States before traveling to London and Paris. This itinerary suggests a premeditated plan of action or, at the very least, a clear-headed appraisal of what measures he needed to take prior to his return to China.

Sun had legitimate reasons to be worried about the Western capitals' response to the actions of the revolutionaries. Given the millions in loans and unpaid indemnities owed by the Qing government, it was conceivable that the Western powers might intervene against the revolutionaries in order to prop up a weak Qing monarchy. With this perspective, Sun's primary goal was twofold: 1) to assure the Western governments that the new republican government would honor all treaties and debts to foreign powers; and

TONGMENG HUI (REVOLUTIONARY ALLIANCE SOCIETY)—A political group forged out of several competing parties in 1910. By joining forces they became the largest Chinese revolutionary party and the forerunner of the Nationalist party, the Guomindang.

WUHAN—The tri-city area of Wuchang, Hankou and Hanyang situated at the confluence of the Yangzi and Hanshui Rivers. Site of the October 10, 1911 Wuchang uprising which sparked the Chinese Revolution.

WUCHANG UPRISING (1911)—The uprising that began on October 10, 1911 as a result of the accidental detonation of explosives by Tongmenhui members. It started the Chinese revolution, which led to the fall of the Qing dynasty and the founding of the Republic of China.

NATIONAL DAY—The Wuhan Uprising on October 10 (or "Double-10"), 1911 marked the beginning of the Chinese Revolution and is still celebrated as National Day in the Republic of China [Taiwan]. The anniversary of the founding of the PRC on October 1, 1949, is National Day in the People's Republic of China.

2) to lay the groundwork for diplomatic recognition, and where possible, future loans for the fledging government. Sun stopped in Chicago where he showed his fundraising prowess by raising $10,000 from Chinese Americans to promote the revolution. His efforts with the Western governments were not as successful. He received no firm financial or political commitments from the American, British, or French leaders. He did extract a useful promise from the British and French not to make any additional loans to the Qing government. After doing what he could overseas, Sun arrived in Shanghai on December 25, 1911. A week later, on New Year's Day, he took the train to Nanjing, the new capital of China, and that afternoon was sworn in as the provisional president.

Today, both the People's Republic of China (mainland) and the Republic of China (Taiwan) revere Sun as the "Father of the Nation" (*guofu*). However, there is debate among many scholars as to how the events of 1911/1912 should be portrayed given the fact that the "revolution" involved relatively little military conflict.

In early 1912, Sun Zhongshan and the Provisional Government in Nanjing faced several unpleasant realities. Their leadership and support was almost entirely composed of southerners with virtually no assistance from the Qing military based in the greater Beijing area. Nor, as they had hoped after the Wuchang Uprising, did the political events compel the Qing emperor to abdicate and acknowledge Nanjing as China's new government. The National Assembly in Beijing continued to assert that they were China's legitimate constitutional body. Although the provinces had exhibited uniformity in their declarations of independence, there was virtually no agreement on what form the Republic of China should take, or if Nanjing should continue as the capital. The reluctance of the emperor to abdicate confused the situation further.

Many key individuals of the new provincial government soon began to wonder if the skills Sun Zhongshan had employed as a revolutionary agitator were sufficient to lead modern China through its difficult initial phases of nationhood. He had spent most of his adult life outside China and had no military or political experience in an established government. There were serious organizational issues needing to be resolved.

With this political stalemate, **Yuan Shikai,** a political and military official who had broad ties with both the Qing court and the military forces, emerged as the only individual who, it seemed, could break the deadlock, negotiate an end to the Qing dynasty and transform China into a republic. In exchange for taking on this critical role, he demanded the office of president. Many Chinese felt he was the only person capable of peacefully bringing an end to Qing rule as well as preventing a civil war. And so Yuan Shikai assumed leadership as China's first president. His leadership proved to be a political disaster that did not save China, but only served to hasten China's political disintegration and to usher in a period of deep disunion. As the pressure mounted, and just six weeks after accepting the provisional presidency, Sun Zhongshan agreed to resign from office to make way for Yuan Shikai. He would never serve as president of a unified China. He would, however, remain active in China's political development.

1911 REVOLUTION

The suddenness of the October 1911 revolution surprised virtually every constituency vying for power within China. Each political group, from the radical revolutionaries to the conservative constitutional monarchists, scrambled to position themselves and profit

YUAN SHIKAI (1859–1916)—Staunch Qing loyalist and commander of the powerful Beiyang Army which allowed him, in 1912, to broker the abdication of the Qing in exchange for the presidency of the new republic. His term as president was plagued by corruption, extortion and a misguided attempt to proclaim himself emperor before his death in 1916.

from the Wuchang Uprising. In November the National Assembly, a body formed by the imperial court in accordance with the Constitutional timetable but not yet given full parliamentary rights, promoted the creation of a political structure similar to the constitutional monarchies of Japan and Great Britain (7.1). The revolutionaries, who had focused on abolishing the Qing dynasty and forestalling any monarchy, had no common vision of the future or of how to force the abdication of the Qing emperor (7.3). Within six months of the Wuchang Uprising, China's first attempts to form a solid democracy would falter and quickly disintegrate into disunity and infighting among the revolutionaries, provincial leaders, and the former imperialists.

7.1 DEMANDS OF THE NATIONAL ASSEMBLY, SUBMITTED IN A MEMORIAL TO THE THRONE (NOVEMBER 3, 1911)

In the weeks after the Wuchang Uprising, the National Assembly sought to persuade the imperial court to make parliamentary concessions by agreeing to maintain the monarchy and to establish the emperor as the ceremonial head of government. For most revolutionaries, however, the time for such half-measures had already passed. As the memorial below suggests, the National Assembly sought to attain legitimacy through an imperial mandate, and not through popular or "revolutionary" activity. This approach would produce a China with two competing political bodies: the National Assembly, maintaining a connection with the Qing, and the Provisional Government, rooted in revolution and headed by Sun Zhongshan in Nanjing. The two political groups claimed authority through radically different processes, and neither was based on an open and comprehensive selection process.

Questions

1. **What aspects of the following demands would have been threatening to the throne? Why?**
2. **Why does the National Assembly seek to retain the emperor?**

1. The Qing Dynasty shall be maintained in perpetuity.
2. The person of the Emperor shall be inviolable.
3. The prerogative of the Emperor shall be limited by the Constitution.
4. The succession to the Throne shall be prescribed in the Constitution.
5. The Constitution shall be drafted and determined by the National Assembly and promulgated by the Emperor.
6. All amendment of the Constitution lies within the province and power of Parliament.
7. Members of the Upper House of Parliament are to be elected by the people from specially qualified classes.
8. Parliament will elect but the Emperor shall appoint the Prime Minister, on whose recommendation the

other members of the Cabinet shall be appointed by the Emperor; but Imperial princes shall be ineligible for any ministerial office or for the governorship of a province.
9. The Prime Minister may be impeached, whereupon either he shall ask for a dissolution of Parliament or shall resign.
10. The Emperor shall be in supreme control of the army and the navy, but when this control is exercised in respect of domestic matters it shall be subject to such limitations as may be imposed by Parliament.
11. Imperial Edicts shall not have the force of law except in emergencies, and even then under special provisions and only for the carrying out of what has already been determined by law.

12. No treaty with a foreign Power shall be concluded without the authority of Parliament, but the conclusion of a peace or the declaration of a war may be made during the session of Parliament without the consent of Parliament being obtained until afterwards.

13. Standing orders of an administrative character shall be settled by Acts of Parliament.

14. If the budget should fail to be accepted by Parliament the Government shall act upon the preceding year's budget, but no further expenditure shall be added thereto and no special financial measures shall be adopted.

15. The determination of the revenues and expenditures of the Imperial Household shall be within the power of Parliament.

16. The Imperial Household Laws shall not violate the Constitution.

17. The two Houses of Parliament shall jointly establish Administrative Courts.

18. The Emperor shall promulgate all the laws enacted by Parliament.

19. The National Assembly shall exercise all the authority vested in Parliament by Articles 8, 9, 10, 12, 13, 14, and 18, until Parliament is duly elected and opened.

7.2 FIRST PROVISIONAL PRESIDENT'S PROCLAMATION (JANUARY 2, 1912)

Sun was sworn into office the day before issuing his first proclamation. His speech clearly sought to remold his *Three Principles of the People* (5.11) to fit the immediate exigencies facing the nascent Chinese Republic. While it may seem a smooth summary of the events, it offered little in the way of concrete measures to resolve the challenges facing a nation that did not have a consensus for shaping its political future. Having no public mandate and a non-existent military force to leverage his position, Sun had no viable means for leading China to accept the political framework he outlined.

Questions

1. **What did Sun see as the major challenges facing China?**
2. **What actions did he intend to make to resolve these problems?**

In the beginning of the formation of the Chinese Republic [I], though unworthy, have been elected the provisional president and I am day and night taking great care, fearing I could not meet the desires of our People. The abuses of the despotic Government of China have been going from bad to worse during the past two hundred years. When, however, once our people determined to overthrow it, it has taken only several dozen days in restoring over a dozen provinces to our cause, which success is unprecedented in any history.

Without any organ to control or any body to meet with foreign Powers it is impossible to carry on our work and therefore we have to organize a Provisional Government. I am not going to do a thing by professing my own individual merit but I do not hesitate to attend to the organization of the Provisional Government to serve the People by carrying out our duties. By serving the People we can wipe out the bad habits of despotism and establish Republican government to

benefit the People, to attain the aim of the Revolution, to satisfy the minds of the People commencing from today. Thus I proclaim my own idea frankly. I say the foundation of a state is the People. The different races such as Hans, Manchus, Mongols, Muslims, and Tibetans are now to be united as a nation. This is what I call the unity of our Races.

Since the fighting at Wuchang commenced, over a dozen provinces have proclaimed independence, and by independence has been meant to be independent from the yoke of the Manchu Qing dynasty; but to join hands with the provinces which are on the same side, and to amalgamate Mongolia and Tibet for our cause, are part of the same plan and therefore it becomes necessary to form a Government to unite them. This is what I call the unity of our Territories.

Once the righteous army commenced fighting for our cause many men of arms arose in the said provinces, but the armed forces are not under one control and they are not in uniform organization though their arms are the same. They should be combined under common command and for common cause. This is what I call the unity of our Military Administration.

The area of the State is wide and the various provinces have their own ways and the Manchu Government has tried to effect centralization of power under the false name of constitutional government, but now it is to be arranged that each province be self-governed, and all shall be federated under a common central Government. This is what I call the unity of our Internal Administration.

Under the Manchu Government, in the name of enforcing constitutional Government, many taxes have been raised from poor people, but hereafter the national expenditure will be fixed in accordance with the principles of finance with a view to maintaining the happiness of the People. This is what I call the unity of Finance.

These are our principal policies and we are going to carry these principles out properly. The principle of revolution is the same all the world over and revolutionary movements have failed often, yet foreigners all took notice of our real aim.

Since we first rose in October last all the friendly nations have maintained strict neutrality and the newspapers and public opinion of foreign countries are quite sympathetic with our cause, for which I have to express our deep thanks.

With the establishment of Provisional Government we will try our best to carry out the duties of a civilized nation so as to obtain the rights of a civilized state. Under the Manchu Government China has been obliged to be under humiliation and had anti-foreign feeling, but all these should be wiped out and we should aim at the principle of peace and tranquility and to increase our friendship with friendly nations so as to place China in a respectable place in international society, to follow in the steps of the other Powers of the world. Our foreign policy is based on this point.

In establishing a new Government for a country there are many affairs to deal with, either international or internal, and how could I be able to carry on these important complicated affairs? Yet this is a Provisional Government. This is a government in a time of revolution. In the past decades all those who have been engaged in the revolutionary movements have been doing their work with a spirit honest and pure, and we have fought many difficult obstacles; and the further we proceed the more difficulties will lie before us, but we shall continue with our revolutionary spirit to carry out our aim to the last and if we could establish the foundation of the Chinese Republic, the duties of the Provisional Government would be at an end; then we may be pronounced to be "not guilty," in the eyes of the nation and the world. On this day when I meet our People I frankly declare what is my view.

7.3 THE LAST EMPEROR'S ABDICATION EDICT (FEBRUARY 12, 1912)

The following is one of several carefully orchestrated exchanges of edicts between Yuan Shikai and the imperial throne. Yuan Shikai had commanded the **Beiyang Armies** and been a firm proponent of the imperial throne. By the end of 1911, as the dominant military leader in northern China, many revolutionaries believed that only he could prevent the disintegration of China into competing regional armies. His long service to the throne also positioned him as one of the few people who could persuade the young emperor (and his advisors) of the need to abdicate. In exchange for such services, Yuan Shikai demanded that Sun Zhongshan step aside and allow him to replace Sun as the provisional president. Although Yuan Shikai issued a statement pledging loyalty to the republic, promising not to move the new capital back to Beijing, and pledging to allow China to adopt a full constitutional government—within months he would go back on each of these assurances.

BEIYANG ARMY—A Western-style army forged from Li Hongzhang's Anhui Army in the 1880s and led by Yuan Shikai after Li Hongzhang's death in 1901. It was funded by North China customs' revenues, first used to build the Beiyang ("Northern Ocean") fleet, hence the name. The Beiyang Army remained intact until the Republican era, first led by Yuan Shikai, then the conservative warlord general Zhang Xun.

Questions

1. **What reasons does the Qing leadership give for succumbing to the rising political pressures?**
2. **What role does Yuan Shikai play as presented in the edicts below?**

25th day, 12th month, 3rd year of the Xuantong reign [February 12, 1912]

We have today received from the Empress Dowager Longyu an Edict stating that on account of the uprising by the Army of the People, with the cooperation of the people of the Provinces, the one answering to the other as the echo does to the sound, the whole Empire has been as a boiling cauldron and the People have endured much tribulation. We therefore specially appointed Yuan Shikai to instruct Commissioners to confer with the representatives of the Army of the People for the summoning of a National Convention at which the future form of Government should be decided. There was wide divergence of opinion between the North and the South, and each strongly maintained its own views, and the general consequence has been an entire stoppage of trade and suspension of ordinary civil life. So long as the form of government remains undecided, so long will the disturbed condition of the country continue. It is clear that the minds of the majority of the people are favorable to the establishment of a republican form of government, the Southern and Central provinces first holding this view, and the officers in the North lately adopting the same sentiments. The universal desire clearly expresses the will of Heaven, and it is not for us to oppose the desires and incur the disapproval of the millions of the People merely for the sake of the privileges and powers of a single House. It is right that this general situation should be considered and due deference given to the opinion of the People. I, the Empress Dowager, therefore, together with the Emperor, hereby hand over the sovereignty to be the possession of the whole People, and declare that the constitution shall henceforth be republican, in order to satisfy the demands of those within the confines of the nation, hating disorder and desiring peace, and anxious to follow the teaching of the sages, according to which the country is the possession of the People.

Yuan Shikai, having been elected some time ago president of the National Assembly at Beijing, is therefore able at this time of change to unite the North and the South; let him then, with full powers so to do, organize a provisional Republican Government, conferring thereon with the representatives of the Army of the People, that peace may be assured to the People whilst the complete integrity of the territories of the five races, Chinese, Manchus, Mongols, Muslim Chinese [Hui], and Tibetans, is at the same time maintained, making together a great state under the title the Republic of China. We, the Empress Dowager and the Emperor, will retire into a life of leisure, free from public duties, spending Our years pleasantly and enjoying the courteous treatment accorded to Us by the People, and watching with satisfaction the glorious establishment and consummation of a perfect Government.

7.4   SUN ZHONGSHAN'S REPLY TO YUAN SHIKAI AND RESIGNATION (FEBRUARY 12, 1912)

Sun Zhongshan, on February 12, 1912, resigned his position as provisional president. His contradictory feelings toward Yuan Shikai are manifest in the following documents. Like many of his revolutionary cohorts, he saw no alternative to allowing Yuan Shikai to replace him as president. Sun's fears that Yuan Shikai had little commitment to a democratic government were quickly validated when Yuan Shikai failed to honor numerous promises and moved the capital back to his powerbase in Beijing. Yuan's presidency was characterized by placing his cronies in power, bribing those outside his control, and assassinating those resistant to his despotic leadership.

Questions

1. **What elements of his resignation disturbed Sun Zhongshan?**
2. **Why do you think Sun only lasted six weeks as leader of China?**

Dr. Sun to Yuan Shikai, dated Nanjing, 12th February, 1912.

Tang Shaoyi has telegraphed me that the Qing Emperor has abdicated and that you will support the Republic. The settlement of this great question is a matter of the utmost joy and congratulation. I will report to the National Assembly that I agree to resign the office of President in your favor. But the Republican Government cannot be organized by any authority conferred by the Qing Emperor. The exercise of such pretentious power will surely lead to serious trouble. As you clearly understand the needs of the situation, certainly you will not accept such authority. I cordially invite you to come to Nanjing and fulfill the expectations of all. Should you be anxious about the maintenance of order in the North, would you inform the Provisional Government by telegraph whom you could recommend to be appointed with full powers to act in your place as a representative of the Republic? Expecting your reply to this telegram, hereby again extend to you our cordial welcome to Nanjing.

Resignation of First Provisional President. Dr. Sun to the National Assembly at Nanjing, 12th February, 1912.

Today I present to you my resignation and request you to elect a good and talented man as the new President.

The election of President is a right of our citizens, and it is not for me to interfere in any way. But according to the telegram which our delegate Dr. Wu was directed to send to Beijing, I was to undertake to resign in favor of Mr. Yuan when the Emperor had abdicated, and Mr. Yuan has declared his political views in support of the Republic. I have already submitted this to your honorable Assembly and obtained your approval. The abdication of the Qing Emperor and the union of the North and South are largely due to the great exertions of Mr. Yuan. Moreover, he has declared his unconditional adhesion to the national cause. Should he be elected to serve the Republic, he would surely prove himself a most loyal servant of the state. Besides, Mr. Yuan is a man of political experience, to whose constructive ability our united nation looks forward for the consolidation of its interests. Therefore, I venture to express my personal opinion and to invite your honorable Assembly carefully to consider the future welfare of the state, and not to miss the opportunity of electing one who is worthy of your election. The happiness of our country depends upon your choice. Farewell.

WARLORD ERA

Yuan Shikai's death in 1916, although welcome in many quarters, further destabilized China's already precarious political situation. In the months after his demise a power struggle for political control of the government in Beijing ensued. There was even one attempt to restore the emperor to his throne (7.6). The following year, Sun Zhongshan founded the Military Government of the Republic of China with its capital in Guangzhou. Numerous other provinces instituted various degrees of self-rule, often headed by military leaders (commonly known as **warlords**). The political situation worsened to the point that no political entity could speak for China as a whole. There was no clear consensus, either domestically or internationally, as to which of the many governments being established during this period held the political authority to act as China's bona fide government.

Into this political vacuum arose a class of autonomous military commanders [*dujun*]. A period of nearly unending military conflict and political fragmentation lasted from 1916 to 1928 and is loosely referred to as "the Warlord era." These warlords controlled large swaths of China, with the tides in their control ebbing back and forth. Warlords sought to portray themselves as fighting for the reunification of China (or as one scholar humorously put it, "warlords against warlordism"). The public viewed the warlords with extreme interest often using nicknames to remember each warlord (e.g. the "Pigtail General," the "Scholar General," or the "Dogmeat General").

7.5   CONVENTION BETWEEN GREAT BRITAIN, CHINA AND TIBET: SIMLA (1914)

Similar to the effect China had on many Europeans, Tibet inspired considerable hopes among the British as a potential market for Britain's manufactured goods and India's tea. As early as 1861 British colonial officials were plotting missions to learn more about the Tibetan plateau. By the 1870s and 1880s, exploratory, and later military and diplomatic forays, made their way into Tibet. While the Qing government acquiesced to British demands to open up "treaty ports" and trade markets in Tibet, the Tibetan government was never party to any of the negotiations and refused to accept such diplomatic agreements. It became clear to the British that China, for all intents and purposes, no longer exerted any control over Tibet. Seeking to engage the Tibetan government in talks that would formalize trade and a British presence in Tibet, the British sent an expeditionary force to Tibet, ultimately entering Lhasa on August 3, 1904. A series of bilateral conventions between Tibet and Great Britan were signed, but it left the question of China's control over Tibet ambiguous. After the fall of the Qing in 1911, the Thirteenth Dalai became increasingly intent on formalizing Tibet's independence through diplomatic agreements with Britain that would formally indicate Tibet's separate suzerainty from China. As negotiations began between China, Tibet, and Great Britain, it became clear that Tibet sought a convention acknowledging their independence, China sought a convention acknowledging Tibet as a part of China, and Great Britain sought Tibetan autonomy but not independence. The resulting Simla Convention (1914) reflects the cross purposes of the three nations. China, in the end, refused to sign the convention. While many accepted the Simla Convention as an indication of Tibet's de facto independence, no nation took the final step of formally recognizing Tibet's status as such.

Questions

1. What purpose did establishing an "inner" and "outer" Tibet serve (or not serve) each of the participating nations?
2. Why did Great Britain balk at creating an independent Tibet?

WARLORDS (JUNFA)—A term applied to the military governors and commanders who battled for political control usually through the use of regionally based armies from 1911 to the late 1920s.

His Majesty the King of the United Kingdom of Great Britain and Ireland and of the British Dominions beyond the Seas, Emperor of India, His Excellency the President of the Republic of China, and His Holiness the Dalai Lama of Tibet, being sincerely desirous to settle by mutual agreement various questions concerning the interests of their several States on the Continent of Asia, and further to regulate the relations of their several Governments, have resolved to conclude a Convention on this subject and have nominated for this purpose their respective Plenipotentiaries, that is to say:

> His Majesty the King of the United Kingdom of Great Britain and Ireland and of the British Dominions beyond the Seas, Emperor of India, Sir Arthur Henry McMahon, Knight Grand Cross of the Royal Victorian Order, Knight Commander of the Most Eminent Order of the Indian Empire, Companion of the Most Exalted Order of the Star of India, Secretary of the Government of India, Foreign and Political Department;

> His Excellency the President of the Republic of China, Monsieur Ivan Chen, Officer of the Order of the Jia He;

> His Holiness the Dalai Lama of Tibet, Lonchen Ga-den Shatra Pal-jor Dorje; who having communicated to each other their respective full powers and finding them to be in good and due form have agreed upon and concluded the following Convention in eleven Articles:

ARTICLE 1

The Convention specified in the Schedule to the present Convention shall, except in so far as they may have been modified by, or may be inconsistent with or repugnant to, any of the provisions of the present Convention, continue to be binding upon the High Contracting Parties.

ARTICLE 2

The Governments of Great Britain and China recognizing that Tibet is under the suzerainty of China, and recognizing also the autonomy of Outer Tibet, engage to respect the territory integrity of the country, and to abstain from interference in the administration of Outer Tibet (including the selection and installation of the Dalai Lama), which shall remain in the hands of the Tibetan Governent at Lhasa.

The Government of China engages not to convert Tibet into a Chinese province. The Government of Great Britain engages not to annex Tibet or any portion of it.

ARTICLE 3

Recognizing the special interest of Great Britain, in virtue of the geographical position of Tibet, in the existence of an effective Tibetan Government and in the maintenance of peace and order in the neighborhood of the frontiers of India and adjoining States, the Government of China engages, except as provided in Article 4 of this Convention, not to send troops into Outer Tibet, nor to station civil or military officers, nor to establish Chinese colonies in the country. Should any such troops or officials remain in Outer Tibet at the date of the signature of this Convention, they shall be withdrawn within a period not exceeding three months.

The Government of Great Britain engages not to station military or civil officers in Tibet (except as provided in the Convention of September 7, 1904, between Great Britain and Tibet) nor troops (except the Agents' escorts), nor to establish colonies in that country.

ARTICLE 4

The foregoing Article shall not be held to preclude the continuance of the arrangements by which, in the past, a Chinese high official with suitable escort has been maintained at Lhasa, but it is hereby provided that the said escort shall in no circumstance exceed 300 men.

ARTICLE 5

The Governments of China and Tibet engage that they will not enter into any negotiations or agreements regarding Tibet with one another, or with any other Power, excepting such negotiations and agreements between Great Britain and Tibet as are provided for by the Convention of September 7, 1904, between Great Britain and Tibet and the Convention of April 27, 1906, between Great Britain and China.

[. . . .]

ARTICLE 10

The English, Chinese and Tibetan texts of the present Convention have been carefully examined and found to correspond, but in the event of there being any difference of meaning between them the English text shall be authoritative.

ARTICLE 11

The present Convention will take effect from the date of signature.

If token where of the respective Plenipotentiaries have signed and sealed this Convention, three copies in English, three in Chinese, and three in Tibetan.

Done at Simla this third day of July, A.D. one thousand nine hundred, and fourteen, corresponding with the Chinese date, the third day of the seventh month of the third year of the Republic, and the Tibetan date, the tenth day of the fifth month of the Wood Tiger year.

Initial of Lonchen Shatra.
(Initialled) A.H.M.
Seal of the Lonchen Shatra.
Seal of the British Plenipotentiary

7.6   ZHANG XUN'S REASONS FOR RESTORING THE MONARCHY (1917)

In 1916, a dispute broke out between China's President Li Yuanhong and Premier **Duan Qirui** over China's entrance into World War One. The parliament voted for his removal, and President Li Yuanhong obligingly dismissed Duan Qirui. A supporter of Duan Qirui, General **Zhang Xun** (1854–1923), marched with his military forces into the capital on the pretext of reinstating Duan Qirui as premier. Zhang Xun was a fervent monarchist who retained his queue and was known as the "Pigtail General." Instead of helping Duan, General Zhang Xun decided to reinstate the former emperor, Puyi. On July 1, 1917 a coronation ceremony officially restored the emperor to the throne. Within a week the military tide had shifted again, and Duan Qirui defeated Zhang Xun's forces. On July 12, Puyi was, for the second time in his life, forced to abdicate. Zhang Xun sought and received asylum in the Dutch consulate. He was eventually pardoned the following year for his "treasonous" anti-parliamentary acts. The following is a long manifesto posted by Zhang Xun on July 3, 1917.

> ### Questions
> 1. **What critical characteristics does Zhang Xun attribute to the parliamentary system?**
> 2. **What does Zhang Xun suggest is as "great as the distance between heaven and earth?"**

Ever since the uprising at Wuchang and the establishment of the republic peace and order have been cast to the winds and good reliable people have been nowhere to be seen. Anarchists have been holding sway while unscrupulous people have been monopolizing the power. Robber chiefs are called heroes and dead convicts are worshiped as martyrs. Parliament relied on rebels for support while Cabinet Ministers used biased parties as their protection. Unscrupulous borrowing of foreign money is called finance; and bleeding the people is termed revenue-raising. Oppression of innocent people is considered self-government; and defaming old scholars is considered civilization. Some spread rumors under the pretext that they are public opinion while others secretly finance foreigners and call it diplomacy. All these are treason practiced under the fine name of statesmanship, and corruption under the mask of legislation. They even advocate the abolition of Confucianism and thus call down the wrath of God. … In name we are a Republic but nothing is known of

DUAN QIRUI (1864–1936) — A prominent warlord whose power base was centered in Beijing. He served as China's premier during Yuan Shikai's presidency. His later political activities were tainted by his close relationship with Japan, though he continued to be active politically in the Beijing government as well as in the Anhui warlord clique.

ZHANG XUN (1854–1923) — A prominent warlord during China's Republican era and a noted Qing-loyalist known as the "Pigtail General" who attempted to restore the last Qing emperor to the throne in 1917.

the citizens. People are called citizens but they know nothing about their country. Now the people are poor and financial resources exhausted, the foundations of the country begin to shake. All this is the result of the bad form of government.... Look at the matter at its root, we find that Republicanism is the source of all the evil....Compare this with the continuous reign of a monarchy, wherefrom the people may enjoy peace for tens or hundreds of years, the difference is at once seen to be as great as the distance between heaven and earth.... Carefully weighing present conditions and the tendency of the people it is preferable to expel party politics and establish a firm monarchy than to invite ruin by adopting the empty name of a Republic.... Our Emperor, who is in his boyhood, has devoted himself to study and learning to be calm in obedience to the demand of the day. The country has passed many great upheavals but in the palace there has always reigned peace and calm. Recently His Majesty has made marked progress in his sacred studies and his virtuous reputation has spread far and wide. It can thus be seen that Heaven has smiled on the Qing dynasty by conferring His Majesty with unusual wisdom so that he might be able to rise at the proper moment to stop disorder and revert to right.... [Zhang] Xun and others have been accumulating their energy with their weapons near at hand for the last six years.... On this day we have jointly memorialized His Imperial Majesty to again ascend the throne in order to establish the foundation of the country and to consolidate the minds of the people.

7.7 GENERAL WU PEIFU AND OTHER WARLORDS (1924)

By 1924, China's internal hostilities had been ongoing for more than ten years. Articles would periodically appear in the Western press discussing the latest peace proposals. At the time this article was written, Wu Peifu seemed the most likely warlord (or "dujun" as the article refers to them) able to cobble together an alliance between the northern and southern cliques within a government of national unity. Known as the "Scholar General" because of his literary background (he had passed the provincial level *xiucai* degree under the Qing), Wu Peifu appeared by 1924 to have finally brokered an agreement between the major military and political factions. His success prompted *Time* magazine to publish a feature article on China's warlords with Wu Peifu gracing the magazine's cover—the first Chinese ever to appear there. Just weeks after the article was published, one of Wu's allies, Feng Yuxiang, suddenly reversed his military offensive into northeast China and attacked Wu Peifu's army in Beijing. The breakdown of Wu Peifu's alliance with Feng was typical of the period, in that warlords relied on military allegiances forged through weak personal ties rather than alliances based on the construction of coherent political programs. The following document shows both the "score card" mentality needed to keep track of the shifting warlord scene and the growing American interest in Chinese politics.

Questions

1. What area of China seems most affected by the inter-warlord violence?
2. What role does Sun Zhongshan play in the warlord conflict? Did any area escape warlord rule or excesses?

WU PEIFU (c. 1874–1939)—A major figure and leader of the Zhili clique during the Warlord era, often referred to as the "Scholar General." In 1924, Wu was nearly able to broker a peace agreement among the various factions, but ultimately failed. He resisted overtures from both the Guomindang and Japanese during the 1930s and died in suspicious circumstances in 1939.

China was threatened last week by a civil war of considerable size. Troops were massed upon the border between Zhejiang and Jiangsu, two maritime Provinces in the middle of China's long seacoast. Reports were issued to the effect that fighting had started, but no confirmation was obtainable.

Actors

Gen. Wu Peifu, Dujun of Zhili Province. He is the ablest military mind of China. Under his control is the whole north and centre of China, except Manchuria. He is the Lord Protector of Beijing, which is in his province. Although a democrat, he aims at reunifying China by the sword, which policy has brought him into conflict with the Dujun of Manchuria and Dr. Sun Zhongshan, of the South. One of the anomalies of the situation in Beijing is that President Cao Kun was once an enemy of Gen. Wu. At the time Cao Kun was made President of the Chinese Republic, Gen. Wu made no opposition and it was alleged that he had been "bought off." Apart from being a military genius, he is a man of culture, scientific and literary. He studies hard. Recently he began to learn English, employed a tutor, gave him his only spare hour — 4:30 a.m. to 5:30 a.m. He is known as a "man who speaks softly and carries a big stick."

Gen. Qi Xieyuan, Dujun of Jiangsu, friend of Gen. Wu.

Gen. Lu Yongxiang, Dujun of Zhejiang, once military commissioner of Shanghai, an enemy of Gen. Qi. He is about 57 years of age. After he became Dujun of Zhejiang, he had Gen. He Fenglin appointed to the Shanghai post, although Shanghai is not in his Province.

Gen. He Fenglin, Military Commissioner of Shanghai, in the Province of Jiangsu. He is about 47 years of age and is under the influence of Gen. Lu.

*Marshal **Zhang Zuolin,*** Dujun of Manchuria, an avowed Imperialist — that is, a Monarchist. He is a young man of great brains and tremendous power, but no match for Gen. Wu, who once sadly defeated him. Manchuria is about the size of Texas and Colorado, forming enough territory in northern China to make Marshal Zhang's title of War Lord of the North no empty epithet.

The Row

The cause of the present trouble in China centers in Shanghai. So numerous have been the reasons for the rumpus that they have varied with the political complexion of each sinologue interpreter.

The immediate cause is that Gen. Qi wants Shanghai under his thumb. As it is, he thinks the Military Commissioner in Shanghai ought to be a man of his choice. Having tried peacefully to oust Gen. He from the Commissionership, he is now resolved to do it by force, which brings him into conflict with Gen. Lu, who is equally determined to preserve his influence in Shanghai.

The general cause of the dispute is inherent in the political chaos which besets China. The Dujuns, who exercise almost sovereign power in their Provinces, are split up in many factions, due largely to personal jealousies. The immense power which the Dujuns wield is naturally the greatest obstacle to the reunification of China. China as such is internationally little more than a geographical expression. Nothing short of a civil war between the Centre under Gen. Wu, "biggest man in China," the South under Dr. Sun Zhongshan, and the North under Marshal Zhang can ever clear away the political strife which for years has thrown the country into annual turmoil.

Warning

Sir Ronald Macleay, British Minister to China and Acting Dean of the Diplomatic Corps. sent the Chinese Foreign Office a note from the Powers reminding the Government of China that it would be held responsible for loss of life and damage to property of foreign nationals. The note read:

ZHANG ZUOLIN (1875–1928) — Warlord nicknamed the 'Old Marshal' who controlled most of northeast China (Manchuria) from 1916 until 1928 when he was assassinated by a Japanese military forces.

"We, the undersigned representatives of Great Britain, Japan, France, and the United States, learning of the grave danger of hostilities breaking out between the provincial authorities of Jiangsu and Zhejiang, feel it our duty to repeat and reaffirm in the most solemn manner the obligations of the Chinese Government in the present crisis, to prevent loss of life and property to members of the foreign community in and around Shanghai."

Foreign Forces

The principal Powers that are diplomatically represented in Beijing keep military and naval forces in China for the protection of foreigners, who are not subject to the laws of China but to the laws of their own countries, and who are under the jurisdiction of their consulates.

With trouble brewing around Shanghai, ten warships were sent to the harbor to watch over the inhabitants of the city and its outlying area. Rear Admiral David Murray Anderson, of the British Navy, was designated Commander-in-Chief of all foreign vessels: four American, three British, three Japanese.

Peace

It has been said, perhaps too often, that money has frequently stopped a Chinese War. Perhaps with that in view, the Shanghai merchants essayed to bring about agreement between the threatening troops. The chances of success were said to be small.

Attempts were also made to induce both sides to designate a neutral zone surrounding Shanghai. It was not known if they were successful.

7.8 REMEMBERING THE BRUTAL AND CORRUPT WARLORD ZHANG ZONGCHANG (1936)

In an era known for its ruthless behavior, the brutal exploits of Zhang Zongchang, the "Dogmeat General," were conspicuous for their sheer callousness. He ruled as warlord of Shandong province for nearly three years, from 1925 to 1928, and was assassinated in 1932 by the son of a man killed in one of Zhang's assaults. Among his many nicknames was the "Three-Unknowns General," a nickname alluding to rumors that he did not know how many concubines, how many guns, or how much money he possessed, as they were too numerous to count. The following article was published in a Chinese magazine soon after Zhang's death. The editors had publicly invited readers' contributions in describing his evil behavior. The selected vignettes appeared in this column specially designated "The Smelly Tale of the Dead Tiger."

Questions

1. What aspects of Zhang's rule most affected the local populace?
2. To what did the phrase "listening to the telephone" refer?

Early Life of Zhang Zongchang

Zhang Zongchang, often teasingly called the "Dogmeat General" or "Long Legged General," was born in Yexian of Shandong province. His father was a funeral musician and a barber. His mother worked as a traditional healer. At the age of twelve or thirteen, he accompanied his father playing the cymbal. At fifteen or sixteen, he followed his mother to Yingkou [Liaoning Province], working at a gambling house, where he became friendly with a group of thieves. His reputation caught up with him and members of the local gentry drove him out of town. He fled to Manchuria and joined up with the bandits there. His mother remained in Yingkou, living with a public bathhouse owner, a shoe cobbler and an itinerant street merchant of cloth. Out of jealousy, the cloth merchant killed the shoe cobbler and was arrested by the police.

Thus Zhang's mother was washed up. She had no money left so she prostituted herself as payment to a man who drove her back to Yexian where she reunited with the musician. The musician was too poor to support a family so he sold his wife to a grain merchant named Jia. That was why it was known that Zongchang had two fathers.

[. . . .]

Damage to Shandong by Zhang Zongchang (1)

Soon after his arrival in Shandong [1925], he wasted little time to display his true face. Under his 'rule of iron sword' (*gangdao zhengce*), the thriving student associations disappeared and the top students fled. The provincial parliament, which represented the people, was terrified. The clever people turned around quickly and heeded his every whim. "Living in chaos, why not take the opportunity to thrive and divide the profit?" Thus a new wave of people took over as prefects, county commissioners, etc. acting imperious and haughty. The typical lackeys, when they got to their post, exploited the local people and worked hard to extort as much profit as possible in order to please their superiors. Soon all one could see were obese corpulent officials or skinny and emaciated people. The situation reached such extremes that the rich behind their red gates had far too much to eat and drink while emaciated bodies lay by the side of the road. In the three years when Zhang was in power in Shandong, from the day he arrived June of 1925 to the night of April of 1928 when he hastily fled under the cover of darkness, he extorted more than 350,000,000 yuan from the people

[. . . .]

Damage to Shandong by Zhang Zongchang (2)

Heavy taxation—In his nearly four years of control in Shandong, Zhang collected taxes on a daily basis. His method of collection—besides the normal taxes—was to add taxes and then to add tolls. If today he wanted so much money, he would simply write a note to several counties to appropriate the desired amount. Then he would spend it all as he pleased. During that period, the people of Shandong truly lived in deep hardship and their suffering was among the greatest in the country. . . . After the success of the **Northern Expedition** according to the report of provincial department of finance: "From Zhang's arrival until his departure, of all types of taxations that he collected, some had been collected in advance through the year of 1939."

Loans—After Zhang's period of control came to an end. The formal government (under Chen Diaoyuan in 1930) was established. The provincial department of finance reported the following loans given to Zhang Zongchang.

1. Under the auspices of the provincial department of finance Zhang procured loans from the Bank of China (including interest) in the amount of 563,300 yuan; and from the Bank of Transportation, in the amount of 377,000 yuan.
2. The provincial department of finance guaranteed a loan to the provincial bank from the Bank of China in the amount of 283,000 yuan and from the Bank of Transportation in the amount of 283,000 yuan.

[. . . .]

Uncontrolled Distribution of Paper Money—Under his authority, his government printed the following types of currency: 1) a paper script issued in the name of the Bank of Shandong; 2) Military script; 3) Gold-backed Bonds, issued with a total value of several tens of millions without any actual gold backing the true value assigned to the money. Due to military failures, the money often devalued quickly causing further financial disorder. When soldiers used such money in markets, they became very unreasonable and rude. They might beat people up if there was any disagreement. Such fights happened often and caused great hardship on businessmen. It was said that there was a store that refused to accept military script. When Zhang heard of it, he ordered the owner arrested and had him tortured and finally executed.

NORTHERN EXPEDITION (1926–1927)—A military campaign led by Jiang Jieshi and the Guomindang (Nationalists) in 1926 that began in southern China and advanced northward reuniting much of eastern China. It brought an end to the worst of the warlord excesses—often by simply co-opting the warlords into Jiang's government.

Firing Cannon towards the Sky—In summer of 1927 there was an extended drought and all the crops dried up in the fields. Zhang issued an order that forbid butchering any animal. He then personally conducted a prayer at the Dragon King Temple for water, which failed. Incensed, Zhang shook his fists towards the Dragon King and later ordered the cannons at the Zhangzhuang fort be fired towards the sky every couple of hours to express his anger towards the heaven. The rains still did not come.

Public Sale of Opium—Zhang ordered that opium be allowed to be sold publicly. There were opportunists who opened opium shops on the second floor of the newly built commercial building in Baotu

Fountain district [Jinan city], and dubbed it the "Quit Smoking Shop." Opium sales taxes were paid directly to Zhang monthly.

Drafting Soldiers—In Jinan, under Zhang's regime, people would commonly be arrested on the street and sent directly to the military front. There they often ended up being killed. During that period, pedestrians on the street were under constant threat of being 'drafted' in this manner. The captured ones were all healthy men. Students from school were often detained and could only be released after negotiations to have them released. To prevent such incidents, schools made a special cloth badge pinned to their chest for students to wear with their names and school's official stamp in order to distinguish them from the non-students.

MAY FOURTH MOVEMENT

As the military and political crises deepened, intellectually charged movements arose. These movements advocated publicly for a unified response by China's fragmented political and military leaders. The **May Fourth Movement** is best understood as a popular movement unified by a desire to *intellectually* redefine China's traditional culture and society, even its language (7.11). The catalysts for these changes were varied, such as the humiliating political and economic demands imposed on China by Japan, the demeaning treatment China received in the Versailles settlement of World War One, and the debilitating effect of the rampant Warlord militarism (7.9). The May Fourth Movement, though a response to these kinds of external pressures, was first and foremost an internal, intellectual movement that sought to alter what it meant for anything or anyone to be Chinese. Journals such as *New Youth,* intellectuals such as **Chen Duxiu,** and literary figures like Lu Xun were all part of a broad public dialogue that sought to reshape the basic building blocks of Chinese society. This dialogue covered political ideology, literature, and the composition of Chinese "national essence" (*guocui*). In many of the following documents we see the political, social and cultural seeds of China's future, though the context in which these events took place gave little evidence of their eventual success.

MAY FOURTH MOVEMENT—A movement narrowly defined as events sparked by the student-led demonstrations of May 4, 1919 against the Treaty of Versailles. More often it is used to identify the broad intellectual and cultural transformations that took place after Japan's Twenty-One Demands (1915) lasting well into the 1920s.

CHEN DUXIU (1880–1942)—A gifted May Fourth intellectual who helped launch and edit *New Youth* in 1915, was appointed as Dean to the School of Arts at Beijing University in 1917, and was a founding member and first party secretary of the Chinese Communist Party in 1921.

NEW CULTURE MOVEMENT (c. 1917–1923)—A movement roughly equivalent to the "May Fourth Movement," though some suggest the New Culture Movement indicates a more "thought" oriented movement compared to the "action" agenda of the May Fourth Movement. The conflation of the terms has made them interchangeable in popular discourse.

7.9 JAPAN'S TWENTY-ONE DEMANDS (JANUARY 18TH, 1915)

On January 18, 1915, Eki Hoiki, the Japanese minister in Beijng, handed President Yuan Shikai the following list of twenty-one demands grouped into five sections. The timing of the demands took full advantage of Great Britain's recent entrance into the First World War. The Japanese calculated that Britain would be hard pressed to hold Japan to the terms of the Anglo-Japanese Alliance of 1905 which stated that both countries would be bound to the "preservation of the ... independence, and integrity of the Chinese Empire." On May 7, the Japanese minister presented an ultimatum including a revised series of demands (in particular the postponement of the demands in Group 5 (see below) and the threat that if these terms were not accepted within 48 hours the Japanese government would "take such steps as they deem necessary." The next day, Yuan Shikai accepted the demands and on May 25, 1915 he officially signed treaties and diplomatic notes acknowledging China's assent to the terms. His acceptance set off a furor and sparked popular anti-Japanese movements throughout China.

Questions

1. Rank the five groups of demands into what you surmise China (and the Chinese people) found most to least objectionable?
2. In what ways are Japan's twenty-one demands similar or different from the unequal treaties China was forced to sign with Western powers during the nineteenth century (Chapter 4)?

GROUP I

The Japanese Government and the Chinese Government being desirous of maintaining the general peace in Eastern Asia and further strengthening the friendly relations and good neighborhood existing between the two nations agree to the following articles:

ARTICLE 1—The Chinese Government engages to give full assent to all matters upon which the Japanese Government may hereafter agree with the German Government relating to the disposition of all rights, interests and concessions which Germany, by virtue of treaties or otherwise, possesses in relation to the province of Shandong.

ARTICLE 2—The Chinese Government engages that within the Province of Shandong and along its coast, no territory or island will be ceded or leased to a third power under any pretext.

ARTICLE 3—The Chinese government consents to Japan's building a railway from Yantai or Longkou to join the Jiaozhou-Jinanfu Railway.

ARTICLE 4—The Chinese Government engages in interest of trade and for the residence of foreigners, to open by herself as soon as possible certain important cities and towns in the province of Shandong as commercial ports. What places shall be opened are to be jointly decided upon in a separate agreement.

GROUP II

The Japanese government and the Chinese government, since the Chinese government has always acknowledged the special position enjoyed by Japan in South Manchuria and Eastern Inner Mongolia, agree to the following articles:

ARTICLE 1—The two contracting parties mutually agree that the term of lease of Port Arthur

[Lüshun] and Dalian and the term of lease of the South Manchurian Railway and the Andong-Shenyang Railway shall be extended to the period of 99 years.

ARTICLE 2—Japanese subjects in South Manchuria and Eastern Inner Mongolia shall have the right to lease or own land required either for erecting suitable buildings for trade and manufacture or for farming.

ARTICLE 3—Japanese subjects shall be free to reside and travel in South Manchuria and Eastern Inner Mongolia and to engage in business and in manufacture of any kind whatsoever.

ARTICLE 4—The Chinese government agrees to grant to Japanese subjects the right of opening the mines in South Manchuria and Eastern Inner Mongolia. As regards what mines are to be opened, they shall be decided upon jointly.

ARTICLE 5—The Chinese government agrees that in respect of the (two) cases mentioned herein below the Japanese Government's consent shall be first obtained before action is taken:

a. Whenever permission is granted to the subject of a third power to build a railway or to make a loan with a third power for the purpose of building a railway in South Manchuria and Eastern Inner Mongolia.
b. Whenever a loan is to be made with a third power pledging the local taxes of South Manchuria and Eastern Inner Mongolia as security.

ARTICLE 6—The Chinese government agrees that if the Chinese Government employs political, financial or military advisers or instructors in South Manchuria or Eastern Inner Mongolia, the Japanese government shall first be consulted.

ARTICLE 7—The Chinese government agrees that the control and management of the Jilin-Changchun shall be handed over to the Japanese government for terms of 99 years dating from the signing of this agreement.

GROUP III

The Japanese government and the Chinese government, seeing that Japanese financiers and the Hanyeping Co.

have close relations with each other at present and desiring that common interests of the two nations shall be advanced, agree to the following articles:

ARTICLE 1—The two contracting parties mutually agree that when the opportune moment arrives the Hanyeping Company shall be made a joint concern of the two nations and they further agree that without the previous consent of Japan China shall not by her own act dispose of the rights and property of whatsoever nature of the said company nor cause the said company to dispose freely of the same.

ARTICLE 2—The Chinese government agrees that all mines in the neighborhood of those owned by the Hanyeping Company shall not be permitted, without the consent of the said Company, to be worked by other persons outside of the said Company; and further agrees that if it is desired to carry out any undertaking which, it is apprehended, may directly or indirectly affect the interests of the said Company, the consent of the said Company shall first be obtained.

GROUP IV

The Japanese government and the Chinese government with the object of effectively preserving the territorial integrity of China agree to the following special article:

The Chinese government engages not to cede or lease to a third power any harbor or bay or island along the coast of China.

GROUP V

ARTICLE 1—The Chinese Central Government shall employ influential Japanese as advisers in political, financial and military affairs.

ARTICLE 2—Japanese hospitals, churches and schools in the interior of China shall be granted the right of owning land.

ARTICLE 3—Inasmuch as the Japanese Government and the Chinese Government have had many cases of dispute between Japanese and Chinese police which caused no little misunderstanding, it is for this reason necessary that the police departments of important places (in China) shall be jointly administered by

Japanese and Chinese or that the police departments of these places shall employ numerous Japanese, so that they may at the same time help to plan for the improvement of the Chinese Police Service.

ARTICLE 4 — China shall purchase from Japan a fixed amount of munitions of war (say 50 percent or more of what is needed by the Chinese government) or that there shall be established in China a Sino-Japanese jointly worked arsenal. Japanese technical experts are to be employed and Japanese material to be purchased.

ARTICLE 5 — China agrees to grant to Japan the right of constructing a railway connecting Wuchang with Jiujiang and Nanchang, another line between Nanchang and Hangzhou, and another between Nanchang and Chaozhou.

ARTICLE 6 — If China needs foreign capital to work mines, build railways and construct harborworks (including dockyards) in the Province of Fujian, Japan shall be first consulted.

ARTICLE 7 — China agrees that Japanese subjects shall have the right of missionary propaganda in China.

7.10 MAY FOURTH MANIFESTO (MAY 4, 1919)

China, like many non-Western European nations, had placed considerable confidence in President Wilson's Fourteen Points. Many non-Western countries took Wilson's Fourteen Points to mean he advocated equality among all nations in the World War One peace proceedings at Versailles outside of Paris. When word finally reached China that Germany's holdings would be given to Japan instead of reverting to Chinese control, public outrage boiled over. Students in Beijing took to the streets to protest the peace negotiations. One of the student leaders, Luo Jialun, wrote the following manifesto which was the only publication printed that day. The demonstration by today's standards was small—only 3,000 students from Beijing's thirteen colleges. However the impact was immediate and sparked a countrywide reaction against the treaty and against Japan. The Treaty of Versailles, formally signed eight months after the war's end in June 28, 1919, did not include China's signature.

Questions

1. **At what target is the anger of the May Fourth demonstrations directed?**
2. **What political and military contingencies (within China) made it difficult for the Chinese (Beijing) government to oppose the Versailles Peace Treaty?**

At the Paris Peace Conference, Japan's request to occupy and control Shandong, is about to be granted! Their diplomacy has triumphed completely while ours has failed utterly! The loss of Shandong can only denote the end of China's territorial integrity. The end of China's territorial integrity can only mean China is done for! Therefore today, we, the students, form a procession and demonstrate in front of every embassy of every country, and demand that they defend justice. We hope people in industry, business and every walk of life all over the country will hold citizens meetings to fight; internationally for China's sovereignty, and domestically to rid the country of traitors. China's survival depends on this next move! Today we take two oaths with all our fellow countrymen:

China's territory can be conquered, but not given away!

The Chinese people may be killed, but they will not submit!

The country will be lost! Fellow citizens, rise up!

7.11 CHEN DUXIU'S "NEW YOUTH" MANIFESTO (DECEMBER 1, 1919)

The leading journal of the May Fourth Movement was *New Youth* (*Xin Qingnian*). Founded in 1915, it was in the vanguard of an intellectual movement promoting science, vernacular Chinese literature, and an often leftist political ideology. In late 1919 the journal issued a novel and idealistic manifesto, which captured the rapidly shifting political mood in China. This was unlike anything it had printed before. Among other things, this manifesto exhibited a far more radical attitude towards political parties than had been previously published. It captured the sharp shift in thought that transpired in the post-May Fourth period, and it asserted that Chinese citizens must begin to participate in political change.

> **Questions**
> 1. Who in 1919 would disagree that "politics, ethnic science, the arts, religion, and education should meet all practical needs... for present and future social life"?
> 2. What is the editorial's final paragraph suggesting? Why?

We believe that the moral progress of mankind should expand to a standard above the life based on animal impulse (i.e., aggressive and possessive); therefore, we should extend a feeling of friendship and mutual assistance to all peoples of the world. But toward aggressive and possessive warlords and plutocrats, we have to be hostile.

We advocate mass movement and social reconstruction, absolutely cutting off any relations with past and present political parties.

Although we do not believe in the omnipotence of politics, we recognize that politics is an important aspect of public life. And we believe that in a genuine democracy, political rights must be distributed to all the people. Even though there may be limitations, the criteria for the distribution will be whether they work or not, rather than whether they own property or not. This kind of politics is really inevitable in the process of introducing the new era and a useful instrument for the development of the new society. As for political parties,

we also recognize them as a necessary device for political practice, but we shall never tolerate membership in parties that support the interests of the few or of one class rather than the happiness of the whole society.

We believe that politics, ethics, science, the arts, religion, and education should all meet practical needs in the achievement of progress for present and future social life.

We have to give up the useless and irrelevant elements of traditional literature and ethics, because we want to create those needed for the progress of the new era and new society.

We believe that it is requisite for the progress of our present society to uphold natural science and pragmatic philosophy and to abolish superstition and fantasy.

We believe that to respect women's personality and rights is a practical need for the social progress at present, and we hope that they themselves will be completely aware of their duty to society.

[....]

7.12 LU XUN'S CALL TO ARMS (DECEMBER 3, 1922)

No single literary figure more accurately captured the mood, aspirations, and musings of the May Fourth era than **Lu Xun** (1881–1936). Still revered in China today (especially

LU XUN (1881–1936)—A prominent twentieth-century Chinese author, a major proponent of vernacular (*baihua*) literature, and a major figure in the May Fourth Movement in 1919. While leftist in his political thought he never joined the CCP.

for his sardonic tale of a village idiot in "The True Story of A Q"), Lu Xun actively pushed his leftist agenda in his writings. His clear affinity with the lower classes and his ability to capture the choices facing all Chinese in his writings transcended standard political divisions. The following excerpt is taken from his preface to a collection of short stories entitled *Call to Arms*. The autobiographical themes he describes would have resonated among many of the May Fourthers and with the growing numbers of politically disaffected Chinese.

Questions

1. **From his preface can you deduce why Lu Xun entitled his collected works *Call to Arms*?**
2. **What are the parallels between the "iron house" metaphor and the May Fourth generation?**

When I was young I, too, had many dreams. Most of them I later forgot, but I see nothing in this to regret. For although recalling the past may bring happiness, at times it cannot but bring loneliness, and what is the point of clinging in spirit to lonely bygone days? However, my trouble is that I cannot forget completely, and these stories stem from those things which I have been unable to forget.

For more than four years I frequented, almost daily, a pawnshop and pharmacy. I cannot remember how old I was at the time but the pharmacy counter was exactly my height and that in the pawnshop twice my height. I used to hand clothes and trinkets up to the counter twice my height, then take the money given me with contempt to the counter my own height to buy medicine for my father, a chronic invalid. On my return home I had other things to keep me busy, for our physician was so eminent that he prescribed unusual drugs and adjuvants: aloe roots dug up in winter, sugar-cane that had been three years exposed to frost, original pairs of crickets, and an ardisia [shrub] that had seeded ... most of which were difficult to come by. But my father's illness went from bad to worse until he died.

It is my belief that those who come down in the world will probably learn in the process what society is really like. My eagerness to go to N—and study in the K—seems to have shown a desire to strike out for myself, escape, and find people of a different kind. My mother had no choice but to raise eight dollars for my traveling expenses and say I might do as I pleased. That she cried was only natural, for at that time the proper thing was to study the classics and take the official examinations. Anyone who studied "foreign subjects" was a social outcast regarded as

someone who could find no way out and was forced to sell his soul to foreign devils. Besides, she was sorry to part with me. But in spite of all this, I went to N— (**translator's note:** Nanjing) and entered the K—Academy (**translator's note:** Jiangnan Naval Academy where author studies in 1898); and it was there that I learned of the existence of physics, arithmetic, geography, history, drawing and physical training. They had no physiology course, but we saw woodblock editions of such works as *A New Course on the Human Body* and *Essays on Chemistry and Hygiene*. Recalling the talk and prescriptions of physicians I had known and comparing them with what I now knew, I came to the conclusion that those physicians must be either unwitting or deliberate charlatans; and I began to feel great sympathy for the invalids and families who suffered at their hands. From translated histories I also learned that the Japanese Reformation owed its rise, to a great extent, to the introduction of Western medical science to Japan.

These inklings took me to a medical college in the Japanese countryside. It was my fine dream that on my return to China I would cure patients like my father who had suffered from the wrong treatment, while if war broke out I would serve as an army doctor, at the same time promoting my countrymen's faith in reform.

I have no idea what improved methods are now used to teach microbiology, but in those days we were shown lantern slides of microbes; and if the lecture ended early, the instructor might show slides of natural scenery or news to fill up the time. Since this was during the Russo-Japanese War, there were many war slides, and I had to join in the clapping and cheering in the lecture hall along with the other students. It was a long time since I had seen any compatriots, but one day I saw a news-reel slide of a number of Chinese, one of them bound and the rest standing around him. They were all sturdy fellows but appeared completely apathetic. According to the commentary, the one with his hands bound was a spy working for the Russians who was to be beheaded by the Japanese military as a warning to others, while the Chinese beside him had come to enjoy the spectacle.

Before the term was over I had left for Tokyo, because this slide convinced me that medical science was not so important after all. The people of a weak and backward country, however strong and healthy they might be, could only serve to be made examples of or as witnesses of such futile spectacles; and it was not necessarily deplorable if many of them died of illness. The most important thing, therefore, was to change their spirit; and since at that time I felt that literature was the best means to this end, I decided to promote a literary movement. There were many Chinese students in Tokyo studying law, political science, physics and chemistry, even police work and engineering, but not one studying literature and art. However, even in this uncongenial atmosphere I was fortunate enough to find some kindred spirits. We gathered the few others we needed and after discussion our first step, of course, was to publish a magazine, the title of which denoted that this was a new birth. As we were then rather classically inclined, we called it *Vita Nova* (New Life).

When the time for publication drew near, some of our contributors dropped out and then our funds ran out, until there were only three of us left and we were penniless. Since we had started our venture at an unlucky hour, there was naturally no one to whom we could complain when we failed; but later even we three were destined to part, and our discussions of a future dream world had to cease. So ended this abortive *Vita Nova*.

Only later did I feel the futility of it all. At that time I had not a clue. Later it seemed to me that if a man's proposals met with approval, that should encourage him to advance; if they met with opposition, that should make him fight back; but the real tragedy was for him to lift up his voice among the living and meet with no response, neither approval nor opposition, just as if he were stranded in a boundless desert completely at a loss. That was when I became conscious of loneliness.

And this sense of loneliness grew from day to day, entwining itself about my soul like some huge poisonous snake.

But in spite of my groundless sadness, I felt no indignation; for this experience had made me reflect and see that I was definitely not the type of hero who could rally multitudes at his call.

However, my loneliness had to be dispelled because it was causing me agony. So I used various means to dull my senses, to immerse myself among my fellow nationals and to turn to the past. Later I experienced or witnessed even greater loneliness and sadness which I am unwilling to recall, preferring that it should perish with my mind in the dust. Still my attempt to deaden my senses was not unsuccessful—I lost the enthusiasm and fervor of my youth.

In S—Hostel was a three-roomed house with a courtyard in which grew a locust tree, and it was said that a woman had hanged herself there. Although the tree had grown so tall that its branches were now out of reach, the rooms remained deserted. For some years I stayed here, copying ancient inscriptions. I had few visitors, the inscriptions raised no political problems or issues, and so the days slipped quietly away, which was all that I desired. On summer nights, when mosquitoes swarmed, I would sit under the locust tree waving my fan and looking at specks of blue sky through chinks in the thick foliage, while belated caterpillars would fall, icy-cold, on to my neck.

The only visitor to drop in occasionally for a talk was my old friend Jin Xinyi. Having put his big portfolio on the rickety table he would take off his long gown and sit down opposite me, looking as if his heart was still beating fast because he was afraid of dogs.

"What's the use of copying these?" One night, while leafing through the inscriptions I had copied, he asked me for enlightenment on this point.

"There isn't any use."

"What's the point, then, of copying them?"

"There isn't any point."

"Why don't you write something? ..."

I understood. They were bringing out *New Youth*, but since there did not seem to have been any reaction, favorable or otherwise, no doubt they felt lonely. However I said:

"Imagine an iron house having not a single window and virtually indestructible, with all its inmates sound asleep and about to die of suffocation. Dying in their sleep, they won't feel the pain of death. Now if you raise a shout to wake a few of the lighter sleepers, making these unfortunate few suffer the agony of irrevocable death, do you really think you are doing them a good turn?"

"But if a few wake up, you can't say there is no hope of destroying the iron house."

True, in spite of my own conviction, I could not blot out hope, for hope belongs to the future. I had no negative evidence able to refute his affirmation of faith. So I finally agreed to write, and the result was my first story "A Madman's Diary." And once started I could not give up but would write some sort of short story from time to time to humor my friends, until I had written more than a dozen of them.

As far as I am concerned, I no longer feel any great urge to express myself; yet, perhaps because I have not forgotten the grief of my past loneliness, I sometimes call out to encourage those fighters who are galloping on in loneliness, so that they do not lose heart. Whether my cry is brave or sad, repellent or ridiculous, I do not care. However, since this is a call to arms I must naturally obey my general's orders. This is why I often resort to innuendoes, as when I made a wreath appear from nowhere at the son's grave in "Medicine," while in "Tomorrow" I did not say the Fourth Shan's Wife never dreamed of her little boy. For our chiefs in those days were against pessimism. And I, for my part, did not want to infect with the loneliness which I had found so bitter those young people who were still dreaming pleasant dreams, just as I had done when young.

It is clear, then, that my stories fall far short of being works of art; hence I must at least count myself fortunate that they are still known as stories and are even being brought out in one volume. Although such good fortune makes me uneasy, it still pleases me to think that they have readers in the world of men, for the time being at any rate.

So now that these stories of mine are being reprinted in one collection, for the reasons given above I have chosen to entitle it *Call to Arms*.

Beijing
December 3, 1922

7.13 HU SHI'S LITERARY REVOLUTION AND RENAISSANCE IN CHINA (1926)

While it is possible to see the May Fourth Movement in largely political terms, it is important to recognize its diverse intellectual dimensions as well. **Hu Shi**'s aggressive promotion of the "vernacular movement" is one of his greatest legacies. Many intellectuals sought to promote a written language that reflected the spoken language (*baihua*). Up until this point, the bulk of the written literature was "classical Chinese" which differed considerably from the type of Chinese spoken on the street. The foremost proponent of this linguistic revolution was Hu Shi. Educated in the United States on a Boxer Indemnity scholarship, Hu Shi returned to China in 1917 and became a prominent philosophical force among intellectuals. Although liberal in thought, Hu Shi's focus on language reform put him at odds with the socialists and anarchists that dominated many of the May Fourth groups. By the time he delivered this talk he had become a strong supporter of the **Guomindang** (calling it the "only political party worthy of the name"). His talk offers a forthright assessment of the challenges China faced in the first two decades of the twentieth century.

HU SHI (1891–1962)—Born in Shanghai and educated at Cornell University with funds from the Boxer Indemnity Scholarship Program, he returned to China to become a leading intellectual luminary, in particular advocating vernacular Chinese. Hu Shi supported the GMD and in 1949 retreated to Taiwan where he became the president of the Academia Sinica.

GUOMINDANG (NATIONALIST PARTY)—The party founded by Sun Zhongshan in 1912 after the founding of the Republic of China. It ruled China from 1928 until 1949. Defeated by the CCP, it retreated to Taiwan where it remains an important political force.

Questions

1. **In what ways does Hu Shi argue that language is the foundation of the "Chinese Renaissance?"**
2. **Why would Hu Shi's emphasis on vernacular reform be such a key step in altering China's education system?**

In 1914, 1915, and 1916 there was an all-pervading sense of despair. A number of young men committed suicide because they could think of no way out, could see no ray of light ahead. It was not like those last years of the Manchu Dynasty, when people knew that somewhere and some time a rebellion would come. Now it had come, had been swept out of the path and had left only depression and despair. One of my young friends jumped into the West Lake at Hangzhou, leaving letters of farewell to his friends expressing his joy at escape from a situation without hope. In those years people began at last to realize the futility of superficial political change, and to seek some new factor which could be made the corner-stone of a new age.

May I read to you an extract from a letter of Huang Yuanyong, one of the leading publicists of the day, written just before leaving the country in 1915 at the height of Yuan Shikai's power. "Politics are in such confusion that I am at a loss to know what to talk about. Ideal schemes will have to be buried for future generations to unearth .... As to fundamental salvation, I believe its beginning must be sought in the promotion of a *new literature*. We must endeavor to bring Chinese thought into contact with the contemporary thought of the world and thus accelerate its radical awakening. And we must see to it that the basic ideals of the modern world produce some direct effect upon the life of the average man. The method seems to lie in using simple language and literature for the wide dissemination of ideas among the people. Have we not seen that historians regard the European Renaissance as the foundation of the overthrow of medievalism in Europe?"

[....]

It was at that time that the new movement began which forms the title and topic of my address tonight. In the years 1915 and 1916 groups of Chinese students in American universities were carrying on a controversy on problems of literature. The results of the controversy were published in the early days of 1917, and formed the first declarations of a movement which has created a revolution in Chinese literature. This literary revolution marks the first stage in the Chinese Renaissance, for here will be found a spirit essentially different from the earlier stages of modernization.... We have realized at last that certain things must be given up if China is to live. If we really want education, general and universal education, we must first have a new language, a language which can be used and understood by tongue and ear and pen, and which will be a living language for the people. For years and years we tried to have education, but we feared to use the spoken language. We tried to compromise in various ways, but we clung as scholars to the scholarly language. It was impossible to preach a language, to ask people to accept a language, which was not good enough for us. China went through a stage of contradictions and remained unconscious of the fact.

At last the new movement began in earnest, the Literary Revolution. It advocates the adoption of the spoken language, the vulgar tongue of the people, as the lay medium for all official and literary composition. Its aim is to elevate the despised vulgar tongue of the people to the dignified position of the literary language of the nation. It is a revolution in a sense because it has involved a reassessment of the vulgar literature of the past and of the classical tradition. It seeks to introduce the spoken language of the people as the medium of expression in all textbooks, in all the newspapers, in all the respectable branches of literature.

[....]

This Literary Revolution formed the first phase of the Chinese Renaissance. It marked a new phase, a new life. It was not a complete breaking from the past, it was an historical development; it was a conscious effort to make articulate all the valuable elements we already possessed. At the same time the methods were modern, the inspirations were modern. It thus presented to the people a new and living idea.

As language is the most important vehicle of thought and of expression, any radical and fundamental change in a national language could not but involve a great change in a national language, could not but involve a great change in other phases of social and intellectual life. So during the past ten years, this

Literary Revolution has spread and has affected various phases of Chinese life. I shall not describe those different phases in great detail. I shall confine myself to two particular phases: first, the intellectual changes, and secondly, the social and political developments.

However multifarious these tendencies may seem, there are certain general characteristics which unite them more or less into one great National Movement. The whole movement may be characterized, in the words of Nietzsche, as a movement of the transvaluation of all values. It is a movement in a way to make everything upside down; to try to judge, to criticize, to doubt, to revalue old things according to new standards. Nothing is too high or too low to be subjected to this process of transvaluation. Marriage, concubinage, widowhood, Confucianism, Christianity—nothing is too sacred to be allowed to pass without criticism. It is for us an age of doubt, of criticism, of protest.

CHAPTER 8
CHINA IN THE TWENTIES: THE STRUGGLE FOR UNITY

VISUAL SOURCE
Selling a New Image of 1920s China: Chinese Advertisements

GONGPING TOBACCO POSTER: China Gongping Tobacco Company (top) Hoping that our fellow citizens will try to promote (right) Smoking only domestic tobacco (left) A Top Quality, Low Price Product (bottom)

NATIONAL GOODS CAMPAIGN: In the 1920s boycotts against foreign (particularly Japanese) goods became increasingly common. In 1925 a "national goods campaign" sought to promote Chinese products over foreign goods. In order to boost their own sales (over foreign competition) Chinese companies often prominently included references to the campaign in their own ads. Some scholars have shown however that such overt use of patriotism in the advertisements was highly suspect given the integrated nature of the global economic system and the difficulty of determining the exact "national" content of any product.

1920s ADVERTISING: By the 1920s, there existed three primary types of print advertising in Republican China: wall posters, wall calendars, and in newspapers. The posters and calendars were often given away to clients and would often serve as an inexpensive way to embellish the home, stores, or office. Chinese newspapers looked quite different from the typical modern western papers since advertisements often exceeded 60% of the paper's total content (and much of the cover page).

CORPORATE ADVERTISERS: The main advertisers in 1920s China tended to be tobacco, cosmetic, and chemical companies. These companies often had their own team of artists, painters, and draftsmen who worked full time producing an array of ads. The two advertisements here are typical both in the sponsorship and the fact that the products themselves (and even the trademarks) are visually marginalized within the advertisement.

1920s Advertisement for Gongping Tobacco Company

c. 1930 Advertisement for BM & Company (Buneimen) Fertilizer

BUNEIMEN FERTILIZER: Please use Buneimen Fertilizer! (top) Emei Yue Brand sulfate fertilizers works well on all types of plants (right) An excellent Emei Brand fertilizer, An abundant Harvest and Good Profit (left)

WOMEN IN ADVERTISING: Stylish young women figured prominently in 1920s advertisements regardless if the product's target audience was women or not. Ads that featured young faddish women underscore the fact that femininity became a defining feature of modernity in 20th century China. Companies were seeking to use these pictures of "liberated" women to promote themselves as progressive and proponents of a new age.

CHINESE OR FOREIGN?: Similar to advertisers today, advertising companies sought to create ads that promoted their product but remained as socially neutral as possible. In the 1920s, the notion of a product being foreign remained sensitive. Among more conservative segments of society many products were still viewed as foreign and not Chinese. Products such as matches, cigarettes, makeup, and chemical fertilizer in a traditional context all were categorized as non-Chinese. To counteract this potentially negative connotation when advertising such products, advertisers commonly mixed modern with traditional Chinese themes as in the fertilizer advertisement.

Sober obituaries announcing the death of another Communist Party octogenarian appear with some frequency in China's daily newspapers. But in the summer of 2005, the obituary of Gu Yue (1937–2005) was unusually emotional and reverent. Not a typical party minion, Gu Yue had made a career as an actor starring as one man, Mao Zedong, China's most famous revolutionary leader. A household name (even if a second-rate actor), Gu Yue appeared in over eighty movies and television series and, aside from one or two forgettable exceptions, always as Mao. The obituaries inevitably commented on Gu Yue's uncanny ability to capture Mao's unique Hunan accent, mimic his body language, and of course Mao's distinctive receding hairline. Although Gu was the first, and arguably the most famous, of the Mao impersonators, today there exists a stable of twenty or so actors who make a living off their resemblance to Mao and other top Chinese leaders from the past. These Chinese-leader look-alikes, aside from appearing in feature films and television series, are available for hire to appear at factory openings, large conferences and variety shows where even an ersatz version of a famous leader lends a veneer of credibility.

As the prominent and reverent coverage of his death suggests, Gu Yue and his fellow impersonators are perceived in an entirely different light than that of Western impersonators such as the scathing lampooning of political leaders on NBC's *Saturday Night Live* or the kitschy Las Vegas-style Elvis impersonators. Their representation of the political leader is done without any irony, humor, or psychological depth. In this way, Gu Yue is similar to the interchangeable World War II movies that John Wayne starred in where the enemy (German or Japanese) was less a realistic depiction of that country than a one-dimensional foil to depict the United State's own heroic view of itself. The difference of course is that Gu Yue starred repeatedly as Mao, seriously eroding the separation of fiction and reality. The cinematic versions of Mao's life create a type of selective pastiche. Actors like Gu Yue play a crucial part since their physical resemblance adds a layer of authenticity or verisimilitude to the past. That is to say, they also cover up the messy side of history. And without a doubt the history of 1920s China was messy.

Cinematic representation of Chinese Communist earlier years is particularly fraught with problems. As should be clear from the previous chapter, the Chinese Communist Party emerged as a political force in the 1920s, deeply influenced by the intellectual ferment of the May Fourth Movement. Yet, unlike the many films in which Gu Yue featured, the success of the CCP was hardly assured. More specifically, the victory of the CCP was the result of a series of unforeseeable events. When examining any event in the 1920s, it is imperative to remember the broad array of challenges facing China. There are at least four distinct factors any analysis should take into consideration: 1) China's emergent political parties, 2) the continuing control of warlords over most of China up until 1927, 3) the explicit and implicit threat of Japanese diplomatic and military actions, and 4) the global post-World War I economic depression. The intricacy of each of these factors makes tracing the historical trajectory of China in this period extremely awkward.

The presence of such contingencies is central to any understanding of 1920s China period. Given the cultural, political, and military complexity of this era it is tempting to adopt the notion of historical inevitability in order to make a path through the confusing array of competing events. Is it inevitable that the Communists would emerge from the 1920s as a major alternative to the Nationalists? Can we reduce the events of the 1920s and 1930s to a stepping-stone that lead only to an invasion of Japanese onto Chinese soil? One antidote to these and other narratives of Republican China is to attempt to view the array of possible paths from the viewpoint of Chinese of the period (or conversely try and imagine the diversity of Chinese viewpoints of the period: peasant, urban worker, soldier, etc.).

For example, few Chinese during the 1920s and early 1930s could have even told you the main political goals of the CCP, let alone be able to list their top leaders. Indeed, far more meaningful to most Chinese in this period was whether you were a "revolutionary" at all. To most Chinese, the revolutionaries occupied such a small portion of the political stage there was little point in distinguishing between anarchists, communists, socialists, and the newly emergent Nationalists (except obviously for those participants active in such movements). In the 1920s, the average Chinese citizen, regardless of their ideology, agreed on the major issues facing China. Virtually every political party was anti-imperialist (usually meaning anti-Western imperialist), anti-feudalist (generally interpreted to mean anti-warlord), and anti-Japanese. The prominent sentiment of 1920s China then is one of uncertainty, questioning the past, but unsure of what road China should follow to shed the nation of the numerous afflictions it suffered. The success of the Russian Revolution in 1917 led the new government to give up all holdings in China making a positive impression on many Chinese (though in reality Russia would go back on such promises). Japan, on the other hand, appeared just as intent on pursuing its own interests in China.

What emerges as the most prominent characteristic of the period is a vast number of false-starts, missteps, and political adjustments which coexisted with an idealism, intuitiveness, and sheer willfulness that belied the circumstances. Or put much more simply, China in the 1920s is far more about the complexities (and even the failed efforts) rather than the ideologies themselves.

ORIGINS OF THE CCP

In the 1920s, many aspects of Marxism appealed to Chinese revolutionaries across the political spectrum. On a theoretical level, it offered a unified framework to resolve the social, political and economic predicaments that faced China. On a practical level, the success of the Russian Revolution and the formation of the Soviet Union only years earlier offered hope to many Chinese that China would benefit from Marxist revolution. Yet, when Chinese communists began to apply the Marxist model to Chinese conditions several problems emerged. Marxism's emphasis on an alienated industrial working class simply had little traction in a country that remained overwhelmingly agrarian. Famously, Marx once referred to peasants as like a "sack of potatoes" unable to throw off their oppressors. Or, put another way, attempting to start a revolution with peasants as your primary revolutionary catalyst was a non-starter. As a result, an early point of contention among the Chinese Communists revolved around whether the CCP should focus its diminutive resources on the urban centers or concentrate on the rural countryside.

Regardless of what Marx speculated, the CCP's most striking successes occurred in their peasant movements while their stunning defeats uniformly took place in the urban centers. Marxist theory offered little guidance for an agrarian-based revolution and the USSR **Comintern** advisors tended to disparage such efforts as misguided. The CCP experience in the 1920s and early 1930s comes across as a bit confused with several branches of the party some more active in the cities with other active in the countryside. Yet with the Guomindang party strongest in the cities, the CCP had more success in the countryside.

COMINTERN—Founded in Moscow in 1919, the Comintern (short for Communist International) played a guiding role in the global Communist movement, including China.

8.1 FIRST MANIFESTO OF THE CCP ON THE CURRENT SITUATION (JUNE 15, 1922)

The spring of 1922 was a confusing period for the CCP. Chinese Communists were intensely interested in the emerging international leadership taken on by the Soviet Union. In particular, many Chinese were inclined to view the Soviet government favorably since the **Karakahan Manifesto** (1919) renounced all of Russia's unequal treaties with China. However, there existed considerable dissension among the Chinese Communist Party over Soviet Union's directive for all Chinese Communists to join Sun Zhongshan's Guomindang (GMD) government. Specifically, many argued that the GMD with its plan to establish alliances with warlords and form an army to unify China the GMD differed little from the warlords themselves. Under pressure from the Comintern representative, the CCP agreed to the notion of an alliance with the GMD whereby communists on an individual level could join the GMD. The following declaration is the first public CCP pronouncement adhering to the notion that the Guomindang can be considered "revolutionary."

Questions

1. What positive attributes does the CCP ascribe to the GMD?
2. How do they describe the warlord situation? How do they suggest it be resolved?

The struggle for democracy is struggle of one class, a struggle which aims to overthrow the dominance of another class; it is the replacement of one system by another, and in no event can it be regarded as a struggle of one individual or one group for the overthrow of another individual or group.

A real democratic party must possess two characteristic elements: (1) its principles must be correlated with the concepts of democracy; and (2) its actions must consist in an active struggle against feudalism in the form of the military. Of all the political parties existing in China, only the GMD can be characterized as a revolutionary party, yet it possesses only a relative amount of democratic and revolutionary spirit. The program of this party has not yet been fully elaborated. But its three principles, "of the people, for the people, and by the people" [evidently an oblique reference to Sun Zhongshan's Three People's Principles], in conjunction with plans for the industrial development of China [cp. Sun's *International Development of China,* 1922 (1919)] reflect the democratic spirit of the GMD. In addition to this party's participating in the revolutionary

struggle through it parliamentary members, the GMD has offered a number of other proofs of its democratic spirit, namely: the Guangzhou government [headed by Sun Zhongshan, 1921–22] has not been restricting the labor movement; it has abolished police regulations in regard to "public order and national security"; and it has abolished the law by which workers were deprived of the right to strike. Not infrequently, however, this party's actions have been contradictory in nature. On occasion the GMD manifests a friendly attitude even with respect to ... monarchists, and an inclination for a rapprochement "for tactical reasons" with the Beiyang military clique. If the GMD, as a party, wishes to play definite role in the revolutionary struggle for the consolidation of democracy in China, it must renounce once and for all every policy of vacillation, compromise, and endless zigzags.

With respect to the present situation, the view is very popular that the convening of the old parliament [at Beijing] and the restoration of Li Yuanhong as President [June 1922] are cardinal events which assure the solution of the political problems confronting

KARAKHAN MANIFESTO (1919)—A manifesto issued on July 25, 1919 by Russian Foreign Minister Lev Karakhan relinquishing all Tsarist Russian claims to special rights and privileges in China. The Soviet Union did, however, continue to pursue special rights and privileges.

China. This point of view cannot stand criticism and is in complete contradiction of the facts. Is there any basis for asserting that parliament will be able to realize its "legal power" when there is a dominance of a feudal power of the "Beiyang" party type, a power which pursues the idea itself as a group of "relatives" who fell heir to the "Beiyang" military clique? The account of past experience has testified plainly that Li Yuanhong during his presidency in the recent past (1915–17) [this should be 1916–17] did not manage to resolve a single political task or any problem as a whole. What reasons are there for asserting that Li Yuanhong will be able to organize a democratic government when—in the face of all the unfavorable historical circumstance—Li Yuanhong's term of office, as such, has already expired? So long as the military dominates in China and over China, the organized struggle against democracy will not end, nor will the struggle end among the militarists themselves.

[. . . .]

The military is the cause of civil war in China. So long as the military exists and rules, the creation of a so-called "good government" will be out of the question. In the present circumstances no government in China can be stable and firm, and the life and property of Chinese citizens are subject to destruction every time the militarists clash.

[. . . .]

Members of the GMD! You were originally revolutionary fighters for the triumph of democracy. You should also conduct a revolutionary struggle now for democracy and prefer to perish in this struggle than to vanish from the socio-political arena in consequence of a policy of compromise. During the first year of the existence of the Chinese Republic [1912] you were deceived by Yuan Shikai, who tried his best to demonstrate his loyalty to the republic. You were cruelly deceived also by Duan Qirui, when he proposed the restoration of parliament and of the constitution [1916–17]. Do not let yourselves be deceived now by all this talk about restoring parliament, abolishing the *dujun* system, demobilizing provincial troops, for the sake of concluding another compromise with the military of North China. Does the present constitutional parliament differ in any way from the parliament of the fifth and the sixth year of the Republic [1916–17]? Aren't the hopes for abolishing the *dujun* system and for demobilization merely hopes that the tiger may shed its own skin? Does the title of "troop commander" as distinct from or other than *dujun*—a phenomenon which can be observed in the provinces of Yunnan, Sichuan, and Hunan—differ

essentially from the *dujun* institution and the conditions which existed prior to the nominal abolition of the *dujun*?

[. . . .]

Workers, peasants, students, soldiers, policemen, and merchants! So long as the authority of the military is not overthrown, there will be no hope of disarming the provincial armies and abolishing the *dujun* system. So long as the authority of the military is not overthrown, there will be no hope of reducing the demands for national funds, which are used to cover war expenses and further to disrupt the entire national and local financial system. So long as the authority of the military is not overthrown, all conditions will be present to allow the military to secure new loans from foreigners and thus bring about an intensification of foreign influence in China. So long as the authority of the military is not overthrown, there will be no hope that the military will cease imposing heavy imposts on the citizens of China; there will be no hope that looting may cease, no hope that order may be restored in all regions of China. So long as the authority of the military is not overthrown, there will be no hope of a broad development of education in China and of industrial progress in our country. So long as the authority of the military is not overthrown, there will be no hope that the struggle among militarists for the expansion of their own spheres of influence may cease. Peasants and merchants are always war victims. These wars will be inevitable and endless if they are not stopped by the people themselves.

For all of us, the only way by which we can liberate ourselves from the hard yoke of the military is to join the democratic struggle against the relics of the past—a struggle for freedom and peace. The government opposition game, played by the bourgeoisie, the intelligentsia, and the politicians, cannot be trusted. We all want peace, but real peace rather than false peace. We welcome a war to achieve the triumph of democracy, to overthrow the military and the militarists and to liberate the Chinese people.

The CCP, as the vanguard of the proletariat, struggles for working class liberation and for the proletarian revolution. Until such time as the Chinese proletariat is able to seize power in its own hands, considering the present political and economic conditions of China's development and all the historical processes now going on in China, the proletariat's urgent task is to act jointly with the democratic party to establish a united front of democratic revolution to struggle for the overthrow of the military and for the organization of a real democratic government.

8.2 MAO ZEDONG'S REPORT ON AN INVESTIGATION OF PEASANT MOVEMENT IN HUNAN (MARCH 1927)

Of the communist writings from this period, the following report by **Mao Zedong** on the Peasant Movement in the province of Hunan is a classic. It represents Mao's own emphatic defense of the need for a peasant-based revolutionary struggle. There is little doubt that Mao, originally from Hunan himself, was in his element. The CCP party leaders, headed by Chen Duxiu, equally adamantly believed that only an orthodox revolution following the more traditional urban-based revolution would succeed. The following are the first four sections from the report.

Questions

1. **What does Mao Zedong suggest is the main target of peasant discontent?**
2. **What does Mao Zedong mean when he states "It's terrible!"**

THE IMPORTANCE OF THE PEASANT PROBLEM

During my recent visit to Hunan I made a first-hand investigation of conditions in the five counties of Xiangtan, Xiangjiang, Hengshan, Liling, and Changsha. In the thirty-two days from January 4 to February 5, I called together fact-finding conferences in villages and county towns, which were attended by experienced peasants and by comrades working in the peasant movement, and I listened attentively to their reports and collected a great deal of material. Many of the hows and whys of the peasant movement were the exact opposite of what the gentry in Hankou and Changsha are saying. I saw and heard of many strange things of which I had hitherto been unaware. I believe the same is true of many other places, too. All talk directed against the peasant movement must be speedily set right. All the wrong measures taken by the revolutionary authorities concerning the peasant movement must be speedily changed. Only thus can the future of the revolution be benefited. For the present upsurge of the peasant movement is a colossal event. In a very short time, in China's central, southern and northern provinces, several hundred million peasants will rise like a mighty storm, like a hurricane, a force so swift and violent that no power, however great, will be able to hold it back. They will smash all the trammels that bind them and rush forward along the road to liberation. They will sweep all the imperialists, warlords, corrupt officials, local tyrants and evil gentry into their graves. Every revolutionary party and every revolutionary comrade will be put to the test, to be accepted or rejected as they decide. There are three alternatives. To march at their head and lead them? To trail behind them, gesticulating and criticizing? Or to stand in their way and oppose them? Every Chinese is free to choose, but events will force you to make the choice quickly.

GET ORGANIZED!

The development of the peasant movement in Hunan may be roughly divided into two periods with respect to the counties in the province's central and southern parts where the movement has already made much headway. The first, from January to September of the last year, was one of organization. In this period, January to June was a time of underground activity, and July to September, when the revolutionary army was driving out Zhao Hengdi, one of open activity. During this period, the membership of the peasant

MAO ZEDONG (1893–1976) — Born in Hunan, he became involved in the nascent CCP in Beijing during the May Fourth era. Played an increasingly prominent role in the Jiangxi Soviet in the early 1930s before rising to prominence during the Long March (1934). He successfully guided the CCP through the War of Resistance Against Japan and the Chinese Civil War before founding the PRC in 1949. His legacy is a mixed one of significant social and economic development as well as of policies that led to the deaths of tens of millions Chinese citizens.

associations did not exceed 300,000–400,000, the masses directly under their leadership numbered little more than a million, there was as yet hardly any criticism of the associations in other circles. Since its members served as guides, scouts and carriers of the Northern Expeditionary Army, even some of the officers had a good word to say for the peasant associations. The second period, from last October to January of this year, was one of revolutionary action. The membership of the associations jumped to two million and the masses directly under their leadership increased to ten million. Since the peasants generally enter only one name for the whole family on joining a peasant association, a membership of two million means a mass following of about ten million. Almost half the peasants in Hunan are now organized. In counties like Xiangtan, Xiangxiang, Liuyang, Changsha, Liling, Ningxiang, Bingjiang, Xiangyin, Hengshan, Hengyang, Leiyang, Zhenxian, and Anhua, nearly all the peasants have combined in the peasant associations or have come under their leadership. It was on the strength of their extensive organization that the peasants went into action and within four months brought about a great revolution in the countryside, a revolution without parallel in history.

DOWN WITH THE LOCAL TYRANTS AND EVIL GENTRY! ALL POWER TO THE PEASANT ASSOCIATIONS!

The main targets of attack by the peasants are the local tyrants, the evil gentry and the lawless landlords, but in passing they also hit out against patriarchal ideas and institutions, against the corrupt officials in the cities and against bad practices and customs in the rural areas. In force and momentum the attack is tempestuous; those who bow before it survive and those who resist perish. As a result, the privileges which the feudal landlords enjoyed for thousands of years are being shattered to pieces. Every bit of the dignity and prestige built up by the landlords is being swept into the dust. With the collapse of the power of the landlords, the peasant associations have now become the sole organs of authority and the popular slogan "All power to the peasant associations" has become reality. Even trifles such as quarrel between husband and wife are brought to the peasant association. Nothing can be settled unless someone from the peasant association is present. The association actually dictates all rural affairs, and, quite literally, "whatever it says, goes." Those who are outside the associations can only speak

well of them and cannot say anything against them. The local tyrants, evil gentry and lawless landlords have been deprived of all right to speak, and none of them dares even mutter dissent. In the face of the peasant associations' power and pressure, the top local tyrants and evil gentry have fled to Shanghai, those of the second rank to Hankou, those of the third to Changsha and those of the fourth to the county towns, while the fifth rank and the still lesser fry surrender to the peasant associations in the villages.

"Here's ten yuan. Please let me join the peasant association," one of the smaller of the evil gentry will say.

"Ugh! Who wants your filthy money?" the peasants reply.

Many middle and small landlords and rich peasants and even some middle peasants, who were all formerly opposed to the peasant associations, are now vainly seeking admission. Visiting various places, I often came across such people who pleaded with me, "Mr. Committeeman from the provincial capital, please be my sponsor!"

In the Qing Dynasty, the household census compiled by the local authorities consisted of regular register and "the other" register, the former for honest people and the latter for burglars, bandits and similar undesirables. In some places the peasants now use this method to scare those who formerly opposed the associations. They say, "Put their names down in the other register!"

Afraid of being entered in the other register, such people try various devices to gain admission into the peasant associations, on which their minds are so set that they do not feel safe until their names are entered. But more often than not they are turned down flat, and so they are always on tenterhooks; with the doors of the association barred to them, they are like tramps without a home or, in rural parlance, "mere trash." In short, what was looked down upon four months ago as a "gang of peasants" has now become a most honorable institution. Those who formerly prostrated themselves before the power of the gentry now bow before the power of the peasants. No matter what their identity, all admit that the world since last October is a different one.

"IT'S TERRIBLE!" OR "IT'S FINE!"

The peasants' revolt disturbed the gentry's sweet dreams. When the news from the countryside reached the cities, it caused immediate uproar among the gentry. Soon after my arrival in Changsha, I met all sorts of people and picked up a good deal of gossip. From the middle social strata upwards to the Guomindang right-wingers, there was not a single person who did not sum up the whole business in the phrase, "It's terrible!" Under the impact of the views of the "It's terrible!" school then flooding the city, even quite revolutionary-minded people became downhearted as they pictured the events in their mind's eye; and they were unable to deny the word "terrible." Even quit progressive people said, "Though terrible, it is inevitable in a revolution." In short, nobody could altogether deny the word "terrible." But, as already mentioned, the fact is that the great peasant masses have risen to fulfill their historic mission and that the forces of rural democracy have risen to overthrow the forces of rural feudalism. The patriarchal-feudal class of local tyrants, evil gentry and lawless landlords has formed the basis of autocratic government for thousands of years and is the cornerstone of imperialism, warlordism, and corrupt officialdom. To overthrow these feudal forces is the real objective of the national revolution. In a few months the peasants have accomplished what Dr. Sun Zhongshan wanted, but failed, to accomplish in the forty years he devoted to the national revolution.

This is a marvelous feat never before achieved, not just in forty, but in thousands of years. It's fine. It is not "terrible" at all. It is anything but "terrible." "It's terrible!" is obviously a theory for combating the rise of the peasants in the interests of the landlords; it is obviously a theory of the landlord class for preserving the old order of feudalism and obstructing the establishment of the new order of democracy, it is obviously a counter-revolutionary theory. No revolutionary comrade should echo this nonsense. If your revolutionary viewpoint is firmly established and if you have been to the villages and looked around, you will undoubtedly feel thrilled as never before. Countless thousands of the enslaved–the peasants–are striking down the enemies who patterned on their flesh. "What the peasants are doing is absolutely right; what they are doing is fine!" is the theory of the peasants and of all other revolutionaries. Every revolutionary comrade should know that the national revolution requires a great change in the countryside. The Revolution of 1911 did not bring about this change, hence its failure. This change is now taking place, and it is an important factor for the completion of the revolution. Every revolutionary comrade must support it, or he will be taking the stand of counter-revolution.

8.3   LAND LAW OF THE JIANGXI SOVIET (1932)

In 1927, the Guomindang conducted a multi-city round-up and execution of all communists (and suspected communists) forcing the CCP leadership to flee to remote areas to set up autonomous areas under direct communist rule (called **soviets**). The communists would not have a substantial urban presence again for nearly two decades. The key communist leaders set up armed bases in the mountainous areas of Jiangxi. There the CCP experimented with a variety of land reforms seeking to attract peasant support while maximizing agricultural production. The Land Law of the **Jiangxi Soviet** marks a major shift from an urban to rural-based revolution. The Jiangxi era also marked the emergence of a darker more radical phase forcefully carrying out land reform that became extremely violent killing tens of thousands of people. It would mark a phase of the CCP evolution in which there existed considerable tensions among the leadership leading to political campaigns hastily conceived and often confused in execution.

SOVIET—The term "soviet"(*suweiai*) in the Chinese context designated CCP bases in Jiangxi, Anhui, Hunan, Fujian, and later in Shaanxi and Gansu during the late 1920s and early 1930s. The term refers to areas under the direct control of Communists. Western papers at the time referred to them as "red bases."

JIANGXI SOVIET—A CCP controlled area (or "soviet") founded in 1931 and governed by a council headed by Mao Zedong. The soviet's threat to the GMD lead to a series of "extermination campaigns" eventually causing the CCP to flee on a year long "Long March."

Questions

1. **What aspects of the Land Law do you think were most popular among the lower classes?**
2. **What factors do you think would lead to such violence that the CCP itself was forced to halt many aspects of the reform?**

A. Whose Land Should Be Confiscated?

1. Land (including land rented to tenants), houses, and all other forms of property, including household items, that belonged to members of the gentry and landlords are to be confiscated.

2. Land, houses, and all other forms of property, including household items, that belong to family shrines, Buddhist or Daoist temples, clan or social organizations are to be confiscated.
[. . . .]

4. Land owned by rich peasants should be confiscated.

B. Who Should Receive Land?

5. The amount of land to be distributed is the same for all tenant farmers and poor peasants. Whether the land of the middle peasants should be redistributed so as to assure that they have the same amount as that of tenant farmers and poor peasants depends upon the decision to be made by the middle peasants themselves. If the majority of them so desires, the land of the middle peasants will be redistributed, even though the minority does not agree. If the majority of the middle peasants does not want its land to be redistributed, its land will not be redistributed and it can keep the land it presently has; but its decision, in this case, does not bind the minority of the middle peasants which, if it so chooses, can participate in the redistribution program. This provision, however, does not affect land distribution among the middle peasants that had been completed before December 31, 1931. The completed distribution should remain effective and should not be altered in any fashion.

6. The relatives of a farm laborer shall receive land. He himself should also receive land if he is unemployed. (By unemployment is meant the lack of employment for most of the year. It does not include temporary unemployment that lasts only a short period of time)

7. Independent artisans (including artisans who have apprentices working for them but excluding those who have hired workers), physicians, and teachers are to receive land if they have been unemployed for six months or longer.

8. Shop owners and their relatives shall not receive any land.

9. Rich peasants will receive poor land in accordance with the size of their respective households as well as the number of able-bodied workers in them. If a rich peasant household has able-bodied workers, each of them will receive a certain amount of poor land as his share. If none of its members can work, a subsidy in the form of poor land will be provided, but this subsidy shall not be more than two-thirds of the land granted to others.

10. Beginning with the operation of this statute, members of the gentry, landlords and members of counterrevolutionary organizations will not be entitled to land distribution. Nor are former wives, daughters-in-law, or daughters of rich peasants who have in the past assumed the leadership in opposing land distribution of their own accord, even though they are presently married to farm laborers, tenant farmers, poor or middle peasants.

11. There are cases in which members of the gentry, landlords, and counterrevolutionary rich peasants have adopted the method of "invitation marriage" by marrying their wives or daughters to farm laborers, tenant farmers, poor or middle peasants for the sole purpose of preserving their own properties. The properties in question, including houses, shall be confiscated by the government forthwith.

However, the farm laborers, tenant farmers, poor or middle peasants who have been thus married will receive their fair share when the confiscated properties, including houses, are redistributed.

12. As for the adopted sons or daughters of members of the gentry, landlords, and those rich peasants who have in the past been members of counter-revolutionary organizations, they are not entitled to land distribution if they have lived the same kind of the life and have had the same kind of education as their foster parents. If on the other land they have been treated like slaves even though they are adopted sons or daughters, they are entitled to land distribution.

13. As for Buddhist monks and nuns, Daoist priests, magicians and sorcerers, fortunetellers, geomancers, and other feudal remnants as well as Protestant ministers and Catholic priests, they are not entitled to land distribution if religion is their main means of earning a livelihood. If land has been granted to them, it should be returned. If on the other hand religion is only their avocation and farming is in fact their main occupation, they are entitled to land distribution if people in their respective communities approve.

14. Beginning with the operation of this statute, the sons or daughters of the members of the gentry or landlords are no longer entitled to land distribution even though they have been adopted by poor laborers or peasants as their own children.

15. Members of the gentry, landlords, and those rich peasants who have in the past assumed the leadership in opposing land distribution of their own accord, together with all of their relatives, are not entitled to land distribution. If land has been granted to them, it shall be returned to the government.

16. Rural merchants who, prior to the revolution, had been able to support their families through trade and commerce are not entitled to land distribution. If land has been granted to them, it shall be returned to the government. They will be granted land in the same fashion as independent artisans, however, had they become unemployed after the revolution.

17. Unemployed peddlers are entitled to land distribution.

18. A woman can dispose of her land the way she wishes when she is married.

[. . . .]

8.4   THREE MAIN RULES OF DISCIPLINE AND SIX POINTS FOR ATTENTION (1928)

Mao Zedong first drafted the following rules in the spring and summer of 1928 while in the Jinggang Mountains of Jiangxi for all Communists and Communist troops. He made several small revisions in 1929 (changing Rule 2, for example, from "don't take anything from the workers and peasants" to "don't take a single needle or piece of thread from the masses"). In later years he would add two more points to the "Six Points for Attention": 1) "Don't bathe within sight of women" and 2) "Don't search the pockets of captives." While these may seem self-evident, one only needs to compare these rules with the behavior of Zhang Zongchang and other warlord armies to realize the distinctiveness that such guidelines (and the adherence to them) would have had upon the people with whom they interacted.

Questions

1. **What goal do you believe Mao had in mind when he instituted the following rules?**
2. **Why might these rules have made the CCP a popular presence among the rural populace?**

Three Rules of Discipline

1. Obey orders in your actions
2. Don't take anything from the workers and peasants
3. Turn in all things taken from local bullies.

Six Points for Attention

1. Put back the doors you have taken down for bed-boards
2. Don't take a single needle or piece of thread from the masses.
3. Speak politely
4. Pay fairly for what you buy
5. Return everything you borrow
6. Pay for anything you damage

RISE OF THE GUOMINDANG

With Yuan Shikai's death in 1916, most Chinese political activists and revolutionaries had come to the realization that politically the 1911 revolution had failed. In spite of this, in the minds of most Chinese, Sun Zhongshan remained the only hope of bringing an end to the warlords' dominance in the political sphere. In 1920, Sun met with members of the Comintern who sought a more mainstream (and numerically stronger) political party under which the CCP might thrive. Sun's ideology had always tended to be progressive, but through his interactions with the CCP and Comintern, Sun's politics took on a much more militaristic and leftist tone (8.5, 8.6). More to the point, the Soviet Union proved to be the only European nation to recognize Sun Zhongshan's government and provide financial support. Sun also worried that if he did not accept the Comintern's offer they would throw their support behind one of the other warlords (or push for the CCP to take a more active political stand).

The Guomindang and Communists jointly cooperated with Comintern oversight from 1923 until 1927. The founding of the **Huangpu Military Academy** in 1924, is perhaps the single most prominent example of CCP-GMD collaboration with members of both parties served in positions of leadership. In early 1925, even as he prepared for a military expedition to unite northern and southern China, Sun traveled to Beijing. There he hoped to negotiate with the warlord government officials. While in Beijing, Sun discovered that he was in the advance stages of liver cancer. On March 12, 1925, he passed away in Beijing. His imminent death set off a scramble for control of both his political party and for his ultimate legacy (8.7). Later, **Jiang Jieshi** would have Sun's body interred (according to Sun's own wishes) in a massive mausoleum outside of Nanjing called Zhongshanling.

8.5 THE THREE PRINCIPLES OF THE PEOPLE (MARCH 6, 1921)

Sun Zhongshan delivered the following speech on his Three Principles at an executive meeting of the Guomindang in March 6, 1921. His three principles (or at least what he emphasized within each of the three principles) had evolved considerably over the years

HUANGPU (WHAMPOA) ACADEMY—A military academy founded by Sun Zhongshan in 1924 (often romanized according to Cantonese pronunciation as Whampoa) outside of Guangzhou. Many of China's top military leaders of the 1920s and 1930s, regardless of party affiliation, were educated or served at the academy.

JIANG JIESHI (1887–1975)—Born in Zhejiang, he attended numerous military schools before joining the GMD, serving as commandant of Huangpu Military Academy in 1924. After Sun Zhongshan's death in 1925, Jiang Jieshi became the military commander who organized and led the Northern Expedition. From 1928 until 1949 he served as President of China. After the GMD's retreat to Taiwan he served as president from 1952 until his death in 1975.

(compare with 5.11). Gone are the references to ridding China of the Manchus, and in its place are calls to keep all parts (Tibet, Xinjiang, Mongolia) of "China" unified. Sun deftly weaves in the popular appeals of the May Fourth Movement and rising demands for redistribution of land. His notion of "People's Livelihood" remains essentially unchanged from his earlier versions, yet it takes on a much more prominent place in this speech.

Question

1. Do you find Sun's solutions more or less realistic than those he proposed fifteen years earlier (5.11)?
2. What does Sun suggest by his term "equal appraisal of land" with regard to his land reforms?

Dear Comrades:

[. . . .]

Three Principles of the People. What are the Three Principles of the People? They are Nationalism, Democracy and Livelihood of the People. When the Manchus occupied China, revolutionaries focused exclusively on achieving a nationalist revolution with little attention given to democracy and livelihood. A constitution composed of five powers is an imperative policy to establish a country. Prior to the overthrow of the Manchus, our Party members assumed once the Manchus had been deposed, the goal to achieve the national power and people's welfare would occur spontaneously. Only now is it finally understood that the mistake came from the earlier single-minded focus on the nationalism while neglecting the other two principles of democracy and livelihood. This is our Party's unrealized duty. It is important to understand that without implementation of the other two principles, even if nationhood is achieved it will not be stable; not to mention, we have not yet reached our goal of nationalism!

I. *People's Nationalism.* What do we mean when we say that we have failed to achieve the goal of nationalism? When the Manchus conquered China over 200 years ago, we—the Han Chinese people—were subjugated. Today, even though the Manchus have been overthrown and a Han-rule reinstated, our people (*minzu*) have still not achieved their independence. This is because our Party continues to play only a passive instead of active role [in the revolution]. . . . Our Party must take the blame for this. Since the [1911] revolution, only the former Qing officials, recalcitrant conservatives and the revisionist parties, clustering together and claiming to have founded a Republic of Five Nationalities (*wuzu gonghe*).

Few fully comprehend that the fundamental misunderstanding lies precisely on this point. For when one speaks of the five peoples, there are only four or five millions Tibetans; less than one million Mongolians; several million Manchus; and a large number of Muslims; but the majority [of China's population] are the Han Chinese. If we examine the current situation, Manchuria is under Japan's sphere of influence; Mongolia is under Russian influence; and Tibet is almost completely under British control. Obviously they are unable to defend themselves and we Han must come to their aid. There are four hundred million or more Han Chinese, if we cannot establish an independent all-Han nation, it is truly a great disgrace to us as a Han people. This is why our Party has not succeeded in achieving our goal of nationalism.

It is for this reason, our party must continue to work hard to achieve nationalism, to ensure that the Manchus, Mongolians, Muslims and Tibetans are assimilated into the Han Chinese, in order to create a great nationalist country.

[. . . .]

II. *People's Democracy. . .* Direct democracy includes the following four electoral rights: universal suffrage, the referendum, the initiative and the rights of recall.

III. *People's Livelihood.* Here again let me speak about People's Livelihood. Today People's Livelihood means socialism. Gentlemen, reflect for a moment, when did I first begin to broach the notion of People's Livelihood? It is already too late to start to talk about socialism today. But the theory of socialism arrived in China not too long ago, so that is it quite proper for me to have translated "**socialism**" as "people's livelihood" in the past.... The solution is in "land" and "capital". People who are aware of the current situation nowadays often say there are no capitalists in China that there is no need to talk about socialism; or let's not start to talk about socialism until we have capitalist production. This is not the right approach.

[....]

As far as People's livelihood concerns, I already have one solution that is "equal distribution" (*pingjun diquan*) of land. When the Republic of China was established in Nanjing, I advocated the proportional distribution of the land, trying to implement our Party policy of People's Livelihood, which met opposition from some of our comrades. I asked them: haven't you all taken oaths to uphold Party's ideology?

Because of inequality, we must implement People's Livelihood. What do we mean by inequality? In ancient times, although the distinction between rich and poor existed, the difference was not as marked. Today the rich own all the land, while the poor do not even own a little piece to step his feet on. The reason for this inequality is the huge difference in productive power. For example, in ancient times tools that timber-cutters used were axes, knives and saws. That the ancient saying goes, to accomplish one's work, one must first sharpen the tools. Whereas nowadays industry is greatly developed, machines have replaced human labor, and the result is that a much greater quantity of products is obtained with much less human energy....

[....]

Now that we have established the Guangzhou branch of the Guomindang Party, which has been designated as the primary office to carry out propaganda. From this we can expect the future to be unlimited. Guangdong province will become the experimental center for us to implement our party's policy and the starting point for democracy. We can push our Party's ideology from Guangdong to the whole country, the Yangzi and Yellow River regions. You gentlemen must understand we have to practice and propagandize our Party's ideology promptly because, although the Republic is ten years old, common people do not understand the meaning of republic and they do not consider themselves as citizens, but subjects. They are still waiting for the Son of Heaven [the emperor] to appear and preparing to become royal subjects in a peaceful world. I ask you to try to imagine how could we even implement a popular election for a county commissioner? To avoid future failure, we must actively practice Three Principles of the People, rely on Our Party members to govern Guangdong. All is depending on our party members' effort and the familiarity of Three Principles of the People. After that we must actively implement the Constitution of Five Powers. The 'Three Principles of the People' and the 'Constitution of Five Powers' are the fundamental ideology of our Party, which from Guangdong we must spread throughout the country.

8.6   MANIFESTO ON THE NORTHERN EXPEDITION (SEPTEMBER 18, 1924)

In the months after the Huangpu Academy first admitted cadets, Sun Zhongshan began to advance his plans for a military reunification of China. A central component of his plan was a military expedition striking northward from Guangzhou in order to defeat the major warlord armies and finally realize the Revolution's unfulfilled potential. Sun hoped that many of the warlords would in the face of this threat accede to his demands and join him under the Nationalist government. Many warlords did, in the end, become members of his GMD party. Many, however, would not. Sun would not live to see the Northern Expedition or more importantly to him, a reunited China.

SOCIALISM—A socio-economic system in which wealth, services, and production are controlled by the community or government. For Karl Marx, socialism would be the socio-economic system that later progressed into communism.

Questions

1. How does Sun Zhongshan characterize the warlords still active in China in 1924?
2. What goals does Sun suggest will achieve by this military reunification?

The People's Revolution aims at the protection of a free, independent nation. Such a free, independent nation might have come into existence after the campaign of 1911, which destroyed the despotic and aristocratic rule of the Manchus. If, at that time, the members of our party, a party based upon the interests of the nation and of the common people, had destroyed all existing counter-revolutionary influences, we would have had political stability during the last thirteen years, and would have made considerable progress in the task of national reconstruction along economic, educational, and other lines. So, even if the success of the Revolution could not have been instantaneously complete, at least we should have traveled in the right direction and every day's work would have brought us closer to the ultimate goal.

But the counter-revolutionary influences have survived! They have brought irreparable losses to our nation and to our people due to their internal maladministration and diplomatic defeats. Inheriting antiquated despotic ideas, the counter-revolutionists have struggled to maintain the traditional position of privilege. Yuan Shikai tried to make himself emperor; Zhang Xun tried to restore the boy emperor to the throne; Feng Guozhang and Xu Shichang Destroyed the Republican Constitution; and Cao Kun and Wu Peifu came into power through bribery and other illegal means.

For thirteen years there has been one plot after another for destroying the Republic. Although there were changes of personnel at the head of the militarist government, the same old feudalistic ideas were handed down from one to another through the whole line of them. These counter-revolutionaries have used Beijing as their base and from there have spread their influence throughout the provinces. What is worse, a great many revolutionists, because of lack of determination to work for the national and people's interests, have fallen in line with these corrupt elements and consequently have caused the present disintegration and disorganization within the camps of the revolutionary forces.

The counter-revolutionaries have been able to survive because of the support of foreign imperialists; there is abundant evidence to prove the truth of this statement. In 1913 when Yuan Shikai decided to suppress the revolutionary movement by force in order to make himself the emperor of China, the Consortium Loan of two hundred and fifty million dollars was put through; and so Yuan was given a huge sum for military expenditure.

Afterward, throughout the regimes of Feng Guozhang and Xu Shichang, each period of civil war was preceded by huge foreign loan. Recently, just as Cao Kun and Wu Peifu decided to send a punitive expedition to the southeastern provinces, the Gold France Case, which had been pending for a long time, was suddenly settled. All these facts serve to show without the least doubt that the direct cause of our civil wars during the last thirteen years has been militarism, and the indirect cause has been imperialism.

Now our allied armies in Zhejiang have declared war against Cao Kun and Wu Peifu; and Shenyang is taking a concurrent action with Zhejiang. The Revolutionary Government hereby proclaims that the northern expedition is being undertaken in order to co-operate with the rest of the country in destroying Cao Kun, Wu Peifu, and other traitors. But we solemnly declare before the people and the allied forces that aim of our punitive expedition is the destruction of not only Cao and Wu, but of all other persons who choose to follow the example of Cao and Wu. Moreover, this war is not only directed against militarism, but against imperialism, whose support has made the existence of militarism possible. Not until then will the root of the counter-revolution be permanently eradicated and China elevated from the position of a sub-colony to that of a free, independent nation.

The ultimate aim of the Chinese Guomindang is the realization of the *San Min* [Three Peoples] Doctrine. We, therefore, solemnly declare before the people and the allied forces that after overthrowing the northern military clique, we shall demand the immediate adoption of the first part of the *San Min* Doctrine.

We have entered the preset civil war as fighters against militarism. The first duty after the battle is won will be to use the power of the Revolutionary Government to clean out all sinister influences of counter-revolution in order to prepare a clear road toward freedom and self-government. We shall then demand the revision of unequal treaties and the abolition of all special privileges in order to protect our national interests in foreign relations and to eradicate the imperialist influence in China. New treaties will be concluded in accordance with the principles of international equality and mutual respect of sovereignty. After China has achieved her political equality, we may expect the following developments:

1. National freedom from external restrictions will enable China to develop her national economy and to increase her productivity.
2. Industrial development and rural reform will improve the livelihood of China' farmers and laborers.
3. The increase of China's productivity and the unionization of the working class will afford opportunities for improving the living conditions of the working class.
4. The development of agriculture and industry and the consequent increase of the people's purchasing power will give new chances for the rapid growth of commerce.
5. Economic development and the increase of national dividends will easily provide sufficient funds for cultural and educational purposes.
6. After the abolition of unequal treaties, China's new laws will be applied throughout her territories, including the existing leased settlements; and in this way nowhere will the counter-revolutionary influences find a strong hold for their sinister activities.

All these developments will, no doubt, lead to the creation of a sound economic foundation, national unification, and a democratic political machinery working for the welfare of the common people. We urge, therefore, that our people take a determined stand against militarism in the present struggle and that they help to carry out the minimum political projects just mentioned as the initial step of the *San Min* Doctrine.

8.7 SUN ZHONGSHAN'S LAST WILLS AND TESTAMENT (MARCH 11, 1925)

Given Sun's own broad political framework, it is not surprising that in his death there existed considerable efforts on both the right and the left to commandeer his legacy. Upon his death Sun left three documents: a personal will, a political will, and a "Letter of Farewell." It is commonly agreed that Wang Jingwei drafted the political will (known in Chinese as the "**Premier's Will**") several weeks before Sun's death. The "Farewell Testament to the Soviet Union" was drafted by Chen Youren and approved of by Comintern representative Michael Borodin. All three documents were signed by Sun on the night before his death. Only the first two wills were published in Chinese papers in the days after his death, with Sun's "Final Farewell" being published in Pravda (the central party newspaper in the Soviet Union) on March 14, 1925.

Questions

1. **How does each of these three documents reflect a different dimension of Sun's legacy?**
2. **What is Sun's legacy? Why did Sun's legacy become so important for all political parties?**

PREMIER'S WILL—The "Premier's Will" became a staple of Chinese life in the decade after Sun's death. Employed in a manner similar to the "Pledge of Allegiance" in the United States, all school children recited the will every Monday morning throughout the 1930s and 40s.

Sun Zhongshan's Personal Will

I have devoted myself to matters of the nation, instead of making a fortune. I bequeath all my belongings, including books, clothing, houses, etc., to my wife Song Qingling. My children are fully grown and independent. I hope each of them will carry on their good behavior and continue my goals. This is my will.

Sun Zhongshan's Political Will

For forty years I have devoted myself to the cause of the national revolution, the objective of which is to achieve the liberty and equality for China. The forty years' experience has convinced me that to realize such goal, we must awake our people, to unite with peoples of the world who treat us equally, and together to carry out our common fight.

Today the success of the revolution has not been achieved. All my comrades must follow my writings, *The Plan for National Reconstruction, The Fundamentals of National Reconstruction, Three Principles of the People,* and *Manifesto of the First National Convention,* as well as continue their endeavors and accomplishments. Recent proposals to set up a National Convention and to abolish unequal treaties especially need to be accomplished in the shortest time possible. This is my heartfelt charge to you.

Sun Zhongshan's Farewell Testament to Soviet Union

Dear comrades of the Central Committee in the Union of Soviet Socialist Republics:

As my body is afflicted with a terminal illness, my mind and heart turns toward you, and the future of my Party and country. You are the leader of this great union of the liberated republics [USSR]. This great union of liberated republics is Lenin's enduring legacy and the oppressed peoples of the world true inheritance. There the fugitives from imperialists powers can find protection and freedom, and liberate themselves from the unjust international system built on unequal wars.

With my death, I leave the Guomindang, a party I hope will continue to cooperate together with you to liberate China and other countries invaded by imperialists. Fate is forcing me to lay down my uncompleted mission, and so I pass to you who would adhere to Guomindang Thought and Teachings to organize our faithful comrades. Consequently, I have asked the Guomindang to pursue the national revolution, so that China can break out of the semi-colonial restraints imposed by the imperialists. To fulfill this task, I have already instructed the Guomindang to continue our long-term collaboration with you. I have confidence that your government will also continue the support you have offered us in the past.

Dear comrades! In bidding farewell to you, I wish to express my fervent hope that the day will soon dawn when the Soviet Union, as a friend and ally, will welcome a powerful and independent China. And that the two countries will, hand in hand, move forward to realize the victory in fighting for the liberation of all the oppressed peoples in the world. Here as a brother, I wish you peace!

8.8 "QINGDANG"–PURGE THE PARTY OF ALL UNDESIRABLE ELEMENTS (APRIL 1927)

When the Northern Expedition reached Shanghai in April 1927, Jiang Jieshi turned on the Communists and all leftist sympathizers carrying out a bloody purge first in Shanghai (also known as "White Terror"), and then in all other major urban centers under GMD control. Jiang clearly believed that the GMD gained little from the alliance between Communists and the Nationalists. Equally, it suggests that Jiang believed the GMD party no longer needed the financial and international prestige offered by relations with the USSR. Although the purge was clearly orchestrated by Jiang (and the threat largely ignored by the Comintern), the following official statement clearly seeks to present the purge as a breach of faith on the part of the Communists. If anything, the Chinese Communists had aided the Northern Expedition by harnessing the power of the labor unions and other factory workers help control cities on the approach of the Northern Expedition. Although there is no denying that Communist party expanded and strengthened themselves during their cooperative period with the GMD. Communist party members were especially successful in penetrating the military hierarchy in ways that had otherwise been completely barred from them. More significantly, Jiang needed to secure financial support from Shanghai entrepreneurs and his pro-capitalists tactics (and anti-labor) were key factors in obtaining support from Western countries.

Questions

1. **What does the following statement accuse the Communists of doing?**
2. **Who besides the Communists does Jiang suggest are being targeted by the purge?**

To understand clearly the objects of the movement for the purification of the Guomindang Party, it is necessary to know first the actual conditions of the present time. We have not yet accomplished the aims of the Revolution. We are only at the beginning of the task; and while victory is already in sight, it is of the utmost importance at this juncture to carry on the Revolution to a successful end. We must stand together and face the common cause with a united mind. The slightest neglect on our part will not only defeat the Revolution, but will also make it impossible to attain the objects of liberty and equality for the Chinese nation.

Therefore, all members of the party must know the gravity of their responsibility. At this critical moment, the undesirable elements are unscrupulously and untiringly doing the work of destruction, and if we do not check it in an effective manner, it will not only mean the fall of the Party but also the failure of the Revolution. With this in view, we adopt the following for the purification of the Party. First, to purge the Party of the Communists, and secondly, to purge the Party of the opportunists and other undesirable elements.

It will be remembered that when Dr. Sun Zhongshan admitted members of the Communist Party into the Guomindang, he was quite aware of the fact that Communism was not fit for China. But as the Communist Party members were ready to give up their Communistic belief, and willing to be directed by the Guomindang in order to cooperate in the work of the Revolution, it was only natural that they should be admitted into the Party. But since the beginning of the Northern Expedition, while members of the Guomindang have been laboring faithfully either on the field of battle or elsewhere, and while the militarists of the country have been gradually eliminated, the Communists, taking advantage of our success, have seized important cities as their centers for propaganda and usurped the power of the Party. Our military successes are being utilized by them to inflame the undesirable sections of the populace to undermine our forward move and to create disturbances in the rear.

Aside from the Communistic members who are to be condemned, there are also the opportunists and other undesirable elements in the Party. It is they who shamefully steal the name of the Party for their selfish gains, and it is also they who falsely use the power of the Party for their personal activities and aggrandizement. Theirs is a crime no less serious than that of the Communists.

For the welfare of the Revolution as well as that of the Guomindang, we are forced to adopt this strong measure to purge the Party of all the undesirable elements.

8.9   GMD'S PURGE THE PARTY SLOGANS (MAY 1927)

In the wake of the "White Terror" purge of Communists in urban centers, the Guomindang began to amplify its anti-Communist propaganda. While certainly the Guomindang had political differences with the Chinese Communists, the intensity also was based in fact that the CCP posed the biggest threat to the GMD. Without any other major parties offering serious competition, the GMD (with the communists largely in remote rural areas) ruled atop a one-party system. The following slogans were prepared by the Publicity Committee in Guangdong province, and suggest the rapidity with which the political spirit shifted from one (ostensibly at least) of political unity to one of political exclusivity.

> ### Questions
> 1. What relationship do the following slogans suggest the GMD is seeking with the CCP?
> 2. What role does Sun Zhongshan play in the slogans?

May 1927

1. Down with the Chinese Communist Party, which is treacherous to our late director, Dr. Sun Zhongshan.
2. Down with the Chinese Communist Party which is against the *Sanmin Zhuyi*, "The Three Principles of the People."
3. Down with the Chinese Communist Party which is destroying the People's Revolution.
4. Down with the Chinese Communist Party which is undoing the work of the Northern Expedition.
5. Down with the Chinese Communist Party which is utilizing bandits and labor usurpers to oppress the Peasants and Laborers.
6. Down with the Chinese Communist Party which is insulting and disgracing our late Director, Dr. Sun.
7. Down with the Chinese Communist Party which is plotting the downfall and destruction of the Guomindang.
8. To be against "The Three Principles of the People" is to be a Counter-Revolutionary.
9. To be against the Guomindang is to be a Counter-Revolutionary.
10. All power and authority belongs to the Guomindang.
11. All true and loyal comrades of the Guomindang must unite and rise.
12. Down with all Counter-Revolutionaries.
13. Down with all Opportunists.
14. Concentrate the powers of the Guomindang.
15. Down with all forms of Imperialism.
16. Down with the Fengtian clique of Militarists.
17. Eradicate all corrupt officials, greedy gentry, and unscrupulous merchants.
18. Purge the Guomindang of all anti-revolutionists.
19. To call a strike against the Guomindang is Counter-Revolutionary.
20. Those who refuse to come under the direction and guidance of the Guomindang are not Revolutionaries.
21. The masses of the people must rise and clean up the Counter-Revolutionary Chinese Communist Party.
22. The masses of the people must rise and support the Chinese Guomindang.
23. Support the Central Government at Nanjing.
24. Support the advancing Nationalist Forces.
25. Down with the bogus governments at Wuhan and Beijing.

8.10 A PROCLAMATION FROM THE HEADQUARTERS OF THE 26TH ARMY (APRIL 22, 1927)

In the wake of the April 12th purge of the Communists in Shanghai, the GMD sought to solidify their urban base, with a public offensive against labor organizations. Fearful of the left's general success among the working class, the GMD moved to turn public opinion against labor organizers greatest weapon, strikes. The author of the document, Zhou Fengzi (1904–1928), was a graduate of Huangpu Academy's illustrious first graduating class and a leading figure in the Northern Expedition. He likely would have risen even farther had he not died suddenly of a disease in 1928.

Questions

1. **Why would the GMD fear the ability of the workers to strike?**
2. **What beside the CCP might have encouraged the GMD to take such an anti-labor stance?**

Our Chinese workmen have been admired by the world for their endurance and obedience, but with increase in industrial activity there has come a menace in the form of strikes and walkouts.

When Shanghai was recently taken by our armies, many workmen were induced or forced by mutineers to leave their employment and to parade and join various unlawful associations, and to otherwise countenance unlawful activities.

Through my advice to workers and other steps which have been taken many factories are again running. There are cases, however, where simple-minded workers are still deluded by agitators. To them I wish to offer this advice:

1. The manufacturing and commercial conditions of China are quite different from those of Europe and America. Because of this difference the treatment accorded to workmen must be different. Chinese workmen, consequently, cannot expect the same treatment as that accorded to workmen in other countries.

2. Chinese workmen are fortunate in that they can if they wish make China a real industrial nation by gaining full knowledge of the industries with which they are affiliated. This fact was apparently been lost sight of in following professional agitators who are very selfish and who are seeking to sacrifice the laboring classes only for their own benefit.

3. If, in the following advice of these agitators, and law violators, a strike occurs, the loss of valuable time and the money which that valuable time would bring to the workmen is the only result. Although some of the workmen who go on strike have money for the rainy day, others

have not. These last starve themselves and starve their families. It is absolutely foolish to strike, for it is both unlawful and a loss of livelihood.

4. When a strike is in effect the factories are closed. Consequently the Nationalist government and the Nationalist armies are forced to buy foreign made goods merely because there are no native productions. This is death not only to the country's commerce, but to patriotism as well.

From the above four points it is plain that strikes are not only harmful, but they have not a single advantage.

The Nationalist Government is now facing and executing the task of clearing away the bacteria which causes the disturbances in the laboring classes—and making the source of this disturbance clear.

Hereafter when professional agitators or others in the laboring classes plan to induce otherwise good workmen to strike, commit unlawful acts or violence we ask that the factories and the good workmen report them to the headquarters of this army that they may be severely punished. Only by doing this may we be able to protect the good workman and see that they are well treated.

April 22, 1927

Zhou Fengqi

Commander of the Twenty-Sixth Nationalist Army and Vice-Commander of the Shanghai and Songjiang Defense Area

LITERARY CURRENTS IN 1920s CHINA

The literature of the "May Fourth Era" exerted a deep influence on the Chinese people. In particular, the literature of this era reflects a wide generation gap between traditional Chinese beliefs of the late imperial period and the more "modern" practices of the "May Fourth Youth" (8.11). The desire to have premarital relationships and marry according to one's own wishes was a common theme not only in the 1920s, but on into the 1940s. Arranged marriages decrease but remain common for several more decades and as Ba Jin's *Family* throws into sharp relief, it was not only the women who suffered from such arrangements, but also the men (8.13). The advent of daily newspapers, weeklies, and other periodicals, provided ample avenues for the dissemination of these new beliefs. While novels and short stories might appear quite conventional, it should be remembered that stories written in a colloquial manner (and about young love) were perceived in the 1920s still as quite innovative and even risqué (8.12).

8.11 YANG ZHIHUA'S *LOVE AND SOCIALIZING BETWEEN MEN AND WOMEN* (JULY 1922)

Yang Zhihua (1900–1973), a prominent feminist author of the May Fourth Movement and communist labor organizer, wrote many short articles for various newspapers. A well-known proponent of women adopting a more prominent voice in love relationships and marriage, Yang's own love life was particularly open for her era. When she fell in love with Qu Qiubei (a well-known writer) while married to another man, she orchestrated a meeting between herself, her husband and Qu to work out their individual wants and desires. As a result, on a single day, three announcements appeared side-by-side in the daily newspaper. The first announced that Yang and Qu Qiubei had married, the second declared that Yang and her first husband were divorced, and the third that Qu Qiubei and Yang's first husband had become good friends. A stylish dresser and a striking beauty, she was a leading figure in 1930s Shanghai. The following article, published in *Women's Critic* as an insert of the *Republican Daily,* typifies her mixture of personal experiences with more generalized changes occurring in Chinese society.

Questions

1. In what ways do Yang Zhihua's ideas about love break with those in China's past?
2. What does Yang Zhihua suggest is the basic problem(s) with the way dating occurs in 1920s China?

There stood several young men, who all wore new-style clothes, hats, and shoes, and usually spoke and wrote in a brand new language and fancy style. Suddenly, one of them came up to me and said: "Your relationship with so-and-so is already known to us all. Aha, you two are in love!" I simply laughed. If he had been smart, he would have instantly known what my laughter meant. What did I laugh at? I simply laughed at his "newness" and the fact that he was new on the outside but old on the inside. His mixture of old and new is even older than the old and dirtier than dirt. Then he continued to ask me: "Why don't you tell us more about it, since you two are indeed in love?" Once again, I laughed coldly. He had no idea.

How many people who are supposedly engaged in the New Culture movement these days truly mean business? Far too many of them are just wearing masks! As it is, there are more destroyers than builders; if this continues, our future is really in grave danger!

Open socializing between men and women is a very important issue. There has been a lot of public demand for that since the May Fourth Movement. Unfortunately, it has not been easy to carry out. Why not? In my opinion, it is due to the obstacles created by the men and women involved. On the one hand, they advocate open socializing between men and women; on the other hand, they are doing things to hinder it. This is a real self-contradiction; it is like blocking one's own way with rocks.

This is where the obstacles lie.

First, when a man and a woman start to socialize by speaking and writing to each other, going to the parks together, or studying together, people jump to the conclusion that this young man and this young woman are in love, even though they are actually just friends. Consequently, some young men and women succumb to these outside pressures and speculations, go ahead and push themselves into the "business of love," and then have sex. After that, they break up, agonize, and part ways. The whole process usually lasts a very short time because their relationship has the wrong foundation to begin with. This kind of love is caused by outside pressure, so it is not true love. It is not a personal choice, so it usually does not last long. It is certainly not a good thing for society when couples separate, though divorce is an expedient means to deal with problems caused by the old marriage system. Any society that allows people to copulate and then casually separate is a primitive one and exists only in periods of barbarism. Now that such things happen in our society, it is no wonder that those old moralists feel disgusted.

As I have shown, this situation results from the fact that some people who have been steeped in the old tradition resent and make a fuss about socializing between men and women. This is an objective obstacle.

The second obstacle—one that is caused by the men and women themselves. Often, one feels excited when one meets a stranger of the opposite sex. When this happens, people behave strangely, assuming that the purpose of socializing with someone of the opposite sex is to "love and marry." For the sole purpose of speeding up the game of love, they discard their personal integrity and try all sorts of tricks to seduce the opposite sex. They never question whether love should be achieved that way and whether this kind of union between the sexes is natural or everlasting. This is completely wrong! This kind of union has nothing to do with love. It is nothing but animal desire. With this kind of animalistic socializing going on, it is no wonder that those old moralists curse the absurdity of the New Culture Movement and prevent their own children from going to public gatherings.

Third, there are some who tend to misunderstand the intention of the other party, assuming that even the slightest agreement in language and thought signifies "love." They then seek love without trying to understand the other party. Suffering from "unrequited love," many of them end up becoming ill, insane, or suicidal. Those who are smarter may come back to their senses in time. Observation of these kinds of encounters may cause pessimism and loneliness in other people, and keep them from going out and socializing.

The above are the obstacles that hinder the socializing between men and women.

Love is sacred and should not be spoken of lightly. It is a union of character. Anybody who misinterprets the concept of character, fails to distinguish between the part and the whole, or fails to understand the significance of character is not qualified to talk about "love."

I respect my own and others' character. If I actually fall in love with someone, I will not be afraid to talk about it. If not, however, I will certainly curse those who don't respect the character of others. Who can sway my will? Who can force me? Who would dare to control me? I have the right to control my own life and would never allow anybody else to control me. I sincerely advise young people: Raise your consciousness, never take lightly your own character or others', never try to destroy our New Culture Movement, and avoid hindering our progress. It is my hope that there will be more discussion on socializing between men and women. I also welcome comments and criticisms.

8.12   DING LING'S *MISS SOPHIE'S DIARY* (1928)

Ding Ling (1904–1986), the pen-name of Jiang Bingzhi, was perhaps the most prominent female author of twentieth-century China. Highly influenced by May Fourth thought and sympathetic to the communist cause, she joined the Chinese Communist Party in 1932. Her husband, Hu Yepin, also a communist, was detained and executed along with other communists by the GMD in 1931. Ding Ling herself was arrested in 1933 by the GMD and held under house arrest until 1936. The story "Miss Sophie's Diary," was only Ding Ling's second published story, yet it typifies her highly successful early style and bold expression of her sexual feelings. The story takes place in Beijing with the characters, Yufang and Yunlin, being two close friends of the main character, Miss Sophie.

Questions

1. Why would "Miss Sophie's Diary" be considered innovative literature for the period?
2. Would you describe the relationships as radical? Would many of the emotions she illustrates still be true today?

12 January

Yufang has moved in, but Yunlin has moved out. Can there be another couple like them in the universe? They won't live together for fear of having a child. I imagine that they can't be certain that if they lay in each other's arms in bed they wouldn't do other things too, which is why they're taking this precaution against that sort of physical contact. Hugging and kissing when they're alone isn't dangerous, so the occasional discreet bout doesn't come within the scope of their ban. I couldn't help laughing at them for their asceticism. Why shouldn't you embrace the naked love of your beloved? Why repress that manifestation of love? How can the pair of them think of those irrelevant and worrying things before they're even under the same quilt? I don't believe that love can be so rational and scientific.

They didn't get angry with me for teasing them. They're proud of their purity, and they laughed at my childishness. I can understand their state of mind, but there are so many strange things in the world that I can't fathom at all.

I stayed at Yunlin's (or Yufang's, as I should now say) till 10 before coming back. We talked a lot about ghosts.

I got used to talk about ghosts when I was tiny. I often used to sit on my aunt's lap listening to my uncle telling stories from *Liaozhai* [Pu Songling's Tales from the Studio], and I loved listening till late at night. As for being frightened, that was another matter. I'd never tell anyone about it, because if I'd admitted being frightened I'd never have heard the story to the end, my uncle would have gone into his study, and I'd not have been allowed to get out of bed. When I went to school I learnt a little science from the teachers. Because I was completely convinced by our teacher Pockmarked Zhou I believed the books too, whereupon ghosts weren't frightening any more. Now I'm more grown up I still say that I don't believe in ghosts, but my disbelief doesn't stop the goose-pimples or my hair standing on end. But whenever the conversation gets on to ghosts other people don't realize that I'm wanting to change the subject because I'm afraid of lying alone in my quilt at night being sad at missing my dead aunt and uncle.

When I came back and saw that dark alley I did feel a little scared. I wouldn't have been at all surprised if a great yellow face had appeared in some corner or if a hairy hand had stretched out in that alley that seemed to be frozen solid. But that tall man Ling Jishi seemed a reliable bodyguard to have beside me, so when Yufang asked me I said I wasn't scared.

Yunlin came out with us and went back to his new place. As he went south and we went north the sound of his rubber-soled shoes on the footpath died out within three or four paces.

He put out a hand and took me by the waist.

"I'm sure you're frightened, Sophie."

I tried to struggle but I couldn't break free.

My head rested against his ribs. I wondered what sort of creature I'd look like in the light, held by the arms of a man over a head taller than me.

I ducked down and got out. He let go and stood beside me as we knocked at the front gate.

The alley was very dark, but I could see very clearly where he was looking. My heart was pounding somewhat as I waited for the gate to open.

"You're frightened, Sophie," he said.

There was the sound of the bolts being drawn as the porter asked who was there. I turned to him and started to say, "Goodnight." He seized my hand fiercely and I couldn't finish the word. The porter showed his astonishment as he saw the tall man behind me.

When the two of us were alone in my room my boldness was not needed any longer. I deliberately tried to make some politely conventional remarks but just couldn't. All I could manage was, "Do sit down." Then I began washing my face.

Goodness knows how, but I'd forgotten all about ghosts.

"Are you still interested in studying English, Sophie?" he asked suddenly.

So he was coming to me, and he was the first to bring up the English. Of course he wouldn't necessarily be pleased at having to sacrifice his time for nothing to give some extra classes: he couldn't fool me, a woman of twenty, about what he had in mind. I smiled, though only in my head.

"I'm too stupid," I said. "I'm worried that I couldn't manage it and would only make a fool of myself."

He said nothing, but picked up a photograph that was standing on my table. It was of my sister's little girl. She's just one year old.

When I'd washed my face I sat down at the other side of the table. He looked first at me, then at the little girl, then back at me again. Yes, she looked very much like me.

"She's nice, isn't she?" I asked him. "Do you think she's like me?"

"Who is she?" His voice clearly showed that he was very serious.

"Don't you think she's sweet?"

He kept asking me who she was.

Suddenly I realized what he was driving at. I wanted to lie to him.

"She's mine." I snatched the photograph and kissed it.

He believed me. I'd actually fooled him. I felt triumphant in my dishonesty.

This triumph seemed to make him less charming and handsome. Why else could I have ignored his eyes and forgotten his mouth when he showed that naïve astonishment? Otherwise this triumph was bound to cool my passion.

But after he'd gone I felt sorry. There'd been so many obvious chances set in front of me. If only I'd made some other expression when he pressed my hand and let him understand that I wouldn't have turned him down he'd certainly have made some bolder moves. When it comes to boldness between the sexes I'm absolutely certain that as long as you don't detest the other person the pleasure you feel must be like the body melting. So why do I have to be prim and proper with him? After all, what did I move into this dilapidated room for?

8.13 BA JIN'S *FAMILY* (1931)

Ba Jin came of age in a large wealthy family in Chengdu (the capital of Sichuan province in western China). The family compound had over 50 family members with at least as many servants. His most famous novel, *Family,* is drawn from many of his own personal experiences (and frustrations). *Family* is the first book of a trilogy (the books *Spring* and *Autumn* followed). While Ba Jin sought to paint the traditional family customs in a dark light, the book was interpreted in a more positive light as pointing out the ways in which a new generation could change China. His work offers a more mainstream, less ideologically informed view of Republican China and is still revered and read in China today. The trilogy is considered one of the best literary works discussing marriage issues

BA JIN (1904–2005)—Pen name of influential May Fourth author Li Feigan who is best known for his novel *Family,* the first in the *Torrents Trilogy* which also included *Spring* and *Autumn.*

from the view of the young generation, under the influence of May Fourth, and how they fight against the traditional Confucian family values.

Questions

1. **How did Juexin's father's decision affect his future aspirations?**
2. **How do you think Ba Jin's depiction of China in the 1920s resonated with Chinese readers?**

To Juemin and Juehui, Juexin was "Big Brother." Though born of the same mother and living in the same house, his position was entirely different from theirs. In the large Gao family, he was the eldest son of an eldest son, and for that reason his destiny was fixed from the moment he came into the world.

Handsome and intelligent, he was his father's favorite. His private tutor also spoke highly of him. People predicted that he would do big things, and his parents considered themselves fortunate to be blessed with such a son.

Brought up with loving care, after studying with a private tutor for a number of years, Juexin entered middle school. One of the school's best students, he graduated four years later at the top of his class. He was very interested in physics and chemistry and hoped to go on to a university in Shanghai or Beijing, or perhaps study abroad, in Germany. His mind was full of beautiful dreams. At that time he was the envy of his classmates.

In his fourth year at middle school, he lost his mother. His father later married again, this time to a younger woman who had been his mother's cousin. Juexin was aware of his loss, for he knew full well that nothing could replace the love of a mother. But her death left no irreparable wound in his heart; he was able to console himself with rosy dreams of his future. Moreover, he had someone who understood him and could comfort him – his pretty cousin Mei, "mei" for "plum blossom."

But then, one day his dreams were shattered, cruelly and bitterly shattered. The evening he returned home carrying his diploma, the plaudits of his teachers and friends still ringing in his ears, his father called him into his room and said:

"Now that you've graduated, I want to arrange your marriage. Your grandfather is looking forward to having a great-grandson, and I, too, would like to be able to hold a grandson in my arms. You're old enough to be married; I won't feel easy until I fulfill my obligation to find you a wife. Although I didn't accumulate much money in my years away from home as an official, still I've put by enough for us to get along on. My health isn't what it used to be; I'm thinking of spending my time at home and having you help me run the household affairs. All the more reason you'll be needing a wife. I've already arranged a match with the Li family. The thirteenth of next month is a good day. We'll announce the engagement then. You can be married within the year…"

The blow was too sudden. Although he understood everything his father said, somehow the meaning didn't fully register. Juexin only nodded his head. He didn't dare look his father in the eye, although the old man was gazing at him kindly.

Juexin did not utter a word of protest, nor did such a thought ever occur to him. He merely nodded to indicate his compliance with his father's wishes. But after he returned to his own room, and shut the door, he threw himself down on his bed, covered his head with the quilt and wept. He wept for his broken dreams.

He had heard something about a match with a daughter of the Li family. But he had never been permitted to learn the whole story, and so he hadn't placed much credence in it. A number of gentlemen with unmarried daughters, impressed by his good looks and his success in his studies, had become interested in him; there was a steady stream of matchmakers to his family's door. His father weeded out the applicants until only two remained under consideration. It was difficult to make a choice; both of the persons serving as matchmakers were of equal prestige and importance. Finally, he decided to resort to divination. He wrote each of the girls' names on a slip of red paper, rolled the slips up into the balls, then, after praying for guidance before the family ancestral tablets, picked one.

Thus the match with the Li family was decided. But it was only now that Juexin was informed of the result.

Yes, he had dreamed of romance. The one in his heart was the girl who understood him and who could comfort him – his cousin Mei. At one time he was sure she would be his future mate, and he had congratulated himself that this would be so, since in his family marriage between cousins was quite common.

He was deeply in love with Mei, but now his father had chosen another, a girl he had never seen, and said that he must marry within the year. What's more, his hopes of continuing his studies had burst like a bubble. It was a terrible shock to Juexin. His future was finished, his beautiful dreams shattered.

CHAPTER 9
FRACTURED VISIONS: MANCHURIA, NANJING, AND YAN'AN IN THE 1930s

VISUAL SOURCE
A Map of the Long March

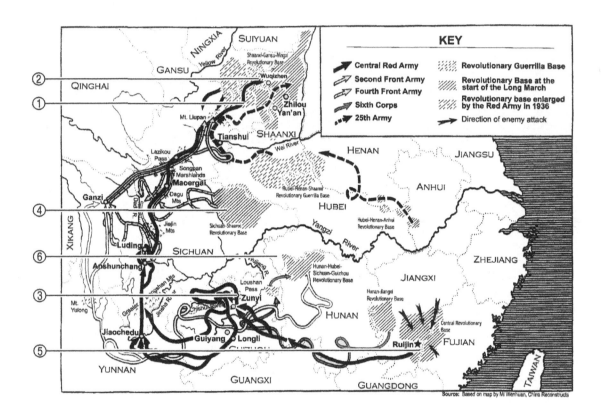

① LONG MARCH: In response to increased Nationalist (GMD) attacks on the Jiangxi soviet in southeastern China,100,000 members of the Central Red Army (also known as the First Army) left in October of 1934 arriving little over a year later with only 8,000 in the northwestern city of Yan'an due to attrition, desertion, and deaths.

② LENGTH: The Long Marchers are traditionally said to have traversed a distance of "25,000 li" or about 8,000 miles though some have estimated the distance as little as 3,700 miles. Regardless, the Long March was no small feat (like walking from Los Angeles to New York and then continuing down to Miami). But as this map highlights perhaps it is even more accurate to talk of multiple "Long Marches" since there were several other Communist forces taking different routes with all the veterans considered "Long Marchers."

③ ZUNYI (January 15–17, 1935): The Central Army marched into Zunyi, a city in northern Guizhou, in mid-January. It was the first rest from near constant military pressure since their departure from Jiangxi several months earlier. Aside from time to clean up their equipment, gather supplies, and recruit men to join their army the top ten, CCP leaders met to discuss military strategy. Mao Zedong delivered a strong critique of the leader's military tactics leading to his promotion to the Standing Committee, and thus marking the beginning of his ascent to leadership of the CCP.

④ GMD PURSUIT & CCP TACTICS: The Guomindang's encirclement campaigns (or "blockhouse" strategy) sought to cut off the Jiangxi Soviet economically, politically, and militarily from all outside contact and aid. Although the Central Army successfully broke out of that encirclement, GMD troops harassed, pursued, and out-flanked the Communists throughout the retreat. As the Communists evaded his troops the GMD called on their allies (often local warlords) to come to his aid, though most local troops sought to protect the major population centers instead of engaging the Communists.

⑤ LONG RETREAT?: Many scholars question the Communist glorification of the march suggesting at best it should be considered a desperate reaction to a desperate situation. The CCP's main military force was reduced by 90%, the march took the CCP leadership from a relatively heavily populated and strategically significant location to a remote and relatively sparsely populated hinterland where their position remained threatened by Jiang Jieshi's armies.

⑥ MYTHOLOGIZING OF THE LONG MARCH: The Long March as a watershed event in the history of the Chinese Communist Party has been embellished in both Chinese and western accounts. Today Chinese school children still learn about the physical hardships, harrowing victories, and great distances traveled by the Long Marchers. The term "Long March" is applied as a superlative to describe revolutionary work units, special express trains, and even China's latest rockets to the moon.

In the early morning hours of December 12, 1936, troops under the command of the "Young Marshal," **Zhang Xueliang,** entered the guesthouse outside Xi'an where Chinese president Jiang Jieshi was sleeping. Jiang Jieshi, awakened by the shots fired by his guards, fled out a back door leaving his dentures, and some say his pajamas, behind. He hid behind a large boulder on the hillside for nearly half an hour before he was discovered and whisked away to a secret location by Zhang Xueliang's troops. In a telegram sent to the Nanjing government later that day Zhang Xueliang demanded: 1) an immediate declaration of war against Japan, 2) a pledge by the Nanjing government to recover all lost territories, including Manchuria, and 3) the reorganization of the Guomindang Party to allow the readmission of Communists to membership on the same basis that existed before the anti-Communist purge began in 1927. Almost two weeks later on Christmas Day, Jiang Jieshi was suddenly released with the announcement that he had agreed in principle to Zhang Xueliang's demands. He immediately flew back to Nanjing with his wife, Song Meiling and brother-in-law Kong Xiangxi, who had helped negotiate his release. Zhang Xueliang returned with Jiang Jieshi to Nanjing seeking to prove his actions were made out of his loyalty to Jiang Jieshi not in defiance of him.

Upon their arrival in Nanjing, Zhang Xueliang issued a public apology stating: "I am naturally rustic, surly, and unpolished. This has led me to commit an impudent and criminal act." For his part, Jiang Jieshi, incensed by what he felt was a traitorous deed, immediately arrested, court-marshaled, and eventually sentenced Zhang Xueliang to house arrest. Jiang Jieshi never forgave Zhang Xueliang. He kept him under house arrest for the next fifty-three years—first on the Chinese mainland, and later Taiwan when the GMD retreated there—earning him the unwelcome distinction of being the longest-serving political prisoner in the world. Given his harsh treatment by Jiang Jieshi, Zhang Xueliang seems like an improbable candidate to earn the sobriquet by both the Chinese Communist and Nationalist governments as a "hero of history" (*qiangu gongchen*) for his efforts in coaxing Jiang Jieshi not to exterminate the Communists in favor of defending China against the Japanese encroachment.

Historians have long debated Zhang Xueliang's motives in kidnapping Jiang Jieshi. Zhang Xueliang's father, Zhang Zuolin, had controlled Manchuria (northeastern China) and ruled there for well over a decade until assassinated by Japanese agents in 1928. Only twenty-eight years old at the time, Zhang Xueliang struggled in his inherited role to modernize Manchuria while pursuing a profligate lifestyle of drugs, majiang, and womanizing. In 1931, while Zhang Xueliang was in a Beijing hospital attempting to break his opium addiction, Japanese forces invaded Manchuria and established a puppet state of "Manchukuo" (installing the last Qing emperor, Puyi, on the throne). Jiang Jieshi's refusal to send Nationalist troops to defend the region was a major factor in Zhang Xueliang's hasty departure to Europe the following month. There he earned a reputation for fast cars, dancing, all-night poker games and an entourage that included scores of beautiful women. His extravagant lifestyle made him a regular feature in the European papers' gossip columns, with the press invariably referring to him as the "Dancing Despot." He returned to China in 1934, conforming to a spartan lifestyle. Jiang Jieshi quickly appointed him to the post of Vice-Commander of Nanjing's anti-Communist forces (largely his own former Manchurian army) on the outside of the northwestern city of Xi'an.

ZHANG XUELIANG (1900–2001)—Son of Manchurian warlord Zhang Zuolin and mastermind behind the kidnapping of Jiang Jieshi in 1936 convincing him to fight Japan rather than the CCP.

On his return to China, Zhang Xueliang encountered a politically charged situation. Jiang Jieshi, with the help of German advisors, had embarked on his fifth (and final) encirclement of Chinese Communist forces in Jiangxi. Encountering numerically superior and better-equipped troops, the Chinese communist army was forced to **march** 6,000 miles across southern and western China to the northwestern province of Shaanxi. Japan continued to edge menacingly towards northern China. Jiang Jieshi claimed that "the Japanese were a disease of the skin, while the Communists were a disease of the heart," and thus there was a need first to exterminate the Communist threat to his Nationalist government, and only then to focus attention on the Japanese. His stance ran counter to the popular sentiment of intense enmity towards Japan that had existed ever since Japan's Twenty-one Demands in 1915. The decision for most Chinese was self-evident when faced with a choice between exterminating fellow Chinese, of whatever political hue, and resisting Japanese advances. Jiang Jieshi's reluctantance to engage Japan was ultimately forced by Japan's invasion of China in the summer of 1937.

In retrospect, the Xi'an Incident is perhaps the most critical juncture in Republican China (1912–49). Without such a dramatic turn in Nationalist policy, Yan'an (the final refuge of the Chinese Communists), would have almost certainly been eliminated. In 1936 Communist forces totaled about 20,000 men, while Nationalist forces were at least ten times that many. Equally significant, this event galvanized the Chinese people into unifying behind Jiang Jieshi and toughened them for a long battle against the Japanese. Zhang Xueliang, under house arrest for over five decades, would never again be allowed to play an active political or military role. Though, in what he must have considered a hollow victory, Zhang Xueliang outlived both Jiang Jieshi and his son Jiang Jingguo. He was finally released from house arrest in 1990 and spent his last years living with his son in Honolulu, Hawaii where he died at the age of 101.

MANCHUKUO: JAPAN IN MANCHURIA

In the last decades of the Qing, China, Russia, and Japan vied for control of northeastern China, or Manchuria. After the fall of the Qing, Manchuria, like many areas of China, came under warlord control—namely Zhang Zuolin and later, his son Zhang Xueliang. In this decentralized state, Japan's sphere of influence began to expand from Korea, which had become a colony under Japanese control in 1910. Japan invested heavily in the region hoping to benefit industrially, agriculturally, and militarily. In 1931, Japan invaded and assumed total control of northeastern China, a region three times the size of Japan's homeland, and one rich in minerals and fertile farmland. They created the puppet state of **Manchukuo** in 1932, and placed Puyi, the last Qing emperor, as the titular head. Two years later they made him emperor of the state, though with virtually no real control over administrative and political affairs. Outraged, the Nationalist Nanjing government took the case to the League of Nations, forerunner of today's United Nations, but refused to take military action.

LONG MARCH (1934–35)—A series of CCP marches from their bases in the southeast to northwestern China. The main route ran 6,000 miles from Jiangxi to Shaanxi and took one year to complete. Casualties and desertions reduced the original 100,000 marchers by more than 90 percent to fewer than 10,000.

MANCHUKUO—The puppet government formed by the Japanese in 1932 in northeastern China. The last Qing emperor, Puyi, was named its chief executive and remained titular head until the end of the Second World War in 1945.

9.1 JAPANESE ASSERTION THAT CHINA IS NOT AN ORGANIZED STATE (FEBRUARY 19, 1932)

In their statement before the League of Nations general assembly, Japan defended their actions in Manchukuo by principally asserting that China's chaotic political situation necessitated such a step. Japan claimed that without their intervention the entire region could become destabilized, endangering all of Northeast Asia, including Japan and their Korean colony, hence their actions were purely self-preservation. Few nations failed to see through Japan's incongruent claim, below, that twelve years earlier (in 1921) at the height of warlord control, China was more stable than under the Nanjing regime. There was no acknowledgement that many of Japan's earlier interventions (e.g., military maneuvers, loans to warlords, etc.) fueled such "anarchy."

Questions

1. What does Japan suggest results from China's "condition of complete chaos and incredible anarchy"?
2. In what ways does Japan suggest that its position is "similar to that in which several Powers have found themselves in the last few years"?

The preamble to the Covenant of the League specifies distinctly that the Covenant applies to organized peoples. It regulates the relations between such peoples. I am obliged to state that in the Far East we have to deal with a country—I regret to have to say so, but it is the truth—which has for more than ten years been in a state of civil war, in a condition of complete chaos and incredible anarchy.

Such are the circumstances in which difficulties arose between Japan and China. Had such difficulties arisen in another country which had a properly organized and efficient administration, our action would have been different. There would have been no need for us to go to the point we have reached now. We would have accepted any peaceful settlement of the dispute. We could have observed literally the provisions of the Covenant.

China was admitted to membership of the League twelve years ago because she was regarded as an organized country with a regular administration. It was in that capacity that she was admitted. Events, however, have brought about a complete change in China. There have been wars between the Chinese generals and this has led to a state of complete anarchy, with the result that the rights and interests of foreigners ensuing from various treaties and conventions have ceased to be protected. That is why the countries with interests in China have been compelled to employ methods which would not have been permitted if the same difficulties had

occurred elsewhere in a really organized country. We do not lack precedents in this connection. Our position is similar to that in which several Powers have found themselves in the last few years. We are obliged to take the protection of the lives and rights of our nationals into our own hands. If the use of a method of legitimate defense, or protection, was admitted and recognized as permissible for one Power a few years ago, Japan can claim the same right today. If we are censured for having committed acts of aggression, similar acts should have been censured when committed by certain other Powers having interests by China. If the Council censures the acts of hostility committed by Japan, it must first tell us what view it takes of similar acts we all have in mind that took place previously. All that is the outcome of the circumstances now existing in China. Had the position been normal in China, the Powers which in the past had recourse to extreme measures would not have done so. They would not have found it necessary to do so. They would have appealed to the League Council to settle their dispute by pacific and regular methods. The fact that they were unable to do so proves that the League—and the Council in particular—could not, as would have been natural and normal in other circumstances, apply the Covenant to its full extent and in accordance with the strict interpretation of its wording.

Japan today is under the same imperious necessity. It is solely to protect our interests that we have had to act as we have done.

9.2 PRINCIPLES FOR THE ORGANIZATION OF THE "MANCHUKUO" GOVERNMENT (1932)

As international pressure increased, Japan sought to justify its dominant economic, political and military power within the newly established Manchukuo state. The League of Nations, as part of its investigation into China's charges against Japan, asked Japan to provide statements explicating its presence in Manchuria. The following document is Japan's own portrayal of its role in Manchukuo and justifying why Japanese oversight was needed in the region. It must be acknowledged that Japan's actions in Manchuria were quite successful, though not popular with the members of League of Nations. Between 1931 and 1945 nearly 500,000 Japanese immigrated to Manchuria, with most of them working as farmers in the region's fertile farmland. It was not just the Japanese who were attracted to Manchukuo, Japanese-Americans, frustrated with the limited opportunities in pre-war America, immigrated to Manchuria in substantial numbers. The ease with which Japan gained control of Manchukuo, and its subsequent economic success, led Japan to use it as a model for subsequent puppet states in China and Asia.

Questions

1. **Japan suggests that Manchukuo is an independent state. What aspects in the following list support that claim?**
2. **What elements suggest that Japan is not simply interested in protecting Manchukuo from potential external threats?**

1. Japan, with a view to maintaining and developing her rights in Manchuria, shall establish organs, to direct the affairs of the "Manchukuo." The organ shall, in addition, be given sufficient power so that the new state may rely upon the Japanese for guidance and follow the lines of development as laid down by Japan who, on her side, shall exercise her control with sincerity and goodwill in order that the new state may not have any feelings of distrust. Our attitude should be just and fair.

2. The form of the government shall not be republican. Established on the basis of the "kingly principle," the new state shall adopt a monarchical form of government.

3. The new state shall exercise absolute authority over its internal affairs, and under the direction of Japan, it shall carry out policies based on monarchical principles.

4. With a view to realizing the above object, Japan shall provide the royal family ruling over the new state with sufficient military power to control Manchuria and Mongolia.

5. The political system of the new state and its various organization shall be modeled after those of Japan with modifications according to local conditions in the new state. This principle holds good not only for organizations of a political nature, but also for social institutions as, for instance, customs and usages, which should be gradually assimilated with those of Japan. In the execution of this principle, however, simplicity and practicability should be emphasized so as to avoid the complexity of Japanese laws.

6. The Chinese people do not have the same sense of loyalty to the Imperial House as the Japanese. The authorities should therefore be severe in their rule of the people so that they may have reverence and awe towards their rulers.

7. If the necessity of drafting the Constitution arises, the Constitution shall be modeled after that of Japan. The representative assembly shall be nothing more than an advisory council and an organ to publish statements respecting the finance of the state. (Toward the last decade of the Qing dynasty, the evils of the Advisory Council which was established to prepare for a constitutional government were too obvious).

8. Legislative and executive powers shall reside with the supreme authorities, but the judicial power

shall be respected in accordance with laws so that its independent spirit may be maintained.

9. With regard to the laws, Japanese laws, and particularly Japanese procedural laws, shall be made use of. As to the laws of the family, the authorities shall take into consideration the special customs and usages of the population. In cases where the foreign nationals are involved, it seems better that Japan should assume the responsibility of supervising the final decision.

10. All executive acts shall be performed in accordance with the existing customs and usages, and simplicity and practicability shall be emphasized. The complexity of Japanese local organizations shall be avoided and the corruption of officials shall be eliminated.

11. The police force of the new state shall be under the control of a strong organ which shall also be given the power of bandit suppression. The force shall be organized on a semi-military basis and well distributed in the state so that under strict supervision and able direction bandit activities may be eliminated.

12. The national defense of the new state shall be left entirely to Japan. In order to complete its nationhood, the new state is not yet in a position to defend itself from China and Russia under its present conditions. Moreover, the national defense of the state coincides with that of Japan; therefore, under no circumstance, shall the new state have the right of defending itself.

13. The foreign relations of the new state shall be entrusted to Japan so that serious diplomatic blunders may be avoided and national safety assured.

14. The military forces shall be maintained to a degree sufficient to suppress internal disorders. The royal family ruling over the new state shall directly command the forces so that the symbol of authority may be deeply impressed upon the imagination of the people. But the ultimate strength of the new state resides in the military power of Japan, so that there is no necessity of maintaining a large force. Whenever the need of suppressing internal disorders arises, the new state can always apply to Japan for aid, because she has special rights and duties of maintaining order in Manchuria.

15. The South Manchuria Railway shall have the exclusive right of railway enterprises in Manchuria. The new projected railways shall be always in the form of joint enterprises so that the spirit of the idea of "mutual dependence to promote mutual glory" may be realized.

16. As regards the right of existence in Manchuria, the Japanese people shall enjoy the same rights and privileges at the nationals of the new state. Besides concluding treaties with the new state to that effect, Japan shall devise means to facilitate Japanese immigration.

17. Because of many complications, Japan will consider carefully the desirability of appointment of Japanese people as the officials of "Manchukuo." But in any case, Japan shall exercise actual control and disciplinary supervision in the execution of the basic policies of the government in order to prevent corruption and achieve political success. The present organization should be submitted for revision, but in the selection of the personnel, if sufficient care is not taken, there will be grave consequences. Japan shall therefore take very seriously consideration of the matter.

18. With regard to military organs, there shall be careful selection of Japanese people to enforce discipline and supervise the training of the soldiers. As regards matters relating to the distribution of Japanese officials in the various executive organs, to their appointment and dismissal, their control and supervision, the new unified Japanese organ in Manchuria shall assume full responsibility of deciding upon them.

9.3 LYTTON COMMISSION REPORT (OCTOBER, 1932)

In 1931 the League of Nations sent a commission to China and Manchukuo headed by Lord Lytton, the former Viceroy of India, to investigate both Japan's and China's claims. The **Lytton Report,** or officially "The Report of the Commission of Enquiry," ran over 400 pages, including supplementary documents. The commission initially sought to offer

LYTTON REPORT (1932)—A League of Nations report indicting Japan for its role in seizing, subjugating and continuing to manage the northeastern area of China under the puppet Manchukuo government. Japan withdrew from the League a month after the international body voted to accept its conclusions.

recommendations amenable to both the Chinese and Japanese. When it realized this would be impossible, in October 1932 it issued its full report which was adopted by the League the following February. Upon receiving the report the General Assembly issued statements of facts regarding the Sino-Japanese disputes and followed with the adoption of ten principles and conditions (such as the evacuation of Japanese troops from Manchuria). Finally, the Assembly approved a recommendation to all League of Nations members not to recognize the existing Manchukuo regime. Eventually, a total of ten nations—virtually all wartime allies of Japan—and the Vatican, extended diplomatic relations to Manchukuo.

Questions

1. **What does the Lytton Report suggest motivated Japan's "actions and policies" in Manchuria?**
2. **What solutions does the report offer to resolve the situation?**

We recognize the great importance of Manchuria in the economic development of Japan, nor do we consider unreasonable her demand for the establishment of a stable government which would be capable of maintaining the order necessary for the economic development of the country. But such conditions can only be securely and effectively guaranteed by an administration which is in conformity with the wishes of the population and which takes full account of their feelings and aspirations. And equally it is only in an atmosphere of external confidence and internal peace, very different from that now existing in the Far East, that the capital which is necessary for the rapid economic development of Manchuria will be forthcoming.

In spite of the pressure of increasing overpopulation, the Japanese have not as yet fully utilized their existing facilities for emigration, and the Japanese Government has not hitherto contemplated a large emigration of their people to Manchuria. But the Japanese do look to further industrialization as a means to cope with the agrarian crisis to further industrialization as a means to cope with the agrarian crisis and with the population problem. Such industrialization would require further economic outlets and the only large and relatively sure markets that Japan finds are in Asia and particularly in China. Japan requires not only the Manchurian, but the whole Chinese market, and the rise in the standard of living which will certainly follow the consolidation and modernization of China should stimulate trade and raise the purchasing power of the Chinese market.... This economic *rapprochement* between Japan and China, which is of vital interest to Japan, is of equal interest to China, for China would find that a closer economic and technical co-operation with Japan would assist her in her primary task of national reconstruction....

It may, however, be less economic considerations than anxiety for her own security which has determined the actions and policy of Japan in Manchuria. It is especially in this connection that her statesmen and military authorities are accustomed to speak of Manchuria as 'the life line of Japan.' One can sympathize with such anxieties and try to appreciate the actions and motives of those who have to bear the heavy responsibility of securing the defense of their country against all eventualities. While acknowledging the interest of Japan in preventing Manchuria from serving as a base of operations directed against her own territory, and even her wish to be able to take all appropriate military measures if in certain circumstances the frontiers of Manchuria should be crossed by the forces of a foreign Power, it may still be questioned whether the military occupation of Manchuria for an indefinite period, involving, as it must, a heavy financial burden, is really the most effective way of insuring against this external danger; and whether, in the event of aggression having to be resisted in this way, the Japanese troops in Manchuria would not be seriously embarrassed if they were surrounded by a restive or rebellious population backed by a hostile China. It is surely in the interest of Japan to consider also other possible solutions of the problem of security, which would be more in keeping with the principles on which rests the present peace organization of the world, and analogous to arrangements concluded by other Great Powers in various parts of the world. She might even find it possible, with the sympathy and goodwill of the rest of the world, and at no cost to herself, to obtain better security than she will obtain by the costly method she is at present adopting.

Apart from China and Japan, other Powers of the world have also important interests to defend in this Sino-Japanese conflict. We have already referred to existing multilateral treaties, and any real and lasting solution by agreement must be compatible with the stipulations of these fundamental agreements, on which is based the peace organization of the world. The considerations which actuated the representatives of the Powers at the Washington Conference are still valid. It is quite as much in the interests of the Powers now as it was in 1922 to assist the reconstruction of China and to maintain her sovereignty and her territorial and administrative integrity as indispensable to the maintenance of peace. Any disintegration of China might lead, perhaps rapidly, to serious international rivalries, which would become all the more bitter if they should happen to coincide with rivalries between divergent social systems. Finally the interests of peace are the same the world over. Any loss of confidence in the application of the principles of the Covenant and the Pact of Paris in any part of the world diminishes the value and efficacy of those principles everywhere.

9.4 JAPANESE DECLARATION AND WITHDRAWAL FROM LEAGUE (MARCH 27, 1933)

On February 24, 1933, the League of Nations Assembly adopted the Lytton Report on Manchuria with Japan casting the only dissenting vote. Most damning was the Lytton Report's conclusion that it was "indisputable that without any declaration of war, a large part of Chinese territory has been forcibly seized and occupied by Japanese troops, and that in consequence of this operation, it has been separated from and declared independent of the rest of China." Japan's response to the League of Nations' resolutions was swift. On the same day the League Assembly adopted the report, Japan's entire delegation walked out of the Assembly chambers. A month later, on March 27, 1933, Japan officially announced its intention to withdraw from the League of Nations citing a failure of the League to grasp the realities of the East Asia situation.

Questions

1. **In what ways does Japan believe the League has misunderstood its actions in Manchuria?**
2. **Why would the Japanese Government find it more beneficial to leave the League than to remain a member?**

The Japanese Government believe that the national policy of Japan which has for its aim to ensure the peace of the Orient and thereby to contribute to the cause of peace throughout the world, is identical in spirit with the mission of the League of Nations, which is to achieve international peace and security. It has always been with pleasure, therefore, that this country has for thirteen years past, as an original member of the League, and a permanent member of its Council, extended a full measure of its high purpose. It is indeed a matter of historical fact that Japan has continuously participated in the various activities of the League with a zeal not inferior to that exhibited by any other nation. At the same time, it is and has always been the conviction of the Japanese Government that in order to render possible maintenance of peace in various regions of the world, it is necessary in existing circumstances to allow the operation of the Covenant of the League to vary in accordance with the actual conditions prevailing in each of those regions. Only by acting on this just and equitable principle can the League fulfill its mission and increase its influence.

Acting on this conviction, the Japanese Government, ever since the Sino-Japanese dispute was, in September, 1931, submitted to the League, have, at meetings of the League and on other occasions, continually set forward a consistent view. This was, that if the League was to settle the issue fairly and equitably, and to make a real contribution to the promotion of peace in the Orient, and thus enhance its prestige, it should acquire a complete grasp of the actual conditions in this quarter of the globe and apply the Covenant of the League in accordance with these conditions. They have repeatedly emphasized and insisted upon the absolute necessity of taking into consideration the fact that China is not an organized State,—that its internal conditions and external relations are characterized by extreme confusion and complexity and by many abnormal and exceptional features,—and that, accordingly, the general principles and usages of international law which govern the ordinary relations between Nations are found to be considerably modified in their operation so far as China is concerned, resulting in the quite abnormal and unique international practices which actually prevail in that country.

However, the majority of the members of the League evinced in the course of its deliberations during the past seventeen months a failure either to grasp these realities or else to face them and take them into proper account. Moreover, it has frequently been made manifest in these deliberations that there exist serious differences of opinion between Japan and these Powers concerning the application and even the interpretation of various international engagements and obligations including the Covenant of the League and the principles of international law. As a result, the report adopted by the Assembly at the Special Session of 24 February last, entirely misapprehending the spirit of peace in the Orient, contains gross errors both in the ascertainment of the facts and in the conclusions deduced. In asserting that the action of the Japanese army at the time of the **incident of 18 September** and subsequently did not fall within the just limits of self-defense, the report assigned no reasons and came to an arbitrary conclusion, and in ignoring alike the state of tension which preceded, and the various aggravations which succeeded, the incident—for all of which the full responsibility is incumbent upon China—the report creates a source of fresh conflict in the political arena of the Orient. By refusing to acknowledge the actual circumstances that led to the foundation of Manchukuo, and by attempting to challenge the position taken up by Japan in recognizing the new State, it cuts away the ground for the stabilization of the Far Eastern situation. Nor can the terms laid down in its recommendations—as was fully explained in the statement issued by this Government on 25 February last—ever be of any possible service in securing enduring peace in these regions.

The conclusion must be that in seeking a solution of the question the majority of the League have attached greater importance to upholding inapplicable formulae than to the real task of assuring peace, and higher value to the vindication of academic theses than to the eradication of the sources of future conflict. For these reasons, and because of the profound differences existing between Japan and the majority of the League in their interpretation of the Covenant and of other treaties, the Japanese Government have been led to realize the existence of an irreconcilable divergence of views, dividing Japan and the League on policies of peace, and especially as regards the fundamental principles to be followed in the establishment of a durable peace in the Far East. The Japanese government, believing that in these circumstances there remains no room for further cooperation, hereby give notice, in accordance with the provisions of Article 1, paragraph 3, of the Covenant, of the intention of Japan to withdraw from the League of Nations.

THE NANJING DECADE

The ten-year period between the end of the Northern Expedition in 1927 and the start of the War of Resistance in 1937 is often referred to as the "Nanjing Decade." Under Jiang Jieshi's leadership the Nanjing government unified China to an extent not seen since the fall of the Qing. Superficially, China seemed to modernize quickly. Chinese cities across the nation, Shanghai and Nanjing in particular, emerged as the vanguard of China's new cosmopolitanism. Shanghai became the "Paris of the Orient" with an urban renaissance that seemed to prosper under GMD rule. Jiang Jieshi and his wife Song Meiling sought to provide a moral underpinning to this emergent Chinese identity with their

MUKDEN (SHENYANG) INCIDENT (SEPTEMBER 18, 1931)—Japan's Kwantung Army blew up a portion of the Southern Manchuria Railway, and used the incident to justify an attack on the city of Shenyang and then on the whole of Manchuria.

"New Life Movement" (9.6). However, pervasive corruption, runaway inflation, and only minimal economic aid for the largest and poorest segments of the population, made the regime increasingly unpopular. Politically and militarily, Jiang Jieshi maintained an intense loathing of Chinese communists. He stepped up military actions against both the Communists and remaining warlords in a series of campaigns that lasted well into the 1930s. In this regard, the Nanjing Decade preserved a distinctly military flavor very similar to the same period in Italy and Germany. Undermining this relatively popular and prosperous era was Jiang Jieshi's reluctance to confront the Japanese militarily which sought to take advantage of every opportunity to further its interests in China.

9.5 EMERGENCY LAW FOR THE SUPPRESSION OF CRIMES AGAINST THE SAFETY OF THE REPUBLIC (1931)

Between 1929 and 1934, Jiang Jieshi's military forces were almost constantly engaged in campaigns against warlords, the Communists, and any internal party dissent. The general public did not completely embrace Jiang's new brand of governance. Protests against his passive stance towards Japan's aggression in northeast China, diatribes against the government in the press, and political agitation amongst the student and working classes, were all prevalent during the first decade of GMD rule. Jiang Jieshi reacted to this by enacting a set of laws severely restricting personal rights. Promulgated by the Nationalist government on January 31, 1931, these Emergency Laws were implemented a month later on March 1st. As the military tone of the laws suggests, the GMD government was still attempting to reintegrate many areas of China under their authority. By 1937, Jiang had only managed to bring two-thirds of China's territory back under Nanjing's centralized administration.

Questions

1. Taking the Emergency Laws as a whole, what are Jiang Jieshi's primary goals in instituting the new regulations?
2. One historian of the "Nanjing Decade" suggested that Jiang's rule was neither democratic nor totalitarian, but somewhere in between. If you were to judge his administration by this set of laws how would you describe his government?

ARTICLE 1

Whoever, with a view to subvert the Republic, commits one of the following acts, shall be punished by death:

1. Disturbing peace and order,
2. Entering into secret relationship with a foreign country in order to disturb peace and order,
3. Associating with rebels in order to disturb peace and order,
4. Instigating a military person to commit a non-disciplinary act or cause him to fail in the performance of this duty, or to associate with rebels.

ARTICLE 2

Whoever, with a view to subvert the Republic, commits one of the following acts shall be punished with death or life imprisonment:

1. Instigating another person to disturb peace and order or to associate with rebels,
2. Conducting a campaign of propaganda against the State by writing, sketching, or speech-making.

ARTICLE 3

Whoever, with a view to subvert the Republic, commits one of the following acts, shall be punished by life imprisonment or imprisonment of not less than ten years:

1. Committing a non-disciplinary act, failing in the performance of his duty, or associating with rebels on the instigation of the criminal indicated Par. in 4 of Article 1,
2. Disturbing peace and order or associating with rebels on the instigation of the criminal indicated in Par. 1 of Article 2,
3. Conducting propaganda on the instigation of the criminal indicated in Par. 2 of Article 2.

Whoever, having committed one of the crimes specified in the preceding paragraphs, on immediately and voluntarily reporting, shall receive an attenuation or exoneration of the penalty.

ARTICLE 4

Whoever, having knowledge that a certain individual is a rebel, shelters him without giving notification to the competent authorities, shall be punished by imprisonment of not less than five years.

Whoever, having committed the crime specified in the preceding paragraph, immediately and voluntarily reports, shall receive an attenuation or exoneration of the penalty.

ARTICLE 5

Whoever, with a view to subvert the Republic commits one of the following acts, shall be punished with death, or life imprisonment or imprisonment of not less than ten years:

1. Obtaining or transporting military supplies for rebels,
2. Revealing or transmitting to rebels military and political secrets,
3. Destroying means of communication.

ARTICLE 6

Whoever, with a view to subvert the Republic organizes associations or unions or spreads doctrines incompatible with the "Three Principles of the People," shall be punished by imprisonment of from five to fifteen years.

ARTICLE 7

Whoever commits one of the crimes specified by the present law in a region under a state of siege shall be tried by the highest military organ in that region. If he commits the crime within the limits of the suppression of banditry, he shall be tried by a provisional court composed of the magistrate of the district and two judicial officials.

The provisional court shall be established in the district and the magistrate shall be designated as the president of the court.

ARTICLE 8

In case a suspect is tried by a military organ in conformity with the present law, that organ shall submit a statement of the trial to the competent superior military organ and the sentence shall be executed only after approval by the latter. If the suspect is tried by a provisional court, the court shall submit a statement of the trial to the superior court and the sentence shall be executed only after approval by the latter; the case shall also be reported to the provincial government for reference.

The competent superior military organ or the superior court, if it doubts the judgment passed by the organ which is its subordinate, can give to that organ an order for re-examination, or designate a special delegate to be present at the reconsideration of the judgment.

ARTICLE 9

The military organ or police which arrests a person suspected of having committed one of the infractions specified by the present law, shall report the matter immediately to the interested competent authorities.

ARTICLE 10

To all offenses that do not fall within the limits of the present law, the provisions of the Penal Code are applicable.

ARTICLE 11

The duration of the application of the present law and the date of its enforcement shall be fixed by ordinance.

The provisional law suppressing anti-revolutionary plots shall be repealed from the date of the enforcement of the present law.

9.6 SONG MEILING ON NEW LIFE MOVEMENT (1934)

Established in 1934, the New Life Movement was a calculated attempt by Jiang Jieshi and Song Meiling to instill the government with an element of traditional Confucianism. Framed in the moral language of China's traditional society, the primary tendencies of the New Life Movement mirrored the social movements popular in 1930s Fascist Italy and Nazi Germany, though they were far from identical or as successful. The program had neither the hefty fiscal backing nor institutional depth of its European counterparts and, despite extensive propaganda, drew little public support or widespread interest. Initially, Jiang Jieshi focused the program on those segments and areas of the country he felt were most opposed to his rule: the Communists and labor organizers. Like many such programs, it was light on substance and heavy on idealism. Many critics suggest it displayed Jiang Jieshi's detachment from the true problems facing China.

Questions

1. **What does Song Meiling identify as the problems facing China? How does she suggest the New Life Movement will resolve such issues?**
2. **How does she respond to the criticism that the government should first find a solution to feeding people before promoting a program like the New Life Movement?**

China, like almost every other nation during the past few years, has felt tremendous enervating effects of world depression. Each nation, according to its lights, has sought to find a way out of stagnation into normalcy. Italy has its Fascism, Germany its Nazism, the Soviet Union its first and second five-year plans, and America its New Deal. The primary aim of each is to solve the economic problems involved and to bring material prosperity to the people. China, like the rest of the nations, is confronted with a similar problem, added to which is the necessity of rescuing the people from cumulative miseries of poverty, ignorance, and superstition, combined with the after effects of communistic orgies and natural calamities, and last but not least, the grave consequences of external aggression.

To this end, what is known as the New Life Movement has been launched, to strike at the very roots of the several evils. Conditions obtaining in China are so different from those facing any other country that it would be impossible for the average foreign mind to comprehend the reasons for the New Life Movement, its program, its actual working result, and its future, without a brief explanation of the background of the psychological and social state in which China finds herself after some three hundred years of oppression and neglect by the rulers of the Manchu Dynasty, followed by the chaos consequent upon the revolution which overthrew that regime.

[...]

Gradually, however, the leaven of the Republic began to work, and relatively great and far-reaching reforms and improvements took place through these changes were mostly confined to seaboard cities and to a number of the larger cities in the interior. But the country at large went unchanged, or difficult to change, and because of this fact communist agents soon discovered that here they had a more fertile field in which to work than any other country could provide. They seized their advantage and, before their activities were realized, they had contrived to impose upon the ignorance of the people to such an extent that they were firmly established in several regions. Military efforts against them became necessary.

The idea of the New Life Movement became crystallized in the mind of Generalissimo Jiang Jieshi during the anti-communist campaign. He realized that military occupation of recovered territory was not enough; that it must be followed up by social and economic reconstruction in the devastated areas; and that, to be effective, a national consciousness and spirit of mutual co-operation must be aroused. He saw that the immediate need was the development of the vitality of the spirit of the people, which seemed to have been crushed. He contemplated the perspective of history in the light of existing conditions about him; he realized how much depended upon the people's consciousness of their heritage from the past; the conviction came to him that the four great virtues of old China, *Li, Yi, Lian,* and *Chi* constituted a remedy that could rescue the country from stagnation and ruin, because at the time when those principles were practiced, China was indeed a great nation. He decided then and there to base a New Life Movement upon them, to try to recover what had been lost by forgetfulness of this source of China's greatness. For it has become obvious that mere accumulation of wealth is not sufficient to enable China to resume her position as a great nation. There must also be a revival of the spirit, since spiritual values transcend mere material riches.

What significance lies behind these four principles which hold so much good in them for China, if they can be carried out in the spirit intended?

First is *Li,* which in the ordinary and most accepted form of translation means courtesy. And by courtesy is meant that which emanates from the heart—not a formality which merely obeys the law.

The second is *Yi,* which, roughly translated, means duty or service, toward the individual's fellow men and toward himself.

The third is *Lian,* meaning a clear definition of the rights of the individual and of the degree in which those rights may be enforced without infringing upon those of others. In other words, honesty. A clear demarcation between what is public and what is private, what is yours and what is mine.

The fourth is *Chi,* which denotes high-mindedness and honor.

Some people have criticized the New Life Movement on the ground that, since there is not sufficient food for everyone in the land, it is useless to talk about or seek spiritual regeneration. We reject the argument by pointing out the very evident fact that, if everyone from the highest official to the lowest wheel barrow man would conscientiously practice these principles in everyday life, there would be food for all. If we have the right conception of *Li,* we recognize not outward

pomp but the sterling native qualities of our fellow men. If we practice *Yi,* we feel an obligation not to hold wealth and enjoy it wastefully while our fellow countrymen may be on the verge of starvation or suffering from sickness or other misfortunes. Again with *Lian:* If officials recognize the rights of the people under them, they do not try to benefit themselves at the expense of the people just because the latter are too powerless and ignorant to fight in their own defense. And if *Chi* is a reality no one is shameless or stoops to mean or underhanded deeds.

Being a realist, the Generalissimo recognized that conditions in China are entirely different from what they were centuries ago when China was a great nation. At that time China could well afford to stand aloof, shut herself within the confines of her own boundaries, and keep out all intruders; but today she is part of a world-wide scheme of things, and in order to maintain and improve her present position, she must keep in step with world progress.

So the New Life Movement is based upon the preservation of these four virtues, and it aims to apply them to actual, existing conditions, in order that the moral character of the nation shall attain the highest possible standard. The Generalissimo observed that communism crushed the spirit of the people, in addition to robbing them of material things; that it struck at all the fundamental principles of moral character. He found the people bereft of ideas or ideals concerning either humanity in general or in their fellow men in particular. Communism was, indeed, the last abrasive in the destruction of a sense of law and order, unselfishness, loyalty and those other qualities necessary for the development of human kindness and the maintenance of a high national consciousness. It tortured and degraded the status of man and dispossessed human life of value. In the face of this dismal prospect, the Generalissimo decided that the New Life Movement could sow the first seeds of an effort to awaken the people an urge for a more-satisfying life.

9.7 ZHANG XUELIANG'S XI'AN INCIDENT SPEECH (DECEMBER 13, 1936)

In 1936, Zhang Xueliang kidnapped Jiang Jieshi who was about to engage in what Jiang Jieshi hoped would be the final extermination campaign against the Communists. After Jiang Jieshi's capture, Zhang Xueliang gave a speech to the nation outlining his motivation for the kidnapping and the terms for Jiange Jieshi's release. In this way he hoped to rally the nation (and Jiang) to the need for unity against the Japanese invaders. Zhang Xueliang's tone and his ability to capture the mood of the entire nation in his plea for Jiang Jieshi's resistance seem to support his later claims that he sought to save the nation through his actions. Regardless, the means by which he sought to achieve his ends must be considered highly unorthodox, as was his willingness to accompany Jiang Jieshi back to Nanjing to face trial for his actions. Even Jiang Jieshi's own account of the event suggests that anything less drastic would have failed.

Questions

1. What does Zhang Xueliang suggest motivated him to kidnap Jiang Jieshi?
2. Does Zhang Xueliang indicate his attitude towards Jiang Jieshi? Is he anti-GMD?

I have not come to work in the office for more than a month and consequently to speak with you. The reason I have not attended to my official duties is my dissatisfaction with them—namely, I no longer want to fight the Communists. At a time when the nation is in peril at the hands of a foreign aggressor [Japan], we, instead of facing our real enemy, choose to fight among ourselves. This grieves me greatly.

I presume that by now all of you have heard about yesterday's events. Let me explain for you the rationale for my action.

Prior to yesterday's events I had repeatedly expressed to the Generalissimo [Jiang] my belief that we must stop the civil war and form a united front to face Japan. Unfortunately I was not able to change his mind. He said that I was wrong; yet he gave me no guidance as to why I was wrong.

As his view and mine became irreconcilable and as this dispute must be put to an end, I decided that there were only three courses of action open to me. First, I could resign. Second, I could continue my persuasion in the hope that I someday I would be convinced of the correctness of my proposals. Third, I could do what I did yesterday—namely, use force to drive home a point.

I could have easily taken the first course of action and returned to the Northeast [Manchuria] to fight the enemy on my own had it not been for the fact that Japan was as much as an enemy to me personally as she was to the nation, that I shouldered great responsibility for the state, and that, finally, all of my subordinates shared my opinion with regard to Japan. It was extremely doubtful, however, that my resignation could bring about the same result as choice number three hopefully would.

As for the second course of action, I have pursued it consistently for the past month. I searched for every approach and used every argument to convince the Generalissimo of the correctness of my views. My motive was pure; my intention was selfless. I journeyed twice to Luoyang to see him; and, to convince him of the purity of my motives, I did not bring any bodyguards with me. But I failed in my persuasion. I was his second in command; yet he not only refused to accept my proposals but also would not allow me to complete my presentation. He only listened to those who agreed with him.

As the first and second courses of action could not and would not yield any result, the only choice open to me was the third. Let me explain the immediate causes that finally prompted me to take action.

First, seven leaders of the patriotic movement were arrested in Shanghai. What crimes did they commit? Well, according to Shen Chunyu [1874–1963], an old professor who was one of the arrested, their crime was patriotism. Once when I spoke on behalf of the seven arrested, the Generalissimo's response was: "Of all the people in the nation only you look at this matter differently." Second, on December 9 when the students in Xi'an planned a massive demonstration for patriotism, Governor Shao Lizi [1882–1967] and I did our utmost to persuade them not to proceed with the implementation of their plan. We suggested that any opinion they wished to express could be done in writing. When they insisted on carrying out the demonstration, we said that under no circumstances could they be allowed to demonstrate before the Generalissimo's headquarters in Linguan [a suburb of Xi'an]. Had the police not opened fire and thus aroused public anger, I doubt very much that the students would have gone to Linguan in the first place. After their arrival at Linguan, I went there to talk with them; eventually I was able to persuade them to return to the city. Instead of a word of approval or appreciation, the Generalissimo accused me of having failed to use more effective means to suppress the students. His accusation convinced me that he would never change his policy toward Japan. Third, the Generalissimo wanted me to punish some of my subordinates whose conduct and behavior he regarded as improper. I declined. I prefer sacrificing myself rather than punishing innocent subordinates.

In taking the action that we did yesterday, personal considerations—glory or shame, life or death—never entered into our minds. We did this for our country and our people. We shall never do anything harmful to the country and the people; neither shall we refrain from taking such actions as judged to be beneficial to them. We realize that our action may have an adverse effect on national order. In the long run, however, it will be most beneficial.

The Generalissimo is safe; we have no personal hatred or resentment of him. We do not oppose him as an individual; we do oppose his policies and the way he carries them out. By giving him the opportunity to reexamine himself, we are inspired by our love for him. Should he decide to abandon his past policies by rallying the nation to resist Japan, we shall of course continue to support him and remain his most loyal subordinates. He may punish us as a group of mutineers, but that is quite all right with us. What we are fighting for is the adoption of a policy of resisting Japan. If that policy is adopted, we have achieved our purpose. Other considerations simply do not matter.

CCP: LONG MARCH TO THE UNITED FRONT

As the GMD's political hold on China strengthened, Jiang Jieshi moved to eradicate the last Communist strongholds. Employing a "blockhouse strategy," Jiang Jieshi established a perimeter around the Jiangxi soviet and slowly choked off all contact and supply routes. In the autumn of 1934, the CCP held a series of contentious strategy meetings over whether to stay or flee. In October, a majority finally agreed it was not longer viable to remain in Jiangxi. They decided to fight their way through the GMD lines and join Communist forces in other parts of China. In what would later be referred to as the "Long March" (9.8), the CCP crossed southern and western China, arriving a year later in the northwestern province of Shaanxi, a mere shadow of their former strength. It was during this period that Mao Zedong rose to the dominant position within the CCP, and the CCP emphasized an anti-Japanese policy. This led to their participation in the Xi'an Incident which forced Jiang Jieshi to promise a similar strategy (9.9). Once again united with the GMD, the CCP sought to promote themselves as the political party most interested in China's survival (9.10).

9.8 OTTO BRAUN ON THE LONG MARCH (1934–1935)

Sent to China in 1932 by the Comintern, **Otto Braun** arrived in the Jiangxi soviet primarily to serve as a military advisor. Only 32 years old at the time, with virtually no knowledge of China or the Chinese language (aside from his Chinese name, Li De), Braun exercised considerable control over the CCP's political and military decisions. He was the Comintern representative until early 1935 when he was stripped of his powers at the **Zunyi conference** by the anti-Soviet faction led by Mao Zedong. He remained a key member of the top political structure until 1939, then returned to the Soviet Union and, later, lived out his life in East Germany. As the only foreigner to complete the entire Long March, his impressions are unique, though his inability to speak Chinese and non-participation in

OTTO BRAUN (1900–1974)—Served as Comintern advisor to the CCP leadership from 1932 until he left China in 1939. Sometimes known by his Chinese name Li De, he was the only foreigner to complete the entire Long March.

ZUNYI CONFERENCE (JANUARY 15–17, 1935)—A meeting held in the southwestern province of Guizhou during the Long March by the CCP leadership, it marked the rise of Mao Zedong and his supporters to top leadership positions.

the decision making process during the latter-half of the Long March make some of his assessments questionable. The following document is translated from his autobiography published late in his life and offers a rare first-hand remembrance of the "strategic retreat" of the CCP to Shaanxi.

Questions

1. **Why might the Long March loom large in the history of the CCP as a type of "foundational myth"?**
2. **Why did the CCP traverse such inhospitable terrain?**

A few days after the Politburo meeting, both columns set out on the new march. First on the right one moved northwards, then the left turned to the northwest. The right column's route, the only one I can describe from experience, led back into mountainous terrain. This quickly changed into a high plateau, about 4,000m above sea level. Here began the most difficult part of the march. A deceptive green cover hid a black viscous swamp, which sucked anyone who broke through the thin crust or strayed from the narrow path. I myself witnessed the wretched death of a mule in this fashion. We drove native cattle or horses before us which instinctively found the least dangerous way. Grey clouds almost always hung just over the ground. Cold rain fell several times a day, at night it turned to wet snow or sleet. There was not a dwelling, tree, or shrub as far as the eye could see. We slept in squatting positions on the small hills which rose over the moor. Thin blankets and large straw hats, oil-paper umbrellas or, in some cases, stolen capes, were our only protection. Some did not awaken in the morning, victims of cold and exhaustion. And this was the middle of August! Our sole nourishment came from the grain kernels we had hoarded or, as a rare and special treat, a morsel of stone-hard dried meat. The swamp water was not fit to drink. Still it was drunk, for there was no wood to purify it by boiling. Outbreaks of bloody dysentery and typhus, which had subsided somewhat in Xikang, again won the upper hand. These harrowing conditions lasted over a week. We were fortunate that the enemy could attack us neither from the air nor on land.

We finally began our descent into friendlier surroundings with gardens, fields, houses, and enormous lama temples resembling castles. Here too most of the inhabitants had fled. Before us lay Songpan, a small town with thick walls. Enemy troops had already advanced from the Min River and occupied it so we veered westward. A few days later we reached Baxi, our first goal south of the Gansu border, and called a halt. In this area, where there were more than a few towns with lamaseries, we supplied ourselves with food. We harvested the nearly ripe grain and vegetables, and slaughtered every head of livestock we could find. It was already the end of August. Before us, in the distance, we saw the snowy peaks of the Min mountains, an obstacle difficult to surmount in autumn, and nearly impossible in winter. We made our preparations for the next few months with the utmost haste.

[....]

Shaanxi was not devoid of enemy forces either: quite the opposite! Xi'an was the headquarters of the 10,000-man strong Northeast Army under Zhang Xueliang, whom Jiang Jieshi had withdrawn from Manchuria in 1931. In the Gansu-Shaanxi border region and on the north bank of the Wei River there were two or three divisions commanded by the provincial governor of Shaanxi, General Yang Hucheng. The political morale of these two armies, however, left much to be desired. From the soldiers to the highest commanders, they would have much preferred to fight the Japanese than the 'Reds.' They therefore limited themselves to the defense of strategic points and fortifications.

All of this argued so strongly for the march to Shaanxi that an alternative was not even considered. The Xinjiang variant was renounced once and for all. I was immensely relieved.

While we conferred, Lin Biao led the 1st Corps to the Tianshui River where the 25th Corps had set up a bridgehead to ensure our crossing. We put the river behind us at the end of September, shortly before the Guomindang troops reached the crossing point.

We proceeded in a northeasterly direction, roughly following the Gansu-Shaanxi border. In a sense the

25th Corps acted as our vanguard. It routed a cavalry unit of General Ma Hongbin near Pingliang, then turned eastwards towards Heshui and Qingyang to engage Yang Hucheng's and Zhang Xueliang's troops from the rear. The 1st Army continued to the northeast without meeting serious resistance.

Chinese Muslims predominated in the part of Gansu we crossed and I must say that their religious constraints were strictly observed. The political administration issued instructions forbidding, for example, entering houses and mosques, using the cooking and eating utensils of the people, and eating pork. Our deportment did not go unrewarded. We had no logistical problems and there were enough big landlords to expropriate. The inhabitants, severely oppressed and exploited by Gansu warlords, gave us much useful advice. Since our passage through Lolo [Yi] territory this was our first benign contact with, not strictly national, but a religious minority. This was to have an enduring impact as was evident when the Red Army extended the soviet domain, or rather its sphere of influence, to this area in 1939.

[. . . .]

On October 20, 1935, almost a year to the day we broke through the blockade in Jiangxi we entered Wayaobao. The Long or Great March, as it was henceforth called, had ended for the 1st Army. Originally planned as a large-scale operation, militarily speaking it dissolved into a strategic retreat, not turning into an advance until its last phase. It had demanded extraordinary sacrifices. When it entered northern Shaanxi the 1st Army numbered 7,000 to 8,000 men, of whom 5,000 to 6,000 were in the regular divisions. These were battled-steeled cadres who later formed the backbone of the party and Army in the anti-Japanese War and in the subsequent People's Liberation War. At its critical turning-point, after the auspicious union of the 1st and 4th Armies, the Army and Party were torn asunder. Finally, and this was to have disastrous consequences, the March helped consolidate the peasant and soldier brand of communism preached by Mao Zedong. It obscured, perhaps even deliberately, the day-in and day-out struggle of the Chinese urban working class, which was no less dedicated or heroic and ran even greater risks.

Despite these grave and negative moments, the Long March did represent a political victory for the Chinese Red Army. It had braved an enormously superior enemy force, penetrated its fortifications and encirclements, defeated it a dozen times and out-maneuvered it hundreds. It had covered 10,000 km, been through twelve provinces, traversed eighteen mountain ranges, five of which were covered with perpetual snow and ice, and had crossed twenty-four broad rivers. This is an enduring accomplishment which testifies to the great courage, stamina, and revolutionary spirit of the fighters of the Chinese Red Army, a peasants' army under the leadership of the Communist Party.

9.9   MAO ZEDONG'S STATEMENT ON JIANG JIESHI'S STATEMENT (DECEMBER 28, 1936)

As the days passed after the Xi'an Incident, Jiang Jieshi issued no public statement regarding the compromises he had promised during his captivity—namely that he would cease military operations against the CCP and move to resist the Japanese advances in the northeast. Mao Zedong issued the following declaration at this point with Jiang Jieshi's reticence playing into the CCP claim that they were the only major political force pushing for anti-Japanese measures. Mao Zedong almost surely sought to publicize Jiang Jieshi's promises in an effort to preempt any attempt by Jiang Jieshi to repudiate them. As a result of their role in the Xi'an Incident and the adamant (and publicly) anti-Japanese stance, many Chinese citizens began to adopt a more open and positive attitude towards the CCP.

Questions

1. How does Mao characterize Jiang's behavior and public statements in the days after the Xi'an Incident?
2. What does Mao mean when he states "Promises must be kept and action must be resolute"?

In Xi'an Jiang Jieshi accepted the demand for resistance to Japan put forward by Generals Zhang Xueliang and Yang Hucheng and the people of the Northwest and, as an initial step, he has ordered his civil war troops to withdraw from the provinces of Shaanxi and Gansu. This marks the beginning of Jiang's reversal of his wrong policy in the past decade. It is a blow to the intrigues conducted by the Japanese imperialists and the Chinese "punitive" group [taofa pai] to stage-manage a civil war, foment splits and get Jiang killed in the Xi'an Incident Their disappointment is already apparent. The indication that Jiang Jieshi is beginning to wake up may be considered a sign of the Guomindang's willingness to end the wrong policy it has pursued for ten years.

On December 26 Jiang Jieshi issued a statement in Luoyang, the so-called "Admonition to Zhang Xueliang and Yang Hucheng", which is so ambiguous and evasive as to be an interesting specimen among China's political documents. If Jiang really wants to draw a serious lesson from the incident and try to revitalize the Guomindang, and if he wants to end his consistently wrong policy of compromise in foreign affairs and of civil war and oppression at home, so that the Guomindang will no longer stand opposed to the wishes of the people, then as a token of good faith he should have produced a better piece of writing, repenting his political past and setting a new course for the future. The statement of December 26 cannot meet the demands of the Chinese masses.

However, it does contain one praiseworthy passage, in which Jiang asserts that "promises must be kept and action must be resolute". This means that, although he did not sign the terms set forth by Zhang [Xueliang] and Yang [Hucheng] in Xi'an, he is willing to accept such demands as are beneficial to the state and the nation and will not break his word on the grounds that he did not sign. We shall see whether, after he has withdrawn his troops, Jiang will act in good faith and carry out the terms he has accepted. The terms are:

1. to reorganize the Guomindang and the National Government, expel the pro-Japanese group and admit anti-Japanese elements;

2. to release the patriotic leaders in Shanghai and all other political prisoners, and guarantee the freedoms and rights of the people;

3. to end the policy of "suppressing the Communists" and enter into an alliance with the Red Army to resist Japan;

4. to convene a national salvation conference, representing all parties, groups, sections of the population and armies, to decide on the policy of resisting Japan and saving the nation;

5. to enter into co-operation with countries sympathetic to China's resistance to Japan; and

6. to adopt other specific ways and means to save the nation.

The fulfillment of these terms requires above all good faith, and also some courage. We shall judge Jiang [Jieshi] by his future actions.

But his statement contains the remark that the Xi'an Incident was brought about under the pressure of "reactionaries." It is a pity that he did not explain what kind of people he meant by "reactionaries," nor is it clear how the word "reactionary" is defined in Jiang's dictionary. However, what is certain is that the Xi'an Incident took place under the influence of the following forces:

1. the mounting indignation against Japan among the troops of Generals Zhang [Xueliang] and Yang [Hucheng] and among the revolutionary people of the Northwest;

2. the mounting indignation against Japan among the people of the whole country;

3. the growth of the Left forces in the Guomindang;

4. the demand by the groups in power in various provinces for resistance to Japan and for the salvation of the nation;

5. the stand taken by the Communist Party for a national united front against Japan; and

6. the development of the world peace front.

All these are indisputable facts. It is just these forces that Jiang calls "reactionary"; while other people call them revolutionary, Jiang calls them "reactionary"—that is all. Since he declared in Xi'an that he would fight Japan in earnest, presumably he will not resume violent attacks on the revolutionary forces

---

PUNITIVE FACTION—A group within the GMD lead by He Yingqin and Dai Jitao who some claimed sought to kill Jiang Jieshi in the Xi'an Incident (1936) in order to destabilize the political situation by promoting a civil war and delaying engagement with the Japanese.

immediately after leaving Xi'an; not only does his own political life and that of his group hang upon his good faith, but they now have confronting them and obstructing their political path a force which has expanded to their detriment—the "punitive" group which tried to get him killed in the Xi'an Incident. We therefore advise Jiang Jieshi to revise his political dictionary, changing the word "reactionary" to "revolutionary," for it is better to use terms corresponding to the facts.

Jiang should remember that he owes his safe departure from Xi'an to the mediation of the Communist Party, as well as to the efforts of Generals Zhang and Yang, the leaders in the Xi'an Incident. Throughout the incident, the Communist Party stood for a peaceful settlement and made every effort to that end, acting solely in the interests of national survival. Had the civil war spread and had Zhang and Yang kept Jiang Jieshi in custody for long, the incident could only have developed in favor of the Japanese imperialists and the Chinese "punitive" group. It was in these circumstances that the Communist Party firmly exposed the intrigues of the Japanese imperialists and of Wang Jingwei, He Yingqin, and other members of the Chinese "punitive" group, and firmly advocated a peaceful settlement, which happened to coincide with the views of Generals Zhang Xueliang and Yang Hucheng and such members of the Guomindang as Song Ziwen. This is exactly what the people throughout the country call for, because they bitterly detest the present civil war.

Jiang was set free upon his acceptance of the Xi'an terms. From now on the question is whether he will carry out to the letter his pledge that "promises must be kept and action must be resolute," and strictly fulfill all the terms for saving the nation. The nation will not permit any further hesitation on his part or allow him any discount in fulfilling the terms. If he wavers on the issue of resisting Japan or delays in fulfilling his pledge, then the nation-wide revolutionary tide will sweep him away. Jiang and his group should bear in mind the old saying: "If a man does not keep his word, what is he good for?"

If Jiang can clean up the dirt created by the Guomindang's reactionary policy over the past ten years, thoroughly correct his fundamental errors of compromise in foreign affairs and of civil war and oppression at home, immediately join the anti-Japanese front uniting all parties and groups and really take the military and political measures that can save the nation, then of course the Communist Party will support him. As early as August 25, the Communist Party promised such support to Jiang and the Guomindang in its letter to the Guomindang. The people throughout the country have known for fifteen years that the Communist Party observes the maxim, "Promises must be kept and action must be resolute." They undoubtedly have more confidence in the words and deeds of the Communist Party than in those of any other party or group in China.

9.10 COMMUNIST CO-OPERATION BY THE CENTRAL COMMITTEE OF THE COMMUNIST PARTY OF CHINA (JULY 15, 1937)

In the months after the Xi'an Incident, the CCP, with their anti-Japanese position, continually worked to position themselves as patriotic and on the moral high ground. Significantly, the policy announced by Zhou Enlai is said to have been drafted on July 4, 1937 three days before the Lugouqiao Incident (also known in English as the Marco Polo Bridge Incident) on July 7, 1937. This incident began China's eight-year War of Resistance against Japan. Although the CCP and GMD were officially united, near-constant friction existed and, at times, there was unmitigated hostility between the two forces. There is little doubt that the war benefited the Chinese Communist Party and helped them to establish a foothold in northwest China, to hone their own military strategies, and to develop their military forces for the future civil war.

Questions

1. What aspects of the "co-operation" with the GMD does the CCP emphasize?
2. Why does the CCP stress the battles against Japan?

Dear Fellow-Countrymen,

With the greatest enthusiasm, the **Central Committee** of the Communist Party of China announces to our elders, brothers, and sisters all over the country that to save our motherland at a time when it is faced with a most serious crisis and its very fate is at stake, we have reached an understanding with the Guomindang on the basis of peace, unification, and united resistance to foreign aggression and have joined together with them to meet the crisis. This has enormous significance for the future of our great Chinese nation! For, as we all know, with our nation facing extreme peril today, it is only through internal unity that we can defeat Japanese imperialist aggression. Now that the foundation has been laid for national unity and the basis created for the independence, freedom and liberation of our nation, the Central Committee of the Chinese Communist Party salutes the splendid future of our people. However, we know that the task of turning bright promise into reality and creating a new China, independent, happy and free, will demand tenacious, dauntless struggle on the part of our countrymen and, indeed, of every patriotic descendant of our common ancestor, the Yellow Emperor Huangdi. On this occasion, the Communist Party of China would like to set forth to all our countrymen the general objectives of our struggle. They are the following:

1. To strive for the independence, freedom and liberation of the Chinese nation. First of all, it is necessary earnestly and speedily to prepare and launch a national revolutionary war of resistance, in order to recover our lost lands and restore our territorial integrity and sovereignty.
2. To put democracy into effect and convene a national assembly to frame and adopt a constitution and draw up a policy of national salvation.
3. To enable the Chinese people to lead a happy and prosperous life. Effective measures must first be

taken to provide famine relief, ensure a stable livelihood, develop a defense economy, deliver the people from suffering and improve their living conditions.

These are China's urgent needs and they constitute the goal of our struggle. We are convinced that they will receive the warm support of all our countrymen. The Communist Party of China wishes to attain these general objectives by joint effort with all our countrymen.

The Chinese Communist Party is fully aware that in marching towards this lofty goal, we need to overcome many obstacles and difficulties, and that, first of all, we will encounter obstruction and sabotage by the Japanese imperialists. To strip the enemy of any pretext for his intrigues and to remove any misunderstanding among all well-intentioned doubters, the Central Committee of the Communist Party of China finds it necessary to proclaim its sincere devotion to the cause of national liberation. Therefore, it once again solemnly declares to the whole nation:

1. That Dr. Sun Zhongshan's Three People's Principles being what China needs today, our Party is ready to fight for their complete realization;
2. That we shall give up our policy of encouraging insurrection to overthrow the Guomindang regime, call off the Sovietization movement, and discontinue the policy of forcible confiscation of the land of the landlords;
3. That we shall abolish the present Soviet governments and call for the practice of democracy in the hope that state power will be unified throughout the country; and
4. That the Red Army will give up its present name and designation, that it will be reorganized as part of the National Revolutionary Army and placed under the Military Council of the National Government and that it will be ready for orders to march to the anti-Japanese front and do its duty.

CENTRAL COMMITTEE—A committee limited to the highest-ranking CCP members, ranging in size from 100 to 300 members and from which the powerful Politburo and Standing Committee are selected.

Dear fellow-countrymen! Our Party has long since shown in word and deed before the whole country an open, selfless attitude and a readiness to compromise for the common good, which have won the commendation of all. Now, with a view to uniting with the Guomindang in good faith, consolidating the peace and unity of the whole country and carrying out a national revolutionary war against Japan, we are ready to honor forthwith those of our promises which have not yet been formally carried out—for example, to abolish the Soviet areas and to redesignate the Red Army—so that the united strength of the entire country may be used to resist foreign aggression.

The Japanese aggressors have driven deep into our country and disaster is imminent. Fellow-countrymen, arise and unite as one! Our great, ancient Chinese nation is indomitable. Arise and fight for national unity! Fight to overthrow Japanese imperialist oppression! The Chinese nation will surely triumph.

For victory in the War of Resistance Against Japan!

For a new China, independent, happy and free!

CHAPTER 10
CHINA AT WAR (1937–1949)

❧

VISUAL SOURCE
Drawing People's Attention to Politics: Political Cartoons in 1930s and 1940s

GERMANS & JAPANESE: The cartoon depicts two figures, one a German (with the head on a sword sporting a cap that reads "Austria") and the other a Japanese (with a skull on a sword) that reads "Occupied China." Underneath the caption is a well-known line from Confucius' Analects which reads "Virtue will never be left to stand alone, He who practices it will always attract neighbors." The cartoon puns on the Chinese character for "virtue" (de) and Germany (deguo).

CHINESE MANHUA: The term "manhua" (borrowed from the Japanese "manga") or "cartoon" was first used in China by Feng Zikai in May 1925. When the war against Japan began in 1937, Chinese cartoonists produced a wave of potent images that profoundly depicted the war as well as the emotions of the Chinese themselves.

BOMBING VICTIMS: The cartoon depicts a woman carrying a baby on her back running for shelter, in which the baby has been struck by a bomb (or shrapnel) and whose head is flying through the air. The short poem that accompanies it reads: When the fierce bombings begin, a woman carrying her baby, flees. Before reaching the shelter, the baby's tiny head is thrown into the air; hot blood gushes out like a raging torrent.

Gao Longsheng, " 'De' bugu, bi you lin" (Analects, IV 25)

Feng Zikai

POST-WAR PEACE: The calligraphy in the corner could literally be translated as "Spring has arrived" but is more accurately translated as "good times have arrived." It pictures a family (notably missing the father) watching two kites which read "equality" (r) and "freedom" (l).

CIVIL WAR BOMB: In the center of the cartoon Jiang Jieshi is depicted sitting atop a bomb labeled "All out civil war" while lighting a fuse labeled "Central China." The caption (in the upper right corner) reads "Watch Yourself."

THEMES & POLITICS: The cartoons during the war against Japan and the civil war addressed predictable themes of patriotism, wartime atrocities, and corruption. Chinese cartoonists addressed these themes in ways that print articles were not allowed to do during the war. In the post-1945 period, cartoons became fiercely anti-government reflecting the Nationalists steady loss of popular support.

FENG ZIKAI: Feng Zikai (1898–1975) was perhaps the best known of the first generation of Chinese cartoonists (and drew the two center cartoons). He studied and taught fine art before going to Japan to continue his studies in 1921. He began to publish his own work in 1926, but his fame came from his deceptively simple cartoons that were sought by a wide array of popular and political journals, periodicals, and newspapers.

Feng Zikai, "Spring Has Arrived"

Kong Ping, "Watch Yourself"

The Western perspective of the reoccupation of the Rhineland, the annexation of Austria (Anchluss), and the Dunkirk Evacuation evoke a very specific time and place in twentieth-century history. Even though these events occurred decades ago, the form in which the events at the beginning of the Second World War in Europe are remembered usually falls into a predictable and emotion-charged narrative. A similar remembering process surrounds the outbreak of Japan's hostilities towards China in 1937. As with Western memories of the Second World War, the mention of Japan's invasion of Manchuria, the Lugouqiao Incident, and the Rape of Nanjing evoke a well-established narrative within a fixed emotional context to most Chinese. The problem with both of these narratives (and the collective memory of any nation about its past), is that they are built around a heroic representation of the nation's history which encourages a type of "collective forgetting." Few conventional histories of any country dwell on the unpleasant, but very real, occurrence of military retreats, collaborations, and traitors. Yet as several documents below attest, perceiving the more disreputable side of the war between China and Japan can help to provide a more balanced understanding of China's past.

The beginning of the War of Resistance against Japan is usually dated July 7, 1937, with the exchange of shots between Japanese and Chinese troops near **Lugouqiao Bridge** (often referred to as Marco Polo Bridge), about thirty miles west of Beijing. By the end of July, Japan had begun a wholesale invasion of China. The northern Chinese cities of Beijing and Tianjin fell in quick succession to Japanese forces on July 29th and 31st. By mid-August, the Japanese opened a second front by attacking Shanghai, China's financial and commercial center. The Guomindang troops defended the city for 13 weeks, until finally the city succumbed to the Japanese on November 9, 1937. One month later the Nationalist capital, Nanjing, surrendered, marking a swift end to the decade of GMD control over eastern China. Retreating up the Yangzi, Jiang Jieshi and his government eventually made the inland city of Chongqing China's wartime capital.

As it was reported in nationalistic histories, China spent the next eight years courageously resisting Japan's overwhelming military machine. This depiction of China's war with Japan is accurate, but it fails to describe the manner in which Japan occupied China's heartland for eight years. Most significant was Japan's governance over the occupied territory with a succession of collaborationist governments. Yet historical accounts of occupied China typically focus on brave acts of resistance and harsh condemnations of Chinese collaboration. Such characterizations emphasize only the two extremes of conduct typical under Japanese occupation. These historical accounts barely touch on the mundane, yet difficult choices many Chinese made on a daily basis while under Japanese rule. The nature and consequences of this rule was complex and uneven across the occupied areas.

Japan's Manchukuo regime had functioned in northeastern China since 1932, and Japan had long planned to set up similar collaborationist governments in the wake of its military victories in eastern China. These plans were realized in December 1938 when Japan successfully attracted the second most influential GMD leader,

LUGOUQIAO (MARCO POLO BRIDGE) INCIDENT—An incident that transpired on the outskirts of Beijing near the Lugouqiao Bridge on July 7, 1937, traditionally marking the beginning of the War of Resistance Against Japan.

WAR OF RESISTANCE AGAINST JAPAN (1937–1945)—Sometimes referred to as the "Anti-Japanese War," fought between China and Japan before and during World War II. Beginning in 1937, Japan occupied all major urban and communication centers in eastern China by 1938 and forced the Nationalist government to move its capital inland to Chongqing until Japan's defeat in 1945.

Wang Jingwei to their side. A "Reorganized National Government of China" was formally established in March 1940 with Wang Jingwei as president. Nazi Germany's victories in Europe and Japan's considerable success in Asia provided a persuasive backdrop for Wang Jingwei to promote his government as the future of China and as the true heirs to Sun Zhongshan's GMD party. These claims are often falsely discounted in post-war histories as the demented ramblings of a deluded and bitter political also-ran who sold his political soul to the Japanese. A truly autonomous government, free of Japanese interference, did not transpire (10.3), Wang Jingwei's government did bring some relief to the Chinese under Japanese control.

Traditional historical narratives of the war against Japan reveal little about the experiences of ordinary Chinese. Most suggest that the eight years of occupation were ones of determined and continuous resistance, the reality was more mundane. But as with any extended foreign occupation, the local Chinese population was forced to engage with their Japanese occupiers in order to survive. As famed Chinese director Jiang Wen made apparent in his film *Devils on the Doorstep* (*Guizi laile*)—a poignant and humorous depiction of this period—the Chinese living under Japanese collaborationist rule were caught between a desire for normality and the reality that their country was occupied. In the film, the villagers are forced by Communist insurgents to aid in concealing a captured Japanese officer and his translator and eventually to participate in the men's execution. As the villagers squabble among themselves and seek to avoid detection by both the Japanese army and the Chinese resistance, the claim of constant resistance is exposed as romanticized half-truths (10.4). For most of occupied China the occupation was a complex mixture of fear, confusion, and hard choices.

OCCUPIED CHINA

Japan's first military offensives into China-proper culminated in the capture of Nanjing in December 1937. That victory was followed by an extended riot of violence, murder, and rape that shocked the world (10.1). The fear that China would capitulate were greatly enhanced when the Japanese enticed Jiang Jieshi's rival Wang Jingwei to serve as the president of occupied China (10.2). Japan hoped that their move would force Jiang Jieshi to join the newly formed collaborationist government. Jiang Jieshi with increasing financial and military support from the United States adamantly refused Japan's repeated overtures.

10.1   LETTER TO THE JAPANESE EMBASSY FROM NANJING SAFETY ZONE (DECEMBER 18, 1937)

After capturing Nanjing, Nationalist China's capital, Japanese troops went on a six-week rampage commonly referred to as the "Rape of Nanjing." It is generally acknowledged that some 300,000 Chinese civilians and POWs were massacred. These atrocities were reported in both the Western and Chinese press at the time. Later, these events became the centerpiece in the war trials after Japan surrendered in 1945 and continue to be a flash point in Sino-Japanese relations to the present day. The following account is one of many letters written by John H.D. Rabe, a German businessman, director of the Siemens office, and leader of the Nanjing branch of the Nazi party. He served as the head of a war relief committee known as the International

Committee of the Nanjing Safety Zone that communicated with the Japanese in an effort to protect civilians from robbery, rape, and other atrocities by Japanese troops.

Dear Sirs:

We are very sorry to trouble you again but the sufferings and needs of the 200,000 civilians for whom we are trying to care make it urgent that we try to secure action from your military authorities to stop the present disorder among Japanese soldiers wandering through the Safety Zone.

There is no time or space here to go into the cases that are pouring in faster than we can type them out. But last night Dr. Bates of our Committee went to the University of Nanjing dormitories to sleep in order to protect the 1,000 women that fled there yesterday because of attacks in their homes. He found no Gendarmerie on guard there nor at the new University library building. When at 8 p.m. Mr. Fitch and Dr. Smythe took Rev. W.P. Mills to Jinling College to sleep in the house near the gate (as one or more of us have been doing every night since the 14th in order to protect the 3,000 women and children, yesterday augmented to 4,000 by the panic), we were seized roughly by a searching squad and detained for over an hour. The officer had the two women in charge of Jinling College, Miss Minnie Vautrin and Mrs. Chen, with a friend, Mrs. Twinem, lined up at the gate and kept them there in the cold and the men pushed them around roughly. The officer insisted there were soldiers in the compound and he wanted to find them and shoot them. Finally, he let us go home but would not let Rev. Mills stay so we do not know what happened after we left.

This combined with the marching off of the men at the Ministry of Justice on December 16 ..., among which were several hundred civilian men to our positive knowledge and 50 of our uniformed police, had made us realize that, unless something is done to clear up this situation, the lives of all the civilian men in our Zone are at the mercy of the temperament of searching captains.

With the panic that has been created among the women who are now flocking by the thousands to our American institutions for protection, the men are being left more and more alone. (For instance, there were 600 people in the old Language School at Xiao Taoyuan up till December 16. But because so many women were raped there on the night of December 15, 400 women and children moved to Jinling College, leaving 200 men.) These public institutional buildings were originally listed to accommodate 35,000 people; now, because of panic among the women, this has increased to 50,000, although two buildings have been emptied of men: the Ministry of Justice and the Supreme Court.

If this panic continues, not only will our housing problem become more serious but the food problem and the question of finding workers will seriously increase. This morning one of your representatives, Mr. K. Kikuchi, was at our office asking for workers for the electric light plant. We had to reply that we could not even get our own workers out to do anything. We are only able to keep rice and coal supplied to these large concentrations of people by Western members of our Committee and Staff driving trucks for rice and coal. Our Food Commissioner has not dared leave his house for two days. The second man on our Housing Commission had to see two women in his family at 23 Hankou Road raped last night at

NANJING MASSACRE (DECEMBER 1937–JANUARY 1938) — A six-week assault carried out in and around the capital of Nanjing after it fell to the Japanese army in 1937. Upwards of 300,000 non-combatants were killed, including tens of thousands of women and children. The army committed numerous atrocities, including looting, rape and arson, with the seeming consent of their officers. Also referred to as the "Rape of Nanjing."

supper time by Japanese soldiers. Our Associate Food Commissioner, Mr. Sone (a Theological Professor), has had to convey trucks with rice and leave the 2,500 people in families at his Nanjing Theological Seminary to look out for themselves. Yesterday, in broad daylight, several women at the Seminary were raped right in the middle of a large room filled with men, women, and children! We 22 Westerners cannot feed 200,000 Chinese civilians and protect them night and day. That is the duty of the Japanese authorities. If you can give them protection, we can help feed them!

There is another matter that is in the minds of the Japanese officers searching the Zone: they think the place is full of "plain-clothes soldiers." We have notified you several times of the presence of soldiers who, disarmed, entered the Zone on the afternoon of December 13. But now we can safely assure you that there are no groups of disarmed Chinese soldiers in the Zone. Your searching squads have cleaned out all of them and many civilians along with them.

For the good of all concerned, we would beg to make the following constructive suggestions:

I. *Control of Soldiers.*

1. We repeat our request of yesterday for patrols of Gendarmerie for the Zone night and day.
2. In our letter of December 16, we asked that guards be placed at entrances to the Zone to keep out wandering soldiers at night. This has not been done. But we hope the Japanese Army will find some way to prevent soldiers from robbing, raping, and killing the civilian population, especially at night when soldiers might be confined to their barracks.
3. Until general order can be restored among the soldiers will you please station sentries at the entrances to our 18 larger concentrations of refugees. These sentries should be instructed to be responsible for preventing soldiers climbing over the walls of the compounds as well. . . .

II. *Searching.*

1. Since our refugee camps seem to be misunderstood by captains of searching squads, we suggest that today we will be glad to have a high officer of the Japanese Army accompany one of our housing men to each of the 18 refugee camps and see them in daylight.
2. Since we know there are no groups of disarmed soldiers in the Zone and there has been no sniping in the Zone at any time; and since, furthermore, search of both Refugee Camps and

private houses has been carried out many times and each time means robbery and rape; we would venture to suggest that the Army's desires to prevent any former Chinese soldier's hiding in the Zone can now be accomplished by the patrol of the Gendarmeries mentioned above.

3. We venture to make these suggestions because we sincerely believe that if the civilian population is left alone for two or three days, they will resume their normal daily life in the Zone, food and fuel can be transported, shops will open, and workers will appear looking for work. These workers can then help start the essential service of electricity, water, and telephones.

III. *Police that have been taken away.*

Yesterday we called your attention to the fact that 50 uniformed police had been taken from the Ministry of Justice, and that 46 "volunteer police" had also been marched off. We now must add that 40 of our uniformed police stationed at the Supreme Court were also taken. The only stated charge against them was made at the Ministry of Justice where the Japanese officer said they had taken in soldiers after the place had been searched once, and, therefore, they were to be shot. As pointed out in the accompanying "Memorandum on the Incident at the Ministry of Justice," Western members of our Committee take full responsibility for having put some civilian men and women in there because they had been driven out of other places by Japanese soldiers.

Yesterday, we requested that the 450 uniformed police assigned to the Zone be now organized into a new police force for the city under Japanese direction. At the same time, we trust the above mentioned 90 uniformed police will be restored to their positions as policemen and that 46 volunteer police will either be returned to our office as workers, or we be informed of their whereabouts. We have on file a complete list of the 450 uniformed police assigned to the Zone, so can help you in this process.

Trusting that you will pardon our venturing to make these suggestions, and assuring you of our willingness to cooperate in every way for the welfare of the civilians in the city, I am

Most respectfully your,

JOHN H. D. RABE

Chairman

10.2 WANG JINGWEI'S TELEGRAPH TO JIANG JIESHI INDICATING HIS COLLABORATION WITH THE JAPANESE OCCUPIERS (1938)

An early confidant and friend of Sun Zhongshan, Wang Jingwei (1883–1944) entered the revolutionary fray in 1910 when he attempted to assassinate the last emperor's father and regent Zaifeng (Prince Chun) and played a prominent role in advocating for a republican-style government (5.12). Wang remained close to Sun after the 1911 Revolution and his stature within the party was such that many assumed that he, and not Jiang Jieshi, would assume leadership of the GMD after Sun's death in 1925. In the years after Sun's death, he remained an influential figure. He served as administrative head of the National Government, but frequently feuded with Jiang Jieshi over government policy. After the fall of Wuhan in October 1938, Wang increasingly questioned China's ability to maintain a protracted war against Japan. As the situation deteriorated in late December he flew to Hanoi (in French Indochina). On December 29th he issued the following telegram that was taken to Hong Kong by his followers and published by the "South China Daily" on December 31st.

Questions

1. **How does Wang Jingwei promise to bring about an end to the War of Resistance?**
2. **Why is Wang Jingwei convinced Japan would pursue a policy of peace?**

Dear Comrades of Chongqing Central Party Committee, President Jiang, and Members of Central Executive Committees:

In April, the manifesto of the provisional National Congress explained the rationale for the War of Resistance and stated:

> "Since the **Tanggu Agreement** our people have born the humiliation and burden of dealing with Japan, hoping for nothing more than ending the military combat. Only peaceful means should be employed to secure the northern provinces; furthermore, actions should be taken to properly resolve the issues of the four northeastern provinces; politically the minimal acceptable conclusion of negotiations is to maintain sovereignty and administrative integrity of China; economically cooperation must be based on the principle of equality and mutual benefit."

Since the Lugouqiao Incident in July of last year, China has come to realize that such aspirations are untenable and has been forced into a war of resistance. On the 22nd of this month, Japan readjusted the fundamental policy on Sino-Japanese relations, stating:

I. On Becoming Friendly Neighbors.

Japan sincerely declares that it does not demand any Chinese territory nor does it insist upon payment for military expense. Japan not only respects China's sovereignty, but also plans to model their actions on those of the Meiji Reformation; that is to say in exchange for permission of free trade in China's interior, Japan will return all treaty settlements, abolish

---

TANGGU TRUCE (1933) — An agreement signed on May 31, 1933 between China and Japan establishing a demilitarized zone south from the Great Wall to Beijing.

extraterritoriality, all so that China can achieve her independence.

With such a sincere declaration from the Japanese government, if we follow the peaceful approach, not only will the northern provinces be safeguarded, the territory lost since the War of Resistance can be regained, allowing Chinese sovereignty, administrative independence and integrity to be maintained. In this way, we ought to have confidence and pursue [Japan's] declaration to seek proper resolution for problems involving the four northeastern provinces.

II. On Mutual Prevention of Communism.

For several years, the Japanese government has repeated this proposal. We worry they will take this opportunity to intervene in military and internal affairs.

Today the Japanese government has clearly declared Japan should model its behavior on the united anti-Communist spirit of Japan, German and Italy, to create a Sino-Japanese anti-communism agreement. In this way, our worries can finally be brought to an end. The purpose of anti-communism is to prevent the Comintern's internal collusion and interference, which would not alter the relationship with the Soviet Union. Since the Chinese Communists have declared they would fight for the realization of Three Principles of the People, they should immediately give up their organization and propaganda, abolish their special government, military bases, and completely abide by the legal system of Republic of China. The Three Principles of the People is the highest principle in the Republic of China. We all must freely and actively punish any organizations or [Communist] propaganda which violate this highest principle, in order to fulfill our responsibility of protecting the Republic of China.

III. On Economic Cooperation.

For several years, the Japanese government has repeatedly proposed this. Up until now, we did not accept economic cooperation, as our political dispute was not resolved. Today, the Japanese government has genuinely declared to respect China's sovereignty and administrative independence and integrity. They have also stated they have no intention of controlling China's economy alone, nor are they asking China to restrict their activities with third party nations.

[. . . .]

China's and Japan's lands are connected. It is natural and necessary for them to become friendly neighbors. The two have gone in opposite directions in the past years, and so need to explore the reasons and clarify the responsibilities of each. In the future, although China will implement an education policy of becoming friends with neighbors, Japan should specifically order her people to give up their traditional belief that they need to invade and humiliate China. They should start an education policy of befriending China, to establish the foundation of long-term peace between the two nations. This is the effort we ought to make for obtaining the happiness of East Asia. Meanwhile, together with other nations, we must strive to secure Pacific and world peace, to maintain and strengthen friendship and mutual interest.

This is merely a proposal, waiting to be adopted!

Wang Zhaoming [Jingwei], **yan**

10.3   [OCCUPIED] CHINA-JAPAN: TREATY CONCERNING BASIC RELATIONS-ANNEXED PROTOCOL (NOVEMBER 30, 1940)

Wang Jingwei did not immediately assume leadership of occupied China after leaving Chongqing in 1938. He spent over a year in negotiations with top Japanese officials. Not until March 30, 1940 did Japan formally announce the creation of a new national government, the Republic of China. Negotiations moved slowly because Wang Jingwei

YANDIAN (YAN TELEGRAM)—During this era, telegrams used an abbreviated system of dating consisting of one character to represent the date. In this case, the date is represented by the character *yan* 艳, and therefore the telegram became known as *yandian*, telegram of *yan* date.

was not Japan's first choice to head their collaborationist government. Japan originally believed Jiang Jieshi could be coaxed into peace negotiations if he saw Japan's interest in Wang Jingwei. As a result, Japan withheld establishing formal diplomatic relations between Japan and Wang's new Nanjing regime until they had exhausted all attempts to negotiate with Jiang's Chongqing government. Negotiations were finally completed almost two years after Wang Jingwei had severed his ties with the Nationalist Chongqing government. Wang Jingwei remained optimistic that he had made the right choice through the early 1940s as Japan and Germany's military victories mounted. Wang Jingwei died in 1944 from the lingering complications of a 1935 assassination attempt. His death allowed him to escape the ignominious fate of the other collaborationist leaders who were executed within weeks if not days of Japan's defeat.

Questions

1. **What rights in the Annexed Protocol does Japan still retain during wartime?**
2. **Why do you think Japan was interested in consolidating the collaborationist regimes into a single regime with Wang as the president?**

In proceeding this day to the signature of the treaty concerning the basic relations between Japan and China, and the plenipotentiaries of the two countries have agreed as follows:

ARTICLE 1

The Government of the Republic of China, understanding that, during the period in which Japan continues warlike operations it is at present carrying on in the territory of China, there exists a special state of affairs attendant upon such warlike operations, and that Japan must take such measures as are required for the attainment of the object of such operations, shall accordingly, take the necessary measures.

Even during the continuation of the said warlike operations, the special state of affairs referred to in the preceding paragraph shall, in so far as there is no obstacle to the attainment of the object of the operations, be adjusted in accordance with the changing circumstances and in conformity with the treaty and its annexed documents.

ARTICLE 2

While the affairs previously administered by the Provisional Government of the Republic of China, the Reformed Government of the Republic of China and others have been taken over and temporarily maintained as they are by the Government of the Republic of China, those which require adjustment but are not yet adjusted shall be adjusted in conformity with the purpose of the treaty and its annexed documents through consultation between the two countries, as promptly as circumstances may permit.

ARTICLE 3

When general peace is restored between the two countries and the state of war ceases to exist, the Japanese forces shall commence evacuation with the exception of those which are stationed in accordance with the treaty concerning the basic relations between Japan and China signed today and the existing agreements between the two countries, and shall complete it within two years with the firm establishment of peace and order, and the Government of the Republic of China shall guarantee the firm establishment of peace and order during the period.

ARTICLE 4

The Government of the Republic of China shall compensate for the damages to rights and interests suffered by Japanese subjects in China on account of the China affair since its outbreak.

The Government of Japan shall with respect to the relief of the Chinese rendered destitute by the China affair, cooperate with the Government of the Republic of China.

ARTICLE 5

The present protocol shall come into effect simultaneously with the treaty.

In witness whereof the plenipotentiaries of the two countries have signed this protocol and have affixed thereto their seals.

Done in duplicate, in the Japanese and Chinese languages, at Nanjing the 30th day of the 11th month of the 15th year of Showa, corresponding to the 30th day of the 11th month of the 29th year of the Republic of China.

10.4 JIANG WEN'S *DEVILS ON THE DOORSTEP* (2000)

Jiang Wen's film *Devils on the Doorstep* (*Guizi Laile*) takes a morbidly humorous look at the complexities of nationalism in the context of the War of Resistance Against Japan. The film follows events in a north China village that is suddenly caught between dealing with the Japanese or with the Communist insurgents. Jiang Wen's underlying point is that neither of the alternatives—the Communist resistance or Japanese collaboration—was particularly appealing as each entailed considerable risks for those involved. The film, shot in black and white, takes the well-worn theme of China's war against Japan and breathes new life into it by showing the vagaries of politics during wartime. The film's ambivalent stance towards the Communist movement led the current Chinese government to ban the film and forced the director Jiang Wen into a two-year hiatus from making films. While the film was not a commercial success, *Devils on the Doorstep* received critical acclaim at the Cannes Film Festival, winning the Jury's Grand Prize in 2000. The film begins with the scene described below of two men—a Japanese officer and his Chinese translator (as they are later identified)—who are unceremoniously deposited in Ma Dasan's home.

Questions

1. **Why are the villagers at a loss over what to do with the two men dropped off in the middle of night?**
2. **What aspects of this scene would make the Chinese censors nervous enough to seek to recall the print of the film from the Venice Film Festival?**

(*In 1945 in a village by the Bohai Sea. The scene opens late at night in Ma Dasan's home with Ma Dasan and a young widow Yuer engaged in a late night tryst when there is a knock on the door.*)

Scene I

MA DASAN: Who is it?

MAN: Me.

MA DASAN: Who?

MAN: Me.

YUER: (*speaking to Ma Dasan*) Quick, put your clothes on.

MA DASAN: What about you?

YUER: I will hide in the usual place.

(*Yuer, naked, runs across the room and climbs into a trunk. Ma Dasan throws a quilt over her and closes the trunk. Ma Dasan walks towards the door*)

MA DASAN: Who is it?

MAN: Me.

(*Ma Dasan opens the door and a gun points straight to his forehead as he moves back into the room.*)

MAN: Close your eyes. What's your name?

MA DASAN: Ma Dasan.

MAN: What's the name of the village?

MA DASAN: Baojiatai.

MAN: So late at night, why is your lamp still lit?

MA DASAN: I was mulling things over.

MAN: Then, you think hard. Listen, we have two things to leave with you. Neither can go lost or missing. And don't let the [Japanese] devils know about it. If anything goes wrong, you'll be dead.

MA DASAN: Well… There is a [Japanese] blockhouse at the end of the village. It probably won't work?

MAN: What's not working? It's called "the dark spot under the light." Understand?

MA DASAN: Understood. Uh, what if something goes wrong, who is responsible?

MAN: You!

(*The man quickly runs off into the dark night. Ma Dasan opens his eyes, seeing the front door wide open and two large canvas bags on the ground. He closes the door. Yuer opens the trunk and gets out*)

YUER: Who was it?

MA DASAN: Not a clue.

(*They light a match and untie the bag*)

YUER (suppressed yell): Yikes! It's a live person.

(*Ma Dasan opens the other bag, inside is another man. Ma Dasan moves quickly towards the door*)

MA DASAN: I will go and find them.

(*The paper on window next to Ma Dasan is slowly cut through by a blade*)

MAN: Ma Dasan.

MA DASAN: Yes?

MAN: Listen! Question those two for us when you have time. At midnight on New Year's Eve, we will come and pick them up. We'll take them along with their confession! Understand?

MA DASAN: Understood! Then… who will come to pick them up?

MAN: Me!

Scene II

(*In a room with a few villagers, Ma Dasan is describing what has happened.*)

MA DASAN: Like this, this, and this. Zoom! Zoom! Zoom! Jumped over the wall and ran away.

VILLAGE ELDER: Then, what was his name?

MA DASAN: Didn't say. He just said "Me."

VILLAGE ELDER: Then… what did he look like?

MA DASAN: Couldn't tell. My eyes were closed.

VILLAGER I: What was he wearing? How tall was he?

MA DASAN: My eyes were closed. If your eyes are closed, can you see me?

VILLAGER II: (*squatting on the ground*) How many of them?

MA DASAN: Didn't I say my eyes were closed? I dared not to look.

VILLAGE ELDER: Then what exactly did he say?

MA DASAN: He just said, "We will leave these two at your village." They will come back and pick them up on New Year's Eve midnight.

YUER: Yeah, those people sounded very scary.

MA DASAN: They also said "it's called 'the dark spot under the light'."

FENG QIYE: I'll kill you, you damn bastard.

VILLAGE ELDER: Deal with your family problems later.

VILLAGER II: The affair between your daughter-in-law and Dasan has been going on for more than a couple days.

VILLAGE ELDER: We are discussing something serious.

(*Yuer quickly moves the rifle away from the old man and hands him a bowl of water*)

FENG QIYE: With these two, how can anything be serious?

VILLAGER I: Go to sleep.

YUER: Dad, have some water.

FENG QIYE: I am not your dad. You shameless slut.

VILLAGE ELDER: Does that sound like anything a father-in-law should say?

MA DASAN: (*Getting excited and trying to hand the rifle to Feng Qiye*) Just shoot me please, elder. I am so worried and have no way out anyway. Just shoot me.

FENG QIYE: I'll kill you, damn bastard…

VILLAGE ELDER: (*ordering both*) Sit down! Lie down! (*continues to talk after all calmed down*) Just as

---

FENG QIYE—Literally means "Crazy Seventh Grandpa" – Yuer's father-in-law, who is lying in bed ranting against Ma Dasan who he reviles for sleeping with his daughter-in-law

It is difficult for fortune to turn into misfortune, it is difficult to avoid misfortune.

MA DASAN: Then is it fortune or misfortune? Elder, what on earth shall we do?

VILLAGER II: (*squatting on the ground stands up*) Well! Let's take them to the blockhouse. I know the *sensei.*

MA DASAN: What did you say?

VILLAGER II: Hand them over to the Japanese!

MA DASAN: That won't work! That…then, when those people come for them on New Year's Eve, what do we say?

VILLAGER II: Let them go and ask the Japanese. What do they dare do to the Japanese?

MA DASAN: The Japanese? The Japanese was tied up and put in the bag by them! You tell me what they dare to do.

VILLAGER I: (*to villager II*) Won't you be a collaborator?

MA DASAN: That's right.

(*Villager II squats down*)

FENG QIYE: I will choke them both, one with each hand, then dig a hole to bury them.

VILLAGER I: Eh? That sounds good. Just dig a hole. I'll dig.

MA DASAN: You dig? Those people said if we lose or miss one, or let the Japanese find out, then… they would not want them back, instead they want lives!

VILLAGERS: Want lives? Whose lives?

MA DASAN: Lives, the lives of our entire village.

VILLAGER II: (*Standing up*) Well?… No, that's no good! (*He squats down again*)

VILLAGER I: What? You tell us, tell us!

VILLAGER II: No.

VILLAGE ELDER: Tell us!

VILLAGER II: I'll say it. The entire village should run away. We'll all run away, and just leave those two and see whose lives they will take?

VILLAGE ELDER: Sit back down!

VILLAGER II: I said it was no good. And you made me say it anyway. What a waste!

FENG QIYE: (*pointing to Ma Dasan*) I'd better shoot you now. Otherwise the whole village is going to die sooner or later because of you.

VILLAGER I: Stop it! Stop it! Or I will leave!

VILLAGE ELDER: Come back here! Sit down! Didn't you hear what he said, they want to kill the entire village?

FENG QIYE: I will choke them both, one with each hand, then kill 'em both. Dig a hole and bury them.… dig a hole and bury them.

VILLAGE ELDER: What's coming is no good! Nothing good is coming! Common people would not do such a thing. We cannot afford to piss off either side: those who live in the mountains [the Communists] or by the water [the Japanese]. In five days it'll be New Year's Eve. On New Year's Eve, they will come and take them away. Nobody knows about it. We'll send them away, along with the misfortune. San'er [Ma Dasan], in the next few days, you need be careful and watchful. This is for the whole village.

(*Ma Dasan nods*)

VILLAGE ELDER: (*to villager II*) Erbozi,

VILLAGER II: Yes, fifth great uncle.

VILLAGE ELDER: Don't say a word to your mother. She has a big mouth.

ERBOZI: I will keep it to myself, OK?

VILLAGE ELDER: Then… Let's go.

MA DASAN: Ah?… Don't go. It's not over yet. Those people asked us to question those two when we have time.

VILLAGE ELDER: Question them? What will we ask them?

LIFE IN YAN'AN

From 1936 to 1947, Yan'an was the political, military, and symbolic center of the Chinese Communist Party (CCP). Located on a bleak loess plateau in northern Shaanxi Province, the steep Yan'an valley is dominated by the now famous Baota Pagoda. This period is often looked at as the ideologically pure era of the CCP. Edgar Snow's groundbreaking study of Yan'an accurately portrayed the exhilarating thrill, felt by many who passed through the communist soviet, of participating in the dawn of a new political age (10.5). Yet, Yan'an was

SENSEI—Japanese term of respect when referring to a teacher or official.

no idyllic communist paradise. Even famous and well-respected communist writers such as Ding Ling and Wang Shiwei learned how quickly the political winds could shift (10.6, 10.7). Part of the insecurity of Yan'an came from the CCP leaders' perilous circumstances. Engaged in a perilous game of brinksmanship with the GMD, Japan and the Soviet Union, they sought to retain a political, ideological and practical footing. This was no simple task given the demands of waging a war against Japan, withstanding constant GMD censure and trying to interpret the Soviet Union's constantly shifting directives.

10.5 EDGAR SNOW'S SOVIET SOCIETY (1937)

Edgar Snow studied journalism at the University of Missouri before traveling to China. There he was swept up by the gripping political and social changes of 1930s China. In 1936 he became captivated by the stories trickling out from Communist Yan'an. Snow succeeded in traveling to the northwestern Communist outpost and gathering first-hand observations. His narrative below was part of the first book length description of the Chinese Communists and life in Yan'an written in any Western language. The book became an immediate success and attracted international attention. By the 1950s, though, his pro-Communist views brought him under intense scrutiny during the McCarthy era.

Questions

1. **What reforms does Snow hail as positive improvements over life outside of the Communist-controlled area?**
2. **Why would Snow's comment that "marriage was by mutual consent, the legal age had been moved up sharply to twenty for men and eighteen for women" have been surprising to Western readers?**

Whatever it may have been in the South, Chinese Communism as I found it in the Northwest might more accurately be called rural equalitarianism than anything Marx would have found agreeable as a model child of his own. This was manifestly true economically, and although in the social, political, and cultural life of the organized Soviets there was a crude Marxist guidance, limitations of the material conditions were everywhere obvious.

[....]

The co-operative movement was being vigorously pushed. These activities extended beyond production and distribution co-operatives, branching out to include co-operation in such (for China) novel forms as the collective use of farm animals and implements—especially in tilling public lands and Red Army lands—and in the organization of labor mutual-aid societies. By the latter device great areas could be quickly planted and harvested collectively, and periods of idleness by individual farmers eliminated. The Reds saw to it that a man earned his new land! In

busy periods the system of "Saturday Brigades" was used, when not only all the children's organizations, and any Red Army detachment that happened to be nearby, were mobilized to work at least one day a week at farming tasks. Even Mao Zedong took part in this work.

Here the Reds were introducing the germs of the drastically revolutionary idea of collective effort—and doing primary education work for some future period when collectivization might become practicable. At the same time, into the dark recesses of peasant mentality there was slowly penetrating the concept of a broader realm of social life. For the organizations created among the peasantry were what the Reds called three-in-one: economic, political, and cultural in their utility.

What cultural progress the Reds had made among these people was, by any advanced Western standards, negligible indeed. But certain outstanding evils common in most parts of China had definitely been eliminated in the score of long-Sovietized counties in north

Shaanxi, and a crusade of propaganda was being conducted among inhabitants of newer areas to spread the same elementary reforms there. As an outstanding achievement, opium had been completely eliminated in north Shaanxi, and in fact I did not see any sign of poppies after I entered the Soviet district. Official corruption was almost unheard-of. Beggary and unemployment did seem to have been, as the Reds claimed, "liquidated." I did not see a beggar during all my travels in the Red areas. Foot-binding and infanticide were criminal offences, child slavery and prostitution had disappeared, and polyandry and polygamy were prohibited.

The myths of "communized wives" or "nationalization of women" are too patently absurd to be denied, but changes in marriage, divorce, and inheritance were in themselves extremely radical against the background of semi-feudal law and practice elsewhere in China. Marriage regulations included interesting provisions against mother-in-law tyranny, the buying and selling of women as wives and concubines, and the custom of "arranged matches." Marriage was by mutual consent, the legal age had been moved up sharply to twenty for men and eighteen for women; dowries were prohibited, and any couple registering as man and wife before a county, municipal, or village Soviet was given a marriage certificate without cost. Men and women actually cohabiting were considered legally married, whether registered or not—which

seems to rule out "free love" —and their offspring were legitimate. No illegitimacy of children was recognized.

Divorce could also be secured from the registration bureau of the Soviet, free of charge, on the "insistent demand" of either party to the marriage contract, but wives of Red Army men were required to have their husband's consent before a divorce was granted. Property was divided equally between the divorcees, and both were legally obliged to care for their children, but responsibility for debts was shouldered by the man alone(!), who was also obliged to supply two-thirds of the children's living expenses.

Education, in theory, was "free and universal," but parents had of course to supply their children with food and clothing. In practice, nothing like "free and universal education had yet been achieved, although old Xu Teli, the commissioner of education, boasted to me that if they were given a few years of peace in the Northwest they would astound the rest of China with the educational progress they would make. Farther on I shall discuss more in detail what the Communists had done and hoped to do to liquidate the appalling illiteracy of this region, but first it is interesting to know how the government was financing not only the educational program, such as it was, but this whole seemingly simple and yet in its way vastly complex organism which I have called Soviet society.

10.6   DING LING'S THOUGHTS ON MARCH 8, WOMEN'S DAY (1942)

Ding Ling's early success as a leftist feminist writer in the 1920s and 1930s (8.12) had made her one of the darlings of the May Fourth Era writers. Yet the traits that might have been admired among the Beijing and Shanghai elite did not have the same effect in Yan'an. Her caustic portrayal of women at the hands of communist **cadres** in Yan'an reflects her tendency to offer an unsparing (if accurate) analysis of life under the CCP. The following column, published by her in 1942, highlights the most common abuses women faced in Yan'an. The column obliquely indicts a pattern among top CCP leaders (including Mao Zedong) to divorce their aging wives in favor of younger women available in Yan'an. The following article originally appeared on March 9, 1942 in the literary section of the *Liberation Daily,* Yan'an's main newspaper. Soon after its publication Ding Ling was accused of taking an overly feminist line in her writing. She (and many other writers) immediately offered self-criticisms and she accepted the party's reproach of her writing as "divisive" in order to be rehabilitated by the party.

CADRE—In the Chinese Communist context, a term meaning functionaries or administrators, often used as shorthand for essential or particularly revolutionary "backbone" members of the CCP.

Questions

1. **What does Ding Ling suggest are the primary problems women face in Yan'an?**

2. **In what ways does she suggest there is a double standard for woman revolutionaries that does not exist for men in Yan'an?**

When will it no longer be necessary to attach special weight to the word "woman" and to raise it specially?

Each year this day comes round. Every year on this day meetings are held all over the world where women muster their forces. Even though things have not been as lively these last two years in Yan'an as they were in previous years, it appears that at least a few people are busy at work here. And there will certainly be a congress, speeches, circular telegrams, and articles.

Women in Yan'an are happier than women elsewhere in China. So much so that many people ask enviously: "How come the women comrades get so rosy and fat on millet?" It doesn't seem to surprise anyone that women make up a big proportion of the staff in hospitals, sanatoria, and clinics, but they are inevitably the subject of conversation, as a fascinating problem, on every conceivable occasion. What's more, all kinds of women comrades are often the target of deserved criticism. In my view these reproaches are serious and justifiable.

People are always interested when women comrades get married, but that is not enough for them. It is impossible for women comrades to get onto friendly terms with a man comrade, even more so with more than one. Cartoonists ridicule them: "A departmental head getting married too?" The poets say: "All the leaders in Yan'an are horsemen, and none of them are artists. In Yan'an it's impossible for an artist to find a pretty sweetheart." In other situations they are lectured at: "Damn it, you look down on us old cadres and say we're country bumpkins. But if it wasn't for us country bumpkins, you wouldn't be coming to Yan'an to eat millet!" Yet women invariably want to get married. (It's even more of a sin not to marry, and single women are even more of a target for rumors and slanderous gossip.) So they can't afford to be choosy, anyone will do: whether he rides horses or wears straw sandals, whether he's an artist or a supervisor. After marriage, they inevitably have children. The fate of such children is various. Some are wrapped in soft baby wool and patterned felt and looked after by governesses. Others are wrapped in soiled cloth and left crying in their parents' beds, while their parents consume much of the child's allowance. But for this allowance (25 yuan a month, equivalent to just over three pounds of pork), many would never get a taste of meat. Whoever they marry, those women who are compelled to bear children will probably be publicly derided as "**Noras** who have returned home." Those women comrades in a position to employ governesses can go out once a week to a prim get-together and dance. Behind their backs there will also be the most incredible gossip and whispering campaigns, but wherever they go they cause a great stir and all eyes are glued to them. This has nothing to do with our theories, our doctrines, and the speeches we make at meetings. We all know this to be a fact, a fact that is right before our eyes, but it is never mentioned.

It is same with divorce. In general there are three conditions to observe when getting married. These are (1) political purity; (2) similar age and comparable looks; and (3) mutual help. Even though everyone is said to fulfill these conditions—as for (1), there are no open traitors in Yan'an; as for (3), you can call anything "mutual help," including darning socks, patching shoes, and even feminine comfort—everyone nevertheless makes a great show of giving thoughtful attention to them. And yet the pretext for divorce is invariably the wife's political backwardness. I am the first to admit that it is a shame when a man's wife is not progressive and retards his progress. But let us consider how backward they really are. Before marrying, they were inspired by the desire to soar in the heavenly heights and lead a life of bitter struggle. They got married partly through physiological necessity and partly as a

A DOLL'S HOUSE—An 1879 play by Norwegian playwright Henrik Ibsen. It traces Nora's realization of her limited role in society and her determination to fight against patriarchal constraints. The play's feminist themes made it popular in May Fourth era China, with Hu Shi praising the play as "nothing but realism."

response to sweet talk about "mutual help." After that they are forced to toil away and become "Noras returned home." Afraid of being thought "backward," those who are a bit more daring rush round begging nurseries to take their children. They ask for abortions and risk punishment and even death by secretly swallowing potions to induce them. But the answer comes back: "Isn't giving birth to children also work? You're just after an easy life, you want to be in the limelight. After all, what indispensable political work have you performed? Since you are so frightened of having children and so unwilling to take responsibility once you have had them, why did you get married in the first place? No one forced you to." Under these conditions how can women escape the destiny of "backwardness"? When women capable of working sacrifice their career for the joys of motherhood, people always sing their praises. But after ten years or so, they inevitably pay the tragic price (i.e., divorce) of "backwardness." Even from my point of view, as a woman, there is nothing attractive about such "backward" elements. Their skin is beginning to wrinkle, their hair is growing thin, and fatigue is robbing them of their last traces of attractiveness. It should be self-evident that they are caught up in a tragedy. But whereas in the old society they would probably have been pitied and considered unfortunate, nowadays their tragedy is seen as something self-inflicted, as their just desserts. Is there not a discussion going on in legal circles about whether divorce should be granted simply on the petition of one party or on the basis of mutual agreement? In the great majority of cases it is the husband who petitions for divorce. If the wife does so, she must be leading an immoral life, so of course she deserves to be cursed!

I myself am a woman, so I understand the failings of women better than others. But I also have a deeper understanding of what they suffer. Women are incapable of transcending the age they live in, of being perfect, or of being hard as steel. They are incapable of resisting all the temptations of society or all the silent oppression they suffer here in Yan'an. They each have their own past written blood and tears, they have experienced great emotions—in elation as in depression, in the lone battle of life or in the humdrum stream of life. This is even truer of the women comrades who come to Yan'an, so I have much sympathy for those fallen and classed as criminal. What's more, I hope that men, especially those in top positions, and women themselves will consider women's mistakes in their social context. It would be better if there were less empty theorizing and more talk about real problems, so that theory and practice are not divorced,

and if each Communist Party member were more responsible for his own moral conduct.

But we must also hope for a little more from our women comrades, especially those in Yan'an. We must urge ourselves on and develop our comradely feeling.

People without ability have never been in a position to seize all. So if women want equality, they must first strengthen themselves. There is no need to stress this, we all know it. Today there are certain to be people who make fine speeches about the need first to acquire political power. I would simply mention a few things that any front liner, whether a proletarian, a fighter in the war of resistance, or a woman, should pay attention to in his or her everyday life:

1. Don't allow yourself to fall ill. A wild life can at times appear romantic, poetic, and attractive, but in today's conditions it is inappropriate. You are the best keeper of your life. There is nothing more unfortunate nowadays than to lose your health. It is nearest to your heart. Keep a close watch on it, pay careful attention to it, cherish it.

2. Make sure that you are happy. Only when you are happy can you be youthful, active, fulfilled in your life, and steadfast in the face of every difficulty; only then will you see a future ahead of you and know how to enjoy yourself. This sort of happiness is not a life of contentment, but a life of struggle and of advance. All of us should every day do some meaningful work and some reading, so that each of us is in a position to give something to others. Loafing about simply encourages the feeling that life is hollow, feeble, and in decay.

3. Use your brain, and make a habit of doing so. Correct any tendency not to think and ponder, or to swim with the tide. Before you say or do anything, think whether what you are saying is right, whether that is the most suitable way of dealing with the problem, whether it goes against your own principles, whether you feel you can take responsibility for it. Then you will have no cause to regret your actions later. This is what is known as acting rationally. It is the best way of avoiding the pitfalls of sweet words and honeyed phrases, of being side-tracked by petty gains, of wasting our emotions and wasting our lives.

4. Resolution in hardship, perseverance to the end. Aware, modern women should identify and cast off all their rosy, compliant illusions. Happiness is to take up the struggle in the midst of the raging storm and not to pluck the lute in the moonlight or to recite poetry among the blossoms. In the absence of the greatest resolution, it is all too easy to falter

in mid-path. Not to suffer is to become degenerate. The strength to carry on should be nurtured through the quality of "perseverance." People without great aims and ambitions rarely have the firmness of purpose that scorns petty advantages and a comfortable existence. Only those who have aims and ambitions for the benefit not of the individual but of humanity as a whole can persevere to the end.

Dawn, August 3, 1942

Postscript

On rereading this article, it seems to me there is much room for improvement in the passage about what we should expect from women, but because I have to meet a deadline, I have no time to revise it. Yet I also feel that there are some things that, said by a leader before a big audience, would probably evoke satisfaction. But when written by a woman, they are more than likely to be demolished. However, since I have written it, I offer it as I always intended, for the perusal of those with similar views.

10.7 WANG SHIWEI'S "WILD LILY" (1942)

Wang Shiwei (1907–1947) attended Beijing University in 1925 and joined the CCP the following year. By the 1930s he had gained a reputation as a talented translator of world literature and as a fiction writer in his own right. With the outbreak of the war against Japan in 1937, he fled to Yan'an. There he translated a large number of philosophical and political works, including works by Marx and Lenin. In the spring of 1942, he published several articles painting life in Yan'an in an unfavorable light. The most famous of these, "Wild Lily" (*Ye Baihehua*), was featured in the literature section of the *Liberation Daily* on March 13th and 23rd, 1942. In response to Wang Shiwei's, Ding Ling's, and others' criticisms, the CCP leaders initiated a political rectification campaign in the spring of 1942. It quickly became clear that he was a main target. He was publicly criticized, then arrested, and finally (some say mistakenly) executed for his views.

Questions

1. What is Wang Shiwei's primary criticism of life in Yan'an?
2. Why would CCP officials be upset by Wang Shiwei's description of Yan'an (and the comparison it made with areas outside of Yan'an)?

While I was walking alone along the riverbank, I saw a comrade wearing a pair of old-style padded cotton shoes. I immediately fell to thinking of Comrade Li Fen, who also wore such shoes. Li Fen, my dearest and very first friend. As usual my blood began to race. Li Fen was a student in 1926 on the preparatory course in literature at Beijing University. In the same year she joined the Party. In the spring of 1928 she sacrificed her life in her home district of Baoqing in Hunan province. Her own uncle tied her up and sent her to the local garrison—a good illustration of the barbarity of the old China. Before going to her death, she put on all her three sets of underclothes and sewed them tightly together at the top and the bottom. This was because the troops in Baoqing often incited riff-raff to defile the corpses of the young women

Communists they had shot—yet another example of the brutality, the evil, the filth and the darkness of the old society. When I got news of her death, I was consumed with feelings of deep love and hatred. Whenever I think of her, I have a vision of her pure, sacred martyrdom, with her three layers of underclothes sewn tightly together, tied up and sent by her very own uncle to meet her death with dignity. (It seems rather out of place to talk of such things in tranquil Yan'an, against the warbled background of [the Beijing Opera] "Yutang Chun" and the swirling steps of the golden lotus dance; but the whole atmosphere in Yan'an does not seem particularly appropriate to the conditions of the day—close your eyes and think for a moment of our dear comrades dying every minute in a sea of carnage.)

In the interest of the nation, I will not reckon up old scores of class hatred. We are genuinely selfless. With all our might we are dragging the representatives of old China along the road with us toward the light. But in the process the filth and dirt is rubbing off on us, spreading its diseases.

On scores of occasions I have drawn strength from the memory of Li Fen—vital and militant strength. Thinking back on her on this occasion, I was moved to write a *zawen* [essay] under the title "Wild Lily." This name has a twofold significance. First, the wild lily is the most beautiful of the wild flowers in the hills and countryside around Yan'an, and is therefore a fitting dedication to her memory. Secondly, although its bulbs are similar to those of other lilies, they are said to be slightly bitter to the taste, and of greater medicinal value, but I myself am not sure of this.

WHAT IS LACKING IN OUR LIVES?

Recently young people here in Yan'an seem to have lost some of their enthusiasm, and to have become inwardly ill at ease.

Why is this? What is lacking in our lives? Some would answer that it is because we are badly nourished and short of vitamins. Others, that it is because the ratio of men to women is eighteen to one, and many young men are unable to find girlfriends. Or because life in Yan'an is dreary and lacks amusements.

There is some truth in all these answers. It is true that there is need for better food, for partners of the opposite sex, and for more interest in life. This is only natural. But one must also recognize that young people here in Yan'an came with a spirit of sacrifice to make revolution and not for food, sex, and an enjoyable life. I cannot agree with those who say that their lack of enthusiasm, their inward disquiet even, are a result of our inability to resolve these problems. So what is lacking in our lives? Perhaps the following conversation holds some clues.

During the New Year holiday I was walking home in the dark one evening from a friend's place. Ahead of me were two women comrades talking in animated whispers. We were some way apart so I quietly moved closer to hear what they were saying.

"He keeps on talking about other people's petty-bourgeois egalitarianism; but the truth is that he thinks he is something special. He always looks after his own interests. As for the comrades underneath him, he doesn't care whether they're sick or well. He doesn't even care if they die, he hardly gives a damn!... Crows

are black wherever they are. Even Comrade XXX acts like that."

"You're right! All this bullshit about loving your own class. They don't even show ordinary human sympathy! You often see people pretending to smile and be friendly, but it's all on the surface, it doesn't mean anything. And if you offend them, they glare at you, pull their rank and start lecturing you."

"It's not only the big shots who act that way, the small fry are just the same. Our section leader XXX crawls when he's talking to his superiors, but he behaves very arrogantly towards us. Often comrades have been ill and he hasn't even dropped in to see how they are. But when an eagle stole one of his chickens, you should have seen the fuss he made! After that, every time he saw an eagle he'd start screaming and throwing clods of earth at it—the self-seeking bastard!"

There was a long silence. In one way, I admired the comrade's sharp tongue. But I also suddenly felt depressed.

"It's sad that so many comrades are falling ill. Nobody wants people like that to visit them when they fall ill, they just make you feel worse. Their tone of voice, their whole attitude they don't make you feel they care about you."

"Right. They don't care about others, and others don't care about them.

If they did mass work, they'd be bound to fail."

They carried on their conversation in animated whispers. At this point our ways parted, and I heard no more of what they had to say. In many ways their views were one-sided and exaggerated. Perhaps the picture they drew does not apply widely: but there is no denying that it is useful as a mirror.

[....]

EGALITARIANISM AND THE SYSTEM OF RANKS

According to what I heard, one comrade wrote an article with a similar title for his departmental wall newspaper, and as a result was criticized and attacked by his department "head" and driven half-mad. I hope this story is untrue. But since there have been genuine cases of madness even among the "little devils" [orphan children who acted as personal assistants to the Communist cadres], I fear there may be some madness among adults. Even though the state of my nerves is not as "healthy" as some people's, I still have enough life in me not to go mad under any circumstances. I therefore intend to follow in the footsteps of that comrade and discuss the question of equality and the ranking system.

Communism is not the same as egalitarianism, and we are not at present at the stage of Communist revolution. There is no need for me to write an eight-legged essay on that question, since there is no cook crazy enough to want to live in the same style as one of the "heads." (I don't dare write "kitchen operative," since it sounds like a caricature; but whenever I speak to cooks I always address them in the warmest possible way as comrade kitchen-operatives' —what a pitiful example of warmth!) The question of a system of ranks is rather more difficult.

Those who say that a system of ranks is reasonable use roughly the following arguments: (1) they base themselves on the principle of "from each according to their ability, to each according to their worth," which means that those with more responsibilities should consume more; (2) in the near future the three-thirds government [the "tripartite system" under which the Communists nominally shared power with the "petit bourgeoisie and the enlightened gentry" in the areas under their control] intends to carry out a new salary system, and naturally there will be pay differentials; and (3) the Soviet Union also has a system of rank.

In my opinion all these arguments are open to debate. As for (1), we are still in the midst of the revolution, with all its hardships and difficulties; all of us, despite fatigue, are laboring to surmount the present crisis, and many comrades have ruined their precious health. Because of this it does not yet seem the right time for anyone, no matter who, to start talking about "to each according to their worth." On the contrary, all the more reason why those with greater responsibilities should show themselves willing to share weal and woe with the rank and file. (This is a national virtue that should be encouraged.) In so doing, they would win the profound love of the lower ranks. Only then would it be possible to create ironlike unity. It goes without saying that it is not only reasonable but necessary that those with big responsibilities who need special treatment for their health should get such treatment. The same goes for those with positions of medium responsibility. As for (2), the pay system of the three-thirds government should also avoid excessive differentials; it is right that non-party officials should get slightly better treatment, but those officials who are Party members should uphold our excellent traditions of frugal struggle so that we are in a position to mobilize even more non-party people to join us and cooperate with us. As for (3), excuse my rudeness, but I would beg those "great masters" who can't open their mouths without talking about Ancient Greece to hold their tongues.

I am not an egalitarian, but to divide clothing into three and food into five grades is neither necessary nor rational, especially with regard to clothes. (I myself am graded as "cadres' clothes and private kitchen," so this not just a case of sour grapes.) All such problems should be resolved on the basis of need and reason. At present there is no noodle soup for sick comrades to eat and young students only get two meals of thin congee a day (when they are asked whether they have had enough to eat, Party members are expected to lead the rest in a chorus of "Yes, we're full"). Relatively healthy "big shots" get far more than they need to eat and drink, with the result that their subordinates look upon them as a race apart, and not only do not love them, but even … This makes me most uneasy. But perhaps it is a "petty bourgeois emotion" to always be talking about "love" and warmth"? I await your verdict.

TAIWAN AND THE GMD'S ROAD TO DEFEAT (1945–1949)

When Japan finally surrendered in August of 1945, the tensions between the GMD and the CCP were extremely high. Despite multiple attempts to bring about reconciliation, two decades of suspicion and mistrust poisoned virtually all efforts to persuade the two sides to govern jointly. In some ways repeating his mistake of the mid-1930s, Jiang Jieshi became fixated on exterminating the CCP while ignoring the economic, social, and political problems that had built up during the war. Negative public opinion over his handling of the country's rampaging inflation, his harsh repression of any political dissent, and his slow response to the needs of a country desperately attempting to piece itself back together left little room for error. Initially, Jiang Jieshi and the GMD appeared to have every advantage over the CCP. With the Cold War heating up, the United States funneled aid almost exclusively to the GMD, which allowed the GMD an overwhelming advantage in troops, weapons and financial reserves. In the end though, it was a litany of errors large and small, as well as inept leadership and a shocking level of corruption by GMD officials that undermined their initial advantage. The CCP, conversely, swiftly and effectively put to work the lessons they had learned during their eight years of warfare. It was by their speedy and decisive military leadership that they were able to defeat the Nationalists quickly and emphatically.

10.8 WEN YIDUO'S EULOGY OF LI GONGPU (JULY 15, 1946)

Wen Yiduo (1899–1946), an erudite and famed scholar of classical Chinese poetry and literature, studied at the Chicago Art Institute, Colorado College, and Columbia University between 1922 and 1925. Upon his return he taught at Qinghua University before the Japanese invasion forced his evacuation to Kunming in southwestern China. In Kunming, despite the huge number of refugees and a scarcity of housing and teaching positions, Wen Yiduo achieved extraordinary productivity during this time. When the war ended and many of the universities returned to their original campuses in eastern and northern China, Wen Yiduo chose to remain in Kunming. There he helped organize the Democratic League office. In 1946, Li Gongpu, one of Wen's closest friends and a fellow political activist, was shot and killed by GMD agents just blocks from Wen Yiduo's home. Despite both veiled and open threats, Wen Yiduo insisted on holding a memorial service for this friend. The following is the eulogy he delivered. Just hours later GMD agents shot and killed Wen as he returned home with his teenage son.

Questions

1. Aside from eulogizing his friend's death, what do Wen Yiduo's words tell us about popular attitudes towards Jiang Jieshi's tactics in retaining political control?
2. What do you think that Li Gongpu and Wen Yiduo mean when they suggest the 'dawn is near?'

A few days ago as we are all aware, one of the most despicable and shameful events of history occurred here in Kunming. What crime did Mr. Li Gongpu commit that would cause him to be murdered in such a vicious way? He merely used his pen to write a few articles, he used his mouth to speak out, and what he said and wrote was nothing more than what any Chinese with a conscience would say. We all have pens and mouths. If there is a reason for it, why not speak out? Why should people be beaten, killed, or, even worse, killed in a devious way? [Applause]

Are there any special agents [Guomindang spies] here today? Stand up! If you are men, stand up! Come forward and speak? Why did you kill Mr. Li? [Enthusiastic applause] You kill people but refuse to admit it and even circulate false rumors that the murder happened because of some sexual scandal or as the result of Communists killing other Communists. Shameless! Shameless! [Applause] This is the shamelessness of the Guomindang but the glory belongs to Mr. Li. Mr. Li participated in Kunming's democratic movement for a number of years. Now he has returned to Kunming and sacrificed his own life. This is Mr. Li's glory, it is the glory of the people of Kunming!

Last year, at the time of the December 1st Incident, the young students of Kunming were slaughtered for demonstrating against the civil war and that was a case of the younger generation sacrificing its precious lives. Now, Mr. Li, striving for democracy and peace, has also suffered assassination by the reactionaries. Let me proudly say, an old comrade-in-arms has now sacrificed his precious life for my generation. Both of these incidents happened here in Kunming and this will be an eternal glory for Kunming. [Applause]

DEMOCRATIC LEAGUE—A political party first formed in 1941 and officially reorganized into the Democratic League in 1944. Intellectuals dominated the league leadership and espoused national unity, open democracy and peace. It remains an active party within the PRC today.

After the news of the reactionary's assassination of Mr. Li spread, everyone was indignant and outraged. I certainly can't understand the heart of those shameless creatures; under these circumstances how can they fabricate false rumors to insult Mr. Li? But in fact it is very simple. The reason they are madly creating terror is because they themselves are in a panic! They are afraid! They create terror because they feel terrified!

Special Agents, think about it, how many days are left for you?

Do you really think that if you hurt a few or kill a few, that you can intimidate the whole people? In fact, you cannot beat all of the people or kill all of the people. For every Li Gongpu you kill, hundreds of millions of Li Gongpu will stand up! [Applause] In the future you will lose the support of hundreds of millions of people.

The reactionaries believe that they can reduce the number of people participating in the democratic movement and destroy its power through the terror of assassination. But let me tell you, our power is great, our power is enormous! [Applause] Look! All of these people today are our people and their power is our power. [Applause]

The power of the people will win and truth will live forever! [Applause] Throughout history, all who have opposed the people have been destroyed by the people! Didn't Hitler and Mussolini fall before the people? Jiang Jieshi, you are so rabid, so reactionary, turn the pages of history, how many days do you think you have left? You're finished! It is over for you! [Enthusiastic applause]

Bright days are coming for us. Look, the light is before us. Just as Mr. Li said as he was dying" "Daybreak is coming!" Now is that darkest moment before dawn. We have the power to break through this darkness and attain the light! The coming of our light marks the final moment for the reactionaries! [Applause]

Mr. Li's blood was not shed in vain! Mr. Li gave his life and we shall demand a price in return. We have confidence and we must have this confidence....

Reactionaries, you have seen one man fall but have you seen hundreds of millions stand up?

Justice can never be killed because truth lives forever! ... [Applause]

To attain democracy and peace, we must pay a price. We are not afraid of making sacrifices. Each of us should be like Mr. Li. When we step through the door, we must be prepared never to return. [Long, enthusiastic applause]

10.9   LI ZONGREN'S "THE DISINTEGRATION OF OUR MILITARY FORCES"

Li Zongren (1891–1969) was born in the southwestern province of Guangxi. He obtained a military education then led a group of dissidents against the warlord who controlled the province. In the mid-1920s he joined the GMD and participated in the Northern Expedition. Throughout this time, however, he remained disdainful of Jiang Jieshi's leadership. During the War of Resistance Against Japan he distinguished himself as one of the most successful GMD generals in battles against the Japanese. In 1948, he was elected vice-president (much to Jiang's disappointment) and in the following year became interim president when Jiang briefly resigned in the face of military defeats on virtually every front. Li's account of the GMD's strategy and leadership against the CCP is a devastatingly accurate account of lost chances and mismanaged resources.

Questions

1. **What leadership decisions by Jiang Jieshi does Li Zongren suggest were faulty and precipitated the GMD's defeat?**
2. **What factors does Li Zongren suggest led to the military failures in 1948?**

After Manchuria had been captured, the Communist forces under Lin Biao, now totaling a million, crossed south of the Great Wall into northern China and launched a massive campaign against General Fu Zuoyi, aimed at capturing Beiping and Tianjin. Fu's Troops in both these cities were overwhelmed and on January 15, 1949, the city of Tianjin was captured and the government commander, General Lin Weichou, taken prisoner. To save the ancient city of **Beiping** from destruction, Fu Zuoyi arranged a peaceful settlement with the Communists. On January 22, 1949, the Communists took over Beiping without a fight.

In the meantime the situation in eastern China had deteriorated with equal speed. The collapse of the government forces started in Shandong early in September 1948, when Governor Wang Yaowu refused to send reinforcements to support the former puppet forces of Wu Huawen, who were surrounded by Communist troops at Yanzhou. Wu thereupon surrendered to the Communist troops without a fight. Siege was immediately laid to Shandong's capital city of Jinan, and on September 25 the Communist captured the city and its governor.

The central army forces in southern Shandong and northern Jiangsu had originally been under the command of General Tang Enbo, but following a series of defeats in the fall of 1947, Tang had been ordered to pull his troops south of the Yangzi. Four miscellaneous unattached units under the command of general Huang Botao were ordered to remain in the area and continue the war against the Communists.

In the summer of 1948, when the situation in Shandong began to deteriorate, Jiang decided to establish two war zones between the Yangzi and Yellow Rivers, with two bandit suppression headquarters at Xuzhou and Wuhan respectively. When I learned of this, I went to Jiang and proposed a unified command of these two war zones. From a strategic point of view, the plains region between the two rivers—from Tongguan and Yichang west of the coast in the east—was an unbreakable geographical unit in which communications were facilitated by three railways—the Long-Hai, the Beiping-Hankou, and the Tianjin-Pukou lines. Thus, it would be better if the war in this area were directed by a single unified command rather than being complicated by two. My proposal, however, was not accepted. Instead Bai Chongxi was appointed to head the Bandit Suppression Headquarter at Wuhan and Liu Shi to head the headquarters at Xuzhou.

Late in 1948 the supreme command sent 300,000 troops, representing the cream of the central armies, to the Xuzhou area. They were equipped with American weapons, including two armored units, and were under the respective command of Xu Tingyao and the generalissimo's younger son Jiang Weiguo. These crack troops were to defend the city of Xuzhou alone, while the four miscellaneous units under Huang Botao were stationed at Caobaji and Nianzhuang, about twenty miles east of Xuzhou. The strategic plan, jointly prepared by Du Yuming and Qiu Qingquan, called for the central army forces to entrench themselves in the suburbs of Xuzhou and set a trap while they waited for the Communists to attack the city.

Although Manchuria and northern China were doomed to Communist capture, the national Government still controlled a region greater than that held by the enemy. The entire valley of the Huai River, southern and western Henan provinces, all of northwest China, the whole of the Yangzi valley, and the entire region south of the Yangzi River were still firmly under the control of the central government. A victory at Xuzhou would have given us a chance to halt the flood tide of Communism in China.

Unfortunately, Du Yuming and Qiu Qingquan were not competent to command such a large-scale campaign. Both were Huangpu graduates and unusually proud men, and the lessons we had learned in Manchuria and northern China had done little to alter their personal pride and exaggerated confidence. They still believed that the Communists could not wage trench warfare on a large scale. While the Communist armies numbering some 600,000 men were closing in upon Xuzhou, the two government commanders failed to draw up a flexible plan for a lightning offensive that might have crushed the enemy. Instead they dug in their troops and lay waiting for the oncoming opponent to strike. They reasoned that the flat, open suburbs of Xuzhou would provide the best possible battleground on which to demonstrate the mobility and firing power of their armored division.

But Liu Bocheng and Chen Yi, the two Communist commanders, were shrewder than the government commanders. Instead of trying to launch a massive attack against the city of Xuzhou, they formed a large circle outside the defense area set up by the government commanders and began to round up the outermost and weakest government units one after the other. Early in November 1948 the army corps under

---

BEIPING—In 1928, the GMD made Nanjing, literally "Southern Capital," the new capital of China and changed the name of Beijing, "Northern Capital," to Beiping, "Northern Peace." In 1949, the CCP captured Beijing, restored both its position as capital of China and its original name.

Huang Botao was surrounded in the Nianzhuang area. Then the Communists called in their strongest forces and launched a ferocious attack against Huang.

After failing to break through the Communist encirclement, Huang signaled for help from General Qiu at Xuzhou but Qiu refused to come to his aid. When the situation at Nianzhuang became critical, Gu Zhutong, then chief of the General Staff at Nanjing, flew to Xuzhou and personally ordered Qiu to assist Huang. I was informed that Qiu flatly rejected Gu's order, saying, "If I send troops to rescue Huang Botao, who will bear the responsibility if the safety of Xuzhou is endangered?" Slapping his breast, Gu replied, "I, the chief of the General Staff, will be responsible if anything should happy to Xuzhou.

[…]

After Huang Botao had been exterminated, over a million Communist troops under the capable command of Chen Yi, Chen Geng, and Liu Bocheng closed in upon Xuzhou in several circles. Their aim was to starve the government forces into surrendering rather than fighting it out to the end. They succeeded in cutting off all the roads connecting Xuzhou with the outside world and forcing the defenders and the population of the city to depend primarily on air drops for daily rations. Bad weather and cold winter added to the difficulties of the defense. The local population and the troops suffered dreadfully from the acute shortage of food, fuel, and winter clothing. The miserable situation in Xuzhou was beyond all description.

Later in November 1948 Jiang ordered Bai Chongxi to transfer sufficient forces from central China to end the siege of Xuzhou. Bai immediately sent an entire group army, about 100,000 strong, under the command of General Huang Wei, toward Xuzhou. Huang was surrounded by Communists at Shuangduiji, south of Suxian in northern Anhui province, and the entire group army perished after several days of bloody fighting. The Communists managed to capture General Huang alive.

Under these desperate circumstances, Jiang had no alternative but to order the government troops to break through the encirclement and pull south. Unfortunately, he repeated the mistake that he had made at Jinzhou only a few weeks before. He personally issued orders to the various commanders to withdraw without any preliminary planning, resulting in great confusion during the withdrawal. At the same time the weather took a turn for the worse, and the unpaved roads around Xuzhou could not be used effectively. The entire army, numbering into the hundreds of thousands, was caught up in terrific congestion and confusion.

Xuzhou was abandoned on December 2, 1948, but the retreating government troops were surrounded anew in the vicinity of Yongcheng, southwest of Xuzhou. The Communists mobilized several hundred thousand local farmers, who in a single night dug several ditches around the position held by the government troops. The latter managed to hold their positions on the open ground, in heavy snow and hail, for several weeks. Their fighting spirit finally collapsed when the Communists set up loudspeakers and called on them to surrender. Thousands laid down their arms and offered to surrender peacefully. General Qiu Qingquan was killed in the confusion, but Du Yuming was captured on January 8, 1949. More than 300,000 of the best equipped and trained government troops, along with several armored divisions, vanished entirely within a period a few weeks. It was the worst defeat the National Army ever experienced.

Throughout his long career Jiang had always considered the armed forces to be his trump card. Now they were nearly all gone. Casting about for a new means of survival, he chose to retreat and announced his temporary retirement.

10.10 REPUBLIC OF CHINA'S DECLARATION OF THE STATE OF SIEGE IN TAIWAN (MAY 19, 1949)

On May 19, 1949 the Guomindang government proclaimed a general state of siege on Taiwan. With this act, the Republic of China suspended the 1947 Constitution and all individual civil rights. The government ordered a permanent state of emergency and instituted martial law. Through the 1950s and 1960s these extra-constitutional arrangements were expanded, which effectively rescinded the presidential two-term limit and extended the terms of incumbent National Assembly members to life. In other words, the declaration of the State of Siege triggered a series of events that quickly legitimized

Jiang Jieshi's presidency for life and instituted a one-party authoritarian government over those areas controlled by the Republic of China.

Questions

1. Why would the imposition of the regulations implemented by the State of Siege be necessary in Taiwan?
2. Why did Jiang Jieshi suspend the 1947 Republic of China constitution rather than alter it? How did his legitimacy rely on his ties to the pre-1949 era?

A. In order to secure public peace and order, a state of siege is hereby declared by this Command over the whole province [of Taiwan], effective zero hour, 20 May [1949].

B. Effective from the same date, all ports shall be closed and strictly off limits, except the three ports of Jilong, Gaoxiong, Magong which shall remain open under surveillance of this Command, which will regulate the maritime communication lines of this province.

C. During this period of the state of siege, the following regulative and prohibitive rules shall be enforced

1. Effective from the same date, a general curfew shall be enforced in the ports of Jilong and Gaoxiong every day from 1:00 a.m. to 5:00 a.m., during which all traffic is forbidden except with special permit.

2. All stores and public entertainment places in Jilong and Gaoxiong must be closed by midnight.

3. All stores and hawkers in this province are forbidden to raise commodity prices, to close their businesses, to stockpile the daily necessities or to disrupt the market.

4. All incoming and outgoing travelers must go through procedures as prescribed by this Command and submit to inspection.

5. Public meetings, strikes, demonstrations or petitions are strictly forbidden.

6. Spreading of rumors by letter, slogan, or other means is strictly forbidden.

7. Carrying by civilians of arms, ammunition, or dangerous articles is strictly forbidden.

8. All inhabitants, whether indoors or outdoors, must carry their identification papers. Those who do not shall be arrested.

D. During the period of the state of siege, those who commit the following acts shall be condemned to death in accordance with law:

1. Circulating rumors and beguiling the public
2. Inciting the public to riot.
3. Disrupting the money market.
4. Forceful theft or robbery.
5. Striking by workers or traders disrupting public order.
6. Encouraging students to strike or publicly inciting others to commit crime.
7. Destroying traffic or communications, or stealing the materials thereof.
8. Disrupting water supplies, or electric or gas services.
9. Setting fires or causing flood and endangering the public safety.
10. Possessing arms, ammunition, or explosives without permission.

10.11 PROGRESS ON FORMOSA (JULY 28, 1952)

In the 1950s a fundamental problem faced both the Guomindang and the Government of the Republic of China (ROC). They needed to resolve the obvious disconnect between the reality of the government's limited territorial jurisdiction (essentially extending over only Taiwan, and the small coastal islands of Mazu, Penghu, and Jinmen) and their theoretical claims of legislative, judicial and executive powers for all of China. By 1952 there was little likelihood that the Republic of China could retake any part of the mainland without considerable military backing from the United States. As a result, during the 1950s and 1960s, Jiang Jieshi's mission focused on securing the island's self-defense and in making the island economically viable. Then (as now) there existed tremendous tension between the Taiwanese and the mainlanders on Taiwan. The mainland Chinese arrived en masse in 1949 and by 1952 dominated both the government and state structures, even though they constituted only about 8 percent of the population. The *Time Magazine* article below highlights those elements of Jiang Jieshi's character and political strategy that would resonate with an American audience. These include his Christianity, spartan lifestyle, and his efforts to balance the national budget. Gimo, a shortening of Jiang's title generalissimo, was the nickname given by American officials to Jiang.

Questions

1. **What mutual self-interest maintained the relationship between the United States and the Republic of China?**
2. **What was life like under the Republic of China government in 1952?**

Visitors arriving at Taibei, capital of **Formosa,** are presented with an illustrated booklet, compliments of the Nationalist government. The booklet explains Nationalist policy: "It is vital for us to do well in Taiwan [Chinese name for Formosa]. It is not only a desirable end in itself; it is also the basis of hope for an eventual return to the mainland." It is now 30 months since the Nationalists were hurled out of China. Last week TIME'S Hong Kong Bureau Chief Robert Neville, after a tour of Formosa, reported on how the Nationalists are doing there:

The Nationalists' accomplishments in Formosa fall somewhat short of miracles, but they are very real. The Nationalist administration, though still top-heavy, has been subject to constant overhauling, until today it is an honest and efficient instrument of government.

Gone are the days when high military commanders could write drafts which the treasury had to honor —usually by turning the printing press a few more times. The Nationalists' budget, 37 percent in the red in 1950, is now close to balancing. Six months ago, one U.S. dollar would buy 30 or more Formosan dollars on the Hong Kong free market; today's rate is around 22.

For the first time in the history of modern China, taxes are levied and collected equitably. The native Formosans, once resenting the intrusion of the Nationalists, have become loyal to Jiang. Last winter, 12,000 young islanders were drafted into the Nationalist army without complaints or repercussions. Formosa's local government, under able Nationalist Administrator K. C. Wu, has become, in the opinion of Americans in Taibei, the soul of rectitude.

The Leader

Generalissimo Jiang Jieshi and Madame Jiang [Song Meiling] resent the notion that they are living in exile. Taipei, they insist, is simply the provisional capital of China, just as Chongqing was during World War II. Although Jiang's vast domain has shrunk to a mere 14,000 square miles, his icy dignity has, if anything, increased. Nobody is now, or ever was, on back-slapping terms with Jiang. At 65, he lives a Spartan life, eats sparingly, and neither drinks nor smokes.

Jiang, member of the Methodist Church since his conversion to Christianity in 1930, rises at daybreak, and before breakfast will have said his prayers and spent a half-hour in meditation, usually with Madame Jiang, in his private chapel. When interviewers ask the inevitable question about returning to the mainland, Madame Jiang answers: "With faith, there is nothing in the world that cannot be accomplished."

FORMOSA—An outdated term formerly used for Taiwan originating from the Portuguese term for the island meaning "beautiful."

The Troops

The Gimo's chief interest remains where it always was—with his fighting men. Statistically, the Nationalists claim an army of 600,000 men; actually, they can muster no more than 150,000 combat-worthy soldiers, organized in twelve divisions. Man for man, the Nationalist troops are in a fine state of training, well-fed, well-clothed and as pugnacious as terriers. U.S. military observers here are sure that they would give an excellent account of themselves if the Reds attacked Formosa. But at present, and certainly for the next year, the decisive factor in the defense of Free China must remain the U.S. Seventh Fleet, patrolling Formosa Strait.

Speculation about Jiang invading the mainland, however, does the Nationalists disservice, and the expression, "Take the wraps off Jiang," disregards the long, hard period of training, the uphill fight for equipment and most of all, the growing military might of the Chinese Reds. An entirely new element has been added to the military situation during the past year: the acquisition by the Reds of a modern, jet-propelled air force. U.S. officers with long experience in Formosa will tell you that morale in the Nationalist air force has very understandably dropped, now that the pilots feel they are flying obsolete planes (U.S. Mustangs, Lightnings, etc.) which would have no chance against Mao's Russian-built MIGs.

On the whole, however, the Chinese Nationalists have regained their confidence to the point where they are now almost cocky. They are fairly certain that, come what may, there will be no international deal to turn Formosa over to the Reds. Generally, they are not notably grateful to the U.S. "They think we are aiding them only because it's in our own interest to aid them," said an American officer. The Chinese not only have long memories, but are notoriously unsentimental. Perhaps it's just as well that U.S. aid to Formosa should be put on the hard-headed basis of mutual self-interest.

Things Are Humming

Around the island, the impression is unmistakable that things are humming. Warehouses are being repaired, repainted and rebuilt in almost every town. Formosa's textile industry (100,000 spindles) now produces half the islanders' clothing needs. But the most impressive and certainly the most vital improvement has been in rice production. Not only has this small island (an area

about equal to Massachusetts and Connecticut combined) fed its own rapidly growing population as well as 2,000,000 Nationalist refugees; it has also kept up its rice exports to Japan, the Nationalists' main source of foreign exchange. No one in Formosa suffers from the Orient's oldest disease: starvation.

The Nationalists' three-pronged agrarian reform program has been largely responsible for fatter harvests. Stage 1 reduced the rents of all tenant farmers from 50% of their cash crop to 37.5%. This has meant a big increase in farm incomes, which in turn has produced a spate of what the islanders now call "37.5% homes" and "37.5% brides."

Stage 2 was the sale, at equitable prices, of the vast public lands once owned by the Japanese. The third stage will be inaugurated next Jan. 1; it will chop up the big estates into individual peasant holdings of not more than two hectares (five acres) of rice-growing land per head. The Nationalists frankly think their land distribution will take the wind out of Mao Zedong's agrarian reform sails.

Proper Perspective

This overall improvement needs to be put in proper perspective. First of all, Formosa is infinitely more manageable than the huge mainland. It was already, as a result of 51 years of Japanese rule, much more highly developed than any similar area on the mainland. Formosa's good macadam roads, its efficient railroad system, its fine harbors and its admirable school system, which has given the island's population a literacy rate approaching 80%—all these things have been kept up and in some cases improved by the Nationalists.

Nor would Formosa's improvement have been possible without U.S. economic aid, which, not counting military expenditures, is now running at roughly $100 million annually—certainly a large sum to spend on a small island with a population of 9,000,000.

Unfortunately, the Nationalists' political and military progress has lagged behind economic improvements. Jiang's propaganda to the Chinese mainland, like U.S. propaganda, simply does not ring the bell. And Formosa retains too rigid a state atmosphere to make it a comfortable place for many loyal anti-Communist Chinese.

Yet, when seen against the background of defeat and disgrace which the Nationalists suffered in 1949, and against the lawless tyranny of the Communist-enslaved mainland, Formosa looks good, and it is steadily getting better.

USEFUL READINGS AND WEBSITES FOR PART TWO

Useful Websites

1. **HISTORICAL PHOTOGRAPHS OF CHINA (1870–CA1955)** http://hahn.zenfolio .com – An exceptional collection of historical photos of temples, sacred mountains, as well as more recent photos of historical sites, collected and maintained by a photography specialist, Thomas H. Hahn.
2. **REVEREND CLAUDE L. PICKENS COLLECTION ON MUSLIMS** http://hcl .harvard.edu/libraries/harvard-yenching/collections/pickens/ – Over 1000 photos of Muslims of Western China taken in the 1920s and 1930s by Reverend Claude L. Pickens, Jr. who served as a Christian missionary in China from 1927 to 1937. The website is augmented by an informative bibliography about Islam in China.
3. **INTERNET GUIDE FOR CHINESE STUDIES** http://sun.sino.uni-heidelberg.de/ igcs/ – One of the best Internet guides on web resources related to China. Remarkably well organized, timely in its updates, and helpful in rating the listed sites.
4. **THE NANKING (NANJING) ATROCITIES** http://www.nankingatrocities.net/ – A sensitive treatment of a complex and politically controversial subject. The website is well organized, nicely designed, and includes a variety of textual, visual and sound files which offer one of the most complete accounts of the Nanjing Massacre on the web.
5. **TALES OF OLD CHINA** http://www.talesofoldchina.com – An eclectic but useful website because of its diverse contents which include photos, full English language sources from early to mid-nineteenth century, and pictures and descriptions of the currency used from the 1920s to 1940s.

Suggested Readings

1. **R. Keith Schoppa, *Blood Road: The Mystery of Shen Dingyi in Revolutionary China* (Berkeley: University of California Press, 1995).** Told in the style of a murder mystery, Schoppa's book unravels the killing of GMD politician Shen Dingyi in 1928 through the lens of the complex cultural, regional and party politics of the era.
2. **Edward J.M. Rhoads, *Manchus and Han: Ethnic Relations and Political Power in Late Qing and Early Republican China, 1861–1928* (Seattle: University of Washington Press, 2000).** Re-examining the events surrounding the fall of the Qing and the rise of the Republic by centering the analysis on the Manchu court and the shifting nature of Manchu identity.
3. **Odd Westad, *Decisive Encounter: The Chinese Civil War, 1946–1950,* (Palo Alto: Stanford University Press, 2003).** A superb analysis of the final military struggle between the CCP and GMD, offering a detailed political and military look at the formation of the PRC.
4. **Germie Barmé, *An Artistic Exile: A Life of Feng Zikai* (Berkeley: University of California Press, 2002).** A biography of one of China's first political cartoonists. Offers a wealth of information about Feng Zikai as well as the turbulent era in which he lived.
5. **Frederic Wakeman, Jr., *Spymaster: Dai Li and the Chinese Secret Service* (Berkeley: University of California Press, 2003).** A chilling account of Jiang Jieshi's top spy, Dai Li, as told by one of the master storytellers of Chinese history, Frederic Wakeman. Reveals the underworld of the Nanjing Decade with verve and an eye to detail that brings the period to life.
6. **Alai (trans. Howard Goldblatt and Sylvia Li-chun Lin), *Red Poppies* (Houghton Mifflin, 2002).** Winner of the prestigious Chinese Mao Dun literary prize, this novel tells the story of local Tibetan rulers along the Sino-Tibetan border areas in the 1930s. An absorbing story that raises knotty questions of ethnic acculturation and modernization along China's borderlands.

PART THREE

POST-1949 CHINA
(1949–PRESENT)

Timeline

World		China
	1949	People's Republic of China established
Sino-Soviet Treaty of Alliance and Friendship	**1950**	New Marriage Law
	1953	China's First Five Year Plan begins
Viet Minh defeat French at Dien Bien Phu	**1954**	
USSR launches Sputnik, the first earth satellite	**1957**	100 Flowers and Anti-Rightist Movement
	1958–59	Great Leap Forward
	1959	Dalai Lama flees Tibet
Krushchev removed from power	**1964**	*East is Red* premieres in Beijing
	1966	Mao launches the Great Proletarian Cultural Revolution
	1967	China detonates first H-bomb
Neil Armstrong, first person on the moon	**1969**	
UN transfers China seat from ROC (Taiwan) to PRC	**1971**	
	1972	President Nixon visits China
	1975	Jiang Jieshi dies and is succeeded by his son Jiang Jingguo as president of ROC
	1976	Zhou Enlai, Zhu De & Mao Zedong die / Tangshan earthquake kills over 250,000
United States recognizes PRC	**1979**	
	1980	One-child policy officially begins
First personal computer launched by IBM	**1981**	Gang of Four found guilty and sentenced
	1988	Li Denghui becomes president of ROC (Taiwan)
Dalai Lama awarded Nobel Peace Prize	**1989**	Tiananmen student demonstrations
Soviet Union collapses	**1991**	
	1994	Three Gorges Dam project begins
	1997	Hong Kong returned to China
	2000	Jiang Zemin's Three Represents
	2003	SARS epidemic
	2008	China hosts Olympics

CHAPTER 11
NEW CHINA – FINDING
A NEW WAY

VISUAL SOURCE
Great Expectations: Examining the Propaganda
of the Great Leap Forward

THE GREAT LEAP FORWARD (1958–1959): In January 1958 Mao Zedong called for a rapid rise in agricultural and steel output through centralized social and economic planning. The government encouraged the use of "revolutionary" methods such a "close planting" of rice and grain and by building "backyard furnaces" to smelt their own steel and iron in order to dramatically raise production.

CHILDREN DANCING ON RICE: This photo appeared in the magazine *China Pictorial* with the caption: Hubei province Macheng county Jianguo No.1 Agriculture commune's first-season rice harvest of 1.016 mu [.16 acre] paddy field, reaped a record 36,956 jin [40,737 lbs] of rice per mu. Look how dense the rice is growing! Children can stand on top of the rice [growing in the field], it is just like stepping on a soft sofa.

COMMUNES: By December 1958, over 99% of all rural families belonged to communes. Private ownership of farming equipment, livestock, and even garden plots were forbidden. Communal kitchens replaced private kitchens in an effort to conserve time, energy, and food. The communal dining halls also greatly augmented the state's presence at the most basic level of society.

SUSPENDED DISBELIEF: Throughout the Great Leap Forward the Chinese people retained an unshakable confidence in the Chinese top leadership—especially Mao Zedong. Part of this misplaced faith came from the widespread publications like those seen here. Widely disseminated news reports convinced people that the much hailed record harvests were true and that their own experiences were an anomaly in a sea of success.

ENVIRONMENTAL IMPACT: The Great Leap Forward had severe economic consequences. Whole areas were stripped of trees and brush to feed the furnaces that needed to be kept going 24 hours a day in order to maintain the constant level of heat. In addition to the backyard furnaces and questionable agricultural practices, another major campaign "Eliminate the Four Pests" (rats, flies, mosquitoes, and sparrows) decimated the sparrow populations in many areas leading to even worse insect infestation.

BACKYARD FURNACES: At the urging of Mao Zedong tens of thousands of "backyard furnaces" were constructed in communes and the cities. The furnaces required a tremendous outlay in labor both for the building and in order to tend them day and night. Where no natural sources of ore (or even those that did) existed all non-essential metal (cooking woks, utensils, nails, pitchforks) were collected to be melted down. The furnaces—often poorly built—produced only low quality pig-iron and non-industrial grade steel. The picture below (right) is from Wulidun, Xinyang City, in the central Chinese province of Henan.

HUMAN CONSEQUENCES: As a result of the Great Leap Forward, China from 1959–1962 experienced a three-year long famine that is estimated to have resulted in about 30 million deaths. Even for those who survived, as a direct result of the famine, many Chinese postponed or were unable to have children, demographically causing a sharp (if temporary) drop in China's birthrate.

On a wintery Beijing afternoon in early December 1949, Mao Zedong boarded an armored train bound for the USSR. It was the first time he had traveled outside China. He would join hundreds of communist leaders from around the globe to celebrate Stalin's seventieth birthday in Moscow. Mao's decision to make his first state visit as China's Party Chairman and President to the Soviet Union seemed self-evident. The Soviet Union was the undisputed leader of the Communist world. But despite all outward appearances, the two largest Communist powers did not have an amicable relationship. Up until his 1949 invitation to Mao, Stalin had repeatedly rebuffed Mao's efforts to meet in Moscow. Stalin's hesitancy struck a sensitive nerve within the CCP leadership since the Soviet Union, from the 1920s onward, had insinuated China was ill prepared for a Communist uprising and doggedly urged them to work within the GMD controlled governments. In addition to these actions, Stalin signed a Sino-Soviet Treaty of Friendship with Jiang Jieshi at the end of the Second World War then pressured Mao Zedong to negotiate the October 10th Agreement (1945). Sino-Soviet differences aside, Mao's trip was even more striking in light of the fact that this two-month trip came within weeks of the founding of the People's Republic, at a time when tens of thousands of GMD troops lingered in areas of mainland China. Mao Zedong's motivations for making the trip were complex, and were based on securing China's future. This future depended on Mao's ability to forge a new relationship with Joseph Stalin and the Soviet Union.

Traveling ten days by train, because of his fear of flying, Mao arrived in Moscow at the stroke of noon on December 16. That same evening, in a gesture meant to demonstrate the Soviet's recognition of Mao's standing, Stalin and members of the Soviet **politburo** received Mao at the Kremlin. Stalin cautiously questioned Mao Zedong about what he hoped to achieve during his visit. Mao replied, "For this trip we hope to bring about something that not only looks nice but tastes delicious." As this was translated into Russian, one of the politburo members burst out laughing. It became clear that Mao's tendency to speak in earthy aphorisms resulted in losing his meaning in the translation. Mao Zedong's own translator stepped in and attempted to straighten out the confusion noting that what Mao meant by "looking nice" was something with a good form, and "tasting good" meant something substantial. It was an inauspicious start to the first meeting between the notoriously brusque Stalin and thin-skinned Mao.

When Mao and Stalin moved on to the more formal discussion, the subject matter quickly turned to the Sino-Soviet Treaty Stalin had signed with Jiang Jieshi after Japan's defeat four years earlier. Earlier that year the USSR had indicated they were willing to nullify the original treaty and negotiate a new treaty with Mao and his PRC government. When Stalin raised the matter, however, he now suggested to Mao he was reluctant to alter the existing treaty. He averred that to make "a change in even one point could give America and England the legal grounds to raise questions about modifying the treaty's provisions concerning the Kurile Islands, South Sakhalin, etc." When Mao sought to take another tack by asking Stalin whether his foreign minister Zhou Enlai should come to Moscow to further discuss such matters, Stalin enigmatically responded "No, this question you must decide for yourselves." Stalin's surprise position on the treaty and evasive response must have been a rude welcome for Mao who had come to the Soviet Union with high expectations for Soviet support. Mao remained calm, humbly acknowledging that he'd not taken the British and American response into account. At the end of the two-hour discussion, however, there could have been little doubt in Mao's mind that his goals for Sino-Soviet relations differed considerably from those of Stalin.

POLITBURO—A shorthand term for "political bureau," it was the principal executive policy-making committee within a Communist Party. The politburo is centralized within the Standing Committee of the Communist Party of China.

Over the course of the next week, national and international delegations swarmed into the Soviet capital to celebrate Stalin's seventieth birthday and left Mao few opportunities to broach the issue again with either Stalin or his top ministers. By the end of December Mao's exasperation turned to indignation as it became clear that Stalin sought to deliberately chasten Mao by leaving him in a dacha outside of Moscow. Several Soviet officials visited Mao and encouraged him to take a trip around the country instead of remaining in the dacha. Mao replied in his typically off-color style that while in Moscow he "only had three tasks: eat, sleep and shit. I did not come to Moscow to congratulate Stalin on his birthday … if you do not want to conclude a treaty of friendship, so be it. I will fulfill my three tasks."

What happened next is not entirely clear, but several factors conspired to prompt Stalin to reconsider his position towards Mao Zedong and China. For one, India, Burma, Denmark, Sweden and Great Britain were all pushing China to establish diplomatic relationships. Stalin realized that to continue the stalemate with Mao would force the USSR to relinquish the prestige of being the first country to formally establish ties with the PRC. The other, more obvious, factor was the embarrassing foreign press reports stating that Stalin had put Mao under house arrest. Chagrined at the impression being given to the world, Stalin swiftly ordered TASS (the official press agency of the Soviet Union) to interview and publish an article on Mao's visit to Moscow. Mao, never one to miss such a golden opportunity, stated in his interview that the foremost goal in his mind was to sign a new Treaty of Friendship between China and the Soviet Union.

The following day, seventeen days after first arriving in Moscow, Stalin broke the standoff and sent his foreign minister, Vyacheslav Molotov to inform Mao Zedong that he should summon Zhou Enlai, China's Foreign Minister, to conclude a new treaty between China and the Soviet Union. The relief for Mao must have been immense. One can sense the levity in his telegram relaying the news back to Beijing informing them not only of the new treaty and instructions for Zhou, but giddily sharing his plans for sightseeing (saying that Molotov recommended visiting the subway and a nearby ordnance factory).

When Stalin, Mao Zedong, and Zhou Enlai met almost three weeks later, Stalin opened the conversation by saying that the previous treaty between China and the Soviet Union was an anachronism and needed to be changed significantly. When Mao timidly sought to verify Stalin's change of heart regarding the impact such a change would have on the Yalta Agreement, Stalin replied "To hell with it! If we make a decision to revise treaties, we must go all the way."

Stalin's gambit was not without its risks, but for the Soviets it was a relatively safe scheme. By jettisoning the security offered by the Yalta Agreement, Stalin knew he had caused China to be deeply indebted to the Soviet Union. The Chinese were appropriately appreciative and allowed the Soviets to retain many of the rights from the 1945 treaty (including considerable authority and supervision over Dalian, Lüshun, and the Changchun Railroad). Mao, however, also got what he needed. He could now return to China with a new Sino-Soviet Agreement, an explicit mutual military commitment (stating that each country would come to the aid of the other in the event of war), and the desperately needed Soviet economic aid to rebuild, fortify and modernize China.

And so, on February 14, 1950, the two sides signed the Treaty of Friendship, Alliance, and Mutual Assistance in the Kremlin. Three days later Mao, after spending more than two months in the Soviet Union, left Moscow with an unambiguous sign of Soviet support in hand that demonstrated to any who might have doubted his acumen at forging an alliance with China's most potent neighbor. Neither Mao nor Stalin realized the speed with which their goodwill and partnership would be put to the test. Within six months after Mao's departure from Moscow, North and South Korea would be at war and China would be pressed by both its Communist Allies, Stalin and Kim Il-Sung, to come to North Korea's aid.

NEW CHINA: EXTERNAL CHALLENGES

At a September 1949 preparatory session of the Chinese Political Consultative Conference, Mao Zedong spoke one of his most remembered statements: "We [the Chinese people] have stood up." Though many Chinese mistakenly attribute these words to his speech marking the founding of People's Republic of China from atop Tiananmen Gate (11.1), the simple phrase is still electrifying over fifty years later. Mao's pronouncement tapped into the Chinese peoples' deep humiliation resulting from a century of occupation and misgovernment. But even as "China stood up," the communist leadership realized their path to establishing themselves as a global power would be a treacherous one in the highly polarized Cold War world. There was little question that China and their fraternal socialist neighbor, the Soviet Union, would remain allies (11.2), but there remained considerable fear (even by Stalin), whether Mao Zedong would pursue an independent path like Joseph Tito of Yugoslavia. As North Korean troops invaded South Korea with Stalin's blessing, Chinese leaders quickly realized that many choices would be made out of necessity rather than their own strategic needs (particularly their desire to mount an invasion of Tibet and Taiwan) (11.4). China's relationship with its Communist neighbors evolved over time—however, its relationship with the United States was preordained, largely as a result of the United States' unyielding commitment to Jiang Jieshi and its role in the Korean War.

11.1 PROCLAMATION OF THE CENTRAL PEOPLE'S GOVERNMENT OF THE PEOPLE'S REPUBLIC OF CHINA (OCTOBER 1, 1949)

On October 1, 1949, surrounded by top CCP military and political leaders, Mao Zedong declared the founding of the People's Republic of China. This must have been a sublime sensation for Mao and the communist leadership who only years earlier had been on the verge of political extinction, living in Yan'an on the borderlands of China. It may seem easy to lampoon Mao's speech with its heavy reliance on phrases such as "liberation," "reactionary rule," and "counter-revolutionary." Even though such terminology may appear timeworn today, at the time they linguistically demarcated the end of the economically depressed and politically fractured world of China's past and the beginning of a bright, new world for the CCP's leadership. For their part, the vast majority of Chinese greeted Mao Zedong's speech with celebratory excitement and eagerness for change. After decades of political infighting and twelve years of near continuous war (1937–1949), Mao Zedong was seen as a savior who had unified China, and was about to usher the nation into a new era.

> **Questions**
>
> 1. Why does Mao qualify some of his statements saying that the war has been "basically won" and "the majority of the people" liberated?
> 2. Why would most Chinese people be excited by Mao's speech?

The people throughout China have been plunged into bitter suffering and tribulations since the Jiang Jieshi Guomindang reactionary government betrayed the fatherland, colluded with imperialists, and launched the counter-revolutionary war. Fortunately our People's Liberation Army, backed by the whole nation, has been fighting heroically and selflessly to defend the territorial sovereignty of our homeland, to protect the people's lives and property, to relieve the people of their sufferings, and to struggle for their rights, and it eventually wiped out the reactionary troops and overthrew the reactionary rule of the Nationalist government.

Now, the People's War of Liberation has been basically won, and the majority of the people in the country have been liberated. On this foundation, the first session of the Chinese People's Political Consultative Conference, composed of delegates of all the democratic parties and people's organization of China, the People's Liberation Army, the various regions and nationalities of the country, and the overseas Chinese and other patriotic elements, has been convened. Representing the will of the whole nation, [this session of the conference] has enacted the organic law of the Central People's Government of the People's Republic of China, elected Mao Zedong as chairman of the Central People's Government; and Zhu De, Lui Shaoqi, Song Qingling, Li Jishen, Zhang Lan, and Gao Gang as vice chairmen [of the Central People's Government];

[....]

The Central People's Government Council of the People's Republic of China took office today in the capital and unanimously made the following decisions: to proclaim the establishment of the Central People's Government of the People's Republic of China; to adopt the Common Program of the Chinese People's Political Consultative Conference as the policy of the government; to elect Lin Boqu from among the council members as secretary general of the Central People's Government Council; to appoint Zhou Enlai as premier of the Government Administration Council of the Central People's Government and concurrently minister of Foreign Affairs, Mao Zedong as chairman of the People's Revolutionary Military Commission of the Central People's Government, Zhu De as commander-in-chief of the People's Liberation Army, Shen Junru as president of the Supreme People's Court of the Central People's Government, and Luo Ronghuan as procurator general of the Supreme People's Procuratorate of the Central People's Government, and to charge them with the task of the speedy formation of the various organs of the government to carry out the work of the government. At the same time, the Central People's Government Council decided to declare to the governments of all other countries that this government is the sole legal government representing all the people of the People's Republic of China. This government is willing to establish diplomatic relations with any foreign government that is willing to observe the principles of equality, mutual benefit, and mutual respect of territorial integrity and sovereignty.

11.2   TWO TELEGRAMS RELATING TO THE KOREAN WAR (1950)

The Korean War began with the invasion of South Korea by North Korean troops in June 1950. Within seventy-two hours, the United States decided to intervene and the UN Security Council had voted to send an international force. The following telegrams from Mao Zedong reveal the hesitant, yet progressive steps the two sides took to aid Kim Il-Sung. When UN troops crossed the 38th parallel on October 7—an act China had indicated would cause them to enter the war—Mao decided to mobilize Chinese troops. However, at this crucial juncture Stalin retracted his offer for Soviet air support, causing the Chinese to rethink their situation and the 1950 Treaty of Friendship. Unbeknownst to the UN troops who rushed northwards believing the Chinese were vacillating over their decision, Marshal Peng Dehuai was amassing Chinese troops along the North Korean border. In late October, Chinese troops crossed the Yalu River surprising the UN forces and driving them all the way back to Seoul. While this battle was presented to the Chinese people as an incontrovertible victory, it cost over 700,000 Chinese casualties (including the death of Mao's son Mao Anying), and diverted critical resources from domestic reconstruction.

Questions

1. **What factors are the Chinese weighing prior to entering the Korean War?**
2. **Why is Mao's assessment of the United States so critical to his decision to aid North Korea?**
3. **Why do you think China went ahead with preparations for the war even when the USSR appeared less willing to offer support?**

Telegram #1: Telegram to Stalin Concerning the Decision to Send Troops into Korea for Combat (Oct. 2, 1950)

1. We have decided to send part of the armed forces into Korea, under the title of **Volunteer Army,** to do combat with the forces of America and its running dog Syngman Rhee and to assist our Korean comrades. We recognize this course as necessary. If we allow the United States to occupy all of Korea, Korean revolutionary strength will suffer a fundamental defeat, and the American invaders will run more rampant, and have negative effects for the entire Far East.

2. We recognize that since we have decided to dispatch Chinese troops to do combat in Korea, first, they must be able to solve the problems; they must be prepared to destroy and expel within Korea itself, the armies of the United States and other countries; second, since Chinese troops will fight American troops in Korea (even though they will be using the title Volunteer Army), we must be prepared for the United States to declare and enter a state of war with China; we must be prepared [for the fact] that the United States may, at a minimum, use its air force to bomb many major cities and industrial centers in China, and use its Navy to assault the coastal region.

3. Of these two problems, the primary problem is whether or not the Chinese Army can destroy the American forces within Korea itself, and effectively resolve the Korean problem. So long as our forces can destroy the American forces within Korea itself, most importantly [as long as they can] destroy the American Eighth Army (an old army with combat effectiveness), while the seriousness of the second problem (America's declaring war on China), will still exist, the situation will already have turned in favor of the revolutionary camp and China. This is to say, if the American forces are defeated, the Korean problem is, in fact, finished ([although] it is possible that formally it may not be over; the U.S. may for a long time not recognize Korea's victory); so, even if the Americans have already openly declared war on China, the scope of this war will probably not be great, and the duration will not be long. We see the least advantageous situation as the Chinese Army being unable to destroy the American forces in large number, the two armies becoming mutually deadlocked, and, in addition, the United States having already entered an open state of war with China, thus leading to resulting destruction of the economic construction plan we have already begun, and moreover, arousing dissatisfaction toward us among the national bourgeoisie and other segments of the people (they are very afraid of war).

4. Under the present situation, we have decided that on October 15 we will begin dispatching the twelve divisions that have been transferred in advance to South Manchuria. They will locate themselves in appropriate districts of North Korea (not necessarily all the way to the 38th parallel). While they do combat with the enemy who dares to advance and attack north of the 38th parallel, in the first period fighting a defensive war to destroy small enemy detachments and gaining a clear understanding of the

PEOPLE'S VOLUNTEER ARMY OF CHINA—In an effort to distinguish their actions from what they considered the imperialist actions of the United States, China's military forces in Korea adopted the name "People's Volunteer Army." It suggested China was voluntarily aiding their Korean neighbors and not imposing external pressure on Korea's domestic affairs.

situation, they will await the arrival of Soviet weapons and the equipping of our Army, and then [they will] coordinate with Korean comrades a counterattack, destroying the invading American army.

5. According to our intelligence to date, an American Army (two infantry divisions and one mechanized division) totals 1,500 pieces of artillery ranging from 7 to 24 centimeter caliber, including tank and anti-aircraft artillery; one of our armies (three divisions) only has 36 pieces of that type of artillery. The enemy has control of the air, and the air force we have begun training will not be able to put 300 planes into the war until February 1951. Because of this, our forces are still unable to assure destruction of the American Army in one blow. And, since we have decided to fight with Americans, we should be prepared so that, at the point in a campaign that the American command assembles its forces on the battlefield to fight with ours, our troop strength should be four times that of the enemy (using four of our armies to counter one of the enemy's) and our firepower should be one and a half to two times that of the enemy (using 2,200-3,000 of every type of artillery piece from seven centimeters and up to counter 1,500 enemy artillery pieces of the same caliber). Thus they will assuredly, cleanly and thoroughly destroy the one army of the enemy.

6. Besides the 12 divisions mentioned above, we are also in the process of transferring twenty-four divisions from south of the Yangzi River and from the ShaanGan [Shaanxi and Gansu] District to take up positions in the LongHai, JinPu, BeiNing lines, in order to form the second and third wave of military forces to assist Korea. We estimate that in the spring and summer of next year, according to the circumstance at the time, they will progressively be employed.

Telegram #2: Telegram to Zhou Enlai [in Moscow] Concerning [Why] Our Troops Should Enter Korea (October 13, 1950)

1. The result of a discussion on the part of comrades in the Politburo is that we unanimously believe that having our troops enter Korea is more advantageous [than the alternatives]. In the first period we can focus on attacking the puppet forces; our troops' countering of puppet forces is certain [of success]; we can open up a base in Korea in the large mountain region north of the Wonson-Pyongyang line, and can inspire the Korean people. In the first period, as long as we can destroy some divisions of the puppet army, the Korean situation can take a turn to our advantage.

2. The adoption of the active policy above will be extremely advantageous for China, Korea, the Far East, and the world; and on the other hand, if we do not send troops, allowing the enemy to press to the Yalu border and [allowing] the arrogance of reactionaries at home and abroad to grow, then this will be disadvantageous to all sides. Above all it will be most disadvantageous to Manchuria; all of the Northeastern border defense forces will be absorbed, and South Manchurian electrical power will be controlled [by the enemy].

In summation, we recognize that we should enter the war; we must enter the war; entering the war will have great benefits; the harm inflicted by not entering the war would be great.

11.3   U.S. IMPERIALISM IS A PAPER TIGER (JULY 14, 1956)

By 1953 a truce had been declared dividing Korea along the thirty-eighth parallel—the original 1945 demarcation. The US involvement (and leadership) in the war along with American support of the GMD, made the United States China's foremost international adversary. Domestically, the United States became the focus of numerous political campaigns. Mao's speech outlines the growing efforts to rally international anti-American support suggesting that the United States was not as powerful as many made them out to be. Despite his popularization of the expression, Mao did not coin the phrase "paper tiger." The term "paper tiger" (*zhi laohu*) dates back to at least the nineteenth century and means simply somebody who appears strong but is actually harmless. The document below recounts comments he gave to two Latin American journalists.

Questions

1. How do you think Mao's anti-Americanism was received among Chinese? Among Latin Americans, Asians and Africans?
2. What does he mean when he refers to the United States as a "paper tiger?"

The United States is flaunting the anti-communist banner everywhere in order to perpetrate aggression against other countries.

The United States owes debts everywhere. It owes debts not only to the countries of Latin America, Asia and Africa, but also to the countries of Europe and Oceania. The whole world, Britain included dislikes the United States. The masses of the people dislike it. Japan dislikes the United States because it oppresses her. None of the countries in the East is free from U.S. aggression. The United States has invaded our Taiwan Province. Japan, Korea, the Philippines, Vietnam and Pakistan all suffer from U.S. aggression, although some of them are allies of the United States. The people are dissatisfied and in some countries so are the authorities.

All oppressed nations want independence.

Everything is subject to change. The big decadent forces will give way to the small new-born forces. The small forces will change into big forces because the majority of the people demand this change. The U.S. imperialist forces will change from big to small because the American people, too, are dissatisfied with their government.

In my own lifetime I myself have witnessed such changes. Some of us present were born in the Qing Dynasty and others after the 1911 Revolution.

The Qing Dynasty was overthrown long ago. By whom? By the party led by Sun Zhongshan, together with the people. Sun Zhongshan's forces were so small that the Qing officials didn't take him seriously. He led many uprisings which failed each time. In the end, however, it was Sun Zhongshan who brought down the Qing Dynasty. Bigness is nothing to be afraid of. The big will be overthrown by the small. The small will become big. After overthrowing the Qing Dynasty, Sun Zhongshan met with defeat. For he failed to satisfy the demands of the people, such as their demands for land and for opposition to imperialism. Nor did he understand the necessity of suppressing the counter-revolutionaries who were then moving about freely. Later, he suffered defeat at the hands of Yuan Shikai, the chieftain of the Northern warlords. Yuan Shikai's forces were larger than Sun Zhongshan's. But here again this law operated: small forces linked with the

people become strong, while big forces opposed to the people become weak. Subsequently Sun Zhongshan's bourgeois-democratic revolutionaries co-operated with us Communists and together we defeated the warlord set-up left behind by Yuan Shikai.

Jiang Jieshi's rule in China was recognized by the governments of all countries and lasted twenty-two years, and his forces were the biggest. Our forces were small, fifty thousand Party members at first but only a few thousand after counter-revolutionary suppressions. The enemy made trouble everywhere. Again this law operated: the big and strong end up in defeat because they are divorced from the people, whereas the small and weak emerge victorious because they are linked with the people and work in their interest. That's how things turned out in the end.

During the anti-Japanese war, Japan was very powerful, the Guomindang troops were driven to the hinterland, and the armed forces led by the Communist Party could only conduct guerrilla warfare in the rural areas behind the enemy lines. Japan occupied large Chinese cities such as Beijing, Tianjin, Shanghai, Nanjing, Wuhan and Guangzhou. Nevertheless, like Germany's Hitler the Japanese militarists collapsed in a few years, in accordance with the same law.

We underwent innumerable difficulties and were driven from the south to the north, while our forces fell from several hundred thousand strong to a few tens of thousands. At the end of the 25,000-*li* Long March we had only 25,000 men left.

In the history of our Party many erroneous "Left" and Right lines have occurred. Gravest of all were the Right deviationist line of Chen Duxiu and the "Left" deviationist line of Wang Ming. Besides, there were the Right deviationist errors committed by Zhang Guotao, Gao Gang and others.

There is also a good side to mistakes, for they can educate the people and the Party. We have had a good many teachers by negative example, such as Japan, the United States, Jiang Jieshi, Chen Duxiu, Li Lisan, Wang Ming, Zhang Guotao and Gao Gang. We paid a very high price to learn from these teachers by negative example. In the past, Britain made war on us many times. Britain, the United States, Japan, France,

Germany, Italy, tsarist Russia and Holland were all very interested in this land of ours. They were all our teachers by negative example and we were their pupils.

During the War of Resistance, our troops grew and became 900,000 strong through fighting against Japan. Then came the War of Liberation. Our arms were inferior to those of the Guomindang. The Guomindang troops then numbered four million, but in three years of fighting we wiped out eight million of them all told. The Guomindang, though aided by U.S. imperialism, could not defeat us. The big and strong cannot win, it is always the small and weak who win out.

Now U.S. imperialism is quite powerful, but in reality it isn't. It is very weak politically because it is divorced from the masses of the people and is disliked by everybody and by the American people too. In appearance it is very powerful but in reality it is nothing to be afraid of, it is a paper tiger. Outwardly a tiger, it is made of paper, unable to withstand the wind and the rain. I believe the United States is nothing but a paper tiger.

History as a whole, the history of class society for thousands of years, has proved this point: the strong must give way to the weak. This holds true for the Americas as well.

Only when imperialism is eliminated can peace prevail. The day will come when the paper tigers will be wiped out. But they won't become extinct of their own accord, they need to be battered by the wind and the rain.

When we say U.S. imperialism is a paper tiger, we are speaking in terms of strategy. Regarding it as a whole, we must despise it. But regarding each part, we must take it seriously. It has claws and fangs. We have to destroy it piecemeal. For instance, if it has ten fangs, knock off one the first time, and there will be nine left, knock off another, and there will be eight left. When all the fangs are gone, it will still have claws. If we deal with it step by step and in earnest, we will certainly succeed in the end.

Strategically, we must utterly despise U.S. imperialism. Tactically, we must take it seriously. In struggling against it, we must take each battle, each encounter, seriously. At present, the United States is powerful, but when looked at in a broader perspective, as a whole and from a long-term viewpoint, it has no popular support, its policies are disliked by the people, because it oppresses and exploits them. For this reason, the tiger is doomed. Therefore, it is nothing to be afraid of and can be despised. But today the United States still has strength, turning out more than 100 million tons of steel a year and hitting out everywhere. That is why we must continue to wage struggles against it, fight it with all our might and wrest one position after another from it. And that takes time.

It seems that the countries of the Americas, Asia and Africa will have to go on quarrelling with the United States till the very end, till the paper tiger is destroyed by the wind and the rain.

To oppose U.S. imperialism, people of European origin in the Latin-American countries should unite with the indigenous Indians. Perhaps the white immigrants from Europe can be divided into two groups, one composed of rulers and the other of ruled. This should make it easier for the group of oppressed white people to get close to the local people, for their position is the same.

Our friends in Latin America, Asia and Africa are in the same position as we and are doing the same kind of work, doing something for the people to lessen their oppression by imperialism. If we do a good job, we can root out imperialist oppression. In this we are comrades.

We are of the same nature as you in our opposition to imperialist oppression, differing only in geographical position, nationality and language. But we are different in nature from imperialism, and the very sight of it makes us sick.

What use is imperialism? The Chinese people will have none of it, nor will the people in the rest of the world. There is no reason for the existence of imperialism.

11.4   SEVENTEEN-POINT PLAN FOR THE PEACEFUL LIBERATION OF TIBET (1951)

With no nations willing to recognize them diplomatically, and militarily no match for the PLA, the Tibetan government sent a delegation to Beijing to negotiate a peaceful resolution. The resulting Seventeen Point Agreement (largely written by the PRC and presented to the Tibetan representatives) established the guidelines by which China and Tibet would engage one another. The document marks the first time both the Chinese and

Tibetan governments explicitly acknowledged that Tibet was under Chinese sovereignty. Mao Zedong believing that Tibet would soon see the benefits of the Communist revolution, agreed to allow the Dalai and Panchen Lamas to retain their religio-cultural positions as the top representatives of the political system. Relative to the political settlements Beijing made with other ethnically non-Chinese regions, Tibet retained considerable autonomy for its traditional government. The Dalai Lama, much to his and his close officials' surprise, only learned of the agreement after it had been signed. After some months of heated discussion, the Dalai Lama sent Mao Zedong a telegram in October 1951 indicating his acceptance of the terms laid out in the **Seventeen-Point Plan.**

Questions

1. **What guarantees did the Seventeen Point Plan promise Tibetans?**
2. **What did China gain from such an agreement?**

THE AGREEMENT OF THE CENTRAL PEOPLE'S GOVERNMENT AND THE LOCAL GOVERNMENT OF TIBET ON MEASURES FOR THE PEACEFUL LIBERATION OF TIBET
23 MAY, 1951
[. . . .]

1. The Tibetan people shall be united and drive out the imperialist aggressive forces from Tibet; that the Tibetan people shall return to the big family of the motherland—the People's Republic of China.
2. The Local Government of Tibet shall actively assist the People's Liberation Army to enter Tibet and consolidate the national defences.
3. In accordance with the policy towards nationalities laid down in the Common Programme of the Chinese People's Political Consultative Conference, the Tibetan people have the right of exercising national regional autonomy under the unified leadership of the Central People's Government.
4. The Central Authorities will not alter the existing political system in Tibet. The Central Authorities also will not alter the established status, functions and powers of the Dalai Lama. Officials of various ranks shall hold office as usual.
5. The established status, functions, and powers of the Panchen Ngoerhtehni shall be maintained.

6. By the established status, functions and powers of the Dalai Lama and of the Panchen Ngoerhtehni is meant the status, functions and powers of the 13th Dalai Lama and of the 9th Panchen Ngoerhtehni when they were in friendly and amicable relations with each other.
7. The policy of freedom of religious belief laid down in the Common Programme of the Chinese People's Political Consultative Conference will be protected. The Central Authorities will not effect any change in the income of the monasteries.
8. The Tibetan troops will be reorganised step by step into the People's Liberation Army, and become a part of the national defence forces of the Central People's Government.
9. The spoken and written language and school education of the Tibetan nationality will be developed step by step in accordance with the actual conditions in Tibet.
10. Tibetan agriculture, livestock raising, industry and commerce will be developed step by step, and the people's livelihood shall be improved step by step in accordance with the actual conditions in Tibet.
11. In matters related to various reforms in Tibet, there will be no compulsion on the part of the Central Authorities. The Local Government of Tibet should carry out reforms of its own accord,

SEVENTEEN-POINT AGREEMENT (1951)—An agreement signed in 1951 between representatives of the Tibetan government with CCP leaders laying out the points by which Tibet would accept Chinese sovereignty over Tibet. Both sides renounced the agreement in 1959, and the Dalai Lama established a government-in-exile in neighboring India.

and when the people raise demands for reform, they must be settled through consultation with the leading personnel of Tibet.

12. In so far as former pro-imperialist and pro-GMD officials resolutely sever relations with imperialism and the GMD and do not engage in sabotage or resistance, they may continue to hold office irrespective of their past.

13. The People's Liberation Army entering Tibet will abide by the above-mentioned policies and will also be fair in all buying and selling and will not arbitrarily take even a needle or a thread from the people.

14. The Central People's Government will handle all external affairs of the area of Tibet; and there will be peaceful co-existence with neighboring countries and the establishment and development of fair commercial and trading relations with them on the basis of equality, mutual benefit and mutual respect for territory and sovereignty.

15. In order to ensure the implementation of this agreement, the Central People's Government will set up a military and administrative committee and a military area headquarters in Tibet, and apart from the personnel sent there by the Central People's Government it will absorb as many local Tibetan personnel as possible to take part in the work. Local Tibetan personnel taking part in the military and administrative committee may include patriotic elements from the Local Government of Tibet, various district and various principal monasteries; the name list is to be prepared after consultation between the representatives designated by the Central People's Government and various quarters concerned, and is to be submitted to the Central People's Government for approval.

16. Funds needed by the military and administrative committee, the military area headquarters and the People's Liberation Army entering Tibet will be provided by the Central People's Government. The Local Government of Tibet should assist the People's Liberation Army in the purchases and transportation of food, fodder, and other daily necessities.

17. This agreement shall come into force immediately after signatures and seals are affixed to it.

Signed and sealed by delegates of the Central People's Government with full powers:

Chief Delegate: Li Weihan (Chairman of the Commission of Nationalities Affairs);

Delegates:
Zhang Jingwu
Zhang Guohua
Sun Zhiyuan

Delegates with full powers of the Local Government of Tibet:
Chief Delegate: Kaloon Ngabou Ngawang Jigme (Ngabo Shape)

Delegates:
Dzasak Khemey Sonam Wangdi
Khentrung Thuptan
Tenthar,
Khenchung Thuptan Lekmuun Rimshi,
Samposey Tenzin Thondup

A NEW SOCIETY IN A NEW CHINA – FARTHER, FURTHER, FASTER

In the months after the founding of the PRC, the central government moved swiftly to transform China's political, economic and cultural landscape in order to create a "**New China.**" A central promise of the CCP throughout its long period of development was to address China's engrained patriarchal culture—that is the customary belief that men should hold power in society (and government) and that women should be excluded from it. The **1950 Marriage Law** (11.5), for the first time in Chinese history, made men and women equal before the law and allowed women equal rights in seeking a divorce. Equally significant, China adopted a centrally planned economy that was organized

NEW CHINA—A term widely employed in China today suggesting a significant demarcation between the traditional practices of "Old China" and those of the People's Republic of China. Many Chinese refer to the PRC-era as "New China."
MARRIAGE LAW OF 1950—One of the first laws promulgated after the founding of the PRC in 1949, it set a minimum age for marriage, legalized divorce, made men and women equal in courts of law, and prohibited concubinage.

around five-year plans largely based on the policies of Stalin's economic planners. Initially the reforms brought about rapid change and increased economic output (both industrial and agricultural). By the mid 1950s, the pace of production slowed, causing the CCP leadership to look for new ways to reenergize China's economy. In 1956, Mao began a campaign known as the "100 Flowers Campaign" which solicited criticisms to improve both the party and country. Unexpectedly negative assessments of the CCP's first five years of rule began to flood in. Mao and the Central Committee, taken aback, reacted by accusing counter-revolutionaries of using the campaign to attack the party and weaken its policies. To root out the rightists, Mao began an "Anti-Rightist Campaign" to purge the party of dangerous elements. This ideological campaign was followed in quick succession by 1958's "Great Leap Forward," a mass movement designed to accelerate China's economic growth and catch-up with the world's global powers. It calamitously sought to double (and then triple) agricultural and industrial production. (11.8, 11.9, 11.11). By the following spring, however, famine and environmental degradation caused Marshal Peng Dehuai to write a note to Mao begging him to reverse his policy (11.10). Furious at what he took to be a personal attack, Mao attacked Peng by stripping him of his office as Defense Minister and continued the disastrous policies for another two years.

11.5   THE MARRIAGE LAW (1950)

On May 1, 1950, the first Marriage Law in the People's Republic of China went into effect. On many levels the law was the first introduction to the methods the Chinese Communist Party sought to employ in their quest to fundamentally alter traditional Chinese society. Although the GMD government had revised many laws regarding marriage and family in 1931, both the impact of those laws and the GMD's ability to implement them were uneven. The 1950 Marriage Law, and the numerous campaigns in 1950–51 to put the laws into effect, radically altered the previously inviolable patriarchy—particularly in the countryside. The law set the legal age of marriage at 18 for women, and at 20 for men. The law formally outlawed "feudalistic practices" like arranged marriage, concubinage and polygamy. Conversely, it encouraged "free choice" in selecting marriage partners while advocating monogamy within marriage. The greatest impact from the law was giving equal authority of divorce to both women and men (though the law mandated mediation prior to granting divorce). After its promulgation, a wave of divorces occurred, doubling in number from 186,167 in 1950 to 409,500 in 1951, which caused many to suggest the law should be called the "Divorce Law" of 1950.

> **Questions**
> 1. In place of "feudalistic practices" previously the norm in China, what new guidelines did the PRC government establish before one can marry?
> 2. How did the state seek to control divorce?

CHAPTER 1. GENERAL PRINCIPLES

Article 1

The feudal marriage system, which is based on arbitrary and compulsory arrangement and the superiority of man over woman and ignores the children's interests shall be abolished.

The New Democratic marriage system, which is based on the free choice of partners, on monogamy, on equal rights for both sexes, and on the protection of the lawful interests of women and children, shall be put into effect.

Article 2

Bigamy, concubinage, child betrothal, interference with the remarriage of widows, and the exaction of money or gifts in connection with marriages shall be prohibited.

CHAPTER 2. THE MARRIAGE CONTRACT

Article 3

Marriage shall be based upon the complete willingness of the two partners. Neither party shall use compulsion and no third party shall be allowed to interfere.

Article 4

A marriage can be contracted only after the man has reached 20 years of age and the woman 18 years of age.

Article 5

No man or woman in any of the following instances shall be allowed to marry:

 a. Where the man and woman are lineal relatives by blood or where the man and woman are brother and sister born of the same parents or where the man and woman are half-brother and half-sister. The question of prohibiting marriage between collateral relatives by blood within the fifth degree of relationship is to be determined by custom.
 b. When one party, because of certain physical defects, is sexually impotent.
 c. When one party is suffering from venereal disease, mental disorder, leprosy, or any other disease which is regarded by medical science as rendering the person unfit for marriage.

Article 6

In order to contract a marriage, both the man and the woman shall register in person with the people's government of the subdistrict or village in which they reside. If the marriage is found to be in conformity with the provisions of this law, the local people's government shall, without delay, issue a marriage certificate.

If the marriage is found to be incompatible with the provisions of this law, no registration shall be granted.

CHAPTER 3. RIGHTS AND DUTIES OF HUSBAND AND WIFE

Article 7

Husband and wife are companions living together and shall enjoy equal status in the home.

Article 8

Husband and wife are in duty bound to love, respect, assist and look after each other, to live in harmony, to engage in productive work, to care for the children and to strive jointly for the welfare of the family and for the building up of the new society.

Article 9

Both husband and wife shall have the right to free choice of occupation and free participation in work or social activities.

Article 10

Both husband and wife shall have equal rights in the possession and management of family property.

Article 11

Both husband and wife shall have the right to use his or her own family name.

Article 12

Both husband and wife shall have the right to inherit each other's property.

CHAPTER 4. RELATIONS BETWEEN PARENTS AND CHILDREN

Article 13

Parents have the duty to rear and to educate their children; the children have the duty to support and assist their parents. Neither the parents nor the children shall maltreat or desert one another.

The foregoing provision also applies to foster-parents and foster-children. Infanticide by drowning and similar criminal acts are strictly prohibited.

Article 14

Parents and children shall have the right to inherit one another's property.

Article 15

Children born out of wedlock shall enjoy the same rights as children born in lawful wedlock. No person shall be allowed to harm or to discriminate against children born out of wedlock.

Where the paternity of a child born out of wedlock is legally established by the mother of the child, by other witnesses, or by other material evidence, the identified father must bear the whole or part of the cost of maintenance and education of the child until it has attained the age of eighteen.

With the consent of the natural mother, the natural father may have custody of the child.

With regard to the maintenance of a child whose natural mother marries, the provisions of Article 22 shall apply.

Article 16

Husband or wife shall not mistreat or discriminate against a child born of a previous marriage.

CHAPTER 5. DIVORCE

Article 17

Divorce shall be granted when the husband and wife both desire it. In the event of either the husband or the wife alone insisting on divorce, it may be granted only when mediation by the district's people's government and the judicial organ had failed to bring about reconciliation.

In the case where divorce is desired by both the husband and wife, both parties shall register with the subdistrict people's government in order to obtain a certificate of divorce. The subdistrict government, after establishing that divorce is desired by both parties and that appropriate measures have been taken for the care of children and prosperity, shall issue the certificate of divorce without delay.

When only one party insists on divorce, the subdistrict people's government may try to effect a reconciliation. If such mediation fails, it should, without delay, refer the case to the district or city people's court for decision. The subdistrict people's government shall not attempt to prevent or to obstruct either party from appealing to the district or city people's court. In dealing with a divorce case, the district or city people's court must, in the first instance, try to bring about a reconciliation between the parties. In case such mediation fails, the court shall render a verdict without delay.

In the case where, after divorce, both husband and wife desire the resumption of matrimonial relations, they should apply to the subdistrict people's government for a registration of remarriage. The subdistrict people's government should accept such a registration and issue a certificate of remarriage.

Article 18

The husband shall not apply for a divorce when his wife is with child. He may apply for divorce only one year after birth of the child. In the case of a woman applying for divorce, this restriction does not apply.

Article 19

The consent of a member of the revolutionary army on active service who maintains correspondence with his or her family must first be obtained before his or her spouse can apply for divorce.

As from the date of the promulgation of this law, divorce may be granted to the spouse of a member of the revolutionary army who does not correspond with his (or her) family for a subsequent period of two years. Divorce may also be granted to the spouse of a member of the revolutionary army who has not maintained correspondence with his (or her) family for a further period of one year subsequent to the promulgation of the present law.

11.6   BIRTH CONTROL AND PLANNED FAMILIES (MARCH 7, 1957)

The 1953 census calculated China's population to be almost 600 million. Worry over the economic and social implications of problems such a large (and growing) population presented soon paved the way for a birth control campaign which gained momentum in 1955. The campaigns of the mid-1950s tended to stress the health, financial and educational advantages of having fewer children. The following excerpts, from a speech given by Ms. Li Dequan, Minister of Health, to the Third Session of the National Committee of the Second Chinese People's Political Consultative Conference marks the highwater point of early birth control campaigns. In 1958, as the Great Leap Forward campaign gained momentum, optimism about China's ability to rapidly develop economically led to the belief that the profits realized by the added labor would exceed the added costs such a rise in the population would incur on the nation (and thus the belief that China did not need to practice birth control). As a result, a confusing period ensued when birth control for health (e.g. to prevent having too many children in quick succession) emerged side-by-side with the belief that China's rapid progress demanded a larger population.

Questions

1. **What are the main family planning features advocated by Li Dequan?**
2. **Does Li Dequan suggest there is opposition to birth control?**

Our birth-rate is really very high. As reported in the *Renmin Ribao,* an investigation of 19 State cotton mills in Shanghai, made by Shanghai public health departments, showed that, of the 609 pregnant women workers, 17 percent conceive twice a year, 53 percent once a year on an average, and 22 percent twice in three years. Such frequent childbirth not only imposes a heavy burden upon one's family and affects one's own health, work and studies, but also makes it difficult to look after and bring up the children satisfactorily. Of the 3,213 families in Tongwenchangge and Anfu Hutong investigated by the comrades of a health center in Beijing, 643, or 20 percent, each have more than four children. The average monthly income of each of these families is about ¥80, which means, on an average, about ¥13 for each person's living expenses (including adults). The average living expenses for each person will be ¥10 in a family with five children and less than ¥5 in a family with many children. Illness caused by malnutrition is serious. For example, Zhao, a worker in the Post Office, who lives in Shuncheng Street, has a monthly income of ¥70. His wife is 28 and has given birth to six children, some of whom are suffering from rickets while one daughter

will become an invalid. Now this woman is pregnant again. Sun, a worker in a joint State-private meat store, who lives in Jinglou Hutong, has a monthly income of ¥40. His wife, afflicted with mental disease, has given birth to nine children (one of whom has been given to another family) and had a miscarriage this year. Although the State, under the present circumstances, can give some relief to such families, they remain in great want and are unable to look after and bring up their children satisfactorily.

Although the living conditions in rural areas are different, the average annual income of a able-bodied worker is only ¥40-¥50, and the problem of frequent childbirth must also be serious. Our 500 million peasant each could have, on an average, three *mu* [half an acre] of land. Now, owing to the growth of population, each can have, on average, only a little over two *mu*. Thus, it can be seen that birth control, contraception, proper adjustment of the frequency of childbirth, and planned childbirth are not only not immoral, but actually indispensable to morality and the State's responsibility to the people.

Some people hold that contraception is only women's business. There are husbands who do not understand their wives' points of view in desiring birth control. They not only fail to co-operate with their wives, but also quarrel and fight with them; this makes matters even worse.

People who oppose contraception on the ground that we now have new methods of delivering babies, are obviously wrong. Contraception is intended to achieve planned pregnancy and childbirth, while the new method of delivery means that babies are delivered by scientific methods to keep the mother and the baby healthy. We must satisfactorily protect and bring up new-born babies according to the Constitution's provision that "mothers and children shall be protected by the State." If we fail to do so, then we are really immoral and violating the fundamental function of public health work.

Henceforth, in order further to make a success of this task, we must develop propaganda on contraception more intensively, so that everyone fully understands the great significance of planned childbirth to the State, the families, the individuals and the young generation. We must make this propaganda achieve the objective of enabling every family, every man and woman to understand contraception, breaking down all obstacles caused by misunderstandings about it.

We have still not done enough in regard to contraceptive guidance. On the one hand, some people regard childbirth after marriage as a "mystery," which cannot be talked about and is shameful. On the other hand, some public health and medical personnel hold that contraceptive guidance does not belong to the scope of medical treatment and public health services, and that they cannot take the initiative to give this guidance energetically. Henceforth we have to abandon these viewpoints. We should understand that childbirth is a natural physiological phenomenon of marriage and that there is nothing "mysterious" or shameful about it. Proper birth control and planned childbirth are legitimate demands. Public health personnel must break away from the narrow scope of merely curing disease and providing health services and come to regard the giving of guidance in planned childbirth, and the satisfying of this demand of the masses, as their duty. As to the performance of operations for purposes of induced abortion and sterilization, all personnel concerned with women's and children's health services and midwives' work should henceforth make the decision whether to perform the operation mainly on the basis of the wish of the individuals, and limitations on its discretion should be abolished. But this does not signify the promotion of induced abortion, which we are compelled to carry out in certain circumstances. Induced abortion is not only harmful to a woman's health, work and studies, but also cannot achieve the purpose of birth control. In the future, we must try to solve such problems as the improvement of the quality of contraceptive medicines and instruments, the increase of their quantities, and the lowering of their prices, so as to enable us to achieve a close co-ordination between this supply on the one hand and our propaganda and guidance on the other to satisfy the requirement of planned childbirth.

11.7   LIU SHAOQI'S BLUE PRINT FOR THE GREAT LEAP FORWARD (1958)

In the wake of the Anti-Rightist Campaign of 1957, the CCP launched the Great Leap Forward, China's ambitious economic development plan. Intended to expand on the PRC's first Five Year Plan—which had elevated China back to pre-1937 production levels—Mao sought to push production to even higher levels. Specifically, Mao wanted to put China on pace to achieve self-sufficiency in grain output and to produce enough steel and iron to surpass outputs in Great Britain, the United States and the Soviet Union. To do this Mao consolidated the 750,000 cooperatives (with an average population of 768) into some 24,000 **communes** (with an average population of 23,600). Self-reliance was the key impetus for the communes, wherein each commune's education, medical, and production systems would be independent of the others. The drawback with such a system was that it required each commune to produce their own basic necessities even if they did not have the appropriate resources or raw

COMMUNE—Seeking to reduce the state economy through consolidation, China merged, as part of the Great Leap Forward, 750,000 cooperatives into 24,000 communes, which became the highest of three administrative levels in rural areas from 1958 until 1983.

materials to do so. This flaw dramatically hindered Mao's goal for communes to increase both their iron and grain production. Such defects were greatly exacerbated by the communes' efforts to prove their loyalty to Mao by attempting to exceed the already excessively high quotas. Liu Shaoqi's speech reveals the central government's inclination to set impossibly high goals and of being disconnected from actual harvest and industrial production levels.

Questions

1. **What are the key targets of the Great Leap Forward?**
2. **What does Liu Shaoqi suggest should occur to for the Great Leap Forward to succeed?**

[...]

The spring of 1958 witnessed the beginning of a leap forward on every front in our socialist construction. Industry, agriculture and all other fields of activity are registering greater and more rapid growth.

To begin with industry. The total value of industrial output for the first four months of this year was 26 percent higher than in the same period last; the April increase was 42 percent. According to estimate made on the basis of the present situation, China's steel output this year will be over 7.1 million tons; coal output will reach 180 million tons; 60,000 machine tools will be produced and irrigation machinery with more than 3.5 million horsepower; the output of chemical fertilizers will amount to 1.35 million tons....

An upsurge is shaping up in capital construction in industry this year. Nearly one thousand above-norm projects will be under construction this year; this is more than the total number of such projects under construction in the first five-year plan period. In addition, construction work has already started on thousands of medium and small-sized coal mines, power stations, oil refineries, iron and steel plants, nonferrous mines, chemical fertilizer plants, cement plants, engineering works, and agricultural and animal products processing plants.

The output of local industry this year will show a considerable increase as a result of widespread industrial capital construction undertaken by local authorities. Take iron and steel for example. The amount of iron to be produced by local enterprises this year will reach 1,730,000 tons (as against the 593,000 tons produced last year) and that of steel will reach 1,410,000 tons (as against the 790,000 tons of last year). The rapid growth of the local industries is one of the outstanding features of this year's industrial upswing....

In agriculture, the most striking leap took place in the campaign of the cooperative farmers to build irrigation works. From last October to April this year, the irrigated acreage throughout the country increased by 350 million *mu*, that is, 80 million *mu* more than the total added during the eight years since liberation and 110 million *mu* more than the total acreage brought under irrigation in the thousands of years before liberation. At the same time, more than 200 million *mu* of low-lying and easily waterlogged farmland was transformed and irrigation facilities were improved on another 140 million *mu* of land. The loss of water and soil was brought under control over an area of 160,000 square kilometers. This gives proof of the power to conquer nature which the masses of the people have demonstrated in the field of agriculture following the great socialist revolution on the economic, political, and ideological fronts and the release on a tremendous scale of our social productive forces.

[...]

Rapid developments are also taking place in the fields of culture, education, and public health. Energetic efforts are being made in many villages throughout the country to eliminate illiteracy and establish large numbers of primary and secondary schools financed by the people. Cultural and artistic activities among the masses are advancing quickly. The public health campaign centered on the elimination of the four pests has already spread to every urban and rural district and achieved notable results.

[...]

In the light of the practical experience gained in the people's struggle and of the development of Comrade Mao Zedong's thinking in the past few years, the Central Committee of the Party is of the opinion that the following are the basic points of our general line, which is to build socialism by exerting our utmost efforts, and pressing ahead consistently to achieve greater, faster, better, and more economical results:

To mobilize all positive factors and correctly handle contradictions among the people;

To consolidate and develop socialist ownership, that is, ownership by the whole people and collective ownership, and consolidate the proletarian dictatorship and proletarian international solidarity;

To carry out the technical revolution and cultural revolution step by step, while completing the socialist revolution on the economic, political and ideological fronts;

To develop industry and agriculture simultaneously while giving priority to heavy industry;

With centralized leadership, overall planning, proper division of labor and coordination, to develop national and local industries, and large, small, and medium-sized enterprises simultaneously; and

By means of all this to build our country, in the shortest possible time, into a great socialist country with a modern industry, modern agriculture, and modern science and culture.

Based on the requirements of this general line, what are the main tasks facing the party and the people in the technical and cultural revolutions?

The main tasks of the technical revolution are as follows:

To put the national economy, including agriculture and handicrafts, systematically and in a planned way on a new technological basis, that is, the technological basis of modern, large-scale production, so that machinery can be used wherever feasible and electrification is brought to all the cities and villages of the country;

To turn all big and medium-size cities throughout the country into industrial cities; and to build up new industrial bases in those places where the necessary conditions exist, to enable all the county towns and many townships to have their own industries, and to increase the value of industrial output of all the provinces and autonomous regions and even most of the special administrative regions and counties so that it exceeds the value of their agricultural output;

[...]

To wipe out illiteracy, to institute compulsory primary education and step by step to bring secondary schools to the townships in general, and higher educational institutions and scientific research bodies to the special administrative regions in general and to many counties;

To complete the work of devising written languages for the national minorities or improving those already in existence and to make energetic efforts to reform the written languages used by the Han people;

To wipe out the "four pests," improve sanitary conditions, promote sports, eliminate the principal diseases, break down superstitions, reform customs and change habits, and invigorate the national spirit;

[...]

Some comrades are worried that, though the development of agriculture can accumulate funds for industrialization, it will for the present at least divert some funds which could be used by the state for industrialization. The upsurges in agriculture in 1956 and 1958 have proved such worries unnecessary. So long as we know how to rely on this great force of our 500 million peasants, we can greatly expand the scope of agricultural construction even if there is no increase in state investments in agriculture. The state has invested 1,450 million *yuan* to harness the Huai River, and completed over 1,600 million cubic meters of masonry and earth work in the past eight years. But by depending mainly on the labor, money and material resources of the peasants themselves, in six months of the winter of 1957 and spring of 1958, more than 12,000 million cubic meters of masonry and earth work were completed in Henan and Anhui provinces alone.

[...]

The party's general line for socialist construction is the application and development of its mass line in socialist construction, we must fully combine centralized leadership with decentralized management, and coordinate the resources of the central government with those of the local authorities, the resources of the state with those of the local authorities, the resources of the size with those of the masses, the giant undertakings with small and medium-size plants, the striving to raise the quality of work with popularization—all this is applicable not only to industry but also to other economic and cultural undertakings, and to the technical and cultural revolutions as a whole.

11.8 CLOSE PLANTING (1950s)

Western farming

Prior to the Great Leap Forward, Mao had complained that "some of our comrades are tottering along like a woman with bound feet, always complaining that others are going too fast." To accelerate China's economic development, Mao sought to jettison traditional economic assumptions while adopting revolutionary ones. Mao's revolutionary practices, while couched in quasi-scientific terms, were not based on scientific reality. In the agricultural realm, Chinese farmers were encouraged to embrace the ideas of "deep plowing" (in order to get closer to the ground water), fertilizing in a thick layer over fields (based on the idea if a little was good, a lot must be better), and "close planting," the topic of the article below. Peasants, even if they were skeptical, did not challenge the cadres' production quotas. The cadres, if dubious, could not diminish their pretense of revolutionary enthusiasm without fear of censure from the central government. To make the façade complete, the communes were forced to deliver the mandated percentages to the central governments. This often left the communes with desperately low levels of supplies to last them through the winter, while their supposed surpluses rotted in inadequately prepared state warehouses. The following account is typical of articles printed in newspapers and other materials distributed to the communes with a mix of factual information, typical village behavior, and new revolutionary ideas all focused on a revolutionary-minded individual upon which all commune members should model themselves.

Questions

1. **Why would such a story be so difficult to contradict in the climate of the Great Leap Forward?**
2. **Why would "close planting" be considered revolutionary?**

Old Beliefs

In the old society, the practice was to leave enough space between cotton plants for a baby to lie in. As things are today, a small dog might just about manage to run between the rows, but not between two plants in the same row. Qiliying commune, after years of testing and popularization, has raised the density of its cotton plants from 2,000 to 7,000 and even 8,000 per mu.

One of the pioneers in achieving this was Du Fating, head of the agro-technical group of the Kangzhuang brigade, another of the ten commune-nominated peasant experts. Enjoying high regard not only in his own village, he now leads a network comprising the agro-technical groups of four brigades. [...]

His interest in close planting arose in the early 1950s, in the mutual-aid period following the land reform. After visiting a state farm, he said to his father one day:

"They get their high yields in cotton by planting 4,000 to the mu. Why shouldn't we?"

Not picturing how close the planting would have to be to get this figure, his father said nothing. But out in the fields, when he saw how densely his son was spacing the plants, he exploded:

"You don't know what you're doing! Who on earth ever planted like that?"

"Let's try it once," said Du Fating. "if it won't work, we'll drop it."

"You'll have all the neighbors laughing at us. Don't expect me to look a fool along with you," snapped the old man, stopping his work and stalking off home.

Young Du sought support from the other old and experienced peasants in the team. But they, too, didn't believe in close planting. Finally he alone tried the new method, his teammates stuck to the old rule. Dense here, sparse there, the resulting average was barely 3,600 plants per mu.

In the field management afterwards, Du faithfully applied what he had learned from the state-farm agronomist. When the plants came up, many people gathered for a look.

"So close," some remarked, shaking their heads. "There'll be stalks and leaves, but not bolls."

"Beautiful!" one said, nodding. Du's heart leaped at this seeming approval. But then the man added, "Like flowers in the mirror, fine to look at but of no use."

Du was so put out, he almost picked a quarrel then and there. Fortunately, the agronomist had warned him that at the start, close planting was bound to meet with mockery, as people weren't used to it. Only a rich yield would convince them.

That year, Du's experimental cotton plot produced a bumper crop of 110 *jin* per *mu,* and became the talk of the whole village.

"Young Du's done it! The yield's really high!" people said to each other.

[. . .] Local Party organizations had often seized on examples like Du Fating's to show the advantages of scientific farming to the peasants. But its application over large areas became possible only after the formation of the co-operatives.

With the founding of the commune, scientific farming rapidly developed in breadth and depth to become a revolutionary mass movement. More and more members came to realize that this was a fight against the force of habit left over from the small-peasant economy that had prevailed in China for thousands of years. In making sweeping reforms in the old methods of cultivation, they have exploded the myth of predestination spread by Confucius and his adherents through the ages, and established a firm belief in continued revolution and in the truth that man can conquer nature.

Particularly noteworthy is the fact that they have learned to apply Marxist dialectics to the solution of many problems arising in scientific farming.

New farming methods aginst Confus.

11.9 ONCE AGAIN OUR COUNTRY SET NEW WORLD RECORD OF FIRST-CROP RICE HARVEST (SEPTEMBER 1958)

Throughout the summer and fall of 1958, communes competed with one another, not simply to meet the already outrageous government targets, but in efforts to see how far they could exceed them. The central government, deluded by their own propaganda, began to believe the communes' boasts, and major newspapers and periodicals all reinforced the extravagant claims. The peasants, not used to challenging the government authority, said nothing. The cadres, fearful of the government's response if they told the truth, worried that if their yields did not match the government estimates they would appear "counter-revolutionary." In the fervor of the period, it appeared that when a lie is repeated a thousand times, it becomes the truth. By September 1958, some communes were reporting "record rice yields" of 30 tons per *mu*—an amount many times the biological limit possible. When central government inspectors came to visit, communes would often temporarily transplant closely together plants from other fields for the inspection, then replant them after the inspectors left. Many of the provinces or counties mentioned in the following article suffered the worst in the famine that hit China in the years to follow.

Questions

1. **What seems to be the motivation in recording record harvests?**
2. **How does the article explain the reason for such phenomenal increases?**

The grain production in our country is making flying progress at a speed that no one has witnessed in human history. After surpassing United States in wheat production, the first-crop rice production achieved unprecedented great harvest. The Changfeng Agriculture Commune in Xiaogan County of Hubei Province created a record harvest of 15,361 *jin* of **first-crop rice** per *mu* in 1.21 *mu* of experiment field, which was followed by an unceasing series of new records. 15,665 *jin* per *mu* of first-crop rice was harvested in

JIN—A unit of weight (often translated as "catty") typically equal to 1.3 pounds or 0.5 kilograms with considerable local variation.

MU—A unit of measure for land equivalent to 0.16 acres.

RICE HARVESTING: In southern China, rice can be harvested two, and sometimes three, times in one year. The first harvest is referred to as "first-crop rice."

1.43 *mu* of an experimental field in Aoxian Agriculture Commune in Liling County of Hunan Province; 16,227 *jin* per *mu* first-crop rice was harvested in a 1.042 *mu* experiment field in Gaofeng Agriculture Commune in Zongyang County of Anhui Province; 16,260 *jin* per *mu* first-crop rice was harvested in an experimental field 1.01 *mu* in No. 2 Agriculture Commune in Pingjing Town, Macheng County of Hubei Province. Furthermore this county's No. 1 Jianguo Agriculture Commune, set a record of harvesting 36,956 *jin* per *mu* first-crop rice in its 1.016 *mu* experiment field.

It is no longer special to see a first-crop rice harvest above 10,000 *jin* per *mu* in our country. Just in Qianrenqiao Agricultural Commune in Shucheng County, Anhui Province there are three places holding such records. Xiaogan Prefecture of Hubei Province has recorded 149.5 *mu* attaining this record, of which 9.4 *mu* has a record over 20,000 *jin* per *mu*.

In our country the first-crop rice harvest not only repeatedly set new records in small area, but also created a record of massive harvest in the larger region. For example, Xiaogan County of Hubei Province has total of over 302,000 *mu* first-crop rice field, and the harvest average at 1,755 *jin* per *mu*, of which 109,000 *mu* produce 2,335 *jin* per *mu*; while the average of 1957 was 617 *jin* per *mu*. In addition, in Anhui Province, the entire province's 6,129,900 *mu* first-crop rice field produced 6,150,900,000 *jin* which averages 1,003 *jin* per *mu*. The total production increased 234% in comparison to 1957, and its average production per *mu* increased 175.5%. In Xingfu Town of Langxi County in this province, the 16,450 *mu* first-crop rice field produced 3,008 *jin* per *mu*, the total product of first-crop rice in one season is more than the total product in the past three years combined.

Similar to the great wheat harvest, this year's extraordinary first-crop rice harvest was achieved as a result of the peasant masses all out effort, aiming high, and defeating the natural disasters under the leadership the of Party. This year many first-crop rice regions suffered disasters of various degrees. For example, during the first-crop rice growing period, Mianyang County in Hubei Province suffered wind and flood disasters on a level unseen for over a hundred years. However, under the leadership of the Party, the peasants of the whole county defeated the severe disaster, and still achieved a harvest greater than ever. The entire county's over 80,100 *mu* first-crop rice field product averaged at 1,018 *jin* per *mu*, which was one and half times increase compared to that of 1957 when the weather was perfect. Another example, can be found in Anhui Province, the first-crop rice field suffered a drought the severity of which has not witnessed for several decades. The entire province mobilized over ten million people to fight continuously for three months against the drought in order to protect the rice seedlings till the harvest.

The great victory in our country's agriculture production has fully displayed the great advantages of the socialist system, largely strengthened the power of the socialist front, and greatly enhanced the cause of world peace. Now, the economy of every socialist country, led by the Soviet Union, is advancing at an even faster rate. It will not be long before the economic power of the socialist front leaves the imperialists far behind while the socialist system is more forcefully proved to the whole world its incomparable advantage.

11.10 PENG DEHUAI'S LETTER TO CHAIRMAN MAO (JULY 14, 1959)

In 1959, as the horrifying (and almost entirely preventable) results of the Great Leap Forward became obvious, leaders began to discuss how to bring relief to those areas hardest hit by famine. After a personal fact-finding trip through many of the regions most affected by the campaign, Peng Dehuai learned of the severe suffering and widespread starvation. **Peng Dehuai,** as a veteran of the Long March, hero of the Korean War, and longtime friend of Mao, felt compelled to broach the issue and to prevent any further deterioration of the situation. A firm believer and battle-hardened communist himself, Peng only presented his findings after the Central Committee had confirmed the "success" of the movement during the Lushan Meeting (July 1959). As the following letter indicates, he did not seek to grandstand (the letter was sent to Mao alone) and went to

PENG DEHUAI (1898–1974) — A PLA general who gained notoriety and prestige for his command of Chinese troops during the Korean War. When he offered Mao Zedong a negative assessment of the Great Leap Forward in 1959 he was denounced and never regained his prominent position within the Party or the government.

great lengths to make his comments constructive. He did, however, point out the failures of the movement in a frank and forthright manner while most of his colleagues chose to remain silent. As a result of Mao Zedong's failure to address the agricultural mistakes the country experienced three years of famine which claimed the lives over 30 million people.

Questions

1. **What does Peng Dehuai suggest are the root reasons for the failures of the Great Leap Forward?**
2. **How does he suggest the Party move forward?**

A number of problems that have developed merit attention in regard to our way of thinking and style of work. The main problems are:

1. A growing tendency towards boasting and exaggeration on a fairly extensive scale. At the Beidaihe Meeting last year, the grain output was overestimated. This created a false impression and everyone thought that the food problem had been solved and that we could therefore go all out in industry. In iron and steel, production was affected with such extreme one-sided thinking that no serious study was conducted on equipment for steel making and rolling and ore crushing as well as for coal mining and other mineral ores and for making coke, on the source of pit-props, on transportation capacity, on the expansion of the labor force, on the increase in purchasing power, on the distribution of market commodities, etc. In sum, we did not have a balanced overall plan.

It was also a lack of realistic thinking that gave rise to these errors. This, I am afraid, was the cause of a series of our problems.

The exaggeration trend has become so common in various areas and departments that reports of unbelievable miracles have appeared in newspapers and magazines to bring a great loss of prestige to the Party.

According to what was reported, it seemed that communism was just around the corner, and this turned the heads of many comrades.

results of new farming

Extravagance and waste grew in the wake of reports of extra-large grain and cotton harvests and a doubling of iron and steel output. As a result, the autumn harvest was done in a slipshod manner, and costs were not taken into consideration. Though we were poor, we lived as if we were rich.

What is particularly serious in all this is that it was very hard for us to get to know the real situation for a fairly long period. We did not have a clear idea of the situation even at the time of the Wuchang Meeting and the meeting of secretaries of provincial and municipal Party committees held in January this year.

The tendency towards boasting and exaggeration has its social cause, which is worth studying. It also has to do with our practice of fixing production quotas without corresponding measures to meet them.

Though Chairman Mao reminded the Party last year of the need to combine soaring enthusiasm with a scientific approach and the principle of 'walking on two legs,' it seems that his instructions have not been grasped by most leading comrades, and I am no exception.

2. Petty-bourgeois fanaticism which makes us vulnerable to "left" errors. In the Great Leap Forward of 1958, I, like many other comrades, was misled by the achievements of the Great Leap Forward and the zeal of the mass movement. As a result, some

BEIDAIHE — A coastal resort town northeast of Beijing used by the CCP's central committee and high level officials for work and meetings during the summer.

WALKING ON TWO LEGS — A phrase Mao used to describe the simultaneous development of both the agricultural and industrial sectors.

"Left" tendencies developed in our heads. We were thinking of entering a communist society in one stride, and the idea of trying to be the first to do this gained an upper hand in our minds for a time. So we banished from our minds the mass line and the working style of seeking truth from facts, which had been cultivated by the Party for a long time.

In our way of thinking, we have often muddled up the relationship between strategic goals and concrete measures, between long-term principles and immediate steps, between the whole situation and part of it, and between big collectives and small collectives. The Chairman's calls such as "strive for a high yield on a smaller area and bring in a big crop," "catch up with Britain in 15 years," etc., are long-term strategic goals. But we have not studied them carefully and have not paid enough attention to the specific current conditions so as to arrange our work on a positive, safe and reliable basis. . . .

By now we have got a basically clear picture of the domestic situation. Particularly because of the recent meetings, most comrades within the Party basically hold the same view. The present task for the whole Party is to unite and keep up the effort. In my opinion, it will be very beneficial to review in a systematic way the achievements and lessons in our work since the latter half of last year to further educate the comrades of the whole Party. The aim

is to make a clear distinction between right and wrong and to raise our ideological level. Generally speaking, we should not go about trying to affix blame; this would be harmful to our unity and our cause. Basing ourselves on our experience and research since the latter half of last year, we can clarify some problems arising from unfamiliarity with the laws governing socialist construction. Other problems can also be grasped after a longer period of study and experiment. As for our way of thinking and work style, the profound lessons we are learning this time help us to realize the problems in them more easily. But we'll have to try very hard before they can be thoroughly rectified. Just as the Chairman has instructed us at the present meeting: "The achievements are great, the problems are many, the experience is abundant, and the future is bright." It is up to us to grasp the initiative. So long as the whole Party is united and works hard, the conditions for continuing the leap forward are present. The plans for this year and next and for four more years will surely be fulfilled successfully. The aim of catching up with Britain in 15 years can be basically achieved in four years, and we can surely surpass Britain in the output of some important products. Hence our great achievements and bright future.

With greetings,

Peng Dehuai (July 14, 1959)

[handwritten: Unclear how to complete]

11.11   TIAN ZHUANGZHUANG'S *BLUE KITE* (1992)

Released in early 1993, the film *Blue Kite* directed by Fifth Generation director Tian Zhuangzhuang captures the life of a family by tracing the members through wave after wave of political campaigns beginning in 1953. The story is told from the perspective of Tietou (or "Iron Head"), and the title comes from a blue kite that he treasured as a child that became entangled in a tree and his father promised to replace. But that was before his father chose an inopportune moment to leave a meeting during which the selection of rightists was taking place. *Blue Kite* reflects the experiences of a generation that encountered government opposition to their political leanings. The film, however, never seeks to place the blame on any particular entity (even his critique of the government tends to be oblique). Rather, Tian Zhuangzhuang focuses on the consequences of such political movements and offers little explicit

FIFTH GENERATION—A group of Chinese filmmakers that emerged after the end of the Cultural Revolution and included Zhang Yimou, Tian Zhuangzhuang, and Chen Kaige. They ushered in an era of considerable international acclaim for Chinese cinema.

interpretation. The scenes below reveal how quickly all aspects of living—entire families and heterogeneous spheres of society (academic, military, etc.)—were affected.

> ## Questions
>
> 1. What changes does the scene below depict occurred within families as a result of the political tensions?
> 2. How does the film depict the selection of the quota for rightists?

[Chen Shujuan and her family are having dinner around the table. Among the family members gathered are her son Tietou ('iron head'), her mother, her elder sister, her older brother (Chen Shusheng), and her younger brother (Chen Shuyan)]

Scene I

TIETOU: (*Standing up making airplane noises*) Duh, duh, duh, duh, flyyyyy!

CHEN SHUJUAN: (*To her son*) Hey, let's eat. Sit down.

(*Tietou sits down before quickly ducking under the table*)

CHEN SHUSHENG: Good boy! (*Picking up the boy*) Little Iron head.

CHEN SHUJUAN: What did you say?

CHEN SHUSHENG: Oh, nothing!

ELDER SISTER: Shuyan, I have told you time and again. Young people should study hard and pay attention to ideological reforms. But you would not listen. You are nonsensical.

CHEN SHUJUAN: Elder sister, can you possibly just stop talking so much? I've got enough to worry about on my mind.

MOTHER: What are you worrying about? Not to mention nothing is happening to Shaolong [her husband]. Even if something happens to him, you still got your son, the little treasure?

CHEN SHUJUAN: What do you know about anything? These are two separate and unrelated matters.

MOTHER: Fine, fine, fine, I am not arguing with you all. There is more food to eat. (*She stands up and leaves the table*)

CHEN SHUYAN: (*To her elder sister*) You don't need to be afraid. If something happens, I won't let it affect anyone else and your glorious reputation will remain untarnished.

(*Big sister stares at him and quickly slaps him on face*)

TIETOU: Elder Auntie hit him!!

(*Chen Shuyan stands up and angrily leaves the room*)

Scene II

(*Meeting at a military office where Chen Shusheng works. Officers sitting around a table*)

OFFICIAL: The following members are being 'washed out' of this department. Staff officer division: Zhang Yunming, Liu Shaofeng; operation division: Yu Jie, Xiao Jun, Su Changjun; military supplies division: Jiang Yicheng, Hou Mingxin, Wang kaiyun. Next is our political division: Hu Jinsheng, Wu Shaoquan, Li Yonggang.

(*At that moment a gunshot is heard, and an officer whose name was just read slumps to the ground as the camera pans to the blood slowly spreading on the floor next to his head*)

ANONYMOUS OFFICER: Yonggang! Yonggang!

Scene III

(*In a big meeting room where Lin Shaolong works several dozen people are sitting around a long table with their leader positioned at the head of the table. He knocks his knuckle on the table to start the meeting*)

LEADER: Comrades! I ask you to reconsider once again more carefully. How could such a big library of ours have only one "rightist," Liu Yunwei? And while

I do not agree with the method of assigning the responsibility of discovering a specific percentage of "rightists" we must be responsible towards our Party's course and treat this political campaign seriously.

(*He pauses and looks around. People remain silent or whisper to one another in very low voices with few willing to make direct eye contact with their leader. Lin Shaolong stands up and quietly walks out of the meeting room to go to the bathroom next door. The sound of water flushing is heard in the background before he returns wiping his hands dry walking into the meeting room. As he stands by the door, all eyes turned towards him without anyone saying a word. He closes the door behind him and returns to his seat. It is clear that Lin Shaolong chose the wrong moment to leave the meeting and that in his absence was selected as a rightist*)

Scene IV

(*Children playing in the courtyard where they live. Chen Shujuan and Lin Shaolong are at home talking to one another immediately after Lin Shaolong returned from the meeting. She was washing clothes and he was watching the pot on stove.*)

CHEN SHUJUAN: Go and talk to your leader once more.... Ohhh, why did you have to go to the bathroom at that moment?

CHAPTER 12
CHINA IN THE 1960s

VISUAL SOURCE
Behold, the East is Red: Images of Mao in the 1960s

GREAT PROLETARIAN CULTURAL REVOLUTION: The Cultural Revolution began in 1966 largely engineered by Mao Zedong as a means to catapult him back into power. The political campaigns were largely an assault on lingering "bourgeois" elements in society, counter-revolutionaries, and anyone disloyal to Mao. Extremely violent in the initial three-year-period, the political consequences reverberated until Mao Zedong's death in 1976.

TIANANMEN RALLIES: On August 18, 1966 Mao Zedong held the first of eight massive rallies in Tiananmen Square with more than 2 million people in attendance. Typically the square would begin to fill up in the dark early morning hours. With deeply symbolic timing, Mao Zedong would arrive just after sunrise, walking through the square before he ascended Tiananmen Gate to address the adoring and, by this time, ecstatic crowd.

RED GUARDS: At this first rally, Mao publicly received the Red Guards thus officially validating their radical and violent tactics. "Chairman Mao's Red Guards" first formed among Beijing middle school students in the spring of 1966. Across the country teenagers formed their own Red Guard units to fight against the Four Olds: Old ideas, old culture, old customs, old habits.

LITTLE RED BOOK: Marshal Lin Biao in 1964 selected, compiled and published the quotations of Mao Zedong. Designed with portability in mind, the "treasured red book," was only about five inches tall and typically bound in a shiny durable red plastic with Mao's likeness on the cover. By 1974 more than a billion copies had been published and translated into eight indigenous languages and 37 foreign languages.

EAST IS RED: The phrase "the East is Red" originally came from a revolutionary song of the late 1930s proclaiming the arrival of Mao and Communism. By 1966, the sun rising in the east had been transformed into a potent symbol representing the arrival of Communism led by Chairman Mao. In the poster above (right), Chairman Mao is superimposed over the sun with the words the "East is Red" in front of his hand. Along the bottom it reads: "Chairman Mao is the red sun in our heart."

PROPAGANDA POSTERS: The public posting of information on walls and public places dates back well into imperial China. With the founding of the People's Republic propaganda posters took on a new dimension. The posters apart from their visually striking style sought to reinforce messages being disseminated in other media forms such as newspapers, speeches, radio, and film. The poster pictured here is originally in black and red on a white background.

INTERNATIONALIZATION: As tensions rose between the Soviet Union and China, the PRC increasingly sought to promote itself as the center of the international communist movement. In this poster, an unmistakably Chinese worker leads China's communist African, Asian, and Latin American comrades along the socialist road (each proudly holding a copy of the "Little Red Book").

In the summer of 1966, China launched the Great Proletarian Cultural Revolution. The Sixteen Point directive adopted on August 8 presented the revolutionary aims with some precision (12.5). This directive instructed the people to "revolutionize people's ideology," and as a consequence to achieve greater, faster, and more economical results in all fields of work. The Chinese people were called upon to remove all traces of traditional culture, to overthrow all remnants of the bourgeoisie, and to make all elements of Chinese society conform to the socialist system. Most ominously, the document anticipated violence by stating explicitly that the masses should expect to encounter resistance. The titles of the campaigns unleashed by Mao and the central government offer a bone-chilling glimpse into the terrifying nature of this period: "Bombard the Headquarters," "Sweeping Away All Monsters and Demons," "Destroy the Four Olds." What is disconcerting is the fact that this was not a campaign unleashed immediately after the CCP had secured power and sought to "purify" the population. This was, rather, a political campaign led by the most powerful individual in China—Mao Zedong—against large segments of the population within his own country who had displayed little indication of political disobedience.

To begin to understand the impact that the Chinese Cultural Revolution era had on any individual it is essential to understand the depth to which the state regulated virtually every aspect of their citizen's lives. A key tool of this central government control was the personal dossier (*dang'an*), which gave them power over each individual. The importance of this dossier for the common Chinese citizen cannot be overstated for it contained every significant document relating to a citizen's personal, academic, and professional life. To a Chinese citizen in the 1960s, the most consequential elements would be **family background** (*jiating chushen*), political appearance (*zhengzhi mianmao*), and the various behavior evaluations of job, political, or personal conduct. Furthermore, since a work unit's (*danwei*) authorization was required to get married, give birth, or transfer jobs—and the fact that those decisions were largely based on the dossier—that dossier to a large extent dictated a future career, an ability to find a partner, and even permission to attend college.

The personal dossier was property of the state and, as such, the individual was not permitted to see it. Only a person's superiors or Communist Party members had the authority to review the file. Any information put in the personal file could only be expunged in exceptional circumstances with considerable effort. The constant fear that any errant behavior could be entered in the dossier served as one of the PRC's most powerful deterrents. Even more worrisome were the ways in which this system could be subverted: by irritated neighbors reporting politically inappropriate comments, by jealous co-workers embellishing any work-related shortcomings, or by a resentful superior knowingly filing half-truths and out-right falsehoods in the dossier. These worries were compounded by radical political campaigns like the Cultural Revolution.

Unlike previous political campaigns that were mostly top-down affairs orchestrated by the central government, the Cultural Revolution gave extensive power to China's youth. With Mao Zedong's explicit authorization, revolutionary youth groups called "Red Guards" (*hongweibing*) were whipped into a revolutionary frenzy to purify the

---

FAMILY BACKGROUND—Depending on the class background of one's parents (and sometimes one's grandparents), each individual was designated as "red" or "black." If one's parents were workers, poor peasants, lower-middle-class peasants, revolutionary cadres, or revolutionary soldiers, they were classified as one of the "five red types" (coming from a "revolutionary" background). If one's parents were landlords, rich peasants, counter-revolutionaries, evildoers, rightists, capitalists or reactionary intellectuals, they were classified as being in one of "seven black categories."

country. They were to attack all suspected counter-revolutionaries and cleanse society of the Four Olds: old culture, old ideas, old customs and old habits. Officially sanctioned by Mao, sporting **Mao buttons,** and quoting from their "Little Red Book" (*Quotations from Chairman Mao*), they spread a public reign of terror such as the nation had never witnessed. Although the earliest **Red Guard** units were from Beijing, revolutionary gangs quickly materialized throughout the country. Seeking to show their commitment, the units would work their way through neighborhood homes searching for evidence of revolutionary crimes. People wearing close-fitting clothes and high-heeled shoes, or having long hair (all considered "improper bourgeois attire," [*zichanjieji qizhuang yifu*]) were accosted on the streets and the offending articles of clothing were removed or hair was cut in a more "appropriate" revolutionary style. Items as innocuous as pre-liberation photos, books in a foreign language, or letters from abroad could be enough to precipitate verbal abuse, physical beating, and incarceration in cells, referred to as **cow sheds** (*niupeng*), for months on end. Those found to be counter-revolutionary would be paraded through the streets and forced to wear oversize dunce-caps and derogatory placards announcing their crimes. These placards labeled them as counter-revolutionaries, traitors, or spies—or worse, "son of a bitch," "whore," or "ox ghost and snake spirits." It was routine for such public humiliations to culminate at massive **struggle sessions** where the accused would be publicly demeaned and frequently beaten. By the end of 1966, thousands of cadres, teachers, and so-called counter-revolutionaries had been rounded up, accused in public struggle sessions, and then killed. Liu Shaoqi, Mao Zedong's former chosen successor, and his wife were paraded through the streets of Beijing and pilloried in public struggle sessions before enormous crowds. He would die alone, naked and devoid of any political standing in a Henan prison cell in 1969.

Chinese society became more and more unhinged as the revolutionary excesses reached new extremes. These excesses altered even the normal rhythms of the day. The day would begin with "morning instructions" (*zaoqingshi*), conclude with "evening reports" (*wanhuibao*), and could be interrupted day or night with Mao Zedong's "highest directives" which people were required to greet with appropriate celebratory behavior. To accidentally sit on a newspaper wherein Chairman Mao's name was printed was a crime. Children mis-writing a slogan on a wall were said to be subversives working against the Communist Party, and their parents arrested. The fierce nature of the political attacks ripped apart the very fabric of Chinese society. Family members would be urged to "draw a distinct line" (*huaqing jiexian*) between themselves and a disgraced family member. Spouses were told to divorce their partners, children told to renounce their parents. People abandoned the habit of writing diaries or letters, terrified that the thoughts and ideas politically acceptable during one campaign could suddenly be used against them in another. Parents, fearful their children might say the wrong thing at school or on the street and bring unwanted attention to their family, self-censored what they said in front of them; they never dared to explain the complex political tides to their children and thus facilitated on some level the excesses that teenagers unleashed on China. Life was chaotic.

MAO BUTTONS—Worn as a symbol of one's loyalty to Mao Zedong during the Cultural Revolution, at least 2 billion badges were manufactured with well over 10,000 different designs.

RED GUARDS—Middle and high school aged students who answered Mao Zedong's call in 1966 to spread his teachings, fight against the "Four Olds," and remove all counter-revolutionary elements from society.

COW SHEDS—A place of confinement chosen by the Red Guards, usually in a vacant classroom, lecture hall or even a bathroom converted for their detainees.

STRUGGLE SESSIONS—Cultural Revolution rallies where individuals accused of "black," or counter-revolutionary, activities would be publicly attacked in sessions lasting many hours held in large auditoriums.

The first and most violent phase of the Cultural Revolution ended in 1969. Some estimate at least half a million people died as a direct result of the initial revolutionary excesses, and it is likely two million were killed in the entire period. Virtually no one emerged unchanged from the Cultural Revolution. Families were split apart as parents were consigned to separate parts of the country (if they were lucky enough to avoid re-education, labor camps, or prison). Teenagers were raised without adult supervision and encouraged by the government to carry out appalling excesses in the name of revolution. They found themselves working in remote parts of the countryside with no indication of when they would be allowed to return to their home cities (12.7). Young children entering school at this period were taught only a "revolutionary education" of Maoist propaganda, and the formal instruction at the universities for all intents and purposes stopped for the duration.

If there was any bright spot to the Cultural Revolution, it was that most Chinese began to realize that the aging Chinese leadership was not infallible. Most Chinese would never again follow the central government with the same blind faith as they did throughout the Cultural Revolution.

PURSUING NEW LOYALTIES

Quite early in the history of the Chinese Communist Party, Mao Zedong sought to pursue a "China-first" policy with regards to China–Soviet Union relations. The relationship established between the two Communist powers in the early 1950s (discussed in the previous chapter) was a partnership of mutual convenience for both Stalin and Mao. Stalin's death in 1953 and Mao's growing disagreement with his successor, Nikita Khrushchev (who sought to pursue a policy of "peaceful co-existence" with the United States) brought China and the USSR a **Sino-Soviet split.** This split culminates in an open letter from the Soviet Central Committee publicly criticizing China. In this climate, accusations of Khrushchev revisionism and charges of Soviet breaks with orthodox Marxist-Leninist thought became the norm (12.1). During this same period China's domestic propaganda began to emphasize model workers like Lei Feng (12.2). Model communes like Dazhai (12.3) would become mainstays of state campaigns well into the 1970s. In the case of Lei Feng, this emphasis was occasionally revived well into the 1990s.

12.1   THE KHRUSHCHEV REVISIONISTS ARE BETRAYERS OF PEOPLE'S WAR (SEPTEMBER 3, 1965)

A brilliant military strategist, PLA General and hero of the Chinese Civil War (1945–49), Lin Biao succeeded Peng Dehuai in 1959 (Mao secretly believed Peng Dehuai was colluding with the Soviets) as Defense Minister. In 1969 Mao officially designated Lin Biao as his successor, but in 1971 he would mysteriously die in a plane crash attempting to escape to the Soviet Union. Although the Chinese had successfully detonated their first nuclear explosion in 1964, Lin Biao, like Mao, believed China's strength lay in a "people's war," with China's massive population as its greatest asset. The following speech by Lin underscores China's growing international strategy of bolstering communist insurgencies

SINO–SOVIET SPLIT (c. 1959) — Relations between the Soviet Union and China soured in the late 1950s with a series of diplomatic disagreements over Taiwan, India and the United States. As a result, the Soviet government withdrew their experts, scientific information, and financial support from China. This lead to an acrimonious 30-year split between China and USSR that ended with Gorbachev's visit in 1989.

and governments throughout the world in the hopes of encircling and thus eventually defeating American imperialism. It also underscores the growing extremism that preceded the Cultural Revolution that would begin the following year.

Questions

1. How does Lin Biao suggest Khrushchev's effort to bring about a rapprochement between the United States and the USSR is a threat to China and the world?
2. Why would China be particularly worried about the United States in 1965 (and thus reluctant to follow the Soviet lead in enhancing Sino-American relations)?

The Khrushchev revisionists have come to the rescue of U.S. imperialism just when it is most panic-stricken and helpless in its efforts to cope with people's war. Working hand in glove with the U.S. imperialists, they are doing their utmost to spread all kinds of arguments against people's war and, wherever they can, they are scheming to undermine it by overt or covert means.

The fundamental reason why the Khrushchev revisionists are opposed to people's war is that they have no faith in the masses and are afraid of U.S. imperialism, of war and of revolution. Like all other opportunists, they are blind to the power of the masses and do not believe that the revolutionary people are capable of defeating imperialism. They submit to the nuclear blackmail of the U.S. imperialists and are afraid that, if the oppressed peoples and nations rise up to fight people's wars and if the people of socialist countries repulse U.S. imperialist aggression, U.S. imperialism will become incensed, they themselves will become involved and their fond dream of Soviet–U.S. co-operation to dominate the world will be spoiled.

Ever since Lenin led the great October Revolution to victory, the experience of innumerable revolutionary wars has borne out the truth that a revolutionary people who rise up with only their bare hands at the outset finally succeed in defeating the ruling classes who are armed to the teeth. The poorly armed have defeated the better armed. People's armed forces, beginning with only primitive swords, spears, rifles and hand-grenades, have in the end defeated the imperialist forces armed with modern airplanes, tanks, heavy artillery and atom bombs. Guerrilla forces have ultimately defeated regular armies. "Amateurs" who were never trained in any military schools have

eventually defeated "professionals" graduated from military academies. And so on and so forth. Things stubbornly develop in a way that runs counter to the assertions of the revisionists, and facts are slapping them in the face.

The Khrushchev revisionists insist that a nation without nuclear weapons is incapable of defeating an enemy with nuclear weapons, whatever methods of fighting it may adopt. This is tantamount to saying that anyone without nuclear weapons is destined to come to grief, destined to be bullied and annihilated, and must either capitulate to the enemy when confronted with his nuclear weapons or come under the "protection" of some other nuclear power and submit to its beck and call. Isn't this the jungle law of survival par excellence? Isn't this helping the imperialists in their nuclear blackmail? Isn't this openly forbidding people to make revolution?

[. . . .]

We want to tell the U.S. imperialists once again that the vast ocean of several hundred million Chinese people in arms will be more than enough to submerge your few million aggressor troops. If you dare to impose war on us, we shall gain freedom of action. It will then not be up to you to decide how the war will be fought. We shall fight in the ways most advantageous to us to destroy the enemy and wherever the enemy can be most easily destroyed. Since the Chinese people were able to destroy the Japanese aggressors twenty years ago, they are certainly still more capable finishing off the U.S. aggressors today. The naval and air superiority you boast about cannot intimidate the Chinese people, and neither can the atom bomb you brandish at us. If you want to send troops, go ahead, the more the better. They will annihilate as many as you can send, and can even give you receipts. The Chinese people are a great, valiant people. We have the courage to shoulder the heavy burden of combating U.S. imperialism and to contribute our share in the struggle for final victory over this most ferocious enemy of the people of the world.

It must be pointed out in all seriousness that after the victory of the War of Resistance Taiwan was returned to China. The occupation of Taiwan by U.S. imperialism is absolutely unjustified. Taiwan province is an inalienable part of Chinese territory. The U.S. imperialists must get out of Taiwan. The Chinese people are determined to liberate Taiwan.

[. . . .]

All peoples suffering from U.S. imperialist aggression, oppression and plunder, unite! Hold aloft the just banner of people's war and fight for the cause of world peace, national liberation, people's democracy and socialism! Victory will certainly go to the people of the world!

Long live the victory of people's war!

12.2   LEI FENG, CHAIRMAN MAO'S GOOD FIGHTER (1963)

As China's Defense Minister, Lin Biao played a central role in educating and building up the People's Liberation Army (PLA). Lin promoted Mao's teachings, eventually collecting and publishing Mao's quotations into a compact red handbook, first for the PLA soldiers and later for all Chinese. As part of this broader campaign to promote Mao Zedong Thought, Lin Biao also promoted a model soldier, Lei Feng, to reinforce the notion of individual sacrifice and commitment to Mao. Mao officially bestowed his blessing on this endeavor in a 1963 speech in which he urged the Chinese masses to "Learn from Lei Feng." According to his official biography, Lei Feng began work as a tractor driver before becoming a steel worker. He finally joined the People's Liberation Army (PLA) and later died in a truck accident in 1962. His undeviating adherence to Mao and China's socialist path, as revealed in his freakishly aseptic diary that was discovered and published, as well as the amazing degree to which Lei Feng's life was photo-documented, has led many to suggest it is all a bit too convenient. Regardless of these suspicions, Lei Feng's pristine class background and his unselfish, and steadfast commitment to Mao's teaching made him an ideal model to be emulated by all Chinese. In China today his name lives on. To tell a friend or colleague to "Learn from Lei Feng" is to suggest that they pursue an overly altruistic (even foolish) course of action.

Questions

1. **What practical lessons did Lei Feng learn from his studies of Mao Zedong's teachings?**
2. **What type of behavior do you think the average Chinese would attempt to emulate after "learning from Lei Feng?"**

To me Chairman Mao's works are like food, weapons and the steering wheel of a vehicle. To live you must have food, to fight you must have weapons, to drive a vehicle you must have a steering wheel, and to work for the revolution you must read Chairman Mao's works.

From Lei Feng's diary

[. . . .]

Lei Feng had begun to regularly study Chairman Mao's writings from 1958. He had made a rule by which he studied one hour every morning and up to ten or eleven o'clock in the evenings. He had made a point of studying the *Selected Works of Mao Zedong* during every spare moment when he worked in the coal yard of the Anshan Iron and Steel Company. After joining the army he had managed to complete volume three of the *Selected Works* while boiling water for the amateur cultural troupe. Then the army leadership called on the men to "study Chairman Mao's works, follow his teachings, act in accordance with his instructions and be good soldiers of Chairman Mao." Lei Feng took this call as a maxim and wrote it down on the front covers of his copies of Chairman Mao's works. But where the leadership had asked the men to "study Chairman Mao's works," he added "every day" so that he would study them more diligently. Lei Feng's job as a driver often took him to various places but wherever he went he always carried a satchel containing different essays by Chairman Mao, which he read at every opportunity. Soon his comrades had described his satchel as a "mobile library."

About this time one of his comrades grumbled, "There's so much work to do we haven't got enough time for our personal affairs, nor for rest." Lei Feng did not agree, and to encourage himself to work and study even harder he wrote this passage in his diary which he remembered from a book he once read:

> How do you put a screw into a piece of wood which is perfectly smooth and has no holes? You use force and screw it in. Then just as a screw has to be forced and screwed in, so when you study you should bore firmly into the subject.

It was with this spirit that Lei Feng was able to complete Chairman Mao's *Selected Works,* from volume one to four. And among many of the essays he repeatedly read were: "In Memory of Norman Bethune," "Serve the People," "Carry the Revolution Through to the End," "On Practice," and "On Contradiction."

[...]

Lei Feng found an inexhaustible source of strength and wisdom in Chairman Mao's works, and he gradually came to understand the meaning of life, of revolution and the laws of social development. He learnt how to treat one's enemy and one's comrades, and what attitude one should take to work. He felt he could see things more and more clearly, that his vision of life was broadening and that a new big world was opening up before him.

[...]

It was about nine o'clock on the morning of August 15, 1962. Lei Feng and his assistant, who had been driving in a drizzle, returned to their barracks. Jumping down from the cabin Lei Feng told his comrade to drive the truck away and get it washed down and cleaned.

Lei Feng's comrade took the driver's seat, got the truck in gear and turned the steering wheel. The truck chugged, shook itself, and backed, splashing mud all round. Meanwhile, Lei Feng waves and shouted, "left, left, back, back...."

The ground was covered with water and the road was slippery. While making a turn the truck bumped into a big wooden post standing by the roadside. Lei Feng was so busy directing the truck that he did not notice the post which crashed on his head knocking him unconscious ...

Within minutes the deputy company commander himself was driving at full speed to Shenyang to bring the city's most competent surgeon to Lei Feng's aid. Not a minute, not a second must be lost, the officer thought to himself as he raced against time for medical help.

Sweat was running down the deputy company commander's face as he returned with the surgeon, but it was too late – Lei Feng had died from a cerebral hemorrhage in spite of emergency treatment by the army doctors. And so Lei Feng parted from those close to him that morning, unable to hear his commander's call, his assistant's cries, his comrades' sobs....

Lei Feng died on duty. He lived only twenty-two years, a short but glorious life. He was born in misery and poverty and brought up in happiness, and his life shed a brilliant light in the era of Mao Zedong.

[...]

Every river has its source, every tree its root. Lei Feng's character also had its source – Mao Zedong's thought and the Party's instructions. Lei Feng knew very well that "the more often and the more intensely you study Chairman Mao's works the clearer will be your mind, the broader your views, the firmer your stand and the more far-reaching your thoughts." He compared Chairman Mao's teachings to food, to a soldier's weapon and to a vehicle's steering wheel. That was why he took to them with such great zeal, not only creatively studying and applying them, but applying them while studying them. This was essentially how Lei Feng, a poor orphan in the old society, became a hero in the new society and a communist fighter.

Lei Feng is immortal. In the words of a poet:
What death does to you;
From one Lei Feng come millions of Lei Fengs.

To remember Lei Feng, Chaiman Mao, our beloved leader, called on us to **"Learn from Comrade Lei Feng."**

Yes, we must listen to what the Party and Chairman Mao say and follow Lei Feng's example. We are now confronted with the heavy task of socialist construction and may face acute class struggle at any moment. Like Lei Feng we must always remember the misery suffered by the proletariat in the old society, take a firm stand in the class struggle, recognize whom to love and whom to hate, and devote ourselves entirely to the revolutionary cause of the proletariat. Like Lei Feng we must be "a screw that never rusts" in our work. Like Lei Feng we must, in our daily work, add brick after brick and stone after stone to the edifice of socialism. Above all, like Lei Feng, we must ceaselessly study Chairman Mao's works, constantly raise our level of class consciousness and Marxism-Leninism, and be good pupils of Chairman Mao.

12.3   WHAT IS DAZHAI SPIRIT?

In 1964, Mao Zedong introduced two new campaigns: "In industry learn from Daqing" and "In agriculture learn from **Dazhai.**" At the base of both campaigns was Mao's desire to emphasize the self-reliance of communes as embodied by Daqing and Dazhai. In an increasingly turbulent society, it appeared to many that the safest way forward was to emulate the Dazhai model. Thus many villages and communes sought to reclaim land, and cadres would refuse central government aid even when it was desperately needed. Regardless of the actual efficacy of this commune campaign, as a propaganda tool it was a stunning success. In the decade following Mao's proclamation, Dazhai received about 10 million visitors. The following document was published in the English-language magazine *China Reconstructs* under a column entitled "Questions and Answers" which was meant to help explain various political movements that might not be self-evident to the foreign readership. As was common in the Cultural Revolution, all quotations from Chairman Mao are in bold.

Questions

1. **What aspects of Dazhai made it a model other agricultural communes should emulate?**
2. **Why do you think the central government relied so heavily on such model campaigns as "Learn from Dazhai" and "Learn from Lei Feng"?**

Dazhai is the name of a production brigade of Dazhai People's Commune which lies at the foot of inhospitable Hutuo Mountain in Xiyang county, Shanxi province.

In 1964 our great leader Chairman Mao issued the call to the nation: **"In agriculture, learn from Dazhai!"** In the years since, and especially since the Great Proletarian Cultural Revolution began, the millions upon millions of China's commune members, filled with militant daring, have carried on a mass movement to learn from and catch up with Dazhai. They vow: "We must resolutely take the Dazhai road and firmly learn the Dazhai spirit!"

What is the Dazhai spirit? Premier Zhou Enlai, in his report on the work of the government at the First Session of the Third National People's Congress in December 1964, said: "The spirit persisted in by the Dazhai brigade is worth promoting—that is, the principle of putting politics in command and proletarian ideology in first place, the spirit of self-reliance and hard work and the communist style of love for the state and the collective." This is both a summary and high appraisal of the Dazhai spirit.

Putting politics in command and proletarian ideology in first place means concretely that the

DAZHAI—A village located in the mountainous Shanxi province which Mao Zedong held up as a model village encouraging all Chinese to "Learn from Dazhai in agriculture."

Dazhai people have used Mao Zedong's thought to arm their minds and, through thoroughly eliminating self-interest and establishing public interest, have revolutionized their thinking.

Over twenty years, under the leadership of the Communist Party branch committee, the heroic Dazhai people have creatively studied and applied Mao Zedong's thought, followed closely Chairman Mao's proletarian revolutionary line and kept to the socialist road in advancing through the mutual-aid team, semi-socialist and fully-socialist cooperatives to the people's commune.

In carrying out the three great revolutionary movements of class struggle, the struggle for production and scientific experiment, they have constantly struggled against nature, against the handful of class enemies, against the counter-revolutionary revisionist line which arch renegade, traitor, and scab Liu Shaoqi pushed in the countryside, and against their own selfishness. Through struggle, they transformed the poor Dazhai into a prosperous, socialist new Dazhai. In the struggle, the Dazhai people have matured into new men of high communist consciousness.

Our great leader Chairman Mao teaches us: **"On what basis should our policy rest? It should rest on our own strength, and that means regeneration through one's own efforts."** This self-reliance and arduous struggle means to carry on socialist revolution and socialist construction in the spirit of the Party's General Line of going all out, aiming high and getting more, faster, better and more economical results in building socialism, bringing into full play the initiative of the masses and relying on collective strength and ingenuity.

Under the leadership of their Party secretary, Chen Yonggui, the Dazhai people resolutely carried out these principles. Over the years they gradually

tamed the mountain by thoroughly transforming seven ravines and eight mountain slopes, and built tier on tier of terraced fields with the heroic boldness of **"daring to make sun and moon shine in new skies."**

Dazhai's average grain yield was just several dozen *jin* per *mu* at liberation. But now it has risen to over 800 *jin*. In the past decade and more, Dazhai suffered severe setbacks on three occasions from heavy rain, drought and hail. The greater the difficulty, the greater their determination. Three times the Dazhai people refused to accept state relief. They resolved to restore their fields in five years and their houses in ten years, all by their own efforts. But in only three years, the face of the village underwent great changes. All the members have new cave houses, and every one has electric light. Chairman Mao's classic teaching that people are the decisive factor displayed its unparalleled power.

Through the creative study and application of Mao Zedong's thought, the Dazhai people have constantly remolded their outlook, cultivated devotion to the public interest and developed a communist spirit. It would take more than three years to eat the grain they produce in one year. But they don't farm just to get more grain for themselves. As their contribution to building the socialist motherland, they sell all their surplus grain to the state. Although the brigade has only some 80 households, the surplus grain they sell to the state every year has always topped 240,000 *jin*. The Dazhai people proudly say, "Here on Hutou Mountain, our eyes on Tiananmen and the whole world in our hearts, we farm for the revolution."

Dazhai is only a small mountain village in Shanxi province. But guided by Mao Zedong's thought, it has become a brilliant example for China's 600 million peasants in building a new socialist countryside.

THE GREAT PROLETARIAT REVOLUTION

The scope, scale and fervor of the Cultural Revolution overshadows virtually every other Chinese political campaign that came before or after it. Despite the horrendous atrocities that were carried out in its name, many Chinese who survived it retain a fond nostalgia for the songs, propaganda and even for the seemingly black and white worldview it provided. The Cultural Revolution had its beginnings in the spring of 1966, but it was Mao's "Big Character Poster" (12.4) and the Sixteen Point decision of the Eleventh Plenum of the Central Committee of the CCP, which became the political campaign's guiding document (12.5). With the publicly visible resurgence of Mao's attack against Liu Shaoqi and other top leaders, events quickly escalated and massive rallies were held for the Red Guards in

August and on into the autumn (12.6). By 1969, with violence disrupting the many basic elements of daily life, the distribution of goods, and generally slowing the economy, Mao ordered China's youth to be "sent down to the countryside" (12.7).

12.4 MAO ZEDONG'S MY BIG-CHARACTER POSTER (AUGUST 5, 1966)

On August 7th at the Eleventh Meeting of the Central Committee, Mao distributed his "Big Character Poster." Although his name is never explicitly mentioned, the poster suggests that China's president, Liu Shaoqi, was the center of the bourgeois base in the Central Committee (or in the language of the poster, the "headquarters"). By divulging his target, Mao signaled his determination to overthrow Liu Shaoqi and many other long-term communist revolutionaries whom Mao considered a threat to his absolute authority. The Central Committee tacitly accepted his radical line, and several days later issued their Sixteen Point Declaration, which signaled the beginning of the attack on Liu Shaoqi and Deng Xiaoping.

Questions

1. **What does Mao mean by "bourgeoisie" and how does he suggest they are harming China?**
2. **What does Mao mean by suggesting the "wrong tendency of 1964" was "Left in form, but Right in essence?"**

China's first Marxist-Leninist **big-character poster** and Commentator's article on it in *Renmin Ribao* are indeed superbly written! Comrades, please read them again. But in the last fifty days or so some leading comrades from the central down to the local levels have acted in a diametrically opposite way. Adopting the reactionary stand of the bourgeoisie, they have enforced a bourgeois dictatorship and struck down the surging movement of the great cultural revolution of the proletariat. They have stood facts on their head and juggled black and white, encircled and suppressed revolutionaries, stifled opinions differing from their own, imposed a white terror, and felt very pleased with themselves. They have puffed up the arrogance of the bourgeoisie and deflated the morale of the proletariat. How poisonous! Viewed in connection with the Right deviation in 1962 and the wrong tendency of 1964, which was "Left" in form but Right in essence," shouldn't this make one wide awake?

12.5 THE SIXTEEN POINTS: DECISION OF THE CENTRAL COMMITTEE OF THE CHINESE COMMUNIST PARTY CONCERNING THE GREAT PROLETARIAN CULTURAL REVOLUTION (AUGUST 8, 1966)

Perhaps no document so clearly lays out the entire scope and goals of the Cultural Revolution than the Sixteen Point Decision of 1966. While Mao's *Little Red Book* may have provided the means by which the Red Guards and other leaders could defend their own actions (and attack those of their rivals), the Sixteen Points provided a road map for what classes to attack, what tools to use in the assault, and offered

BIG–CHARACTER POSTER—Posters often attacking a specific person or type of behavior written in large characters and posted publicly typically on interior and exterior walls.
LITTLE RED BOOK (QUOTATIONS OF CHAIRMAN MAO)—A pocket size collection of Mao Zedong's quotations first published for the PLA in 1964. 900 million copies were ultimately printed.

warnings against potential pitfalls. The document also criticized the elements that Mao had undeniably grown to distrust—intellectuals, science, and education—and instead audaciously adhered to a radical line. Mao's approach may have achieved his goals, but it created a highly unstable political environment. Many of his guidelines seemed unambiguous in print, yet when they were applied, their meaning became far less distinct. The result was considerable friction, in-fighting, and violence—all in the name of Mao's teachings.

Questions

1. **How does Mao Zedong define who are the counter-revolutionaries?**
2. **Who is the enemy? Who are "our friends"? Who might be somewhere in between?**

1. A NEW STAGE IN THE SOCIALIST REVOLUTION

The Great Proletarian Cultural Revolution now unfolding is a great revolution that touches people to their very souls and constitutes a new stage in the development of the socialist revolution in our country, a stage which is both broader and deeper.

At the Tenth Plenary Session of the Eighth Central Committee of the Party; Comrade Mao Zedong said: To overthrow a political power, it is always necessary first of all to create public opinion, to do work in the ideological sphere. This is true for the revolutionary class as well as for the counter-revolutionary class. This thesis of Comrade Mao Zedong's has been proved entirely correct in practice.

Although the bourgeoisie has been overthrown, it is still trying to use the old ideas, culture, customs and habits of the exploiting classes to corrupt the masses, capture their minds and endeavor to stage a comeback. The proletariat must do the exact opposite: it must meet head-on every challenge of the bourgeoisie in the ideological field and use the new ideas, culture, customs and habits of the proletariat to change the mental outlook of the whole of society. At present, our objective is to struggle against and overthrow those persons in authority who are taking the capitalist road, to criticize and repudiate the reactionary bourgeois academic "authorities" and the ideology of the bourgeoisie and all other exploiting classes and to transform education, literature and art and all other parts of the superstructure not in correspondence with the socialist economic base, so as to facilitate the consolidation and development of the socialist system.

[. . . .]

4. LET THE MASSES EDUCATE THEMSELVES IN THE MOVEMENT

In the Great Proletarian Cultural Revolution, the only method is for the masses to liberate themselves, and any method of doing things in their stead must not be used.

Trust the masses, rely on them and respect their initiative. Cast out fear. Don't be afraid of disturbances. Chairman Mao has often told us that revolution cannot be so very refined, so gentle, so temperate, kind, courteous, restrained and magnanimous. Let the masses educate themselves in this great revolutionary movement and learn to distinguish between right and wrong and between correct and incorrect ways of doing things.

Make the fullest use of big-character posters and great debates to argue matters out, so that the masses can clarify the correct views, criticize the wrong views and expose all the ghosts and monsters. In this way the masses will be able to raise their political consciousness in the course of the struggle, enhance their abilities and talents, distinguish right from wrong and draw a clear line between ourselves and the enemy.

5. FIRMLY APPLY THE CLASS LINE OF THE PARTY

Who are our enemies? Who are our friends? This is a question of the first importance for the revolution and it is likewise a question of the first importance for the great Cultural Revolution.

Party leadership should be good at discovering the Left and developing and strengthening the ranks of the Left; it should firmly rely on the revolutionary Left. During the movement this is the only way to isolate the most reactionary Rightists thoroughly, win over the middle and unite with the great majority so that by the end of the movement we shall achieve the unity of more than 95 per cent of the cadres and more than 95 per cent of the masses.

Concentrate all forces to strike at the handful of ultra-reactionary bourgeois Rightists and counter-revolutionary revisionists, and expose and criticize to the full their crimes against the Party, against socialism and against Mao Zedong's thought so as to isolate them to the maximum.

The main target of the present movement is those within the Party who are in authority and are taking the capitalist road.

The strictest care should be taken to distinguish between the anti-Party, anti-socialist Rightists and those who support the Party and socialism but have said or done something wrong or have written some bad articles or other works.

The strictest care should be taken to distinguish between the reactionary bourgeois scholar despots and "authorities" on the one hand and people who have the ordinary bourgeois academic ideas on the other.

6. CORRECTLY HANDLE CONTRADICTIONS AMONG THE PEOPLE

A strict distinction must be made between the two different types of contradictions: those among the people and those between ourselves and the enemy. Contradictions among the people must not be made into contradictions between ourselves and the enemy; nor must contradictions between ourselves and the enemy be regarded as contradictions among the people.

[. . . .]

7. BE ON GUARD AGAINST THOSE WHO BRAND THE REVOLUTIONARY MASSES AS "COUNTER-REVOLUTIONARIES"

In certain schools, units, and work teams of the Cultural Revolution, some of the persons in charge have organized counter-attacks against the masses who put up big-character posters criticizing them. These people have even advanced such slogans as: opposition to the feeders of a unit or a work team means opposition to the Central Committee of the Party, means opposition to the Party and socialism, means counter-revolution. In this way it is inevitable that their blows will fall on some really revolutionary activists. This is an error on matters of orientation, an error of line, and is absolutely impermissible.

A number of persons who suffer from serious ideological errors, and particularly some of the anti-Party and anti-socialist Rightists, are taking advantage of certain shortcomings and mistakes in the mass movement to spread rumors and gossip, and engage in agitation, deliberately branding some of the masses as "counter-revolutionaries." It is necessary to beware of such "pick-pockets" and expose their tricks in good time.

In the course of the movement, with the exception of cases of active counter-revolutionaries where there is clear evidence of crimes such as murder, arson, poisoning, sabotage or theft of state secrets, which should be handled in accordance with the law, no measures should be taken against students at universities, colleges, middle schools and primary schools because of problems that arise in the movement. To prevent the struggle from being diverted from its main target, it is not allowed, under whatever pretext, to incite the masses or the students to struggle against each other. Even proven Rightists should be dealt with on the merits of each case at a later stage of the movement.

8. THE QUESTION OF CADRES

The cadres fall roughly into the following four categories:

1. good;
2. comparatively good;
3. those who have made serious mistakes but have not become anti-Party, anti-socialist Rightists;
4. the small number of anti-Party, anti-socialist Rightists.

In ordinary situations, the first two categories (good and comparatively good) are the great majority.

The anti-Party, anti-socialist Rightists must be fully exposed, refuted, overthrown and completely discredited and their influence eliminated. At the same time, they should be given a chance to turn over a new leaf.

[. . . .]

10. EDUCATIONAL REFORM

In the Great Proletarian Cultural Revolution the most important task is to transform the old educational system and the old principles and methods of teaching. In this great Cultural Revolution, the phenomenon of our schools being dominated by bourgeois intellectuals must be completely changed.

In every kind of school we must apply thoroughly the policy advanced by Comrade Mao Zedong of education serving proletarian politics and education being combined with producing labor, so as to enable those receiving an education to develop morally, intellectually and physically and to become workers with both socialist consciousness and culture.

The period of schooling should be shortened. Courses should be fewer and better. The teaching material should be thoroughly transformed, in some cases beginning with simplifying complicated material. While their main task is to study, students should also learn other things. That is to say, in addition to their studies they should also learn industrial work, farming and military affairs, and take part in the struggle of the Cultural Revolution to criticize the bourgeoisie as these struggles occur.

[. . . .]

14. TAKE FIRM HOLD OF THE REVOLUTION AND STIMULATE PRODUCTION

The aim of the Great Proletarian Cultural Revolution is to revolutionize people's ideology and as a consequence to achieve greater, faster, better and more economical results in all fields of work. If the masses are fully aroused and proper arrangements are made, it is possible to carry on both the Cultural Revolution and production without one hampering the other, while guaranteeing high quality in all our work.

The Great Proletarian Cultural Revolution is a powerful motive force for the development of the social productive forces in our country. Any idea of counterposing the Great Cultural Revolution to the development of production is incorrect.

15. THE ARMED FORCES

In the armed forces, the Cultural Revolution and the socialist education movement should be carried out in accordance with the instructions of the Military Commission of the Central Committee of the Party and the General Political Department of the People's Liberation Army.

16. MAO ZEDONG'S THOUGHT IS THE GUIDE TO ACTION IN THE GREAT PROLETARIAN CULTURAL REVOLUTION

In the Great Proletarian Cultural Revolution, it is imperative to hold aloft the great red banner of Mao Zedong's thought and put proletarian politics in command. The movement for the creative study and application of Chairman Mao Zedong's works should be carried forward among the masses of the workers, peasants and soldiers, the cadres and the intellectuals, and Mao Zedong's thought should be taken as the guide to action in the Cultural Revolution.

In this complex great Cultural Revolution, Party committees at all levels must study and apply Chairman Mao's works all the more conscientiously and in a creative way. In particular, they must study over and over again Chairman Mao's writings on the Cultural Revolution and on the Party's methods of leadership, such as On New Democracy, Talks at the Yan'an Forum on Literature and Art, On the Correct Handling of Contradictions Among the People, Speech at the Chinese Communist Party's National Conference on Propaganda Work, Some Questions Concerning Methods of Leadership and Methods of Work of Party Committees.

Party committees at all levels must abide by the directions given by Chairman Mao over the years, namely that they should thoroughly apply the mass line of "from the masses, to the masses" and that they should be pupils before they become teachers. They should try to avoid being one-sided or narrow. They should foster materialist dialectics and oppose metaphysics and scholasticism.

The Great Proletarian Cultural Revolution is bound to achieve brilliant victory under the leadership of the Central Committee of the Party headed by Comrade Mao Zedong.

12.6 CHAIRMAN MAO JOINS A MILLION PEOPLE TO CELEBRATE THE GREAT CULTURAL REVOLUTION (AUGUST 18, 1966)

From August 18 to November 26, 1966, Mao Zedong greeted more than twelve million Red Guards in eight massive rallies in Tiananmen Square. During those months millions of Chinese youth, Red Guards, middle school and university students, and workers from across the country rushed to Beijing for the chance to behold Chairman Mao. During this period, all Red Guards could ride the trains for free simply by flashing their Red Guard armband. For young Chinese who had never traveled outside the city of their birth, the chance to be in Beijing and see the Chairman was a heady experience. Tens of thousands of revolutionary youth chanted revolutionary slogans and waved their little red books. The rallies were highly orchestrated affairs with participants housed in dormitories or vacant schools, bused in early, and often escorted to the train station in order to ensure their departure (and to make room for the next wave).

Questions

1. **Why would so many young Chinese travel to Beijing to participate in such ceremonies?**
2. **How does the article below suggest Mao (and Mao Zedong Thought) will guide the Cultural Revolution?**

On August 18, at a mass rally to celebrate the Great Proletarian Cultural Revolution, Chairman Mao Zedong, our great leader, great supreme commander, and great helmsman, joined a million revolutionary people from Beijing and other parts of China in the magnificent Tiananmen Square in Beijing, the centre of the proletarian revolution and the capital of our great motherland.

At five o'clock in the morning when the sun had just risen above the eastern horizon and had begun shedding its brilliant rays, Chairman Mao arrived at Tiananmen Square which was covered by a vast sea of people and a forest of red flags. There he met the revolutionary people, who even earlier had converged on the square from all sides. He was dressed in an olive cotton military uniform, and a red star sparkled on his cap. He walked across Jinshui Bridge in front of Tiananmen Gate into the midst of the masses, firmly shook hands with many of them and waved to all the people in the square. The square was seething with excitement. Turning towards Chairman Mao, people raised their hands overhead and jumped up, cheered and clapped. Many clapped till their hands became sore, many shed tears of joy. "Chairman Mao is here!" they exclaimed elatedly. "Chairman Mao has come among us!" And the vast crowd in the square shouted at the top of their voice: "Long live, long live Chairman Mao!" The crescendo of cheers roared up to the sky.

Our great leader Chairman Mao spent more than six hours with the masses that morning. He stood side by side with Comrade Lin Biao on the rostrum on Tiananmen Gate and reviewed the parade of the one-million-strong army of the proletarian Cultural Revolution. Watching the magnificent march-past, he remarked with gratification to Comrade Lin Biao: "This is a movement of a momentous scale. It has indeed aroused the masses. It is of very great significance to the revolutionization of the thinking of the people throughout the country."

Tens of thousands of Red Guards, wearing red armbands and brimming over with high spirit and vigor, caught the eye of all present. The Red Guards are revolutionary mass organizations set up in the Great Proletarian Cultural Revolution by the capital's college and middle school students. Members pledge that they will remain red vanguards defending Chairman Mao, the Chinese Communist Party and their motherland all their lives. Representatives of the Red Guards filled the rostrum on Tiananmen Gate and the reviewing stands on both sides of the gate. Everywhere, on the rostrum, in the square, and on the boulevard running through the square, spirited Red Guards kept order at the rally.

During the rally, a Red Guard from the Girls' Middle School attached to Beijing Normal University mounted the rostrum and put a red arm band of the Red Guards on Chairman Mao. The Chairman warmly shook hands with her. Red Guards on and off the rostrum were beside themselves with joy. Some of them jumped high in the air and cried with great excitement: "Chairman Mao is our supreme commander and we are his little soldiers." Some said: "Chairman Mao joins our Red Guards. This is the greatest support and inspiration to us. With Chairman Mao's backing, we have nothing to fear."

One thousand and five hundred student representatives mounted the rostrum to attend the rally together with Party and government leaders. Chairman Mao and Comrades Lin Biao, Zhou Enlai, Jiang Qing and others received them in groups, talked with them and had pictures taken together with them. When Chairman Mao received them, the students excitedly crowded around him and kept shouting "Long live Chairman Mao!"

The rally began at 7:30 in the morning. As the band played The East Is Red, Chairman Mao appeared on the Tiananmen tower together with Lin Biao and other comrades. The crowd leapt with joy. A great many hands; holding red-covered Quotations from Chairman Mao Zedong, stretched towards the rostrum. A million warm hearts flew out to Chairman Mao and a million pairs of eyes sparkling with revolutionary fervor were turned on him. The crowd became even more excited when they noticed that their respected and beloved leader was wearing a plain cotton uniform. "We feel Chairman Mao is still closer to us in military uniform," they said. "Chairman Mao always fights together with us." Some remarked: "We are wonderfully happy to have such a supreme commander as Chairman Mao. We will always be his good fighters, follow him and make revolution for the rest of our lives."

[. . . .]

12.7   THE ROAD FOR CHINA'S SCHOOL GRADUATES

In the years immediately following Mao's 1966 call for revolution, violence spread throughout the country. Rival factions occupied whole areas of cities and fighting went on for months at a time. In 1969, Mao finally decided to bring the excessive bloodshed to an end. He instructed the country's youth that instead of doing the "teaching," they should go to the countryside and "learn" from the peasants. The so-called "sent-down youth" are an often forgotten chapter of the Cultural Revolution. While Mao succeeded in curtailing the violent excesses of the 1966–1968 period, the harsh living conditions and minimal local resources available to support the newly arrived youths made the transition particularly harsh. The following document is from the magazine *China Reconstructs,* which interviewed Wu Zhangui, a deputy secretary of the municipal Communist Party committee in Zhuzhou, Hunan province. Some youth moved only several hours from their urban homes, while many of the early groups traveled to China's harshest borderlands in the northeast and southwest corners of the country.

Questions

1. **What does Wu Zhangui suggest the youth will acquire from their time in the countryside?**
2. **What do the villages gain?**

Q. Would you discuss the situation with the middle-school graduates who have gone to work and settle in the rural areas and its significance?

A. It is one of the new socialist practices for young people from the city to go and live in the countryside. When in December 1968 during the Cultural Revolution Chairman Mao issued the call, "It is highly necessary for young people with education to go to the countryside to be re-educated by the poor and lower-middle peasants," many young people enthusiastically sent in applications declaring their determination to become peasants of a new type with socialist consciousness and culture.

Since then, in Zhuzhou as in the rest of the country, going to the countryside on graduation has become the thing, a powerful revolutionary tide. So far 10,000 middle school graduates from our area have left the city and settled in the rural areas on the city's outskirts and in surrounding Zhuzhou county.

This is important for producing a new generation which will carry on the revolutionary cause of the proletariat. It provides a force needed to accelerate the building of a new socialist countryside. It has a profound and far-reaching significance in relation to reducing the difference between industry and agriculture, between town and country and between mental and manual labor.

As you know, it took the Chinese people more than a hundred years of struggle until finally, led by the Communist Party and Chairman Mao, they overthrew the reactionary rule of imperialism, feudalism and bureaucrat capitalism. Thus they achieved victory in the new-democratic revolution and ushered in the new historical period of social-ist revolution and the dictatorship of the proletariat. An even more arduous task is to consolidate this new political power and see that socialist China advances according to a Marxist-Leninist line with-out deviating into revisionism and backsliding into capitalism, in other words to achieve communism in the end. It requires a protracted struggle over many generations.

Revolutionaries cannot grow up in a hothouse. They must take part in revolutionary struggle. They must go to places where they face hardships to be tempered and to gain experience. The countryside is such a place. In the countryside, where the great majority of our population live, young people will find plenty of opportunity to educate themselves in the three great revolutionary movements: class struggle, the struggle for production and scientific experimentation.

There their "teachers" are the poor and lower-mid-dle peasants, the most reliable allies of the working class. They have deep hatred for the old society and strong feeling for the new, for socialism, for the collective and for labor. They have a tradition of hard struggle and plain living, and a lot of revolutionary experience. The young people need contact with all of these.

Agriculture is the foundation of our national economy but our agricultural production is still not high. Young people with socialist consciousness and cultural and scientific knowledge are needed in large numbers to help change the situation. Seventy percent of the rural areas in Zhuzhou county and the city's outskirts are hilly. Water takes up another 10 percent of the areas, leaving only 20 percent for farmland. If we are to follow the example of Dazhai, the model agri-cultural brigade in Shanxi province, we must make 130,000 hectares of our barren hills productive. Since 1964 the Zhuzhou municipal Party committee has led the communes in transforming the denuded hills through orchards, tea plantations and afforestation. The young people have done well at this work.

[....]

Q. What role are the young people playing in the countryside? What change have they undergone personally?

A. The young people have become a fresh, vigorous, militant army for socialist construction in the coun-tryside. Enthusiastic propagandists for Mao Zedong Thought, they have become disseminators of new ideas, new culture, new customs and new habits.

During the movement to criticize Lin Biao and Confucius, many of the young people have joined the poor and lower-middle peasants' political theory study groups. From a Marxist-Leninist viewpoint they criticize Lin Biao's utilization of the doctrines of Con-fucius and Mencius and condemn his criminal plot to restore capitalism in China. Some of the young peo-ple have become instructors in the evening political schools.

With the commune members they are reclaiming barren hills. Over the past two years areas where the young people are located have planted 8,000 hectares of hills to fruit trees and Chinese firs and done the work of tending more than 20,000 hectares of young forests. They have scientific experimentation groups in which they study the best methods of caring for young sassafras bushes, cultivating the firs and graft-ing orange and tangerine trees, as well as of soil improvement and prevention of insect pests. Some notable results have already been achieved. Jian Xinwu, a city school graduate now at the Chunfeng commune's forest farm, spent six months in intensive study of the habits of termites and ways of eliminating them and came up with material which will be of value to the entire area.

Through the centuries in China there has been a tendency to look down on agriculture and the tillers of the soil. Always the thing was to study, go to the city, become an official. It was thought there was no future for people with education to go back to the farm. Today China's school graduates, being tempered in the countryside, are experiencing a pro-found change in their thinking and feeling. With a firmer proletarian class stand, they are developing a genuine love for physical labor and the working people. They have high revolutionary ideals which now include the aim of devoting their whole lives to building up the new socialist countryside. Many of the young people have been elected to leading groups of their communes or brigades. Some have become teachers, barefoot doctors or tractor drivers in the communes. A younger generation of an entirely new type is vigorously growing up in China's vast countryside.

12.8 REVOLUTIONARY MASSES OF VARIOUS NATIONALITIES IN LHASA THOROUGHLY SMASH THE "FOUR OLDS" (1966)

In the 1950s, the CCP was optimistic about the government's ability to encourage non-Han ethnic minorities to pursue the same political goals as the majority population, but how to treat them until they reached this decision (often referred to as the "nationalities question") was highly contentious. There were differing opinions among the top leadership over how to rule the autonomous regions of Tibet and Xinjiang where ethnically non-Han citizens vastly outnumbered Han Chinese. Some advocated allowing concessions for local customs and religious practices. Others espoused immediate and total assimilation. With the beginning of the Cultural Revolution such a division disappeared. With pro-assimilation, ideological zealotry became commonplace, often for the first time, in places like Lhasa. The following article appeared in the *Workers Daily* in 1966 and reveals how quickly the Cultural Revolution and its excessive politics spread even to China's most distant regions.

Questions

1. **What aspects of Lhasa are immediately altered at the beginning of the Cultural Revolution? What rationale is given for such changes?**
2. **Why might the concerns of the Chinese government of removing "feudal serfdom" for a "revolutionary society" have been unattractive to some Tibetans?**

Filled with revolutionary sentiments and united, the Red Guards and revolutionary residents of various nationalities in Lhasa are making revolution today in the ancient city of Lhasa. As they removed the old names of streets, places and work units, left from feudal serfdom, they put on revolutionary new ones.

The whole city of Lhasa is permeated in a vibrant revolutionary atmosphere. The Red Guards and revolutionary masses of the Tibet, Hui and other nationalities walked to streets with a strong hatred of feudal serfdom, capitalism and revisionism. Acting on the suggestion of the little Red Guard generals, the broad masses of poor residents living in the confine of the Barkhor Street Residents Committee violently complained against the reactionary serf owners who lived in that district before and against "Langzixia" (the former reactionary Lhasa Municipal Government) for the crimes they committed and against the reactionary elements who continued perpetuate the criminal acts of injuring and exploiting the masses even after the democratic reforms were instituted. The Red Guards and masses submitted written proposals, wrote wall posters and sent happy tidings to the Tibet Autonomous Regional Party Committee and Lhasa Municipal People's Council . They requested the name of "Barkhor Street" be changed into that of "Lixin Main Street." They said that the Barkhor Street was a place for "Zhuanjing [pilgrimage]" (a kind of superstitious

activity) where the laboring people got separated and became homeless vagrants. They declared that they were determined to break with the old world and build a new world, creating the new by smashing the old. The Barkhor Street residents' requests were warmly praised by the Party and Government and enthusiastically supported by the urban residents, revolutionary students, the broad masses of workers, peasants and soldiers and the revolutionary workers and employees. Today, the residents broke the old name plate into pieces and put up a new one bearing the name of "Lixin Main Street."

The Red Guards and revolutionary masses who gathered in the new urban district of Lhasa also changed the name of Menzikang (Medical Accounting Bureau or Lhasa Municipal Tibetan Hospital) into "Labor People's Hospital"; Yaowang (Chakpori) Shan, a key point for the armed rebellion staged by the former Tibetan local government, into "Victory Peak" in commemoration of the quelling of the rebellion; Luobu Linka [Norbulinka], the Dalai's nest of political rule, economic exploitation and religious benumbing for over 200 years, into "People's Park." The revolutionary masses rejoiced in great jubilation when the new name plates in both Tibetan and Han language were placed and the new name tablet went up on the Victory Peak. They said that the liberated serfs' expectations have finally come into reality.

To celebrate this victory of the Great Proletarian Cultural Revolution, the Red Guards and the revolutionary masses of the city residents held a grand garden party in the People's Park this afternoon with a repertoire full of unrestrained revolutionary vigor.

MUSIC, OPERA AND PLAYS – CREATING A CULTURE BEFITTING A REVOLUTION

From the beginning of the communist movement in China, music played a central role in the attempts to attract and retain support among the Chinese. In 1942 Mao's *Forum on Literature and Art* dictated that there were only two categories of literature and art: capitalist or proletarian. As **Jiang Qing** provocatively, if not very imaginatively, asked a group of musicians below (12.9): "Which class do you support?" From the 1950s onward, Mao sought to integrate "realism and romanticism" in order to portray accurately the life of the peasants in their fields, the workers in their factories and the soldiers protecting the nation. For Mao, romanticism meant praise of the proletarian socialism of China (visible in the song lyrics collected in 12.11). Many of China's songs also sought to retell the glorious history of China's revolution, and the difficulties that the Chinese people and Chinese Communist Party had overcome to create the People's Republic of China (12.10). During the Cultural Revolution, China's theaters and stages, as well as amateur productions, were dominated by the "Eight Model Works" (*Yangbanxi*) and other appropriately revolutionary plays, operas or movies.

12.9   JIANG QING'S SPEECH ON THE REVOLUTION IN BEIJING OPERA (JULY 1964)

Born Li Yunhe in 1914, Jiang Qing had an undistinguished career as an actress (under the name of Lan Ping) in Shanghai's fledgling film industry. More famous for her tempestuous relationships than her politics, she left Shanghai before the Japanese attacked the city and made the hazardous trip to Yan'an where she became romantically involved with Mao Zedong. Mao, who was still married to his third wife, He Zizhen, sought a divorce despite stiff resistance from the CCP elite. It is commonly said that the party leaders granted Mao his wish on the grounds that Jiang Qing was to have no political powers or appointments. For the most part, Jiang Qing remained in the background through the 1950s, accepting only an honorary appointment to the Ministry of Culture. In 1964 she was elected as a representative to the People's Congress—a position without any tangible power. The following document is a speech she delivered in 1964 which was not published until May 10, 1967. In the intervening period, Jiang Qing became progressively more powerful—personally supervising the creation and revision of model revolutionary operas and more generally becoming the creative umpire of all things artistic or literary.

Questions

1. Why does Jiang Qing suggest that Chinese should create more art and literature for the proletariat?
2. What does Jiang Qing mean when she suggests "Theatres are places in which to educate the people, but now the stage is dominated by emperors and kings, generals and ministers, scholars and beauties?"

JIANG QING (1914–1991)—Wife of Mao Zedong who advocated a radical line of political thought during the Cultural Revolution. After Mao's death she and her allies, the Gang of Four, were arrested, tried, and in 1981 found guilty. Her death sentence was commuted to life in prison, where she committed suicide in 1991.

[...] We must have unshakable confidence in the staging of Beijing Operas on revolutionary contemporary themes. It is inconceivable that, in our socialist country led by the Chinese Communist Party, the dominant position on the stage is not occupied by the workers, peasants and soldiers, who are the real creators of history and true masters of our country. We must create literature and art which protect our socialist economic base. When we are not clear about our orientation, we must try our best to find the right orientation. Here I would like to give two groups of figures for your reference. These figures strike me as shocking.

Here is the first group: according to a rough estimate, there are 3,000 theatrical troupes in the country (not including amateur troupes and unlicensed companies). Of these, around 90 are professional modern drama companies, 80-odd are cultural troupes, and the rest, over 2,800, are companies staging various kinds of operas. Our operatic stage is occupied by emperors and kings, generals and ministers, scholars and beauties, and on top of these, ghosts and monsters! As for those 90 modern drama companies, they don't necessarily all depict the workers, peasants and soldiers either. They, too, lay stress on staging full-length plays, foreign plays and plays on ancient themes. Therefore we can say that the modern drama stage is also occupied by ancient Chinese and foreign figures. Theatres are places in which to educate the people, but now the stage is dominated by emperors and kings, generals and ministers, scholars and beauties—by feudal and bourgeois stuff. This state of affairs cannot serve to protect our economic base but will undermine it.

Here is the second group of figures: there are well over 600 million workers, peasants, and soldiers in our country, whereas there is only a handful of landlords, rich peasants, counter-revolutionaries, bad elements, Rightists and bourgeois elements. Are we to serve this handful, or the well over 600 million? This question calls for consideration not only by Communists, but also by all those literary and art workers who are patriotic. The grain we eat is grown by the peasants, the clothes we wear and houses we live in are made by the workers, and the People's Liberation Army stands guard at the fronts of national defense for us and yet we do not portray them. May I ask which class stand you artists take? And where is the artists' "conscience" you always talk about? [...]

12.10 SONGS PLAY THEIR PART IN REVOLUTION (JUNE 1965)

When the concept of a Chinese nation, of differing political ideologies, and patriotism were still new in China, songs played an instrumental role in educating and familiarizing the Chinese people to these ideas. Ma Ke's article, written for **China Reconstructs** in 1965, offers a useful survey of songs from the three decades leading up to the Cultural Revolution. Read carefully, this document also shows the themes and attitudes of the era in which the article was written. In particular, it suggests that all of Chinese music is subservient to the political criteria of the CCP. In reality, as Ma Ke correctly points out, much of the music was purloined from popular folk songs, melodies, or operas and merely given a "revolutionary" veneer.

Questions

1. How do songs accurately reflect the phases of China's political campaigns?
2. In his conclusion, Ma Ke suggests that the songs have a style that is "unmistakably of the people?" Do you agree? How would you describe that style?

CHINA RECONSTRUCTS—A magazine established by Song Qingling in 1952, published in five languages and intended to offer positive articles about the People's Republic of China for a foreign audience.

INTRODUCTION

Singing revolutionary songs is a part of the Chinese people's cultural life. In factories and on farms, in army camps, schools and offices, millions of people have formed choruses. Besides practicing in their spare time and giving performances on holidays and at weekends, many of them also join in singing contests, sometimes on a county or city basis. The songs are about the people's life and struggles during different historical periods. Whether spirited or lyrical, they express the people's healthy, optimistic outlook on life and their fighting will to carry on the revolution from generation to generation.

MILITANT THEMES AND MUSIC

Beginning with the two pioneers of China's revolutionary music, Nie Er (1912–1935) and Xian Xinghai (1905–1945), a tradition of composing music to serve the revolution and the workers, peasants and soldiers has been built up by many fine song writers.

From 1931 when Japanese imperialists seize control of China's northeast to the outbreak of the anti-Japanese war in 1937, the Guomindang government followed a two-faced policy of passive resistance to imperialist aggression and active anti-communism, a policy that plunged our country into a state of national crisis. At this time, Nie Er's "March of the Volunteers" resounded like a bugle call throughout the land, summoning the nation to arms with its immortal words, "Arise, all you who refuse to be bond slaves!" This and many other revolutionary songs roused the people to translate their anger against Japanese aggression into action. Still other songs, mirroring the miserable plight of the people, gave them strength and urged them to revolt. This is represented, for example, by Xian Xinghai's "Ploughing Song":

Hei yo__ la yo! Hei yo__ la yo! Hei__ yo_____ la__ yo!

SONGS OF RESISTANCE

During the War of Resistance Against Japanese Aggression (1937–45), many musicians joined the struggle for national liberation. Fighting side by side with the workers, peasants and soldiers, they wrote hundreds of songs which helped to unite the people and inspire them to carry on the struggle.

Middle-aged people today can still remember how Xian Xinghai's famous "Yellow River Cantata" aroused the nation in the war. Its music and words epitomized the Chinese people's invincible spirit. Thousands of young men and women, fired by the power of such songs, took their places in the revolutionary ranks. I was one of them.

The most representative songs of this period, and the greatest in number, are those with militant tunes. Mai Xin's "March of the Broadswords" was typical of the flaming enthusiasm in the early days of the war, its music pouring forth like the roaring torrent of a turbulent river:

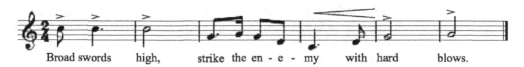

Broad swords high, strike the en - e - my with hard blows.

During the following period of protracted war, when the revolutionary forces had increased their strength, the tunes were characterized by firm steady rhythms and spirited melodies like "Song of the Guerrillas" by He Luding:

First-rate ri - fle-men are we. With ev' ry bul - let we will down an en - e - my. We are

fleet-winged men at__ arms; We fear not moun-tains or ri - vers deep.

The Chinese Communist Party's policy of resistance was a sharp contrast to the Guomindang's capitulationism. Music showing confident hope appeared during these times when the people saw clearly that their future lay with Yan'an, center of the anti-Japanese movement. Their love and respect for the Chinese Communist Party and the heroic **Eighth Route Army** produced songs like "The East is Red," [see 12.14 (#2)] adapted from a northern Shaanxi folk song, and "In Praise of Yan'an" by Zheng Lücheng.

THE WAR OF LIBERATION

Militant tunes remained in the ascendant during the War of Liberation (1945–1949) when the people's armed forces, having defeated the Japanese invaders and grown stronger than ever before, set out to liberate the country from the rule of the U.S. imperialism and Guomindang reaction. The songs pulsated with strength and optimism, as in "March of the Chinese People's Liberation Army," which gives a true reflection of the people's firm belief that they will smash the forces of reaction and liberate themselves.

In the Guomindang areas where the reactionary nature of the Guomindang and the aggressive designs of U.S. imperialism became more and more evident satirical songs were popular. Li Jiefu's "The Jiang Bandits are in a Real Mess" burned with contempt and hatred:

ALONG THE SOCIALIST ROAD

In the 15 years since the founding of the new China, many musicians have gone to factories and mines, to the countryside and to the armed forces. There they live and toil with the working people and express the latter's thoughts and feelings in new songs. The songs they write cover a wide range of themes – in praise of socialism, of the three red banners of the General Line for Socialist Construction, the Big Leap Forward and the People's Communes, of collective and communist spirit, and of the Asian, African and Latin American people's heroic struggles against imperialism.

The music of this period has a free and sweeping spirit and through it shines the resolution of a people who are marching along the socialist road. There are such inspiring works as Meng Bo's "Raise High the Revolutionary Banner," expressing the people's determination to carry the revolution through the end, and Qu Xixian's "Working Men of All Lands, Unite!" voicing confidence in the final victory of the worldwide anti-imperialist struggle:

Often the resolution in the music is blended with the overwhelming joyousness of people who are masters of their own destiny. The brisk and lively tunes of Li Huanzhi's "Socialism is Good" and of Jian Er's "Compare, Learn, Catch Up and Help" which reflects communist-style emulation among workers are two good examples. Lyrical songs have also grown greater in number. The beautiful melody of "The Never-setting Sun Shines Over the Grassland," by Milchik, conjures up visions of the vast pasturelands of Inner Mongolia and of the new life of herdsmen there.

EIGHTH ROUTE ARMY—The main military force of the CCP commanded by Zhu De and nominally a part of the GMD-controlled National Revolutionary Army during the War of Resistance Against Japan.

White clouds cross the sky so blue, Hor-ses gal-lop fast and free.

Wang Yuxi's "The Commune Members are Sunflowers" bring out very well the peasants' love for the commune in a tune both light and gay.

These songs, conveying the soaring enthusiasm of the Chinese people for their socialist construction and revolution, are heard everywhere and at all times—on the street, in the clubrooms, during rest breaks and in the evenings. They inspire both singers and listeners to move forward to new victories.

NATIONAL STYLE

Revolutionary songs have their own national style that is unmistakably of the people. This has been formed through three decades of history during which composers searched for ways to express the revolutionary will and sentiments of the workers, peasants and soldiers.

The national style of the songs can be seen from both their melodies and their forms. Composers sometimes borrow traditional tunes from one or the other of China's many nationalities to give their music definite local or national color. Sometimes their works have no direct relation to existing tunes but one can easily recognize the Chinese character of the new melodies.

Composers consciously study traditional forms. Besides folk songs, work chants are used, sometimes as a theme, sometimes as a refrain. This form is successfully adapted in "Happiness River Cantata," written by four young Shanghai composers in praise of the collective strength that built the great irrigation network on the northern Jiangsu plain. The work chants infuse the music with the spirit that "man, not heaven, determines." Still another form is the music for particular styles of storytelling. This is used to achieve dramatic effects in songs recounting deeds of heroes and model workers.

Adaptation of the singing-dancing form so popular among the Chinese people has led to its further development, particularly to express jubilance and to call up vivid images. Li Jiefu and two other composers have successfully adapted the northeastern folk song-dance form into their choral work, "Victory Flowers Bloom Everywhere."

Our musicians are also experimenting with local operatic forms. China has over 400 styles of local opera which are now beginning to be studied and which will make our revolutionary songs even more expressive and colorful.

12.11   REVOLUTIONARY SONG LYRICS

1. National Salvation March (1936)

Xian Xinghai (1905–45) was an early supporter of the CCP and wrote numerous patriotic songs, including the "National Salvation Song" and "Children of the Homeland" (*Zuguo de haizimen*). His most famous work is the prodigious "Yellow River Cantata" (*Huanghe dahechang*) that, like the following song, sought to create a national narrative, a retelling of China's past through music. Like many of the early musicians from this era (including Nie Er, the composer of the national anthem), Xian Xinghai died young and became a patriotic martyr in the PRC.

Fire at the foe,
Onward march!
Do not harm nor fight,
Your own people!
Our ranks are solid as steel,
Our hearts are iron strong!
Protect the motherland.
Be free, evermore.
Fire at the foe,

Onward march!
Protect the motherland,
Be free, evermore!

Take up your guns,
Aim at the foe!
Each shot hits the mark.
Step by step we gain!
Our ranks are solid as steel.
Our hearts are iron strong!

Protect the motherland.
Be free, evermore.
Take up your guns,

Aim at the foe!
Protect the motherland,
Be free, evermore!

2. East is Red (*Dongfang Hong*)

"The East is Red" is perhaps the best-known revolutionary song in China. Even today, most Chinese can sing this song from memory (not surprising since a good portion of them woke to the song blaring from loud speakers every morning for a decade or more). The song, originally written in 1943 by a peasant farmer in Shaanxi, was reworked in 1964 into a revolutionary play known by the same name, "The East is Red" (*Dongfang Hong*).

The East is red, the sun has risen,
China has brought forth a Mao Zedong.
He works for the people's happiness,
Hu er hai yo, he's the people's great liberator!

Chairman Mao loves the people,
He is our guiding leader,

To build a New China,
Hu er hai yo, he leads us; march on!

The Communist Party is like the sun,
It brightens whatever it shines upon.
Wherever the Communist Party goes
Hu er hai yo, there the people will be liberated.

3. Commune Members are Sunflowers

The Cultural Revolution marked a low point in twentieth-century China's music scene. Several ideologically correct model operas and revolutionary appropriate songs dominated the period. Political leaders demanded that songs be subservient to the political campaigns and narrowly serve the same goals as the ideological campaigns. A prime example of this is the following song, stiffly comparing communes to ripening fruit.

The commune is an ever-growing vine. All its
    members
are the fruit upon the vine. Ripening fruit and vine,
growing there together. Our commune and its
    members,
they all grow together. When the vine is strong,
all the fruit is large and sweet.

The green vine of people's communes joins our
    homes. All our families
work together growing commune crops. More hands
    mean good yields;
unity is strength. When together, we do not fear
either drought or raging flood. When we are as one,
we can hold up the sky.

The commune is a red sun, a big red sun. All the
    members
of the commune are the sun flowers. Flowers face
    the sun,
big as any millstone. Rain or shine or wind or storm,
nothing makes us waver. Never will we leave,
never leave the good commune.

Sunshine of the people's commune lights our homes.
    All the families
join together setting higher aims. We all love our
    commune;
following the Party. Ours is daily happiness,
full as swelling grain. Ours is daily joy,
full as swelling harvest grain.

CHAPTER 13
CHINA REEMERGES (POLITICAL TRENDS IN 1970s)

VISUAL SOURCE
Following Mao: Mao's Funeral and Political Cartoons of the Gang of Four

ANOUNCING MAO'S DEATH: Mao died at just past midnight on September 9, 1976. The Central People's Broadcasting network did not make the public announcement until 4 p.m. that afternoon. Even though his death was expected, many Chinese broke into tears (of grief, relief, or simply because Chinese believed that was what was expected of them). Very quickly, people's mind, turned to what direction the country was headed now that the "Great Helmsman," the only paramount leader China had known, was gone.

PRESERVING MAO ZEDONG: Mao's death caused considerable consternation among the doctors who had been assembled to preserve his body. Although Mao Zedong indicated he wanted to be cremated it was decided to preserve his body in order to place it permanently on display. With little information on how to preserve a body, the doctors assigned to the task injected so much formaldehyde that it oozed from his pores and made Mao's neck as wide as his head. Terrified, the team quickly squeezed out the excess liquid with towels and cotton balls.

MAO'S FUNERAL: At 3 p.m. on September 18, 1976, after a ten-day period of mourning, the entire nation was ordered to observe a three minute period of silence. A million people gathered at his funeral in Tiananmen Square. In 1977, his mausoleum was completed where his embalmed body was placed and can still be visited by the public.

ANTI-POETRY MEETING OF THE "GANG OF FOUR"
(Translation clockwise from upper left corner):
Jiang Qing: "By the river is a blue peak,"
Zhang Chunqiao: "A new 'queen' to replace the old.
(on his fan: Revisionism; on the scroll: Anti-experiencism is the
key) Wang Hongwen: Who says there's no 'fish' to catch"
(on his fish: Make a list of who should be given cabinet posts)
Yao Wenyuan: Establish a long-lasting new dynasty.
(on his hand: Follow the established policy [of Mao Zedong.)

GANG OF FOUR: The Gang of Four was a radical political clique
led by Jiang Qing (wife of Mao Zedong) which in the wake of
Mao's death, attempted to wrest power away from the
moderates like Deng Xiaoping but failed. On October 6, 1976
Mao's designated successor, Hua Guofeng, had the Gang of
Four arrested and launched a massive media barrage against
them, labeling them the "Gang of Four" and blaming the
excesses of the Cultural Revolution on them. Five years later in
1980, a massive (and televised) show trial found them all guilty
anti-party activities.

SATIRIZING THE GANG OF FOUR: A Chinese viewing this
cartoon would have found humor on multiple levels. The first is
that Jiang Qing's words are the first line from a poem she wrote
in 1974 and thus the "anti-poetry" title pokes fun at the
hypocrisy in the Gang of Four's words (they are anti-poetry but
are composing a poem). The second level lies with the deliberate
irony between their "revolutionary" ideals and their constant
pursuit of "feudalistic" power.

While the Cultural Revolution is often dated from 1966 to Mao Zedong's death in 1976, the latter years of the period were characterized more by ideological uncertainty than by the radical violence associated with the early years of 1966–1969. Although the Chinese may have taken some comfort in the reduction of violence and radical politics in the early 1970s, several events caused many to rethink the political assumptions they had built up over the three previous decades.

Since the founding of the PRC in 1949, Mao had appointed and dismissed several of the men who had been carefully selected to succeed him. In 1959, Liu Shaoqi replaced Mao's first heir apparent, Minister of Defense Peng Dehuai. Liu Shaoqi was in turn purged and replaced by Lin Biao. Lin Biao, who had carefully and, some would say, with great calculation promoted the Cult of Mao, was officially designated as Mao's successor in 1969. It was with some bewilderment that the Chinese people abruptly learned of his death on September 13, 1971 in a plane accident over Mongolia. According to the state media, Lin Biao and his associates were accused of plotting to assassinate Mao by blowing up his train, then flying north in a plane piloted by his son, an air force officer, hoping for asylum in the Soviet Union. Before they could reach Soviet airspace, Lin Biao's daughter was said to have exposed their conspiracy to Zhou Enlai who successfully scrambled jet fighters to intercept and shoot the plane down.

In the international arena, Mao Zedong's state of mind seemed equally volatile. China's relationship with the Soviet Union had waxed and waned over the years, but the role of the United States as China's arch-enemy had gone unchanged for decades. All that changed on July 16, 1971 (the time difference made this July 15th in the United States), when the United States and China simultaneously announced that President Nixon would visit China the following spring to seek normalization of relations between the two nations. The Chinese media made far less of this announcement than their American counterparts. The following February President Nixon flew to Beijing where he met with Mao Zedong and Zhou Enlai. The two countries signed a joint communiqué in which the United States agreed "there is but one China and that Taiwan is a part of China." With Nixon's visit, both Americans and Chinese began to view their relationship in a new light. If there was concern among the average Chinese citizen, it was over the aging of China's leadership, most of whom had been more or less in place since the 1930s. As China held its New Year celebrations in 1976, Mao Zedong was 83, Zhou Enlai 78, and Zhu De almost 90.

Of the three, Zhou Enlai, after a long battle with cancer, was the first to, in Mao's famous characterization, "go meet Marx." The level of public grief over Zhou Enlai's death caught the government unprepared. Mao and Zhou had never been close friends, and Mao allowed Jiang Qing and others to stifle the people's mourning for the former premier. This suppression had the added benefit of hampering Deng Xiaoping (Zhou's protégé) from becoming his replacement. Such repressive actions, however, were at variance with the country's mood.

A common sentiment among most Chinese was that Zhou Enlai alone had sought to moderate Mao's excesses. Many Chinese erected a small memorial in their homes with Zhou's portrait draped in black. Few top officials realized the full extent of the public's desire and their need publicly to mourn Zhou's death. The tension this created burst to the surface on April 5th during the traditional day of mourning the dead known as "**Tomb Sweeping Day.**" Seeking to honor Zhou Enlai's memory, hundreds of thousands

QINGMING FESTIVAL (TOMB SWEEPING DAY)—The 15th day after the Spring Equinox, Qingming is a traditional Chinese holiday when families pray at the tombs or graves of their deceased relatives. It is believed that one should offer food and often liquor to the spirits on this day or they will become "hungry ghosts" and disrupt the living.

of people gathered spontaneously at the Memorial to Revolutionary Heroes in Tiananmen Square. There they deposited funeral wreaths, flowers, and poems in a mass display of grief for one of the nation's most beloved leaders. As the crowds grew, the government became uneasy. Police and soldiers were called out to disperse the crowds. In a rare display of spontaneous resistance, the crowd resisted the attempts to deprive them of what they believed was one of their last inviolable rights, the right to grieve openly. Additional troops were summoned and beatings and mass arrests followed. Ultimately the square was cleared of all people and all items left in Zhou's memory. Officially, the public demonstrations were blamed on Deng Xiaoping's emotional eulogy at Zhou Enlai's memorial service, and Deng was dismissed from his posts.

Several months later, just as the country seemed to be returning to its normal routine, the brilliant military strategist of the Chinese Civil War, Zhu De died. Though viewed with respect, Zhu De had long been outside of the corridors of power, hence his funeral did not produce much public response. His death however, in conjunction with growing concern about Mao Zedong's ill health, did cause many Chinese to wonder more openly about the future of China.

Throughout the country Chinese spoke in whispers to relatives, close colleagues, and friends about the "Mandate of Heaven." The Mandate had for millennia been given and then taken back by "Heaven" if a dynasty lost its ethical moorings. Many felt this was precisely the case. Rumors circulated of Communist cadres using their positions to procure scarce goods, to promote their friends and relatives, or even to demand sexual favors in exchange for promotions. All that was missing was a clear sign from Heaven of its displeasure. When in the early morning hours of July 28, 1976 a massive earthquake struck Tangshan several hundred miles southeast of Beijing, it appeared that Heaven had spoken.

The Tangshan earthquake was catastrophic. Official government figures put the number of deaths at just under 250,000, while more recent scholarship suggests the toll was well over a half million people. Either figure makes it the deadliest earthquake of the twentieth century. The entire city of Tangshan was leveled. Roads and railroad tracks leading in and out of the city were impassable. While the state media put a positive spin on the heroic work of rescue and aid workers, most Chinese interpreted the earthquake as an unmistakable sign of Heaven's rage with the Communist regime. A change was needed. Thus, with little surprise but considerable grief, the Chinese public greeted the announcement on September 9 of Mao Zedong's death. As the entire country participated in the state-orchestrated grieving for and burial of Mao Zedong, the underlying question on the mind of most Chinese was who would succeed Mao.

The official announcement, declaring that **Hua Guofeng** had succeeded Mao, appeared to many as a compromise. The choice, undoubtedly preordained by Mao, sought to deny power to both Deng Xiaoping, whom Mao considered a reformist, and the **Gang of Four,** who were considered unstable radicals. Hua Guofeng realized that to remain above these two factions meant that he would have no backing. He accordingly moved quickly to arrest Jiang Qing and the Gang of Four. This move dovetailed with his decision to bring about a necessary and formal closure of the Cultural Revolution, which was officially declared at an end in August of 1977. Without the Gang of Four, the field

HUA GUOFENG (1921–2008) — Chosen by Mao Zedong to replace Zhou Enlai as Premier in 1976, he succeeded Mao Zedong upon his death several months later. He moved quickly to arrest the Gang of Four and end the Cultural Revolution, but was soon eased out of power by Deng Xiaoping. Hua Guofeng was not purged by Deng, setting a new precedent, and retained his party membership until his death nearly two decades later.

GANG OF FOUR — A term coined by Mao Zedong, it referred to top Chinese leaders lead by Mao's wife Jiang Qing as well as Wang Hongwen, Zhang Chunqiao, and Yao Wenyuan, who were accused of being responsible for the Cultural Revolution's worst excesses and were put on trial in 1980. All four were found guilty.

was left open to the more reform-minded officials aligned behind Deng Xiaoping. It was through his astute backroom maneuvering and the broad support for his program of modernization that resulted in ultimately Deng, and not Hua Guofeng, becoming the true inheritor of Mao's legacy and power.

SHIFTING ALLIANCES: THE TWO CHINAS AND THE UNITED STATES

The fiction of a Republic of China government on Taiwan as the government of all China remained a key feature of the ROC's international presence. In 1971, the PRC finally mustered the votes it needed to unseat the Republic of China (Taiwan) in the United Nations (13.1). Jiang Jieshi's response reveals much of the personal bitterness and his unremitting hope that the Republic of China would remain a prominent international player (13.2). This marked the beginning of the diplomatic erosion of the Republic of China's international presence and foreshadowed President Richard Nixon's trip to Beijing in 1972 which culminated in the Shanghai Communiqué (13.3).

13.1 RESOLUTION ON THE RESTORATION OF THE LAWFUL RIGHTS OF THE PEOPLE'S REPUBLIC OF CHINA IN THE UNITED NATIONS (OCTOBER 25, 1971)

After the founding of the PRC in 1949, many countries, Great Britian and France among them, when forced to choose between the PRC and ROC (Taiwan), recognized the PRC. At this time the United States was heavily involved in Vietnam and thus reliant on Taiwan as a strategic base of military action. Convinced that the United States could not afford to turn its back on its old ally, Jiang Jieshi, they refused offers to recognize two Chinas. He did not want the same status of other divided countries such as North and South Korea, and East and West Germany. But by 1971 it was clear to many observers that the United States and Taiwan were fighting a losing battle against international opinion. There had been almost annual votes to pass the China seat in the UN to the PRC. Up until just hours before the actual vote, most thought that the ROC would again retain the votes to keep their seat in the United Nations. At the last moment several countries swung their votes to the PRC and the final count was 59 to 54 in favor of the following resolution.

Questions

1. Why would the United States seek to keep China's UN seat in the hands of the ROC while pursuing the normalization of relations with the PRC?
2. Why was the ROC's loss of the UN seat so critical to the ROC?

The General Assembly,

Recalling the principles of the Charter of the United Nations,

Considering that the restoration of the lawful rights of the People's Republic of China is essential both for the protection of the Charter of the United Nations and for the cause that the United Nations must serve under the Charter.

Recognizing that the representatives of the Government of the People's Republic of China are the only lawful representatives of China to the United Nations and that the People's Republic of

China is one of the five permanent members of the Security Council,

Decides to restore all its rights to the People's Republic of China and to recognize the representatives of its Government as the only legitimate representatives of China to the United Nations, and to expel forthwith the representatives of Jiang Jieshi from the place which they unlawfully occupy at the United Nations and in all the organizations related to it.

1976th plenary meeting,

25 October 1971.

13.2 JIANG JIESHI DECLARATION TO COMPATRIOTS REGARDING THE REPUBLIC OF CHINA'S WITHDRAWAL FROM THE UNITED NATIONS (OCTOBER 26, 1971)

Immediately after the UN vote against Taiwan, Jiang Jieshi issued an acrimonious declaration. Already 84 years old, Jiang Jieshi had grown increasingly isolated and inattentive to shifting global politics. His Cold War mindset and outdated, repressive style of government seemed less and less attractive to observers both inside and outside of Taiwan. Following the UN vote, the countries slowly began to switch their diplomatic recognition from the ROC to the PRC. The question of just what status Taiwan (ROC) holds—sovereign or independent, but with no formal recognition of either—remains one of the biggest unresolved diplomatic questions of Asia.

Questions

1. How does Jiang Jieshi suggest the ROC government is the more legitimate representative of the "700 million China on the mainland?"
2. How does Jiang Jieshi suggest the UN vote will affect the global situation?

Dear compatriots in and outside the country:

The 26th session of the General Assembly of the United Nations violated its Charters and Regulations, and voted for a proposition brought by Albania and other bandit-affiliated countries who led Mao's communist bandits to steal the Republic of China's position in United Nations and its seat on the UN Security Council. To retain our policy to maintain the separation between honorable and the thieves and to protect the dignity of the Charter, we announced our withdrawal from the United Nations that we helped to found, prior to the vote being put forward. At the same time, we declared the Government of the Republic of China and all Chinese people would not acknowledge the validity of the illegal decision passed by this General Assembly which violated its Charter and Regulations.

Mao's communist bandits are a rebellious regime within the Republic of China. Domestically, they have harmed and committed enormous crimes against the people. They are the common enemy of all Chinese people, especially the 700 million people on the mainland. Internationally, they are actively involved in sabotage and engaged in invasions that have been condemned by the United Nations as unlawful invaders. Now despite that the mainland is occupied by the Mao-Communist-bandits, the Government of Republic of China, based in Taiwan, Penghu, Jinmen and Mazu, is the true representative of the 700 million Chinese on the mainland—representing their common will and painful cries and offering them with the most courage and hope in their fight against violent force of Mao's communist bandits to obtain human rights and freedom. Therefore, based on either the principles of United Nations' Charter or on the natural laws of humanism, especially on the common will of all Chinese people, we absolutely will not tolerate Mao's communist bandits' unlawful occupancy of the seat held by the Republic of China in the United Nations and the Security Council.

[....]

For twenty years, the [Communist] bandits have continuously fought for control of China. Recently the fight has become more fierce demonstrating that both the ideology of the Mao bandits and the Communist system are totally bankrupted. People on the mainland, including the majority of the Communist cadres, have turned from disappointment to resistance. As Mao's communist bandits could not suppress the volcano [of popular discontent] that erupted underneath their feet they had no choice but to turn their strategy outwards and hope that through deception they could survive a bit longer. In fact Mao's communist bandits are unable to make any changes to their objectives of "anti-revisionism" "anti-American Imperialism" and "anti all counter-revolutionists." Therefore, their international strategic change will cause them loosing stand either moving forward or backward in ideological and policy front, which will result more severe dispute and chaos in power struggle. Henceforth, the anti-Communism and anti-violence forces on the mainland may take this opportunity to speed up and become stronger. Facing such a change of situation, we must further reinforce our faith, consolidate our strength and intensify our military preparedness so that we shall lose no time in grasping the moment of opportunity, to speed up the spreading of revolutionary forces in struggle against Mao and Communism on the mainland.

Compatriots! The process of the Anti-Communism movement is just like moving ships forward in an unpredictable ocean with changing winds and clouds. We all share common understanding on the basic situation towards anti-Communism, are not misguided by the temporary changes, and stay towards the right direction. We must remain closely united, collaborate with one mind, share fortune and misfortune, hardship and good life alike. We cannot become arrogant and remain alert in peaceful time. We cannot be not scared, disappointed, or delude ourselves during stormy time. The worse the situation, the stronger and more driven we become. Surely we will reach the other side, save our compatriots and revive the mainland.

13.3 JOINT COMMUNIQUÉ OF THE UNITED STATES OF AMERICA AND THE PEOPLE'S REPUBLIC OF CHINA (SHANGHAI COMMUNIQUÉ) (FEBRUARY 28, 1972)

By the time Nixon arrived in China, Henry Kissinger and Zhou Enlai had already agreed on the basic issues surrounding the future normalization between China and the United States. Nixon and Mao needed a formula that would satisfy conservative factions in both China and the United States. The key phrase in the following document is: "there is but one China and that Taiwan is a part of China." It should be remembered that Nixon's visit did not establish diplomatic relations—that event was further delayed by Nixon's resignation in 1974 and Mao's death in 1976. China and the United States finally normalized diplomatic relations in 1979.

Questions

1. The joint Shanghai Communiqué acknowledges substantial differences in how both countries viewed the world. Why do you think both countries decided to seek out talks towards achieving normalization?
2. In many ways the diplomatic formula of there only being "one China and Taiwan is part of China" papers over the remaining problem that two governments both claiming to rule China continue to exist. Why was this solution amenable to both the United States and the PRC?

SHANGHAI COMMUNIQUÉ (1972)—An agreement signed in 1972 between the United States and the PRC pledging further talks towards achieving a normalization of relations and agreeing on the status of Taiwan as part of China.

1. President Richard Nixon of the United States of America visited the People's Republic of China at the invitation of Premier Zhou Enlai of the People's Republic of China from February 21 to February 28, 1972. Accompanying the President were Mrs. Nixon, U.S. Secretary of State William Rogers, Assistant to the President Dr. Henry Kissinger, and other American officials.

[....]

6. The Chinese side stated: Wherever there is oppression, there is resistance. Countries want independence, nations want liberation and the people want revolution—this has become the irresistible trend of history. All nations, big or small, should be equal: big nations should not bully the small and strong nations should not bully the weak. China will never be a superpower and it opposes hegemony and power politics of any kind. The Chinese side stated that it firmly supports the struggles of all the oppressed people and nations for freedom and liberation and that the people of all countries have the right to choose their social systems according their own wishes and the right to safeguard the independence, sovereignty and territorial integrity of their own countries and oppose foreign aggression, interference, control and subversion. All foreign troops should be withdrawn to their own countries. The Chinese side expressed its firm support to the peoples of Viet Nam, Laos and Cambodia in their efforts for the attainment of their goal and its firm support to the seven-point proposal of the Provisional Revolutionary Government of the Republic of South Viet Nam and the elaboration of February this year on the two key problems in the proposal, and to the Joint Declaration of the Summit Conference of the Indochinese Peoples. It firmly supports the eight-point program for the peaceful unification of Korea put forward by the Government of the Democratic People's Republic of Korea on April 12, 1971, and the stand for the abolition of the "U.N. Commission for the Unification and Rehabilitation of Korea." It firmly opposes the revival and outward expansion of Japanese militarism and firmly supports the Japanese people's desire to build an independent, democratic, peaceful and neutral Japan. It firmly maintains that India and Pakistan should, in accordance with the United Nations resolutions on the Indo-Pakistan question, immediately withdraw all their forces to their respective territories and to their own sides of the ceasefire line in Jammu and Kashmir and firmly supports the Pakistan Government and people in their struggle to preserve their independence and sovereignty and the people of Jammu and Kashmir in their struggle for the right of self-determination.

8. There are essential differences between China and the United States in their social systems and foreign policies. However, the two sides agreed that countries, regardless of their social systems, should conduct their relations on the principles of respect for the sovereignty and territorial integrity of all states, non-aggression against other states, non-interference in the internal affairs of other states, equality and mutual benefit, and peaceful coexistence. International disputes should be settled on this basis, without resorting to the use or threat of force. The United States and the People's Republic of China are prepared to apply these principles to their mutual relations.

[....]

11. The two sides reviewed the long-standing serious disputes between China and the United States. The Chinese side reaffirmed its position: the Taiwan question is the crucial question obstructing the normalization of relations between China and the United States; the Government of the People's Republic of China is the sole legal government of China; Taiwan is a province of China which has long been returned to the motherland; the liberation of Taiwan is China's internal affair in which no other country has the right to interfere; and all US forces and military installations must be withdrawn from Taiwan. The Chinese Government firmly opposes any activities which aim at the creation of "one China, one Taiwan," "one China, two governments," "two Chinas," an "independent Taiwan" or advocate that "the status of Taiwan remains to be determined."

12. The US side declared: The United States acknowledges that all Chinese on either side of the Taiwan Strait maintain there is but one China and that Taiwan is a part of China. The United States Government does not challenge that position. It reaffirms its interest in a peaceful settlement of the Taiwan question by the Chinese themselves. With this prospect in mind, it affirms the ultimate objective of the withdrawal of all US forces and military installations from Taiwan. In the meantime, it will progressively reduce its forces and military installations on Taiwan as the tension in the area diminishes. The two sides agreed that it is desirable to broaden the understanding between the two peoples. To this end,

they discussed specific areas in such fields as science, technology, culture, sports and journalism, in which people-to-people contacts and exchanges would be mutually beneficial. Each side undertakes to facilitate the further development of such contacts and exchanges.

13. Both sides view bilateral trade as another area from which mutual benefit can be derived, and agreed that economic relations based on equality and mutual benefit are in the interest of the peoples of the two countries. They agree to facilitate the progressive development of trade between their two countries.

14. The two sides agreed that they will stay in contact through various channels, including the sending of a senior US representative to Beijing from time to time for concrete consultations to further the normalization of relations between the two countries and continue to exchange views on issues of common interest.

15. The two sides expressed the hope that the gains achieved during this visit would open up new prospects for the relations between the two countries. They believe that the normalization of relations between the two countries is not only in the interest of the Chinese and American peoples but also contributes to the relaxation of tension in Asia and the world.

16. President Nixon, Mrs. Nixon and the American party expressed their appreciation for the gracious hospitality shown them by the Government and people of the People's Republic of China.

WHO'S NEXT: CHOOSING A SUCCESSOR

From 1976 until 1978, Deng Xiaoping, Hua Guofeng and other top party officials vied for leadership of China. By 1978, Deng Xiaoping and his supporters had, almost entirely behind the scenes, gained control of the government. Hua, though, would remain active in the government until he quietly retired from the Central Committee in 2002. With his ascent, Deng Xiaoping ushered in a "Beijing Spring," effectively shifting the party from a political focus to reconstructing the country's education system, industries and the economy. Deng's policy sought to repudiate Hua Guofeng's "Two 'Whatevers' Policy" of adhering to "whatever" Mao Zedong had advocated. Deng did not totally reject Mao Zedong Thought for fear that it would create an ideological free-for-all (13.4). More accurately, Deng Xiaoping wanted to move the country away from adhering to any specific ideology and concentrate on actually modernizing the country. His aspirations sprung from the realization that without rebuilding the country's infrastructure and implementing deep-rooted reforms, the PRC, and in fact the entire CCP, could very well collapse. Through his advocacy of the "Four Modernizations" (13.5) Deng sought to repair the decades of neglect, particularly visible in the science and technology sector, through renewed attention to education. He stopped short of achieving this through the liberalization of the political sphere called for by many officials (13.6).

13.4 EDITORIAL IN SUPPORT OF HUA GUOFENG'S "TWO WHATEVERS" POLICY (FEBRUARY 7, 1977)

As Mao's handpicked successor, Hua Guofeng tried to unconditionally carry out Mao's legacy, in part to secure his own position as the Party's leader. He orchestrated the publication of this editorial article simultaneously in the two flagship publications of the state: *People's Daily* and *Liberation Army Daily,* as well as one journal, the *Red Flag.* The "Two Whatevers" Policy quickly met strong resistance from powerful party elite. Many feared that Hua Guofeng's policy would leave the political landscape unchanged. Deng Xiaoping quickly harnessed this sentiment behind the scenes, then orchestrated the removal of Hua Guofeng from key positions of power.

Questions

1. **What are the "Two Whatevers" that Hua Guofeng supports?**
2. **Why does Hua Guofeng intend to continue to promote Mao Zedong Thought?**

[...]

Chairman Mao, our great leader and tutor, led us to fight for over half a century and experience ten significant struggles between the lines [of interpretation] inside the Party. Whenever we adhered to Chairman Mao's revolutionary line and followed Chairman Mao's instruction, revolutionary victory was achieved; whenever we parted from Chairman Mao's revolutionary line, and disobeyed Chairman Mao's instruction, revolution would fail. Chairman Mao's banner is the banner of victory. When Chairman was alive, we united and fought under Chairman Mao's great banner. Today, Chairman Mao has passed away, even more we ought to hold high and firmly safeguard Chairman Mao's great banner. This is the sacred duty of our 800 million people and over thirty million Party members; the political foundation for us to unite and fight continuously; and the fundamental assurance to achieve further victory. Chairman Hua led us to implement Chairman Mao's heritage, and to have fought and still fighting to destroy the "Gang of Four." This is another significant struggle between two lines within our Party. Through this struggle Chairman Mao's great banner was safeguarded which secured our country to continue moving forward along Chairman Mao revolutionary line. This is the significant historical achievement of Chairman Hua. Under the leadership of wise leader Chairman Hua, we have started on the new march to begin the important work of initiating new future while continuing the past. The responsibility on our shoulder is heavy. We are facing many difficulties. We have courage and confidence to bear the heavy responsibility and conquer all difficulties. Chairman Mao used to call upon us to: "Unite together, focus on the key situation, straighten up spirit, and work hard."

Let us hold high the great banner of Chairman Mao, even more voluntarily implement Chairman Mao's revolutionary line. We will resolutely uphold whatever policy decisions Chairman Mao made and unswervingly follow whatever instructions Chairman Mao gave. We will mostly closely united around the Central Committee of the Party headed by Chairman Hua, closely follow the strategic plan of the Central Committee of the Party headed by Chairman Hua. Every single action of ours should follow the leadership of the Central Committee of the Party headed by Chairman Hua, with one heart, one mind, and one coordinated step, to tightly grasp to the core policy of thoroughly unveiling and criticizing the "Gang of Four," to obtain the significant new victory in governing country.

13.5 DENG XIAOPING ON THE FOUR MODERNIZATIONS (MAY 7, 1978)

Consciously seeking to move the country away from Mao's promotion of revolutionary fervor over practical results, Deng Xiaoping's first major campaign picked up and amplified a policy first voiced by Zhou Enlai calling for the "**Four Modernizations.**" Deng Xiaoping clearly recognized China's industrial and economic shortcomings and sought to show that pursuing a vibrant economy did not necessarily require the country to abandon the socialist ideology upon which it was founded. The following speech is an excerpt from a talk given to an economic and trade delegation of the government of the Democratic Republic of Madagascar. It typifies many of the speeches given during this period that tended to pillory the Gang of Four for the excesses of the past and encouraged the modernization of China.

FOUR MODERNIZATIONS—Part of Deng Xiaoping's modernization program emphasizing: agriculture, industry, national defense, and science and technology.

Questions

1. **How does Deng Xiaoping envision China pursuing the "Four Modernizations"? How does he think it will change China?**
2. **What do you think Deng Xiaoping means by "less talk and more action"?**

The entire Chinese nation rejoiced over the downfall of the Gang of Four. Things are better now and the mood of the people has improved. We are soberly aware that it is an arduous task to achieve the four modernizations, but we can manage. First of all, the entire Party is united, as are the people of the whole nation. Our people are hard-working and have a tradition of hard struggle. Second, we have laid a solid material foundation. Third, we have clearly defined principles whereby we shall make use of all the advanced technologies and achievements from around the world. The Gang of Four did not allow us to do so, calling this a slavish comprador philosophy. Science and technology have no class nature; capitalists make them serve capitalism, and socialist countries make them serve socialism. Ancient China had four great inventions [paper, printing, gunpowder and the compass], which later found their way to countries around the world. Why then should we be hesitant about making use of advanced technologies and achievements from around the world? We should make advanced technologies and achievements the starting point for our development. Finally, we have abundant natural resources. To sum up, the tremendous enthusiasm of our people, a substantial material foundation and our enormous resources, in addition to the introduction of state-of-the-art technology from around the world will make it possible for us to achieve the four modernizations. Naturally, the task will be far from easy. The world's advanced technologies continue to develop rapidly, with the rate of development no longer calculated in terms of years, but in terms of months, and even in terms of days, a trend which we call "changes coming with each passing day." Even when we have realized the four modernizations, our output of industrial and agricultural products and our national income will remain relatively low when calculated on a per capita basis. Our current principles and policies are clearly defined, and our motto is "less talk, more action."

At present, we are still a relatively poor nation. It is impossible for us to undertake many international proletarian obligations, so our contributions remain small. However, once we have accomplished the four modernizations and the national economy has expanded, our contributions to mankind, and especially to the Third World, will be greater. As a socialist country, China shall always belong to the Third World and shall never seek hegemony. This idea is understandable because China is still quite poor, and is therefore a Third World country in the real sense of the term. The question is whether or not China will practice hegemony when it becomes more developed in the future. My friends, you are younger than I, so you will be able to see for yourselves what happens at that time. If it remains a socialist country, China will not practice hegemony and it will still belong to the Third World. Should China become arrogant, however, act like an overlord and give orders to the world, it would no longer be considered a Third World country. Indeed, it would cease to be a socialist country. I first addressed these points in a speech delivered at the Special Session of the United Nations General Assembly in 1974. The current foreign policy, which was formulated by Chairman Mao Zedong and Premier Zhou Enlai, will be passed on to our descendants.

13.6 WEI JINGSHENG'S THE FIFTH MODERNIZATION: DEMOCRACY (DECEMBER 5, 1978)

Deng Xiaoping rose to power largely on his policy of reform and openness (*gaige kaifang*). After ten years of Cultural Revolution, tired of the unending sequence of political campaigns, Deng Xiaoping's policies were a welcome return to normalcy. As government control over people's lives loosened, many hoped that the liberalization of the political sphere would also begin. In late 1978, posters began to advocate more democratic reforms and were posted on a wall in the Xidan district of central Beijing near the Forbidden City. **Democracy Wall,** as it came to be known, attracted amazingly frank and philosophically sophisticated discussions around China's ability to democratize. Filled with the hopes of a new era, this "Beijing Spring" seemed full of promise to people like Wei Jingsheng. Wei Jingsheng, a former Red Guard and electrician with no formal education, actively publicized his ideas in articles posted on Democracy Wall. The exploration of China's intellectual freedoms flowered on into 1979 with the self-publication of numerous journals explicitly critical of the government. As the government became increasingly uneasy, one of the most prominent figures, Wei Jingsheng, was arrested on May 29, 1979. During his trial the prosecutor admonished Wei that "[o]ur Constitution clearly stipulates extensive democratic rights. However, our democracy should be a democracy protected by law. It does not mean absolute freedom for one to do as one likes." In October 16, 1979, he was sentenced to 15 years in prison for sedition and the leaking of state secrets. Released in 1994, he again spoke critically of government policies and was re-arrested. In 1997, Wei Jingsheng was suddenly released from prison, escorted to the Beijing airport where he flew to the United States and began an enforced exile abroad.

Questions

1. What does Wei Jingsheng mean by suggesting Deng Xiaoping's "Four Modernizations" are analogous to the Chinese proverbs "feeding the people by painting cakes," or "quenching thirst by contemplating plums"?
2. Why does Wei Jingsheng believe that democracy is a prerequisite to modernization?

If newspapers and the radio have now stopped bashing our ears with their deafening propaganda catchwords on the theme of "class struggle," it is partly because this was the magic abracadabra of the "Gang of Four." But mostly because the masses were fed up with it; you cannot make people march anymore to that tune.

There is a law of history according to which as long as the old does not disappear, the new cannot come into existence. Now that the old is gone for good, everyone is scanning the horizon in the hope of seeing the emergence of the new. As the saying goes: "God would never disappoint the faithful." Hence, a fantastic new formula was invented and is being served to us now. They call it "The Four Modernizations." Chairman Hua [Guofeng] (our "wise leader") and Vice Chairman Deng [Xiaoping] (who, in the eyes of some people, is even wiser and greater) managed to defeat the "Gang of Four," thus making it possible again to dream of democracy and prosperity—a dream for which heroic people shed their blood in Tiananmen Square, on April 5, 1976.

After the arrest of the "Gang of Four," the people ardently hoped for the return of Deng; and in their delusion that he would "restore capitalism," they turned him into the living symbol of their movement. Eventually, Deng was reinstalled in the central leadership of the State and of the Party; and this event was greeted by entire nation with indescribable enthusiasm and emotion.

After that, alas! Our odious political system was not amended in the slightest.

[...]

There is an old Chinese saying that tells of "feeding the people by painting cakes," and there is another one of "quenching thirst by contemplating plums." The satirical spirit of this old wisdom truly reflects long political experience. If history is actually a constant progression, how could one still hope today to swindle the public with those same crude stratagems that had already been exposed long ago by our ancestors? And yet there are still people who believe they can cheat

DEMOCRACY WALL—A wall located in central Beijing and covered in Big Character Posters advocating political reform from 1978 until 1980 when the wall was declared off limits to such postings and relocated to the outskirts of the city.

the world with such tricks, and who actually proceed in this fashion.

[. . . .]

And yet, what is actually happening now? Some gentlemen come to warn us earnestly: "Marxism-Leninism and Mao Zedong Thought remain the foundation of all there is on earth; no valid utterance can be formulated without referring to it." Or again: "Chairman Mao is the savior of the people," and "Without the Communist Party, there would be no New China" which amounts to saying, "Without Chairman Mao, there would be no New China." Now, if anyone questions these affirmations, there are good medicines to cure him of his skepticism! Some others lecture us: "The Chinese people need to be led by a strong man. If the modern despot is even tougher than his feudal predecessors, this merely shows his greatness. The Chinese people have no need for democracy, except when it comes properly 'centralized'; in any other form, it is not worth a penny. You have little faith? As you wish. For your kind of people, there is always room in our jails. …"

Nevertheless, they still leave you one open path. *Forward march!* Within the framework of the "Four Modernizations," close all ranks, and cut out the nonsense, all you dutiful packhorses of the Revolution! At the end of the road you will reach Paradise—the utopia of Communism—with the "Four Modernizations." Furthermore, well-meaning persons still come forward to lavish their wisdom on us: "If these perspectives still fail to stir your enthusiasm, apply yourselves seriously to the study of Marxism-Leninism and Mao Zedong Thought! Your lack of enthusiasm results from your deficient theoretical understanding, and the very fact that you do not understand the theory precisely proves its sublime depth. Come on, be good fellows now— anyway, the authorities that be, ordained by history, will not allow you any alternative. …"

I beg you all—do not let these political swindlers cheat you yet again! Rather than swallow what we know to be a dupery, why not, for once, simply rely on our own resources? The cruel experiences of the Cultural Revolution have opened our eyes. Let us try to discover by ourselves what is to be done.

[. . .]

Forward Toward Modernization: Establishing Democracy

If the Chinese people wish to modernize, they must first establish democracy, they must first modernize

China's social system. Democracy is not what Lenin says, a mere consequence of a certain stage of development of society. It is not merely the necessary product of a certain degree of development of the productive forces and the production relations. It is also the condition on which depends the very survival of the productive forces (and the production relations in this phase of development, or in situation of superior development). Without democracy, society would sink into a stage of stagnation, and economic growth would encounter insuperable obstacles. Thus, as is shown by historical precedents, a democratic social system was always the prerequisite for any real development. Without this preliminary condition, it would not only be impossible to achieve any progress, but it would even be difficult merely to preserve the achievements obtained at a given level of development. The best evidence is provided by the situation to which our great country has been reduced after these last thirty years.

[. . .]

Can the struggle for democracy mobilize the Chinese people? During the Cultural Revolution, for the first time they became aware of their own strength when they saw all the reactionary powers shaking with fear. But at that time the people still did not have a clear idea of the way they should proceed, and thus the democratic trend could not predominate. Hence it was all too easy for the tyrant to dominate, manipulate, and divert most of these struggles; he neutralized the movement by using in turn provocations, seductions, lies, and violent repression. Since the people, at that time, still had a religious respect for despots, they became the powerless toys and victims of the ruling tyrant as well as of all the other tyrants to come.

Twelve years later, however, the people have now identified their goal, they see clearly the way they should follow, they finally acknowledge their true banner—the flag of democracy.

The Democracy Wall in Xidan became their first fortress in the struggle against all reactionary forces. In this struggle, we shall overcome. As the propaganda phrase used to say: "The people will certainly liberate themselves"; but this time that worn-out slogan is being given a new meaning. Blood will be shed, there will be new martyrs, persecution will become even more sinister; but the reactionary forces will never again succeed in obliterating our democratic flag in their poisonous mist. Let us all unite under this flag, which is great and true; let us march forward to secure peace and happiness for the people, to win our rights and our freedom, and to make our society truly modern!

13.7 TRIAL OF LIN BIAO AND JIANG QING CLIQUES (OCTOBER 1980)

Arrested soon after Mao Zedong's death in 1976, the **Gang of Four** (Jiang Qing, Zhang Chunqiao, Yao Wenyuan, and Wang Hongwen) was only put on trial four years later on November 20, 1980. The trial was broadcast live across the country. It was little more than a show trial that fulfilled Deng Xiaoping's efforts to leave Mao Zedong unsullied while laying blame for the excesses of the Cultural Revolution primarily with the Gang of Four and the associates of Lin Biao. At that time, many Chinese found the trial cathartic and joined Deng Xiaoping in blaming the defendants for China's suffering. Others viewed the trial simply as a demonstration of "victor's justice" by Deng and his supporters towards those who opposed him. While most of the defendants sat sullenly playing their proper role, Mao's widow, Jiang Qing, famously said, "I was merely the Chairman's dog. Whatever he asked me to bite, I bit." Her theatrics, while entertaining, had little affect on the verdict of guilty which was preordained from the outset.

Questions

1. **Why do you think Deng Xiaoping decided to try the Gang of Four publicly?**
2. **What crimes did the government prosecutors charge the Gang of Four?**

Principal Culprits of the Counter-Revolutionary Cliques of Lin Biao and Jiang Qing to Be Tried

The Supreme People's Procuratorate will soon start a public prosecution against the counter-revolutionary cliques of Lin Biao and Jiang Qing. This was announced by Huang Huoqing, Chief Procurator of the Supreme People's Procuratorate, at the 16th meeting of the Standing Committee of the Fifth National People's Congress on September 27. At the meeting he gave a report concerning this case and proposed to the N.P.C. Standing Committee that a special procuratorate of the Supreme People's Procuratorate and a special court of the Supreme People's Court be set up to try the principal culprits of the two counter-revolutionary cliques.

The ten principle defendants to be prosecuted are Jiang Qing, Zhang Chunqiao, Yao Wenyuan, Wang Hongwen, Chen Boda, Huang Yongsheng, Wu Faxian, Li Zuopeng, Qiu Huizuo and Jiang Tengjiao.

According to the regulations of China's Law of Criminal Procedure, no prosecution will be instituted against those defendants who are dead.

Huang Huoqing said that the procuratorate had examined the case file and evidence submitted by the Ministry of Public Security which had concluded its investigation into the case, and had interrogated the accused. He added that ample evidence proved that the Lin Biao and Jiang Qing counter-revolutionary cliques were guilty of grave crimes.

The ten principal accused will be prosecuted and tried on the following four counts:

- Sedition and conspiracy to overthrow the political power of proletarian dictatorship;
- Frame-up and persecution of Party and state leaders and usurpation of Party leadership and state power;
- Persecution and suppression of cadres and the masses of the people and practice of the fascist dictatorship; and
- Plotting to murder Chairman Mao and engineering a counter-revolutionary armed rebellion.

In a word, their crimes were those of usurping Party leadership and state power and bringing calamity to the country and the people.

GANG OF FOUR TRIAL (1980) — Jiang Qing's death sentence was commuted to life in prison, but while on medical parole in 1991 she committed suicide. The youngest gang member, Wang Hongwen, died of liver cancer in 1992 while serving a life sentence. Zhang Chunqiao's death sentence was commuted to life in prison where he died of cancer in 2005. The last member of the Gang of Four, Yao Wenyuan died of diabetes in 2005, having been released from prison in 1996 after serving his full jail term.

The prosecution against Lin Biao, Jiang Qing and company involves only their counter-revolutionary crimes which violated the Criminal Law, and does not touch upon their errors in work, including those related to political line. Huang Huoqing noted.

The case of Lin Biao and the gang of four is being handled seriously and prudently. Huang Huoqing said. The leading group under the Central Commission for Inspecting Discipline to examine the case of Lin Biao and the gang of four has done a great deal of work. The Ministry of Public Security began in late April this year the investigation and pre-trial of those members of the Lin Biao and Jiang Qing cliques who are now in custody. The results of the investigation showed that they had violated the Criminal Law and that they should be dealt with by the judicial department according to law. Since the case was of an extraordinary and grave nature, functionaries of the Supreme People's Procuratorate were assigned to take part in and supervise the whole process of the investigation and pre-trial from the very beginning.

Huang Huoqing stated that the two counter-revolutionary cliques of Lin Biao and Jiang Qing will be prosecuted as one case. This is because the two cliques colluded with and made use of each other. During the first five years of the "cultural revolution," the two cliques acted in collusion and committed crimes in usurping Party leadership and state power, plunging the country and people into calamities. The criminal activities of the two cliques were interrelated and inseparable from each other. After Lin Biao died in an air crash in September 1971 while fleeing the country, the Jiang Qing counter-revolutionary clique recruited his followers and carried on conspiratorial activities.

Huang Huoqing said: The crimes Lin Biao, Jiang Qing and their followers committed during the ten years of the "cultural revolution" brought untold calamities to our country and nation. But we will confine our suit against them to their direct and principal crimes and their responsibility for these crimes.

He added that a detailed study was made during the process of investigation, pre-trial and procuratorial preparations. He stressed: "We lay stress on evidence and do not readily believe confessions. We base ourselves on facts and use the law as our criterion. In the criminal proceedings against Lin Biao, Jiang Qing and their followers, we base ourselves on ascertained and verified original material evidence such as dossiers, letters, diaries, notes, records and tape recordings."

The other accomplices involved in the case will be tried separately by the Supreme People's Court, local people's courts and military courts. [...]

LIFE IN THE 1970s

Life in 1970's China fundamentally changed as a direct result of Deng Xiaoping's policies. Perhaps no event marked those changes and the new opportunities available to the common citizen more than the reestablishment of university entrance exams to select students on the basis of test scores rather than on class and revolutionary background (13.8). An often–overlooked consequence of the government's de-politicization of society was the emotional relaxation that occurred as a result. In the Cultural Revolution, any reflection about one's individual needs or desires outside of the country's was labeled as "bourgeois behavior" and if discovered, harshly punished. The ability to express and even write about such feelings brought forth a wave of literature and articles dissecting what work, careers and even love should be about. The need to articulate these sentiments openly and publicly, questioning the value of the wasted years of the Cultural Revolution, was as important to Chinese society as witnessing the Gang of Four on trial. Equally significant was the emergence of the humor and even openly joking about the absurdity of the top leaders' view of popular culture (13.10).

13.8   UNIVERSITY ENTRANCE EXAMINATIONS (1977)

Beginning in 1957, access to universities, and often even to high school, was denied to children of families with bad, or "black," class backgrounds. The Cultural Revolution further perverted the traditional university system to political ends, with many universities simply closing their doors during much of the period. The return to standard and open entrance exams in 1977 had a deep symbolic impact on Chinese society. Although there were cases of students being denied admission to university in 1977, the following year the official policy demanded that no student be denied the opportunity to enter university based purely on one's family political background. Given the pent up demand, Chinese of all ages under 30, and in special cases even older, took the entrance exams—often with considerable support of their work units. The following account appeared in *China Reconstructs* and captures the widespread excitement surrounding the exams.

Questions

1. Why do you think Deng Xiaoping's decision to open the entrance exams was so popular among common Chinese?
2. What were the various motivations of the students profiled in the article for taking the entrance exams? How did their reasons conform to Deng Xiaoping's new policies?

Ask anyone in China to name ten major events of 1977 and he is sure to include the new reforms in the university enrollment regulations.

Since the announcement last October on extending eligibility, holding entrance examinations, and selecting the best according to an all-round appraisal, this has been *the* topic of conversation everywhere. In buses and restaurants even people who did not know each other would get into warm discussions about it. Bookstores quickly ran out of books helpful for reviewing middle school subjects. Factories, communes and government organizations allowed applicants two weeks off to prepare. Some units also engaged teachers to help.

Middle school teachers worked as hard as the applicants. Many who had retired returned to open special classes. A classroom seating fifty was often packed with twice the number, many of them applicants living nearby and working in factories or stores. A math teacher came home after a long day in her school and before she could sit down to supper, students were already coming in for help. Telling them to be seated, she answered their questions while she ate. Asked if she was tired, she said, "Yes, but I'm glad to help. These are kids who hope to get into university so they'll be better equipped to help modernize our country."

The general atmosphere of hard work in studies extended even to junior middle and primary schools. Youngsters became more attentive in class and there were fewer idlers after school. Many more stayed on in school for extracurricular science activities or went straight home to do homework.

A special kind of atmosphere prevailed in Beijing between December 10–12 when entrance examinations were held. At crowded bus stops people smilingly let young people obviously headed for the exams get on first. In restaurants they received extra quick service. First aid stations and food stalls were set up next to the 200 examination sites. Outside the gate of Beijing Middle School No. 150 a retired woman worker stood with drawing compasses and triangles in her hands. "Waiting for somebody?" she was asked. She held up the things in her hands and said, "Just in case some kids forgot these."

"NOW WE'RE MOVING!"

One couldn't help thinking of the notorious incident during the university entrance examinations of 1973. That summer a young man named Zhang Tiesheng sat for the examinations in Liaoning province. When he couldn't answer most of the questions he filled a whole page of the exam papers with complaints against examinations. The "gang of four," looking for troublemakers to mess up the country in their bid for power, lost no time in setting him up as "a hero who dares to go against the tide." He was not only admitted into university but also given wide publicity as an example for young people. This caused great confusion among the students. Entrance examinations were all but scrapped and there was a growing trend to try to get into university "through the back door," that is, through pull and connections or bribing people with influence, while vast numbers of really promising young people were kept out. The quality of students in the next few years dropped markedly. In all fields of work there is now a severe lack of young and competent trained personnel. If this situation had continued, modernizing the country by the end of the century would have been hopeless. People were deeply worried about the future of China.

With the "gang of four" out of the way, Chairman Mao's hope of seeing China a strong modern socialist country by the end of the century is being made possible again. Plans to train scientists and technicians have been drawn up. Now the reforms in the enrollment regulations are opening the way to more talent and raising the quality of education. Thus when they were announced, people enthusiastically said, "Now we're moving ahead!"

THE APPLICANTS

Asked how they felt about the chance to enter university, many applicants said, "Chairman Hua has made it possible." These were sincere words. First, Chairman Hua halted the "gang of four." Second, the new regulations initiated by the Party Central Committee give all young people under 25 in good health and with a schooling of or equivalent to senior middle school a chance to be selected. Naturally they must love socialism and work and are willing to study hard. The age limit for those with some special skill and good job experience is extended to 30. This extension especially made entrance possible for young people who graduated from senior middle school in 1966 and 1967, the two years at the beginning of the cultural revolution when all universities and colleges were closed. There have never been so many applicants from among workers, peasants, armymen, barefoot doctors, rural school teachers, school graduates already working in the countryside and new senior middle school graduates. By again selecting the best according to an all-round standard consisting of political, intellectual and physical qualifications, including appraisals given by the applicants' places of work, the universities are admitting a large number of very promising young people.

What are some of them like and what are their aims in getting a university education?

One worker, going on thirty, turned in a composition (for his examination in Chinese) that revealed one kind of driving force behind the thirst for knowledge. "Here I am," he wrote, "seemingly at odds with my age, burying myself in something I should have done a dozen years ago—cramming for university entrance exams. Of course there were all kinds of reactions to my decision—encouragement, support, also ridicule, even sneers." But one small incident spurred him on. In the factory where he worked there was an imported chromatograph that had broken down and been gathering dust for several years. For months he and his colleagues tried to get it working. But they failed. The factory had to get the foreign company that manufactured it to send people to repair it. They worked on it for several days and the machine began to run normally. Yet, he never found out what went wrong and how it was fixed. Shamed and humiliated, he made his mind to master his specialization and a foreign language in a year. He studied late into the night every day, and the difficulties were great. "The circuit diagrams began to look like cobwebs and I forgot the vocabulary faster than I learned it." But the memory of the chromatograph incident always made him go on. He would splash his face with cold water and continue until daybreak. He made some progress in six months, but longed for more systematic training in school.

"You can imagine how excited I was when I learned that I, a man turning thirty, still had a chance to go to college. I picked up my middle school textbooks and they were like old friends newly met. When I took up a pencil to work out problems, it seemed as if my old teacher was standing behind me, and I could hear my own heart throb."

At first he didn't want to take his middle school textbooks to the factory, but the thought of the chromatograph incident erased all feeling of embarrassment. "There's no need to be ashamed of being older than most or starting from a low level. The thing to be ashamed of is failing to come up to par at crucial moments, of disgracing the country...."

Younger applicants also showed this desire to do more for the country. Chen Li, a 20-year-old girl working as a pig raiser in the Dongbeiwang commune outside Beijing, said, "I hope to enter university so I can learn more in the science field and serve the people better. But whether I'm admitted or not, I'm going to keep up my studies and do my bit to help modernize our country." As soon as the exams were over she returned to her commune to work while she waited for the results.

Chen Li went to the countryside in the spring of 1976 after graduating from senior middle school, carrying a small bedroll and a big bag of books. She was assigned to the pig farm where everything was still done with manual labor. With a hundred pigs to look after, she had to carry a hundred double-loads of pig mash a day. But no matter how tired she was after a long day's work she would study before going to bed. She concentrated on mathematics and English and always carried a small English-Chinese dictionary in her pocket.

When Chen Li announce her intention to take the entrance exams, her fellow commune members took over her work so she could give all her time to reviewing her lessons. "Remember all the heavy loads you carried," they said to her. "If you get admitted, study to bring us mechanization sooner."

Zhu Xiangdong, 19, a new graduate of Beijing Middle School No. 35, hopes to get into Beijing University and major in physics. Why physics? "It's a basic science subject," he said, "indispensable if we're to modernize in any field. I want to dedicate myself to what the country needs most." His boyish face became eager when he added, "In ancient times our scientists invented the compass, papermaking, gunpowder and printing. But in modern times our science and technology have lagged. It's our generation's responsibility to catch up with the best in the world, and do even better. Chairman Mao said that young people are like the sun at eight or nine o'clock in the morning and he put great hope in us. We must live up to that."

Zhu makes strict demands on himself in every aspect. Even during the time when the "gang of four's" misrule in education caused many students to neglect studying, Zhu didn't waver. He prepared each lesson well, listened attentively in class and raised questions whenever he didn't understand. He did a lot of extra reading related to the subjects he was learning. Before he finished middle school he had already studied first-year college math and physics and started on derivatives and differential and integral calculus. He consistently got good marks in all his subjects. He was also monitor of his class, a sports activist and well liked for his readiness to serve the collective.

A WELCOMED PRESSURE

More than one college professor has spoken of their gratification at discovering so many promising and talented young people. The feeling was especially strong at the Central Music Conservatory.

The conservatory had planned to admit 130 students—then found it had to choose from among 17,000 applicants! After stringent screening, qualified applicants still exceeded the original quota by several times. The teachers then submitted a joint request to the leaders to extend the quota. The conservatory finally accepted nearly three hundred.

"In my twenty-eight years of teaching," said Yu Yixuan, vice-director of the conservatory and an accomplished soprano in her own right, "I have never had to choose from such a great number of applicants, and from so many who are already technically competent, or even proficient." She couldn't help comparing what she saw this time with the admittance work under the cultural dictatorship of Jiang Qing and her followers. At that time the conservatory was allowed to enroll students only from certain specified districts where children were "sure to come from families who suffered bitterly in the old society and have a deep class hatred" (the "gang of four's" ultra-leftism). All other districts were ruled out. Even within the specified districts, unreasonable requirements—one of which was to investigate the applicants' family background back three generations—deprived many promising youngsters of the chance even to apply. With this method invariably the school had been unable to meet its enrollment quota. In 1975 the voice department under Professor Yu planned to enroll 14 students. After seven months of such investigations it selected only five tenors and four sopranos.

This time the entrance examinations turned out to be grand review of musical talent. Applicants for the violin class played difficult pieces by both Chinese and foreign composers. Among those applying for piano was Nekt Igar, a ten-year-old girl of the Owenk nationality from Inner Mongolia who had been learning to play for a little over a year. Playing a prelude by Bach, the Czerny etude No. 599 and a piano adaptation of the Tibetan folk song "There's a Golden Sun in Beijing," she showed sensitive musical feeling and unusual expressiveness, especially in the folk piece.

In one classroom, music played on the traditional instrument *pipa* was still heard at ten o'clock in the evening, past exam time. When a 14-year-old girl from Hangzhou finished her piece, the teacher said, "Play another one." He seemed to have forgotten this was an exam and was as enthralled as at a concert.

For his examination for the composition class, a middle school graduate working in the countryside outside Guangzhou developed a musical theme into variations for the piano in three hours. He had learned composition entirely in his spare time.

The admittance of so many talented young people eager to make music serve socialism put pressure on the music teachers. It meant harder work to cope with the new situation. "This is the kind of pressure we like," they said.

13.9   SHEN RONG'S *AT MIDDLE AGE* (1980)

First published in a literary journal in 1980, the story *At Middle Age* poignantly depicted the sacrifices of those who came of age in the 1960s with little or no recognition of their achievements. Then in the 1970s this group was expected to redouble their efforts to help China modernize. Most Chinese professionals saw no salary increase during the 1960s or early 1970s. Constantly in danger of being labeled rightist or as a counterrevolutionary for their education in "Western sciences," even the most dedicated workers emerged emotionally and physically depleted. Shen Rong's story twists the common idealization of individual sacrifice (like Lei Feng [12.2]) by laying bare the negligible material rewards and the lingering political suspicion intellectuals still encountered even after the end of the Cultural Revolution. The story recounts the life of Dr. Lu through flashbacks after she has suffered a physical collapse in the hospital where she works.

Questions

1. **What critique does Shen Rong offer of Dr. Lu's sacrifices? Is it ultimately a story of reaffirmation or criticism of China's past?**
2. **Why do you think some doctors in the story chose to leave the country or were planning to leave?**

"Can't you see with it at all?"

The patient shook his head.

"Did you see a doctor before?"

As she rose to examine his eye, she remembered he named a hospital. Then his wife, who was sitting beside him, politely stopped her.

"There's no hurry. Dr. Lu. Sit down, please. We ought to go to your clinic for an examination." Smiling, Qin Bo turned to Director Zhao. "Since he developed eye trouble, I've become something of an ophthalmologist myself."

Though Lu didn't examine him, she stayed a long time. What had they talked about? Qin had asked her many personal questions.

"How long have you been here, Dr. Lu?"

She hadn't kept track of the years. She only remembered the year she had graduated. So she answered, "I came here in 1961."

"Eighteen years ago." Qin counted on her fingers.

Why was she so interested in this? Then Director Zhao chipped in, "Dr. Lu has a lot of experience. She's a skilled surgeon."

Qin went on. "You don't seem to be in good health, Dr. Lu."

What was she driving at? Lu was so busy caring for others that she had never given any thought to her own health. The hospital didn't even have her case-history. And none of her leaders had ever inquired after her health. Why was this stranger showing such concern? She hesitated before answering, "I'm very well."

Zhao added again, "She's one of the fittest. Dr. Lu's never missed a day's work for years."

Lu made no answer, wondering why this was so important to this lady, and fretting to get back to her patients. Jiang couldn't possibly cope with so many alone.

Her eyes fixed on Lu, the lady smiled and pressed, "Are you sure you can remove a cataract easily, Dr. Lu?"

Another difficult question. She had had no accidents so far, but anything could happen if the patient didn't cooperate well or if the anesthetic was not carefully applied.

She couldn't recollect whether she had made a reply, only Qin's big eyes staring at her with doubt, unsettling her. Having treated all kinds of patients, she had got used to the difficult wives of high cadres. She was searching for a tactful answer when Jiao moved impatiently and turned his head to his wife, who stopped and averted her gaze.

How had this trying conversation finished? Oh, yes, Jiang had come to tell her that Uncle Zhang had come for his appointment.

Qin quickly said politely, "You can go, Dr. Lu, if you're busy."

Lu left the big bright room, which was so suffocating. She could hardly breathe.

She was suffocating.

[. . . .]

That day, after Lu's departure, Qin had asked, "Director Zhao, is Dr. Lu the vice-head of her department?"

"No."

"Is she an attending doctor?"

"No."

"Is she a Party member?"

"No."

Qin said bluntly, "Excuse my outspokenness since we're all Party members, but I think it's rather inappropriate to let an ordinary doctor operate on Vice-minister Jiao."

Jiao stopped her by banging his walking-stick on the floor. Turning to her he said angrily, "What are you talking about. Qin Bo? Let the hospital make the arrangements. Any surgeon can operate."

Qin retorted heatedly, "That's not the right attitude. Old Jiao. You must be responsible. You can work only if you're healthy. We must be responsible to the revolution and the Party."

Zhao quickly butted in to avoid a quarrel, "Believe me, Comrade Qin, although she's not a Communist, Lu's a good doctor. And she's very good at removing cataracts. Don't worry!"

"It's not that, Director Zhao. And I'm not being too careful either." Qin sighed, "When I was in the **cadre school,** one old comrade had to have that operation. He was not allowed to come back to Beijing. So he went to a small hospital there. Before the operation was through his eyeball fell out. Jiao was detained by the followers of the gang for seven years! He has just resumed work. He can't do without his eyes."

"Nothing like that will happen, Comrade Qin. We've very few accidents in our hospital."

Qin still tried to argue her point. "Can we ask Dr. Sun, the department head, to operate on Jiao?"

Zhao shook his head and laughed, "Dr. Sun's almost seventy and has poor eyesight himself! Besides, he hasn't operated for years. He does research, advises the younger doctors and teaches. Dr. Lu's a better surgeon than he."

"How about Dr. Guo then?"

Zhao stared, "Dr. Guo?" She must have made a thorough investigation of the department.

She prompted, "Guo Ruqing."

Zhao gestured helplessly, "He's left the country."

Qin wouldn't give up, "When is he coming back?"

"He's not."

"What do you mean?" This time she stared.

Zhao sighed, "Dr. Guo's wife returned from abroad. When her father, a shopkeeper, died, he left his store to them. So they decided to leave."

"To leave medicine for a store? I can't understand it." Jiao sighed too.

"He's not the only one. Several of our capable doctors have left or are preparing to go."

CADRE SCHOOL—Often known as May 7th Cadre School. It is a type of farm camp started in 1968 by many government agencies, schools, and research institutes. Officials, regular cadres, and intellectuals were sent to these countryside Cadre Schools for re-education and improvement. The practice wound down towards the end of Cultural Revolution and was officially concluded in 1979.

Qin was indignant, "I don't understand their mentality."

Jiao waved his stick and turned to Zhao, "In the early fifties, intellectuals like you overcame many difficulties to return here to help build a new China. But now, the intellectuals we've trained are leaving the country. It's a serious lesson."

"This can't go on," said Qin. "We must do more ideological work. After the gang was smashed, the social status of intellectuals was raised a lot. Their living and working conditions will improve as China modernizes."

"Yes. Our Party committee holds the same view. I talked with Dr. Guo twice on behalf of the Party and begged him to stay. But it was no use."

Qin, who was about to continue, was stopped by Jiao who said, "Director Zhao, I didn't come to insist on having an expert or a professor. I came because I've confidence in your hospital, or to be exact, because I have a special feeling for your hospital. A few years ago, the cataract in my right eye was removed here. And it was superbly done."

"Who did it?" Zhao asked.

Jiao answered sadly, "I never found out who she was."

"That's easy. We can look up your case-history."

Zhao picked up the receiver, thinking that Qin would be satisfied if he got that doctor. But Jiao stopped him, "You can't find her. I had it done as an out-patient. There was no case-history. It was a woman with a southern accent."

"That's difficult." Zhao laughed, replacing the receiver. "We have many women doctors who speak with a southern accent. Dr. Lu also comes from the south. Let her do it."

The couple agreed. Qin helped Jiao up and they left.

Was this the cause of Lu's illness? Zhao couldn't believe it. She had performed this operation hundreds of times. She wouldn't be so nervous. He had gone over before the operation and found her confident, composed and well. Why this sudden attack, then?

Zhao looked again at Lu with concern. Even on the brink of death, she looked as if she were sleeping peacefully.

13.10 ADVERTISEMENT: MODERN CLOTHES FOR PANTS CREATED IN LINE WITH GOVERNMENT'S POLICY (APRIL 1, 1979)

During the Cultural Revolution, people's commitment to the revolution was demonstrated in the avoidance of "bourgeois clothing." As a result, Chinese of both sexes reverted to wearing plain, often army-style clothing with little or no variation between what men and women wore. In the 1970s, for the first time in decades, foreign styles began to be available, often arriving via Hong Kong and seen on television. People could, and did, dye and perm their hair. The following parody reflects the unexpected social tensions unleashed by Deng's reforms causing him to remark critically in one speech about "trumpet pants" (bell-bottomed pants). In response, the following politically correct "advertisement" was posted on Democracy Wall.

Questions

1. What does the advertisement seek to suggest regarding China's clothing (past and present)?
2. Why would the government even worry about what clothing the Chinese people wore?

In accordance with a directive from the leadership, in line with the propaganda in our press organs, and in order to uphold the boycott on trumpet pants coming in from abroad, our firm has solicited the opinions of all social groups and has newly created a pair of trousers in true Chinese style. We have decided to call them "crutch-covers" or anti-trumpet trousers.

Our product has the following advantages. The model does not differ in any way whatsoever for men or women, for fat people or thin. It can be worn either back to front or front to back. It is suitable for people of all ages and of all body shapes. The color is dark, solemn, tasteful, and dirt-resistant. The model can be worn at all times of the year and by all members of the family.

The cut is practical, the manner of production is simple, and no individual measurements need to be taken, so our crutch-covers are cheap and correspond to the modern system of low wages.

Please buy! A thousand thanks to our leaders, who have forbidden the sale of trumpet pants and thus freed the way for our new product.

Folk-Costumes Shop,

70 Clean Country Alley,

Nostalgia Street,

Resurrection Gate,

Beijing.

CHAPTER 14
LIFE IN CHINA UNDER DENG XIAOPING (1980s AND 1990s)

❧

VISUAL SOURCE
Making Sense of Tiananmen: Photos of the 1989 Student Demonstrations

GATE OF HEAVENLY PEACE: The Chinese term "Tiananmen" literally means the "Gate of Heavenly Peace." The gate marks the entrance to the Imperial City. The square in front of the massive Gate of Heavenly Peace was relatively small up until the 1950s. At the insistence of Mao Zedong and other CCP leaders, the original square was enlarged so that it could hold a million people for the massive rallies.

GODDESS OF DEMOCRACY: As the demonstrations extended into late May, the initial enthusiasm, and intense media interest, began to fade. In order to re-instill the original zeal (and force the government to destroy a potent symbol if they chose to enter the square), students from the Central Academy of Fine Arts conceptualized, constructed and erected the Goddess of Democracy in only four days time.

TIANANMEN SQUARE DEMONSTRATIONS: Tiananmen Square has been the site of public demonstrations since the early 20th century. The first major demonstrations began in earnest in 1919 with the May Fourth demonstrations and again as the site of a mass memorial for former premier Zhou Enlai on April 5, 1976. As student discontent rose in the spring of 1989 it was the natural setting.

1989 STUDENT DEMONSTRATORS: The Tiananmen protests began on April 18, 1989 when thousands of students gathered in the square to mourn and memorialize the passing of Hu Yaobang. The government's April 26th front page editorial threatening to oppose any "turmoil" only incited larger numbers of demonstrators to flock to Tiananmen Square. On May 4th, the seventieth anniversary of the first May Fourth demonstrations, the number of demonstrators topped 100,000.

JUNE 4, 1989: On May 20th due to growing numbers of student demonstrations throughout Beijing, the Chinese government declared martial law. On the evening of June 3, PLA troops moved into the city and opened fire on those attempting to block their advance. By early the next morning the square had been forcibly cleared. Estimates of the deaths in the city of Beijing range from several hundred to several thousand.

TANK MAN: On June 5, 1989 international media captured images of a young man stridently walking out to the middle of Chang'an Avenue to prevent a line of tanks from continuing towards Tiananmen. As the tanks slowed and then sought to go around him, the young man waved his bag and stepped side-to-side impeding their progress. As the tanks came to a stop, he climbed up on top of the tank and spoke with the driver. Anxious bystanders then quickly whisked him away, as the tanks continued forward. The true identity of the young man remains unclear to this day.

GOVERNMENT ACCOUNT: In the state media, government leaders attempted to paint the incident as instigated by a belligerent and misguided small group of agitators. Chinese leaders insist that no lives were lost in Tiananmen Square itself and take incidents such as "tank man" to show how the military displayed considerable self-restraint and respect for the Chinese people. Mostly, however, the incident is simply forgotten with few young Chinese even able to clearly describe the events which occurred during "Tiananmen Incident."

Deng's rise to power marked a slow relaxation of the central government's strict oversight of social trends in music, clothing and entertainment. The de-politicization process led to a general liberalization of life for ordinary citizens, though it did not result in the government completely relinquishing its control of Chinese society. Since the 1930s the Chinese Communist Party had used the control of information, theatrical performances, and media for setting the cultural and ideological parameters of the nation. The emergence of television in the 1980s allowed a new and immensely powerful tool for propagating and controlling popular discourse among most Chinese citizens. Up until the late 1970s, China's primary television channel CCTV (China Central Television) broadcast only one channel. Before that period very few private individuals owned a television, so the question of what was broadcast mattered little. That quickly changed in the early 1980s as television purchases increased dramatically in urban areas.

The Spring Festival, like many traditional **Chinese holidays,** conforms to the lunar calendar. As a result, the festival can fall as early as mid-January and as late as the end of February. Officially, the holiday lasts for three days—but little work occurs days, or even weeks, before and after as people prepare for the holiday and then arrange their journeys home. Train and air tickets for the dates surrounding the holiday are often bought up months in advance. In the late Imperial era, the end of the lunar New Year was the day upon which all debts were due, and according to the traditional reckoning the day on which everyone (no matter what day you were born) was considered to be a year older. By the 1980s, many of the customary traditions associated with the holiday had been stripped away leaving it primarily as the longest national holiday of the year and when all Chinese work units were granted a three-day holiday. During the first years of Deng Xiaoping's leadership, with less emphasis on political campaigns, an increasingly large number of families were able to celebrate the Spring Festival together.

Beginning in 1983, CCTV began broadcasting a *Spring Festival Eve Television Gala* (*chunjie lianhuan wanhui*) comprised of singing, dancing, comedy skits, and comedic cross-talk (*xiangsheng*). The success of the program was almost immediate. Usually lasting between four and five hours on the Lunar New Year's Eve when families are typically all gathered together, the show offered a variety of entertainment unprecedented for most Chinese. It quickly became a set part of every family's Spring Festival activities along with playing Majiang (Mahjong), cards, or other traditional family activities. The performers, skits, and singers would be the topic of subsequent discussions between friends and colleagues for weeks (if not months!).

Over the course of the 1980s, the show evolved but never deviated from the successful formula of an elaborate variety show. The holiday special would perennially achieve a domestic audience share of well over 90 percent (and at the height of the show's popularity in the mid to late 1980s it likely was close to 100 percent). The massive audience size meant that both advertisers and stars cajoled, jockeyed and bribed their way onto the show. In 2005 it was reported that some advertisers paid $1.2 million for prime spots on the show. There exist numerous examples of singers and performers being propelled from virtual obscurity to instantaneous stardom after a single appearance on the show. Perhaps no example is

CHINESE NATIONAL HOLIDAYS—Until 2008, every Chinese had seven days off per year. In 2008 this was raised to eleven days per year: New Years Day (1 day), Spring Festival (3 days), Qingming Festival (1 day); May Day (1 day), Dragon Boat Festival (Duanwu Jie, 1 Day), Mid-Autumn Festival (1 day) and National Day (3 day).

XIANGSHENG—A fast-paced stand-up comedy routine typically with two people similar to the famous Abbot & Costello "Who's On First" sketch that relies heavily on puns and humorous wordplay. Often translated into English as "Crosstalk."

more well known than **Fei Xiang** (Kris Phillips), who, after his appearance, became a household name selling more cassette tapes than any other Chinese singer of that era.

On the surface the *Spring Festival Gala* reflected China's increasing openness to outside influences and its rising consumerism, but on a deeper level the *Gala* was a throwback to many of the CCP's earliest efforts to merge entertainment with party propaganda. In addition to the humorous skits and popular entertainers, there were a sizeable number of unmistakably, and unadulterated, military, patriotic, and government elements included in the gala. The combination of these two elements—what some have called "indoctri-tainment"—appears to Western eyes as somewhat bewildering. One skit hilariously portrayed a father on the run from state officials with his seven daughters while still hoping his again-pregnant wife will give birth to a boy is followed by revered (but clearly past their prime) singers in military uniforms singing martial hymns backed up by dancers, all in fighter pilot outfits, holding model jet fighters. The *Spring Festival Gala's* outward disjuncture, however, demonstrates the Chinese state's flair for adapting the mode in which it delivers its political messages from outright propaganda campaigns to a more seductive delivery via a spectacular television program.

From its first broadcast in 1983 to today, the *Spring Festival Gala* has reflected the complex changes occurring in Chinese society. In particular, a maturing sophistication and growing audience diversification demanded that the show aspire to please an increasingly disparate populace—often with less than satisfactory results. The *Gala* production has evolved by displaying impressive leaps in technology and staging, however, many of the country's middle-aged and senior viewers, including many government officials, have wanted nostalgic and comforting program content that reminds them of past Spring Festivals. The younger population segments yearn for a television spectacular that would entertain them, and would showcase new, and if not cutting edge, talent that were not singers only their grandmothers could enjoy.

The rapid social changes occurring in the 1980s and 1990s underscores the cavernous generation gap and widening urban-rural dichotomy that characterizes contemporary China. Today's *Spring Festival Gala* is less the platform for new talent and excitement seen in the mid-1980s, than a show everyone loves to hate, and in many ways reflects the myriad internal differences within modern China.

POLICIES

In 1980, Deng made a series of speeches regarding Mao Zedong, Mao Zedong Thought, and the guiding principles of the party. Differences of opinion on how the CCP should officially handle Mao's legacy caused Deng Xiaoping to repeatedly emphasize China's **Four Cardinal Principles.** Deng Xiaoping sought to qualify his endorsement of Mao Zedong's legacy by disengaging the "original features" of Mao Zedong Thought. Deng Xiaoping's intent was to acknowledge Mao's contributions as primary, while at the same time recognizing Mao's mistakes (14.1). Deng Xiaoping's other strategy was to turn the country's energies to revitalizing and opening the economy in order to engage more effectively with international markets. With his backing in 1980, the People's Congress

FEI XIANG (1960–)—A child of a Taiwanese mother and an American father, Fei Xiang/Kris Philips became one of the best known Chinese celebrities of the 1980s and 1990s after appearing on the 1987 Spring Festival Television special.

FOUR CARDINAL PRINCIPLES—On March 30th 1979, Deng Xiaoping outlined the Four Cardinal Principles: 1) keeping to the socialist road, 2) upholding the people's democratic dictatorship (dictatorship of the proletariat), 3) upholding leadership by the Communist Party and 4) upholding Marxism, Leninism, and Mao Zedong Thought.

established a series of **Special Economic Zones** (SEZs) in Shenzhen, Zhuhai and other locations primarily along China's southeastern coastline. Each zone took advantage of their geographical locations near Hong Kong, Macao, and Taiwan respectively. In 1992, seeking to underscore his continued support of the SEZs, Deng traveled to southern China promoting the success of the SEZ experiment (14.2).

14.1 BUILDING SOCIALISM WITH A SPECIFICALLY CHINESE CHARACTER (JUNE 30, 1984)

Mao Zedong's death, the arrest of the Gang of Four, and Deng Xiaoping's liberalizing policies all generated considerable reflection among the Chinese people about China's past and future, as well as the role of Marxism as a guiding principle. Deng Xiaoping had to walk a fine line to ensure his leadership did not totally discredit Mao Zedong's legacy and risk losing the support of core CCP powerbrokers, while still turning the nation in a new direction. In the following speech, Deng Xiaoping outlines the trials and tribulations China had successfully overcome in the first decades after Liberation in 1949, and also indicates the hurdles that China still faced on its road to modernization. Deng's speech highlights his rather singular notion of socialism, while emphasizing economic reform.

Questions

1. What is "socialism with Chinese characteristics"?
2. What reasons does Deng Xiaoping give for China's lack of development and modernization?

Since the defeat of the Gang of Four and the convocation of the Third Plenary Session of the Party's Eleventh Central Committee, we have formulated correct ideological, political and organizational lines and a series of principles and policies. What is the ideological line? To adhere to Marxism and to integrate it with Chinese realities — in other words, to seek truth from facts, as advocated by Comrade Mao Zedong, and to uphold his basic ideas. It is crucial for us to adhere to Marxism and socialism. For more than a century after the Opium War, China was subjected to aggression and humiliation. It is because the Chinese people embraced Marxism and kept to the road leading from new-democracy to socialism that their revolution was victorious.

You may ask, what if the Chinese people had taken the capitalist road instead? Could they have liberated themselves, and could they have finally stood up? Let us review the history. The Guomindang followed the capitalist road for more than 20 years, but China was still a semi-colonial, semi-feudal society, which proved that that road led nowhere. In contrast, the Communists, adhering to Marxism and Mao Zedong Thought, which integrates Marxism with actual conditions in China, took their own road and succeeded in the revolution by encircling the cities from the countryside. Conversely, if we had not had faith in Marxism, or if we had not integrated Marxism with Chinese conditions and followed our own road, the revolution would have been a failure, and China would have remained fragmented and dependent. So faith in Marxism was the motive force that enabled us to achieve victory in the revolution.

At the founding of the People's Republic, we inherited from old China a ruined economy with virtually no industry. There was a shortage of grain, inflation was acute, and the economy was in chaos. But we solved the problems of feeding and employing the population, stabilized commodity prices and unified financial and economic work, and the economy rapidly recovered. On this

SPECIAL ECONOMIC ZONES (SEZs)—Areas and cities with special economic status to encourage foreign investment and increase foreign exports. First created under Deng Xiaoping in the late 1970s and 1980s with cities of Shenzhen and Zhuhai (situated next to Hong Kong and Macau respectively) being particularly successful examples.

foundation we started large-scale reconstruction. What did we rely on? We relied on Marxism and socialism. Some people ask why we chose socialism. We answer that we had to, because capitalism would get China nowhere. If we had taken the capitalist road, we could not have put an end to the chaos in the country or done away with poverty and backwardness. That is why we have repeatedly declared that we shall adhere to Marxism and keep to the socialist road. But by Marxism we mean Marxism that is integrated with Chinese conditions, and by socialism we mean a socialism that is tailored to Chinese conditions and has a specifically Chinese character.

[. . . .]

Proceeding from the realities in China, we must first of all solve the problem of the countryside. Eighty percent of the population lives in rural areas, and China's stability depends on the stability of those areas. No matter how successful our work is in the cities, it won't mean much without a stable base in the countryside. We therefore began by invigorating the economy and adopting an open policy there, so as to bring the initiative of 80 percent of the population into full play. We adopted this policy at the end of 1978, and after a few years it has produced the desired results. Now the recent Second Session of the Sixth National People's Congress has decided to shift the focus of reform from the countryside to the cities. The urban reform will include not only industry and commerce but science and technology, education and all other fields of endeavour as well. In short, we shall continue the reform at home and open still wider to the outside world.

We have opened 14 large and medium-sized coastal cities. We welcome foreign investment and advanced techniques. Management is also a technique. Will they undermine our socialism? Not likely, because the socialist sector is the mainstay of our economy. Our socialist economic base is so huge that it can absorb tens and hundreds of billions of dollars' worth of foreign funds without being shaken. Foreign investment will doubtless serve as a major supplement in the building of socialism in our country. And as things stand now, that supplement is indispensable. Naturally, some problems will arise in the wake of foreign investment. But its negative impact will be far less significant than the positive use we can make of it to accelerate our development. It may entail a slight risk, but not much.

Well, those are our plans. We shall accumulate new experience and try new solutions as new problems arise. In general, we believe that the course we have chosen, which we call building socialism with Chinese characteristics, is the right one. We have followed this road for five and a half years and have achieved satisfactory results; indeed, the pace of development has so far exceeded our projections. If we go on this way, we shall be able to reach the goal of quadrupling China's GNP by the end of the century. And so I can tell our friends that we are even more confident now.

14.2 DENG XIAOPING TALKS ON THE IMPORTANCE OF SPECIAL ECONOMIC ZONES (SEZs) (1992)

None of Deng Xiaoping's key reforms reflect Deng's economic frame of mind more than his creation and promotion of the SEZs. Intentionally deviating from Mao Zedong's tendency to implement all policies nationally (in a one-size-fits-all approach), Deng Xiaoping's goal with the SEZs was to initiate reforms in a more controlled fashion within a geographically delimited area. In 1992, after considerable internal debate caused in part by the 1989 Tiananmen "disturbances" (as they were referred to by Deng), Deng Xiaoping went on a "southern tour" to reaffirm the government's determination to foster market reforms. Deng was nearly 90, so the public nature of his tour and his speeches, well covered in the state media, amplified Deng's adherence to socialism as well as a market-oriented, but, according to him, *not* a capitalist economy.

Questions

1. If Deng Xiaoping's reforms, as he suggests, are not a "peaceful evolution towards capitalism," how does he differentiate a capitalist from a socialist economy?
2. What is Deng Xiaoping's speech seeking to encourage?

I

I was here in Guangdong in 1984. At that time rural reform had been under way for several years, and we were just beginning to introduce urban reform and to establish special economic zones. Eight years have passed since then. This time, during my trip here, I have found that the rapid growth in the Shenzhen and Zhuhai special economic zones and some other areas has exceeded my expectations. After what I have seen, I am even more confident.

[....]

III

If we are to seize opportunities to promote China's all-round development, it is crucial to expand the economy. The economies of some of our neighboring countries and regions are growing faster than ours. If our economy stagnates or develops only slowly, the people will make comparisons and ask why. Therefore, those areas that are in a position to develop should not be obstructed. Where local conditions permit, development should proceed as fast as possible. There is nothing to worry about so long as we stress efficiency and quality and develop an export-oriented economy. Slow growth equals stagnation and even retrogression. We must grasp opportunities; the present offers an excellent one. The only thing I worry about is that we may lose opportunities. If we don't seize them, they will slip through our fingers as time speeds by.

In developing the economy, we should strive to reach a higher level every few years. Of course, this should not be interpreted as encouraging unrealistic speed. We should do solid work, stressing efficiency, so as to realize steady, coordinated progress. Guangdong, for example, should try to mount several steps and catch up with the "**four little dragons**" of Asia in twenty years. In relatively developed areas such as Jiangsu Province, growth should be faster than the national average. Shanghai is another example. It has all the necessary conditions for faster progress. It enjoys obvious advantages in skilled people, technology and management and can have an impact over a wide area. In retrospect, one of my biggest

mistakes was leaving out Shanghai when we launched the four special economic zones. If Shanghai had been included, the situation with regard to reform and opening in the Yangtze Delta, the entire Yangtze River valley and, indeed, the whole country would be quite different.

[....]

It seems to me that, as a rule, at certain stages we should seize the opportunity to accelerate development for a few years, deal with problems as soon as they are recognized, and then move on. Basically, when we have enough material wealth, we shall have the initiative in handling contradictions and problems. For a big developing nation like China, it is impossible to attain faster economic growth steadily and smoothly at all times. Attention must be paid to stable and proportionate development, but stable and proportionate are relative terms, not absolute. Development is the absolute principle. We must be clear about this question. If we fail to analyze it properly and to understand it correctly, we shall become overcautious, not daring to emancipate our minds and act freely. Consequently, we shall lose opportunities. Like a boat sailing against the current, we must forge ahead or be swept downstream.

[....]

V

The implementation of the correct political line must be ensured by a correct organizational line. In a sense, whether we can manage our domestic affairs well, whether we can keep to the socialist road and adhere to reform and the open policy, whether we can develop the economy more rapidly and whether we can maintain long-term peace and stability will all be determined by people.

The imperialists are pushing for peaceful evolution towards capitalism in China, placing their hopes on the generations that will come after us. Comrade **Jiang Zemin** and his peers can be regarded as the third generation, and there will be a fourth and a fifth. Hostile forces realize that so long as we of the older generation are still alive and carry weight, no change is possible. But after we are dead and gone, who will ensure that there is no peaceful evolution? So we must educate the army,

FOUR LITTLE DRAGONS—A phrase first employed by the Chinese to refer to the four largest East Asian economies (after Japan): South Korea, Taiwan, Singapore and Hong Kong.

JIANG ZEMIN (1926–)—Born in Jiangsu, he grew up during the Japanese occupation and graduated in 1947 with a degree in electrical engineering. He rose through the ranks to become mayor of Shanghai in 1985 before being chosen by Deng Xiaoping to replace Zhao Ziyang in 1989 and ultimately replace Deng Xiaoping after his death in 1997. In 2003, he stepped down from the Politburo to make way for a new generation of leaders.

persons working in the organs of dictatorship, the Communist Party members and the people, including the youth. If any problem arises in China, it will arise from inside the Communist Party. We must keep clear heads. We must pay attention to training people, selecting and promoting to positions of leadership persons who have both ability and political integrity, in accordance with the principle that they should be revolutionary, young, well educated and professionally competent. This is of vital importance to ensure that the Party's basic line is followed for a hundred years and to maintain long-term peace and stability. It is crucial for the future of China.

This is a pressing problem that has not yet been solved satisfactorily, and I hope it will be. I began to think about it when I resumed work after the "cultural revolution." When we found that it was impossible for our generation to ensure long-term peace and stability, we tried hard to find a third generation to succeed us and recommended a few persons. But that didn't solve the problem. Two persons who were chosen failed, and not with regard to economic issues; they stumbled over the question of opposing bourgeois liberalization. That was something we could not tolerate. In late May 1989 I said that we should boldly choose for the new leadership persons who were generally recognized as adhering to the line of reform and opening up and who had some achievements in that respect to their credit. This would convince the people that we were wholeheartedly committed to that line. The masses judge from practice. When they come to the conclusion that socialism is good and that reform and the open policy are good, our cause will flourish forever. [. . .]

14.3 PANCHEN LAMA'S SPEECH TO THE TIBET AUTONOMOUS REGION STANDING COMMITTEE MEETING OF THE NATIONAL PEOPLE'S CONGRESS IN BEIJING (1987)

After delivering his **"Poisoned Arrow" petition** in 1962, the Panchen Lama again leveled a broadside at the Chinese government in 1964 by giving a speech supporting the exiled Dalai Lama that resulted in a seven-week interrogation, nine years of imprisonment and, finally, five years of house arrest. Released in 1978, the Panchen Lama continued to speak out on the need for less repressive and draconian treatment of Tibet and Tibetan customs. In 1983, he married a Han Chinese woman who later gave birth to their daughter. Despite this violation of his monastic vows, most Tibetans never wavered in their fervent support of him and their belief that he was their greatest advocate in Beijing. In January of 1989, a crowd of over 30,000 Tibetans greeted his return to Shigatse where he participated in religious ceremonies at the Tashilunpo monastery. Under what some considered suspicious circumstances, he died five days later at the age of fifty-one, following another speech critical of Chinese policies in Tibet. The following 1987 speech was typical of the Panchen Lama's undaunted desire to force the Chinese political bureaucracy to face the reality of Tibet's continuing difficulties under Chinese rule.

Questions

1. **What themes does the Panchen Lama highlight as major threats to Tibetan culture?**
2. **What does the Panchen Lama mean when he says that China and the Chinese have tended to: "Criticiz[e] the old system from the perspective of a new ideology."?**

POISONED ARROW PETITION (1962)—A 70,000 word petition written by the Panchen Lama documenting the hardships, substandard living conditions, and forced labor which had befallen Tibetans all in the name of "socialist reform." Mao Zedong reacted by calling the petition a "poisoned arrow" shot at the Party by reactionary feudal overlords. The Panchen Lama was arrested and detained for 15 years.

Ours is a country of many nationalities. Apart from the [Han] Chinese, there are fifty-five nationalities which are in the minority. The leftist trend before, and especially after the time of the Cultural Revolution, has caused the minorities to suffer in many ways. Just recently a story entitled *Pasang and Her Relatives* was intentionally published in a journal to ridicule Tibetans. Last year our representatives from Tibet raised their objections to this story when it was a film script. We even asked Vice Chairman Ngabo Ngawant Jigme to express our misgivings about this story to the concerned departments. However, the film was awarded a first prize. Another film of this nature, entitled *Compassion Without Mercy,* was also given an award. Things like this have been done to other nationalities as well.

[. . . .]

The Chinese Migrants in Tibet

The expense of keeping one Chinese in Tibet is equal to that of keeping four in China. Why should Tibet spend its money to feed them? Instead, we should think carefully on how best the money can be used for the development of Tibet. Tibet has suffered greatly because of the policy of sending a large number of useless migrants. The [Han] Chinese population in Tibet started with a few thousand and today it has multiplied manifold. That is the reason why many old Chinese personnel who worked very hard in the initial period are left without any career now. Today, the Chinese personnel come to Tibet accompanied by their families. They are like the American mercenaries. They fight and die for money. This is ridiculous.

Tibetans are the legitimate masters of Tibet. The wishes and feelings of the people of Tibet must be respected. It is widely believed that Wu Jinhua is going to be replaced. I have been instructed to submit an honest report on him. My report is that he is one of the best officials in Tibet. Amongst other things, he has successfully implemented the nationalities, religious, and United Front policies. Since economic development is our over-riding priority at the moment, we must take a long-term view. We cannot ignore the problems of minority nationalities.

[. . . .]

Nurturing Language and Culture

The government has announced four modernization plans. It is important that we learn from the developed countries. But what we must learn from them is their technological know-how and scientific way of management. Whoever has the highest standard of living has the best system. I have not thought much on this point. The Japanese way of life is rather complicated. They have a very highly developed educational system to teach culture, science and technology. If a new book is published anywhere in the world, within thirty days one can read it in their language.

In Tibet we have very deplorable translation facilities, especially when it comes to the European languages. It is much worse than in Eastern Turkestan [Xinjiang] or Inner Mongolia. Last year, when I went abroad for a visit, I could not find anyone capable of interpreting between Tibetan and English. Therefore, I had to use a Chinese interpreter and speak in Chinese. This must have given a very bad impression to outsiders. This fact proves how poor the standard of education is in Tibet.

In the whole of the Tibet Autonomous Region [TAR] no one has been able to translate physics books into Tibetan. What are the authorities in TAR doing? In Qinghai, they have translated everything, whatever the quality. They are also willing to help the TAR. But the authorities of the TAR have not even responded to this gesture. These officials, in effect, are trying to neglect the Tibetan language completely. This is really a very sad thing. Vice Chairman Ngabo Ngawant Jigme is scheduled to visit Tibet this year. I am wondering if you can find a way to enact a law for the development of the Tibetan language. If such a thing is done, I can assure you that things will improve even within the next two or three years. Ninety five percent of Tibetans do not speak or understand Chinese. The use of the Chinese language for administrative work in Tibet is aimed only at making things convenient for Chinese officials. Can't you see that using Tibetan for administrative works will greatly help the Tibetan masses? Some people complain that I talk too much. Maybe, yes. But many people have expressed similar discontentment. So angry was Ngabo Ngawang Jigme with the situation, as I have outlined just now, that he banged his fist on the table during a meeting last year. I hope everyone will think seriously over this matter. Development of the Tibetan language is no small matter. It is directly related to politics.

[. . . .]

Owning Up to Mistakes

What Rigzin Wangyal said regarding the handling of unrest in Tibet was quite true. In 1959 there were rebellions in Tibet. Forces were dispatched to quell the disorder, which was a right decision and should not be [denied].

However, a lot of innocent people were also persecuted. Many mistakes were made in the way the crack-down operations were mounted. The authorities did not make any distinction between those guilty and those not guilty of participation in the disturbances. People were arrested and jailed indiscriminately. There were no interrogations. On sight Tibetans were taken to jail and beaten. Things like this are still commonplace in Tibet. We should consider this a serious matter.

We should examine and investigate these practices and bring the guilty to book. This is the way by which we will be able to assuage people's resentment. Isn't this what we are here to discuss? [...]

TIANANMEN

The death of reformer **Hu Yaobang** on April 15, 1989 sparked an outpouring of grief that quickly grew into demonstrations—first of students, then with the growing support of workers and other segments of the population. The government quickly labeled the actions of the students as illegal, but with the world attention already drawn to public demands for democratic reforms and a reduction in government corruption, the central leadership gave pause to any consideration of the use of unnecessary force. In addition, there existed an inner circle of officials, led by Zhao Ziyang, who supported the students and many of their goals. Seeking to take a new tack, one of the hardliners, Prime Minister **Li Peng,** agreed to a televised meeting with the student leaders (14.4). The students' refusal to bow before state pressure only further antagonized the hardliners. In the days immediately following the meeting, martial law was declared, Zhao Ziyang was dismissed from his post as the Secretary General (typically seen as the position held by Deng's successor). At the end of May and the first days of June, public support for reform soared. Demonstrations spread to virtually every major city in China, and rock stars visited the square offering free concerts in support of the student-movement (14.6). Word also arrived that troops were being brought into the capital, and despite efforts (and warnings) from many different groups sympathetic to their cause, many students refused to clear the square. In the early morning hours of **June 4, 1989,** the military entered the city *en force* with tanks and troop carriers shooting and crushing those who refused to disperse. In the aftermath, with the top student leaders fleeing underground and often overseas, the government issued a variety of responses to the demonstrations in an attempt to counter the intense international condemnation and to justify their actions to the Chinese people themselves (14.5).

14.4 TRANSCRIPT OF MAY 18 MEETING BETWEEN PREMIER LI PENG AND STUDENTS (MAY 18, 1989)

In an effort to appease the student hunger strikers by appearing to be concerned with the student demands and "listening to the people," Prime Minister Li Peng agreed to meet with the top student representatives. Among the student leaders were Wang Dan of Beijing University and Wuerkaixi (Erkesh Devlet), a Uyghur from the northwestern

HU YAOBANG (1915–1989)—A key reformer under Deng Xiaoping who served as Secretary General. His support for students in 1987 led to his removal from office and his death triggered student demonstrations in 1989.

LI PENG (1928–)—Raised by Zhou Enlai, educated in the Soviet Union, and rose to prominence under Deng Xiaoping, he was a key advocate and orchestrator of the harsh suppression of demonstrators in the June 4, 1989 Tiananmen Incident. He is the key architect of the Three Gorges Dam project.

TIANANMEN SQUARE MASSACRE (JUNE 4, 1989)—The bloody military suppression of the 1989 student movement on June 4th that brought an end to two-months of student demonstrations, hunger strikes, and unprecedented international media attention. Several hundred unarmed students and civilians died in the early morning military attack.

autonomous region of Xinjiang. They sensed that popular opinion was on their side as the students displayed little patience for the standard government platitudes. Throughout the meeting the student leaders did not soften their delivery, interrupting Li Peng, lecturing and deliberately addressing him by titles other than Prime Minister. Wuerkaixi even attended the meeting wearing his pajamas, a clear breach of etiquette. Li Peng and the hard liners were not amused and felt their efforts at reconciliation received only insulting responses. Two days later the Central Committee voted to impose martial law with **Zhao Ziyang** as the only dissenting vote.

Questions

1. **What is Premier Li Peng's primary goal as stated in the transcript below?**
2. **Why are Wang Dan and the student leaders so concerned with the movement being labeled as a disturbance?**

[PREMIER] LI PENG: I am very glad to meet you all. For today's meeting, we are going to talk about only one subject: that is, how to get the hunger strikers out of their present plight. The Party and the government are very concerned about this matter. We are also deeply disturbed by it and fear for the health of these students. Let us solve this problem first; afterward, all matters can be easily settled through discussion. We say this not out of any ulterior motives, but mainly because we are concerned. You are all very young, the oldest among you is no more than twenty-three. Even my youngest child is older than you all. I have three children and none of them is involved in profiteering by officials. But all of them are older than you. You are like our own children, our own flesh and blood.

WUER KAIXI [INTERRUPTING]: Premier Li, it doesn't seem that we have enough time for this kind of talk. We must enter into a substantive discussion as quickly as possible. Now, I would like to say what we have to say. Just now you have said that we were going to talk about only one subject. But the real situation is not that you invited us to this discussion, but that we, all these many people in the Square, asked you to come and talk. How many subjects to discuss, therefore, ought to be up to us. Fortunately, our views here happen to be in agreement.... We have heard and read Comrade Zhao Ziyang's talk that came out in writing yesterday [in which Zhao, on behalf of the Politburo, stated that the students demands for democracy were reasonable and patriotic, and promised there would be no retaliation]. So why haven't the students gone back [to their campus]? Because we believe that it was still not enough,

far from enough. I am sure you are aware of the conditions that we have put forth [for ending the hunger strike] as well as developments in the Square.

WANG DAN: Let me give a report on the situation in the Square. More than two thousand people have already lost consciousness. As for how to make them end the hunger strike and leave the Square, all the conditions we have stipulated must be fully met.... In this regard, our position is very clear: the only way to make the hungry strikers leave the Square is to satisfy the two demands that our students have presented to you.

WUER KAIXI: For your age, sir, I feel it might be appropriate if I call you Teacher Li. Teacher Li, the issue at this time is not at all how to persuade the group of us present here. We would very much like to have the students leave the Square. [But] right now, what's happening in the Square is not so much a case in which the minority follows the majority, but the one in which 99.9 percent follow 0.1 percent so if a single hunger striker refuses to leave the Square, then the other several thousand will not leave either.

WANG DAN: Yesterday, we conducted a poll among over a hundred students, asking, whether or not they would agree to withdraw from the Square after our conversation with Secretary Yan Mingfu [member of the Central Secretariat who sought to avoid using force]. The poll showed that 99.9 percent of the students voted against withdrawing from the Square. Here, we would like to make clear once again what our demands are: one, that the current student movement be recognized as a patriotic Democracy Movement, not a disturbance,

---

ZHAO ZIYANG (1919–2005) — A leading reformer under Deng Xiaoping and seen by many as his anointed heir, but his support for the student demonstrations in 1989 caused him to be stripped of all titles and he spent the last 15 years of his life under house arrest until his death in 2005.

as it has been called; and two, that a dialogue be arranged as quickly as possible and broadcast live. If the government can quickly and satisfactorily respond to these two demands, we then will be able to go and work on the students, to get them to leave the Square. Otherwise, it will be very difficult for us to do this task.

WUER KAIXI: ... Up to the present, still no one has stated that the student movement is not turmoil. The nature of this movement must be [properly] defined. Then, we can work on several [specific] methods for [conveying this message]: (1) Comrade Zhao Ziyang or Comrade Li Peng, Zhao Ziyang would be best, could go to the Square and speak directly to the students; or (2) the *People's Daily* could print another editorial repudiating the one published on April 26, one that apologizes to the people across the country and acknowledges the great significance of the current student movement. Only if this is done can we make our best efforts to persuade the students to convert the hunger strike into a sit-in protest. After we reach this point, we can proceed to solve other problems. We on our part will try our best to persuade the students, but we cannot say for sure that we will succeed.

[STUDENT LEADER] XIONG YAN: We believe that whether or not the government or some other party acknowledges that this is a patriotic democracy movement, history will recognize it as such. But why do [we] especially need the acknowledgement of the government and the others? Because this represents a desire of the people, that is, [a desire] to see if our government is, after all, our own government.... Second, we are people who are struggling for the sake of communism, people of conscience, people with humanity. To resolve this kind of problem, [the government] ought not to care about "losing face," or whatever other thing....

LI PENG: Let me raise one point. When we are talking, I hope you will be kind enough not to interrupt. When we are finished, whomever has more to say can speak again, there will be plenty of opportunities....

YAN MINGFU: ... The only issue that I am concerned with is that of saving the children who are hunger striking in the Square, who are now in a very weakened state, their lives gravely threatened. In my opinion, the final resolution of the issues [between us] and the issue of the hunger strike should be separated. In particular, these students who have not participated in the hunger strike must show care for the hunger strikers. I am confident that in the end we can solve all

our problems.... We should reach an agreement that these two issues ought to be discussed separately, for the evolving situation, as I pointed out to Wuer Kaixi and Wang Dan on the evening of May 13, has already gone beyond the good intentions of those who initiated the hunger strike. They are already out of your control....

LI PENG: Let me make a few points. Since you said you would like to discuss matters of substance, I will begin by discussing a matter of substance. I suggest that China Red Cross and Beijing Red Cross be put in charge of getting the students who are participating in the hunger strike safely to hospitals. I hope that other students in the Square will support and assist this operation. This is my specific proposal. In the meantime, I will ask all the medical personnel under the jurisdiction of the Central Committee and Beijing Municipality to do their best to rescue and take care of the student hunger strikers, so as to ensure the absolute safety of their lives. Regardless of how many common points of view, or disagreements we have, saving human lives is our top priority for the moment....

Second, neither the government nor the Party has ever stated that the masses of students were creating turmoil. We have always regarded the patriotic enthusiasm and wishes of the students as positive and good. Many of the things you have done are quite correct; many of your criticisms correspond to what the government sees as problems and hopes to resolve. To be frank, you have definitely provided impetus for finding solutions to these problems.... Now that our students have so sharply pointed out these problems, [their criticisms] can help the government overcome obstacles on the road to progress. This I think is positive. However, the way the present situation is developing does not depend on your good intentions, your idealistic visions, or patriotic enthusiasm. The fact is that disorder has already appeared in Beijing and is spreading across the entire country. I do not mean to pin responsibility for disorder onto our students, absolutely not. The present state of affairs is already objective reality. Let me tell you, my students, yesterday the Beijing Guangzhou railway line around the Wuhan area was blocked for more than three hours, this caused one of our major railway transportation lines to cease operation. And right now, all sorts of idlers and riff-raff from many cities are descending on Beijing in the name of the students. In the past few days, Beijing has basically fallen into a state of anarchy. Let me just reiterate, I do not mean to pin responsibility on our students. I just hope that our students will turn this over in their minds and think about what consequences will follow if things [are allowed to] go on like this.

The government of the People's Republic of China is one responsible to the people, and we cannot sit and watch idly. We must protect the safety of our students, protect our factories, protect the achievement of socialism and protect our capital. Whether or not you are willing to listen to these words, I am very glad to have had such an opportunity to tell everyone, China has experienced many episodes of turmoil. Creating turmoil was not the original intent of many people, but in the end, turmoil was what occurred.

Third, presently there are some government employees, city residents, workers, even staff from certain departments of our State Council who have taken to the street to show their support for the students. I hope you will not misunderstand why they are doing so. It is out of their concern for you and out of the hope that you will not harm your health. However, I do not completely approve of the methods of many of these people. If they try to persuade you to eat and drink a little, in order to protect your health, if they try to persuade you to leave the Square and express whatever you have to say to the government by way of discussion, that [kind of behavior] is completely correct. But there are also many who have gone to the Square to encourage you to continue with the hunger striker. I will not say what their motives are, but I do not approve of this kind of behavior. As Premier of the government, I must make my position clear....

[STUDENT] WANG ZHIXIN: This is not a dialogue but a meeting.

YAN MINGFU: Correct, a meeting.

14.5 THE TRUTH ABOUT THE BEIJING TURMOIL (1989)

In 2007, a group of American journalists met with a group of Chinese university students to discuss the views of China's youth. When questioned about the Tiananmen Incident, the students responded by asking the reporters why the Western media continued to focus on this event when there were so many more positive aspects about China in the last two decades. Westerners tend to be surprised how little Chinese youth of today know about the Tiananmen incident. The following government account (published bilingually in Chinese and English) offers valuable insight into how the Chinese public has been reeducated about the Tiananmen Square demonstrations. While much of the following article might ring false to Western ears, the overriding concern with stability and suppression of violent elements is viewed as quite legitimate by most Chinese.

Questions

1. **In what ways does the article attempt to vilify the students and demonstrators involved in the 1989 Tiananmen events?**
2. **What aspects of the demonstrations does the government emphasize? What aspects do you find are underemphasized or not mentioned?**

In 1989 when spring was passing to summer, a shocking turmoil happened in Beijing, which has attracted the close attention of people at home and abroad. Influenced by foreign media, people have many questions, guesses, and misunderstandings. What really happened in China? What is the situation now like in Beijing? This album, with its abundant pictures, will help our readers understand the whole story of and truth about the turmoil and the present situation in Beijing.

This turmoil was not a chance occurrence. It was a political turmoil incited by a very small number of political careerists after a few years of plotting and scheming. It was aimed at subverting the socialist People's Republic. By making use of some failings in the work of the Chinese government and the temporary economic difficulties, they spread far and wide many views against the Constitution, the leadership of the Chinese Communist Party, and the People's

Government, preparing the ground for the turmoil ideologically, organizationally, and in public opinion. The former general secretary of the Central Committee of the Chinese Communist Party Zhao Ziyang supported the turmoil and thus has unshirkable responsibility for its formation and development. The various political forces and reactionary organizations abroad had a hand in the turmoil from the very beginning. Some newspapers, magazines and broadcasting stations, especially the Voice of America, fabricated rumours to mislead people, thus adding fuel to the flames.

When Hu Yaobang suddenly died on April 15, a handful of people, thinking that their time had come, stirred up a student upheaval on the pretext of "mourning" for Hu Yaobang. The student unrest had been taken advantage of by the organizers of the turmoil from the very beginning. In violation of the Constitution, laws and regulations, some people put up big-character posters everywhere on the college campuses, preaching bourgeois liberalization and calling for the overthrow of the Communist Party and the legal government. They held many rallies, made speeches, boycotted classes and organized demonstrations, all without permission; they stormed the seat of the Party Central Committee and the State Council; they forcibly occupied the Tiananmen Square on many occasions and organized various illegal organizations without registration for approval. In Changsha, Xi'an, and other cities, some people engaged in grave criminal activities such as beating, smashing, looting and burning stores, and even broke into the compounds of provincial government seats and set fire to the motor vehicles there.

In view of this turmoil, the People's Daily issued, on April 26, an editorial exposing the nature of the turmoil. Even under this circumstance, the Party and the government exercised great restraint towards the students' extremist slogans and actions and had all along given due recognition to the students' patriotic enthusiasm and reasonable demands. At the same time, the Party and the government warned the students not to be made use of by a handful of people and expressed the hope for solving the problems through dialogues and by normal, democratic and legal procedures. However, on May 13, the illegal student organization started a general hunger strike involving over 3,000 people and lasting for seven days. Party and government leaders, on the one hand, went to see the fasting students at Tiananmen Square and met with students' representatives on many occasions, asking them to value their lives and stop the hunger strike, and on the other hand, they lost no time in organizing on-the-spot rescue teams and providing all kinds of materials so as to relieve the suffering of the fasting students. Thanks to efforts of the government and other quarters not a single student died in the hunger strike. But all this failed to win active response.

On the contrary, some media, taking the cue from a small number of people, wrongly guided the public opinion, escalating the turmoil and throwing Beijing and even the whole country in a serious anarchic situation, something that cannot be tolerated in any other country. In Beijing, demonstrations were held continuously, slogans insulting and attacking leaders and openly calling for overthrowing the government could be heard and seen everywhere. The traffic was seriously congested and difficulties were created for Beijing's production and daily supplies. The police were unable to keep normal social order. Gorbachev's schedules in China were also seriously hampered. The small handful of people attempted to take the chaos as an opportunity to seize political power and threatened to "set up a new government in three days."

On May 19, the Party Central Committee held a meeting attended by cadres from the Party, government and military institutions in Beijing, At the meeting, Premier Li Peng and President of the People's Republic of China Yang Shangkun announced the decision to adopt resolute measures to stop the turmoil. But Zhao Ziyang, then general secretary of the Party Central Committee, refused to attend this important meeting.

On May 20, Li Peng signed a martial law order as empowered by Clause 16 of Article 89 of the Constitution of the People's Republic of China. The martial law was to be enforced at 10 a.m. on the same day in parts of Beijing. The small handful of people took fright and coerced those residents who were in the dark about the truth to set up roadblocks at major crossroads to stop the advance of army vehicles and prevent the martial law enforcement troops from getting to designated places according to plan. Besides, they threatened to mobilize 200,000 people to occupy Tiananmen Square and organize a nation-wide general strike. Using the funds provided by reactionary forces at home and abroad, they installed sophisticated communication facilities and illegally purchased weapons. They gathered together hooligans and ruffians to set up terrorist organizations such as the "Dare-to-Die Corps" and the "Flying Tiger Team," and threatened to kidnap or put Party and government leaders under house arrest. They offered high prices in recruiting thugs and fabricated rumours to deceive people.

All the facts proved that, no matter how tolerant and restrained the government was, such people would not give up their wild scheme; on the contrary they threatened to "fight to the end" against the government.

On the evening of June 2, a handful of people bent upon inciting a riot used a traffic accident to spread rumours and mislead people, lighting the fuse of a rebellion. In the small hours of June 3, rioters set up roadblocks at every crossroad, beat up soldiers and armed police, seized weapons, ammunition and other military materials. Mobs also assaulted the Great Hall of the People, the Central Propaganda Department, the Ministry of Public Security, the Ministry of Radio, Film and Television and the west and south gates of **Zhongnanhai.** The seat of the Party Central Committee and the State Council. At about 5 p.m., the illegal organizations distributed kitchen knives, daggers, and iron bars, to the crowd on Tiananmen Square and incited them to "take up weapons and overthrow the government." A group of ruffians banded together about 1,000 people to push down the wall of a construction site near Xidan and seized large quantities of tools, reinforcing bars and bricks, ready for street fighting. They planned to incite people to take to the streets the next day, a Sunday, to stage a violent rebellion in an attempt to overthrow the government and seize power at one stroke.

At this critical juncture, the martial law troops were ordered to move in by force to quell the antigovernment rebellion. At 6:30 p.m., on June 3, the Beijing municipal government and the headquarters of the martial law enforcement troops issued an emergency announcement, asking all citizens to keep off the streets and stay at home. The announcement was broadcast over and over again. At about 10 p.m., the martial law troops headed for Beijing proper from various directions. The rioters, taking advantage of the soldiers' restraint, blocked military and other kinds of vehicles before they smashed and burned them. They also seized guns, ammunitions and transceivers. Several rioters seized an armoured car and fired guns as they drove it along the street. Rioters also assaulted civilian installations and public buildings. Several rioters even drove a public bus loaded with gasoline drums towards the Tiananmen gatetower in an attempt to set fire to it. At the same time, rioters savagely beat up, kidnapped and killed soldiers and officers. On the Chang'an Avenue, when a military vehicle suddenly broke down, rioters surrounded it and ferociously crushed the driver with bricks. At Fuchengmen, a soldier's body was hung heel over head on the overpass balustrade after he had been savagely killed. At Chongwenmen, another soldier was thrown down from the flyover and burned alive. Near a cinema, an officer was beaten to death, disembowelled and his eyes gouged out. His body was then strung up on a burning bus.

Over 1,280 vehicles were burned or damaged in the rebellion, including over 1,000 military trucks, more than 60 armored cars, over 30 police cars, over 120 public buses and trolley buses and over 70 motor vehicles of other kinds. More than 6,000 martial law officers and soldiers were injured and scores of them killed.

Such heavy losses are eloquent testimony to the restraint and tolerance shown by the martial law enforcement troops. For fear of injuring civilians by accident, they would rather endure humiliation and meet their death unflinchingly, although they had weapons in their hands. It can be said that there is no other army in the world that can exercise restraint to such an extent.

The martial law troops, having suffered heavy casualties and been driven beyond forbearance, were forced to fire into the air to clear the way forward. During the counter-attack, some rioters were killed, some onlookers were hit by stray bullets and some wounded or killed by armed ruffians. According to reliable statistics, more than 3,000 civilians were wounded and over 200, including 36 college students, were killed.

At 1:30 a.m. on June 4, the Beijing municipal government and the martial law headquarters issued an emergency notice asking all students and other citizens to leave Tiananmen Square. The notice was broadcast repeatedly for well over three hours over loudspeakers. The students on Tiananmen Square, after discussion among themselves, sent representatives to the troops to express their willingness to withdraw from the square and this was approved by the troops. Then at about 5 a.m., several thousand students left the square in an orderly manner through a wide corridor in the southeastern part of the square vacated by the troops, carrying their own banners and streamers. Those who refused to leave were forced to leave by the soldiers. By 5:30 a.m., the clearing operation of the square had been completed.

During the whole operation not a single person was killed. The allegations that "Tiananmen Square was plunged into a bloodbath" and "thousands of people were killed in the square" are sheer rumours, and the true state of affairs will eventually be clear to the public.

ZHONGNANHAI—A compound just west of the Forbidden City in the center of Beijing, which in the first decades of the PRC housed its top leaders and today serves as the headquarters of the party and top government officials.

After the decisive victory in quelling the riot, order in the capital was basically restored to normal and the situation throughout China soon became stable. The measures adopted by the Chinese government to stop the turmoil and put down the rebellion have not only won the acclaim and support of the Chinese people, but they have also won the understanding and support of the governments and people of many other countries. The Chinese government has announced that it will unswervingly carry on the policy of reform and opening to the outside world, the policy of developing friendly cooperation with different countries of the world on the basis of the five principles of peaceful coexistence, and the policy towards Hong Kong, Macao, and Taiwan. We will continue to strive for the realization of the socialist modernization. We are fully confident of our future.

14.6   SONGS AND TIANANMEN

A significant dimension of the 1989 student demonstrations was the astounding level of popular support it attracted among Beijing's ordinary citizens. Many street vendors distributed free food and drink to students. Local residents lined the streets and applauded the students' frequent processions from the university district in northwest Beijing into Tiananmen Square in the center of the city. Even soldiers posted at intersections or blocked by demonstrators in trucks carried on friendly banter, which was part of the reason that non-Beijing based troops were brought in to carry out the final strike on June 4th. Two songs, along with the rock stars who sang them, Hou Dejian and Cui Jian, became closely associated with the demonstrations. Both songs are famous in their own right, but their message and tone captured the emotions and spirit of Tiananmen and became virtual anthems of the demonstrations.

Questions

1. **Which song do you find more appropriate as an anthem for the Tiananmen demonstrations?**
2. **Why do you think that Cui Jian's "Nothing to My Name" became so popular among the students of 1989?**

Song #1 - Hou Dejian, Descendents of the Dragon (*Long de chuanren*)

In the Far East there is a river,
Its name is the Yangzi River;
In the Far East there is a river,
Its name is the Yellow River.

Although I have never seen the beauty of the
   Yangzi River,
In dreams I often swim in the Yangzi River;
Although I have never heard the roars of the Yellow
   River,
In dreams there are the fierce waves of the River.

In the ancient Far East there is a dragon,
Her name is China;

The ancient Far East there lives a group of people,
They are all descendents of the dragon.

I grew up beneath the feet of the giant dragon,
I grew up to become a descendant of the dragon;
Black eyes, black hair, and yellow skin;
Forever and ever, a descendant of the dragon.

A hundred years ago one serene night,
In the deep night on the eve of a vast change;
The sound of gunfire and cannon shattered the
   serene night,
Enemies on all sides and menacing swords.

A great many years, the explosions still rumble,
A great many years and yet many more years;
Giant dragon, giant dragon, open your eyes bright,
Forever, forever, open your bright eyes.

ENEMIES ON ALL SIDE — The Chinese term *"simian Chu-ge"* comes from a tale known to most all Chinese from the third century BCE regarding Xiang Yu, a famous general. When surrounded on all sides he and his soldiers heard the enemy troops singing songs from his native region of Chu. This caused them to believe that their homeland had already fallen. In Chinese today, the saying means that defeat is near and all hope is lost.

Giant dragon, giant dragon, open your eyes
   bright,
Forever, forever, open your bright eyes.

Song #2 - Cui Jian, "Nothing to My Name" (*yiwu suoyou*) (1986)

I used to ask non-stop,
When are you coming with me?
But you always laugh at me,
For I have nothing.
I want to give you my pursuit
And my freedom,

But you always laugh at me,
For I have nothing.
Oh, when are you coming with me?
Oh, when are you coming with me?

The earth under the feet is moving,
The water next to me is flowing,
But you keep laughing,
For I have nothing.

Why do you keep laughing,
Why am I always after something,
How come in front of you,
I always have nothing.

I am telling you I waited for so long,
I am telling you my last request.
I want to hold your hands,
And take you with me now.

Now your hands are shaking,
Your tears are running,
Aren't you telling me you love me
For I have nothing.

Oh … you will come with me. [repeat]

SHIFTING ROLES AND REPRESENTATION OF WOMEN IN POLICY, CINEMA, AND LITERATURE

As the nation with the largest population in the world, the Chinese leaders quickly realized the urgency of implementing clear policies to forestall the country's population from overwhelming their resources. In the Chinese context, the question of family planning, delayed marriage and the one-child policy is inevitably, if inequitably, one largely about women. The rationale for stringent birth control has evolved from one of revolutionary and socialist concerns, to the social repercussions of a one-child policy (14.7 and 14.8). As a part of the PRC's quest for the integration of women into the workplace, its success unquestionably altered the position of women in Chinese society. By comparison this policy has worked far better in China than in India or other parts of Asia. The ambivalent feelings towards the changes brought about by these policies are sharply underscored in one of the most popular literary works of the 1980s, Zhang Jie's "Love Must Not Be Forgotten" (14.10). The author's unvarnished depiction of women in Chinese society created considerable controversy that was reminiscent of Ding Ling's work in the twenties and forties (8.12 and 10.6). Ultimately, literary and cinematic depictions of women in the 1980s and 1990s shifted from the one-dimensional revolutionary heroes typical of the 1960s and 1970s. In one of her most striking yet unglamorous roles, China starlet Gong Li portrays a Shaanxi peasant in Zhang Yimou's, *The Story of Qiu Ju*. The film challenges both government portrayals of their new legal reforms as much as the complex position of women in rural society (14.9).

14.7   ONE COUPLE, ONE CHILD (1980)

By the 1970s, the Chinese government had growing concerns regarding China's population growth and the effect it would have on its modernization and economic goals. From the outset the **one-child policy** was a controversial policy. In response to wide-

ONE CHILD POLICY—A policy adopted in 1979 allowing each couple only one child. The policy was enforced with an array of incentives and punishments, which varied according to your ethnicity and residency.

spread concerns, the Central Party Committee took the extraordinary step of issuing an "open letter" to clarify the program for restraining the country's population growth. The concerns faded, but never entirely disappeared. Many Chinese worried about the social effects of an entire generation of "only children," raised without siblings, and of having more males than females when they reached maturity. The situation, like many dimensions of modern Chinese society, is complicated by the widely varying conditions in urban and rural sectors of society. The one-child policy tended to be more strictly enforced in the city, including numerous disincentives such as school fees and insurance for all children beyond the first. On the other hand, rural families who exceeded local quotas or sought to have children without the approval of the village leaders, could be, and often were, severely punished by local officials. The following is a synopsis that appeared in the *Beijing Review.*

Questions

1. **In what ways does the family planning policy differ from that of 1957 (11.6)?**
2. **What concerns does the article raise if the population is not brought under control?**

The Central Committee of the Communist Party of China has issued an open letter calling on all members of the Party and the Communist Youth League to take the lead to respond to the call of "one couple, one child." The letter has also urged them to publicize among the people the importance of this call. The aim is to keep the population within 1,200 million [1.2 billion] by the end of this century.

The letter said: "The State Council has already issued a call to the people of the whole country, encouraging each couple to have only one child. This is an important measure which concerns the speed and future of the four modernizations and the health and happiness of the future generations. It is a measure that conforms to immediate and longer-term interests of the whole people."

The letter recalled that in the 30 years since the founding of the People's Republic in 1949, China's net populations increase was 430 million. This was the result of the improvement of health work and people's living standards, which greatly reduced the mortality rate. In those years, the state did not take adequate measures to control the birth rate. The rapid growth of population is causing increasing difficulties for the people in food, clothing, housing, transportation, education, public health, and employment, and makes it difficult for the state to bring about a change to the country's poverty and backwardness within a short time.

What is even more aggravating is the fact that young people under 30 now account for 65 percent of the total population. This means that in the coming years an average 20 million people will reach the marriageable and

childbearing age every year. If efforts are not made to bring the population growth under control, China's population will swell to 1,300 million [1.3 billion] after 20 years and will surpass 1,500 million [1.5 billion] in 40 years if the present rate of 2.2 children per couple continues. This will definitely hinder the modernization program and give rise to difficulties in improving the people's standards of living.

Such being the case, the letter said, the most effective way to solve this question is for one couple to have one child only.

Some people worry that if each couple has only one child, new problems will arise, such as the average age of the population will increase, the male population will outnumber the female population and a large number of old people will have to be supported. Some of these worries result from their misunderstanding while others can be solved if necessary measures are taken in good time. For example, the phenomenon of the population getting older will not appear in this century because at present half of the population are under 21 and those over 65 are less than 5 per cent. The problem of the population getting older will crop up only after 40 years. But of course measures can be taken in advance to prevent such an occurrence.

The Party and the government have decided to take concrete steps to control the population growth, the letter said. Special considerations will be given to the only children and their families. These include enrollment in nurseries and schools, special medical care, priority in getting employment and housing, equal pay for equal work.

In conclusion, the letter stressed that family planning is a matter that concerns the interests of every household and that the method of persuasion and education should be adhered to. In the case of people having actual difficulty in meeting policy requirements, they may be allowed to have two children. The practice may be relaxed among the people of minority nationalities.

Remin Ribao and other newspapers with a nationwide circulation have all published the full text of this letter.

14.8 OVER-THE-LIMIT OF BIRTHS GUERRILLA UNIT—NEW YEAR'S EVE TELEVISION GALA COMEDY SKETCH (1990)

In the 1990 New Year's Gala, two comedians presented a skit about a couple with three young daughters and about to have a fourth child. The skit on the one-child state policy played heavily on out-dated political terminology—old enough not to be too sensitive, but current enough that the entire audience would find it humorous. However, like all good comedy, in numerous instances it skated precariously close to the truth. To avoid being apprehended, many women who did become pregnant, often deliberately in an attempt to have a son, fled to areas where they might not be discovered. The comedy sketch, far from offending state officials, became one of the most recognizable and repeated comedy sketches of the era and was often given encore performances at state sponsored galas for years afterwards.

Questions

1. **Why do you think this skit became so famous in China?**
2. **How would you describe its stance toward the one-child policy?**

[*A man and a woman wearing typical peasant clothes stealthily sneak onto stage each carrying an obviously fake baby doll on their back*]

WOMAN: It's you! Is it safe here?

MAN: According to my reconnaissance, there is no sign of the enemy.

WOMAN: Oh my gosh! [I'm] so exhausted.

MAN: Not so loud!

WOMAN: What's wrong?

MAN: Don't you see the old woman over there!

WOMAN: Where?

MAN: [She] even looks like the head of a **neighborhood committee.** They are very strict about this type of case now.

WOMAN: If we are caught, then that's that. I don't care any more. Hiding here or there every day, I feel like thieves, all for what?

MAN: All will be better in a couple of days after delivering the baby.

WOMAN: Delivery, delivery! It's such misery being married to you. Married for four years, and given birth to three girls. Its nonstop, either No. 1 is crying, or No. 2 is screaming.... Oh me gosh! No. 3 is peeing.

MAN: Here, let her pee into this (taking off his hat).

WOMAN: Doesn't it leak?

MAN: There is a piece of plastic inside. Ordinarily it protects me from the rain, but at critical moments like this, it's used to catch urine. A hat with dual purposes. I'm telling you, there are too many problems in cities. The fine for spitting is 50 cents, so this pee would surely cost us a ten-er [10 *yuan*]!

WOMAN: I'm telling you, our quality of life is getting lower and lower with every birth. I can't even afford the things I've been craving for during my pregnancy.

MAN: Food is not important. *Exercise* is the most important thing in life. Get up, let's go for a stroll.

NEIGHBORHOOD COMMITTEE—The lowest administrative unit in urban China, it keeps updated records of all residents within a defined neighborhood.

WOMAN: Get lost! We've been walking for a whole day! What would going for a stroll achieve?

MAN: If you're lazy and don't move it, it means you're gonna have a girl. It's good for you, come on... let's go for a stroll.

WOMAN: We don't even have any fruit to eat.

MAN: Didn't I get you two bunches of green onions!

WOMAN: How can you compare a big bunch of green onions to fruit!

MAN: The scientific value of green onion is the same as fruit.

WOMAN: Get lost! How can you compare green onion eaters with fruit eaters? The children of the fruit eaters are all of red cheeks and fresh looking. Now look at our three, all are green-onion-color.

[....]

WOMAN: Since we had these kids, our living quality has rapidly deteriorated every day. Even the way the city people look at us is not right. The truth is even how we feel ourselves is ruining the city view. It's a bit better during the day, but at night, we don't even have a place to live and have to crawl into these cement pipelines. My heart is broken to watch the children freezing and shivering. Now, come on let's go home, Okay?

MAN: You know, there are times I want to go home, too. But what can we do when we return to the village? The fine for No. 1, 2 and 3 almost cleaned us out, what's left for No. 4?

WOMAN: But at least, we have a home. Let's acknowledge our mistakes to the village head, so that it can be counted as voluntary confession. That way he has to give us a more lenient punishment. If he's not willing to be lenient and still wants to fine us, let's give him an IOU for No. 4. We will promise not to have any more children, no matter if it [is a] boy or girl. In the future, we will work hard to make more money and raise these kids. Let the two of us find the happiness we once shared again. Don't you think it's better?

MAN: Great! You know, I was thinking more than once, this is such place of strangers to us and what troubles we would be in if we got caught?

WOMAN: Right, of course.

MAN: Especially there are so many people in the city, walking on the street ... oh my gosh, the **bound-feet inspectors** are coming!

WOMAN: Now, retreat!

MAN: You retreat first, while I cover you!

14.9　ZHANG YIMOU'S *THE STORY OF QIUJU* (1992)

Based on the novella *The Wan Family's Lawsuit* (*Wanjia Susong*) by Chen Yuanbin, the film was Zhang Yimou's first film directly addressing issues relevant to contemporary China. Set in the rural northwestern province of Shaanxi, the film traces the pregnant Qiu Ju's effort to work through the different, newly established legal framework. Almost documentary in style, the film captures the daily drudgery, complicated village politics, and the yawning gap between urban and rural China. In many ways, Qiu Ju represents a type of modern China anti-hero, unwilling to bow either to the village head's arrogant behavior or be intimidated by China's notoriously convoluted and opaque bureaucracy.

> ### Questions
> 1. **What event causes Qiu Ju to seek out the police?**
> 2. **Why doesn't Qiu Ju accept the village chief's payment?**

POLICEMAN: Who are you looking for?

QIUJU: Policeman Li.

POLICEMAN LI: Come over, come over, have a seat. Eh, you two sit over there first, I am busy here. What's up?

POLICEMAN LI: Wan Qinglai. What's wrong with Qinglai?

QIUJU: He was kicked.

POLICEMAN LI: You are Qinglai's wife?

BOUND-FEET INSPECTORS—A derogatory reference to the neighborhood committee staff since they were often elderly women.

QIUJU: Yea.

POLICEMAN LI: Aiya, I didn't get to go to Qinglai's wedding. Everyone said his wife is quite beautiful. So it's you, hmmm? Wow, about to have a baby already. Sit, sit. Wound of soft tissue on the right side. Minor swollen of testicle on left side. Qinglai is not a trouble-maker, how could he have been kicked so that it was swollen? With whom?

QIUJU: The village head.

POLICEMAN LI: Who? Wang Shantang?

QIUJU: Ah-huh.

POLICEMAN LI: What for?

QIUJU: My family grows chili peppers, um, you know that?

POLICEMAN LI: Hm-mm.

QIUJU: We wanted to build a chili pepper shed and even had the bricks ready, but the village head simply wouldn't approve it. There was no other way, so we thought we could use the edge of the self-cultivated field my family contracted, and we just build it there. But the village head still said he would not approve it. He said it was not permitted [to build]. I said, fine you have the regulations, show me the regulations. He said he didn't need to show it to me. He said *he* is the reg-ulations, and he wouldn't show me.

POLICEMAN LI: Regardless, there is truly such a policy. The fields are for growing crops, if everyone builds something on it, what are we going to eat?

QIUJU: But the policy doesn't say to hit people. He is the village head, one or two hits are fine, but he sim-ply shouldn't be allowed to kick him "where it counts."

POLICEMAN LI: One hand cannot clap. He wouldn't hit anyone for no reason? What was it really for? What for?

SISTER: My brother was very angry and cussed him out.

POLICEMAN LI: Who are you?

SISTER: Qinglai is my older brother.

POLICEMAN LI: What did your brother say to him?

SISTER: Said he would have no heir to carry on the family ... that he only hatched a flock of hens.

POLICEMAN LI: Ah, that was Qinglai's wrongdo-ing. Everyone knows that [the village headman] Wang Shantang has four daughters and no boys. Those words hit the old man hard. Family planning just pre-vented him [from having more kids], how could this be mentioned?

QIUJU: Whatever [the reason], he was wrong to hit people. He is the village head, how could he just kick him "where it counts?" So I went to ask for an expla-nation, he said he didn't care, he felt like kicking him, so he kicked. I said you kicked him, if you are not responsible, who is? You are the village head and you hit people, you were wrong.

POLICEMAN LI: This is it? Right?

QIUJU: Uh-huh.

POLICEMAN LI: I tell you he was undoubtedly wrong to hit people.

QIUJU: He sure was wrong. How could he kick him "where it counts." He was damaged, he ...

POLICEMAN LI: I just told you, he was undoubt-edly wrong. How about you go home first. In a day or two, I will come to your village to investigate. Okay?

QIUJU: Uh-huh.

POLICEMAN LI: Both sides will need to self-criticize. Clear?

QIUJU: Uh-huh.

POLICEMAN LI: You go home first. I am very busy today. I will keep this here for now.

QIUJU: When will you come?

POLICEMAN LI: In a couple of days.

QIUJU: Okay. Policeman Li, you come in a couple of days.

[. . . .]

[*Qiuju and Policeman Li walk to the grinding house where village head was*]

VILLAGERS: Policeman Li, come in and warm up by the fire.

POLICEMAN LI: [To the villagers] Ah, I need to talk to Old Wang, you guys go outside first.

VILLAGE HEAD: You came.

POLICEMAN LI: Grinding corn?

VILLAGE HEAD: Uh-huh.

POLICEMAN LI: Ah, Old Wang, I have seen the proof from the hospital and Qinglai's injury. He was wrong to insult you. I have criticized him. No matter what, you are a [village] elder and the village head, hitting people is simply wrong.

VILLAGE HEAD: I am handling [their case] according to the policy you gave me.

POLICEMAN LI: The policy does not say you can hit people.

VILLAGE HEAD: Think it over carefully, why do you think was he beaten?

QIUJU: You are the village head, to hit him just once or twice would have been okay. But you cannot kick him "where it counts."

VILLAGE HEAD: So I kicked him, I kicked him so he wouldn't say such nonsense any more.

POLICEMAN LI: Alright, alright. Qiuju, you go out first, I need to talk to the village head.

QIUJU: Uh-huh.

[*Qiuju walked outside and waited. Policeman Li was walking out*]

POLICEMAN LI: Old Wang, so it's solved. Qiuju.

QIUJU: Ah?

POLICEMAN LI: You see, it's like this. He was wrong to hit people, and I have criticized him. But Qinglai's words were quite terrible. Both sides need to do more self-criticism. The result of mediation is like this: Medical expenses and the costs incurred from missing work are Wang Shantang's responsibilities, which totals 200 yuan. What do you think?

QIUJU: I am not after money, but an apology.

POLICEMAN LI: He is a stubborn man and the village head, you just give him some face. Plus Qinglai's injury was not such a big deal.

QIUJU: There is still no apology.

POLICEMAN LI: He is willing to pay, which proves you are right and he is wrong. Isn't this an apology. So this will suffice. Tomorrow, bring the medical receipt and a proof of payment to him. You two make the exchange face to face, then it's over.

[*Qiuju approaches the village head's home*]

QIUJU: Village head.

VILLAGE HEAD: Did you bring the receipt and proof of payment?

QIUJU: Uh-huh. Take a look.

VILLAGE HEAD: This is 200 yuan. It's yours now.

[*The village head then throws it into the air so that the money flies all over causing Qiuju to run around bending over to pick them up off of the ground*]

QIUJU: Village head, what's that for?

VILLAGE HEAD: What for? It's not so simple to take other's money.

QIUJU: I am not after your money today. I just want what's right.

VILLAGE HEAD: Right? You think I am soft? I merely did it for sake of Policeman Li and as it was a long way for him to come and so was giving him face. There were a total of twenty bills. Each time you picked one up, you bowed to me once. You picked one up–you bowed to me once. After twenty bows, then this is over.

QIUJU: It's not up to you if it is over or not.

[*Qiuju returns to the town police station*]

QIUJU: I want to see Policeman Li.

POLICEMAN: He's gone to the district for a meeting.

QIUJU: Gone for a meeting. When is he coming back?

POLICEMAN: Not sure.

[*Qiuju and Qinglai talking at home*]

QIUJU: Originally it was to be over. He threw the money on the ground and said those mean words. I can't believe there is not an apology.

QINGLAI: Our family members are not good at talking. I cannot move around well. The road to the county is not easy. You are getting heavier and I do worry.

QIUJU: Eh, nothing to worry about. If it's meant to drop, it will drop. If it's not meant to drop, you cannot roll it out with a rolling pin.

QINGLAI: Don't forget to take some money with you tomorrow.

QIUJU: We have no cash. We will take a cart of chili peppers.

QINGLAI: It's not the right season and you probably won't get a good price for them.

QIUJU: I don't care about the money. I just need an apology.

14.10   ZHANG JIE'S LOVE MUST NOT BE FORGOTTEN (1979)

Born in 1937, Zhang Jie experienced the harshest of the country's political campaigns. Her stories, while not autobiographical, tapped into the experiences and frustrations of her generation. Her 1985 novel, *Leaden Wings,* won the Mao Dun literary prize. Her writings aroused considerable controversy by challenging the patriarchal, socially amoral, and often corrupt underside of Chinese society. The story excerpted here, "Love Must Not Be Forgotten," called into question the basis of love and marriage in China. As one of the first to dare suggest marriage could and did exist without love (or conversely that love could endure outside marriage), the story was condemned in government circles as subverting the country's morality by defending love outside of marriage. But the author was viewed by the Chinese public as one of China's first novelists to openly express feminist ideas in the post-Cultural Revolution period. Her books were among the country's top sellers.

Questions

1. **Why is the main character in a quandary over her suitor Qiao Lin?**
2. **Do you find the story more idealistic or realistic? Why?**
3. **Why might some Chinese officials be disturbed by the story?**

I am thirty, the same age as our People's Republic. For a republic thirty is still young. But a girl of thirty is virtually on the shelf.

Actually, I have a bona fide suitor. Have you seen the Greek sculptor Myrong's Discobolus? Qiao Lin is the image of that discus thrower. Even the padded clothes he wears in winter fail to hide his fine physique. Bronzed, with clear-cut features, a broad forehead and large eyes, his appearance alone attracts most girls to him.

But I can't make up my mind to marry him. I'm not clear what attracts me to him, or him to me. I know people are gossiping behind my back, "Who does she think she is, to be so choosy?" To them, I'm a nobody playing hard to get. They take offense at such preposterous behavior.

Of course, I shouldn't be captious. In a society where commercial production still exists, marriage like most other transactions is still a form of barter.

I have known Qiao Lin for nearly two years, yet still cannot fathom whether he keeps so quiet from aversion to talking or from having nothing to say. When, by way of a small intelligence test, I demand his opinion of this or that, he says "good" or "bad" like a child in kindergarten.

Once I asked, "Qiao Lin, why do you love me?" He thought the question over seriously for what seemed an age. I could see from his normally smooth but now wrinkled forehead that the little grey cells in his handsome head were hard at work cogitating. I felt ashamed to have put him on the spot.

Finally he raised his clear childlike eyes to tell me, "Because you're good!"

Loneliness flooded my heart. "Thank you, Qiao Lin!" I couldn't help wondering if we were to marry, whether we could discharge our duties to each other as husband and wife. Maybe, because law and morality would have bound us together. But how tragic simply to comply with law and morality! Was there no stronger bond to link us?

When such thoughts cross my mind I have the strange sensation that instead of being a girl contemplating marriage I am an elderly social scientist.

Perhaps I worry too much. We can live like most married couples, bringing up children together, strictly true to each other according to the law. . . . Although living in the seventies of the twentieth century, people still consider marriage the way they did millennia ago, as a means of continuing the race, a form of barter or a business transaction in which love and marriage can be separated. Since this is the common practice, why shouldn't we follow suit?

But I still can't make up my mind. As a child, I remember, I often cried all night for no rhyme or reason, unable to sleep and disturbing the whole household. My old nurse, a shrewd though uneducated woman, said an ill wind had blown through my ear. I think this judgment showed prescience, because I still have that old weakness. I upset myself over things which really present no problem, upsetting other people at the same time. One's nature is hard to change.

I think of my mother too. If she were alive, what would she say about my attitude to Qiao Lin and my uncertainty about marrying him? My thoughts constantly turn to her, not because she was such a strict mother that her ghost is still watching over me since her death. No, she was not just my mother but my closest friend. I loved her so much that the thought of her leaving me makes my heart ache.

She never lectured me, just told me quietly in her deep, unwomanly voice about her successes and failures, so that I could learn from her experience. She had evidently not had many successes—her life was full of failures.

During her last days she followed me with her fine, expressive eyes, as if wondering how I would manage on my own and as if she had some important advice for me but hesitated to give it. She suddenly blurted out, "Shanshan, if you aren't sure what you want, don't rush into marriage—better live on your own!"

Other people might think this strange advice from a mother to her daughter, but to me it embodies her bitter experience. I don't think she underestimated me or my knowledge of life. She loved me and didn't want me to be unhappy.

"I don't want to marry, mother!" I said, not out of bashfulness or a show of coyness. I can't think why a girl should pretend to be coy. She had long since taught me about things not generally mentioned to girls.

"If you meet the right man, then marry him. Only if he's right for you!"

"I'm afraid no such man exists!"

"That's not true. But it's hard. The world is so vast, I'm afraid you may never meet him." Whether married or not was not what concerned her, but the quality of the marriage.

"Haven't you managed fine without a husband?"

"Who says so?"

"I think you've done fine."

"I had no choice...." She broke off, lost in thought, her face wistful. Her wistful lined face reminded me of a withered flower I had pressed in a book.

"Why did you have no choice?"

"You ask too many questions," she parried, not ashamed to confide in me but afraid that I might reach the wrong conclusion. Besides, everyone treasures a secret to carry to the grave. Feeling a bit put out, I demanded bluntly, "didn't you love my dad?"

"No, I never loved him."

"Did he love you?"

"No, he didn't."

"Then why get married?"

She paused, searching for the right words to explain this mystery, then answered bitterly, "When you're young you don't always know what you're looking for, what you need, and people may talk you into getting married. As you grow older and more experienced you find out your true needs. By then, though, you've done many foolish things for which you could kick yourself. You'd give anything to be able to make a fresh start and live more wisely. Those content with their lot will always be happy, they say, but I shall never enjoy that happiness." She added self-mockingly, "A wretched idealist, that's all I am."

Did I take after her? Did we both have genes which attracted ill winds?

"Why don't you marry again?"

"I'm afraid I'm still not sure what I really want." She was obviously unwilling to tell me the truth.

CHAPTER 15
CHINA IN THE TWENTY-FIRST CENTURY

VISUAL SOURCE
The Future Be Dammed:
China's Three Gorges

① NEARLY A CENTURY IN THE MAKING: Serious consideration of a Yangzi dam began with Sun Zhongshan's proposition in 1919. Only under the Nationalist (GMD) government were surveys, feasibility studies, and models completed. As the Chinese Civil War flared up again in 1946 all work came to an abrupt end. Although Mao Zedong gave the dam project his blessing (and many smaller hydroelectric projects were completed), the dam never made headway during his lifetime.

② CONSTUCTION: In the 1980s, the Chinese government again began feasibility studies for a massive single dam that would offer flood control, power generation, and improved navigation. Physical construction of the dam began in 1997 and was completed in 2008, a year ahead of schedule. The dam wall is 7,575 feet long and over 600 feet high. It creates a narrow reservoir 412 miles long with an average width of .7 miles.

③ RELOCATION: A controversial aspect of the dam is the relocation of residents affected by the mammoth reservoir. With the water level at its current height 1.4 million residents from 13 cities, 140 towns, and 1,352 villages (including about 650 factories) have been displaced. While residents were moved and many given compensation packages, often the new settlements lacked the arable land, local industry, or even adequate drinking water for the relocated residents.

④ YANGZI RIVER: The third longest river in the world, the Yangzi twists and turns for over 3,900 miles from the edge of the Tibetan plateau, through China's heartland until exiting into East China Sea near Shanghai. Ocean-going cargo vessels can sail inland 1,700 miles to several in-land ports. For centuries, the river caused great destruction often breeching the dykes and flooding vast areas of the middle and lower Yangzi (including major floods in 1996, 1998, and 2002).

⑤ THREE GORGES: The Three Gorges (Qutang, Wuxia, and Xiling) are a 125-mile stretch of the Yangzi downriver from Chongqing. The narrow gorges have demarcated for thousands of years the border between the up-river Sichuanese inland basin from the down-river central Chinese plains. The granite and limestone cliffs that lined the gorges are among China's most exquisite nature beauties and have been the object of Chinese poems and legendary tales for millennia.

⑥ ENVIRONMENTAL IMPACT: The Three Gorges Dam has resulted in an array of environmental problems. Landslides along the edges of the reservoir are more numerous and more severe than initially expected. Some landslides have been reported to unleash waves 165 feet high. The reduced flow of water is causing pollutants, which were previously flushed downstream and ultimately out to sea, to accumulate behind the dam at alarming levels.

On the tenth anniversary of the founding of the People's Republic of China, October 1, 1959, Mao Zedong drove down Chang'an Avenue in the back seat of China's first domestically produced car, a black Red Flag (Hongqi) sedan. According to revolutionary lore, the sleek Red Flag (Hongqi) in which he rode had been rush-ordered especially for the occasion and built in thirty-three days. In an era when owning a bicycle was considered a luxury, the extravagance of a private car would have been considered feudalistic and counter-revolutionary for all but the Party elite. As a result of this attitude, domestic car production in China was negligible, with only two thousand cars produced, for the exclusive use of the party leaders, in two decades. Their massive frames, abysmal handling, and poor mileage finally brought production of the original Red Flags to an end in the 1980s.

Twenty-five years after the last model rolled off the assembly line, First Auto Works (FAW) introduced a distinctly retro-chic Red Flag sedan. Unveiled in a Beijing car show, the version on display included East-is-Red style, Sun-shaped hubcaps, a grill evocative of the Gate of Heavenly Peace, and the marquee Red Flag hood ornament. Just as unattainable for China's masses as the first Red Flag sedan, this newly released special model had a sticker price of well over a quarter of million dollars. But unlike 1959 when there were few or no options for the ordinary Chinese, China's burgeoning middle class can today choose from over two-dozen domestic manufacturers and virtually every major global car producer.

China's love affair with cars is not unlike what exists in the West. Chinese have embraced personal automobiles as a sign of upward mobility and they increasingly view them as a necessity of life and an extension of their personality, much as any American or European does. Automobiles provide convenience, privacy and status in a way few other commodities do. For decades, China remained a land where the bicycle was the primary mode of transportation. In metropolitan China, separate bike lanes as wide as those allocated for autos ran along all major roads. By the late 1980s the era of the bicycle was rapidly coming to an end. Today bicycles remain an integral part of Chinese life, but bicyclists must share their (increasingly smaller) lane with mopeds, electric scooters, and even automobiles trying to squeeze through. With the rising number of cars on the road, bicycles on the streets of urban China are rapidly dwindling in numbers.

In June of 2007, China had nearly 53 million cars on the road, and it is estimated that China will triple that number within the next 10 years. (By comparison, the United States, with less than a quarter the population of China, had 150 million cars on the road by 2000). The rise of automobiles in China has resulted in a host of other changes within China. In 2005, McDonald's opened its first drive-thru and by 2007 there existed over three dozen drive-thrus in ten different cities across the country. Car clubs have sprung up in most every large city. They sponsor long-distance trips with their members traveling in convoys along China's rapidly expanding highway network. China's swift adoption of the automobile has also wrought an equally abrupt rise in the number of automobile accidents. On average, roughly 90,000 Chinese per year have died in traffic accidents. To put this another way, although Chinese vehicles make up only 3 percent of the world's total, they account for 21 percent of the world's traffic deaths.

The possibility of an individual being able to buy a car underscores the massive social changes generated by Deng Xiaoping's economic reforms begun in the 1980s. These reforms were expanded by Jiang Zemin in the 1990s and sustained by Hu Jintao in the first decade of the twenty-first century. The policies deeply altered Chinese society. In the first decades of the People's Republic of China, virtually every Chinese living in a town or city belonged to a work unit. One's housing, workplace, cafeteria, and infirmary were often all located within a fifteen minute walk of each other. But as the centralized system of controls were rolled back, the work units no longer provided such amenities and Chinese began to find their own careers, buy their own (often much larger) apartments, and purchase their own cars. The trade-offs for the individual citizen were complex and remain difficult to discern, particularly while the economy remains profitable for most Chinese.

What is unambiguous is the disappearance of the "**iron rice bowl**" (*tie fanwan*). The iron rice bowl is a Chinese idiom referring to the Chinese government's original promise (in the 1950s) of cradle-to-grave social security, housing, and employment (regardless of job performance). Under Deng Xiaoping, the country sought to modernize and abandon much of the inefficient, over-staffed, and unprofitable state-run industry (much of it the soviet-modeled heavy industry sectors) through privatization. By the time that Jiang Zemin took office in the early 1990s, the central government had begun to force the closures of inefficient and out-dated state industries across the country. This resulted in millions of workers either being laid off (*maiduan*), whereby workers would receive a lump-sum severance payment but no pension or medical insurance, or receiving internal retirement (*neitui*), whereby the workers would cease working but receive a minimal salary with minimal contributions towards their pension and medical benefits (the size of which would depend upon the financial situation of the individual work unit). It was left to **Hu Jintao** who took office in 2003 to remedy the resulting unemployment and growing disparity between China's urban rich and the rural poor. To this end, Hu Jintao sponsored legislation that promoted insurance for all Chinese citizens and instituted a new labor law that restricts the use of temporary laborers and strengthens the protection of workers from dangers in the workplace and unjust termination. The central government's role in the privatization process juxtaposed with their focus on urban commercialization stands in sharp contrast to the CCP's original focus on China's industrial laborers and rural peasants. Both Jiang Zemin and Hu Jintao were apprehensive about this seeming move against the traditional core constituents of China's communist roots. This apprehension has led them to consistently reiterate the Deng Xiaoping slogan emphasizing "socialism with Chinese characteristics." The shift in government has not gone unnoticed or uncontested by those most affected. In 2004 there were more than 74,000 separate protests (compared to 10,000 in 1994) involving 3.76 million people. Despite this simmering discontent, the vast majority of Chinese appear content, or at least resigned, to the new direction of the country. In large part, there exists a consensus that the central policies implemented under Jiang Zemin and Hu Jintao have ushered in an era of economic prosperity not seen in China since the mid-eighteenth century, the golden age of the Qianlong emperor.

For most Chinese, both in the cities and in the rural areas, the recent economic benefits are perceived to offset any negative elements of the current administration such as rampant corruption, limited social justice, and minimal freedom of political expression. The CCP leadership and the Chinese people are clearly of one mind on most things. Neither wants to replicate the harsh economic privations that struck Russia in the wake of the Soviet Union's dissolution, privations that resulted in only limited political freedom and widespread economic stagnation. According to the World Bank, more than 280 million Chinese lifted themselves out of poverty between 1978 and 2003. In the short term, it appears that the Chinese people are content to allow for the centralized economy and party-controlled political state to remain as long as it provides the economic and social incentives desired—like the chance to purchase their own automobile and maybe even a Big Mac at a McDonald's drive-thru.

IRON RICE BOWL—A term describing guaranteed or "unbreakable" jobs, housing, and social security in the decades immediately after the founding of the PRC.

HU JINTAO (1942–)—Born in Anhui, he received a degree in hydraulic engineering from Tsinghua University and rose through the ranks with posts in Guizhou and Tibet. He became President of the PRC in 2003 and has pursued conservative economic and political reforms.

POLITICAL CURRENTS

In the first decade of the twenty-first century, China's leadership continued to seek for new ways in which to balance adherence to their communist roots while pushing for modernization. Both Jiang Zemin and Hu Jintao, as China's paramount leaders, have created new ideological formulas that seek to bridge external and internal inconsistencies. Jiang Zemin's "Three Represents" sought to update past party doctrine so as to acknowledge the realities of an economically vibrant China (15.1). Hu Jintao's "Scientific Outlook on Development" reflects the efforts of a party run by technocrats rather than ideologues to emphasize the maintenance of social harmony (15.2). Despite new slogans and recent CCP ideologies (often impenetrable to the common Chinese), many traditional goals of the central government remain. None looms larger than the problems of Taiwan (Republic of China) and Tibet. Taiwan's citizens continue to wrestle with the reality of de facto independence, and the façade of a unified China, a façade established with the "One China Policy" agreement between Mao Zedong and President Nixon in 1972. While stopping short of declaring Taiwan's independence, **Chen Shuibian** has tirelessly sought to find alternate avenues to end Taiwan's decades of diplomatic isolation, including inclusion in many international organizations under titles other than the ROC (15.3). The Tibetan resistance to the Chinese presence in Tibet and the power of the Dalai Lama within the Tibetan regions of China continues to challenge the PRC who struggle to find effective and appropriate responses (15.4).

15.1 JIANG ZEMIN'S THREE REPRESENTS (JULY 1, 2001)

Jiang Zemin's "Three Represents" became a formal component of CCP's official ideology, with Marxist-Lenism, Mao Zedong Thought, and Deng Xiaoping Theory, during the Seventeenth Political Congress (2001). Although "Three Represents" makes as little grammatical and philosophical sense in Chinese as it does in English, it suggests that the Chinese Communist Party *represents* three things: 1) the majority of the people—not just the worker, peasant, soldier—the triumvirate of the traditional communist theory; 2) advanced culture—which Jiang equates with Marxism; and 3) advanced technology—or as Deng Xiaoping put it far more succinctly, modernization. In essence, Jiang Zemin's political philosophy, like his leadership, sought to update both the "revolutionary language" and to legitimize the actions of the growing business, or "capitalist" class, and to integrate both into a mainstream political culture. On a functional level, Jiang's doctrines attempted to refocus China's ideology on economic and technological advances while keeping the party machinery in place as the dominant bureaucratic structure.

Questions

1. How does Jiang Zemin's policy deviate from that of Deng Xiaoping? Does he emphasize or include any new or different policies?
2. What aspects of Chinese development do you think most concerned Jiang Zemin?

TAIWAN AND ROMANIZATION: The question of how Taiwanese Romanize their names is fraught with efforts to express linguistic, cultural, and historical preferences. Many of Taiwan's political leaders do not Romanize their names conforming to any single system. Thus the leader of the GMD, Lian Zhan, Romanizes his name as Lien Chan, Chen Shuibian as Chen Shui-bian, and Song Chuyu as Soong Chu-yu (and often in English language sources as James Soong). For the sake of uniformity, but at the risk of disregarding personal choice, all names have been converted to pinyin system.

[. . . .] The meaning of the important thought of Three Represents

Representing the development trend of China's advanced productive forces.

The Party's basic nature determines that it must represent the development trend of China's advanced productive forces. Productive forces are the most revolutionary and dynamic factors in a social mode of production, and they are the forces that ultimately determine how human society develops. The competition among all the forces in the world today is, in the final analysis, a competition in overall national power, including economic, scientific, and technological strength and national cohesiveness. China's productive forces have grown fairly rapidly over the 50 plus years since the People's Republic was founded in 1949, especially over the 20 plus years since the policies of reform and opening up were introduced in the late 1970s. However, their overall level is still much lower than in the developed countries in the West. China must vigorously develop its productive forces and improve its economy so that it can gain greater initiative and a more favorable position in future competition in science and technology and solve its present economic and social problems. All the Party's battles during the 80 plus years since its founding have been waged to emancipate and develop the productive forces. The Party must ground itself on China's realities, conform to the trend of the times, stay focused on economic development, and make developing the productive forces its basic task.

Representing the orientation of China's advanced culture.

Socialist society means a society that develops and progresses comprehensively. A society is truly socialist only when its economic, political, and cultural development is balanced and a good job is done in both material and spiritual civilization. Only by always representing the orientation of China's advanced culture and working hard to develop a socialist culture with Chinese characteristics can the CPC achieve this goal. In present-day China, developing advanced culture means developing a national, scientific, and popular culture that is geared to the needs of modernization, the world and the future. The fundamental task of socialist culture is to educate citizens to have lofty ideals, moral integrity, good education, and a strong sense of discipline. We must always take Marxism as our guide, clearly discern the orientation of advanced culture, and resolutely oppose wrong, anti-Marxist ideas. At the same time, we must clearly understand that Marxism is a developing science. It cannot be regarded as a rigid dogma; new experience and understanding gained from practice must be constantly assimilated and used to enrich and develop Marxism.

Representing the fundamental interests of the overwhelming majority of the Chinese people.

Ever since our Party was founded, its primary aim has been to serve the people wholeheartedly. Over the past 80 plus years, all our successes in both revolution and development have been attributable mainly to the fact that we represent the interests of the overwhelming majority of the people and are able to unite with them in their struggles for their own interests. In the circumstances of carrying out the reform and opening up and expanding the socialist market economy, our Party must emphasize working for the interests of the people more than ever before. The Party's greatest political strength is that we have maintained close ties with the masses, and the greatest danger since assuming political power has lain in the possibility of being estranged from them. Whether the line, principles, and policies the Party formulates conform to the fundamental interests of the overwhelming majority of the people must be taken as the highest criterion for judging them, and whether the people are satisfied with and agree with them must be taken as their basis and goal. Our cadres must maintain the work style and the way of thinking of "from the masses, to the masses". They must be concerned about the people's hardships, listen to their opinions and protect their interests. Party officials, especially leaders at all levels, must be incorruptible and self-disciplined and share weal and woe with the masses. At all times and under any circumstances, Party officials must follow the Party's mass line, adhere to the objective of serving the people wholeheartedly, and take benefiting the people as the starting and end points of all their work. They must carefully study the new character of mass work in the new situation and integrate strengthening and improving mass work into all their work relating to Party building and consolidating political power.

The Three Represents are mutually related, complement each other, and constitute a unified whole.

The unity of the Three Represents is a unity not only in theoretical logic but also in practice. Developing advanced productive forces is a fundamental condition for developing advanced culture and materializing the fundamental interests of the overwhelming majority of the people. At the same time, the development of advanced productive forces is inseparable from cultural issues such as ideology, ethics, education, and science because the general ideological and cultural levels of a given society directly affect the quality of the work force. The same is true of the relationship between the people and the development of advanced productive forces and advanced culture. The people are the main creators of advanced productive forces and advanced culture as well as the basic force to achieve their own interests. At the same time, the basic reason to develop advanced productive forces and advanced culture is to satisfy the ever-growing needs of the people's material and cultural lives and to continually ensure that their fundamental interests are fulfilled. Just as Jiang Zemin pointed out, "All Party members must continue to integrate the fulfillment of the requirements of the Three Represents with all aspects of Party building and with the Party's leadership of the people in the whole process of carrying out the reform, opening up and the socialist modernization drive."

In short, the important thought of Three Represents is developing and advancing. The whole Party must continuously emancipate their minds, make theoretical progress, and break new ground in practice. They must infuse the important thought of Three Represents into all areas of the socialist modernization drive and into all aspects of Party building so that our Party always advances with the times and shares weal and woe with the people.

15.2 HU JINTAO PROPOSES SCIENTIFIC OUTLOOK ON DEVELOPMENT FOR TACKLING CHINA'S IMMEDIATE WOES, CHALLENGES (OCTOBER 15, 2007)

The promotion of Hu Jintao (1942–) to the paramount leader of China marks the full transition from revolutionary leaders to more pragmatic technocrats who occupy the top tier of the CCP. Like Jiang Zemin before him, Hu Jintao has formulated his own ideology to give a more modern shape to the notion of Socialism with Chinese Characteristics, a notion heralded by Deng Xiaoping three decades earlier. Generally referred to as "Scientific Outlook on Development" (*kexue fazhanguan*), Hu Jintao's guiding vision emphasizes the creation of a "Harmonious Society," sustainable development, social welfare, and a more egalitarian society. Within Hu's concept is the distinct effort to move the country into a post-revolutionary era where China's economic markets, its legal framework, and its institutional/bureaucratic infrastructure define the parameters of political life.

Questions

1. **How does Hu Jintao's Scientific Outlook on Development seek to guide China's political evolution and economic growth?**
2. **A central element of Hu Jintao's Scientific Outlook on Development is his notion of developing a "harmonious society." What concrete elements does he put forth as contributing to such a society?**

Hu Jintao, on behalf of the 16th CCP Central Committee, expounded on Monday on the political concept, which was put forward in 2003, in the political report to the 17th CCP National Congress that opened Monday morning.

"In light of the basic reality that China is in the primary stage of socialism, the Scientific Outlook on Development has been formulated to meet new requirements of development by analyzing China's own practice and drawing on the experience of other countries in development," Hu told more than 2,000 delegates at the live telecast meeting.

Some of the major features of the preliminary stage include:

- The economic strength has increased markedly, but the overall productivity remains low, the capacity for independent innovation is weak, and the long-standing structural problems and the extensive mode of growth are yet to be fundamentally addressed.

- The socialist market economy is basically in place, but there remain structural and institutional obstacles slowing down development, and further reform in difficult areas is confronted with deep-seated problems.

- A relatively comfortable standard of living has been achieved for the people as a whole, but the trend of a growing gap in income distribution has not been thoroughly reversed, there are still a considerable number of impoverished and low-income people in both urban and rural areas, and it has become more difficult to accommodate the interests of all sides.

- Efforts to balance development have yielded remarkable results, but the foundation of agriculture remains weak, the rural areas still lag behind in development, and the country faces an arduous task to narrow the urban-rural and interregional gaps in development and promote balanced economic and social development.

- Socialist democracy has continued to develop and we have made steady progress in implementing the rule of law as a fundamental principle, but efforts to improve democracy in the legal system fall somewhat short of the need to expand people's democracy and promote economic and social development, and political restructuring has to be deepened.

- Socialist culture is thriving as never before, but the people have growing cultural needs and have become more independent, selective, changeable, and diverse in thinking, setting higher requirements for the development of an advanced socialist culture.

- The society has become evidently more dynamic, but profound changes have taken place in the structure of society, in the way society is organized and in the pattern of social interests, and many new issues have emerged in social development and management.

- China is opening wider to the outside world, but international competition is becoming increasingly acute, pressure in the form of the economic and scientific dominance of developed countries will continue for a long time to come, both predictable and unpredictable risks are increasing, and the need to balance domestic development and opening to the outside world is greater than ever.

All the above-mentioned features boil down to the fact that "the reality that China is still in the primary stage of socialism and will remain so for a long time to come has not changed," he said.

"Stressing recognition of the basic reality is not meant to belittle ourselves, wallow in backwardness, or encourage unrealistic pursuit of quick results," Hu said. "Rather, such recognition will serve as the basis of our endeavor to advance reform and plan for development."

The cure for such challenges and woes lies in the Scientific Outlook on Development, which Hu said it "takes development as its essence, putting people first as its core, comprehensive, balanced and sustainable development as its basic requirement, and overall consideration as its fundamental approach."

Hu said to thoroughly apply the Scientific Outlook on Development "we must work energetically to build a harmonious socialist society," which features democracy and the rule of law, equity and justice, honesty and fraternity, vigor and vitality, stability and order, and harmony between man and nature."

"We will spare no effort to solve the most specific problems of the utmost and immediate concern to the people and strive to create a situation in which all people do their best, find their proper places in society, and live together in harmony, so as to provide a favorable social environment for development," Hu said.

15.3   ASSOCIATED PRESS INTERVIEW WITH PRESIDENT CHEN SHUIBIAN (DECEMBER 10, 2007)

Born in rural southern Taiwan, Chen Shuibian (1950–) received a law degree from National Taiwan University in 1974. In 1994, he became the mayor of Taibei, Taiwan's provincial capital. His popularity as mayor catapulted him to national fame as the first non-GMD president and later into a second term, which ended in 2008. In an effort to conciliate the GMD, he pledged not to move Taiwan closer to independence, though he has mounted campaigns to raise Taiwan's status in many international organizations, including WHO, WTO, and the United Nations, from which Taiwan was expelled when the PRC was acknowledged as the representative for China (13.1). Chen Shuibian's effort to gain admission to the UN has garnered considerable displeasure from the PRC and the United States as defying the "One China Policy" instituted under President Nixon and Chairman Mao Zedong in 1972. In the last months of 2007, President Chen Shuibian solicited interviews with several top media outlets. The following are excerpts from an interview with a reporter from the Associated Press.

Questions

1. **Why is the use of "Taiwan" instead of the "Republic of China" such a sensitive issue for Taiwanese, Chinese, and the world?**
2. **Does Chen Shuibian support the notion that to become Taiwanese an individual must incontrovertibly lose one's Chinese identity?**

ASSOCIATED PRESS (AP): I would like to start by asking President Chen how he would characterize his efforts to advance the rights of Taiwan's people in international organizations like the UN and the WHO during his eight years in office. Some of his critics say that, on the international stage, Taiwan remains more isolated than ever before, now. How does he respond to these criticisms?

PRESIDENT CHEN: One must not forget that it was during my presidency, at the end of 2001, that Taiwan finally acceded to the World Trade Organization (WTO), formally becoming the 144th member of the organization on January 1, 2002. Of course, it was only after years of hard work that an opportunity finally arrived at the end of 2001. On January 1, 2002, Taiwan then followed close on the heels of the People's Republic of China to become a formal member of the WTO.

We are pleased to see that, even though we have yet to succeed in gaining membership in the World Health Organization (WHO), our efforts toward this end have attracted increasing attention and support from the international community. The European Parliament, US Congress, as well as parliaments of other countries have passed resolutions in support of Taiwan's bid to gain observership in the World Health Assembly (WHA). In 2004, the issue was put to a vote, and I was very grateful to the US and Japan, neither of which enjoys formal diplomatic

relations with Taiwan, for voting in favor of Taiwan's observer status.

Since 2005, many European and American countries have given us much encouragement. They do not wish to see Taiwan remain the only loophole in the global disease prevention network, so they have supported Taiwan's meaningful participation in the WHO.

This year saw Taiwan's first ever application for membership in the UN under the name "Taiwan," and we are especially grateful that so many of our allies spoke out on our behalf. Even though the letter I sent to the UN Secretary-General Ban Ki-moon on behalf of our 23 million people to apply for UN membership was, unfortunately, rejected, with the help of our allies, 140 out of the 192 UN member states registered to take part in the discussion on the issue of Taiwan's participation during the second plenary session of the UN General Assembly. The discussion lasted for 4 hours and 15 minutes. Indeed, this year, the question of Taiwan's participation in the UN received unprecedented attention and space for debate.

We estimate that there were at least four to five times more international media reports and comments regarding Taiwan's UN participation this year than there were last year, reflecting a growth of support for Taiwan's UN membership within the international community. Therefore, even though we have yet to gain UN membership, we have taken a promising first step.

China has employed a "three alls" strategy against Taiwan—that is, to take all of Taiwan's diplomatic allies, block all channels for Taiwan internationally, and crush all Taiwan's international room for maneuver. Currently, Taiwan has 24 diplomatic allies, and this is not the lowest number of allies we have ever had. At one point during the Guomindang (GMD) era, Taiwan only had 19 diplomatic allies. Internationally, we face the "China factor" and China's suppression [of our country], which create many difficulties for us. But we still believe that we will find our way through.

So, during my administration, we have proactively sought to promote and enhance Taiwan's diplomatic relations. For example, this year marked the sixth time Taiwan held a summit with its Central American allies and the Dominican Republic. Also this year, we held the second summit with our Pacific allies, and hosted, for the first time, a summit with our African allies.

Therefore, not only do we wish to participate in international organizations; we also want to expand our circle of friends in the international arena; and apart from strengthening bilateral relations, we are also constantly trying to consolidate multilateral relations.

AP: I'm wondering if I could follow up now by talking a little bit about the campaign to enter the United Nations. President Chen has invested a huge amount of political resources in pursuit of this goal, despite the fact that because of China's veto power there is no chance that Taiwan can enter the United Nations. And at the same time, the cost of this effort in terms of Taiwan's relations with the United States, its most important diplomatic partner, has been very, very substantial. I wonder, given the fact that it's very difficult, if not impossible, to overcome the Chinese veto, and the cost to relations with the United States seems to be so high, how President Chen can justify this effort.

PRESIDENT CHEN: Joining the UN is a strong aspiration, expectation, and hope of the 23 million people of Taiwan, who want to enjoy the basic political rights and collective human rights accorded to formal UN members. In Taiwan, people may hold very divergent views on various issues, but regarding the issue of Taiwan's joining the UN, we have support from both the governing and opposition parties, and we have a vast majority of more than 70—up to 80—percent support from the general public.

Right now, the two referendum proposals regarding UN membership—that of the Democratic Progressive Party (DPP), using the name "Taiwan" to join the UN, and the GMD's version, using the name "Republic of China" to return to the UN—have both received enough support and garnered enough petition signatures for a referendum to be held. It is very rare in Taiwan for such an issue to garner such a high degree of support irrespective of party affiliation. This case, therefore, represents the majority voice of the people of Taiwan, and their wish that their voice be heard by the international community.

There is a threefold significance in holding a referendum on joining the UN under the name "Taiwan." First of all, my view is that referendums are a basic human right and a universal principle, and one should not compromise or apply different standards to such universal human rights and principles. The 23 million people of Taiwan deserve to enjoy the basic right to referendum. They should not be deprived of this right or have it restricted. We wish to follow such a democratic procedure and voice our aspiration to the world. It is only reasonable to expect our rights to be respected and supported.

Second, the people of Taiwan consider their nation to be an independent sovereign country. And our sovereignty rests with the 23 million people of Taiwan. Our sovereignty does not belong to the People's Republic of China. Taiwan and the PRC are two separate sovereign countries. Neither exercises jurisdiction over the other. Therefore, Taiwan has the full right to become a member of the UN.

Third, using the name "Taiwan" to apply for UN membership is to differentiate ourselves from China, from the PRC, because internationally, many regard Taiwan as part of China. Instead of using "Republic of China," we want to use "Taiwan" to apply for UN membership so as to avoid [seeming to] compete with the PRC on this issue of representing "one China" in the UN, an issue that was dealt with in 1971 by Resolution 2758 of the General Assembly. Using the name "Taiwan" to apply for UN membership demonstrates that we have no intention of fighting with the PRC over the representation of China. Instead, we want to seek appropriate representation for the 23 million people of Taiwan in the UN.

Using the name "Taiwan" to apply for UN membership does not mean changing the national moniker, nor does it violate the "**four noes**" (*sibu*) pledge I made. About 40 percent of the 192 UN member states do not use their formal national moniker as their name in the UN. Likewise, Taiwan uses "Chinese Taipei" to participate in the Asia-Pacific Economic Forum, and "the Separate Customs Territory of Taiwan, Penghu, Jinmen and Mazu" to participate in the WTO.

So if we use names other than our national moniker to participate in other international organizations, surely it can be done in the UN. Where is the sense in saying that using the name "Taiwan" to apply for UN membership constitutes a change of the national moniker? I think some people have tried to distort and misinterpret our UN bid as amounting to altering the status quo and changing our national moniker. We certainly cannot agree with their claims.

We use the name "Taiwan" because we think it is the most familiar, most beautiful, most endearing name that we have, and one that is associated with this land and our people. It is the name of the motherland of the 23 million people of Taiwan. That's why we want to use the name "Taiwan."

As to whether or not we will manage to gain UN membership, in the past 15 years, we have tried very hard to participate in the UN, but we have failed, largely because we were using the wrong strategy. We used the name "Republic of China" in our attempts to rejoin the UN, but by using this name, we were [giving the misimpression of] competing with China for the right to represent China in the UN, a question which was dealt with by Resolution 2758. That is why Taiwan did not stand a chance in the past. But now we are employing a new strategy. We want to acquire a new seat for the 23 million people of Taiwan instead of [seeming to] compete for the old China seat in the UN.

The PRC fought for 21 years before it was admitted to the UN, and Taiwan has only fought for 15 years. Previously, we employed the wrong strategy, but now we have come up with a new strategy with which to seek new membership. I believe that we will not waste another 15 years. Although we understand that success cannot be achieved overnight, we have taken the right first step, and now we have the opportunity to take the second, third, and further steps forward. As long as we work hard, persevere, and do not give up

too easily, I don't think we will need to wait another 15 years. I think we will succeed before then.

During the time when the PRC was trying to join the UN, the ROC was a permanent member of the UN Security Council, and had veto power. In the end, however, it did not succeed in stopping the PRC from joining the UN.

I think the key to Taiwan's success in its UN bid lies not in the international community or external factors but in internal factors—whether we are united and have the same goal at heart. The common goal of all our people should be to join the UN under the name "Taiwan." This is more important than any external factors. As long as we are united in expressing our aspiration and have enough internal strength, we will succeed.

[....]

AP: I wonder, I'm just looking at this beautiful *caoshu* [cursive Chinese calligraphy], and I want to ask President Chen why he's working so hard to "desinify" Taiwanese culture. Isn't Taiwanese culture Chinese culture? I'm referring, for example, to initiatives in the educational system to deemphasize the role of China in Taiwan's culture, things like that.

PRESIDENT CHEN: We have not tried to "desinify" our culture. We have merely tried to emphasize that there is a culture of Taiwan that incorporates not only Chinese culture but also other cultures. Chinese culture is a continental culture, whereas Taiwanese culture is oceanic in nature.

The ocean receives water from many rivers and unites them. Taiwan is an oceanic nation, and the people of Taiwan are an oceanic people. Ours is a society of immigrants. The culture that came from China constitutes just one part of the whole of Taiwanese culture.

Let's look at the example of Singapore. It is an independent sovereign country. Though it has been heavily influenced by Chinese culture, Singaporean culture cannot be called Chinese culture. The United States provides another example. It is enriched with numerous cultures from around the world that together have created a rich and pluralistic cultural melting pot. We cannot say that just because in an earlier period of its history the United States was heavily influenced by Anglo-Saxon culture, today we should equate American culture with

---

FOUR NOES—Chen Shuibian's 2000 promise not to: 1) declare Taiwanese independence, 2) change the official title of the country from the Republic of China (R.O.C.) to the Republic of Taiwan, 3) enforce a "state-to-state" framework of "cross-strait" relations, or 4) endorse a referendum on formal independence.

English culture. Nor does it make sense to ask why Americans "de-Anglicize" American culture. English culture only constitutes one part of American culture.

We can't say that just because China and its culture are very strong and powerful today, it can negate the existence of other cultures in the world. Taiwan has its own identity and culture. Just as we have an independent economy, so too do we have our own cultural identity.

If our culture lost its Taiwan-centric quality and Taiwan became one of China's appendages, or one of China's marginal, peripheral cultures, then we would lose our own cultural identity. And if we lost that, our roots would be gone and we would become a people without a culture or a country.

15.4   INTERVIEW WITH HIS HOLINESS THE DALAI LAMA (APRIL 4, 2007)

The West's view of Tibet and the Dalai Lama is a complex one. On the one hand, the Dalai Lama has access to virtually every head of state—despite China's expression of deep displeasure over such visits. He is friends with some of Hollywood's most famous stars and has had a full-length feature film made about his life, *Kundun,* directed by Martin Scorsese. While it would be difficult to pay for such publicity even if one could, it does have a downside. It leads to a misrepresentation of Tibet in the popular imagination. The "Free Tibet" stickers, so prolifically displayed, are often more an attempt to declare oneself a 'liberal' than to engage with the knotty problems facing Tibet. In the following interview with the Dalai Lama in 2007, Polish reporter Ewa Kedzierska asks penetrating questions and receives sharp, realistic responses which puncture many of the false beliefs about the Tibet movement as it is perceived by the Dalai Lama.

Questions
1. How would you characterize the Dalai Lama's position vis-à-vis Chinese control of Tibet?
2. Does he believe violence is needed to improve the situation in Tibet?

EWA KEDZIERSKA: Is there one or more Chinese policy on Tibet? Phuntsok Wangyal, a Tibetan communist (who led Chinese troops into Tibet decades ago) in three letters sent to President Hu Jintao condemned hawks for thriving on their opposition to You, Your Holiness, and for blocking Your return home. "They make a living, are promoted, and are becoming rich by opposing splittism," he said. Is there within the Chinese government a debate among the leftists, the hardliners, and the more liberal lobby? What are the perspectives?

H.H. THE DALAI LAMA: Yes, within the central government, among the top leaders, there are different views. So the central government itself is not clear about its policy. As far as the local level is concerned, as China is an authoritarian state, unless some blessing comes from the central government, the local authorities cannot act freely. They must follow wishes or instructions of the superior. Sometimes it looks a little contradictory: the local authorities' behavior and the central government's attitude, but it is difficult to understand...I don't know.

EWA KEDZIERSKA: Methods to obtain whatever from China can be violent or non-violent. As a Buddhist, you are, Your Holiness, sincerely committed to non-violence. However, the definition of this word should be clarified. Can You explain, Your Holiness, what, from the Buddhist point of view, violence is? Is a legitimate self-defense a violence? Does non-reaction to a permanent violence not legitimate violence somehow? In what cases, following the Buddha's teachings, is violence admitted?

H.H. THE DALAI LAMA: Theoretically speaking yes, violence or non-violence are methods. The motivation and the result are more important than the methods. So theoretically speaking, under certain circumstances violence could be possible or permissible. But then, in a practical level, violence is always dangerous and negative. For me I feel it is absolutely essential not to go with violence. If things become desperate, [and a] majority of the people want violence, I will withdraw, resign.

EWA KEDZIERSKA: Your Holiness, would it be taboo, or politically incorrect, to ask the Dalai Lama about the potential insurrection in Tibet? I spoke with some politicians, who told me, that "they cannot help Tibet, because Tibet does not move." Of course, we are aware of the objective conditions, yet, please, let me ask, these may be extremely naïve questions — Would China morally survive — now — in the eyes of the world a massacre of hundreds of thousands of the Tibetan insurgents? Would the world ignore this up to refraining from any move? Does historical responsibility of the Head of State, towards past and future generations, not request sometimes a sacrifice of human lives, in order to preserve, the national identity?

H.H. THE DALAI LAMA: I think in the past at least few hundred thousand Tibetans sacrificed their lives, but what was the result? And equally, few hundred thousand Chinese lives also diminished. So one million people were killed. What did it bring? More oppression. And moreover if the Tibetan side kills a few Chinese, then will support or solidarity shown by Han Chinese [be] reduced? If there will be a real hatred between the Chinese and the Tibetan people, then this problem will remain forever. Up to now the Chinese people, as the Chinese people have a very close feeling with us, because we are strictly following non-violence. So more and more Chinese are now very critical about their own government policy. The governments change, yet the people always remain. So I consider the Chinese public support, public sympathy towards us is very essential. If the Tibetans create more bloodshed, since … it is not a civil war, bloodshed means the Chinese blood … beside, in Tibetan case violence would almost be like a suicide.

[….]

EWA KEDZIERSKA: What significance does China's booming economic growth have for Tibet and the world?

H.H. THE DALAI LAMA: China is a poor and populated country, so economic development is good. But meantime, the Chinese military development is also increasing. That increase engenders more fear, more doubts, especially in the neighborhood states, including India, Japan, and eventually U.S. I think Poland is not in a direct danger (laughs). But Poland is an important member of EU, so your voice also makes a difference. Anyway, one thing I am always telling people: that the democratic China with a free press is in interest of everyone and that is very important. Once China becomes an open society, with the rule of law, then China becomes more predictable, and this will be of an immense benefit for everybody. It will reduce fear. Otherwise what? The authoritarian military power, including military weapons means a danger, not only for 6 million Tibetans, but for the whole planet, 2.5 billion human beings. For example, to improve Sino-Indian relationship (what China wants to obtain), the Tibetan issue is very essential. The present Chinese policy regarding Tibet is just suppression, Rule of terror. With this policy the Tibetan issue, or the Tibetan resentment will remain forever. This means the Chinese soldiers have to be stationed in Tibet forever. That brings more suspicion in the mind of India. This is logical. China wants to have close relations with India, but at the same time ignores the Tibetan problem, so it has to keep large numbers of Chinese soldiers next to the Indian borders. This is contradictory.

[….]

EWA KEDZIERSKA: Your Holiness repeats You are nothing more (or less) than a Buddhist monk. Yet, 6 million Tibetans and enough of others think differently. Are they all just making projections of their own visions and wishes?

H.H. THE DALAI LAMA: (laugh) Yes, mainly. Then? …

EWA KEDZIERSKA: Your Holiness, what would you say to the Western "Buddhists" for whom the Tibetan political issue is completely distant from the religion, which they have so enthusiastically adopted?

H.H. THE DALAI LAMA: (lively and with determination) Oh, that is wrong! Tibetan freedom is very much linked with the Tibetan Buddhism. Without Tibetan freedom, the Tibetan Buddhism cannot survive.

EWA KEDZIERSKA: Thank You, Your Holiness.

CONTEMPORARY ISSUES IN CONTEMPORARY CHINA

When China appears in the news today, the items tend to group around a core set of topics. These include censorship, the Three Gorges Dam, religious freedom, the impact of China's one-child policy, and the shifting mores of China's youth. The articles below offer a Chinese perspective of these topics, not as unadulterated propaganda, but as showing the complexity of the problems facing China today. One of the most famous censorship cases in recent years was the case involving the *Freezing Point Weekly* (15.5). The editor's ability to publicize his side of the story over the Internet reveals the growing difficulty the government has in controlling information released to the public. Similarly, the government's position regarding the massive Three Gorges Dam project and its decision about how to accept its shortcomings (15.6) reveal a nuanced approach not often seen, even five years ago. Allowing one of China's new generation of directors to shoot a feature length film (15.7) and documentary at the dam site and to show it at top film festivals is a far cry from the strict discipline imposed on earlier directors. But none of these issues compares with the breadth and consistency with which the government has maintained its one-child policy and dealt with the social fallout engendered by that policy (15.9). All these issues suggest that while the central government still exerts a firm grip on the circulation of information, the variety of topics and freedom to express opinions on those topics is improving.

15.5 OPEN LETTER PROTESTING DECISION ON *FREEZING POINT WEEKLY* (JANUARY 25, 2006)

Freezing Point is a weekly supplement published by the *China Youth Daily* newspaper. Well known for its spirited intellectual analysis of contemporary issues, the weekly had a wide readership which was largely a result of the unflinching editorial board which challenged unstated (but apparent) restrictions on sensitive topics typically censored by the Propaganda Department. The aggressive editorial stance taken by the weekly, however, eventually resulted in the dismissal of its editor, Li Datong and the magazine being "stopped for reorganization." The professed reason for closing the supplement was an essay by Yuan Weishi, a professor at Zhongshan University, that accused government-approved history textbooks of whitewashing specific historical movements (such as the Second Opium War and the Boxer Rebellion) for patriotic and political purposes. The dismissal met with a wave of negative publicity and international condemnation. As result of this negative reaction, the Propaganda Department allowed the supplement to resume publication, but without its two top editors and with a requirement to publish a criticism of Yuan Weishi's article. The following is a complete translation of the letter posted by Li Datong on his website after he was removed as editor.

Questions

1. What is the primary focus of Li Datong's indignation? Is it the issue of censorship, party-oversight, or his dismissal?
2. Why would Yuan Weishi's article be a sensitive topic for the Chinese government and the Chinese Communist Party?

Journalist colleagues, academic associates, friends from legal circles, and *Freezing Point* readers around the world:

As the deadline for the January 25 issue of *Freezing Point Weekly* approached, on Tuesday, January 24, 2006, following the typical routine, the Beijing editors and reporters gathered in the editorial department intently proofreading the next issue. A little after 4 p.m., the galley proofs were completed and delivered to the editor-in-chief for review and printing. But surprisingly, we received no reply. We heard that the entire leadership of the newspaper had been called to an emergency meeting, so there was no one to look over anything. This was our clue that something out of the ordinary was about to unfold.

Even when the sky comes crashing down, a newspaper's publication has to go on as usual. This is the responsibility owed towards all subscribers and readers. We corrected all the identified errors in the proof and waited quietly for what was to happen. There had been endless criticisms and attacks toward the *Freezing Point Weekly* from the Central Propaganda Department. So on Monday as we read their ruthless attack (from the news critics group of the Central Propaganda Department) which employed a Cultural Revolution-style tactic of magnifying insignificant problems appearing in Professor Yuan Weishi's *Freezing Point* article "Modernity and History Textbook," I, as the chief editor, expected my dismissal was near.

However, the degree of their despicableness is still beyond the imagination of normal people. Around 5 p.m., friends from other media centers around the country began to phone me telling us they had received notices from the Central Propaganda Department, News Office of State Council, and Beijing Municipal News Bureau "forbidding them to publish any news or commentary on the suspension and reorganization of *Freezing Point*," "Forbidding them to participate in the news conference of *Freezing Point's* editors and reporters," "Forbidding them from making it into a media frenzy," and "To maintain distance" etc. A steady stream of phone calls from overseas media reporters followed, asking me to verify the situation. Up until 7 p.m. I received no official notice of any kind. The top leaders of the newspaper had returned from their meeting with the Youth League Central Committee but remained sequestered in a meeting. I, on the other hand, became the last person to learn of this decision. All information suggests that their action had been carefully planned by

several senior Party officials for a long time, which goes against the will of the people. This action not only lacks any constitutional or legal basis, but also grievously violates and tramples on the Party's constitution and the principles of political life within the Party.

As a professional journalist, the suspension of the *Freezing Point Weekly* is beyond my comprehension, something I simply cannot accept. Because a newspaper is a civic tool, there is a contract between the newspaper and the public—that is to say the buyer expects an information product, and the newspaper must honor this agreement—no matter the fate of any one individual, the *Freezing Point Weekly* should reach the subscribers on time. But for those who made this decision, what does social influence matter? What does broad readership matter? What does the reputation of a large mainstream newspaper matter? What does the Party Constitution and the country's law matter? What does the image of China's "reform and opening to the outside world" matter? What does the image of the governing Party matter? They think They can use this civic tool as their own private property, to manipulate as they please.

At 7:30 p.m., I received a call from the publisher and the editor-in-chief asking me to come up for a conversation. They notified me that the Communist Youth League Central Propaganda Bureau had made a decision consisting of several groundless charges against the article by Mr. Yuan Weishi, after which they announced that the publication of *Freezing Point Weekly* would be "stopped for reorganization." In addition to publishing criticism of the editor-in-chief and myself, a "monetary penalty" would also be assessed. Who gave them this kind of power! Such a despicable mindset leaves one not knowing whether to laugh or cry.

Under the conditions described above, the conversation became a farce. Obviously, the Youth League Central Committee was assigned to play the role of the clown on the stage, while a small number of "superiors" manipulated them from behind the scenes. I condemned this "decision" in front of the publisher and editor-in-chief, as well as the absurdity of the Central Propaganda Department's "News Commentary and Criticism." I also announced that I would formally bring charges against such illegal activities to the Party's Central Disciplinary Inspection Committee with illegal activities.

Today just as the *Freezing Point Weekly* is being shut down, the newspaper is receiving a large number of calls from readers for clarification, with many of them, upon learning of the *Freezing Point Weekly's* suspension, angrily going to the Post Office to cancel their subscriptions.

The elimination of *Freezing Point Weekly* by a few "superiors" had been plotted far in advance. On June 1 2005, prior to the sixtieth anniversary celebrating the victory of the Second World War, the *Freezing Point Weekly* published an article entitled "The **Campaign of Pingxingguan** and Victory of Pingxingguan." The article factually documented the close cooperation between Communist and Guomindang military forces that bravely fought together in a period of great danger for the nation. Differing from previous propaganda, *Freezing Point,* for the first time in a mainstream publication, objectively and truthfully reported the Guomindang's sacrifice of several tens of thousands of officers and soldiers in the battle.

This fact-based description received churlish criticism from the journalist-criticism group of the Central Propaganda Department. What was their evidence for criticism? They had not one iota of historical fact; instead, they based their critique on the "Narratives on the Victory of Pingxingguan in the History of Communist Party of China, published by XX Press in 19XX year, on XX page." The *Freezing Point Weekly,* they went on to proclaim, "glamorized the Guomindang and debased the Communist Party." In the end, however, at the sixtieth anniversary celebration of the victory of the Second World War, Comrade Hu Jintao, General-Secretary of the Central Committee of the Party, fully confirmed the contributions of the Guomindang officers and soldiers in the main battlefields of the Resistance War Against Japan. It is obvious who was right and who was wrong.

When [GMD Chairman] Lian [Zhan] and [PFP Chairman] Song [Chuyu] were visiting the mainland [separately,] Ms. Long Yingtai, the well-known Taiwanese writer published a long article in *Freezing Point,* "The Taiwan You May Not Know." Supported by abundant references to factual sources, the article for the first time, objectively and truthfully revealed to mainland Chinese the changes in and the development of Taiwan over the past few decades. The article generated strong response and received positive comments among readers, as well creating an essential conduit connecting the peoples from both sides of the strait. However, some people from the Central Propaganda Department, whose viewpoints and mindset were astonishingly narrow, condemned the article as "anti-Communist Party on every level."

On November 18 of last year, the Central Committee of the Party held a solemn meeting to commemorate the 90th birthday of Comrade Hu Yaobang, the great proletariat revolutionist. On behalf of Central Committee of the Party, Comrade Zeng Qinghong introduced Comrade Hu Yaobang's glorious achievements and great character at length, a presentation that was warmly received by the people. However, some individuals from the Central Propaganda Committee prohibited media from publishing articles commemorating Comrade Hu Yaobang and limited publications to articles exclusively from Xinhua News Agency with no alterations permitted.

On December 7 2005, *Freezing Point* published Comrade Hu Qili's unabridged reminiscence, "[Hu] Yaobang in My Heart." The article generated a deep felt response in many domestic and international Chinese-language media outlets, which republished the article. As well, many Internet readers posted comments in which they said the article was so touching it brought them to tears. Despite receiving singularly positive popular reactions, the Central Propaganda Department condemned the newspaper agency, claiming it violated the rule of "publishing without approval!" Among these people there is not a single ounce of recognition of the true feelings and reminiscences expressed towards Comrade Hu Yaobang!

There have been many more irrational derisions and criticisms from a few people in the Central Propaganda Department towards the *Freezing Point Weekly.* For example, on November 30, 2005, an investigation by a *Freezing Point Weekly* reporter revealed the academic plagiarism of law Professor Zhou Yezhong of Wuhan University. While being interviewed by the reporter from *Freezing Point,* this professor impudently suggested the reporter should not be concerned with this matter, stating, "You'd better not be involved with the case. People from the Central Propaganda Department will be contacting you tonight! Your editor-in-chief will soon be getting in touch with you!" When the report was published, sure enough, some people from the Central Propaganda

---

PINGXINGGUAN CAMPAIGN—One of the largest battles carried out by Communist military forces during the War of Resistance Against Japan.

Department ferociously denounced the report, attacking it by claiming it typified the problem of the media misleading the people.

Under pressure, the next installment of the report was withdrawn from the *Freezing Point Weekly*. As a result, on December 28 2005, *Freezing Point Weekly* for the first time was reduced to a three-page issue. Let's ask, what kind of behavior are the people from the Central Propaganda Department safeguarding?

Now they are finally making the *Freezing Point Weekly* pay the price! Using Yuan Weishi's article as a basis for attack is just a false pretense. Professor Yuan is among the most preeminent scholars in the field of modern history whose influence among intellectuals worldwide is quite large. He bases his articles on historical documents, and his arguments employ an open-minded rationality. After his articles were published, they generated considerable discussion. Traditionally, examination of historical questions demands a level, dispassionate, and grounded approach towards sources and various points of view before one can gradually reach a common understanding. Amongst many of the comments given online, many online readers took issue with Yuan Weishi's article, and by adopting a conscientious approach, they offered substantive criticisms of the article. I myself gave some of these web postings to Mr Yuan to examine, and after reading them, he responded: "The methodology of these articles is truly rigorous. I will give their viewpoints serious consideration and respond with any relevant comments." This is one type of a healthy and normal academic exchange. Yet, the journalist-criticism group of the Central Propaganda Department offered nothing other than Cultural Revolution-style humiliation, stigmatization, and attacks.

This incident again reveals the fundamental shortcomings of our country's news management. A small minority in the Central Propaganda Department employ a narrow minded view, using an intolerant, autocratic and peremptory style, to control what ought to be "a hundred flowers bloom, and a hundred schools of thought contend." This creates a tightly controlled atmosphere where people stand by unwilling to offer an opinion. These people want obedience, not equality. Which article in the Chinese Communist Party's constitution grants them this monopoly of power?

[. . . .]

With heartfelt thanks!

Li Datong

Chief Editor of *Freezing Point Weekly, China Youth Daily*

January 25, 2006

15.6 CHINA WARNS OF ENVIRONMENTAL "CATASTROPHE" FROM THREE GORGES DAM (SEPTEMBER 26, 2007)

The Yangzi River flows from the Tibetan Plateau for nearly 4,000 miles through the heart of China before depositing nearly 960 billion cubic meters of water annually into the East China Sea. Since the 1920s Chinese officials, including Sun Zhongshan and Jiang Jieshi, have dreamed of tapping the river's hydroelectric potential as well as harnessing the often devastating flood waters that perennially threaten some of China's most fertile flatlands on the lower stretches of the river. In 1992, the Seventh National People's Congress made its official decision to erect a massive dam in Xiling Gorge, the first gorge of the famous **Three Gorges** region. Construction began two years later in 1994 and was scheduled to take seventeen years to be completed. International condemnation and concern over the ecological affects of the dam prompted one Chinese official associated with the project to say that, unlike the Americans who try to "preserve" the environment, the Chinese approach is to "correct" existing ecological shortcomings. After years of failing to concede the environmental consequences of building the dam, in 2007 Chinese officials began to acknowledge the severe repercussions of the dam's construction.

THREE GORGES DAM—A massive hydroelectric dam on the Yangzi River at the head of the Qutang, Wuxia, and Xiling gorges. The dam was completed in 2008 a year ahead of schedule supplying much-needed electricity, but with severe environmental consequences.

Questions

1. **What types of adverse impact does the article point out might occur (or are already occurring) as a result of the Three Gorges Dam?**
2. **Does the article offer any insight into what Chinese officials see as a strategy to rectify the problems?**
3. **In what ways does the government see the ecological costs as simply part of the larger need for electricity and flood control?**

Chinese officials and experts have admitted the Three Gorges Dam project has caused an array of ecological ills, including more frequent landslides and pollution, and if preventive measures are not taken, there could be an environmental "catastrophe."

While the dam has served as a barrier against seasonal flooding threatening the lower reaches of the Yangtze River and the electricity generated by hydropower has led to a decrease of 100 million tons of carbon emissions, the benefits have come at an ecological and environmental cost, officials said.

All the participants in a two-day forum held in Wuhan on Tuesday agreed that the project had exerted a "notably adverse" impact on the environment of the Three Gorges reservoir, with a total circumference of 600 km, and along the Yangtze since last year, when the project began operation.

They said the huge weight of the water behind the Three Gorges Dam had started to erode the Yangtze's banks in many places, which, together with frequent fluctuations in water levels, had triggered a series of landslides.

"If no preventive measures are taken, the project could lead to catastrophe," they said.

Tan Qiwei, vice mayor of Chongqing, a sprawling metropolis next to the reservoir, said the shore of the reservoir had collapsed in 91 places and a total of 36 km had caved in.

Frequent geological disasters have threatened the lives of residents around the reservoir area, said Huang Xuebin, head of the Headquarters for Prevention and Control of Geological Disasters in the Three Gorges Reservoir.

At the forum he described landslides around the reservoir that had produced waves as high as 50 meters, which crashed into the adjacent shoreline, causing even more damage.

Clear water discharged from the Three Gorges Dam has also threatened the safety of the protective embankments downstream, according to Hubei Vice Governor Li Chunming.

Both Tan and Li said the quality of water in the Yangtze tributaries had deteriorated and outbreaks of algae or aquatic weeds had become more common.

"We can by no means relax our vigilance against ecological and environmental security problems or profit from a fleeting economic boom at the cost of sacrificing the environment," said Wang Xiaofeng, director of the office of the Three Gorges Project Committee of the State Council.

[. . . .]

"We have to make concerted efforts to attain the dual goals of constructing a first-rate hydraulic project and making it into a top-level showcase for the environment," said Wang, "we will work harder to turn the Three Gorges Reservoir Area into an environmentally-friendly society."

The government has invested heavily in programs designed to restore and conserve the ecology of the Three Gorges area in recent years, including 12 billion yuan (about 1.5 billion U.S. dollars) spent on trying to harness geological disasters such as landslides.

It has also closed or relocated 1,500 manufacturing ventures, constructed more than 70 sewage disposal and waste treatment plants and resettled about 70,000 people from disaster-prone areas.

The participants in the forum in Wuhan also called for the establishment of a long-term mechanism on the prevention and control of geological disasters in the Three Gorges Reservoir Area, and a ban on fish farming in cages in the reservoir area to prevent an excess of nutrients degrading the water quality.

The Three Gorges Project, the world's largest water control facility, was launched in 1993, with a budget of 180 billion yuan (about 22.5 billion U.S. dollars). Located on the middle reaches of the Yangtze River, the project boasts a 185-meter-high dam, completed in early 2006, and a five-tier ship lock. It has necessitated the resettlement of at least 1.2 million people.

Seventeen turbines—14 on the northern bank of the Gorges and three more on the southern bank—are now in operation. They produced 23.77 billion kwh of electricity in the first half of the year, 2.65 billion kwh more than the same period last year.

To cut pollutant emissions, more than 1,600 factories have been closed down while 190,000 people moved elsewhere. So far, the State Council has approved the allocation of 52.9 billion yuan ($7.15 billion) to subsidize people moving out of the reservoir area, he said.

"We also encouraged other provinces and cities to help the development of their resettlement area and the support fund from them had reached 34.1 billion yuan ($4.6 billion) by the end of last year," Wang Xiaofeng said.

All the money has been used directly on migrants, including relocation compensations, an annual allowance of 600 yuan to each migrant from rural areas and investment in roads, schools and hospitals around their new homes, he said.

In the future, Wang said, the priorities of ecological and environmental protection would focus on the sustainable use of Three Gorges Dam and water pollutant prevention in the Dam areas and its upper reaches, as well as the protection of bio-diversity.

15.7   JIA ZHANGKE'S *STILL LIFE* (2006)

Chinese director Jia Zhangke began a documentary on the Three Gorges Dam project but realized the human stories unfolding were perfect for a feature length film entitled *Still Life*. (Jia Zhangke ultimately also released a documentary about life in the Three Gorges under the title "East" [*Dong*]). The film follows two individuals who separately return to the region looking for their respective spouses. With a discerning eye for the lives of ordinary people developed in many of his early films, Jia Zhangke highlights the choices of ordinary Chinese, as well as the larger forces shaping those choices, that often lead to dislocation rather than accommodation. The film effortlessly displays the scenery and life along the Yangzi without entering into a political commentary about the dam. Upon its release, the film won numerous prizes at top film festivals, including the Golden Lion, the top prize of the Venice Film Festival (2006). Jia Zhangke has been compared to Fifth-generation director Zhang Yimou (whose films *The Story of Qiuju* (14.9) and *Not One Less* also won the Golden Lion), and this has led many people to suggest that he is the torchbearer of China's new Sixth Generation of filmmakers. In the scene below, a middle-aged coal miner from the province of Shanxi (who shares the same name of the actor, Han Sanming), arrives in Fengjie to search for his ex-wife and daughter.

Questions

1. Unlike the glamorous portrayal of China in many films, how does the flowing dialogue evoke a much more normal style of life?
2. Why is Han Sanming confused about where he should go look for his wife Ma Yaomei?

[SCENE #1: *Han Sanming, one of the central characters in the film, disembarks from the Yangzi ferry and walks several steps to the landing where motorcycle drivers are trying to get customers to taxi them to nearby destinations.*]

MOTORCYCLIST: Hey, brother, where are you going? Can I take you? Where are you going to?

HAN SANMING: Here.

[*Showing the young motorcyclist his address on a piece of paper*]

MOTORCYCLIST: [*Reading address*] Sichuan Province, Fengjie County, Qingshi Street No. 5. ... Okay, let's go. Five yuan.

HAN SANMING: How about three yuan?

1ST MOTORCYCLIST: Come on, everyone charges five yuan.

2ND MOTORCYCLIST: Alright, let's go.

[SCENE #2: *The Motorcycle slows to a stop up the river but curiously there is no town.*]

1ST MOTORCYCLIST: Brother, here we are.

HAN SANMING: Here?

MOTORCYCLIST: See? To the left of the clump of grass grows over there. That's Qingshi Street, No. 5. Get off.

HAN SANMING: How come it's all under water?

MOTORCYCLIST: Fengjie town has already been flooded. Do you watch news? Do you know about Three Gorge Dam Project?

HAN SANMING: Where are the people?

MOTORCYCLIST: Dispersed. Relocated and moved away.

HAN SANMING: You knew it was flooded, but you still brought me here? You cheated me out of 5 yuan.

MOTORCYCLIST: I didn't order it flooded.

HAN SANMING: Do you know Ma Yaomei?

MOTORCYCLIST: All the girls are called Yaomei here. Which one are you looking for? Are you looking for a person or looking for work?

HAN SANMING: A person.

MOTORCYCLIST: Brother, I tell you what. For three more yuan, I will take you to the Relocation Office. Give them her house number and their computer can check and find everything. How about it?

HAN SANMING: OK.

MOTORCYCLIST: See, that ferry marooned over there? My home was originally underneath that. It's long gone now.

[SCENE #3: *People are arguing inside the hallway of the relocation office. An official is surrounded by many residents who are all complaining to him simultaneously.*]

OFFICIAL: We are implementing that policy. It is Policy No. 195 which is posted on the wall over there.

MAN: I say, we are all under the leadership of the same Communist Party. And there is only one policy for relocation subsidies.

OFFICIAL: Right, the same one.

MAN: How come it is implemented differently?

OFFICIAL: Where is it different?

[*Once again the small crowd all talk at once.*]

OFFICIAL: Watch what you say. Watch what you say.

WOMAN: You officials have pocketed the relocation fund. There are problems here.

OFFICIAL: Of course there are problems. How can there be no problems? A 2000-year old city was razed in two years. There are problems. They can only be solved slowly.

[*Han speaking with a female staff inside the office*]

HAN SANMING: Qingshi Street No.5.

STAFF: Sichuan Province, Fengjie County. How long have you been out of touch?

HAN SANMING: Sixteen years.

STAFF: No wonder. Fengjie hasn't been part of Sichuan Province for quite some time. It belongs to Chongqing since Chongqing became an independently administered Municipality in 1997.

HAN SANMING: I heard that.

STAFF: Is she still in Fengjie now?

HAN SANMING: She should be. Where else can she go?

STAFF: It's not certain. Since they are building the Three Gorges Dam we belong to the area which will become the reservoir. So many people have migrated to Guangdong, Liaoning and everywhere.

HAN SANMING: Hmm.

STAFF: Damn computer! Come back to pick up the information tomorrow.

HAN SANMING: Why?

STAFF: The computer is dying.

HAN SANMING: Dying?

STAFF: Dying.... not working.

[*The official shown earlier walks into the office still followed by the woman demanding an answer to her demands.*]

OFFICIAL: You should go home first. Go home. Its no use talking to me.

OLD WOMAN: You must resolve this for us.

OFFICIAL: I am telling you. I have lots of work to do.

[SCENE #4 - *The same motorcyclist is driving Han Sanming through town. Along the street some workers are writing big red characters on the wall of a building: Water Level for Phase Three: 156.5 meters. At a cheap hotel, the manager of the hotel greets Han Sanming and the motorcyclist.*]

OLD MAN: You came from Shanxi [province]? Three yuan per day. Three yuan per day. Alright?

MOTORCYCLIST: What? Three yuan a day? The Three Gorges tourism market is messed up by people like you.

OLD MAN: Alright, alright, for this young man's sake, one and half yuan, one and half yuan.

MOTORCYCLIST: One yuan and twenty cents, let's go.

OLD MAN: Alright. One yuan and twenty cents, so one yuan and twenty cents.

[*Han walks away towards his room and the young motorcyclist returned to the old man at the door.*]

MOTORCYCLIST: Give me my money

OLD MAN: You are best at helping the others. Here is one yuan. Here you are.

15.8 FUDAN UNIVERSITY RELAXES SEX RULES FOR STUDENTS (JULY 19, 2005)

In the early eighties, a male and female Chinese holding hands in public was a rarity. Given the pressure to succeed on university entrance examinations, dating in high school was looked upon harshly and outward physical contact forbidden. As the article below suggests, attitudes have moderated somewhat in the past decade. Young Chinese are increasingly willing to engage in premarital sex despite the lingering puritanical rules at the universities. Government and university officials are also coming under fire for the lack of sex education and the rising number of cases of AIDS. In the 1990s numerous high profile cases had students being expelled for having sex, becoming pregnant, or simply having a long-term relationship. It is one of the contradictions of Chinese society that while sex is not condoned, it is acknowledged in the society at large to the extent that condom vending machines can be found on most any city block.

Questions

1. What is the rationale used by Chinese universities for their harsh stance towards student's intimate behavior?
2. Why do you think Fudan is no longer immediately expelling students for having sex?

Unmarried students at Fudan University will no longer be immediately expelled for having sex, according to a draft version of a revised campus regulation posted on the school's Website last week.

Students will still be punished if they are caught between the sheets with a lover, however.

The school is looking for feedback on the draft, and the rule will go into effect this September after necessary revisions.

Students caught having sex, whether on campus or off, will receive a warning and a bad report on their personal record. Students can be expelled after two warnings.

The new rule comes in response to the Ministry of Education's decision to end a ban on students getting married.

"The revised draft is designed to be in line with the Ministry of Education's new university student management rule," the Website announcement said.

The ministry's new rule, which was issued in March, didn't say anything about students engaging in sex.

Earlier this month, Chongqing Normal University set off a controversy when it issued a rule saying students would be immediately expelled for improper sexual behavior.

The rule specifically forbids female students from engaging in adulterous affairs with married men, but didn't mention male students having sex.

Fudan officials refused yesterday to say what constitutes improper sexual activities, or what is allowed.

Many students question whether schools should have the authority to ban sex, and suggested the rule can't be enforced.

"The sex ban goes against the law and therefore violates students' rights," said Shan Min, a graduate student at Tongji University.

In China, men are allowed to marry at the age of 22 and women can tie the knot at the age of 20, he said. Since many students are older than that, their sex lives are no one else's business, Shan added.

Shen Yaxin, a Fudan university student, said that the ban is simply to show an attitude that the school opposes students having sex and won't be enforced.

"No one would let the secret out if they have sex," Shen said. "How could the school know if they have no evidence?"

Earlier this year, a male student at Shanghai University was expelled after he allowed his girlfriend to spend the night in his dorm room to look after him while he was sick. His expulsion raised a great deal of controversy among many people in the city.

15.9 CHINA VOWS TO HALT GROWING SEX RATIO IMBALANCE (JANUARY 22, 2007)

China's one child policy has, in the last several decades, dramatically affected Chinese society. The vast majority of Chinese children grow up with no siblings, thus creating a generation of "little emperors." As the first generation of these children are now in their mid-twenties, the government and society at large have begun to reflect on the deeper implications of the policy. There remains in some areas of China, and in some segments of Chinese society, a lingering belief that a family must have a male child to carry on the family name. As the technology for identifying the sex of a fetus has become increasingly available, sex-selective abortions have lead to an imbalance between the number of male and female babies born. The article below points out that the sex ratio imbalance varies not only between rural and urban areas, but also geographically within China, for reasons that remain unclear.

Questions

1. What reasons does the article suggest for the sex ratio imbalance? Does it offer any indication of the ways in which the state might seek to rectify this imbalance?
2. Does the article suggest that the social preference for a male offspring is changing? Is this the only factor influencing a family's desire for more than one child?

Chinese authorities have vowed to take tough measures to control fetus gender testing and sex-selective abortions to hold back the rising sex ratio imbalance. "People who conduct illegal gender testing of fetuses and sex-selective abortions should face serious punishment," according to a document jointly issued by the Central Committee of the Communist Party of China and the State Council. The authorities also pledged to improve protection of baby girls, saying that people who kill, abandon, or injure infant girls or ill-treat their mothers, should be severely punished.

Medical institutions that use ultra-sound technology and abortion medicines will be more closely supervised, according to the document. China's gender ratio for new born babies in 2005 was 118 boys for every 100 girls, compared with 110:100 in 2000. In some regions, the figure has reached 130 boys born for every 100 girls. The decision said the gender-ratio imbalance which has been developing for some time amounts to "a hidden danger" for society that will "affect social stability."

In an attempt to halt the growing imbalance, China launched a "care for girls" campaign nationwide in 2000 to promote equality between men and women. The government has also offered cash incentives to girl-only families in the countryside. The authorities said such programs will continue to fight discrimination against girls and to adopt more policies to ensure the healthy growth of girls. The authorities also pledged to "firmly" continue the 33-year-long family planning policy, as the country is still facing huge challenges from growing population.

Formulated in the early 1970s, China's family planning policy encourages late marriages and late childbearing, and limits most urban couples to one child and most rural couples to two. The government has employed 520,000 people, including 160,000 technicians, to implement family planning policies and provide services. The family planning policy is credited with preventing 400 million new births. However, authorities warn the country is still facing an "unprecedented" situation.

The key and difficult area is the country's rural region, where the social security network is underdeveloped and people's traditional preference for male heirs has not changed. The authorities promised to continue to improve family planning services in rural areas and will offer more assistance to girl-only families. It also said those who violated the family planning policy, especially Party members and government officials, should be fined and punished according to law. Violators of the policy will be subject to Party or administrative discipline and held legally responsible, the document said.

"Maintaining a low birth rate is the priority of family planning during the next phase," the document said adding that the next four years is a "crucial" period. China's government has pledged to keep the mainland population under 1.36 billion by 2010 and under 1.45 billion by 2020. "Over the coming decades, China's overall population will increase by eight to 10 million a year," bring unprecedented challenges to the country's social and economic development, the document said. "China's overall population, along with its working population and its aging population, will peak in the first half of the twenty-first century," noted the document.

China currently has 1.3 billion people. China will further increase its public investment in population and family planning, according to the document. By 2010, China is expected to spend 30 yuan (3.84 U.S. dollars) per person up from 10 yuan (1.28 U.S. dollars) per person in 2005, said the document. China is also encouraging enterprises, non-governmental organizations, and individuals to provide financial assistance for the country's family planning programs, said the document. China will also study the causes of birth defects and try to alter the key factors that cause them. The document blamed unhealthy lifestyles, environmental factors, and heredity for causing genetic defects in newborns. The document also urged Chinese couples to complete physical examination before they marry and women to give birth in hospital and to breast feed.

Relevant departments and hospitals are urged to provide consulting and health care services for pregnant women. More comprehensive training will be given to family planning staff to improve their knowledge not only in policies and techniques, but also in public health, psychology, consulting and social services. With China's migrant worker population reaching close to 150 million, ensuring they are covered by family planning is extremely important to maintaining a stable, low birth rate, said the document. Eighty percent of migrant workers are former farmers and they are permitted to have two children if their first is a girl.

The document commits China to improving family-planning services for migrant workers and strengthening the registration system for migrant workers to better track their family planning choices. The document also said family planning associations will be set up in communities and enterprises with large numbers of migrant workers.

15.10 WEI HUI'S *SHANGHAI BABY* (1999)

In the late 1990s, several books by young urban Chinese women burst onto China's literary scene. The following quasi-autobiographical story by Wei Hui describes 25-year old "Nikki" (also known as Coco to her friends) and her postmodern life in Shanghai. Open about both her sexual and emotional needs, the book explores the meaning of freedom, love, and loneliness in the cosmopolitan context of China's most trendy city. With hardly a reference to socialism, revolutionary goals, or political concerns, the story is a sharp break from China's literary tradition (like that displayed in Zhang Jie's "Love Must Not be Forgotten"). But the world it describes is in many ways closer to the reality of life for China's urban youth than the idealized stories typical of the previous decades.

Question

1. **What relationship does Nikki have with her parents?**
2. **How does Nikki's view of love differ from that of Zhang Jie's story?**

What sort of person am I? To my mother and father, I'm an evil little thing devoid of conscience. (By five I'd learned how to stomp out, haughtily clutching my lollipop.) To my teachers or ex-boss and colleagues at the magazine, I'm smart but hardheaded, a skilled professional with an unpredictable temperament who can guess how any film or a story will end from the way it begins. To most men, I qualify as a little beauty, as pleasing as spring light on a lake's rippling surface, with a pair of oversize eyes right out of a Japanese cartoon and a long Coco Chanel neck. But in my own eyes, I'm just an ordinary woman, even if I become famous one of these days.

When my paternal great-grandmother was alive, she often said: "A person's fate is like a kite string. One end is here on the earth, and the other is in the heavens. There's nowhere to hide from fate." Or: "Which part of life is the part worth living for?"

This old lady with snow-white hair and a tiny frame would sit all day, like a ball of white wool, in her rocking chair. Many people believed she had second sight. She correctly predicted the 1987 Shanghai earthquake which registered 3.0 on the Richter scale, and told her relatives of her impending death three days before it happened. Her photograph still hangs on the wall of my parents' house, and they believe that she continues to protect them. In fact, it was my grandmother who predicted that I would be a writer. With a literary star shining down on me and a belly full of ink, I would, she said, make my mark one day.

At the university I often used to write letters to boys I was secretly in love with, rich in expression and affection, almost guaranteeing conquest. At the magazine, the interviews and stories I wrote were like something out of a novel, with their twisted plots and rarefied language, so that the real seemed false, and vice versa.

When I finally realized that everything I had done until then was just a waste of my talent, I gave up my highly paid job at the magazine. My parents despaired of me once again, because my father had had to pull a lot of strings to get me the job in the first place.

"Child, are you really my daughter? Why does your head grow horns and your feet grow thorns?"

said Mother. "Tell me, why all these wasted efforts?" Mother is a pretty, frail woman who has spent her life ironing shirts for her husband and seeking the right road for her daughter's happiness. She can't accept the idea of sex before marriage and absolutely cannot bear the shape of a girl's nipples when she wears a tight T-shirt and no bra.

"The day will come when you realize that a steady, down-to-earth life is the most important thing. Even **Eileen Chang** says that human life needs a stable foundation," said Daddy. He knows I admire this famous author. Daddy is a slightly chubby history professor who likes cigars and heart-to-heart talks with young people. A well-mannered man, he spoiled me from the start. By the time I was three, he had trained me to appreciate operas such as *La Bohème*. He always worried that when I grew up I'd lose my body and soul to a sex maniac. I'm his most precious baby, he says, and I should treat men cautiously and never shed tears over them.

"The way we think is just too different. We're separated by a hundred generation gaps. We'd best respect one another rather than argue our cases," I said. "Anyway, it's a waste of time. I'm twenty-five, and I want to be a writer. Even though the profession's totally passé, I'm going to make writing up-to-date again."

When I met Tian Tian and decided to move out, there was an uproar in my family fit to roil the Pacific Ocean.

"I don't know what to do about you. We'll just have to wait and see how you'll turn out. I might as well pretend I didn't raise you," said Mother, almost shouting. She looked as if she had been struck hard on the face.

"You've hurt your mother's feelings," said Daddy. "And I'm disappointed, too. A girl like you is bound to be taken advantage of. You say that boy's family is odd. His father died in strange circumstances. Is he normal himself? Is he reliable?"

"Believe me, I know what I'm doing." I said. I grabbed my toothbrush, some clothes, CDs, and a box of books, and left.

ZHANG AILING (EILEEN CHANG) (1921–1995) — A well-known female writer of the 1940s whose writings remain immensely popular in China today.

USEFUL READINGS AND WEBSITES FOR PART THREE

Useful Websites

1. **MORNING SUN:** http://www.morningsun.org/ – A companion website to the film by the same name, the site is an unparalleled and visually stunning examination of the Cultural Revolution. Seeks to move beyond the purely political dimensions of the event by examining how political campaigns shaped culture, family, and art.

2. **GATE OF HEAVENLY PEACE:** http://tsquare.tv/ – A resource for the film *Gate of Heavenly Peace,* co-directed by Carmen Hinton and Richard Gordon is an engaging multi-layered look at the 1989 Tiananmen Incident. Includes primary and secondary sources as well as a wealth of film and sound clips.

3. **CHINA IN THE RED:** http://www.pbs.org/wgbh/pages/frontline/shows/red/ – Filmed between 1998–2001, *China in the Red* traces the stark economic and political changes occurring in China by following the lives and experiences of individuals affected by the changes. Includes links to background articles, teacher's guides, and news reports related to contemporary China. Streaming-videos of the entire program also available.

4. **VISIONS OF CHINA: 50 YEARS OF THE PEOPLE'S REPUBLIC:** http://edition.cnn.com/SPECIALS/1999/china.50/ – A website created by CNN celebrating the PRC's 50th anniversary in 1999. The expansive, if slightly dated, website includes pictorial galleries, interactive maps, timelines, and a Mao quotation generator.

5. **CHINESE PROPAGANDA POSTERS:** http://www.iisg.nl/~landsberger/ – An amazingly comprehensive collection of Chinese propaganda posters, organized into helpful categories with basic introductions and explanations of the posters and the political campaigns for which they were produced.

Suggested Readings

1. **Philip Short, *Mao: A Life.* (New York: Henry Holt & Company, 2000).** The most thorough and detailed biography of Mao Zedong written to date. The book is more than a tally of Mao's good or bad acts; it is an explication of his role in history.

2. **Anita Chan, Richard Madsen, and Jonathan Unger, *Chen Village Under Mao and Deng.* (Los Angeles: University of California Press, 1992).** An insightful and penetrating village level view of the first three decades of political reforms from the 1950s through the early 1980s. Using their extensive interviews with the inhabitants, the authors reveal the impact of national politics on a single village in south China.

3. **Yan Yunxiang, *Private Life Under Socialism: Love, Intimacy, and Family Change in a Chinese Village, 1949–1999.* (Stanford University Press, 2003).** A rural ethnography of a northeastern Chinese village. Exceptional in its details of the rarely addressed private areas of romance, sex, birth control, and gender dynamics within a family, a village and the nation.

4. **Melvyn C. Goldstein, Dawei Sherap, and William R. Siebenschuh, *A Tibetan Revolutionary: The Political Life and Times of Bapa Phüntso Wangye.* (Berkeley: University of California Press).** The biography of a founder of the Tibetan Communist Party who later coordinated the merger with the CCP in the 1950s and then served as the translator for the Dalai Lama during his meetings with Mao Zedong.

5. **Andrew J. Nathan and Perry Link, eds., With Liang Zhang, compiler, *The Tiananmen Papers: Chinese Leadership's Decision to Use Force Against Their Own People – In Their Own Words.* (New York Public Affairs).** The most complete collections of government documents about the 1989 Tiananmen Incident available with insightful and useful introductions.

SOURCES

Chapter 1

GRAPHIC: Yang Lin: "Memorial to Kangxi" (China National Tourist Office) — in Zhongguo di 1 lishi dang'anguan, *Yubi zhaoling shuo Qingshi* (Jinan: Shandong jiaoyu chubanshe, 2003), p. 76. Reprinted with the permission of Zhongguo Di 1 Lishi Dang'an Guan.

1.1 Shunzhi, "Head-shaving Decree," in Dun J. Li, *The Civilization of China: The Formative Period to the Coming of the West* (New York: Scribner, 1975), p. 310. Reprinted with the permission of Scribner, a Division of Simon & Schuster Adult Publishing Group, from *The Civilization of China: From the Formative Period to the Coming of the West* by Dun J. Li. Copyright © 1975 by Dun J. Li. All rights reserved.

1.2 Zhou Zhenhe, *Shengyu guangxun: jijie yu yanjiu* (Shanghai: Shanghai shudian chubanshe, 2006) [Frontpiece].

1.3 Kangxi, "Imperial Edict Regarding Wu Sangui" in Zhongguo di 1 lishi dang'anguan, *Yubi zhaoling shuo Qingshi* (Jinan: Shandong jiaoyu chubanshe, 2003), p. 63.

1.4 Evelyn Rawski, *The Last Emperors: a Social History of Qing Imperial Institutions,* (Berkeley: University of California Press, 1998), pp. 36–44. Copyright © 1998. Regents of the University of California. Reprinted by permission of University of California Press.

1.5 Fu Kang'an, Kyirong Hutuku and Dzaza Lama, "The 29 Imperial Regulations" in Ya Hanzhang, *Dalai Lama zhuan* (Beijing: Renmin chubanshe, 1984), pp. 72–83.

1.6 Kangxi, "Edict of Toleration" in Couvreur, Séraphin, *Choix de Documents: Lettres Officielles, Proclamations, Édits, Mémoriaux, Inscriptions* (Ho Kien Fou: Imprimerie de la Mission Catholique, 1906), p. 105.

1.7 King George III, "A Letter to the Emperor of China" in Hosea Ballou Morse, *The Chronicles of the East India Company trading to China, 1635–1834* (Cambridge: Harvard University Press, 1926), vol. 2, pp. 244–247.

1.8 Helen Henrietta Robbines, *Our First Ambassador to China: an Account of the Life of George, Earl of Macartney, with Extracts from His Letters, and the Narrative of His Experiences in China, as Told by Himself, 1737–1806, from Hitherto Unpublished Correspondence and Documents* (London: J. Murray, 1908), pp. 299–300; 303–304; 308–310; 332–334.

1.9 Qianlong, "An Edict to King George III of England" in *An Embassy to China: Being the Journal Kept by Lord Macartney During His Embassy to the Emperor Ch'ien-lung, 1793–1794*, edited by J.L. Cramner-Byng.

1.10 Jiaqing, "Heshen's Twenty Crimes" in *Da Qing Renzong Rui (Jiaqing) huangdi shilu* (Taibei: Hualian chubanshe, 1964), vol. 1, pp. 388–389.

1.11 Yuan Mei, "Scholar Qiu" and "Revenge of the Wronged Wife" in *Censored by Confucius: Ghost Stories by Yuan Mei*, edited and translated by Kam Louie and Louise Edwards (New York: M.E. Sharpe, 1996), pp. 16–17; 189.

Chapter 2

GRAPHIC #1: Guangzhou Factories in Hosea Ballou Morse (China National Tourist Office) — *The Chronicles of the East India Company Trading to China, 1635–1834,* (Oxford: Clarendon Press, 1926.)

GRAPHIC #2: Chinese depiction of American and British Factories — in *Yue Haiguan Zhi,* (c. 1840.)

GRAPHIC #3: Map of Pearl River Delta (from Guangzhou to Hong Kong) — in Hosea Ballou Morse, *The Chronicles of the East India Company Trading to China, 1635–1834,* (Oxford: Clarendon Press, 1926.)

2.1 William C. Hunter, *The "Fan-kwae" at Canton before the Treaty, 1825–1844,* (London: K. Paul, Trench & Co., 1882), pp. 20–22.

2.2 *Qingdai waijiao shiliao* (Beiping: Gugong Bowuyuan, 1932), juan 4:4–5.

2.3 "Rules Regulating Foreign Trading in Guangzhou" in *British Relations with the Chinese Empire* (London: Parbury, Allen & Co., 1832), pp. 143–47; *Chinese Repository* 3, (August 1834): 191–192.

2.4 Hosea B. Morse, *The International Relations of the Chinese Empire* (London: Longmans & Green, 1910), p. 90–91, 209–210; Michael Greenberg, *British Trade and the Opening of China, 1800–1842* (Cambridge: Cambridge University Press, 1951), p. 81.

2.5 Wenqing, *Chouban yiwu shimo, Daoguang chao,* (Taibei: Guofeng chubanshe, 1963), 2:4a–9b.

2.6 *The Chinese Repository,* 5 (January 1837): 123, 297.

2.7 Lin Zexu, "Edict to the Foreigners" in Zhongguo di 1 lishi dang'anguan, *Yapian zhanzheng lishi dang'an shiliao* (Tianjin: Tianjin Guji, 1992), vol. 1, pp. 513–15.

2.8 Charles Elliot, "Public Notice to British Subjects," *London Times* (August 9 1839): 6.

2.9 Lin Zexu, "Letter to Queen Victoria" in *Portfolio Chinensis: or a Collection of Authentic Chinese State Papers* (Macao: New Washington Press of ff. de Cruz, 1840), pp. 128–49.

2.10 Qi Sihe, *Yapian zhanzheng* (Shanghai: Shanghai Renmin chubanshe, 2000), vol. 4, pp. 12–13.

2.11 House of Commons, *Hansard's Parliamentary Debates vol. 63 (3rd Series),* (London: Thomas Curson Hansard, 1843), pp. 362–470.

2.12 *Treaties, Conventions, Etc., Between China and Foreign States* (Shanghai: Statistic Dept. of the Inspectorate General of Customs, 1917), vol. 1, pp. 351–56.

Chapter 3

GRAPHIC: Taiping Seal (National Museum of China)

3.1 Yang Xiuqing and Xiao Chaogui, "Anti-Manchu Proclamation" in Luo Ergang, ed., *Taiping Tianguo wenxuan* (Shanghai: Shanghai renmin chubanshe, 1956), pp. 77–80.

3.2 Chang Ju-nan, "The Days When the Taipings Arrived at Nanking" Based on: Dun J. Li, *China in Transition: 1517–1911* (New York: Van Nostrand Reinhold, 1969), pp. 121–125. (Source: *Zhongguo Jinbainian shi ziliao,* vol.2, pp. 73–93) [with slight alterations]

3.3 Wang Zhongmin, *Taiping Tianguo* (Shanghai: Shanghai renmin chubanshe, 2000), vol. 1, pp. 78–80.

3.4 "The Taiping Plan for Reorganizing Chinese Society," in J. Mason Gentzler, ed., *Changing China: Readings in the History of China from the Opium War to the* (New York: Preager Publishers, 1977), pp. 55–57, 59–60. © 1978. Reproduced with permission of Greenwood Publishing Group, Inc., Westport, CT.

3.5 Du Wenxiu, "Summons to Arms" in Bai Shouyi, ed, *Huimin qiyi* (Shanghai: Shenzhou guoguang chubanshe, 1952), vol. 2, p. 131.

3.6 T. L. Bullock, "The Great Mahomedan Rebellion in Yunnan," *China Review* 16:2, (September 1887): 92–94.

3.7 Mulla Musa Sayrami, "Rumors of a Massacre" in Hodong Kim, *Holy War in China* (Stanford: Stanford University Press, 2004), pp. 4–7. Excerpt from Hodong Kim *Holy War In China* Copyright © 2004 by the Board of Trustees of the Leland Stanford Jr. University.

3.8 "Royal Geographical Society," *London Times* No. 26688 (Mar 03, 1870): 4.

3.9 *Xuxiu siku quanshu* (Shanghai: Shanghai guji), vol. 952, pp. 540–41.

3.10 Zeng Guofan, "Founding the Shanghai Arsenal" in Ssu-yü Teng and John K. Fairbank *China's Response to the West* (Cambridge: Harvard University Press, 1965), pp. 64–65. Reprinted by permission of the publisher from *China's Response to the West: A Documentary Survey, 1839–1923* by Ssu-yü Têng and John King Fairbank, pp. 64–65, Cambridge, Mass.: Harvard University Press, Copyright © 1954, 1979 by the President and Fellows of Harvard College, Copyright renewed 1982 by Ssu-yü Têng and John King Fairbank.

3.11 Li Hung-chang, "The need for Foreign Language Training" in J. Mason Gentzler *Changing China: Readings in the History of China from the Opium War to the Present* (New York: Praeger, 1977), p. 74. © 1978. Reproduced with permission of Greenwood Publishing Group, Inc., Westport, CT.

3.12 Wo-jen, "No Need for Western Learning," in Dun J. Li *China in Transition: 1517–1911* (New York: Van Nostrand Reinhold, 1969), pp. 161–63.

Chapter 4

GRAPHIC: Map of Treaty Ports (China National Tourist Office)

4.1 T. L. Behan, *Bulletins and Other State Intelligence for the year 1857* (London: London Gazette Office, 1859), pp. 46–48.

4.2 Lord Elgin, *Letters and Journals of James, Eighth Earl of Elgin, Governor of Jamaica, Governor-General of Canada, Envoy to China, Viceroy of India* (London: John Murray, 1872), pp. 253–254.

4.3 G. J. Wolseley, *Narrative of the War with China in 1860* (London: Longman, Green, Longman and Roberts, 1862), pp. 397–411.

4.4 J. L. McGhee *How We Got to Pekin: A Narrative of the Campaign in China of 1860,* London: Richard Bentley, 1862. pp. 283–289.

4.5 G. J. Wolseley, *Narrative of the War with China in 1860* (London: Longman, Green, Longman and Roberts, 1862), pp. 224–241.

4.6 Thomas F. Wade, "Murder of Mr. Margary, and the Chefoo Convention," in Harley MacNair, *Modern Chinese History Selected Readings* (Shanghai: Commercial Press, 1923) pp. 459–61.

4.7 Cen Yuying, *Cen Yuying ji* (Nanning: Guangxi minzu chubanshe, 2005), pp. 171; 180–181.

4.8 *Treaties, Conventions, etc. Between China and Foreign States* (Shanghai: Statistical Dept. of the Inspectorate General of Customs, 1917), vol. 1, pp. 491–498.

4.9 Robert Hart, *These From the Land of Sinam* (London: Chapman and Hall, 1901), Appendix I, pp. 171–81.

4.10 United State, Dept. of States, *Papers Relating to the Foreign Relations of the United States* (Washington: G.P.O., 1894), p. 54.

4.11 Harley MacNair, *Modern Chinese History Selected Readings* (Shanghai: Commercial Press, 1923), pp. 530–31.

4.12 "The Treaty of Shimonoseki," *the American Journal of International Law* 1: 4, (October, 1907) Supplement, Official Documents: 378–84.

4.13 United State, Dept. of States, *Papers Relating to the Foreign Relations of the United States* (Washington: G.P.O., 1899), pp. 129–30.

Chapter 5

GRAPHIC: Boxer Photographs

#1: Chinese Boxer troops, the "Company of Boxers" in Tien-Tsin (Tienjin), China. (Getty Images Inc./ Hulton Archive Photos)

#2: (© Corbis, All rights reserved.)

5.1 K'ang Yu-wei, "Institutional Reform from Above" in J. Mason Gentzler, *Changing China: Readings in the History of China from the Opium War to the Present* (New York: Praeger, 1977), pp. 86–87. © 1978. Reproduced with permission of Greenwood Publishing Group, Inc., Westport, CT.

5.2 Anonymous Editorial, "The Examination System as an Obstruction to Reform," in J. Mason Gentzler, *Changing China: Readings in the History of China from the Opium War to the Present* (New York: Praeger, 1977), pp. 88–89 © 1978. Reproduced with permission of Greenwood Publishing Group, Inc., Westport, CT.

5.3 Zuo Shunsheng, *Zhonguo jinbainianshi ziliao* (Beijing: Zhonghua shuju, 1966), vol. 2, pp. 421–22.

5.4 Chen Zhensjiang, *Yihetuan wenxian jizhu yu yanjiu* (Tianjin: Tianjin renmin chubanshe, 1985), pp. 26–27.

5.5 *Yihetuan shiliao* (Beijing: Zhongguo shehui kexueyuan chubanshe, 1982), vol. 1, p. 18.

5.6 Gugong Bowuyuan, *Yihetuan dang'an shiliao* (Beijing: Zhonghua shuju, 1959), vol. 1, pp. 162–63.

5.7 Gugong Bowuyuan, *Yihetuan dang'an shiliao* (Beijing: Zhonghua shuju, 1959), vol. 1, pp. 214–15.

5.8 "Final Protocol between the Powers and China, signed September 7, 1901," *The American Journal of International Law* 1:4, (Oct., 1907): 388–396.

5.9 "The Joint Proposals of Liu K'un-I and Chang Chih-tung, 1901" in Ssu-yü Teng and John K. Fairbank, *China's Response to the West* (Cambridge: Harvard University Press, 1965), pp. 199–200. Reprinted by permission of the publisher from *China's Response to the West: A Documentary Survey, 1839–1923* by Ssu-yü Têng and John King Fairbank, pp. 199–200, Cambridge, Mass.: Harvard University Press, Copyright © 1954, 1979 by the President and Fellows of Harvard College, Copyright renewed 1982 by Ssu-yü Têng and John King Fairbank.

5.10 John C. Ferguson, "The Abolition of the Competitive Examinations in China," *Journal of the American Oriental Society* 27, (1906): 79–87.

5.11 Julie Lee Wei, *Prescriptions for Saving China, Selected Writings of Sun Yat-sen* (Stanford: Hoover Press, 1995), pp. 41–50. Reprinted from *Prescriptions for Saving China: Selected Writings of Sun Yat-sen,* edited by Julie Lee Wei, Ramon H. Myers, and Donald G. Gillin, with the permission of the publisher, Hoover Institution Press. Traslation copyright 1994 by the Board of Trustees of the Leland Stanford Junior University.

5.12 Wang Ching-wei, "We Want a Republic, Not a Constitutional Monarchy," in Dun J. Li *China in Transition: 1517–1911* (New York: Van Nostrand Reinhold, 1969), pp. 319–24.

Chapter 6

GRAPHIC: Examination Hall—Etienne Zi, *Pratique des Examens Littèraires en Chine* (Shanghai: Imprimerie de la Mission Catholique, 1894) (National Museum of China)

6.1 Wells Williams, *The Middle Kingdom: a Survey of the Geography, Government, Education, Social Life, Arts, Religion, etc.* (New York: John Wiley, 1849), pp. 441–43

6.2 Wells Williams, *The Middle Kingdom: a Survey of the Geography, Government, Education, Social Life, Arts, Religion, etc.* (New York: John Wiley, 1849), pp. 438–39, 443.

6.3 Pu Songling, "Three Genii" in *Strange Stories from a Chinese Studio,* trans., Herbert A. Giles (London: Thomas De la Rue & Co., 1880), vol. 1, pp. 214–16.

6.4 "Chinese family Life," *The China Review,* 11:6, (May 1883): 364–65.

6.5 "Advice to the Troops by Wong Cheuk-T'ong, Intendant of Liu-Chow and K'ing-Chow," *The China Review,* 13:2, (1884): 88–89.

6.6 "Practical Illustrations of the Application of the Law Regarding the Fraudulent Sale of Lands and Tenements," *The China Review,* 18:1, (July 1889): 35–36.

6.7 Pu Songling, "The Boatmen of Lao-lung" in *Strange Stories from a Chinese Studio,* trans. Herbert A. Giles (London: Thomas De la Rue & Co., 1880), vol. 2, pp. 348–50.

6.8 *Lu Chow, "Neu Heo (Female Instructor) (*nüxue)" Chinese Repository, *9,* (December 1840): 543–44.

6.9 "Cases in Chinese Law: Marriage," *The China Review,* 10:6, (May 1882): 357–365.

6.10 Shen Fu (1763–1825), "Wedded Bliss," *Six Chapters of a Floating life,* trans. Lin Yutang (Shanghai: Xifeng she, 1939), pp. 3–15, 69–77.

6.11 Qiu Jin, *Qiu Jin Ji* (Shanghai: Shanghai guji, 1979), pp. 4–6.

Chapter 7

GRAPHIC: May Fourth Pictures—University of Minnesota, Kautz Family, YMCA Archives.

7.1 Rev. G. H. Bondfield, *The China Mission Year Book* (Shanghai: Christian Literature Society for China, 1912), Appendix C, pp. 10–11.

7.2 Rev. G. H. Bondfield, *The China Mission Year Book* (Shanghai: Christian Literature Society for China, 1912), Appendix C, pp. 13–16.

7.3 Rev. G. H. Bondfield, *The China Mission Year Book* (Shanghai: Christian Literature Society for China, 1912), Appendix C, pp. 16–21.

7.4 Rev. G. H. Bondfield, *The China Mission Year Book* (Shanghai: Christian Literature Society for China, 1912), Appendix C, pp. 23–24.

7.5 Melvyn C. Goldstein, *A History of Modern Tibet, 1913–1951* (Berkeley: University of California, 1989), p. 832–35.

7.6 Reginald F. Johnston, *Twilight in the Forbidden City* (New York: D. Appleton-Century, 1934), pp. 137–38.

7.7 "Foreign News: China," *Time* 4:10, (September 8, 1924): 12–13. Copyright TIME INC. Reprinted by permission. TIME is a registered trademark of Time Inc. All rights reserved.

7.8 Gong Yao, "Huoguo yangmin tanwu canbao zhi Zhang Zongchang," *Yijing wenshi banyuekan* 6, (May 20, 1936): 316–320.

7.9 Wunsz King, *V. K. Wellington Koo's Foreign Policy, Some Selected Documents* (Shanghai: Kelly and Walsh, 1931), pp. 87–90.

7.10 Luo Jialun, "Wusi Xuanyan," Originally published at *Meizhou pinglun* (May 11, 1919).

7.11 Chow Tse-tsung, *The May Fourth Movement: Intellectual Revolution in Modern China* (Cambridge: Harvard University Press, 1962), pp. 174–176. Excerpts from "Invigorated Programs of New Youth and New Tide" reprinted by permission of the publisher. Copyright © 1962 by the President and Fellows of Harvard College.

7.12 Lu Xun, "Preface to Call to Arms," *Lu Xun, Selected Works,* trans. Yang Xianyi and Gladys Yang (Beijing: Foreign Languages Press, 1980), vol. 1, pp. 33–38. Beijing: Foreign Languages Press. Reprinted with permission of the publisher.

7.13 Hu Shih, "The Renaissance in China," *Journal of the Royal Institute of International Affairs* 5:6, (Nov., 1926): 269–273.

Chapter 8

GRAPHIC: 1920s Advertisement—University of Minnesota, Art History Collection, College of Liberal Arts.

8.1 "First Manifesto of the CCP on the Current Situation," Conrad Brandt, Benjamin Schwartz and John K. Fairbank, *Documentary History of Chinese Communism* (New York: Atheneum, 1966), pp. 54–63. "First manifesto of the CCP on the current situation, June 10, 1922" from *A Documentary History of Chinese Communism* by Conrad Brandt, Benjamin Schwartz, and John K. Fairbank, pp. 51–62, Cambridge, Mass.: Russian Research Center Studies, 6, Harvard University Press, 1952.

8.2 Mao Tse-tung, *Selected Works of Mao Tse-tung* (Beijing: Foreign languages Press, 1967), vol. 1, pp. 23–30. Beijing: Foreign Languages Press. Reprinted with permission of the publisher.

8.3 "Land Law of 1932," Dun J. Li, *The Road to Communism: China Since 1912* (New York: Van Nostrand Reinhold, 1969), pp. 143–45.

8.4 Mao Tse-tung, *Selected Works of Mao Tse-tung* (Beijing: Foreign languages Press, 1967), vol. 4, p. 155. Beijing: Foreign Languages Press. Reprinted with permission of the publisher.

8.5 Sun Zhongshan, *Sun Zhongshan Quanji* (Beijing: Zhonghua shuju, 1985), vol. 5, pp. 472–81.

8.6 Leonard Hsu, *Sun Yat-sen: His Political and Social Ideals* (Los Angeles: University of Southern California Press, 1933), pp. 142–45.

8.7 Sun Zhongshan, *Sun Zhongshan quanji* (Beijing: Zhonghua shuju, 1986), vol. 11, pp. 639–41.

8.8 Secretariat, the Kuomintang of China, *Nationalist China* (Canton: Central Political Council of Kuomintang, Canton Branch, April 1927), pp. 14–15.

8.9 Secretariat, the Kuomintang of China, *Nationalist China* (Canton: Central Political Council of Kuomintang, Canton Branch, April 1927), pp. 25–26.

8.10 Secretariat, the Kuomintang of China, *Nationalist China* (Canton: Central Political Council of Kuomintang, Canton Branch, 1927), pp. 15–17.

8.11 Yang Zhihua, "Love and Socializing Between Men and Women," Hua R. Lan and Vanessa L. Fong, eds., *Women in Republican China, a Sourcebook,* (Armonk, NY: M.E. Sharpe, 1999), pp. 44–46.

8.12 Ding Ling, *Miss Sophie's Diary and Other Stories,* trans. W.J.F. Jenner (Beijing: Panda Books, 1985), pp. 29–32. Panda Books, reprinted with the permission of Foreign Languages Press, 24 Baiwanzhuang Road, Xicheng District, Beijing 100037, China, flp.com.cn

8.13 Ba Jin, *The Family,* trans. Sidney Shapiro (Beijing: Foreign Languages Press, 1958), pp. 24–26. Beijing: Foreign Languages Press. Reprinted with permission of the publisher.

Chapter 9

GRAPHIC: Map of Long March

9.1 "Japanese Assertion that China is not an Organized State," Westel W., Willoughby, *The Sino-Japanese Controversy and the League of Nations* (Baltimore: The John Hopkins Press, 1935), pp. 245–46. © 1935 The Johns Hopkins University Press Reprinted with permission of The Johns Hopkins University Press.

9.2 Memorandum on Japan's Attempts to Monopolize the Railways in the Three Eastern Provinces, Document No. 15, Peiping, June 1932, in *Memoranda Presented to the Lytton Commission* (New York: Chinese Cultural Society, 1932), pp. 47–50.

9.3 "Lytton Commission Report, (October, 1932)" Westel W. Willoughby, *The Sino-Japanese Controversy and the League of Nations* (Baltimore: The John Hopkins Press, 1935), p. 96–97. © 1935 The Johns Hopkins University Press Reprinted with permission of The Johns Hopkins University Press.

9.4 "Japanese Declaration and Withdrawal from League (March 27, 1933)," Westel W. Willoughby, *The Sino-Japanese Controversy and the League of Nations* (Baltimore: The John Hopkins Press, 1935), pp. 595–96. © 1935 The Johns Hopkins University Press Reprinted with permission of The Johns Hopkins University Press.

9.5 T'ang Leang-Li, ed. *Suppressing Communist Banditry in China* (Shanghai: China United Press, 1934), pp. 111–13.

9.6 *General Chiang Kai-shek and the Communist Crisis; Madame Chiang Kai-shek on the New Life Movement* (Shanghai: China Weekly Review Press, 1937), pp. 55–60.

9.7 "Chiang Kai-shek, Chang Hsueh-liang and Chang Kuo-t'ao/Three Views on the Sian Incident," Dun J. Li, *Modern China: Mandarin to Commissar* (New York: Scribner, 1978), pp. 240–42. Reprinted with the permission of Scribner, a Division of Simon & Schuster Adult Publishing Group, from *Modern China: From Mandarin to Commissar* by Dun J. Li. Copyright © 1978 by Dun J. Li. All rights reserved.

9.8 Otto Braun, *A Comintern Agent in China 1932–1939* (Stanford: Stanford University Press, 1982), pp. 136–37, 143, 146. Reprinted with permission of C. Hurst & Co. (Publishers) Ltd.

9.9 Mao Tse-tung, *Selected Works of Mao Tse-tung* (Beijing: Foreign Languages Press, 1967), vol. 1, pp. 255–58. Beijing: Foreign Languages Press. Reprinted with permission of the publisher.

9.10 Zhou Enlai, *Selected Works of Zhou Enlai* (Beijing: Foreign Languages Press, 1981), vol. 1, pp. 93–95. Beijing: Foreign Languages Press. Reprinted with permission of the publisher.

Chapter 10

GRAPHIC: (China National Toursit Office)

#1: Gao Longshang, "'De' bugu, bi you lin." (Analects, IV 25), *Quanguo manhua zuojia kangzhan jiezuo xuanji,* Huang Miaozi, n.p.: Zhanwang shuwu, 1938, p. 61.

#2: Feng Zikai, "A Baby's Head Thrown Into the Air," *China Weekly Review* 88, 7 (April 15, 1939): 207, Shanghai.

#3: Feng Zikai, Zhoubao 10 (November 15, 1945): front cover, second impression, Shanghai.

#4: Kong Ping, "Watch Yourself," *Xiaoxi* [News], No. 12 (May 16, 1946), p. 178.

10.1 John H.D., Rabe, "Letter to the Japanese Embassy," Timothy Brook, ed., *Documents on the Rape of Nanking* (Ann Arbor: University of Michigan Press, 1999), pp. 18–23.

10.2 "Wang Jingwei's Telegram (*yandian*)," Chinese document accessed: http://www.omnitalk.com/miliarch/messages/2660.html

10.3 China-Japan: Treaty Concerning Basic Relations-Annexed Protocol," *American Journal of International Law* 35:3, Supplement, Official Documents (July 1941): 127–28.

10.4 Jiang Wen (Director), *Devils on the Doorstep* (DVD, Japan: Pioneer LDC, 2000).

10.5 Edgar Snow, *Red Star Over China* (New York: Random House, 1938), pp. 211, 218–20. Copyright © 1968 by Edgar Snow. Used by permission of Grove/Atlantic, Inc.

10.6 Ding Ling, "Thoughts on March 8, Women's Day," Hunter, Alan, *Wild Lily, Prairie Fire* (Princeton: Princeton University Press, 1995), pp. 78–82. Copyright © 1995 Princeton University Press Reprinted by permission of Princeton University Press.

10.7 Wang Shiwei, "Wild Lily," Hunter, Alan, *Wild Lily, Prairie Fire* (Princeton: Princeton University Press, 1995), pp. 69–71, 73–75. Copyright © 1995 Princeton University Press Reprinted by permission of Princeton University Press.

10.8 Wen Yiduo, "The Poet's Farewell," Pei-kai Cheng, Michael Lestz with Jonathan D. Spence, *The Search for Modern China: a Documentary Collection* (New York: W. W. Norton, 1999), pp. 337–38. "18.1 — Wen Yiduo: The Poet's Farewell, 1946," from *The Search for Modern China, A Documentary Collection* by Pei Kai Cheng, Michael Letsz and Jonathan Spence. Copyright © 1999 by W. W. Norton & Company, Inc. Used by permission of W. W. Norton & Company, Inc.

10.9 Te-kong Tong and Li Tsung-jen, *The Memoirs of Li Tsung-jen* (Boulder, Co: Westview Press, 1979), pp. 474–78.

10.10 Peng Ming-min, "Political Offences in Taiwan: Laws and Problems," *China Quarterly* 47, (July-September 1971): 472–73. Reprinted with the permission of Cambridge University Press.

10.11 "Progress on Formosa," *Time,* (July 28, 1952): 25. Copyright TIME INC. Reprinted by permission. TIME is a registered tradmark of Time Inc. All rights reserved.

Chapter 11

GRAPHIC: Two photos of the Great Leap Forward Campaigns

#1: *Renmin Hua bao* 9 (September 1958): 3. Reprinted with the permission of Xinhua News Agency.

#2: (ChinaStock Photo Library)

11.1 Michael Y.M. Kau, and John K. Leung, ed., *The Writings of Mao Zedong,* (Armonk, NY: M. E. Sharpe, Inc., 1986), p. 10–11.

11.2 Thomas J. Christensen, "Threats, Assurances, and the Last Chance for Peace: The Lessons of Mao's Korean War Telegrams," *International Security* 17:1 (1992): 151–53. Reprinted with permission of MIT Press.

11.3 Mao Tse-tung, *Selected Works of Mao Tse-tung* (Beijing: Foreign Languages Press, 1977), vol. 5, pp. 308–11. Beijing: Foreign Languages Press. Reprinted with permission of the publisher.

11.4 "Seventeen-Point Plan for the Peaceful Liberation of Tibet," International Committee of Lawyers for Tibet, *Legal Materials on Tibet,* (Berkeley, California: International Committee of Lawyers for Tibet, 1997), pp. 182–185. Reprinted with permission of Tibet Justice Center.

11.5 "The Marriage Law of the People's Republic of China," in J. Mason Gentzler, ed., *Changing China: Readings in the History of China from the Opium War to the* (New York: Preager Publishers, 1977), pp. 268–70. © 1978. Reproduced with permission of Greenwood Publishing Group, Inc., Westport, CT.

11.6 Li Dequan, "Birth Control and Planned Families," *Communist China 1955–1959: Policy Documents with Analysis* (Cambridge: Harvard University Press, 1965), pp. 297–98. Excerpts from "Birth Control and Planned Families" reprinted by permission of the publisher from *Communist China 1955–1959: Policy Documents with Analysis* by Robert R. Bowie and John K. Fairbank, pp. 297–298, Cambridge, Mass.: Harvard University Press, Copyright © 1962 by the President and Fellows of Harvard College. *English text is taken from CB 445, translated by the U.S. Consulate General, Hong Kong, from the People's Daily of March 8. 1957.*

11.7 Liu Shaoqi, "A Blue Print for the Great Leap Forward" in Mark Selden, *The People's Republic of China, a Documentary History of Revolutionary Change* (New York: Monthly Review Press, 1979), pp. 389–95.

11.8 Chu Li and Tien Chieh-yun, *Inside a People's Commune: A Report from Chiliying* (Beijing: Foreign Languages Press, 1974), pp. 40–42. Beijing: Foreign Languages Press. Reprinted with permission of the publisher.

11.9 "Woguo zaodao youchuang shijie gaochan jilu," *Renmin Huabao* 9 (September 1958): 3.

11.10 *Memoir of a Chinese Marshal* (Beijing: Foreign Languages Press, 1984), pp. 515–20. Beijing: Foreign Languages Press. Reprinted with permission of the publisher.

11.11 Tian Zhuangzhuang (Director), *Blue Kite* (DVD, New York: Kino, 2002).

Chapter 12

GRAPHIC: Photo of Mao in Tiananmen (Corbis/Bettmann)/Cultural Revolution Poster (Swim Ink/Corbis)

12.1 *Long Live the Victory of People's War!* (Beijing: Foreign Languages Press, 1965), pp. 58–68. Beijing: Foreign Languages Press. Reprinted with permission of the publisher.

12.2 Chen Kuang-sheng, *Lei Feng, Chairman Mao's Good Fighter* (Beijing: Foreign Languages Press, 1968), pp. 60–62, 99–102. Beijing: Foreign Languages Press. Reprinted with permission of the publisher.

12.3 "What is the Tachai Spirit?" *China Reconstructs* 18, (April 1969): 19. Reprinted with permission of China Today (Formerly China Reconstructs).

12.4 Mao Zedong, "My First Big-Character Poster," ed., David Milton, Nancy Milton, and Franz Schurmann, *People's China: Social Experimentation, Politics, Entry onto the World Scene 1966 through 1972* (New York: Random House, 1974), p. 271.

12.5 *Carry the Great Proletarian Cultural Revolution Through to the End* (Beijing: Foreign Languages Press, 1966), pp. 1–14. Beijing: Foreign Languages Press. Reprinted with permission of the publisher.

12.6 *Carry the Great Proletarian Cultural Revolution Through to the End* (Beijing: Foreign Languages Press, 1966), pp. 15–20. Beijing: Foreign Languages Press. Reprinted with permission of the publisher.

12.7 "The Road for China's School Graduates" *China Reconstructs* 25, (January 1976), Supplement: 64–70. Reprinted with permission of China Today (Formerly China Reconstructs).

12.8 Ling Nai-min, *Tibet, 1950–1967* (Hong Kong: Union Research Institute, 1968), pp. 604–605. (Originally published in Gongren Ribao August 28, 1966).

12.9 "Chiang Ching's Speech on the Revolution in Peking Opera, July 1964," Winberg Chai, *The New Politics of Communist China: Modernization Process of a Developing Nation* (Pacific Palisades, CA: Goodyear Publishing Company, 1972), 253–54.

12.10 Ma Ge, "Songs Play Their Part in Revolution," *China Reconstructs* 14, (June 1965): 31–33. Reprinted with permission of China Today (Formerly China Reconstructs).

12.11 "National Salvation March (*Jiuguoyun Ge*)," *China Reconstructs* 12, (May 1963): 28–29; "Commune Members are Sunflowers" *China Reconstructs* 14, (June 1965): 34–35. Reprinted with permission of China Today (Formerly China Reconstructs).

Chapter 13

GRAPHIC: Photo (AP Wide World Photos) & Cartoon (China National Tourist Office): Mao Zedong's Funeral/Gang of Four—*Lishi de shenpan* (Shanghai renmin meishu, 1979), p. 8, 27.

13.1 *Resolutions Adopted by the General Assembly during Its 26th session, 21 September–22 December 1971*, GAOR, 26th sess., Suppl. no. 29, (New York: Oceana), p. 2.

13.2 Jiang Jieshi, "Declaration to Compatriots Regarding the Republic of China's Withdrawal from the United Nations," Chinese text accessed: http://zh.wikiwource .org/wiki/.

13.3 "Shanghai Communiqué, February 28, 1972," accessed: http://usinfo.state.gov/eap/ Archive_Index/joint_communique_1972.html.

13.4 Editorial, "Study the Documents Well and Grasp the Key Link," *People's Daily,* (February 7, 1977), A1.

13.5 Deng Xiaoping, "Realize the Four Modernizations and Never Seek Hegemony" (May 7, 1978) accessed: http://english.peopledaily.com.cn/dengxp/vol2/text/b1200. Reprinted with permission of Beijing: Foreign Languages Press.

13.6 Wei Jingsheng, "The Fifth Modernization: Democracy," Simon Leys, *The Burning forest: Essays on Chinese Culture and Politics* (New York: Holt, Rinehart, and Winston, 1985), pp. 224–239.

13.7 "Principal Culprits of the Counter-Revolutionary Cliques of Lin Biao and Jiang Qing to be Tried" *Beijing Review* 46, (October 6, 1980): 3–4. Reprinted with permission of Beijing Review.

13.8 "University Entrance Examinations, 1977," *China Reconstructs,* Vol. 27 (April 1978): 9–12. Reprinted with permission of China Today (Formerly China Reconstructs).

13.9 Shen Rong, *At Middle Age* (Beijing: Panda Books, 1987), pp. 24–30. Panda Books, reprinted with the permission of Foreign Languages Press, 24 Baiwanzhuang Road, Xicheng District, Beijing 100037, China, flp.com.cn.

13.10 Hunter, Alan, *Wild Lily, Prairie Fire* (Princeton: Princeton University Press, 1995), p. 227. Copyright © 1995, Princeton University Press. Reprinted by permission of Princeton University Press.

Chapter 14

GRAPHIC: Tiananmen Square Incident Photos

#1: Alon Reininger/Contact Press Images Inc.

#2: Jeff Widener/AP Wide World Photos

14.1 Deng Xiaoping, *Selected Works of Deng Xiaoping* (Beijing: Foreign Languages Press, 1994), vol. 3, pp. 72–75. Beijing: Foreign Languages Press. Reprinted with permission of the publisher.

14.2 Deng Xiaoping, *Selected Works of Deng Xiaoping* (Beijing: Foreign Languages Press, 1994), vol. 3, pp. 358–70. Beijing: Foreign Languages Press. Reprinted with permission of the publisher.

14.3 Panchen Lama, "Speech to the Tibet Autonomous Region Standing Committee Meeting of the National People's Congress in Beijing," *From the Heart of The Panchen Lama,* (Dharamsala: Department of Information and International Relations, 1998), p. 36.

14.4 Xinhua News Agency, "Transcript of May 18 meeting between Premier Li Peng and Students" Han Minzhu, *Cries for Democracy* (Princeton University Press, 1990), pp. 242–48. Reprinted by permission of Princeton University Press. Copyright © 1990, Princeton University Press.

14.5 *The Truth about the Beijing Turmoil* (Beijing: Beijing Publishing House, 1990), pp. 3–5.

14.6 Hou Dejian, "Descendents of the Dragon"; Cui Jian, "Yiwu Suoyou," *Rough Guide to the Music of China: Ancient Traditions to Beijing Punk,* (CD, London: World Music Network, 2003.)

14.7 "One Couple, One Child," *Beijing Review* 46 (October 6 1980): 4–5. Reprinted with permission of Beijing Review.

14.8 Huang Hong and Song Dandan (actors,) "Chaosheng youjidui," *1990 New Year's Eve Television Gala Compilation Set,* (DVD, CCTV, 2007).

14.9 Zhang Yimou (Director), Chen Yuanbin (Script), *"Story of Qiuju,"* (DVD, Sony Pictures, 2006).

14.10 Zhang Jie, *Love Must Not Be Forgotten* (Beijing: Panda Books, 1987), pp. 1–4. Panda Books, reprinted with the permission of Foreign Languages Press, 24 Baiwanzhuang Road, Xicheng District, Beijing 100037, China, flp.com.cn.

Chapter 15

GRAPHIC: Yangzi Three Gorges Dam

#1: Photo (© Du Huaju/Xinhua/Corbis/All rights reserved)

#2: Map (Source: International Rivers Network. © Eureka Cartography, Berkeley, CA)

15.1 "Three Represents," *News of the Communist Party of China,* Accessed: http://english.cpc.people.com.cn/66739/4521344.html Xinhua, reprinted with the permission of the Xinhua News Agency.

15.2 Xinhua, "Scientific Outlook on Development," *17th CPC National Congress.* Accessed: http://news.xinhuanet.com/english/2007-10/15/content_6883135.htm Xinhua, reprinted with the permission of the Xinhua News Agency.

15.3 Office of the President, Taiwan (R.O.C.) December 10, 2007 http://www.mac.gov.tw/english/english/macpolicy/ch961210e.htm Office of the President, Taiwan (R.O.C.) "Associated Press Interview with Chen Shuibian," December 10, 2007. Accessed: http://www.president.gov.tw/en/. Reprinted with permission of the Associated Press.

15.4 Ewa Kedzierska, "Interview With His Holiness the Dalai Lama" for the Polish newspaper *Gazeta Wyborcza,* Dharamsala, April 4, 2007. Accessed on January 5, 2008: Phayl.com. Reprinted with permission of Ewa Kedzierska.

15.5 Li Datong, "Open Letter to the Public: Protesting Decision on *Freezing Point Weekly.*" Accessed: http://angrychineseblogger.blog-city.com.

15.6 Jiang Yuxia, ed. "China Warns of Environmental "Catastrophe" from Three Gorges Dam" Xinhua, Accessed: http://news.xinhuanet.com/english/2007-09/26/content_6796234.htm Xinhua, reprinted with the permission of the Xinhua News Agency.

15.7 Jia Zhangke (Director), *Still Life,* DVD (Xstreem Pictures, Shanghai Film Group, 2006).

15.8 "Fudan University relaxes Sex Rules for Students," *China Daily* (July 19, 2005). Accessed: http://www.chinadaily.com.cn/english/doc/2005-07/19/content_461372.htm.

15.9 Xinhua, "China Vows to Halt Growing Sex Ratio Imbalance." Accessed: http://news.xinhuanet.com/english/2007-01/22/content_5637693.htm. Xinhua, reprinted with the permission of the Xinhua News Agency.

15.10 Wei Hui, *Shanghai Baby* (New York: Pocket Books, 2001), pp. 17–19. Reprinted with the permission of Pocket Books, a Division of Simon & Schuster, Inc., from Shanghai Baby by Wei Hui. Translated from the Shinese by Bruce Humes. English translation Copyright © 2001 by Simon & Schuster, Inc.

GLOSSARY

AMBAN – A Manchu term meaning high official, but in the Tibetan context refers to the Qing imperial residents first assigned to Lhasa in 1727. Typically, two Ambans were assigned to Tibet to supervise the region's political situation.

AMIOT, FATHER MARIA (1718–1793) – A Jesuit missionary born in France and sent to China in 1740, he quickly won the trust of the young Qianlong emperor and learned to speak Manchu and Chinese fluently.

ANDIJAN – Located in the Central Asian Republic of Uzbekistan, roughly half way between Kashgar and Kokand.

ANTI-RIGHTEST CAMPAIGN – A political campaign launched in July 1959 immediately following the Hundred Flowers Movement to purge those labeled as rightist and not adequately supportive of the CCP.

BA JIN (1904–2005) – Pen name of influential May Fourth author Li Feigan who best known for his novel Family the first in the Torrents Trilogy which also included Spring and Autumn).

BANNERMEN (QIREN) – "Banners" were large civil-military units, organized along ethnic (Manchu, Mongol or Han) and hereditary lines, though during the Qing the term "bannermen" became synonymous with being Manchu.

BAOJIA – A neighborhood mutual security system in which every ten houses were organized into a unit of ten households and every one hundred households into a jia. Jia leaders were given authority to maintain local order, collect taxes and organize civil projects and were equally responsible for any outbreaks in violence, tax shortfalls, and civil disturbances.

BEIDAIHE – A coastal resort town northeast of Beijing used by the CCP's central committee and high level officials for work and meetings during the summer.

BEIJING CONVENTION (1860) – A set of three separate treaties signed by China with Great Britain, France and Russia after the Second Opium War.

BEIPING – In 1928, the GMD made Nanjing, literally "Southern Capital," the new capital of China and changed the name of Beijing, "Northern Capital" to Beiping, "Northern Peace." In 1949, the CCP captured Beijing, restored both its position as capital of China and its original name.

BEIYANG ARMY – A Western-style army forged from Li Hongzhang's Anhui Army in the 1880s and led by Yuan Shikai after Li Hongzhang's death in 1901. I It was funded by North China customs' revenues, first used to build the Beiyang ("Northern Ocean") fleet, hence the name. The Beiyang army remained intact until the Republican era, first led by Yuan Shikai, then the conservative warlord general Zhang Xun.

BIG CHARACTER POSTER – Posters often attacking a specific person or type of behavior written in large characters and posted publicly typically on interior and exterior walls.

BOXER PROTOCOL (1901) – An extremely harsh peace treaty imposed by the Eight Nation Alliance upon the Qing government, including a 250 million taels ($333 million dollar) indemnity, almost twice the annual Qing budget of 450 taels, and with interest totaling nearly 1 billion taels over 33 years.

BOXER UPRISING (1900) – Originating in Shandong province, the Boxer movement was anti-foreign, anti-Christian, and dedicated to expelling all foreigners from China. Boxers combined martial art techniques ("boxing") with beliefs in traditional spirit possession.

BRITISH EAST INDIA COMPANY – Founded in 1600, the East India Company was granted a monopoly on all British trade from western India to eastern China. The company lost its exclusive monopoly on Asian trade in 1813 and was dissolved in 1874.

CADRE – In the Chinese Communist context, a term meaning functionaries or administrators, often used as shorthand for essential or particularly revolutionary "backbone" members of the CCP.

CADRE SCHOOL – Often known as May 7th Cadre School. It is a type of farm camp started in 1968 by many government agencies, schools, and research institutes. Officials, regular cadres, and intellectuals were sent to these countryside Cadre Schools for re-education and improvement. The practice wound down towards the end of Cultural Revolution and was officially concluded in 1979.

CAI YUANPEI (1868–1940) – Born in Zhejiang, Cai Yuanpei was appointed to Hanlin Academy in 1894, joined the Tongmenghui in 1905 and served as Chancellor of Beijing University (1916–1926). A major proponent of the May Fourth Movement advocating the progressive ideals of Anarchism and women's rights.

CAPITALISM – An economic system in which production, distribution and markets are in the private sphere, where corporations and businesses succeed or fail according to free market forces.

CEN YUYING (1829–1889) – A native of Guangxi, he rose rapidly through official ranks in Yunnan province during the Panthay Rebellion by pursuing an anti-Hui policy, later becoming Governor-General of Yunnan and Guizhou for much of the 1870s and 80s.

CENTRAL COMMITTEE – A committee limited to the highest-ranking CCP members, ranging in size from 100 to 300 members and from which the powerful Politburo and Standing Committee are selected.

CHEN DUXIU (1880–1942) – A gifted May Fourth intellectual who helped launch and edit the New Youth in 1915, was appointed as Dean to the School of Arts at Beijing University in 1917, and was a founding member and first party secretary of the Chinese Communist Party in 1921.

CHEN SHUIBIAN (1950–) – Born in southern Taiwan, he served as the first non-GMD President of the Republic of China (Taiwan) from 2000-2008 and as chairman of the DPP (Democratic Progressive Party).

CHIN-CHIN – A type of "pigeon English" phrase used in Chinese ports, it is a greeting or salute. It is likely a corruption of the Chinese phrase qing-qing, a response akin to "salutation," or "with regards."

CHINA RECONSTRUCTS – A magazine established by Song Meiling in 1949, published in five languages and intended to offer positive articles about the Peoples Republic of China for a foreign audience.

CHINESE COMMUNIST PARTY (CCP) – Founded in 1921 by a small group of intellectuals. Following orders from the Soviet Union, the CCP allied themselves with the GMD during the War of Resistance Against Japan before splitting irrevocably in 1945 and founding the PRC in 1949.

CHINESE NATIONAL HOLIDAYS – Until 2008, every Chinese had seven days off per year. In 2008 this was raised to eleven days per year: New Years Day (1 day), Spring Festival (3 days), Qingming Festival (1 day); May Day (1 day); Dragon Boat Festival (Duanwu Jie, 1 Day), Mid-Autumn Festival (1 day) and National Day (3 day).

CITY GOD – Each city had a deity, said to serve the same purpose as his "earthly" counterpart, but in the "other worldly" realm. This partnership between city gods and magistrates is one of the most common intersections between the spiritual world and the temporal world. The city god temple would be the first official visit any magistrate or official made upon taking up an official posting.

CIXI (1834–1908) – An imperial courtesan of the Xianfeng emperor, she gave birth to his only son, the Tongzhi emperor. After the Xianfeng emperor's death, she served as regent to the Tongzhi emperor and, after his death, to the Guangxu emperor. She remained a driving, if controversial, force within the Qing government until her death in 1908.

COMINTERN – Founded in Moscow in 1919, the Comintern (short for Communist International) played a guiding role in the global Communist movement, including China.

COMMUNE – Seeking to reduce the state economy through consolidation, China merged, as part of the Great Leap Forward, 750,000 cooperatives into 24,000 communes, which became the highest of three administrative levels in rural areas from 1958 until 1983.

COMPRADORE – The top Chinese agent serving in the factories in Guangzhou. The term was also used to apply to Chinese representatives on foreign sailing vessels.

COW SHEDS (NIUPENG) – A place of confinement chosen by the Red Guards, usually in a vacant classroom, lecture hall or even a bathroom converted for their detainees.

CULTURAL REVOLUTION (GREAT PROLITARIAN CULTURAL REVOLUTION) – A political movement launched by Mao Zedong in 1966 to rid China of "liberal bourgeoisie" and to abolish the Four Olds. Though Mao Zedong officially ended its most radical phase in 1969 it continued to affect China until his death in 1976.

COMMUNISM – A system of government in which the economy, production and governance is controlled by a single party that rules in the name of the people, property is to be held in common, class divisions disappear and society works for the common good of the people.

DALAI LAMA – Conventionally viewed as one of the two highest reincarnated lamas of Tibet's main Buddhist order (Gelugpa). Since the seventeenth century, the Dalai Lama has been the head of the Tibetan government based in Lhasa. In 1959, the Fourteenth Dalai Lama fled China and established a government in exile in neighboring India.

DANWEI – A Chinese term meaning "work unit" or one's place of employment. Until the 1990s each danwei controlled housing, child care, schools, clinics, etc. and held considerable power over travel, marriage, and having children.

DAOGUANG (1782–1850) – Seventh emperor of the Qing dynasty, ruling from 1821 to 1850 during a period of tremendous internal turmoil and external threats to the empire.

DAOTAI – A sub-provincial level civil official, often translated as "intendant," he oversaw various sections (or "circuits") of a province or particular waterways, monopolies, and transportation networks.

DAZHAI – A village located in the mountainous Shanxi province which Mao Zedong held up as a model village encouraging all Chinese to "Learn from Dazhai in agriculture."

DEMOCRACY WALL – A wall located in central Beijing and covered in Big Character Posters advocating political reform from 1978 until 1980 when the wall was declared off limits to such postings.

DEMOCRATIC LEAGUE – A political party first formed in 1941 and officially reorganized into the Democratic League in 1944. Intellectuals dominated the league leadership and espoused national unity, open democracy and peace. It remains an active party within the PRC today.

DENG XIAOPING (1904–1997) – Born in Sichuan, educated in France and a veteran of the Long March, he rose to be General Secretary of the Central Committee before 1949. After 1949, Deng Xiaoping held numerous significant posts, and was purged twice times, before rising, after Mao Zedong's death, to become China's "paramount" leader and launched broad economic reforms. His decision to violently suppress the Tiananmen Movement and his inability to control government corruption tarnished an otherwise popular era of governance.

A DOLL'S HOUSE – An 1879 play by Norwegian playwright Henrik Ibsen. It traces a woman's realization of her limited role in society and her determination to fight against patriarchal constraints. The play's feminist themes made it popular in May Fourth era China, with Hu Shi praising the play as "nothing but realism."

DOWAGER EMPRESS – Dowager indicates the empress is widowed. In Cixi's case the term is an oversimplification since she was the widowed mother of the Tongzhi emperor, the aunt of the Guangxu emperor and the great-aunt of the Xuantong emperor (better known as Puyi, the last emperor).

DU WENXIU (1823–1872) – Hui leader of the Yunnan Panthay Rebellion from 1856–1872. Born in western Yunnan, he passed the civil exam at age sixteen. In 1856, after helping capture the western Yunnan city of Dali he was selected to rule the new rebel regime. He died in 1872 after surrendering to Qing troops.

DUAN QIRUI (1864–1936) – A prominent warlord whose power base was centered in Beijing. He served as China's premier during Yuan Shikai's presidency. His later political activities were tainted by his close relationship with Japan, though he continued to be active politically in the Beijing government as well as in the Anhui warlord clique.

EIGHT NATION ALLIANCE – An alliance of eight nations—Austria-Hungry, France, Germany, Italy, Japan, Russia, United Kingdom, and the United States— who came together to quell the Boxer Rebellion.

EIGHTH ROUTE ARMY – The main military force of the CCP commanded by Zhu De and nominally a part of the GMD-controlled National Revolutionary Army during the War of Resistance Against Japan.

ELGIN, LORD JAMES (1811–1863) – British diplomat who in 1857 led British expeditionary force during the Second Opium War and ordered the destruction of the Yuanming Yuan.

ELLIOT, CHARLES (1801–1875) – A British diplomat serving as Chief Superintendent of Trade and British Minister to China from 1835 until 1841,when recalled from his position for not extracting harsh enough concessions in the Convention of Chuanbi (1841).

EXAMINATION DEGREES – The three imperial exam degrees relate to the modern system as follows: the shengyuan (or "Budding Genius") is a bachelor's degree (BA), the juren (or "Promoted Gentleman") is a master's degree (MA) and the jinshi ("Achieved Scholar") is a doctorate (Ph.D.). The average age for passing was 24 years old for the shengyuan degree, 31 for the juren, and 35 for the jinshi.

EXAMINATION QUOTAS – Unlike modern university entrance or SAT exams on which the test taker is given an objective score, each sitting of the imperial exams had a specific quota of degrees to be offered that year with each province designated a pre-determined number of degrees to be issued to those candidates who scored highest on the examination.

EXTRATERRITORIALITY – A legal practice that gives individuals from foreign countries immunity from local laws. In theory, an individual's home country would try the person for a crime under their country's laws, but in practice this rarely occurred.

FAMILY BACKGROUND – Depending on the class background of one's parents (and sometimes one's grandparents), each individual was designated as "red" or "black." If one's parents were workers, poor peasants, lower-middle-class peasants, revolutionary cadres, or revolutionary soldiers, they were classified as one of the "five red types" (coming from a "revolutionary" background). If one's parents were landlords, rich peasants, counter-revolutionaries, evildoers, rightists, capitalists or reactionary intellectuals, they were classified as being in one of "seven black categories."

FEI XIANG (1960–) – A child of a Taiwanese mother and an American father, Fei Xiang/Kris Philips became one of the best known Chinese celebrities of the 1980s and 90s after appearing on the 1987 Spring Festival Television special.

FENG GUIFEN (1809–1874) – A precociously bright scholar, he achieved his jinshi degree at the age of 32 and was immediately appointed to the prestigious Hanlin Academy. A reformer who advocated using Western methods within a Chinese context, he is best known for championing a school to teach Western languages and sciences.

FIFTH GENERATION – A group of Chinese filmmakers that emerged after the end of the Cultural Revolution and included Zhang Yimou, Tian Zhuangzhuang, and Chen Kaige. They ushered in an era of considerable international acclaim for Chinese cinema.

FIFTH MODERNIZATION – In the wake of Deng Xiaoping's Four Modernizations, Wei Jingsheng most famously advocated for a "fifth modernization," democracy.

FOOTBINDING – By the nineteenth century footbinding for women had been practiced within China among the rich and the poor for many centuries. The foot was bound by breaking the bones in the foot's arch, then curling the outer toes underneath by wrapping long cloth bindings tightly around the foot. If done correctly, this produced feet 3 to 5 inches in length.

FORMOSA (TAIWAN) – An outdated term formerly used for Taiwan originating from the Portuguese term for the island meaning "beautiful."

FOUR BOOKS – The core of classical learning in late imperial China included: Confucius' Analects (Lun Yu), Mencius (Mengzi), The Doctrine of the Mean (Zhong Yong), and the Great Learning (Da Xue)

FOUR CARDINAL PRINCIPLES – On March 30th 1979, Deng Xiaoping outlined the Four Cardinal Principles: 1) keeping to the socialist road, 2) upholding the people's democratic dictatorship (dictatorship of the proletariat), 3) upholding leadership by the Communist Party and 4) upholding Marxism-Leninism and Mao Zedong Thought.

FOUR LITTLE DRAGONS – A phrase first employed by the Chinese to refer to the four largest East Asian economies (after Japan): South Korea, Taiwan, Singapore and Hong Kong.

FOUR MODERNIZATIONS – Part of Deng Xiaoping's modernization program emphasizing: agriculture, industry, national defense, and science and technology.

FOUR NOES – Chen Shuibian's 2000 promise not to: 1) declare Taiwan independence, 2) change the official title of the country from the Republic of China (R.O.C.) to the Republic of Taiwan, 3) enforce a "state-to-state" framework of "cross-strait" relations, or 4) endorse a referendum on formal independence.

FOUR OLDS – Referring to broad categories denounced during the Cultural Revolution: Old Customs, Old Culture, Old Habits, and Old Ideas.

GANG OF FOUR – A term coined by Mao Zedong, it referred to top Chinese leaders lead by Mao's wife Jiang Qing as well as Wang Hongwen, Zhang Chunqiao, and Yao Wenyuan who were accused of being responsible for the Cultural Revolution's worst excesses and were put on trial in 1980. All four were found guilty.

GATE OF HEAVENLY PEACE (TIANANMEN) – The main gate and entrance to the Forbidden Palace, erected during the Ming dynasty and rebuilt in 1651. Over one hundred feet tall, the gate has five arched portals through the base; the middle and largest being exclusively for the emperor.

GELUGPA – The dominant school of the four main branches of Tibetan Buddhism in Tibet often imprecisely referred to as the "Yellow Hats" headed by the Dalai Lama.

GONGHANG (COHONG) – A merchant guild authorized in 1720 by the central government as the only organization through which western merchants were allowed to trade with China and designated to collect duties on Western trade. It was abolished by the Treaty of Nanjing in 1842.

GORDON, CHARLES "CHINESE" (1835–1885) – A British officer serving in China during the Taiping Rebellion. He initially fought with British forces, then was appointed to head a joint force of Europeans and Asians known as the "Ever Victorious Army."

GUANGXU (1871–1908) – The ninth emperor of China, selected at the age of four by his aunt Cixi. He initiated the Hundred Days' Reform of 1898, which was abruptly halted by Cixi who stripped him of all power, privileges and honors. He died on November 14, 1908, a day before Cixi.

GUOMINDANG (NATIONALIST PARTY) – The party founded by Sun Zhongshan in 1912 after the founding of the Republic of China. It ruled China from 1928 until 1949. Defeated by the CCP, it retreated to Taiwan where it remains an important political force.

HAKKA (KEJIA) – An ethnic minority prominent in southern China. Many of China's most prominent leaders were Hakka, including Taiping leader Hong Xiuquan, the Song family, and Deng Xiaoping.

HAN CHINESE – The term Han Chinese today refers to the ethnic majority of China's population. In imperial times "Han Chinese" often referred to individuals viewed as culturally Chinese regardless of their ethnicity.

HESHEN (1750–1799) – A high Manchu official and favorite of the Qianlong emperor later accused of numerous crimes, including corruption, extortion and the violation of imperial protocol, and he was sentenced to death.

HONG KONG – An island south of Guangzhou, ceded to Great Britain in 1842 after the Opium War as part of the Treaty of Nanjing and returned to China in 1997.

HONG XIUQUAN (1814–1864) – Leader of the Taiping Rebellion (1851–1864). Born in the southern Chinese province of Guangdong of Hakka ethnicity. Failed to pass the civil service exam in four attempts, before he formed the Society of God Worshippers in Guangxi. He proclaimed himself the Heavenly King of the "Heavenly Kingdom of Great Peace" leading his followers in a failed rebellion against the Qing. Died, likely from suicide on June 1, 1864.

HU JINTAO (1943–) – Born in Jiangsu, he received a degree in hydraulic engineering from Tsinghua University and rose through the ranks with posts in Guizhou and Tibet. He became President of the PRC in 2003 and has pursued conservative economic and political reforms.

HU SHI (1891–1962) – Born in Shanghai and educated at Cornell University with funds from the Boxer Indemnity Scholarship Program, he returned to China to become a leading intellectual luminary, in particular advocating vernacular Chinese. Hu Shi supported the GMD and in 1949 retreated to Taiwan where he became the president of the Academia Sinica.

HUA GUOFENG (1921–2007) – Chosen by Mao Zedong to replace Zhou Enlai as Premier in 1976, he succeeded Mao Zedong upon his death several months later. He moved quickly to arrest the Gang of Four and end the Cultural Revolution but was soon eased out of power by Deng Xiaoping. Hua Guofeng was not purged by Deng, setting a new precedent, and retained his party membership until his death nearly two decades later.

HUANG JUEZI (1793–1853) – A powerful Qing official and leader of a prohibition faction that promoted the outlawing of opium enforced by harsh penalties instead of the legalization sought by other officials.

HUANGPU – A deep water anchorage 12 miles downstream from Guangzhou serving as the primary port for sailing vessels involved in the China trade during the 19th century.

HUANGPU (WHAMPOA) ACADEMY – A military academy founded by Sun Zhongshan in 1924 (often romanized according to Cantonese pronunciation as Whampoa) outside of Guangzhou. Many of China's top military leaders of the 1920s and 1930s, regardless of party affiliation, were educated or served at the academy.

HUBU (HOPPO) – Nineteenth-century Western accounts of trade in Guangzhou refer to any customs officer (and sometimes to the Superintendent of Maritime Customs) as the "hoppo." The term is a corruption of the Chinese designation for the Board of Revenue (hubu) to which all revenue from maritime customs was remitted.

HUI – A Chinese ethnic group largely defined by their practice of Islam and often referred to as "Chinese Muslims" though the label does not include other Muslim groups within China such as the Uigur, Kazakhs, or Kyrgyz peoples.

HUMEN – The mouth of the Pearl River, known in Chinese as "Humen" or literally "Tiger's Gate." Early European sailors labeled it "Bocca Tigris" or "Mouth of the Tiger" which was later called the "Bogue" by British sailors.

HUNDRED DAYS REFORM (1898) – A period that lasted from June 11 to September 21, 1898 when the Guangxu emperor, on advice from Kang Youwei and other top reformers, issued a series of decrees instituting far-reaching reforms. The reform movement ended when Cixi, Dowager Empress, staged a coup, executed several reformers, and effectively removed the emperor from power.

HUNDRED FLOWERS MOVEMENT (1956–1957) – A short-lived government sponsored campaign to encourage suggestions and critiques of the government's performance during its first Five Year Plan. The overwhelmingly negative criticism led to its swift conclusion in the summer of 1957.

IRON RICE BOWL – A term describing guaranteed or "unbreakable" jobs, housing and social security in the decades immediately after the founding of the PRC.

JESUITS (SOCIETY OF JESUS) – A Christian religious order of the Roman Catholic Church that first established Chinese missions in the sixteenth and seventeenth centuries. Successfully operating in the Ming and early Qing era, the Jesuits actively transmitted European knowledge to China and Chinese learning to Europe. Their influence ended when Pope Clement XI decided that Chinese Confucian practices and offerings to the emperor constituted idolatry.

JIANG JIESHI (1887–1975) – Born in Zhejiang, he attended numerous military schools before joining the GMD, serving as commandant of Huangpu Military Academy in 1924. After Sun Zhongshan's death in 1925, Jiang Jieshi became the military commander who organized and led the Northern Expedition in 1927. From 1928 until 1949 he served as President of China. After the GMD's retreat to Taiwan he served as president from 1952 until his death in 1975.

JIANG QING (1914–1991) – Wife of Mao Zedong who advocated a radical line of political thought during the Cultural Revolution. After Mao's death she and her allies (Gang of Four) were arrested, tried, and in 1981 found guilty. Her death sentence was commuted to life in prison, where she committed suicide in 1991.

JIANG ZEMIN (1926–) – Born in Jiangsu, he grew up during the Japanese occupation and graduated in 1947 with a degree in electrical engineering. He rose through the ranks to become mayor of Shanghai in 1985 before being chosen by Deng Xiaoping to replace Zhao Ziyang in 1989 and ultimately replace Deng Xiaoping after his death in 1997. In 2003, he stepped down from the Politburo to make way for a new generation of leaders.

JIANGXI SOVIET – A CCP controlled area (or "soviet") founded in 1931 and governed by a council headed by Mao Zedong. The GMD carried out a series of "extermination campaigns" that eventually caused the CCP to flee the soviet on a "Long March."

JIN – A unit of weight (often translated as "catty") typically equal to 1.3 pounds or 0.5 kilograms with considerable local variation.

JINSHI – The highest degree of the imperial civil service. Examinations were held every three years in Beijing thus called "metropolitan exams" until the system was abolished in 1905. The average age of successful candidates passing the exam was 35, and only 9 out of every million Chinese held the degree.

JOSS – A term used by Europeans to mean a religious icon or statue. Likely a Chinese corruption of the Portuguese Deos, "God," the term was re-adopted by Europeans who thought it was a Chinese word. A "joss house" was any Chinese temple whether Buddhist, Confucian or Daoist.

JUELO (GIORO) – Imperial kinsmen who, because of their relationship to the imperial line, received special treatment and titles

JUREN – The second-highest degree of the imperial civil service. Examinations were held every three years in each provincial capital (colloquially called "provincial exams"). The average age of successful candidates passing the exam was 31.

KANG YOUWEI (1858–1927) – A prominent late-Qing classically trained scholar who advocated modernization and reform within a Confucian framework. His influence peaked during the 100 Days Reform when the Guangxu emperor selected his proposals as the framework for reforms. He was forced to flee China when Empress Dowager Cixi abruptly seized power and executed Kang Youwei's younger brother and five other top reformers.

KANGXI (1654–1722) – The second emperor of the Qing dynasty. His 61 year long reign oversaw the consolidation of Qing rule over China, including the defeating the renegade General Wu Sangui and other rebel generals of the Three Feudatories.

KARAKHAN MANIFESTO (1919) – A manifesto issued on July 25, 1919 by Russian Foreign Minister Lev Karakhan relinquishing all Tsarist Russian claims to special rights and privileges in China. The Soviet Union did, however, continue to pursue special rights and privileges.

KASHGAR – Located in the modern autonomous region of Xinjiang in western China, Kashgar was the meeting point between two trading routes around the Taklamakan Desert. Today, it remains populated by Uigur, Kazak and Uzbek peoples.

KETTELER, KLEMENS von (1853–1900) – German ambassador to China killed by pro-Boxer soldiers. His death became a cause célèbre among the foreign powers.

KOKAND – Located in the Central Asian Republic of Uzbekistan, Kokand was positioned at the juncture of two of Central Asia's main trade routes, one into the fertile Ferghana Valley and the other to Tashkent.

KOWTOW – From the Chinese term ketou or koutou, meaning to ritually prostrate and knock one's forehead to the ground. A gesture of respect and deference used in China before the Emperor, one's elders, or when worshipping.

LATE IMPERIAL CHINA – A period of Chinese history traditionally defined as beginning with the end of Mongol rule in 1368 and concluding with the fall of the Qing dynasty in 1911.

LI – A unit of measure equivalent in distance to about 1/3 mile or half a kilometer.

LI DAZHAO - (1888–1927) – A Chinese intellectual, head librarian at Beijing University, who is traditionally attributed with helping co-found the Chinese Communist Party in 1921 though he was not physically present at the inaugural meeting.

LI DENGHUI (Lee Teng-Hui) (1929–) – Born in Taiwan and educated in Japan and the United States he joined the GMD in 1971, was appointed mayor of Taibei in 1981 and succeeded Jiang Jingguo after his death in 1988. He became the first popularly elected ROC president in 1996.

LI HONGZHANG (1823–1901) – A major figure in the Self Strengthening Movement, Li Hongzhang rose to prominence under the tutelage of Zeng Guofan and commanded the Anhui (Huai) Army. In the 1870s, he promoted the adoption of Western technology such as railways and arsenals as well as by Western-style education. In the last decades of his life, Li Hongzhang became the Qing empire's preeminent (if unappreciated) diplomat.

LI PENG (1928–) – Raised by Zhou Enlai, educated in the Soviet Union, and rose to prominence under Deng Xiaoping, he was a key advocate and orchestrator of the harsh suppression of demonstrators in the June 4th Tiananmen Incident (1989). He is the key architect of the Three Gorges Dam project.

LIANG – A unit of weight generally said to be equal to one ounce and often referred to as a tael in western sources. However, it should be noted that there were local variations and the official weight fluctuated over the eighteenth, nineteenth and twentieth centuries.

LIJIN – A form of local taxation first introduced by Zeng Guofan to fund his Hunan (Xiang) Army. The tax was levied on goods in transit, on shops, and was a tax many foreigners believed a barrier to import goods.

LIN BIAO (1907–71) – A Chinese Communist military leader and hero of the Chinese Civil War. In the 1960s, he compiled Quotations from Chairman Mao Zedong and was named Mao Zedong's successor in 1969. He died in a 1971 plane crash, after allegedly attempting to wrest power from Mao Zedong.

LIN ZEXU (1785–1850) – A scholar-official who passed the highest (jinshi) civil exam at age 26, he was a favorite of the young Daoguang emperor (r. 1821-1850) and a member of Huang Juezi's "prohibition faction." In 1838 he headed the empire's anti-opium efforts, until he was banished to Xinjiang after failing to resolve China's confrontation with Britain.

LITTLE RED BOOK (Quotations of Chairman Mao) – A pocket size collection of Mao Zedong's quotations first published for the PLA in 1964. 900 million copies were ultimately printed.

LIU SHAOQI (1898–1969) – Born in Hunan, he joined the CCP in 1921 gaining notoriety as a key party theoretician. In the 1960s he fell out of favor with Mao Zedong who denounced and stripped him of all his positions then expelled from the Party in 1968.

LONG MARCH (1934–35) – A series of CCP marches from their bases in the southeast to northwestern China. The main route ran 6,000 miles from Jiangxi to Shaanxi and took one year to complete.. Casualties and desertions reduced the original 100,000 marchers by more than 90% to fewer than 10,000.

LORCHA – A sailing vessel of about 100 tons, with a European built hull and Chinese masts and sails.

LUGOUQIAO (MARCO POLO BRIDGE) INCIDENT – An event outside of Beijing near the Lugouqiao Bridge on July 7, 1937 which sparked the beginning of the War of Resistance Against Japan.

LU XUN (1881–1936) – A prominent 20th century Chinese author, a major proponent of vernacular (baihua) literature, and a major figure in the May Fourth Movement in 1919. While leftist in his political thought he never joined the CCP.

LYTTON REPORT (1932) – A League of Nations report indicting Japan for its role in seizing, subjugating and continuing to manage the northeastern area of China under the puppet Manchukuo government. Japan withdrew from the League a month after the international body voted to accept its conclusions.

MACARTNEY, GEORGE (1737–1806) – Served as the British envoy to China in 1793 where he met with Emperor Qianlong and controversially refused to kowtow before him. The mission failed to achieve a permanent embassy in Beijing or a reduction of restrictions on British trade with China.

MANCHUKUO – The puppet government formed by the Japanese in 1932 in northeastern China. The last Qing emperor, Puyi, was named its chief executive and remained titular head until the end of the Second World War in 1945.

MANCHURIA – An area roughly coterminous with northeastern China and the ancestral lands of the Manchu peoples that established the Qing dynasty. Japan occupied the territory in the 1930s and established the puppet state of Manchukuo.

MAO BUTTONS – Worn as a symbol of one's loyalty to Mao Zedong during the Cultural Revolution, at least 2 billion badges were manufactured with well over 10,000 different designs.

MAO ZEDONG (1893–1976) – Born in Hunan, he became involved in the nascent CCP in Beijing during the May Fourth era. Played an increasingly prominent role in the Jiangxi Soviet in the early 1930s before rising to prominence during the Long March (1934). He successfully guided the CCP through the War of Resistance Against Japan and the Chinese Civil War before founding the PRC in 1949. His legacy is a mixed, one of significant social and economic development as well as of policies that lead to the deaths of tens of millions Chinese citizens.

MARRIAGE LAW OF 1950 – One of the first laws promulgated after the founding of the PRC in 1949, it set a minimum age for marriage, legalized divorce, made men and women equal in courts of law, and prohibited concubinage.

MAY FOURTH MOVEMENT – A movement narrowly defined as events sparked by the student-led demonstrations of May 4, 1919 against the Treaty of Versailles. More often it is used to identify the broad intellectual and cultural transformations that took place after Japan's Twenty-One Demands (1915) lasting well into the 1920s.

MEXICAN DOLLAR – A silver coin minted in the Spanish Empire (later in Mexican mints) and the source of nearly all silver on the global markets during the sixteenth, seventeenth and eighteenth centuries. The Mexican dollar (also referred to as the Spanish dollar or "pieces of eight") was the preferred international currency external to European commerce. Most treaties that indicate "dollars" referred to this currency.

MIGRANT LABORERS – Until recently, the place of residency for every Chinese was tightly controlled. Those who moved around illegally were referred to as "mang liu" ("wanderers" or migrants) or "min gong" (migrant laborers). A highly exploited group of people, they are hired illegally but in constant danger of arrest and being sent back to their official place of residence.

MOST FAVORED NATION STATUS – Under terms first granted by China to Britain in the 1842 Treaty of Nanjing, and in 1844 extended to all the foreign powers present in China, the Most Favored Nation status stipulated that any concessions given to one Western country would automatically entitle other Western countries to seek (and likely be granted) the same concessions.

MU – A unit of measure for land equivalent to 0.16 acres.

MUKDEN INCIDENT (September 18, 1931) – Japan's Kwantung Army blew up a portion of the Southern Manchuria Railway, and used the incident to justify an attack on the city of Shenyang and then on the whole of Manchuria.

NANJING MASSACRE (December 1937–January 1938) – A six-week assault carried out in and around the capital of Nanjing after it fell to the Japanese army in 1937. Upwards of 300,000 non-combatants were killed, including tens of thousands of women and children. The army committed numerous atrocities, including looting, rape and arson, with the seeming consent of their officers. Also referred to as the "Rape of Nanjing."

NATIONAL DAY – The Wuhan Uprising on October 10 (or "Double-10"), 1911 marked the beginning of the Chinese Revolution and is still celebrated as National Day in the Republic of China [Taiwan]. The anniversary of the founding of the PRC on October 1, 1949, is National Day in the People's Republic of China.

NEIGHBORHOOD COMMITTEE – The lowest administrative unit in urban China, it keeps updated records of all residents within a defined neighborhood.

NEW CHINA – A term widely employed in China today suggesting a significant demarcation between the traditional practices of "Old China" and those of the People's Republic of China. Many Chinese refer to the PRC-era as "New China."

NEW CULTURE MOVEMENT (c. 1917–1923) – A movement roughly equivalent to the "May Fourth Movement," though some suggest the New Culture Movement indicates a more "thought" oriented movement compared to the "action" agenda of the May Fourth Movement. The conflation of the terms has made them interchangeable in popular discourse.

NEW LIFE MOVEMENT (1934–c.1937) – A program of moral renewal with distinct fascist overtones launched in 1934 by Jiang Jieshi and his wife Song Meiling to counter Communism by promoting Confucianism, Nationalism, and Christianity.

NEW POLICIES (1901–1910) – A series of political reforms set in motion by Cixi in an effort to erect a modern administrative bureaucracy.

NORTHERN EXPEDITION (1926–1927) – A military campaign led by Jiang Jieshi and the Guomindang (Nationalists) in 1927 that began in southern China and advanced northward reuniting much of eastern China. It brought an end to the worst of the warlord excesses—often by simply co-opting the warlords into Jiang's government.

ONE CHILD POLICY – A policy adopted in 1979 allowing each couple only one child. The policy was enforced with an array of incentives and punishments, which varied according to your ethnicity and residency.

OPIUM WAR (1839–1842) – A war between China and Great Britain fought over the importation of opium into China by British merchants. Following imperial orders, Lin Zexu seized and destroyed some 1,300 tons of opium stored in Guangzhou resulting in military hostilities. The conflict came to an end in 1842 with the signing of the Treaty of Nanjing. The war was a military disaster for China and marked the beginning of a century of Western imperialism in China.

OTTO BRAUN (1900–1974) – Served as Comintern advisor to the CCP leadership from 1934 until he left China in 1939. Sometimes known by his Chinese name Li De, he was the only foreigner to complete the entire Long March.

PALANQUIN – A chair for conveying one person. Often enclosed by a curtain, it is fastened to two horizontal poles projecting outward on either side and carried by two, four, or sometimes six men.

PANCHEN LAMA – A reincarnated Tibetan Buddhist religious leader in Tibet's Gelugpa Buddhist order, second only to the Dalai Lama. The Panchen Lama is traditionally based at the Tashilhunpo Monastery near Shigatse.

PENG DEHUAI (1898–1974) – A PLA general who gained notoriety and prestige for his command of Chinese troops during the Korean War. When he offered Mao Zedong a negative assessment of the Great Leap Forward in 1959 he was denounced and never regained his prominent position within the Party or the government.

PEOPLE'S LIBERATION ARMY (PLA) – Established in 1927 as the "Red Army" the PLA became the official name of China's military forces during the Chinese Civil War. In popular culture and propaganda, the army was portrayed as a true "people's army" – from the people, of the people, and for the people.

PEOPLE'S VOLUNTEER ARMY OF CHINA – In an effort to distinguish their actions from what they considered the imperialist actions of the United States, China's military forces in Korea adopted the name "People's Volunteer Army." It suggested China was voluntarily aiding their Korean neighbors and not imposing external pressure on Korea's domestic affairs.

PINGXINGGUAN CAMPAIGN – One of the largest battles carried out by Communist military forces during the War of Resistance Against Japan.

PLENIPOTENTIARY – A person, especially a diplomatic agent, vested with full power to transact any business, such as negotiating a treaty with a foreign power.

POISONED ARROW PETITION (1962) – A 70,000 word petition written by the 10th Panchen Lama documenting the hardships, substandard living conditions, and forced labor which had befallen Tibetans all in the name of "socialist reform." Mao Zedong reacted by calling the petition a "poisoned arrow" shot at the Party by reactionary feudal overlords. The Panchen Lama was arrested and detained for 15 years.

POLITBURO – A shorthand term for "political bureau," it was the principal executive policy-making committee within a Communist Party. The politburo is centralized within the Standing Committee of the Communist Party of China.

PREMIER'S WILL – The "premier's will" became a staple of Chinese life in the decade after Sun's death. Employed in a manner similar to the "Pledge of Allegiance" in the United States, all school children recited the will every Monday morning throughout the 1930s and 40s.

PUNITIVE FACTION – A group within the GMD lead by He Yinqin and Dai Jitao who some claimed sought to kill Jiang Jieshi in the Xian Incident (1936) in order destabilize the political situation by promoting a civil war and delaying engagement with the Japanese.

PUYI (1905–1967) – More formally known as the Xuantong emperor, he was tenth and last emperor of the Qing dynasty. He became emperor at the age of three, abdicated at the age of 7 in 1912, and was the titular head of Manchukuo, the Japanese puppet state in northeastern China at the age of 27 in 1932.

QIANLONG (1711–1799) – The fourth emperor of the Qing dynasty. He officially abdicated in the sixtieth year of his reign in order to not surpass the sixty-one year reign of his grandfather, the Kangxi emperor though he retained de facto power until his death in 1799. Under his reign, Qing armies enlarged the empire to its greatest territorial scope, Qing scholars compiled the 36,000 volume Four Treasuries, and the emperor's artisans greatly expanded the Yuanming Yuan.

QING DYNASTY (1644–1911) – The last Chinese imperial dynasty, founded in 1644 by Manchus from northeastern China. It fell in 1911 after the Wuchang Uprising.

QINGMING FESTIVAL (Tomb Sweeping Day) – The 15th day after the Spring Equinox, Qingming is a traditional Chinese holiday when families pray at the tombs or graves of their deceased relatives. It is believed that one should offer food and often liquor to the spirits on this day or they will become "hungry ghosts" and disrupt the living.

RED GUARDS – Middle and High School-aged students who answered Mao Zedong's call in 1966 to spread his teachings, fight against the "Four Olds," and remove all counter-revolutionary elements from society.

RONG HONG (1828–1912) – More familiar to Western readers as Yung Wing, Rong Hong traveled to the US in 1847, became a US citizen in 1852, graduated from Yale in 1854 and served as an early emissary between China and the United States.

RUYI – A Chinese scepter made of jade, or other precious material, given as a sign of respect. Traditionally, it has a stylized head of a cloud and a long curved handle.

SACRED EDICT – A list of Confucian rules of moral conduct and social relations compiled by the Kangxi emperor in 1670.

SECOND OPIUM WAR (1856–1860) – Known by a variety of names, including the Arrow War, the Second Anglo-Chinese War, as well as the Second Opium War, the war is traditionally understood as taking place in two parts: the first began with the Arrow Incident in 1856 and ended with the signing of the Treaty of Tianjin in 1858. The second part began with the attack on Tianjin and Beijing and ended when the Qing acquiesced and signed the Conventions of Beijing in 1860.

SELF-STRENGTHENING MOVEMENT (c.1861–1894) – A movement beginning in 1861 largely stemming from the urgent need to counter the mid-nineteenth century Chinese rebellions. Initially, the campaign consisted of military reforms adopted by Zeng Guofan and later broadened to adopt western methods in education, industry and diplomacy.

SEVENTEEN POINT AGREEMENT (1951) – An agreement signed in 1951 between representatives of the Tibetan government with CCP leaders laying out the points by which Tibet would accept Chinese sovereignty over Tibet. Both sides renounced the agreement in 1959, and the Dalai Lama established a government-in-exile in neighboring India.

SHANGHAI COMMUNIQUÉ (1972) – An agreement signed in 1972 between the United States and the PRC pledging further talks towards achieving a normalization of relations and agreeing on the status of Taiwan as part of China.

SHAOLIN TEMPLE – A famous Buddhist temple in Henan province in central China. In popular culture, it is a well-known center of martial arts training by Buddhist monks.

SHENGYUAN – Lowest of the three degrees of the imperial civil service exam, which granted holder's the status of "lower gentry." Examinations were held every three years in one's native districts or prefectures. The average age for passing the exam was 24.

SHIYANG MINE MASSACRE (1854) – One of several instances of Han-Hui violence occurring in the years leading up to the Panthay Rebellion.

SINO-FRENCH WAR (1884–1885) – A war between China and France for control of Vietnam which China continued to view as a tributary state but which France saw as part of its Indochinese colonial holdings.

SOCIALISM – A socio-economic system in which wealth, services, and production are controlled by the community or government. For Karl Marx, socialism would be the socio-economic system that later progressed into communism.

SONG BINBIN (1947–) – A famous Red Guard who was selected to meet Mao Zedong in August 1966 at the start of the Cultural Revolution. When Song Binbin ("bin" meaning refined) was asked her name, Mao told her she should change it to Song Yaowu ("yaowu" meaning "to be militant").

SONG FAMILY – The Song family had an aura akin to the Kennedy family in the United States. Each of the Song sisters married prominent politicians or business leaders. Due to their American education, their faces became the face of China for many Westerners.

SONG JIASHU (1863–1918) – Known in the west as "Charlie" Song, he was born on the southern Chinese island of Hainan and lived in the United States for many years. He converted to Christianity at age 15 before returning to China at age 23 to become a successful businessman. His six children were some of the most influential figures of 1920s, 1930s, and 1940s China.

SONG MEILING (1897–2003) – The youngest of the three Song sisters graduated from Wellesley College in 1917 and married Jiang Jieshi in 1927. Her familiarity with the United States and American customs helped her play a prominent role as a spokesperson for China during the 1930s and 1940s.

SONG ZIWEN (1894–1971) – The third of six Song siblings born to Song "Charlie" Jiashu. Often known in western sources as T.V. Soong, he was Harvard educated, and served as the Finance Minister, Foreign Minister and President of the Executive Yuan in the Guomindang government between 1928-1947.

SINO-SOVIET SPLIT (c. 1959) – Relations between the Soviet Union and China soured in the late 1950s with a series of diplomatic disagreements over Taiwan, India and the United States. As a result, the Soviet government withdrew their experts, scientific information, and financial support from China. This lead to an acrimonious 30-year split between China and USSR that ended with Gorbachev's visit in 1989.

SMALLPOX IN CHINA – Smallpox outbreaks remained quite common during the Qing. This was a particular concern to the Manchus, Mongols and Tibetans who had little natural exposure (and thus resistance) to the disease. As a result, the Qing emperor's often excluded those who had not had the disease from the requirements of appearing at court.

SOVIET – The term "soviet"(suweiai) in the Chinese context designated CCP bases in Anhui, Hunan, Fujian, and later in Shaanxi and Gansu during the late 1920s and early 1930s. The term refers to areas under the direct control of Communists. Western papers at the time referred to them as "red bases."

SPECIAL ECONOMIC ZONES (SEZs) – Areas and cities with special economic status to encourage foreign investment and increase foreign exports. First created under Deng Xiaoping in the late 1970s and 1980s with cities of Shenzhen and Zhuhai (situated next to Hong Kong and Macau respectively) being particularly successful examples.

SPHERES OF INTEREST – Areas of China in which a specific Western power was said to hold particular interest, but no specific powers during the late nineteenth century.

STRUGGLE SESSIONS – Cultural Revolution rallies where individuals accused of "black" or counter-revolutionary activities would be publicly attacked in sessions lasting many hours held in large auditoriums.

SUMMER PALACE (YIHE YUAN) – An imperial garden constructed in 1888 for the Dowager Empress Cixi. In some English language sources, the Yuanming Yuan is also referred to as the "Old Summer Palace."

SUN ZHONGSHAN (1866–1925) [SUN YAT-SEN] – Often called the "Father of Modern China," Sun was a principal revolutionary leader during the last decades of the Qing Dynasty. He served as the provisional president of the Republic of China, but resigned in favor of Yuan Shikai. Over the next two decades he headed the Guomindang party until his death in 1925 from cancer.

TAELS – Technically, a Chinese ounce of silver, but in reality there were numerous different forms of taels, of unequal values. In international treaties the most commonly used tael was the "customs tael" (haiguan tael) equivalent to 37.68 grams of silver. The other commonly used tael was the "kuping tael" or "treasury tael" equivalent to 37 grams.

TAIPING REBELLION (1851–1864) – The largest of China's mid-nineteenth century rebellions, it was led by Hong Xiuquan which at its height ruled over 30 million people and lasted thirteen years before finally being suppressed by Qing military force.

TANGGU TRUCE (1933) – An agreement signed on May 31, 1933 between China and Japan establishing a demilitarized zone south from the Great Wall to Beijing.

TARTARY – A European term for Central Asia. Europeans also referred to the nomadic peoples of the steppes (e.g. Mongol, Turkic, Manchu) as "Tartars."

TASHILHUNPO – One of Tibetan Buddhism's four great monasteries of the Gelugpa schools located in the central Tibetan city of Shigatse. It was founded in 1447 by the First Dalai Lama and is traditionally the seat of the Panchen Lama.

THREE CHARACTER CLASSIC – A Confucian primer, which served as an introduction to Confucian thought for most young children.

THREE FEUDATORIES – Areas granted by the early Manchu emperors in southern China to three Chinese generals – Wu Sangui, Geng Jingzhong and Shang Zhixin – who aided in the Manchu's early conquest of China. All three later rebelled against the Qing rulers with the last rebel forces defeated in 1683.

THREE GORGES DAM – A massive hydroelectric dam on the Yangzi River at the head of the Qutang, Wuxia, and Siling gorges. The dam was completed in 2008 a year of head of schedule supplying much-needed electricity, but with severe environmental consequences.

THREE PRINCIPLES OF THE PEOPLE – A political philosophy developed by Sun Zhongshan grouped into the three guiding principles of Nationalism, Democracy and Livelihood.

TIANANMEN SQUARE MASSACRE (1989) – The bloody military suppression of the 1989 student movement on June 4th that brought an end to two-months of student demonstrations, hunger strikes and unprecedented international media attention. Several hundred unarmed students and civilians died in the early morning military attack.

TONGMENG HUI – A political group, also known as the Revolutionary Alliance Society, founded in 1905 with the merger of several competing parties. By joining forces they became the largest Chinese revolutionary party and the forerunner of the Nationalist party, the Guomindang.

TONGWEN GUAN (Foreign Languages College) – Founded in 1862 to systematically begin foreign language instruction under government oversight, the college taught English, French, German, Russian and Japanese as well as courses in science, philosophy and international law. In 1902 it was consolidated into the Imperial University (which later became Beijing University.

TREATY OF NANJING (1842) – Treaty ending the Opium War between China and Great Britain. It opened five treaty ports, ceded the island of Hong Kong, and imposed a 21 million taels indemnity.

TREATY OF TIANJIN (1858) – Treaty ending the first phase of the Second Opium (Arrow) War. Its terms forced the Qing court to accept a British ambassador in Beijing, as well as the addition of ten cities as treaty ports, and the opening all of interior China to travel, trade and Christian proselytizing. The treaty was ratified in the Beijing Convention by the emperor in 1860, only after British and French forces looted and burned the Yuanming Yuan.

TREATY PORTS – Any city in which foreigners were to be allowed to trade and conduct business within China. In addition to treaty ports, foreign settlements and foreign concessions were carved out of existing Chinese cities. These were under the direct control and rule of resident foreign consuls.

TRIPLE INTERVENTION – Germany, France and Russia, ostensibly seeking to help the Qing empire but acting more in self-interest, forced Japan to return territory in northeastern China in exchange for an additional payment to Japan of 30 million taels. Quickly thereafter, Russia, Germany and France each demanded a territorial concession in exchange for their role in the intervention.

TSONGKHAPA (1357–1419) – Founder of the Gelugpa branch of Tibetan Buddhism.

TULKUS – A designation (in Tibetan *sprul sku*) meaning reincarnated (reborn) soul of former incarnate lama (Living Buddha) with the most famous example being the Dalai Lama.

TUNGAN (DONGGAN) – An ethnic label for Muslim Chinese employed only in northwestern China. Also referred to in late imperial documents as Han-Hui.

TURFAN – A city in the most western province of Xinjiang, famous for its fruit, particularly its grapes.

WADE, THOMAS F. (1818–1895) – A British diplomat and talented linguist who was first posted to China during the Opium War in 1941 and successively promoted to higher positions eventually becoming Britain's representative to China. Upon his retirement from the diplomatic service, he became the first professor of Chinese at Cambridge where he taught until his death in 1895.

WALKING ON TWO LEGS – A phrase Mao used to describe the simultaneous development of both the agricultural and industrial sectors.

WANG JINGWEI (1883-1944) – Born in Guangdong, he joined the Tongment Hui in 1905 and attempted to assassinate the last emperor's father Prince Chun. After his release, he worked closely with Sun Zhongshan and challenged Jiang Jieshi for leadership of the GMD. In 1940 he became the head of state for Japanese-occupied China.

WAR OF RESISTANCE AGAINST JAPAN (1937–1945) – Sometimes referred to as the "Anti-Japanese War," fought between China and Japan before and during World War II. Beginning in 1937, Japan occupied all major urban and communication centers in eastern China by 1938 and forced the Nationalist government to move its capital inland to Chongqing until Japan's defeat in 1945.

WARLORDS (JUNFA): A term applied to the military governors and commanders who battled for political control usually through the use of regionally based armies from 1911 to the late 1920s.

WHITE LOTUS SOCIETY – A secret society based on a mixture of Buddhist, Daoist and local spiritual beliefs prevalent since the 17th century, it was declared heretical and prohibited by the Qing government.

WOREN (1804–1871) – A powerful Qing official who served as head of the influential Hanlin Academy. Woren espoused strong Neo-Confucian views and vigorously opposed the westernized curriculum advocated by the Self-Strengthening Movement.

WUCHANG UPRISING (1911) – The uprising that began on October 10, 1911 as a result of the accidental detonation of explosives by Tongmenhui members. It started the Chinese revolution, which led to the fall of the Qing dynasty and the founding of the Republic of China.

WU PEIFU (c. 1874–1939) – A major figure and leader of the Zhili clique during the Warlord era, often referred to as the "Scholar General." In 1924, Wu was nearly able to broker a peace agreement among the various factions but ultimately failed. He resisted overtures from both the Guomindang and Japanese during the 1930s and died in suspicious circumstances in 1939.

WU SANGUI (1612–1678) – A Ming general who allowed the Manchu army to pass through the Great Wall and capture Beijing. He later revolted against the Qing and later declared himself emperor of the new Zhou dynasty. He died of dysentery in 1678.

XIANGSHENG – A fast-paced stand-up comedy routine typically with two people similar to the famous Abbot & Costello "Who's On First" sketch that relies heavily on puns and humorous wordplay. Often translated into English as "Crosstalk."

YALTA AGREEMENT – An agreement signed near the end of the Second World War between the Allies in which the USSR gained the Kurile Islands, Southern Sakhalin, Lushun and Dalian as well as control of the Chinese-Eastern Railroad and the South Manchurian Railroad.

YAMEN – Refers to the compound that houses the local administrative office of the magistrate, his judicial court and his official residence. It also less frequently refers to the magistrate himself.

YANG RUI (1857–1898) – One of the key reformers in the Guangxu emperor's inner circle during the 100 Days Reform. He was one of six reformers arrested and executed by Dowager Empress Cixi upon her return to power.

YARKAND (YARKENT) – Located in the modern autonomous region of Xinjiang in western China, Yarkand was an important trading city populated predominantly by Uigurs.

YIXIN (1833–1898) – The sixth son of the Daoguang emperor often referred to as Prince Gong. He served as regent for the young Tongzhi emperor and became a strong proponent of the Self Strengthening Movement and the establishment of the Zongli Yamen.

YOUYU – The fifth of China's so-called Five Mythical Emperors (sanhuang wudi) who was said to have established and shaped Chinese culture, society and the beginnings of the Chinese state. Also known as "Shun".

YUANMING YUAN – An immense garden with massive lakes, islands and sprawling palaces begun 1709 and expanded over several decades. The Jesuit priests serving in the Qing court helped design one section that had elaborate fountains and Baroque palaces. Sometimes referred to as the "Old Summer Palace."

YUAN SHIKAI (1859–1916) – Staunch Qing loyalist and commander of the powerful Beiyang Army which allowed him, in 1912, to broker the abdication of the Qing in exchange for the presidency of the new republic. His term as president was plagued by corruption, extortion and a misguided attempt to proclaim himself emperor before his death in 1916.

ZENG GUOFAN (1811–1872) – A strict Confucian who nonetheless championed progressive fiscal and military reforms in the early 1860s helping the Qing to suppress the Taiping Rebellion.

ZHANG AILING (1921–1995) – A well-known female writer of the 1940s whose writings remain immensely popular in China today.

ZHANG XUELIANG (1900–2001) – Son of Manchurian warlord Zhang Zuolin and mastermind behind the kidnapping of Jiang Jieshi in 1936 convincing him to fight Japan rather than the CCP.

ZHANG XUN (1854–1923) – A prominent warlord during China's Republican era and a noted Qing-loyalist known as the "Pigtail General" who attempted to restore the last Qing emperor to the throne in 1917.

ZHANG ZUOLIN (1875–1928) – Warlord nicknamed the "Old Marshal" who controlled most of northeast China (Manchuria) from 1916 until 1928 when he was assassinated by a Japanese military officer.

ZHAO ZIYANG (1919–2005) – A leading reformer under Deng Xiaoping and seen by many as his anointed heir, but his support for the student demonstrations in 1989 caused him to be striped of all titles and spent the last 15 years of his life under house arrest until his death in 2005.

ZHIFU (YANTAI) CONVENTION (1876) – A treaty (sometimes referred to as Chefoo Convention) between China and Great Britain imposed largely because of the Qing government's ostensible complicity in the murder of British translator Augustus Margary.

ZHONGNAN HAI – A compound just west of the Forbidden City in the center of Beijing, which in the first decades of the PRC housed its top leaders and today serves as the headquarters of the party and top government officials.

ZONGLI YAMEN – Established in 1861 following the Convention of Beijing, its primary goal was to handle China's foreign relations in a more systematic manner. Often simply called the "Foreign Office," the office's full title Zongli Geguo Shiwu Yamen translates as "Office for the Management of the Affairs of All Foreign Countries."

ZUNYI CONFERENCE (January 15-17, 1935) – A meeting held in the southwestern province of Guizhou during the Long March by the CCP leadership, it marked the rise of Mao Zedong and his supporters to top leadership positions.

INDEX

Also available from Pearson:

Ruth Dunnell, Chinggis Khan (2010) 0-32-127633-7

Mark Elliott, *The Qianlong Emperor: Son of Heaven, Man of the World* (2010) 0-32-108444-6

David B. Gordon, *Sun Yatsen: Seeking a Newer China* (2010) 0-32-133306-3

Edward Moise, *Modern China, Third Edition* (2008) 0-58-277277-X

N. Harry Rothschild, *Wu Zhao: China's Only Female Emperor, First Edition* (2008) 0-32-139426-7

Albert M. Craig, *The Heritage of Chinese Civilization, Second Edition* (2007) 0-13-134610-5

Edward L. Dreyer, *Zheng He: China and the Oceans in the Early Ming Dynasty* (2007) 0-32-108443-8

R. Keith Schoppa, *Revolution and Its Past: Identities and Change in Chinese History, Second Edition* (2006) 0-13-193039-7

Bruce Elleman and Sally Paine, *History of Modern China* (forthcoming)